CASE STUDIES IN BEHAVIOR MODIFICATION

CASE STUDIES IN BEHAVIOR MODIFICATION

WITHDRAWN

Edited and Introduced by

LEONARD P. ULLMANN
University of Illinois

LEONARD KRASNER
State University of New York at Stony Brook

June, 1966

Holt, Rinehart and Winston, Inc.
New York · Chicago · San Francisco · Toronto · London

June, 1966

PREFACE

This book developed from and reflects current evaluative, conceptual, empirical, and procedural developments in clinical psychology. At an evaluative level, we shared the general dissatisfaction with the efficacy of traditional or evocative psychotherapy (Frank, 1961). We believed that it was ethically incumbent upon psychologists to increase the efficiency of the modification of maladaptive behavior. At a conceptual level, as psychologists we started with a behavioral or psychological model rather than with a medical or disease model. When we did so, we found that we raised questions, which will be discussed in the introductory essay, dealing with the nature of "mental illness," the value of current nosologies, the bases for the practice of psychotherapy, and the proper role of the psychotherapist. On an empirical level, we had read with eagerness and made some experimental contributions to the body of literature on behavior modification that grew rapidly after the Second World War and that was beginning to be transferred from rodents and college sophomores to the clinic, the nursery school, and the psychiatric hospital. In this material, the theories of Hull and Skinner were being applied with increasing usefulness to the sort of problems clinical psychologists sought to deal with in psychotherapy. A group of new techniques developed, and it is the goal of this book to describe the content and scope of these procedures.

The actual preparation and writing of this book grew out of personal forces. At a first level, we were privileged to participate in a continuing symposium in which sixteen psychologists who had contributed to the experimental behavior modification literature presented their empirical work and discussed the possible application of their findings to clinical problems. Some of the authors had already made a start on this endeavor, and of these authors, Bijou on retardates (45),* Bachrach on anorexia nervosa (14), and Patterson on child therapy (31, 50) appear in the present volume. More importantly, we learned of many other efforts in this direction that were either in manuscript form or scattered throughout a wide variety of journals. As teachers of college courses in abnormal psychology, and as a way to answer questions of our fellow practitioners, we wanted an easily accessible reference in which the products of the clinical application of learning concepts might be sampled and evaluated. The sources closest to what we had in mind were two excellent books that will be frequently referred to in the following material: Wolpe's *Psychotherapy by reciprocal inhibition* (1958) and the anthology edited by Eysenck, *Behaviour therapy and the neuroses* (1960). Wolpe's book is a major source for the development and introduction of a number of new techniques, particularly that of systematic desensitization, which will be discussed and illustrated in this book by cases by Cowden and Ford (9), Kushner (18, 24), Lazarus (21, 25), Lang and Lazovik (20), Bond and Hutchison (26), and Wolpe (17) himself. Wolpe's book also is a classic illustration of a series of laboratory studies leading to the development of a psychotherapeutic technique. Eysenck's anthology brought together both theoretical articles and examples of therapy. It is a major source for the understanding of behavior therapy. Finally, there are the excellent review articles by Bandura (1961), Grossberg (1964), Kalish (in press), Mertens (1963), and Mowrer (in press). The authors of the last four mentioned works very graciously provided major assistance by letting us see their material prior to publication.

* Simple numerals in parentheses, as here, refer to cases in this volume.

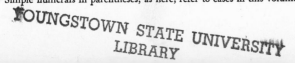

v

With these sources to draw on, why were we so presumptuous as to think that another volume was needed? One of our objectives was to bring together and make far more accessible many of the works mentioned by the authors of review articles. Other purposes are highlighted by the manner in which this volume differs from and supplements that of Eysenck. First, we will devote the majority of our pages to cases in which the subjects are children or schizophrenics. Approximately seventy percent of our material will be devoted to these two groups while less than twenty percent of Eysenck's volume deals with these two groups. Second, none of the articles that appeared in Eysenck's anthology will be reprinted in this volume. In great measure the availability of this much material illustrates the viability of the field. Only six of the fifty articles printed in the present volume were published before 1960, the date of Eysenck's *Behaviour therapy and the neuroses*. Another difference between the present endeavor and Eysenck's volume is one which may be related to our emphasis on children and schizophrenics: where the authors in Eysenck's volume tend far more to a work within Hull's learning theory, the majority of the authors in the present book would, if forced to cite a single allegiance, categorize themselves as influenced by Skinner and operant rather than classical conditioning. Fourth, our format is somewhat different from Eysenck's. Where Eysenck presented pivotal theoretical articles from Watson and Rayner (1920), and Jones (1924a) through Shoben (1949), Yates (1958a), and Eysenck (1959), we have written the introductory material other than that which appears in each article. In so doing we have written for a more application-oriented audience than Eysenck, a matter which may reflect the increasing acceptance of behavior therapy and behavior modification. As we shall discuss below, we believe that this material is important at an undergraduate, nonspecialist level. We have also had in mind colleagues who are practicing psychotherapists, and we have, therefore, discussed matters of nosology, therapist role, values, and future applications that were outside the scope of Eysenck's work. Further, by producing the introductory, background, and theoretical material ourselves, we hope we have achieved a high degree of integration of viewpoint and nonredundant coverage of the available literature. Finally, as implied in the fact that the vast majority of our material was written after the appearance of Eysenck's book, the very quantity of new material called for the present undertaking.

We have had a number of audiences in mind while preparing this book. A first one was composed of advanced undergraduates. The material in current abnormal and clinical psychology textbooks is heavily weighted towards descriptive psychiatry and psychoanalytic hypotheses and there is little if any material dealing with how the patient is actually treated. Collections of outside readings such as Sarbin's *Studies in behavior pathology* (1961) and Quay's *Research in psychopathology* (1963) introduce students to some of the more rigorous inquiries into the nature of disordered and maladaptive behavior, but their emphasis is on methodology and hypothesis testing and not on treatment. When we introduced the type of material presented in this book to our students, we were encouraged by their warm reception. Many of the students in undergraduate psychology courses are interested in careers in teaching, nursing, social work, occupational therapy, and medicine; for them psychoanalytic or evocative therapy concepts are difficult to conceptualize ("What really was done during all those hours when the patient 'worked through?' "). Second, the emphasis on experimental psychology as the basis for treatment procedures brings courses dealing with maladaptive human behavior closer to basic psychology than is currently the case. There should not be any discontinuity between general and experimental psychology on the one hand, and courses in abnormal and clinical psychology on the other. By using case material such as that presented in this book, our students came

to understand why learning theories were important and how they made a difference in therapist behavior. Not only does starting from a behavioral model lead to increased therapeutic
efficiency, but it helped reverse the very unfortunate trend for experimental and clinical psychologists to have increasingly fewer common interests.

A second major audience we had in mind was composed of fellow professional workers
(teachers, psychiatrists, and social workers, as well as clinical psychologists) who were either
looking for new techniques or who had already modified the techniques of evocative therapy
they had been taught and were seeking ways to formulate and communicate their procedures.
We think that many clinical psychologists reading this book will have a shock of recognition
and find some reflection of their own innovations. We have often met fellow professional
workers who apologized for straying from the traditional model on the basis of experience or
common sense. While we can think of few better reasons for altering one's behavior, we hope
that they will find in this book both examples and formulations that will support and help
them.

While we will offer an overview of theoretical considerations and refer to the research
that links theory and practice, for example, Krasner & Ullmann, (1965) *the present book will
present material at an inductive level*. That is, we will present cases as illustrations of what
is being done to mitigate and change maladaptive behavior. Such material, as will be discussed
later, is not evidence or validation in itself. Rather, it provides examples and illustrations. We
have found that students understand and are interested in this material, and that from it they
frequently are led to think critically and ask questions which raise the issues which currently
dominate the psychological and psychiatric literature.

Further, and of major importance, we think that clinical and abnormal psychology are in
the process of a basic change in orientation and content. We hope that this volume of readings
will be part of this change and will reflect its direction. If we are correct, then the students
reading this book will be prepared to understand and take part in the coming debates about
the relationship of psychology to behavior change in the clinical and hospital setting. In providing raw data—that is, cases—the reader will have some opportunity to share and evaluate
one of the major sources for the development of the psychologist's new role.

In short, we hope that this book will be a useful introduction to the application of laboratory findings to the change of behavior in clinics, hospitals, nursery schools, and homes. We
believe that in the near future a knowledge of the fields of clinical, counseling, child, and
abnormal psychology will presuppose some familiarity with articles such as the ones in this
book and in the direction of psychology that they represent.

We are pleased to have this opportunity to acknowledge the assistance of our colleagues,
too numerous to mention, who made this work possible through their encouragement and
suggestions for contributions. We would like, however, to mention the particular assistance
of Drs. Wesley C. Becker, Lloyd G. Humphreys, and Thomas W. Kennelly. Our thanks also
for the facilities provided by Educational Testing Service to L. K. in his year as USPHS
Visiting Scholar. Mrs. Alice Koenig, Mrs. Marguerite Somers, and Miss Elizabeth Rae Larson
were of enormous assistance in the preparation of the manuscript. Our greatest debt is to our
wives Rina and Miriam for their patient support throughout the time we worked on this
volume.

Urbana, Illinois   L. P. U.
Princeton, New Jersey   L. K.
February 1965

CONTENTS

CASE STUDIES IN BEHAVIOR MODIFICATION

INTRODUCTION

What Is Behavior Modification?

In defining *behavior modification* we follow the work of Robert Watson (1962, p. 19), who noted that behavior modification included many different techniques, all broadly related to the field of learning, *but learning with a particular intent, namely clinical treatment and change.*[1]

There are two important aspects of this definition. The first is the insistence that the basis of treatment stems from learning theory, which deals with the effect of experience on behavior, in Hilgard's (1962, p. 623) words: ". . . the process by which new or altered behavior comes about as a result of prior response, provided the changes cannot be attributed to growth or to temporary changes in the state of the organism (as in fatigue or under drugs)." The basis of behavior modification is a body of experimental work dealing with the relationship between changes in the environment and changes in the subject's responses.

The second aspect of behavior modification is a focus on behavior. As Watson notes (1962, p. 16), "Skinner made it possible to see verbal behavior as a response in its own right." Whether the behavior dealt with is verbal or motoric, whether it reflects immediate social needs or is highly symbolic and idiosyncratic, the focus of modification is behavior.

While these concepts may seem so obvious and so general as to be trivial, there are several immediate consequences that distinguish the approaches resulting from them from other forms of treatment. The first consequence is a difference between the methods by which behavior and evocative therapies are developed. Instead of starting with a treatment procedure and bringing in learning theory *after the fact* (compare Shoben, 1949; Dollard and Miller, 1950), it seems much more effective to start with concepts of learning and develop a program for behavior change based on them *before the fact*.

Behavior modification focuses on behavior that may be defined, following Hilgard (1962, p. 614) as: "Those activities of an organism that can be observed by another organism or by an experimenter's instruments." This definition is of vital importance. The working behavior therapist is likely to ask three questions: (a) what behavior is maladaptive, that is, what subject behaviors should be increased or decreased; (b) what environmental contingencies *currently* support the subject's behavior (either to maintain his undesirable behavior or to reduce the likelihood of his performing a more adaptive

[1] We will use the terms *behavior modification* and *behavior therapy* interchangeably in this essay to denote the modification of clinical or maladaptive behavior. *Behavior influence* (Krasner and Ullmann, in press) is the more generic term and includes advertising, brainwashing, institutional pressures, and so forth (as well as psychotherapy) as techniques of altering the subject's behavior, whether to increase adjustive behavior or not.

response); and (c) what environmental changes, usually reinforcing stimuli, may be manipulated to alter the subject's behavior.

In short, in the clinical setting behavior modification starts with the question, "What do we wish to accomplish through our application of learning theory?" If we are told that we should strengthen the subject's ego, we ask how would we know that his ego has been strengthened, what would he *do* differently. If we are then told that the subject would have fewer conflicts and repressions, increased libido, or no longer be fixated, we must ask again how would this be manifested in behavior, what measurable actions would be different.

This focus on behavior has been succinctly stated by Eysenck (1959): "Learning theory does not postulate any such 'unconscious causes,' but regards neurotic symptoms as simple learned habits; there is no neurosis underlying the symptom, but merely the symptom itself. *Get rid of the symptom and you have eliminated the neurosis.*"

These two sentences, like Watson's definition of behavior modification, lead to a number of major issues and differences in procedure. They imply that there is no distinction in the development of adjustive and maladjustive behavior and that both are to be understood through learning theory concepts. They imply a formulation of what is meant by maladjustive behavior or symptomatic behavior that differs markedly from the conceptualizations that have been popular for the last seventy-five years. They imply a therapy focused on overt subject responses and the stimuli that control these responses. They forego intrapsychic conflicts, repressions, and other dynamic explanations. Finally, there are implications as to the proper procedures for affecting behavioral change, particularly concepts of underlying intrapsychic conflicts and return or substitution of symptoms. These issues will be the center of our discussion in the next sections.

To summarize, behavior modification is the application of the results of learning theory and experimental psychology to the problem of altering maladaptive behavior. The focus of attention is overt behavior, and, in terms of both the development and change of behavior, no distinction is made between adaptive and maladaptive responses.

THE MEDICAL MODEL

To appreciate fully the implications of behavior modification, we must discuss the concepts and procedures from which it departs. We shall do so by discussing the medical model in general terms and devoting particular attention to its impact on concepts of maladaptive behavior in terms of symptom formation, categorization, and the process of therapy. The medical model is currently the most widely accepted formulation of maladaptive behavior and the behavior modification viewpoint has developed as an alternative within this context.

By the disease or medical model we mean that the individual's behavior is considered peculiar, abnormal, or diseased, because of some underlying cause. The analogy is made to physical medicine in which germs, viruses, lesions, and other insults foreign to the normal working of the organism lead to the production of symptoms. This approach represented a major breakthrough in physical medicine during the nineteenth century. It permitted effective specific treatment of ailments where before the history of medicine had been almost completely the story of placebo (Shapiro, 1960) or prescription of nonspecific remedies that depended on suggestion and spontaneous remissions. A major statement of the nineteenth-century medical model may make the position clearer and offer some insight into the basis of thinking such as Freud's, which later had such a major impact on evocative psychotherapy.

Freud's first training was in physiology and his major professor was Brucke. To quote Jones (1953, pp. 40–41), "Brucke's institute was an important part indeed of that far reaching scientific movement best known as Helmholtz's School of Medicine. The amazing story of this scientific school started in the early forties with the friendship of Emil Du Bois-Reymond (1818–1896) and Ernst Brucke (1819–1892), soon joined by Herman Helmholtz (1821–1894) and Carl Ludwig (1816–1895). From the very beginning this group was driven forward by a veritable crusading spirit. In 1842 Du Bois wrote: 'Brucke and I pledged a solemn oath to put into effect this truth: No other forces than the common physical-chemical ones are active within the organism. In those cases which cannot at the time be explained by these forces one has either to find the specific way or form of their action by means of the physical-mathematical method or to assume new forces equal in dignity to the chemical-physical forces inherent in matter, reducible to the force of attraction and repulsion.' "

"Within twenty-five or thirty years they achieved complete domination over the thinking of the German physiologists and medical teachers, gave intensive stimulus to science everywhere, and solved some of the old problems forever."

The following account of the physical physiology that captivated the student Freud is abstracted from the introductory pages (of Brucke's Lectures on Physiology):

> Physiology is the science of organisms as such. Organisms differ from dead material entities in action—machines—in possessing the faculty of assimilation, but they are all phenomena of the physical world; systems of atoms, moved by forces, according to the principle of the conservation of energy discovered by Robert Mayer in 1842, neglected for 20 years, and then popularized by Helmholtz. The sum of forces (motive forces and potential forces) remains constant in every isolated system. The real causes are symbolized in science by the word "force." The less we know about them, the more kinds of forces do we have to distinguish: mechanical, electrical, magnetic forces, light, heat. Progress in knowledge reduces them to two—attraction and repulsion. . . .
>
> The spirit and content of these lectures correspond closely with the words Freud used in 1926 to characterize psychoanalysis in its dynamic aspect: "The forces assist or inhibit one another, combine with one another, enter into compromises with one another, etc. . . ."
>
> It has often been assumed that Freud's psychological theories date from his contact with Charcot or Breuer or even later. On the contrary, it can be shown that the principles on which he constructed his theories were those he had acquired as a medical student under Brucke's influence. (Jones, 1953, Pp. 41–45.)

This is what the most dominant medical model looked like, and the background of its most famous exemplar in psychiatry, Freud. The concept of underlying cause, symptom formation as symbolic, fixated libido, and all the rest stem directly from this closed system of conservation of energy, of combinations of forces, and of attraction and repulsion.

Szasz (1960, 1961 a and b) has written extensively on the concepts involved in what he labels the "Myth of Mental Illness," both from an historical viewpoint and from a semantic-philosophical one. Of special importance is that he traces the work of Charcot in bringing neurosis within the realm of medicine. Szasz emphasizes that this event made good sense in the context of the nineteenth century but is, in the twentieth century, an obstacle rather than an aid in the understanding or treatment of this group of people. Szasz would prefer a communication, role, and game-theoretical model approach to the amelioration of maladaptive behavior.

Another description, one centered on the treatment of hospitalized psychiatric patients, stems from Bockoven's work on "Moral Treatment in American Psychiatry" (1963). Bockoven points out that the work of Pinel, Tuke, and their followers in America led to higher remission rates in the early nineteenth century than have since been achieved. Bockoven goes to great length to document the efficacy of this treatment that occurred immediately prior to the advent of the disease model. Some quotes from Bockoven (1963, p. 76) will describe the treatment:

"Moral treatment might be defined as organized group-living in which the integration and continuity of work, play, and social activities produce a meaningful total life experience in which growth of individual capacity to enjoy life has maximum opportunity."

"The moral therapist acted toward his patients as though they were mentally well. He believed that kindness and forebearance were essential in dealing with them. He also believed in firmness and persistence in impressing on patients the idea that a change to more acceptable behavior was expected."

Bockoven quotes from Pinel's "Treatise on Insanity" at length and one excerpt is particularly germane (Bockoven, 1963, p. 34), "The successful application of moral regimen exclusively gives great weight to the supposition, that, in the majority of instances, there is no organic lesion of the brain nor of the cranium."

The breakdown of moral treatment in America was the result of a number of causes, all "enlightened." The first was the introduction of the medical model, reflected in the work (Bockoven, 1963, pp. 40–41) of Dr. John P. Gray:

Dr. John P. Gray was appointed superintendent in 1854, and in 1855 he assumed editorship of the American Journal of Insanity. He held both posts for 30 years. He insisted that insanity was always due to physical lesion, and became the greatest single influence in swinging psychiatry back to the pre-Pinel position.

Dr. Gray was the first to introduce the microscope into American mental hospitals for the study of post-mortem material in the search for the etiology of mental disease. He also took the role of leadership in changing mental hospital organization to treat the mentally ill patient as *physically* ill. He placed great emphasis on rest, diet, proper room temperature, and ventilation. One of his accomplishments was the invention of a rotary fan for the ventilation of the Utica State Hospital. . . . He made a sharp distinction between mind and brain, categorically stating that insanity "is simply a bodily disease in which the mind is disturbed more or less profoundly, because the brain is involved in the sickness either primarily or secondarily. The mind is not, itself, ever diseased. It is incapable of disease, or of its final consequence, death."

This dualism, between body and mind led to *moralistic* arguments, notably that Mind is eternal, superior to bodily structure, and beyond the wear and tear of mortal being. In short, the Soul could not be at fault and obviously, therefore, mental illness was a result of physical disorder.

In the same period, Dorothea Dix's crusade bore fruit and large centralized mental hospitals were built and supplanted smaller structures located in the patients' communities. The waves of immigration of the nineteenth century led to a different type of mental patient, one less readily identified with by the psychiatrist and less responsive to the values of the staff.

But the major factor was a model that, having assumed that the patient was physically sick, directed attention to diagnosis, legal questions, and brain pathology. There could be no cure without first discovering the etiology of the illness, and changes in the patients—spontaneous remissions—were slighted, and one feels at times, considered unfortunate accidents. As the size of hospitals increased the ratio of staff to patients decreased, the expense per patient per day decreased markedly in contrast with the cost of living, and, needless to say, the self-validation of the proposal of the difficulty of treating mental illness was well under way. In this situation, the patient was viewed as physically sick and was expected to fulfill the role of a passive, irresponsible, and rather boring location of an interesting but as yet not understood disease. There was a complete shift from the procedure of treating the patient as fit and expecting more acceptable behavior to the concept that the patient was by definition a danger to himself and others. Normal stimulation was not considered vital or necessary. The space designed for treatment had to be used for custodial purposes because failure of treatment increased the number of patients who remained in the hospital. The outcome was the chronic patient, deprived of sensory stimulation of all types, seated quietly for years in isolation among hundreds of other similarly quiet, withdrawn, uncomplaining cases waiting for a treatment yet to be devised. On the one hand the patient was extinguished for normal behaviors while on the other hand he was trained in the safe, clean, quiet, dependent values of the inmate and patient roles.

At this point, we may summarize some general concepts of the medical model that will be foci of discussion in the immediately succeeding paragraphs. The first is that there is an underlying *cause* and consequently maladaptive behaviors cannot be treated directly because they are products of these causes. Second, changed behavior is not really important unless the "real" trouble has been dealt with. While we shall return to this question when we discuss symptom substitution, it is worth noting that just as in the nineteenth century a patient might not be released because he had not been treated, so it is not uncommon today for a patient to continue to be hospitalized because he has not achieved "insight into his problems." It is instructive that dichotomies are made between "treatment" and "administrative" staffs (Stanton and Schwarz, 1954) with an implied distinction between the medical specialty of the former and the custodial nature of the latter. In actuality, the administrative staff has control over many reinforcing stimuli that could facilitate the work of changing behavior. Third, the distinction between what the subject does, his behavior, and what the clinician expects, or knows to be there, is blurred, and failure to find the expected cause merely confirms the severity of the problem. Aside from the implications for treatment, the medical model may become an obstacle in the way of research through a vast literature of iatrogenic irrelevancies. We will discuss this more fully when we deal with psychodiagnostics.

Symptom Formation within the Medical Model

If, as "mental health" advertisements would have it, "mental illness is like any other illness," then a specific formulation of the meaning and development of maladaptive behavior would follow. We will use material from six popular textbooks on "abnormal psychology" to present this formulation. The medical view of symptoms is pertinently summarized by Thorpe and Katz (1948, p. 166), who write: "Mental symptoms *are signs of disorder or maladjustment* that must be studied and evaluated to determine the reasons for their presence; they are not *the disorder* to be labeled and treated."

The explicit analogy to medical practice involved in this formulation of an underlying cause that must be treated may be observed in another passage from Thorpe and Katz (1948, pp. 161–162):

> At one time the symptoms and syndromes were themselves regarded as constituting a disorder. Many medical doctors endeavored to treat merely the symptoms of both physical diseases and psychological disorders. . . . no attempt was made to discover or remove the causes responsible for the appearance of the symptom. Symptoms are relatively easy to detect. . . . Underlying causes are, however, frequently difficult to locate. . . .
>
> To the clinician the cause—or causes—of a basic personality maladjustment is the all-important factor: to the patient it is the symptoms or syndrome which seem crucial. The complaint concerning which the patient seeks help is the symptomatological description of his disorder. The patient frequently finds it difficult to believe that his symptoms should not be treated directly and that causal factors of a rather complex nature must be located and treated. Most psychological symptoms, as they are known today, are the expressions or reactions of an individual in a difficult or stress-producing situation. . . .
>
> All mental symptoms not of organic origin are significant and meaningful. In the main, they are evidences of psychological danger, or repression, or of threats to the individual's sense of personal worth or feeling of security. . . . It has been deduced from clinical evidence that the symptoms exhibited by a given patient are *the most "economical" mechanisms available under the circumstances* and they are probably the least harmful that he could have "adopted."

This theme is also illustrated by the following quote from Hutt and Gibby (1957, pp. 78–79) which also introduces concepts of the complicated relationship between underlying cause and overt symptom (an association so complicated that it seems to defy experimental verification), the futility of symptom removal because of symptom substitution, repression, childhood developmental experiences still active at an unconscious level, and the partial gratification of unconscious impulses through symptoms:

> But it is the deeper meaning of the symptoms to the individual that is so important to us. . . . Symptoms should be regarded primarily as indications of the fact that there is a malfunctioning of the particular personality. They tell us that an individual is disturbed in some way, in somewhat the same way that a fever may serve as an indicator of some form of somatic illness. . . . There is no simple relationship between the symptoms that a person shows and the basic underlying reason for the development of those symptoms. Two people may show the same symptom, yet there may be entirely different underlying causes; or on the other hand, two people may show markedly different symptoms and yet have the same basic underlying disturbances that result in the symptom production. Often

we may remove symptoms very readily without at all correcting the underlying personality disturbances. To remove the symptom in this manner does not necessarily help the person, as he may often develop different sets of symptoms to enable him to deal with his particular problems. . . .

It was stressed that unacceptable emotional qualities which were traumatic to the individual and which caused him psychological pain were excluded from consciousness through the process of repression. Of course, most of these repressed experiences are centered around the infantile and childhood developmental experiences of the individual. It was also emphasized that, even though these experiences could not consciously be recalled, they were still quite active at the unconscious level of mental life. . . . In general symptoms thus represent substitutes on the part of the person for the id impulses that cannot be directly expressed. The symptoms developed and shown by the individual play a very symbolic part in his life. . . . The unconscious material that cannot be expressed tends to be very deeply repressed. . . . Unconscious impulses are gratified by the individual in a . . . distorted form as symptoms, so that in this changed way they are now acceptable to the ego. There are very strong unconscious drives within the individual toward retention and persistence of the symptoms, since the symptoms symbolically serve to gratify the unattainable, and therefore repressed, wishes.

Another quotation will further document this thesis and will illustrate the concepts that are called into play to buttress the thesis. Cameron (1963, p. 452) writes: "Symptoms are formed, as we have seen, when the balance of forces within the personality system is disturbed, when infantile conflicts are reactivated, and when ego organizations are threatened with disintegration."[2] He further writes: "We shall present the phases of neurotic symptom formation in the following sequence:

1. increased tension and anxiety because of frustration, loss, threat, danger, or increased drive;
2. threat of ego disintegration;
3. partial regression to main levels of fixation;
4. reactivation of infantile conflicts and return of the repressed;
5. defensive transformation and secondary elaboration within the ego; and
6. final emergence of the symptom."

Two further brief quotations will serve to demonstrate that this is not an isolated viewpoint or straw man. Noyes and Kolb (1958, p. 96) write: "To discover the meaning of those unusual personality manifestations that we call symptoms and the functions they are performing in the life history of the patient, we must ascertain the needs and meaningful factors or situations that led to their production." R. W. White (1956, p. 266), states: "Symptoms are the surface phenomena of neurosis. . . . Neurotic breakdown occurs when the patient is driven out of his protective organization and forced back upon the neurotic nucleus."

---

[2] What is involved in "the balance of forces" and "ego disintegration" may be inferred by the reader from Cameron, (1963, p. 452): "When ego functions of energy redistribution within and tension discharge without do not work well the personality system is in for trouble. Untamed id impulses and unconscious ego fantasies threaten to gain expression in preconscious and conscious ego organizations, thus initiating a certain degree of disruption or disintegration. Superego pressures mount, partly in response to the threatening id impulses, partly because of beginning ego disintegration which makes ego boundaries less effectual in all directions."

In short, the current view is that symptoms are the results of underlying causes and not the proper focus of treatment. An immediate deduction from this view is that the causes must be treated, and the form of treatment is what Cameron calls expressive therapy, an interpersonal experience with an accepting therapist. This point has been succinctly put by White (1956, p. 339), "Nothing that we have studied violates the general principle, agreed upon by all schools, that the essence of psychotherapy is a corrective emotional experience."

Coleman (1956, p. 225) is very explicit in deducing the therapeutic position based on the traditional or dynamic viewpoint.

... psychological treatment ... focuses on (1) helping the patient to understand the dynamic significance of his symptoms—how they came about and why he uses them—and (2) helping him to strengthen his personality and find more adequate and effective means of dealing with his problems....

The first major obstacle is the resistance of the patient to being cured. What the neurotic really wants is to be cured of his symptoms without having to face his problems or to give up the more or less unconscious satisfactions which the symptoms obtain for him. Thus he frequently insists on discussing his symptoms at great length, seemingly in a sincere attempt to help the therapist get a clear view of them....

In some cases the patient's symptoms may temporarily disappear so that he is convinced it is unnecessary to return for further treatment. For this reason the immediate disappearance of symptoms is often looked upon as a poor prognostic sign. In still other cases the symptoms may seemingly become intensified and the patient may report that he is becoming worse and has decided to consult another therapist. Thus, it is often very difficult to overcome the patient's resistance to the actual facing of his problems; yet this is required in any effective therapy.

A common pitfall in therapy is the treatment of symptoms rather than underlying personality difficulties.... unless the underlying personality conflicts are properly handled by psychotherapy, the same neurotic symptoms or others designed to defend the patient from his problems will soon appear.

Given this orientation, Coleman (1956, p. 541) ably summarizes the aims of evocative or expressive psychotherapy:

Psychotherapy is directed toward helping the patient to achieve a more adequate personality adjustment. This may mean reinforcing his existing ego defenses or it may mean varying degrees of personality restructuralization....

In general, psychotherapy aims toward personality growth in the direction of maturity, competence, and self-actualization. This usually requires some measure of achievement of the following:
1. increased insight;
2. the resolution of disabling conflicts;
3. increased self-acceptance;
4. more efficient techniques for coping with problems; and
5. the general strengthening of the ego structure of the patient along lines of adequacy and security.

In summary, we may say that given such a model, it follows that the importance ascribed to the overt difficulty or maladaptive behavior will logically follow a medical model. Overt maladaptive behavior is considered to be symptomatic, in the dictionary definition of the medical term, "indicative of the presence of a particular disease." It is the disease then that is treated, and this procedure has a number of consequences. The next part of this section deals with psychiatric categorization or nosology: the identification of the particular disease presumed to be present. Next, we discuss the concept of "symptom substitution." Following a medical model, if the disease is not treated it will continue to be manifested for it is presumed that symptomatic treatment is neither efficient nor enduringly effective. Finally, we will discuss the process of treatment as it relies upon and is affected by a medical model. In later sections the effect of the medical model on the therapist is dealt with in terms of his conception of himself and his treatment, and upon the recipient of the treatment in terms of the subject's role, how he learns it, and how it affects his behavior in therapy.

Classification of Maladaptive Behavior within a Medical Model

Because overt maladaptive behavior is considered in a medical model to be symptomatic or indicative of the presence of a particular disease, and because this disease rather than the overt behavior must be treated, the categorization of the behaviors indicative of diseases becomes of crucial importance. It is these diseases and not the behaviors that are the focuses of treatment. Because it is rare for a person to display all the aspects of the syndrome and no other maladjustive behavior, in practice a limited and variable number of symptoms are considered sufficient to justify the designation of a particular form of mental illness, and those maladaptive behaviors that are present but not considered within the specific syndrome are ignored or rationalized. Once the diagnosis has been arrived at there is a presumption that all people so classified share basic common traits in terms of underlying illness, treatment of choice, and prognosis. It is important to note that the interest and emphasis on psychiatric nosology is a relatively recent trend and is associated with the period of the development of the medical model. The development of major concepts of psychiatric nosology was the work of the latter half of the nineteenth century and is most closely associated with the work of Kraepelin (Zilboorg and Henry, 1941). A general view of both the presumed need for such a system and the typical dissatisfaction of workers in the field with it may be illustrated by the following quote from Cameron (1963, p. 17): "When it comes to communicating with someone else, however, the formulation may be so vague and so inclusive that it only communicates confusion. This, too, is an old tale. About a century ago, experts working in this general area decided that classification was worse than useless. They lumped all psychopathology together and called it by one name. It was not long before this solution proved vain. The groupings began again; and they have continued to evolve up to the present day."

While we shall discuss at length a social reinforcement and role formulation of maladaptive behavior, at this time, the most important point we wish to make is that nosologies are products of medical sociology and reflect social pressures on physicians in terms of the task imposed upon them in given times and places. An important validation of this point is derived from a study of the "Diagnostic and Statistical Manual: Mental Disorders," (1952) prepared by the Committee on Nomenclature and Statistics of the American Psychiatric Association. This book presents the current standard diagnostic system of the American Psychiatric Association. In the Manual's foreword, (pp. vi and vii) we find a piece of history and sociology of the sort so important in Szasz's (1961b) thesis:

> The Armed Forces faced an increasing psychiatric case load as mobilization and the war went on. There was need to account accurately for all causes of morbidity, hence the need for suitable diagnosis for every case seen by the psychiatrist, a situation not faced in civilian life. Only about 10% of the total cases seen fell into any of the categories ordinarily seen in public mental hospitals. Military psychiatrists, induction station psychiatrists, and Veterans Administration psychiatrists, found themselves operating within the limits of a nomenclature specifically not designed for 90% of the cases handled. Relatively minor personality disturbances, which became of importance only in the military setting, had to be classified as "Psychopathic Personality. . . ." The official system of nomenclature rapidly became untenable.

The solution to this difficulty was the development of medical entities that had not previously been recognized such as personality trait disturbance, personality pattern disturbance, and transient situational personality disorders.

Throughout the revised nomenclature, a particular theoretical orientation was accepted as *de facto* truth. For example (p. 13), "For this nomenclature, a psychoneurotic reaction may be defined as one in which the personality, in its struggle for adjustment to internal and external stresses, utilizes the mechanisms listed above to handle the anxiety created." Note the reification of the concept "personality" that *struggles* with stresses and *utilizes* mechanisms to *handle* anxiety. The term, schizophrenic reaction, residual type is applied to "patients," who after a definite schizophrenic reaction, have improved sufficiently to be able to get along in the community, but who continue to show "residual" disturbances. If a person did not have information about the patient's prior history, he would not be able to make this diagnosis, for the person's *behavior* at the time would not differ from a great number of other people. There is then the implication, noted in our discussion of the breakdown of the Moral Treatment, of schizophrenia as an illness that may remit, but which is, at present, not cured or curable.

The concept of underlying causes is also seen in the psychophysiologic disorders where "These reactions represent visceral expression of affect which may be thereby largely prevented from being conscious. The symptoms are due to a chronic and exaggerated state of the normal physiological expression of emotion, with the feeling, or subjective part, repressed." (p. 29.) The concept of symptom and dynamics is nowhere better exemplified than in the definition of "anxiety," the thing the personality "struggles to handle by utilizing mechanisms." On page 31 of the Manual, " 'Anxiety' in psychoneurotic disorders is a danger signal felt and perceived by the conscious portion of the personality. It is produced by a threat from within the personality (for example, by supercharged repressed emotions . . .)." Because it is so central to the concept of the need to treat underlying causes, and the concept of symptom substitution if this is not done, the formulation of phobia deserves to be quoted: "The anxiety of these patients becomes detached from a specific idea, object, or situation in the daily life and is displaced to some symbolic idea or situation in the form of a specific neurotic fear." (p. 33.) Finally, in dealing with the Personality Disorders, "Although the groupings are largely descriptive, the division has been made partially on the basis of the dynamics of personality development. The Personality pattern disturbances are considered deep-seated disturbances, with little room for regression." (p. 34.) In discussing Transient Situation Personality Disorders, we find that in the presence of good adaptive capacity, recession of the symptoms generally occurs when the stress diminishes. However, "Persistent failure to resolve will indicate a more severe underlying disturbance. . . ." (p. 40.) The point is the use of an "underlying cause" as an explanatory device, and that the overt behavior is not used to make the diagnosis. The idea that improper treatment rather than an underlying cause may produce failure to "resolve" a problem is not considered.

Within this schema, observation is distorted. For example, (p. 46) "Some psychiatric diagnoses are incompatible with certain other diagnoses and will not be recorded as existing together, such as psychoneurotic and psychotic reactions." By this concept, the patients in the papers by Cowden and Ford (9),* and Walton (1960b), are inconceivable.

It is not within the scope of this book to deal further with the medical model or the problem of diagnosis. However, it should be pointed out that the application of these diagnostic concepts is far from reliable (Ash, 1949; Schmidt and Fonda, 1956), that deductions based on them are not substantiated (Zimet and Brackbill, 1956; Ullmann and Hunrichs, 1958); and that factor-analytic investigation of actual behavior by patients indicates the heterogeneity of behaviors manifested by subjects with the same diagnoses (Wittenborn, Holzberg, and Simon, 1953; Dreger *et al.,* 1964; Lorr *et al.,* 1962; Zigler and Phillips, 1961).

The point to be made in this section was that the medical model leads to categorization of persons in terms of presumed underlying illnesses. These illnesses, however, are developed on a descriptive basis without the validation of either a clearly defined disease or a definite pattern of behavior. Rather, the classifications that have developed seem to be the result of social and historical pressures and the application of a particular viewpoint that has been presumed but not demonstrated to be valid.

The Process of Therapy within a Medical Model

Adherence to a medical model has distinct effects on therapist behavior. A first effect is the focus on underlying causes. In the present section we wish to discuss the medical model in terms of what the therapist does to alter the underlying causes that are central to his interest.

There is an assumption in the evocative or expressive therapy that follows the medical model that if the therapist establishes the proper atmosphere, *in the very nature of the patient's disorder,* certain therapeutic benefits will result. In both Rogerian and Freudian therapy, the therapist is "permissive," "non-judgmental," and "non-evaluative." The therapist is not critical and is directive only in regard to matters of technique, for example, the fundamental rule of free association. The therapist changes the patient without influencing him. This seeming paradox is explicable only if the patient brings to therapy some basic or underlying problem that will in and of itself generate therapeutically meaningful behavior. In Rogerian therapy there is assumed to be an urge to self-enhancement, self-consistency, and self-actualization. The basic problem is conceptualized as denial of reality and restriction of experiencing. If only given the proper accepting environment, the person will once again continue his growth. In the Freudian school, the basic problem is a biological urge that has been thwarted but that continues

* Simple numerals in parentheses, as here, refer to cases in this volume.

to strive for expression in the form of dreams, slips of the tongue, and the incomplete repression or substitute gratifications that are called symptoms.

It is hypothesized that if the patient is placed in the novel, accepting psychotherapeutic situation, behavior that was previously unlikely, because it had been associated with punishment, will eventually occur. The new behavior, because it meets a different reception, increases in frequency or, if socially unacceptable, is extinguished. This formulation permits the therapist to play a set role and to emit responses that do not vary from patient to patient. While we will discuss later traditional or evocative therapy as a form of behavior therapy, in *theory,* the therapist does not reinforce the subject in any systematic manner. The situation follows a medical rather than a psychological model because therapy, like medicine, is given to the patient who then responds. Just as there are medicines of varying strengths, so there are therapists of varying competence, but the process can no more be changed than that of birth. In birth, the obstetrician may speed up or delay or even terminate the process, but he cannot alter the basic situation. In short, in a medical model, the therapist facilitates and assists a process composed of the underlying cause and the therapeutic situation. This may become clearer through a quotation from Rogers (1951, Pp. 147–149) within which a specific case is discussed.

> One of the most characteristic and perhaps one of the most important changes in therapy is the bringing into awareness of experiences of which heretofor the client has not been conscious. What, psychologically, occurs when the individual thus deals with "repressed" material? Our experience would indicate that it is best described in terms of greater differentiation of perception, and more adequate symbolization. . . . If we examine this sequence from a psychological point of view, it would seem clear that she has all along been experiencing, viscerally, feelings of opposition toward her husband. The crucial missing element is the adequate symbolization of these experiences. . . . It also seems clear that the basic reason for the phenomenon of "repression" or "denial of experience" is that the adequate symbolization of the experience in question would be definitely and often deeply in contradiction to the self concept of the individual. . . . Hence such visceral sensations must be given a distorted symbolization, or not be symbolized at all. It would also appear that the release of "repressions," or the bringing into awareness of denied experiences, is not simply a matter of probing for these, either by the client or the therapist. It is not until the concept of self is sufficiently revised to accept them, that they can be openly symbolized. . . . In practice, it is noted that the first step toward uncovering such material is usually the perception of inconsistencies. . . . *When such discrepancies are clearly perceived, the client is unable to leave them alone.* He is motivated to find out the reason for the discrepancy. . . . Although this process of bringing experience into adequately symbolized awareness is recognized by several therapeutic orientations as being an important and basic element of therapy, there is as yet no objective investigation of it. From a descriptive clinical point of view, however, we may say that successful therapy seems to entail the bringing into awareness, in an adequately differentiated and accurately symbolized way, those experiences and feelings which are currently in contradiction to the client's concept of self. (Italics by the editors.)

Where in the psychological model the therapist actively selects and systematically reinforces specific behaviors, in the medical model the therapist's activity is far more diffuse and not contingent upon the patient's actions. Answers to questions of what the evocative therapist does and how he affects change are given in terms of a *process* within a medical model and involves setting the time and place for changed behavior, but not in fostering or directing it.

The Hypothesis of Symptom Substitution

There is one explicit and critical deduction that can be drawn from the medical model and its emphasis on underlying disease. We shall refer to this hypothesis as symptom substitution. Whereas in behavior modification based on a psychological model maladaptive behavior is treated directly, in the medical model the overt maladaptive responses are presumed to be symptomatic of some underlying problem. We have presented the deduction of symptom substitution in our quotations from Thorpe and Katz (1948), Hutt and Gibby (1957) and Coleman (1956). Dollard and Miller (1950, p. 385) translated the Freudian model into the language of learning theory and in a section entitled "Increased drive from interfering with symptom" write:

"According to our hypothesis, a learned symptom must produce a certain amount of reduction in the state of high drive motivating it. Therefore, interfering with the symptom by any of the foregoing methods will be expected to throw the patient back into a state of high drive and conflict." (By foregoing methods, these authors refer to incompatible responses, hypnosis, punishment, and "transference cures.")

If this hypothesis were true—that there is indeed symptom substitution if only behavior and not "underlying cause" or "drive" is treated—then traditional therapy rather than behavior modification would be the procedure of choice. *The first argument against the theory of symptom substitution is that there is little, if any, evidence for it.* To quote Yates (1958a), "Considering the significant role such a distinction has played in clinical psychology, experimental demonstration of its existence is singularly lacking." Failure to obtain evidence for a theory does not necessarily invalidate it, for in an inductive empirical science one can only reject the null hypothesis and can never prove it. However, as Yates made clear, if the theory is blandly and completely accepted, no conflicting data will be collected. For example, Yates pointed out that while there was considerable evidence for the value of the symptomatic treatment of enuresis, this technique was rarely if ever used in the British Isles because of the acceptance of the concept of symptom substitution. Only by treating maladaptive behavior directly can we find out the facts about symptom substitution. As behavior modification approaches have developed, there has been a steady accumulation of evidence that symptom substitution rarely occurs and when it does, (if indeed it is genuine symptom substitution as will be noted below), it is readily amenable to treatment (Rachman, 1963a).

In the majority of cases of behavior modification, including those reprinted in this volume, we have what Stevenson and Wolpe (1960) have called "white crows," exceptions that indicate that not all crows are black, in other words, that symptom substitution certainly need not be the rule. Eysenck (1959) made a statement on this matter to which five additional years of support may be added at the time of this writing:

How about the return of symptoms? I have made a thorough search of the literature dealing with behaviour therapy with this particular point in view. Many psychoanalytically trained therapists using these methods have been specially on the outlook for the return of symptoms, or the emergence of alternative ones; yet neither they nor any of the other practitioners have found anything of this kind to happen except in the most rare and unusual cases.

A first point, then, is that symptom substitution, which is a direct deduction from the medical model and is very influential in determining the strategy of expressive therapy, is rarely if ever observed. A second point is that if maladaptive behaviors are observed after treatment, there are more parsimonious and reasonable interpretations than ones involving symptom substitution. First there may be a matter of resensitization. There is nothing that precludes a person from undergoing new and trying experiences. Just as a person who goes skiing, breaks a leg, recuperates, and then next year breaks it again either while skiing or walking across a Midwestern college campus during winter, is not properly cited as an example of symptom substitution, so behavior modification does not guarantee a future life free from stress. Behavior modification may lead to a life more resistant to stress as techniques of relaxation, assertion, or other adaptive behaviors generalize, but it never leads to a life free of stress.

Second, the maladaptive behavior that is worked with may be but one of a number of maladaptive patterns of response in the subject's hierarchy. Particularly if extinction (the major technique of evocative therapy as distinct from reconditioning, shaping, chaining, that is, teaching new adaptive responses) is used, it is possible that a succession of maladaptive behaviors will be observed. This is not symptom substitution. For example, one of the authors' students reported a series of behaviors by a child at a summer camp for handicapped children. At first the child was self-punishing, hitting, slapping, and biting himself; when this did not cause the counselors concern, he threw tantrums in which he beat his head against the ground or trees; he gave this up and next took off his clothes in public but this led to no counselor behavior other than putting him to bed (that is, clothes off meant bedtime); giving up the undressing behavior, he stole food off other children's plates even though his own was heaped; to avoid imitation by other children, food stealing led to the child's being placed in a room to eat by himself and in this situation he began defecating and smearing feces over himself, the walls, floors, and his own belongings. Without creating special concern on the part of the counselors, this behavior ceased after five days, and the child took to piling all the children's shoes together. Sorting shoes became a morning game for the group and after a week the shoe game stopped. This was the last of a spectacular series of antisocial behaviors, none of which were reinforced and none of which became permanent. For the remainder of the camp session the child engaged in encouragingly adaptive responses.

The point is that the technique was one of extinction, and a repertoire had to be extinguished, item by item, until adaptive behavior could be reinforced when it occurred. As a subject finds that his prior modes of behavior are no longer successful, he may emit behaviors that have been less likely in the past but that may also be maladaptive.

A frequent statement made by evocative therapists is that the person must be changed in some basic manner before he returns to the situation in which he developed the maladaptive behavior. While we will discuss this matter in greater detail in the section dealing directly with behavior modification, we may note that a different behavior is a genuine change of the person and is likely to alter the situation to which he returns. The person may be taught, as illustrated by Sulzer's article (19) in this volume, to behave in ways that will maximize positive reinforcement. Further, the articles in the present volume will illustrate the direct alteration of behavior by friends, parents, teachers, nurses, and students to provide environmental support for a change by the subject.

Finally, behavior modification is not symptomatic treatment. At a first level, there is simply no place in a psychological model for the concept of symptom. At a more direct level, in terms of the symptom substitution hypothesis, behavior modification deals with stimuli by altering their environmental significance. It is generally far more effective to alter a response to a stimulus than to deal with the response without reference to the stimuli that lead to its emission. A final alternative explanation for the symptom substitution hypothesis is that not all the relevant stimuli have been reconditioned. An illustration of this may be found in the work by Bond and Hutchison (26) reprinted in this volume.

To summarize, a concept of symptom substitution is widely accepted by therapists who follow a medical model. This hypothesis drastically affects their strategy of treatment. However, all the evidence would seem to indicate that symptom substitution is rarely observed. When such occurrences do happen, however, we have offered a number of alternative, more parsimonious explanations for the observed phenomena.

THE PSYCHOLOGICAL MODEL

We have discussed the medical model, currently the most popular formulation of maladaptive behavior. Behavior modification following a psychological or behavioral model is offered as an alternative that has grown up as both a reaction to the medical model and as a form of treatment to replace it. In the following parts of this section, we shall discuss the psychological model, starting with a brief review of elementary learning concepts. This review will be at a level that the student who used an elementary text such as Kendler (1962), Munn (1961), Hilgard (1962), or Morgan (1961) should have no difficulty. Next, we shall take up the major topics we have discussed in terms of the medical model: formulation of maladaptive behavior and the alteration of maladaptive behavior. Specifically, the parts of this section will deal with learning concepts, the formulation of maladaptive behavior, methods of behavior modification, and characteristics of the behavior therapist. The burden of the argument throughout will be that maladaptive behavior is both learned and unlearned in the same manner as all other behavior.

Learning Theory Concepts

At present, only the broadest, most thoroughly established concepts, those common to all learning theories, are used in a clinical setting. This may be supported by two examples of authors writing about the clinical application of learning theory. Dollard and Miller (1950) state: "All that is needed for the present purpose is a reinforcement theory in the broadest sense of those words," and Eysenck (1959): "Those points about which argument rages are usually of academic interest rather than of practical importance . . . there would be general agreement in any particular case about the optimum methods of achieving a quick rate of conditioning, or extinction. . . ."

In this book, most of those authors dealing with hospitalized subjects or children are likely to use terms derived from the work of B. F. Skinner, while authors of articles dealing with adult neurotic or sexual problems are more likely to use the language and concepts of Hull's system. One of the authors (Patterson, 31) in giving the rationale on which he based his treatment, makes use of concepts drawn from Guthrie. The point is that psychologists engaged in behavior modification make use of a variety of learning theories, but their actual operations can be described with ease by any one of a number of learning theories, the fine points that differentiate the theories being relatively minute and not at present reflected in psychologists' behavior in clinical settings.

Basic to concepts of learning is the acquisition of a functional connection between an environmental stimulus and some subject response. Two major, albeit parallel, forms of learning may be noted: classical, or Pavlovian, or respondent conditioning, in which the stimulus elicits the response, and operant conditioning in which the subject must emit the response to the situation prior to the environmental event that becomes associated with and alters its frequency of occurrence in the future either by contiguity or reinforcement.[3]

In the Pavlovian or respondent conditioning situation, a stimulus that initially has no power to elicit a respondent behavior may come to have such power if it is associated with a stimulus that does have the power to elicit the respondent. In this situation, the pairing of the conditioned and the unconditioned stimuli is called *reinforcement* because any tendency for the response to the conditioned stimulus is facilitated by the presence of the unconditioned stimulus and the response to it. Once formed, the conditioned response undergoes systematic changes in strength depending upon the arrangement of the environment. If the unconditioned stimulus is repeatedly omitted, the conditioned response gradually diminishes, and the repetition of the conditioned stimulus without reinforcement is called *extinction*. This is not a passive disappearance, but rather there is learned an inhibition or tendency not to respond. When a conditioned response to one stimulus has been acquired, other similar stimuli will also evoke the response. This observed behavior leads to the concept of *generalization,* a reaction to novel situations in accordance with their degree of similarity to familiar ones. The amount of generalization decreases as the second stimulus becomes less similar to the original conditioned stimulus. A process complementary to generalization is *discrimination*. Conditioned discrimination is brought about through selective reinforcement and extinction so that of two stimuli similar to each other, the one reinforced (followed by the unconditioned stimulus) will elicit the respondent while the one extinguished will not elicit the respondent.

In general, respondent behavior is associated with involuntary musculature and operant behavior is associated with voluntary musculature. From birth, the individual makes massive, random responses, both verbal and motoric. He literally "operates" on his environment, hence the Skinnerian term "operant." An operant behavior that is closely

---

3 Guthrie's concept of contiguity avoids a theoretical difficulty involved in a strict reinforcement theory: we will say that a reinforcing stimulus is one which alters the frequency of an emitted behavior, and then at times imply that a reinforcing stimulus is defined by its effect on the frequency of behavior. This can easily lead to an embarrassing circular definition situation, which, as Dr. Lloyd Humphreys has pointed out to the authors, makes the contiguity theory preferable. While the authors agree, the preponderance of reinforcement theorists among authors in this volume led to the selection of the easier didactic procedure of a reinforcement rather than contiguity frame of reference.

followed by a reinforcing stimulus is likely to be changed in frequency of emission. If the reinforcing stimulus is a pleasant one, for example, one that reduces some current deprivation, it is a positive reinforcement, one that increases the likelihood, when the environmental setting is repeated, of the emission of the act with which it was associated. If the reinforcing stimulus is unpleasant or aversive, the emitted behavior is less likely to occur on repetition of the circumstances. Withdrawal of an aversive stimulus is a positive reinforcing event. It is crucial to state explicitly that frequency of emitted behavior is the prime operational definition of reinforcing stimuli (although latency and amplitude may, at times, be used also). Where positive reinforcement increases emission, and negative reinforcement decreases emission, repeated absence of reinforcement leads to extinction and a return of the rate of response emission to the level observed prior to reinforcement.

We may talk of discriminative stimuli: any stimulus that marks a time or place of reinforcement, positive or negative, being presented or removed, is a discriminative stimulus. A discriminative stimulus marks the time or place when an operant will have reinforcing consequences. A discriminative stimulus does not elicit a response. Elicitation is a characteristic that holds only for respondents, that is, the green traffic light, a discriminative stimulus, does not set people going across the street in the same way that a bright light flashed in their eyes constricts their pupils. A discriminated operant is one controlled by a preceding discriminative stimulus. A person who typically responds under the control of discriminative stimuli is said to be discriminating, and the procedure of bringing an operant under such control is called discrimination. Whenever some particular stimulus, through association with reinforcement, takes on discriminative stimulus properties, then other stimuli (although not directly associated with reinforcement) will also take on discriminative stimulus properties to the extent they are similar to the original discriminative stimulus. This phenomenon is called *operant stimulus generalization.*

Discriminative stimuli may become reinforcing. On highways in California pedestrians are able to press a traffic button that will change the light for them. In order to obtain the discriminative stimulus, the green light, they perform operants, that is, push buttons. Discriminative stimuli become reinforcers with adults and comprise the major environmental stimuli that are systematically associated with reinforcement, for example, money. Reinforcers that have achieved their reinforcing powers through their prior service as discriminative stimuli are called *acquired or secondary reinforcers.*

As will be seen in this volume, particularly in Ayllon's work with hospitalized psychiatric patients (2–5) and in the Harris, *et al.* work (39) with nursery school children, attention is a very strong acquired or secondary reinforcer. For the child, it is usually necessary to obtain an adult's attention before satisfaction of other needs can be obtained. Once established, a secondary reinforcer can strengthen responses other than those used during its original establishment, and can do so with motives other than the motive prevailing during the original training.

The rate at which reinforcements are delivered may follow different patterns, and these patterns are called *schedules of reinforcement.* Reinforcement can be presented upon completion of acts or at the completion of time intervals. A ratio of reinforcement, (one reinforcement for one act, one every two acts, and so forth) or an interval of reinforcement (one every ten seconds, one every minute) may be talked about. Further, these programs may be "fixed" every *n*th act (a fixed ratio) or "variable" (randomly on a one-third or one-tenth ratio). Similarly, there may be fixed interval or variable interval schedules. In general, learning is more resistant to extinction if the reinforcement is intermittent and/or variable.

An important aspect of work applying operant conditioning techniques is the method of *approximations or shaping*. Isaacs, Thomas, and Goldiamond's article (1) in this volume describes and makes use of shaping. The experimenter reinforces only those responses that move in the direction of the final performance, which is the goal, and he extinguishes or does not reinforce all other responses. In shaping the responses, he may, in many instances, only approximate the final desired behaviors. Such selective reinforcement is a powerful tool in bringing about a "new" behavior.

A final note should be made of another technique, that of *response chaining,* in which an increasingly long set of responses is gradually built up prior to the reinforcement. It should be explicit that a schedule of reinforcement, as well as the behavior reinforced, may gradually be changed during the course of time. These procedures, all of which depend eventually upon response contingent reinforcement, both help explain the development of maladaptive behavior and provide tools for its change.

The range of acquired reinforcers, discriminative stimuli, and complex performances is great indeed. Perhaps the most important, and certainly the one given the greatest attention in traditional therapy, is language. While research reports and experimental (as distinct from theoretical) foundations do not fall within the scope of the present work, it is worthwhile to note that the vocal behavior of chickens (Lane, 1961), cats (Molliver, 1963), and dogs (Salzinger and Waller, 1962) have been brought under control of reinforcing stimuli, and that infants' smiling (Brackbill, 1958) and vocalizations (Rheingold, Gewirtz, and Ross, 1959) have been increased through response contingent social reinforcement.

Simple performances, once established, may become parts of more complex ones. Both the increasing demands of the person's society, and his increased range due to language and communicated experience (lectures, readings) lead to increasingly complex performances which become techniques for solving further problems. Skinner (1963) talks of plans and logical analyses as discriminative stimuli, Miller and Dollard (1941) demonstrate the learning of a relationship, imitation in animals, and Berger (1961), Kanfer and Marston (1963) and particularly Bandura and Walters (1963) have investigated, within social reinforcement terms, vicarious reinforcement and modeling.

The learning concepts we have just reviewed are those of Skinner. The most frequent alternative formulation is that of Hull. While for the present purposes, as we have mentioned, the differences between the two schools are of relatively little importance, we will now turn to Hull's formulations. Where Skinner's concepts are based on the frequency of emission of overt behaviors, Hull distinguishes between performance, the overt behavior, and habit, the modification of the central nervous system, which mediates learning and which is not directly measurable. A performance is the product of habit strength and drives such as hunger or thirst. Important concepts for behavior therapy, particularly of tics, are those of reactive inhibition and conditioned inhibition. All activity produces some fatigue and this fatigue produces a drive (reactive inhibition which decreases with rest) and a negative habit (conditioned inhibition). The Hullian system with its concept of drive and mediation through habit is perhaps a stronger explanatory tool than Skinner's system and certainly lends itself more readily (compare Dollard and Miller, 1950) to the translation of psychoanalytic concepts. The Skinnerian system with its orientation to what Boring called "an empty organism" is more likely to focus on the stimulus environment rather than the internal state of the organism. With a concept of mediation and autonomic responses associated with meanings, the Hullian system may rely more heavily on Pavlovian or respondent conditioning than Skinnerian formulations. Hull's system certainly facilitates the comprehension of Wolpe's systematic desensitization procedure in which a conditioned drive, anxiety, may be inhibited by associating the appropriate stimulus with an image or other cue mediating the response to the anxiety provoking stimulus.

In closing this brief section we must add a few related points. The first is that while we have discussed operant and respondent behavior as though they were separate, in reality the two are usually intertwined and operant behaviors have respondent consequences. Especially for the behavior change techniques reported in this book, the concepts of operant and respondent conditioning, role learning and modeling, serve to complement each other. A behavior such as acting pleasantly may have genuine conditioned respondent consequences through prior association with the effects of such behavior, for example, an increase in the positive reinforcing stimuli emitted by other people (Ullmann, Krasner, and Gelfand, 1963). This leads to the concept that an important aspect of the individual's stimulus environment is composed of his own behavior. Performing an appropriate behavior, studying for an exam, may, because of prior experience, lead to an increase in reinforcing stimuli. The operant behavior, studying, may reduce the autonomic consequences of being unprepared. In discussing appropriate behavior of such a molar nature we arrive at a concept of role, a group of behaviors that have been shaped by the environment to meet the expectation of others (that is, to be reinforced) as appropriate for an individual in a given situation. Just as in typing, telegraphy, or piano playing increasing skill leads to larger functional units in which particular enactments may serve as stimuli for subsequent actions, so a complex social response may be developed from fine discriminations of the stimulus situation and generalization from previous situations. The person may learn to identify situations and use his own verbal responses as stimuli, which indicate the similarity or difference of a present situation to ones which were previously punishing or rewarding. This formulation may also include the labeling of patterns of behaviors that have previously been useful such as "Do what the other person is doing" or "It is likely that what happens to him will happen to me" or "This situation—exam—is likely to be painful." The subject responds to the situation with a vocal behavior that in turn is a discriminative stimulus. Finally, just as we noted the complex association of operant and respondent behaviors at the beginning of this paragraph, we should note that the human stimulus situation is considerably more uncontrolled, complex, changeable, and filled with more useful and more irrelevant stimuli than a Skinner box. A small and selected sample of these cues is probably used to match current situations with past ones and provide the self-stimulus of a label. Responses based on self-stimulation are necessary for reasonably prompt social responses, but they may well be inaccurate, superstitious, and self-validating. However, these responses, or the stimuli that control them, may be identified and reconditioned. It is this line of reasoning, the individual's own behavior as a source of stimuli and the patterning of social behavior into roles as units of behavior that we think may offer a fruitful extension of reinforcement theory into increasingly complex areas of social behavior.

Maladaptive Behavior: a Psychological Formulation

Maladaptive behaviors are learned behaviors, and the development and maintenance of a maladaptive behavior is no different from the development and maintenance of any other behavior. There is no discontinuity between desirable and undesirable modes of adjustment or between "healthy" and "sick" behavior. The first major implication of this view is the question of how a behavior is to be identified as desirable or undesirable, adaptive or maladaptive. The general answer we propose is that because there are no disease entities involved in the majority of subjects displaying maladaptive behavior, the designation of a behavior as pathological or not is dependent upon the individual's society. Specifically, while there are no single behaviors that would be said to be adaptive in all cultures, there are in all cultures definite expectations or roles for functioning adults in terms of familial and social responsibility. Along with role enactments, there are a full range of expected potential reinforcements. The person whose behavior is maladaptive does not fully live up to the expectations for one in his role, does not respond to all the stimuli actually present, and does not obtain the typical or maximum forms of reinforcement available to one of his status. The difference between the types of reinforcement that maintain adaptive and maladaptive behavior is that the latter is maintained by more direct and immediate forms of reinforcement than the former. Behavior that one culture might consider maladaptive, be it that of the Shaman or the paranoid, is adaptive in another culture if the person so behaving is responding to all the cues present in the situation in a manner likely to lead to his obtaining reinforcement appropriate to his status in that society. Maladaptive behavior is behavior that is considered inappropriate by those key people in a person's life who control reinforcers. Such maladaptive behavior leads to a reduction in the range or the value of positive reinforcement given to the person displaying it.

In a major article, Scott (1958) reviewed definitions of mental health in order to determine if there was available an operational definition of mental health or illness that could be used for purposes of research. His conclusion was that the current definitions were unworkable and at variance with each other. Such findings are not surprising in view of the questionable model on which a concept of "mental health" is based. Definitions of adjustment must be situation specific. In particular, by definition, a person comes to the therapist or to a hospital because someone wants to change him. That someone may be the person himself, his relatives, friends, employer, or authorities empowered to make the judgment that his behavior is a danger to himself or others so that he or his society would benefit from his treatment. This set of circumstances means that the definition of adjustment is not absolute but shifts from time to time and place to place. Further as the number of mental health professionals increases, it is likely that the number of people specified as requiring treatment will also increase. Jerome Frank (1961, pp. 6-7) summarizes this concept as follows:

> An interesting, if somewhat unfortunate, consequence of the fact that social attitudes play such a big role in the definition of mental illness is that mental health education may

be a two-edged sword. By teaching people to regard certain types of distress or behavioral oddities as illnesses rather than as normal reactions to life's stresses, harmless eccentricities, or moral weaknesses, it may cause alarm and increase the demand for psychotherapy. This may explain the curious fact that the use of psychotherapy tends to keep pace with its availability. The greater the number of treatment facilities and the more widely they are known, the larger the number of persons seeking their help. Psychotherapy is the only form of treatment which, at least to some extent, appears to create the illness it treats.

The next question becomes one of how we can account for the regularities of behavior seen in the "mentally ill" that compose the body of descriptive psychiatry. At a first level, as we have previously implied, these regularities may be far less frequent than is generally supposed. The grouping of people as exemplars of underlying causes or illness is a matter leading to a great deal of argument and constant revision, and expansion under sociological pressures. Textbook cases are hard to find in the psychiatric hospital because most cases manifest only a few of the specific symptoms that compose a syndrome, while many hospitalized people show specific behaviors that belong to more than one syndrome. A factor analytic approach to the question of the covariation of symptomatic behaviors is likely to indicate that classic syndromes are infrequent and may even be labels that do not reflect the behavior actually present. Another instance of this is the increasing use of the concept of premorbid adjustment (Phillips, 1953) or the process-reactive continuum (Ullmann and Giovannoni, 1964) to predict differential responses to stimulus situations either within or across major diagnostic categories. In short, the regularities presupposed by a medical model may not exist.

At a second level there is a matter of role learning. Any behavior that increases positive reinforcement or helps reduce aversive stimuli is likely to be increased. A person who is "sick" is considered unlucky, excused from responsibility, and a proper object of pity and forebearance. In our society, the patient is one who bears or endures suffering without complaint, who is long-suffering, and who is acted upon and receives treatment. At the present time, the person who is a mental patient is frequently considered incompetent legally and yet is in a position to demand attention and forgiveness from his peers. Just as the manifestations of the hypnotic role have changed over time, so have the manifestations of the mentally ill role changed over time and, during the same period, from one social class to another. Illustrations of this are the greater frequency of psychosomatic ills among officers than enlisted men during World War II, the decrease of hysterical symptoms, and the different patterns of maladaptive behavior in different social classes. Kelly (1955, p. 366) notes: "It seemed to the writer, in comparing the complaints of psychologically sophisticated people with those of the psychologically naive, that there was a definite tendency, once a person had chosen a psychological name for his discomfort, to display all of the symptoms in whatever book he had read, even if he had to practice them diligently. It suggested that psychological symptoms may frequently be interpreted as the rationale by which one's chaotic experiences are given a measure of structure and meaning."

The psychiatrist or other mental health professional may do much to foster the regularities supposedly seen in mental illness. During the diagnostic interview, the psychiatrist will focus on, and thereby reinforce with attention, the material that is meaningful to him. Hollingworth (1930, pp. 233–236) makes this point very clearly in his discussion of symptoms rendered vivid by attention. He describes how a medical examination may emphasize complaints: ". . . it is astonishing to find how many bodily sensations have hitherto escaped attention and now clamor for report. Fixation upon them, prolonged attention to them, minute scrutiny of them, increases their vividness, and they now stand out with distinctness. This is the characteristic effect of attention everywhere." (p. 234). If there is pressure to admit a person to the hospital, the psychiatrist will look for behaviors that are symptomatic and permit the statement that a particular syndrome exists. Once this has been accomplished, he can make a medical decision, a diagnosis, and hospitalize the individual. The patient is shaped into giving the physician what is wanted and expected.

Once within the hospital, there are strong pressures on the individual to assume the proper passive, nontroublesome "good patient" role. In particular, the nursing assistants or attendants have the responsibility to keep large groups of patients safe, clean, quiet, and cooperative. The aide culture (Belknap, 1956; Dunham and Weinberg, 1960; Goffman, 1961; Lehrman, 1961) can impose a strong set of explicit reinforcements to obtain expected behavior. Among these are the granting of privileges such as freedom of movement, passes, better accommodations, and the threat of punishment such as electroconvulsive therapy and transfer to a ward peopled by more disturbed patients. The apathy and withdrawal that are the most difficult and prognostically unfavorable symptoms of schizophrenia may well arise from the training given the patient not to be assertive or insistent upon his legitimate human rights. In the typical hospital setting, there is also a marked decrease in normal social contact and sensory stimulation. A number of authors have hypothesized that the social and sensory deficits involved in this situation parallel the production of behaviors similar to psychoses observed in sensory deprivation experiments (McReynolds, Acker, and Daily, 1959). The psychological correlates of playing a particular role and the physical conditions of diet, exercise, and living accommodations may lead to biochemical similarities that are the results and not the cause of hospitalization (Kety, 1960).

While perhaps less severe, there is definite role training observed in out-patient treatment. We shall return to this matter, particularly in the work of Goldstein (1962), when we discuss traditional therapy as behavior therapy. At this point we merely wish to indicate that it is possible to build a case for patients learning the regularities expected of them.

Let us turn to a more intensive analysis of the development of specific symptoms within a learning theory context. Again, for purposes of exposition, we will make distinctions between operant and respondent behavior when in fact the two are intertwined.

In terms of respondent or "surplus conditioned reactions" (Eysenck, 1959), we shall describe the concepts and terminology of Wolpe (1954). However, we have reservations about the usefulness of a drive concept; and the concept of "anxiety" currently has so many extraneous and poorly defined uses as to be a hinderance at times rather than an aid in communication (English and English, 1958, p. 35; Sarbin, 1963). To quote Wolpe (1954): "By 'anxiety' is meant the autonomic response pattern or patterns that are characteristically part of the organism's response to noxious stimulation. . . . An anxiety response is unadaptive when it is evoked in circumstances in which there is objectively no threat." Such responses occur within the paradigm of classic or Pavlovian conditioning. A noxious stimulus is paired with a previously indifferent stimulus, and at a later time the previously neutral stimulus alone elicits the response appropriate to the prior situation (when the noxious stimulus was present), but which is no longer adaptive or appropriate. Watson and Rayner (1920) present the experimental development of a phobia, complete with generalization, by this technique. Moss (1924) used a similar procedure to establish food aversion in two children and anecdotal material illustrative of this point abounds (Burnham, 1924). On a more general level, we may quote Eysenck (1959):

> Many conditioned responses are unadaptive, and consequently may embarrass the individual and even drive him into a mental hospital if sufficiently intense. Yet other conditioned responses are obviously necessary and desirable; indeed, many of them are indispensable for survival. It has been argued very strongly that the whole process of socialization is built up on the principle of conditioning; the overt display of aggressive and sexual tendencies is severely punished in the child, thus producing conditioned fear and pain responses (anxiety) to situations in which the individual is likely to display such tendencies. He consequently refrains from acting in the forbidden manner . . . because only by not indulging, and physically removing himself can he relieve the very painful conditioned anxiety responses to the whole situation. Anxiety thus acts as a mediating drive. . . .

Another way in which this might be put is that the behaviors that reduce the likelihood of aversive stimuli are positively reinforcing and likely to recur. A result is the avoidance of objects, situations, acts, and so forth, that have been associated with noxious stimuli. However, there is likely to be generalization, and in the very nature of withdrawal, a failure to differentiate between those elements of a situation from which it is adaptive to withdraw and those from which it is maladaptive to withdraw. Similarly, a behavior that has been associated with termination of aversive stimuli is likely to be repeated, even if such a behavior had no association with the reinforcement other than contiguity. Other responses may be continued because they were once appropriate to situations that were similar in some aspect irrelevant to the realities of the current situation. The reader's attention is called to our previous comment that the human stimulus situation is uncontrolled, complex, changeable, and filled with cues that are both relevant and irrelevant. This situation leads to responses to situations based on a limited sample of the available cues. Hollingworth's formulation of maladaptive behavior as redintegrated reactions (Hollingworth, 1930, pp. 249–255) is particularly germane. A major difference between physical and mental reactions is the response to symbols of the situation rather than reinstitution of all the original stimuli. "Mental processes . . . are those in which a partial stimulus serves adequately or approximately to provoke responses formerly occasioned only by more elaborate situations." (Hollingworth, 1930, p. 249). The eliciting of a response by a partial detail of its former antecedent is what Hollingworth means by redintegration. Hollingworth (1930, p. 250) writes:

> . . . the response may be overdetermined by the detail, without due regard to other features now occurring with it. The response is thus determined by past contexts rather than by present contexts. It is therefore likely to be bizarre, inutile, maladjusted, and hence neurotic. Prepotency of special cues or fragments of a situation may thus result in ineffective adjustment to that situation. Effective adjustment demands that all present facts be allowed to constellate, to *determine jointly* the nature of the response. Individuals in whom

this synergy or adequate cooperation of all the details of a situation does not effectively take place are lacking in a characteristic which we may for convenience call *scope* or *sagacity*.

For purposes of exposition, we may distinguish between an adaptive response that has not been learned and a maladaptive response that now must be changed.

In terms of deficient prior learning, we may conceive of a person who was isolated and socially withdrawn as a child. Such a person is less likely to have practiced, been reinforced for, and learned effective social skills. This deficit in training may make future social situations less rewarding and lead to the development of a vicious cycle. The development of attention and interest is exemplified by Birnbrauer *et al.* (47) in the present volume. Another example of this area is the treatment of enuresis. The association between bladder tension and wakefulness may be taught within a simple conditioning paradigm. In terms of symptom substitution, it is interesting that Mowrer and Mowrer (1938) who made the major breakthrough in this area write: "Personality changes, when any have occurred as a result of the application of the present method of treating enuresis, have uniformly been in a favorable direction. In no case has there been any evidence of 'symptom substitution.'" Morgan and Witmer (1939), Davidson and Douglass (1950), and Geppert (1953) are among authors who also remark on the general personality improvement associated with overcoming enuresis by conditioning techniques. In short, there may have been a simple failure to learn a particular behavior that can be taught easily.

A second group of maladaptive behaviors may be learned through operant conditioning. The behavior is associated with positive reinforcement of some sort. In the present volume, the child in the report by Wolf, *et al.* (48) found that the maladaptive behavior, vomiting, through misguided kindness, led to release from a potentially uncomfortable situation. When the reinforcement maintaining the behavior, release from the situation, ceased, the maladaptive response to the situation decreased and finally ceased. Mees (1964) summarizes the general principle: "If you want an explanation for this behavior—this monster behavior—I believe we can account for all of it with one general principle: *it pays off*. It pays off for the individual who can't seem to find other, nonmonstrous behaviors to get him what he wants."

Patterns of behaviors are increased, shaped, and maintained through reinforcement. If a person emits a behavior and reinforcement follows soon after, the frequency with which that behavior will be emitted in the future is altered. In terms of the development of maladaptive behavior, we have mentioned the work of Watson and Rayner (1920) and Moss (1924). To this, we may add the Haughton and Ayllon (5) work on the production and elimination of symptomatic behavior printed in this book. In this work, a person for whom cigarettes were reinforcing was handed a broom and given a cigarette. Broom holding became a stimulus associated with being given cigarettes, and the person developed the "bizarre, maladaptive" behavior of holding a broom and refusing to let it go. In another article, Ayllon and Haughton (1964) systematically manipulated the symptomatic verbal behavior of three patients. When the staff responded with interest and attention to bizarre talk, these verbalizations increased in frequency. Withholding social reinforcement (extinction) resulted in a decrease in the frequency of symptomatic verbal responses. The articles in the first section of this book illustrate operant techniques to promote adjustive responses. But, by implication, if adjustive responses are under stimulus control, we may hypothesize that so are maladjustive ones. In studies in which either control groups or periods of no reinforcement (extinction) have been used, Salzinger and Pisoni (1958, 1961) and Weiss, Krasner, and Ullmann (1963) have illustrated that affect self-references and use of emotional words by hospitalized patients may be altered by reinforcement. Many people have posited that a crucial symptom in schizophrenia is disorganization of thinking. Sommer, Witney, and Osmond (1962) have increased, through selective reinforcement of desirable responses, the frequency of common associations of hospitalized patients in a word association situation. Ullmann, Krasner, and Edinger (1964) replicated this result, and perhaps as noteworthy, found that even with long-term schizophrenic patients, the nonreinforced control group decreased in their rate of emission of common associations. Work on nursery school behavior, Allen *et al.* with social isolation (38), Harris *et al.* with regressed crawling (39), and Hart *et al.* with operant crying (40), illustrate with the same paradigm used by Ayllon and Haughton (1964) that these behaviors may be increased or decreased contingent upon adult attention. These three studies of nursery school behavior indicate clearly how a behavior "paying off" may lead to its increase. Finally, avoidance of aversive stimuli is reinforcing: stuttering was instigated in three normally fluent subjects when a persistent shock was introduced and its cessation for a brief period was made contingent upon nonfluent verbal behavior (Flanagan, Goldiamond, and Azrin, 1959). In our introductions to specific groups of case histories, we shall offer additional material, but at the present, we may point to the instigation and manipulation (both increase and decrease) of maladaptive behavior through procedures of reinforcement. While there are relatively few studies that set out to develop maladaptive responses to stimuli, every article that utilizes a psychological technique for the direct alteration of adaptive behavior buttresses by implication this formulation of the development of maladaptive behavior.

A question that follows the development of maladaptive responses is why, or more accurately how, these behavior patterns are maintained. The answer is by the same manner, reinforcement, as they were developed. Some of the evidence for this may be found in the articles cited in the previous paragraph. Further evidence comes from the effect of removing reinforcement (such as attention) in articles such as those of Ayllon (2) and Ayllon and Michael (4). Additional material appears in the Isaacs, Thomas, and Goldiamond article (1) in which a previously mute patient verbalized his wishes with those people who did not respond to his gestures, but continued to be mute with those people with whom the nonverbal behavior was effective. Williams' article on temper tantrums (34) provides an instance of a relapse, a naturalistic experiment similar to the systematic instances reported in the group of nursery school papers previously cited. In Ayllon (3), "emotional responses" which, if reinforced, might have become highly frequent behaviors, did not become so due to being ignored. The current reinforcement obtained for maladaptive behavior need not be the same as the reinforcement that led to the development of the behavior: all that is argued is that the maladaptive behavior is maintained by some reinforcement. An example may make this point clear. A person known to the authors once had a roommate who snored. To drown out the snoring he started using a second pillow to cover his ear. A pillow over the ear was associated with reinforcement, going to sleep, and became a discriminative stimulus for sleeping. Ten years after the original situation he continued to have difficulty going to sleep without a second, covering pillow. Although the original stimulus, the snoring roommate, was no longer present, the behavior continued because it was still associated with a pleasant stimulus, that is, going to sleep. Reinforcing stimuli can, particularly in humans, be different from the stimuli in the original situation. It is neither parsimonious nor necessary to explain behavior by either functional autonomy or underlying causes. It goes without saying that we doubt whether analyzing the dynamics of the comfort pattern of clinging to a soft, white object, such as a pillow, first observed when the subject was separated from his home and mother, would be particularly useful in changing the behavior.

We have noted that because there is no distinction between the development and maintenance of adaptive and maladaptive behavior, what we say of one applies to the other. For this reason, in line with our discussion of the maintenance of maladaptive behavior, we would now like to turn to the generalization of gains made in the professional behavior modification setting to the extra-therapy environment. The explicit techniques for the alteration of maladaptive behavior and fostering of new, more adaptive behavior, will be discussed in the next part of this introduction. But if we assume that the new behavior has developed, we may offer a number of means by which it is maintained.

First and foremost, the new behavior pays off. It is more likely to lead to reinforcement. Lazarus' case (1959) of a boy treated with Wolpe's (1958, pp. 184-185) anxiety-relief technique for sleeping with his mother is an example. The new behavior was welcomed by both parents and the siblings, and the entire family situation was changed. In short, because the subject's behavior leads to responses from other people, a new pattern of behavior by the subject puts him in a new environment. This point is important because evocative therapists typically argue that the person must be "basically" changed (for example, his ego strengthened) before he can withstand the stress of returning to the environment in which he had previously developed a pattern of maladaptive behavior. Using this concept as a solution, alternative, or supplement, expressive therapists are likely to press for the treatment of parents so that they will solve *their* problems.

People who are likely to be important in regard to the maintenance of new adaptive behavior can be taught and literally programed as alternate therapists. In the present volume there are many examples of this. In Ayllon and Michael's (4) and Bachrach, Erwin, and Mohr's articles (14) we will see the nurse being given instructions as to her behavior toward hospitalized patients. In Wolf, Risley, and Mees' article (12), an aide who worked with the child in the hospital went home with him to teach the parents. Davison (13) discusses the training of college undergraduates for work with severely disturbed children. Parents play a key role in selecting and reinforcing behavior in papers by Rickard and Mundy (stuttering) (30), Patterson (school phobia) (31), Williams (temper tantrums) (34), Bentler (phobia) (35), Peterson and London (33), and Madsen (toilet training) (37). School teachers play a key role in the majority of the work with children in social situations, and retardates. Finally, in Sulzer's paper (19) we will see the subject's friends making their reinforcing behavior contingent on his not drinking. It is important to note that this approach is readily understandable to parents and other significant people in the child's environment and thus may lead to a rapid and hearty adoption by them. For example, Jersild and Holmes (1935) discuss the techniques that parents devised to overcome children's fears, and the most effective of these closely parallel the reconditioning techniques that are presented in this book. A second point is that these techniques are more likely to be accepted and utilized by those members of the lower social classes who are likely to have difficulty in utilizing more traditional forms of psychotherapy (Hollingshead and Redlich, 1958). There are many parents who do not value self-insight and neither understand nor believe in the efficacy of working on their basic problems to alleviate their child's maladaptive behavior. For those people, who may well expect prescription and direction, withdrawal from therapy follows a rigid approach which assumes that the focus of difficulty lies in them. By accepting whatever the parent has been doing as evidence of good faith, the person interested in behavior modification can reduce the parents' feelings of inadequacy and pave the way for the development of more effective parental responses to the child's behavior. The therapist's goal is to program the parents to respond to and nurture the desired changes toward adaptive behavior. Behavior therapy may extend the number of cases the therapist is likely to undertake. For example, Phillips (1956, Table 1, p. 47) notes that with his assertion-structured therapy 53 of 59 patients entered therapy and 51 of these 53 obtained benefit in an average of less than eight sessions. In contrast, at the same clinic, and with no noticeable bias of assignment, of 190 cases initially interviewed, 103 were judged unsuitable for treatment by psychoanalytically oriented therapists, 42 refused therapy themselves, and the remaining 45 completed a course of therapy averaging 17 sessions. For approximately 75 percent of these 45 cases, benefit was reported. Aside from the difference in the rate of benefit of those actually undergoing treatment, the assertion-structured approach was found serviceable in a far greater proportion of the population that came for help. Thus behavior therapy may have an additional value in terms of the scope of the population served. Finally, behavior may be maintained by subject feedback. An obvious aspect of this is the increase of positive environmental reinforcement. Another aspect is that certain new behaviors are inconsistent with other maladaptive behaviors. An example may be found in the Ayllon and Michael article (4) in which, with self-feeding and a considerable weight gain, an "untreated" delusion of poisoned food ceased. It seems reasonable to hypothesize that hearty self-feeding is a behavior incompatible with the claim of poisoned food. There is also a matter of generalization: as Eysenck (1959) has noted, removal of one symptom, rather than exacerbating or leading to development of new symptoms, facilitates removal of other maladaptive behaviors. On one level, the person observes that he can be different and can change. On a different level of abstraction, it seems reasonable that if maladaptive responses can generalize, a technique that has been adaptive in one situation will also be tried out as a response to other situations. Finally, as we noted in our discussion of learning concepts, operant and respondent behaviors are intertwined and a considerable portion of the subject's environment is composed of his own behavior. We may hypothesize that this part of the environment is appreciably changed for the better as he emits more adaptive responses. In short, there are many ways in which behavior, whether adaptive or maladaptive, can be maintained without reference to an underlying, historical cause.

The Role of Assessment in a Psychological Model

In dealing with the medical model and in an earlier part of this section, we cast doubt on the disease concept and the pertinence of the regularities of pathology observed in psychiatric settings. This does not mean, however, that there is no place for psychological assessment in behavior modification. It does mean that such assessment focuses on different variables and has different goals. Assessment in behavior modification is directly associated with treatment. A first goal of assessment is to identify the behavior to be modified. This is frequently a difficult task for it involves determining which behavior should be modified first and the subsequent effects such change may have on other behaviors. The focus of treatment is the behavior and not some disease or historical circumstance. It is interesting to note that a not dissimilar step has been taken in much of the chemotherapy of the last decade. Tranquilizers are given for types of behavior such as depression, agitation, anxiety, and the like, and not for diseases such as schizophrenia or neurosis. A second point is that while factor analytic studies of specific behaviors have been valuable as a way of investigating traditional psychiatric nosology and developing methods of measuring the effects of treatment, many maladaptive behaviors are so relatively infrequent that the crucial behavior in a particular case may not be reflected by a factor analytic scale.

Psychological tests may be used in work with an individual case to identify critical situations. Because behavior modification focuses on a specific action, some specific subject response to stimuli must be identified. If the subject claims to be anxious "all the time, of everything" a test such as the Willoughby (1932, 1934) may be used as an interview aid to ascertain areas of particular difficulty. Psychological tests may also play a valuable role in determining relevant subject capabilities. For example, Eysenck (1962) and his colleagues have used the concepts of introversion-extraversion and neuroticism extensively and offer suggestions about the people most likely to respond to certain forms of behavior therapy. In particular, differential predictions of response to conditioning situations have been advanced (Franks, 1961). In general, certain biographical information may be valuable. The process-reactive continuum for example, has been associated with differential response to treatment among hospitalized schizophrenics (Kantor, Wallner, and Winder, 1953; King, 1958; Herron, 1962). In short, because behavior modification deals with overt responses, modification of these responses leads to a strong criterion for the development of new tests and techniques of test administration. Once developed and validated, these techniques in turn may increase the efficiency of behavior modification procedures.

Perhaps the most important area of assessment in behavior modification deals with the subject's social situation. Assessment involves the identification of the stimuli that maintain the maladaptive behavior and the identification of those meaningful aspects of the environment that may be programed to become contingent upon the behaviors that are to be increased or decreased in frequency. The area of psychological evaluation is shifted from the description and measurement of internal dynamics to an evaluation of the total social situation. At this point the clinical psychologist becomes vitally interested in the study of social classes, institutions, and groups as they influence the types of reinforcement and behavior that may be available for manipulation. The psychologist practicing behavior modification is acutely aware of "the demand characteristics of the situation" (Orne, 1962), the personal and professional limitations of the people who comprise the subject's social environment, and the role enactments that are adjustive and realistically reinforced in the situation.

In this section we have outlined a psychological formulation of maladaptive behavior. We introduced some learning concepts and discussed the development and maintenance of adaptive and maladaptive behaviors. Finally we indicated how this formulation affected one of the clinical psychologist's traditional roles, that of assessment. We will now turn to an exposition of the techniques most frequently used at the present time to modify behavior in clinical settings.

Methods of Change: Behavior Modification

The major aspects of behavior modification are the focus on overt behavior and the application of concepts drawn from learning theory to attain change. Up to now we have discussed these concepts theoretically and as departures from the medical model. In this section we shall introduce some of the techniques involved.

There are two principle schools: the one preponderantly using operant conditioning and Skinnerian terms, and the one centering to a greater extent on Pavlovian conditioning and using Hull and Wolpe as theoretical reference points. However, it is at times difficult to place a particular article as illustrative of one school rather than another. Further, as will be illustrated in the cases that follow, with any specific subject, more than one technique may be used.

We should make it clear that while there are many *techniques,* there are few *concepts* or *principles* involved. In terms of techniques, Bandura (1961) ordered his review around extinction, discrimination learning, methods of reward, punishment, and social imitation. Grossberg (1964) organized his material around the procedures of aversion, negative practice, positive conditioning, reinforcement withdrawal, and desensitization. Mowrer (in press) comments aptly that the techniques reduce to extinction and conditioning, and while we will present our review of techniques following the general outline of Wolpe's (1954) review, we wish to agree with Mowrer's point and elaborate on it. Despite differences in approaches and techniques, we would propose that all behavior modification boils down to procedures utilizing *systematic environmental contingencies to alter the subject's response to stimuli.* There are two points that are crucial. The first is the systematic or programmatic nature of the arrangement of the stimulus environment. The second, and more important to the immediate discussion, is that it is the response to stimuli and not the specific response, per se, that is the focus of treatment. Without fully comprehending the nature of behavior therapy, some writers have claimed that behavior therapy involves "symptomatic treatment" and from this, the treatment of responses. We think that the therapist who "removes" maladaptive behavior without helping to replace it with a more adjustive behavior is doing only half his professional job. As the reader will note in the succeeding paragraphs, the subject is taught to make different responses (assertive, relaxed, or new and more adaptive ones) in the same situation in which previously he had made either maladaptive or deficient responses. The goal is to obtain subject behavior in response to stimuli that is different and incompatible with the previous maladaptive behavior.

What follows is a brief description of the major techniques of behavior therapy:

Assertive responses Wolpe (1958) and Metzner (1961) hypothesize that anxiety and the expression of resentment are incompatible, so that if the person can assert himself, anxiety will be inhibited. The therapist provides the motivation by pointing out the irrationality of the fears and encouraging the individual to insist on his legitimate human rights. The technique is given a physiological basis by Wolpe, and by Salter (1961) who refers to its as excitatory. An alternative view is that the therapist sets up a series of progressively more difficult tasks for the person. The behavior therapist uses his relationship with the individual to help him try out a new adaptive response. The therapist may do this by reasoning with him (Ellis, 1962) or assigning tasks as part of a therapy regimen (Herzberg, 1941). He may also do this through practice or role playing directly in the therapeutic situation (Wolpe, 1954, 1958), or through a broader fixed-role technique such as that of Kelly (1955). In any case, the patient makes a new response to the previously threatening stimulus situation and experiences a favorable outcome for his changed behavior. We may hypothesize that there is generalization of the favorable experience based on cues that are common to situations in which the person anticipates aversive consequences. By this procedure the individual is able to enter into and make adaptive responses to progressively more difficult situations. His increasing mastery of these situations is itself rewarding, and this type of reinforcing feedback becomes part of the patient's environment.

In short, the therapist establishes conditions, which may include teaching relaxation responses as well as role playing and exhortation, to increase the likelihood that the person will emit a behavior that will be reinforced. The new pattern of adjustive behavior is likely to be incompatible with the previous maladaptive response to the situation.

Sexual responses If anticipated aversive consequences have become associated with sexual responses, the person is instructed to engage in only those sexual acts which he has an unmistakable desire to perform. While anxiety and sexual responses may well be physiologically incompatible, there is a parallel to the use of assertive responses. A series of increasingly difficult situations (on the one hand, roughly increasing degrees of intimacy, and on the other, similarity to particular sexual objects, that is, types of sexual partners) are identified. By having a successful experience in easier situations, both verbally with the therapist and behaviorally in outside life, the subject not only is reconditioned to specific cues, but, by generalization, to other more difficult but similar situations.

Relaxation responses Jacobson (1938) introduced a method for obtaining muscle relaxation. The theory reasons that a state of relaxation is incompatible with anxiety, defined as muscle tension. Jacobson, and more specifically for psychotherapists, Haugen,

Dixon, and Dickel (1958) taught the use of relaxation in progressively more general life situations.

In our opinion, if a single one of Wolpe's contributions had to be labeled as the most important, it would be the development of systematic desensitization based on relaxation. The key word for behavior modification is *systematic*. In systematic desensitization, the subject is taught to relax, and this state of relaxation is associated with imagined or visualized threatening experiences. The situations are in a series that moves from the least to the most threatening (that is, a "hierarchy"). As each situation of a hierarchy is successively desensitized, or associated with a response incompatible with anticipated aversive consequences, by generalization all other items on the hierarchy are affected. In this technique, Wolpe has developed a positive reinforcer, relaxation, which may be systematically associated with aspects of the threatening situation. The technique may be used in an office setting and permits a wide range of application.

Conditioned avoidance responses Wolpe (1954) notes three techniques under this rubric. The first is that of conditioned inhibition of anxiety through a dominating motor response and is based on a finding by Mowrer and Viek (1948) that when animals were repeatedly exposed to a continuous mild electric shock, those who learned a definite motor response in relation to termination of shock developed less anxiety than those who were not able to learn such a response. Wolpe (1954) illustrates the technique in the case of a woman who was afraid of falling. She was instructed to imagine a mild fall and when she had the image clearly, an electric current was passed into her forearm and ceased upon her making a brisk forearm movement. After a number of times, this movement became an immediate response to shock and the patient reported the idea of falling to be less unpleasant. She was able to attempt an actual fall and then proceeded to more difficult tasks.

A second conditioned avoidance response technique has been called by Wolpe "anxiety-relief" responses. This procedure is based on the concept that if an uncomfortable shock is administered to a person for several seconds and then stopped immediately upon a signal, that signal will become associated with the bodily correlates following cessation of an aversive stimulus, that is, bodily responses incompatible with anticipated punishment or anxiety. A typical response would be the subject saying the word "calm," although a different example will be discussed below in connection with a case by Lazarus (1959).

A third type of conditioned avoidance response is the overcoming of an excessive approach response to stimuli by pairing such stimuli with an aversive stimulus. Wolpe (1954) illustrates the technique with a woman who was obsessed by food and who had been unsuccessfully treated by psychoanalysis and electroconvulsive therapy (ECT). Such aversive conditioning has also been used successfully in the treatment of writer's cramp (Liversedge and Sylvester, 1955; Sylvester and Liversedge, 1960); sexual deviations (see article by Kushner (24) and introduction to it in this volume); alcoholism (Franks, 1958), and enuresis (Jones, 1960b).

An illustration of the combination of concepts within a case of a behavior modification is in Lazarus' (1959) work on elimination of children's phobias. A ten-year-old boy who had a habit of waking up in the middle of the night and entering his mother's bed, imagined his mother's bed, said "mother's bed," and an electric shock started; this shock was terminated when he said, "my bed." One session of fourteen presentations over ten minutes led to dramatic changes in the child's behavior and a consequent general improvement in the home situation. Here we have both a conditioned avoidance response ("mother's bed") and a conditioned anxiety-relief response ("my bed").

Feeding responses   Wolpe (1954) notes that "Presumably, in eating voraciously because of heightened hunger drive, the patient obtains a reciprocal inhibition of any anxiety responses that happen to be occurring within him at that time." Jones (1924b) in the classic example of reconditioning overcame a child's fear of furry animals by pairing a rabbit with food the child liked.

Chemotherapy   Wolpe (1962) discusses the use of carbon dioxide inhalation, Lazarus (1963a) the use of sensory deprivation through hypnotic techniques, and Costello (1964) the use of the drug LSD with patients suffering generalized anxiety. Because these techniques at present are not a clear use of psychological or learning theory concepts, we have considered them outside the scope of the present volume. However, with a three-and-a-half-year-old boy who was afraid of dogs, Lazarus (1959) used a tranquilizing drug to induce relaxation. The feared object was then displayed to the child. Over time, the drug dosage was decreased. The use of a conditioning paradigm brings this procedure within the realm of behavior modification.

Expressive therapy   While we will devote a section to traditional or expressive therapy as behavior therapy, we wish to mention at this point that typical therapy procedures may illustrate either extinction (making the maladaptive response in the presence of a person who does not respond to it) or reconditioning, the discussion of the threatening stimuli in the presence of the calm, relaxing therapist. The difference between behavior modification and expressive therapy is in the rationale for obtaining this behavior and the systematic nature of the therapist's use of the behavior once the person has produced it.

Emotive imagery   The procedure of emotive imagery was introduced by Lazarus and Abramovitz (36) in an article dealing with children's phobias. In this procedure the stimulus to which the individual has made maladaptive responses is woven into the context of stimuli that have been associated with responses incompatible with the maladaptive response. Other examples of this procedure, associating a threatening stimulus with a supportive context, may be found in Walton (1960b), in Burnham (1924, pp. 174–175), and in Jersild and Holmes (1935). As such, the technique of emotive imagery is another instance of reconditioning.

In vivo presentation of disruptive stimuli   The therapist may use himself as a source of relaxing stimuli and pair his presence with progressively difficult stimulus situations. Examples may be found in the work of Freeman and Kendrick (1960), Meyer (1957), Meyer and Gelder (1963), Walton (1960a), and Walton and Black

(1958) in which the Cherry-Sayers approach to stuttering was used to reduce anxiety during progressively more difficult performances.

Modeling   While not frequently used at present, a technique which is likely to find increasing use is that of modeling or imitation in which another person makes and is reinforced for the response to be learned by the subject. An example and discussion of this method may be found in Jones (1924a) in her remarks on the method of social imitation. As with emotive imagery, the stimulus is put in a new context, and in terms of our discussion of learning concepts, the behavior of others may serve as a discriminative stimulus for the subject. Things or situations that other people enjoy usually indicate stimuli worth approaching. However the reverse is also true and Jones (1924a) presents clinical evidence for the dangers as well as the potential usefulness of social imitation. A child who is unafraid of a stimulus when paired with a child who is afraid of it, may develop the latter's fear.

Negative practice   This concept and its therapeutic use are principally the contribution of Dunlap (1932). However, a tighter formulation of the procedure, especially in terms of Hullian reactive inhibition, is primarily the work of Yates (1958b). Practicing a tic, stammer, or undesirable habit such as nail biting, leads theoretically to (a) the extinction of the response in the absence of the "unconditioned stimulus of anxiety," and (b) the inhibition or fatigue associated with having made the response, so that performing the response may be painful and not performing it avoids an aversive situation, that is, becomes a positively reinforced behavior. While in general, negative practice is associated with operant behaviors, Malleson (1959) has offered a case of "reactive inhibition therapy" to supplement Wolpe's "reciprocal inhibition therapy." In Malleson's procedure the most feared outcomes are visualized and discussed till fatigue and boredom are developed and the subject finds it difficult even to think of the dreaded situation. A final example is offered in Walton and Black's (1959) treatment of a case of hysterical aphonia.

Self-disclosure   Mowrer (1964) has advanced the formulation that a person who has acted in contradiction to the internalized standards of his group will try to avoid the consequences of his act by deceiving others. This situation, which we might look at in terms of role-conflict or occurrence of a situation that has previously been associated with aversive consequences, is uncomfortable and the person is dis-eased. In this formulation, Mowrer explicitly rejects a medical model and notes the realistic nature of the dis-ease and the personal responsibility of the subject. Treatment is along the lines of admission of the act, first to a therapist, and then to significant others. Mowrer's concepts cannot be done justice in the space of the present introduction nor can we but mention that the situation he describes is a very common one in our culture. Mowrer's work is appealing for the lines of integration with other professions it offers. In the context of the present discussion we may note that self-disclosure would certainly seem incompatible with deception and the act of disclosure is one likely to alter the stimulus situation.

Extinction   We have mentioned that maladaptive behavior is maintained by current reinforcement and not historical circumstances. By removing the reinforcing stimuli that currently maintain behavior, the person's response to a situation is likely to change and the maladaptive behavior decrease in frequency. New behavior is more likely to occur, and if it is adaptive, may be reinforced. We might even hypothesize that unreinforced behavior may become aversive. An interesting example of an extinction procedure, couched within Hullian theory, is Walton's (1960d) treatment of a case of neurodermatitis. A simpler conceptualization of extinction of a psychophysiological symptom—within a Skinnerian framework—may be found in the present book in Wolf *et al.*'s extinction (48) of a vomiting response. Examples of the use of extinction are perhaps clearest when the subject makes a major physical effort. The reader will find extinction of temper tantrums discussed in this book by Williams (34), Wolf, Risley, and Mees (12), and Zimmerman and Zimmerman (42). Other examples of extinction may be found in the article in this book by Ayllon and Michael (4).

Selective positive reinforcement   This is the prime technique of behavior modification and may take many forms including some of the other specific techniques discussed in the immediately preceding paragraphs. While the papers in this volume will offer many examples, we would like to call particular attention to the articles by Isaacs, Thomas, and Goldiamond (1), King, Armitage, and Tilton (6), and Rickard and Mundy (30) that illustrate the use of reinforcement for progressively more difficult performances. Other work illustrates the development of stimulus control over behavior to eliminate rather than develop a new pattern of behavior and includes work by Ferster, Nurnberger, and Levitt (1962) on overeating and Mertens (1964a; 1964b) on alcoholism. These latter works make use of *lengthening a response chain* so that the chances of stimuli leading to maladaptive behavior are reduced.

Stimulus deprivation and satiation   The likelihood that a subject will change his behavior to alter the frequency of a presumed reinforcing stimulus may be manipulated by depriving him of that stimulus, or making that stimulus so abundant that he becomes satiated thus reducing the reinforcing characteristic of the stimulus. The former, stimulus deprivation, is a common feature of behavior modification programs and is clearly illustrated in the case of anorexia nervosa reported by Bachrach, Erwin, and Mohr (14) in the present volume. Stimulus satiation is illustrated by Ayllon (3) in the treatment of bizarre towel hoarding.

New techniques are constantly being introduced and in a later section we will mention specific ways of applying learning theory concepts that we think are likely to become useful in the near future. These techniques include the explicit use of teaching machines, greater use of the reinforcing properties of group membership, and the more frequent use of intermittent reinforcement. The core of behavior modification, however, rests not on specific methods of application or techniques, but on the planned manipulation of the environment contingent upon the person's responses to stimuli. Many variations of this theme will be illustrated in the case material that follows, but the possibilities for new approaches are limited only by the creativity of experimental psychologists and the ingenuity of clinical workers.

Traditional Therapy and Behavior Therapy

There are three major purposes to this section. The first is to discuss the similarities and differences between behavior therapy and traditional, evocative, or expressive therapies. The second is to point out the amount of behavior influence present in traditional therapy with a view that clinical psychologists should be aware of these aspects of the situation whether it be to maximize or to reduce them. The third purpose is to reformulate some features of traditional therapeutic practice and to point out areas in which behavior therapy techniques might be helpful within the framework of expressive psychotherapy.

The greatest single influence in the area of psychotherapy was Freud. His solitary exploration of the nature of man represents one of the great intellectual adventures of our civilization and reflects the integrity and courage for which he will always be held in esteem. Freud developed his concepts through the clinical investigation of himself, of his disciples, and of a restricted group of patients. A number of psychologists and psychiatrists assumed that Freud had indeed developed an effective method for the treatment of maladaptive behavior and tried to translate his work into psychological terms (for example, French, 1933; Kubie, 1934). The years immediately after World War II saw a number of attempts to bring about an integration of experimental and clinical psychology, and notable among these efforts were those of Shaw (1946, 1948), Shoben (1949), Dollard and Miller (1950), and Magaret (1950). These writers started with a particular clinically derived form of psychotherapy as the "given" to be explained in terms of learning theory. As such, many of the aspects of the situation they described in terms of learning theory might well have been extraneous to the goal of changed behavior. Learning theory was used as a new communication channel to explain psychotherapy as it was, and not as the basis for the practice of psychotherapy as it might become. The point can be made by quoting Shoben (1949) who says "clinical cases share in common (a) anxiety touched off by (b) unverbalized, unsuccessfully repressed impulses to act in ways that have met with punishment, and (c) persistent nonintegrative behavior of many kinds, which reduces the anxiety but does nothing about eliminating its objective causes." The concepts of repression and the need to deal with an underlying cause were carried over from the medical model, and learning theory was a rationalization, after the fact, of the existing therapeutic procedures.

When dealing with treatment Shoben (1949) writes: "It is proposed here that psychotherapy occurs through three interrelated processes: first, the lifting of repression and the development of insight through the symbolic reinstating of the stimuli for anxiety; second, the diminution of anxiety by counter-conditioning through the attachment of the stimuli for anxiety to the comfort reaction made to the therapeutic relationship; and third, the process of re-education through the therapist's helping the patient to formulate rational goals and behavioral methods for attaining them." In the first of these methods we again find concepts of repression, insight, and historical "cause"; in the second method, reconditioning or counter-conditioning, we come close to the techniques that will be exemplified in the present group of readings, but the comfort reaction is that of the rapport that is neither established nor used systematically. Rapport may be contrasted with the teaching of muscle relaxation and its systematic application in Wolpe's desensitization technique. The third method, that of helping the patient formulate rational goals, also presents a vital difference when contrasted with procedures of selectively reinforcing behaviors. A big problem is the development of new behaviors, especially ones observed outside the treatment situation. In a medical or disease model it is assumed that maladaptive behavior is a symptom of the underlying problem and that once the "cause" has been removed, normal, socially adaptive behavior will occur (Yates, 1958a). In behavior therapy a performance must be learned. There must be an alteration of responses to stimuli and an ultimate maintenance of adaptive behavior by positive reinforcement. We have discussed such maintenance earlier in this volume. At present we wish to emphasize that following the medical model adaptive behavior is considered the normal state of the organism, while the behavioral model argues that both adaptive or maladaptive behavior must be learned.

As we shall discuss in succeeding paragraphs, there are direct instigations to altered behavior in an expressive therapy situation. These occur in the differential interest, sympathy, and praise the therapist exhibits to different types of behaviors. The problem of generating new behavior, as we see it, is to have it occur and, once it has occurred, to reinforce it with a meaningful stimulus. Talk of feelings, insight into the etiology of one's problems, analysis of interpersonal relationships, and healthy remarks may all be reinforced by the therapist and lead the patient to have a feeling of improvement that alters his perceptions of social situations. Next, the patient may emit in external situations the behavior he has learned in therapy: he has been trained in new interpersonal techniques and these, and the new view he holds of himself, may lead to an increased likelihood of social reinforcement. The patient may ask himself how his therapist would want him to behave. The training has generated a new *weltanshauung* or set of discriminative stimuli. Another manner in which change may occur is through extinction. If the therapist does not make the typical or anticipated response to a patient maneuver, the maneuver has occurred without being associated with a reinforcing change of the environment. While extinction is a slow and inefficient method of behavior change, it may play a role in traditional therapy by reducing the likelihood of emission of a particular maladaptive behavior so that some other possibly more adaptive behavior may be emitted and reinforced. While it may at first appear odd, complete permissiveness or tender loving care seems to us to be a technique that bears some resemblance to extinction. Although complete acceptance and permissiveness may be a therapist behavior that the patient expects and finds helpful in the establishment of rapport, it is eventually an inefficient technique for behavior change. If one accepts everything and reacts to all behaviors in the same way, one essentially deprives the person of an opportunity to discriminate between his adaptive and maladaptive behaviors. The person who displays complete tender loving care is acting as if what the person is doing made no difference. There is no change in the environment, and it is for this reason that we link permissiveness with extinction.

We may speculate that permissiveness of maladaptive behavior is directly associated with a disease model in which the person is granted tolerance because he cannot help himself. It is interesting to compare work such as that by Allen *et al.* (38) in this book with the more typical procedures in our culture. Instead of the usual added attention for isolate behavior, psychologists interested in the child's development ignored this type of action and reinforced social behavior incompatible with the maladaptive behavior. The result was a decrease in isolate behavior that was later reinstituted when attention was given for withdrawal.

In resumé, learning theory concepts such as reconditioning, modeling, and extinction may be found in expressive therapy. The difference between behavior therapy and evocative therapy is (a) the *a priori* rather than the *post hoc* usage of learning concepts and, (b) the explicit, systematic application of learning concepts to achieve a particular behavioral goal selected at the start of treatment.

We turn now to manifestations of social influence in the process of expressive therapy. Psychotherapy is a social situation in which persons make responses that influence each other. Goldstein (1962) has brought together the considerable literature on this topic. He points out that expectations have an important effect on the likelihood of what behaviors will be manifested and how the behaviors of others will be evaluated. There is an interdependence of the patient's expectations of help and the likelihood of his being helped. In similar fashion the therapist may be influenced in his professional judgment by how well he likes the subject (Masling, 1960). Additionally, there are self-validating hypotheses; for example, the therapist who evaluates the subject as a poor risk for therapy will be less likely to establish good rapport, which will increase the chances of failure, and validate his original belief that the person was a poor bet. Knowledge about social class, and intellectual and verbal abilities may all make the patient more desirable for therapy and lead him to be assigned to a more capable therapist.

The expressive therapist has in mind a series of behaviors that the subject should make. These behaviors may be described as "working on one's problems" and include self-evaluation, discussion of interpersonal difficulties, and expression of negative feelings. However, the procedure is not overtly systematic and the therapist has little way of measuring progress. In private practice especially, a clear, meaningful, and immediate criterion is present: the patient may terminate. Whether prolonged therapy is necessary or not, therapists endeavor to avoid the aversive stimulus of patient termination and may well be shaped to emit behaviors likely to keep the patient in therapy.

The therapist has a "theory" that helps him respond rapidly to patient behavior. We have mentioned his desire to have the patient emit helpful verbalizations. What is helpful or important is decided upon by the professional person. This patient behavior is shaped by the therapist who may compliment his patient for "working" or making progress. In a less direct manner, the therapist may guide the patient's verbal behavior by interest, friendliness, or other nonverbal cues described and utilized in verbal operant conditioning (Krasner, 1955; 1958a; 1962a). Some indication of the extent of this aspect of therapy may be obtained from the Bandura (1956) and Bandura, Lipsher, and Miller (1960) studies of therapists, the research of Lennard and Bernstein (1960), and the content analysis of psychotherapy situations by Murray (1956) and in this volume (23). Whether due to his theory or his personal feelings of comfort with certain material, the evocative therapist trains the patient to emit certain selected correct responses. A psychoanalyst, Marmor (1961), has given a thorough description of the end result of this process:

But what *is* insight? To a Freudian it means one thing, to a Jungian another, and to a Rankian, a Horneyite, an Adlerian, or a Sullivanian, still another. Each school gives its own particular brand of insight. Who shall say whose are the correct insights? The fact is that patients treated by analysts of all these schools may not only respond favorably, but also believe strongly in the insights which they have been given. Even admittedly "inexact" interpretations have been noted to be of therapeutic value. Moreover, the problem is even more complicated than this; for, depending upon the point of view of the analyst, the patients of each school seem to bring up precisely the kind of phenomenological data which confirm the theories and interpretations of their analysts. Thus each theory tends to be self-validating. . . . What the analyst shows interest in, the kinds of questions he asks, the kind of data he chooses to react to or ignore, and the interpretations he makes, all have a subtle but significant suggestive impact upon the patient to bring forth certain kinds of data in preference to others . . . what we call insight is essentially the conceptual framework by means of which a therapist establishes or attempts to establish a logical relationship between events, feelings or experiences that seem unrelated in the mind of the patient. In terms of the analyst's objectives, insights constitute the rationale by which the patient is persuaded to accept the model of more "mature" or "healthy" behavior which analysts of all schools, implicitly or explicitly, hold out to him. Now since interactions that put the patient's material within one frame of reference seem to be just as effective for the patient as interpretations that put it within another frame of reference, it is logical to conclude that the specific insight given *cannot* be the only or exclusive base for the therapeutic reaction.

This brings us to the third point to be made in this section. The process of any therapy is the contingency of patient and therapist behaviors. Any therapeutic procedure carried on without reference to the elements that are really active in it is at best inefficient, at worst magical. The traditional therapist does influence his patients and we think that he should do so consciously and systematically. If he thinks that there is a particular behavior that will help the subject, he should legitimately do everything in his power to maximize the frequency of that behavior. If, for example, he believes that emotional expressiveness is an important deficit in schizophrenics, he may wish to use verbal conditioning to increase the frequency of affect self-references or emotional words (Salzinger and Pisoni, 1958, 1961; Weiss, Krasner, and Ullmann, 1963). If he thinks rational verbal behavior is important, he may wish to increase this in a manner similar to Ayllon and Haughton (1964) or Rickard *et al.* (7, 8) in the articles reprinted in this volume. This rubric may be applied to discussion of "mother" (Krasner, 1958b), "early memories" (Quay, 1959; Craddick and Stern, 1964), active seeking of vocational information (Schroeder, 1964) or ways to get along better with people as in the article by Sulzer (19). A good response with which to work is one that can be reinforced. If the desired behavior, at the start, is so infrequent as to lead to a low level of reinforcement, then the psychologist has chosen poorly or must use a method of approximations. A useful reinforcing stimulus is one that is worth working for and not likely to lead to rapid satiation. There may be training in making particular stimuli, whether tokens or therapist approval, meaningful. We see little conflict between the therapist training the subject in behavior likely to be reinforced and in democratic ideals, for we conceive of freedom and human dignity as the possession of a choice between meaningful alternatives rather than a situation in which all behaviors are equally acceptable and equally inconsequential. While we shall return to this matter when we discuss values in the next section, the present point is that within any particular theory, the therapist can use behavior modification techniques to increase the rate of behaviors he deems adaptive for the subject.

Characteristics of the Behavior Therapist and Social Values

Many adjectives have been used to describe the ideal psychotherapist (Krasner, 1963a). Generally, he sounds like the product of successful treatment by whatever technique the author practices. The basic characteristic of behavior therapists is that their orientation is toward general psychology, particularly learning theory and experimental psychology. The behavior therapist insists on operational definitions and is uncomfortable with internal dynamics and vague concepts that are reversed whenever they fail to account for data in an unreversed form. At times the traditional therapist says the behavior therapist is not interested in people. There is in this an assumption that people can be separated from their behavior and that there is a superficial person involved in behavior who is different and less important than the "real" person. The behavior therapist cannot conceive of this distinction much less act in accordance with it.

The source of much of the experimental learning work stems from lower organisms. The traditional therapists claim that behavior therapists are treating people as if they were rats. The important point is that behavior therapists make use of concepts that apply to lower organisms as well as humans, but *concepts are the basis of treatment and not treatment itself.* Just as scientific endeavor argues against a separate creation, so it seems sounder to deny a discontinuity between organisms, especially as to principles of behavior.

There are thus differences in background, concepts, and values as well as differences in techniques of treatment. These differences in orientation have led the traditional clinical psychologists, including humanists and existentialists, to form a basic premise that the behavior therapist is different from them, hence of less value to the patient. More specifically, Goldstein (1962) has surveyed the literature and found that there seems to be in our culture at present a triad of patient expectancies of the therapist role. These roles are the nurturant, model, and critic roles. Of the nurturant role, Goldstein (1962, p. 57) writes, "Patients falling into this grouping expect a guiding, giving, protective therapist who is neither businesslike, critical, nor expects his patients to shoulder their own responsibilities." Of the model role, Goldstein writes, "Patients of this type expect a well-adjusted, diplomatic therapist who neither judges nor evaluates his patients and who plays the role of a very permissive listener. The therapist is expected to be neither protective nor critical." Of the critic role, he writes, "The third cluster of patient role expectancies involves patients who expect the therapist to be critical and analytical, to want his patients to assume considerable responsibility, and, further, they anticipate he will be neither gentle nor indulgent." These are expectations on the part of *patients,* but they stem from the culture (newspapers, magazines, movies, TV, and even college lectures). That is, these expectations are a result of observation of prior therapist behaviors, and because they influence both the patient and the therapist, they are likely to continue to be important concepts in evocative therapy. It is our hypothesis that negative comment about behavior therapists would come from nurturant and model therapists who can see the critic role therapist as the only alternative to themselves. That is, the reasoning is: "He is A, B, or C; I am an A or a B; he is different; therefore he must be a C and have all the characteristics of a C, and, incidentally, none of the good characteristics which make me an A or B."

Having given some background to the differences that exist between types of therapists, we may now turn to the positive characteristics of behavior therapists. The first area is clinical skill. Clinical skill in a behavior therapist includes a number of elements, an important one being the ability to maintain a standard situation in the face of fluctuating conditions. An example is the administration of an intelligence test, which must be given in a very strict, standard manner; but prior to administration, and just as necessary for validity, is obtaining the subject's cooperation. To do this, the examiner must vary his behavior, the loudness of his voice, the length of the interview preceding the test, and the level of his vocabulary. He must be able to explain his purpose in such a manner that the subject will understand and accept its importance. This ability, to be flexible in achieving a set goal, is an important clinical skill in behavior modification.

The therapist must be centered on the welfare of the patient. This seems a truism. But here it specifically means self-control in fulfilling his own wishes, needs, and responses. Many symptoms are offered during the course of therapy and if not rewarded with attention, drop out. Paying attention may create and prolong symptoms. The behavior therapist must have the self-control to follow a predetermined, albeit flexible program. It is harder for most therapists to be quiet and not respond, than it is to drift, unbusinesslike, with the affairs of the patient. That the behavior therapist is centered on the welfare of his patient, and disciplined, may be contrasted with the concept of therapy as a good way of life for the therapist (Astin, 1961) or as simply "being" (Jourard, 1959). There is genuine self-sacrifice on the part of the behavior therapist.

The behavior therapist has a goal and a procedure, arrived at before the fact, for reaching the goal. He has a behavioristic criterion, frequency of response or progress on a hierarchy, to measure his progress toward that goal. He may evaluate his success toward the goal, decide that his plan is not being effective and change the procedure (note the article by Rafi (29)). There is a scientific training manifested in this constant evaluation. The behavior therapist, unlike either the Freudian or the Rogerian, varies his techniques, and the range of these devices will be manifested by the variety of treatment procedures described in this book. More importantly, he does not start therapy and thereafter let the process of therapy take its course. The behavior therapist explicitly accepts responsibility for the procedure and progress of treatment.

Because the behavior therapist does manipulate the environmental stimuli in a systematic response contingent manner, the behavior therapist has been accused of being cold, dictatorial, and undemocratic.

The goal of therapy is selected because a complaint has been made, either by the patient or by some social agency. We have quoted previously from Thorpe and Katz (1948, p. 161), "The patient finds it difficult to believe that his symptoms should not be treated directly." We have also quoted Coleman (1956, p. 225) on this point: "It is very difficult to overcome the patient's resistance to the actual facing of his problems." If it is improper for the therapist to select the material to be worked with and to guide the learning situation, it seems a graver impropriety to ignore the patient's reason for coming to therapy. It seems fairer to use one's scientific and professional knowledge to help the patient achieve *his* goal than it is to draw him into a process, even if it is called self-actualization, which the patient did not request and which is not firmly validated.

Explicit influence, which the behavior therapist overtly uses in helping the subject achieve his goal, is frowned upon by traditional psychotherapists. However, there is a definite use of social influence and indoctrination in traditional psychotherapy. For example, we have previously quoted Coleman's statement: "Psychological treatment . . . focuses on (1) helping him understand the dynamic significance of his symptoms." That is, there is in expressive therapy a procedure of having the patient accept a particular viewpoint, one which is likely to include the medical model and Freudian psychodynamics.

There is a considerable amount of social influence that occurs in traditional therapy. On a first level, there is the indoctrination of the future psychoanalyst himself (Frank, 1961, pp. 121–129). At a second level, there is the shaping of patients' verbal behavior to conform to therapists' theoretical expectations (Marmor, 1961; Goldstein, 1962). This is probably done by attention, interest, and agreement (the generalized reinforcers used in the laboratory studies of verbal conditioning and illustrated therapeutically in the Rickard *et al.* articles (7, 8)). In short, evocative therapy may involve a considerable amount of response contingent reinforcement, but such social influence procedures are neither consciously nor systematically used in the service of the patient. In this manner, the clinical observations on which traditional therapists build their theories are influenced by the theories themselves and maintain the therapists in their patterns. In terms of the unsystematic use of social influence in traditional psychotherapy, E. J. Murray (1962) has analyzed the behavior of John Rosen, a Freudian, and some client-centered therapy cases (Murray, 1956). Therapist responses are not patient determined; quite the contrary, a point that has been made by Fiedler (1953). Wolpe (1958) has specifically hypothesized that the unsystematic use of reciprocal inhibition is the basis of those successes observed in traditional psychotherapy. To the extent that anxiety provoking material is discussed and paired with the accepting, protective, anxiety reducing atmosphere created by the therapist, there may be counter-conditioning and a direct analogue of the procedures used in Wolpe's desensitization. However, we might add the hypothesis that the unsystematic and unplanned nature of the situation may just as easily lead to resensitization in which a too rapid elicitation of stimuli producing anxiety responses leads to the therapist becoming a stimulus for anxiety responses, rather than anxiety responses being reduced by association with greater therapist calm. Therapists may be prone to demonstrating their skill in uncovering and interpreting material, and it seems more parsimonious to explain patient responses to such interpretative behavior (fear, hostility, emotional reactions) on the basis of resensitization than on a negative transference neurosis due to some prior childhood experience. However, we do not propose this as an explanation for all cases of negative transference: patients may become annoyed or disappointed with the expenditure of time and money that seems to produce no noticeable improvement in their condition. Interpretations that these feelings are due to the patient's resistances or complexes only throws fuel on a fire which seems to be a reasonable and even healthy assertion by the patient that he may expect some return on his investment.

In short, traditional therapists' objection to behavior therapy in terms of the overt application of learning principles seems unwarranted when viewed in the light of their dogmatic application of a theory that overrides the patient's wishes, their actual procedures of indoctrination, and the loss of efficiency by haphazard use of the therapeutic situation. In contrast, the behavior therapist explicitly utilizes all the knowledge and environmental opportunities at his command to modify, alter, or redirect behavior.

Aside from self-referred outpatient adults, there are subjects, usually institutionalized diagnosed schizophrenics, with whom behavior therapy is practiced. We have frequently been challenged whether it is right to change behavior without the person's permission. There are a variety of answers: the first is that the psychologist is a representative of society who does the job he is paid to do as efficiently as he can. We would also claim that a person does not have the *right* to be "sick." That is, if a person's behavior has become a burden to society and if his behavior can be changed, whether he wants it or not, it is right and proper to change the behavior. To the extent that other members of society must support the person who is in a hospital or prison, it is right and proper that the representatives of that society be employed to change the person. If conditions do not permit a person to return to a productive or adaptive role, then we think that there is an obligation to provide for him, but just as we favor training in new techniques to permit industrial reemployment, we think that retraining should proceed in changing conditions that are a barrier to effective living. Szasz's discussion (1963) of the relationship between law, liberty, and psychiatry is most relevant at this point. He calls for a vigilant, democratic, society in which unhappy people are not forced into the behavior controlling mental hospital by indiscriminate labeling of their behavior as "sick" or "mentally ill."

Eventually, however, a person's view of this problem of "values" is determined by whether he considers mental illness or maladaptive behavior to be involved. If the medical model is followed, then the patient's symptoms represent the most economical resolution of psychodynamic conflicts and his symptoms are viewed as defenses and partial gratifications. If however, a behavior modification or learning theory approach is taken, the maladaptive behavior is something that developed and is maintained by environmental consequences.

We find the argument that if the person is happy the way he is, why not leave him be, unrealistic in terms of clinical observation, societal responsibility, and the potential reinforcements that are available through adaptive behavior (better food, more privacy, increased personal liberty and range of alternatives from which he may choose).

In a situation in which little argument on a "value" basis has been raised against insulin coma, electric shock, lobotomy, or drug therapy with varying side effects, we find it strange that problems of "values" should be raised in the case of behavior therapy. An instance in our experience has been the impossibility of depriving patients, who were being subjected to contemporary psychiatric practice, of rich desserts, so that this reinforcement could be made contingent upon adaptive behavior. It seems that many barbarities are permissible in the name of a medical model (including, historically: snake pits, beating, cathartics, blood letting, lobotomies, twirling stools, physical restraints, and dunking), but that there often is little dispensation for psychological model behavior modification. In terms of psychological approaches, it seems that the problem of values did not arise until effective techniques were developed. For example, the same problems raised for behavior modification might well have been raised in the case of psychoanalysis but for its reliance on a medical model and its saving grace of generally being ineffective (Eysenck, 1952).

One of the major contributions of the behavior therapies has been the focusing on the problems of values (Krasner, 1962b, 1963b). The problem of values should be overt so that it may be investigated and guidelines for the appropriate application of behavior influence developed. In view of the increasing efficiency of behavior influence techniques, particularly those of mass media, such an undertaking seems necessary. However, for the interim, the psychologist doing behavior modification with institutionalized or underage subjects must rely on the concept that he is a representative of society with a primary duty to that society. If need be, he may even have to admit that he is in a better position to know what is "good" than a hospitalized patient or a child.

One matter on which there has been some discussion among behavior therapists themselves is that of the need of the therapist to establish rapport. In this particular matter we lean to the view of Meyer and Gelder (1963) that the best results are obtained when the patient and therapist form a good interpersonal relationship. However, this needs to be analyzed and operationally defined. Following the experimental work of Rosenthal (1963), Barber and Glass (1962), Orne (1962), Sarason (1965), and the review work of Frank (1961), Goldstein (1962), and Shapiro (1960), both the subject's and examiner's expectancies, sets, and the like, have a major effect on the individual's response to the situation. As such, a characteristic of the effective behavior therapist is his own self-confidence and his ability to play the professional role. In line with this, the psychologist becomes a reinforcing stimulus. In Patterson's case (31) of a school phobia we see this done by use of a candy reinforcement, and in his case of a hyperactive child (50), there is dramatic evidence of the presence of the psychologist becoming a discriminative stimulus. That is, both the person coming for help and the behavior therapist explicitly expect improvement. The subject's feelings of anxiety, that is, expectations of aversive consequences, are reduced, and the agent removing the aversive stimulus, the psychologist, becomes a reinforcing stimulus. In the very nature of the situation, as well as through use of those reinforcers available in the environment, which include his own behavior as in verbal conditioning (Krasner, 1962a), the psychologist becomes a reinforcer. It is this ability to be a reinforcing stimulus that we would advance as an operational definition of "rapport." This is necessary in general, but particularly when the psychologist uses himself as the stimulus that reduces anxiety as the subject is exposed to real stimuli. Conversely, as Mowrer and Mowrer (1938) point out, a person who wishes to use conditioning techniques in a sadistic manner would easily find other ways to be punishing.

There is genuine skill, as the result of training and practice, in the following tasks: analyzing the situation for the behavior to be changed; finding the reinforcers maintaining the behavior and the reinforcers that may be manipulated to change the behavior; recognizing rapidly the stimuli to reinforce as the patient acts; and programing reinforcement schedules. Some examples may illustrate this. In working with pigeons and rats, it is common knowledge that efficiency in shaping a behavior is greatly improved by practice. There is genuine skill in selecting the area for a hierarchy in reciprocal inhibition, and there is skill in developing the items, their order, and so forth, once the area has been selected. The behavior therapist learns to be flexible and appropriate in terms of the subject while still maintaining discipline and effectiveness in terms of broader aspects of his technique.

Both the patient and the behavior therapist can be and are trained. We have previously noted that the articles in this book will illustrate the programing of students, nurses, and parents. Because the contingencies on which the therapist's behavior rest are explicit, teaching is relatively simple and direct. While all behavior therapy is explicitly training, we can particularly note that the subject is trained in matters such as relaxation responses or new roles.

Even though we take a stand that behavior therapy is easily taught, we do not think that it is a mechanical procedure devoid of either skill or personal warmth. In fact, there are two major aspects to the teaching of behavior therapy. The first includes the specifics of current techniques. But the second, and more important aspect, is the teaching of a way of viewing clinical problems so that the ingenuity of the student can come into play in moving on to even more useful techniques. We believe that any progress in the matter of training people to modify behavior efficiently rests with scientific procedure, particularly adherence to operationally defined concepts. Behavior modification may be contrasted with the statement attributed to a participant in a conference concerned with training in psychotherapy: "Psychotherapy is an undefined technique applied to unspecified problems with unpredictable outcome. For this technique we recommend rigorous training" (Raimy, 1950, p. 93).

Case Histories and the Teaching and Evaluation of Therapy

We can start this discussion of the major content of this volume no better than by quoting from Knight Dunlap (1946): "As for case histories, we can go beyond Janet's statement that no accumulation of case histories can possibly prove a psychotherapeutic theory and say that it requires a sound theory, adequately based on psychology, to validate any case history. For the present, case histories are to be regarded, not as proofs of theories, but as illustrations thereof."

Many points are touched on in this quotation. The first and foremost is the need for the theory before rather than after the fact of the therapeutic endeavor. We have discussed this earlier. The second point is the limited power of case histories to prove a theory. The case history may be, and not infrequently is, the unusual rather than the usual instance. This may be as true for behavior modification as psychoanalysis: both may be offering examples in which a therapist thinks his procedure was decisive when in truth some other factor, unnoticed, unmentioned, and uncontrolled, was operating. However, cases, both successes and failures, comprise the first step in theory building and the validation of applied techniques. Case material, clinical experience as it were, is a first step, inconclusive by itself, perhaps, but necessary. A third point is that while a case history may not prove a theory, it may very well point out an exception that casts major doubt on a different theory. We have mentioned this particular aspect in regard to symptom substitution and the treatment of overt behavior rather than underlying causes. Among the notions that are contradicted by the case histories presented in this volume are that certain patterns of maladaptive behavior are difficult or impossible to treat and that certain people are not proper subjects for therapy. In terms of the former, the reader will find conditions such as phobias and impotence treated as almost "routine." In the traditional psychoanalytic literature these behaviors are considered extremely difficult. Fenichel (1945, p. 170) remarks, "Essentially, impotence and frigidity are not returns of the repressed from the repression but clinical manifestations and bulwarks of the defense itself." In terms of phobias, Lazarus (21) quotes Curran and Partridge (1955) to the effect that "phobic symptoms are notoriously resistant to treatment, and their complete removal is rarely achieved." In terms of subjects, the reader will note that chronic schizophrenics, brain injured children, and retardates respond to behavior modification, although traditionally these people are not considered suitable for psychotherapy. All too frequently, it seems that only the patients with the most favorable prognosis are considered suitable for treatment (Alexander and French, 1946, pp. 96–106; Dollard and Miller, 1950, pp. 233–239; Fenichel, 1945, pp. 573–581). By offering examples that these limiting and self-validating procedures are not necessarily true, case histories such as those in this book perform a genuine service. A fourth point is that case history material serves to answer one of the questions most frequently asked by students: what do psychologists do? The detailed, operationally defined procedures to be presented throughout this book are better answers than either abstract theoretical material or reference to "the patient then was given psychotherapy." For training and didactic purposes the explicit, teachable, and reproducible nature of the material in case histories is of major importance. Fifth, case histories are examples. As such, they illustrate procedures and provide a source of ideas as to how problems may be approached. Further, they serve to link theory and application, to shed light on the meaning of learning concepts and document their import in a manner that may at times be overlooked in academic courses.

Finally, successful case histories may not validate the treatment, but they may certainly generate interest and be highly suggestive. For example, if there has been no earlier improvement after considerable time and treatment, as in the Bachrach, Erwin, and Mohr (14) or the Meyer and Gelder (1963) cases, a rapid change in behavior is dramatic suggestive evidence that the treatment deserves further study. In terms of prior failure to improve followed by a change after the introduction of behavior modification techniques, there will be frequent mention of:

a. Duration of maladaptive behavior;
b. prior forms of treatment;
c. speed with which new behavior became manifest after start of behavior modification;
d. stability of the new, adaptive behavior; and
e. a statement on symptom substitution, or the lack thereof.

To repeat, such instances by themselves do not validate a therapy, but if they become increasingly frequent, particularly with the failures of traditional therapy, there is an argument for the use of behavior modification prior to failure of other forms of treatment. This point is of some importance since a new form of treatment is likely to have to fight for acceptance. Wider acceptance is likely to lead to increased rates of success as the practitioners gain prestige and the patients are referred before they have had opportunity to overlearn maladaptive responses. Aside from a chronic case in which the chance of spontaneous remission has been greatly reduced, and the failure of prior treatment has made a placebo response an unlikely explanation, there is another type of case history that is highly persuasive scientifically. Illustrations of this type of case may be found in this book in the material from the University of Washington nursery school (38, 39, 40) that follow a traditional Skinnerian paradigm.

In these cases, a set of environmental contingencies are devised and the maladaptive behavior decreased; next the contingencies are reversed and the maladaptive behavior increased; and finally the therapeutic contingencies returned and adaptive behavior once more instituted and maintained. This procedure of operant, increase, decrease, and finally increase of adaptive behavior in association with specific environmental conditions demonstrates the degree of stimulus control obtained by the technique.

The presentation of cases stimulates interest and gives instruction in a method that may be replicated by other therapists. In terms of evaluation, the Skinnerian model just discussed is quite persuasive. Efforts at evaluation of behavior modification techniques are in general in their early stages because the widespread use of the procedures is a relatively recent phenomenon. We shall now review some of the various methods that have been used to argue for the merit of these procedures.

A first method depends upon setting up a base rate. In this procedure, data is collected to establish how many cases may be expected to recover in a given period of time without any particular treatment. This base rate then serves as a standard that must be superseded either by more frequent or more rapid success of the technique under evaluation. An illustration of these two related methods may be found in an article by Jones (1960b) on enuresis. Reviewing published reports of over 1000 cases, Jones found the rate of favorable response to a conditioning technique was higher than that of expressive therapy. A second technique illustrated by Jones is that of devising a curve of percentages of individuals at different ages who are enuretic. In this manner the general remission rate from one age to another can be ascertained. It is then easy to demonstrate that the response to conditioning procedures is far faster and that a greater number of individuals respond favorably than would have been expected on the basis of time.

Similar to Jones' work on enuresis is that of Eysenck (1952, 1961) on neurotics. Eysenck reviewed the literature and found that if no treatment was given, as in instances as insurance company workmen's compensation or people placed in state psychiatric hospitals, the remission rate was approximately seventy percent within two years. This rate of remission was found to equal that of traditional psychotherapy, and be somewhat higher than that obtained by patients receiving full psychoanalytic therapy. Directly related to Eysenck's work and the extended quote from Marmor previously given, is that different forms of expressive therapy seem to lead to similar remission rates (Wilder, 1945). With children, a similar result has been documented by Levitt (1957, 1963). Here, after some forty articles, the remission rate for untreated cases would seem to be about sixty-five to seventy percent, and again, little difference is found between no treatment and traditional psychotherapy. In short, the standard is to do better than seventy percent improved in two years, either by a significantly greater percent improved or a significant saving in time.

The point of speed or number of sessions may be made by contrasting the results of two therapists who have recently published surveys of their efficacy over a series of cases. The first is by Heilbrunn (1963), who presented data based on 241 private patients. His conclusions are (p. 435)·

1. Psychoanalytic psychotherapy of whatever duration and intensity had only supportive and managerial value for psychotic and schizoid patients. Sociopathic patients fared just a trifle better.
2. Brief psychotherapy showed impressive results with the symptom neuroses (70 percent) and adjustment reactions of adolescents (83 percent).[4]
3. The personality trait disturbances reached a peak improvement rate of 60 percent with psychoanalysis as compared with 57 percent under extended psychotherapy. Therefore, the treatment of character neuroses should be begun in the form of psychoanalysis, with the reasonable expectation for successful termination before the three-hundredth hour.

Heilbrunn lumped greatly improved and moderately improved patients in one group and slightly improved (which were "improved patients being a mere shade above unimproved") with the unimproved. Across his 241 cases, those seen for 1–20 hours showed 27 percent improvement, those seen between 21–100 hours showed 35 percent improvement, those seen between 101–300 hours showed 39 percent improvement, and those seen 301–1350 hours (average 509 hours) showed 38 percent improvement; 61.7 percent of the psychoneurotics improved in an estimated 55 hours. By contrast, Lazarus (1963b) reports that 78 percent of the 408 individuals who consulted him derived definite and constructive benefit. More germanely, while stringent criteria of improvement were used, Lazarus reports that of his 126 extremely neurotic patients 61.9 percent were rated as markedly or completely improved. The percentage improvements between Lazarus and Heilbrunn are very similar, but a difference is that Lazarus reports that his results were achieved in an average of 14.07 sessions while his slightly and unimproved groups averaged 12.9 sessions. The difference between these two reports is one of speed.

Lazarus in the article just mentioned reports data on twenty follow-up inquiries in which information was obtained from at least one informant other than the patient. The mean follow-up time was two years after therapy. "A special attempt was made to examine the occurrence of 'symptom substitution.' In general, only the most tenuous suggestions of possible 'symptom substitution' were encountered in two cases out of twenty after-study inquiries." In similar fashion Wolpe (1961), selecting thirty-nine cases randomly from his files in which systematic desensitization had been used, reports that six month to four year follow-up of twenty of the successfully treated patients "did not reveal an instance of relapse or the emergence of new symptoms." In this group of cases, there was marked improvement in ninety percent of the cases and a median number of sessions per patient of ten.

The second aspect of base rates, that of remission estimated from percentages in the population, was developed by Shepherd and Gruenberg (1957) and confirms the expectation that approximately seventy percent of the cases should show marked improvement within two years. Wolpe (1954, 1958, 1961) has reported a fairly consistent level of ninety percent marked improvement. Perhaps just as important in terms of ethics is the rapid identification and either termination or change of technique when some form of behavior modification seems to be of dubious value with a person. For example, in his work with a sequence of women who were sexually frigid, Lazarus (1963c) obtained successful results with a majority in an average of less than thirty sessions, but more

[4] This 83 percent was based on six cases.

importantly, all individuals who were not successful had terminated within fifteen or fewer hours. It seems reasonable for the ethical therapist to terminate when he has little hope of treatment being worthwhile. Because behavior modification focuses on overt behavior, the therapist obtains feedback as to progress that permits him to perform his social function not only more efficiently but also more ethically.

The generality of the remission rate across different forms of expressive therapy, as well as untreated individuals, raises a question of the basis of spontaneous remissions and the general functions of therapy. There have been three major lines of explanation.

The first is that all forms of treatment, when they are effective, make use of a common element. As an example, there is Wolpe's concept that reciprocal inhibition, the conditioning of new, incompatible responses to stimuli likely to lead to maladaptive responses, is the common effective element. Included in the present book is an article by Wolpe (17) that offers clinical data to support his contention as to what is the crucial therapeutic element in psychotherapy. The similarity of the remission rate of untreated and traditionally treated cases may be explained by the number of cases resensitized by ineffective psychotherapy being balanced by the cases experiencing (nonsystematic) desensitization.

A second line of explanation considers traditional psychotherapy as a nonspecific one enhancing placebo-like effects. This is the view of authors such as Frank (1961) and Goldstein (1962). The patient's resources are mobilized by the attention of the professional person, and the mutual expectations of patient and therapist that improvement will occur.

A third line of reasoning has been put forward by Eysenck (1960a, 1963a, 1963b). Eysenck argues that there are two patterns of maladaptive behavior. In the first, those of a dysthymic character, which are traditionally called neurotic (anxieties, phobias, depressions, obsessions), it is assumed that the disorder consists of conditioned sympathetic reactions and the treatment consists of reconditioning stimuli to parasympathetic reactions. If there is no underlying "neurosis" but only the maladaptive responses, then in daily life, extinction, the presentation of the conditioned stimulus that defines the learned, maladaptive response without the original unconditioned stimulus will lead to extinction. There will be a curve, which Eysenck approximates from previous studies, of "spontaneous remissions" in which neither symptom substitution nor relapse will be observed. A second type of disorder might be more traditionally called symptom reactions or character disorders and includes alcoholism, fetishism, homosexuality, and the like, in which the conditioned stimulus evokes parasympathetic responses. For these conditions Eysenck suggests aversive conditioning on a continued, overlearned, aperiodic schedule. Here relapse is considered more likely if continued training (roughly twice a year) is not invoked, because the maladaptive behavior usually leads to a gratification more rapidly than the effect of societal disapproval. When such instances occur, extinction of the therapeutic learning is rapid.

Whether in agreement with all of Eysenck's thesis or not, the point becomes that for neurotic or dysthymic or "anxiety" responses, a rate of spontaneous remission is to be expected simply in terms of extinction. The goal of behavior modification, then, is to obtain a greater percentage of remissions, a more rapid rate of remission, or both. Subsidiary problems, which can eventually be settled by random assignment studies, deal with selection of patients (assuming that some problems are more difficult than others) and measures of benefit (assuming that different therapists have different standards of successful outcome). This latter problem arises with particular pertinence in a comparison of traditional and behavioristic therapy because the former minimizes overt (and more readily measured) behavior for psychodynamics and internal motivational systems that are poorly defined and frequently lead to rater unreliability.

While methods such as those of an own-control study with a chronic case, a comparison of different forms of treatment by different therapists, or contrasting results with a base rate may all generate interest and decrease uncertainty to some degree, eventually, there must be experimental validation. This procedure calls for random assignment of cases to forms of treatment and therapists, the use of an overt, highly reliable criteria, and the application of the criterion measures by some rater who is either blind as to the treatment the subject was receiving or who cannot alter the subject's response during the criterion measurement. In the present volume we present three such studies, those of Lang and Lazovik (20), King, Armitage, and Tilton (6), and Lazarus (19). A very complete evaluation of the efficacy of behavior modification techniques has been made by Paul (1964b). College undergraduates were accepted for treatment from a group of students who were highly anxious about giving speeches and requested treatment. While doing an injustice to the scope and thoroughness of the work, the present remarks will be directed to four groups of subjects and a battery of criterion measures. The conditions were a systematic desensitization procedure, an attention-placebo situation that maximized the subjects' expectation of improvement through receiving therapist attention, no treatment, and insight therapy. Insight therapy was defined as the favored and usual practice of the five professional psychologists who served as therapists in all three treatment conditions. In each treatment condition fifteen subjects were seen for five sessions each. There were twenty-nine subjects composing the no-treatment group. Groups were matched on pretreatment measures, and subjects were randomly assigned over therapists. The criterion measure was overt behavior while giving a speech under the stressful circumstance of an audience composed of strangers and psychologists who every thirty seconds rated the presence or absence of some twenty behavioral manifestations of anxiety. The results indicated that significantly greater positive change occurred in the desensitization group than in either the attention-placebo or insight-therapy groups. These last two groups did not differ significantly from each other, but both led to significantly greater improvement than the no-treatment procedure.

While more studies of the type cited in the previous paragraph are needed, the present evidence seems to indicate strongly that behavior modification techniques have merit. Finally, we wish to mention what we consider the basic element validating behavior therapy techniques. The procedures used are devised and tested in laboratory settings before application to clinical populations. The amount of systematic experimentation on behavioral procedures may be contrasted with theories seeking to rationalize clinical experience after the fact. At this point, while we can foresee clinical experience modifying learning concepts, we do not think it probable that clinical experience is likely to negate fundamental concepts in the psychology of learning. We may summarize this section by reiterating our theme that a psychological model is closer to the observed facts and therefore more effective than a disease model.

Behavior Modification: A Perspective in Time

We have described behavior modification in terms of theory and general content. The body of this book will present examples of actual practice. A third approach to behavior modification is historical and will be undertaken in this section.

The major element in behavior modification is the focus on overt behavior and its change through manipulation of the same conceptual variables that led to its development. The subject is exposed to an environment that is manipulated by the therapist to provide meaningful contingencies for the subject's differential responses to stimuli. It is this last rubric, that of systematic response contingent environmental consequences based on the theoretical and empirical work of the last twenty years that is the distinctive mark of contemporary behavior modification. However, there have been many precursors who took the basic attitude—that of retraining behavior—and who utilized, albeit far from systematically, many if not all of the techniques discussed and illustrated in this book.

If we had to signify a single starting point, it would probably be the Greeks whose temple psychiatry (Zilboorg and Henry, 1941) involved an elaborate scheme of social influence including the suggestion of previous cures, rituals, drugs, and so forth, to foster a new course of behavior. The suppliant was considered basically normal and personally responsible, that is, failure to obtain relief was considered an indication of impiety rather than of sickness over which he had no control. While the history of the treatment of persons displaying maladaptive behavior is bleak, we should mention those pioneers who followed naturalistic rather than supernatural approaches and who, in so doing, started by observing behavior: Hippocrates, Erisistratus, Asclepiades, Aretaeus, Vives, Weyer, Plater, and Willis. We have previously mentioned Pinel. His concept of the maladaptive person as one to be treated as normal and responsive to the same treatment as other people led to the concepts of Moral Treatment which we consider a prime example of behavior therapy. In Moral Treatment, as we noted, the person was expected to play a normal rather than sick role. A rewarding environment, but not necessarily a "permissive" one, was developed. As an example of treatment of behavior rather than an underlying cause, we should mention Johan Christian Reil, who at the start of the nineteenth century treated stuporous depressives by infecting them with scabies, or the itch, a procedure that made motor responses reinforcing. More importantly, it was Reil, probably more than any other person, who in his theater for the insane was father of psycho-drama or role-taking as a therapeutic technique (Zilboorg and Henry, 1941, p. 287).

Mesmer's methods in the eighteenth century are in a direct line with both the procedures of the Greeks and the present day discussion of placebo responses as treatment. His procedure, when tested by a committee, including Benjamin Franklin, was found to rest on psychological principles rather than physical or medical ones.

The work of Freud and his followers represents a procedure of environmental change to alter behavior. We have discussed psychoanalysis in a variety of contexts, particularly those elements which are effective methods of behavior modification when systematically applied.

In addition to this general stream of development, there are the direct precursors of behavior therapy. The works of Pavlov, Sechenov, Behkterev, and Bykhov on the one hand, and Thurstone, Hull, Mowrer, and Skinner on the other are considered the foundation of behavior therapy. More clearly than any other person, John B. Watson deserves credit in psychology for pointing out the wide social implications of Pavlov's work, for generating interest among psychologists in it, and for providing early examples with humans of its use.

There are numerous examples of both the approach (that is, William James and L. Witmer) as well as empirical procedures in the English and German language literature from 1890 on. English associationism laid the groundwork for later theories of learning, and German laboratories in the tradition of Fechner, Wundt, and Ebbinghaus, for procedures and discipline by which theories were made to bear fruit. If a single year had to be specified, we would be inclined to point to 1924, and in terms of people, to William Burnham and Mary Cover Jones as the ones who brought together the various backgrounds involved. Because of his review of the previous literature, his discussion of both Pavlov and psychoanalysis, and his emphasis on the value of the meaningful task (which leads to both reinforcement and social role concepts) we are inclined to follow Mowrer (in press) in citing Burnham's volume (1924), *The Normal Mind,* as a major historical landmark.

The extent of Burnham's contribution may best be suggested by quotations from "The Normal Mind" that foreshadow material in the present book. We have previously discussed various methods of change in behavior modification. While, as we noted, these techniques overlap considerably and might be reduced to the single concept of associating new responses to environmental stimuli, we may list a variety of procedures:

1. assertive responses;
2. sexual responses;
3. relaxation responses;
4. conditioned avoidance responses;
5. feeding responses;
6. interview induced emotional responses, including abreaction and emotive imagery;
7. modeling;
8. negative practice and extinction;
9. selective positive reinforcement.

Wolpe's general paradigm, reflected in his formulation of assertive, feeding, sexual, and relaxation responses is that of reciprocal inhibition, the association of a response incompatible with anxiety to the threatening stimulus. Burnham (1924) has a chapter specifically entitled "Inhibition of the inhibitions" and several times gives a basic formulation. For example (Burnham, p. 149); ". . . the essential factor . . . is the associated stimulus that inhibits the inhibition." He writes (p. 623): "In other words, one brings the child definitely to face the cause[5] of its fear, just as the horse trainer, with soothing words, leads the colt face to face with what has frightened it. Then one

[5] Ed. note: in this quote, "cause," as can be seen by the rest, is the "fear inspiring object or idea" (stimulus) and not some "underlying cause" of which the objective stimulus is a displacement.

associates a rival stimulus with the fear-inspiring object or idea. . . . by such discussion, rival stimuli would be associated . . . these associated ideas would inhibit the fear."

A reflection of the use of a dominant motor response is found in Burnham (p. 445): "Coordinated motor activity of any kind, physical or mental, is the universal preventive of fear."

One value of assertive responses is that these behaviors are more likely to be reinforced. Burnham notes (p. 471): "If a child believes that he can do a thing he is likely to attempt it; and, if he begins, the amount of effort put forth depends largely on his belief in the power to succeed."

In terms of the sexual responses, which Wolpe uses primarily in the treatment of impotence, the form of the technique is clearly present (albeit not the specific physical modality) in Burnham's (1924, pp. 431–432) reference to a case presented by Gehring (1893). In this case a literary woman was unable to work, for when she sat down to do so "the foreign emotion of anger would steal in and take possession of consciousness. . . . She was instructed to sit down at her table prepared to write; and if the ideas would not come, merely to continue sitting there. It was not to matter if she did not write a sentence during the hour, but under no circumstances was she to yield to any feeling except that of perfect serenity. She was to feel responsible only for the maintenance of the proper mental attitude." It is reported that in ten days she was able to achieve her normal output.

Burnham was interested in education, mental hygiene, and training adaptive behavior so that maladaptive behavior would be less likely to occur and be reinforced. For example, he writes (p. 562): "The great means of preventing misconduct is the providing of suitable tasks." These suitable tasks are what we would call socially appropriate behavior, activity that is socially meaningful and leads to an experience of success. In providing (manipulating, if one will) an environment, one feature that underlies effective reinforcement schedules is noted (p. 470): "But the maxim for the teacher should be to make the work so easy at first that the child will believe that he can do it. . . ." This leads to a general statement of normal behavior and the role of the modifier of behavior (p. 532): "In the wider sense discipline is a systematic attempt to develop conditioned reflexes and habits adjustant to the tasks of the school and of life." In a manner similar to the concepts of value and freedom that we proposed above, he gives principles (p. 244) that are the purposes of training: the performance of social duty in a natural group; the development of integration in the face of distracting stimuli; individual responsibility in the group; and, the development of conditions that give the opportunity for social success. A fifth statement, following these, is the simple one, "All this implies freedom." That is, the object of freedom is to make meaningful and useful choices rather than to behave without guidance or constraint.

Another technique, anticipating later reciprocal inhibition concepts and procedures of Wolpe and his followers, for example, the emotive imagery of Lazarus and Abramovitz (36) and Walton's (1960b) treatment of a schizophrenic, is the embedding of a threatening concept in a neutral or positive context. A "case" from Burnham (pp. 174–175) will illustrate the point and may be contrasted with Freud's case of Little Hans (compare, Wolpe and Rachman, 1960):

The Genesis of a Conditioned Reflex and an Association Complex.—A boy 22 months old was left to be cared for by a neighbor, while the mother was away, on a stormy day in April with high winds and driving snow. The neighbor went to the store taking the child. On the way home the boy saw a horse slip and fall. He was extremely interested, to the extent that the neighbor was obliged to face the storm with the child and watch men take the harness off and lift the horse up. When the father returned for the evening meal, the first thing the child said was: "Horse fall down." The neighbor explained the circumstances and said that the child had repeated these words at least three times during the afternoon. For several days the child repeated these words at least fifty times a day. The father noted the nascent obsession and thought these words should be replaced by some other phrase or at least modified; and thereafter whenever the boy repeated the words, the father added: "Yes, horse fall down, but man picked it up." Several days later, when the mother returned, the first greeting was: "Horse fall down." Gradually the child added: "but man picked it up." This addition was emphasized every time the child repeated the words. Also whenever the child saw a picture of a horse in a magazine, he always said: "Horse fall down," and a picture of an automobile breaking through a fence and dashing into the river called forth the words: "Automobile fall down," and any picture that could be interpreted in this way was explained as "fall down." Even when a team passed the house the child said: "Horse fall down." Every time he said this the parents emphasized the words "man picked it up." A neighbor showed the child a comic section of a newspaper and talked about "Uncle Munn." The child added this to his horse complex and said: "Uncle Munn picked horse up." The child still continued to say: "Horse fall down," but only perhaps once or twice in several days, and now usually adds: "man picked it up." At first these words were uttered in a doleful tone, but now in a matter-of-fact way.

A final point on the matter of association is that Burnham notes how thinking of the appropriate image or situation may lead to the desired response. As an example he mentions how the poet Southey, to cure his insomnia, would think of his undergraduate classroom.

Positive reinforcement may serve as a stimulus to increase behaviors incompatible with maladaptive behavior. Burnham (p. 479) calls this concept *success*. "The business of the social worker also in large part is to give concrete tasks to those who are chronic failures, to give the opportunity for success so that the stimulus of success may be a help to further activities." Specifically, what we would call verbal conditioning is involved in his analysis of the potential bases of the effectiveness of psychoanalysis. He writes (p. 632): "The sixth factor is the reinforcement of the stimulus to a new course of thinking and acting, the new course of behavior in general, by the statement of the psychoanalyst in emphasizing the value of it, especially if he is an individual in whom one has confidence. Every one feels this reinforcement from the approval of one's opinion or one's action by another person, however humble. One feels it much more when the approval is by one deemed an expert in the matters in question."

Perhaps the most "modern" aspects of Burnham's work occur in his analysis of the psychoanalytic situation. Burnham notes that through dreams, free associations, and the gathering of autobiographical material, the patient in psychoanalysis is provided with a social role which is reinforced or, in his terms, is a meaningful task. The psychoanalytic procedure makes these tasks interesting and builds up the expectation of therapeutic benefit. This is done by finding relations between sets of data important

to the patient, especially his dreams, free associations, and life history. Next (p. 628):
"The psychoanalyst makes the task the more interesting and the more significant to
the ordinary patient by giving some account of the unconscious. This, which is sometimes merely a form of psychological astrology, gives to most people a suggestion of
the transcendent significance of the whole matter." Perceptively, and anticipating later
critiques, Burnham writes (p. 633): "From a psychological point of view this elaborate
philosophy of the Unconscious is hardly needed except, perhaps, to impress the patient,
and give inspiration and enthusiasm to the psychoanalyst. This whole doctrine is at
once romance, philosophy, and poetry. Psychologically, it does not matter whether it is
true or not...."

It is worth noting that the statement is that of giving "inspiration and enthusiasm
to the psychoanalyst." The psychoanalyst's attention and interest are the prime generalized reinforcers at his command, and his attitude of confidence and devotion to his
method are major factors in any success. A procedure that maintains his interest, enthusiasm, confidence, and so forth, is of great therapeutic value even if it may be objectively false. It is a truism that medicines should be given before they lose their
power (that is, therapists become disenchanted with them) and that frequently young
therapists are more effective than older therapists whose experience has given them
some contact with reality. The therapist is the major feature of the therapy and the
stimuli he emits major conditioned cues. Burnham gets at this concept when he writes
(p. 605): "In many cases the cure seems to be the result, not so much of the remedy
given, as of the form in which it is applied. As Heilbronner points out, the psychiatrist
may fail in his efforts until he decides to resort to some measure which, as the patient
says, has always helped. . . . As soon as the psychiatrist adopts this method—that is,
applies the associated stimulus that has become useful in producing certain healthful
conditioned reflexes—the cure is effected."

Finally, many of these concepts are brought together when Burnham summarizes
as follows (p. 638): "In a minor way psychoanalysis is helpful because of the interesting
tasks it prescribes for patients. . . . Just as in physical disease the taking of the medicine
and regimen prescribed by the physician, with the attitudes and associations involved
in it, has its value as a task, whether the medicine be a mere *placebo* or really potent,
so active participation in the methods of the psychoanalyst has its value as a significant
task in itself, whether the philosophy of the method be true or false."

In terms of behavior modification, the conceptualization of symptom formation or
maladaptive behavior is crucial. In 1920 Watson and Rayner established a conditioned
emotional response to a rat in an eleven-month-old boy by pairing its presentation with
a sudden loud sound. "Transfer" or generalization of the fear to other furry objects and
stability of the fear over time were noted. The development of a phobia without reference to unconscious mechanisms or displacement was observed. Burnham cites other
examples of the development of maladaptive or "bizarre" behavior by association or
conditioning. He cites J. V. Haberman's (1917) discussion of the development of a
symptom of vomiting in a child through the rushing of breakfast one morning with
associated feelings of scolding, humiliation and fear of being kept in after school if late.
When the child arrived at school there was vomiting. Next day, although the rushing
and anticipation of punishment were not present, the child again vomited. This was explained through association of the events of the previous day. However, the positive

reinforcements which might have also occurred after vomiting (sympathy and attention for the sick role) might also have played a part. The work by Wolf *et al.* (48) in this volume is germane to this point. Other material on the development of maladaptive behavior has already been cited.

In the same year as Burnham's *The Normal Mind,* two important articles were written by Mary Cover Jones (1924a, 1924b). In the first of these, a three-year-old child whose fear of a white rat extended to a rabbit, a fur coat, a feather, cotton, wool, and so forth, was treated by direct conditioning, the association of a rabbit with food the child liked. At times, other children were present to foster imitative responses. In a second article, Jones discussed empirical trials of a variety of techniques in the elimination of children's fears. The methods of elimination through disuse (that fears would disappear with time if the stimuli were avoided), of repression (ridicule, social teasing), and verbal appeal were ineffective. Negative adaptation (extinction) in which familiarity breeds contempt was found to eliminate the fear, but not to reestablish a normal interested response. A method of distraction, which as Jones states, passes over into the method of direct reconditioning, in which the feared object was placed in the context of a desired goal, was found to be fairly effective. Another useful technique was the method of direct reconditioning, the association of the feared object with a stimulus capable of arousing a pleasant reaction. This is similar to Burnham's inhibition of inhibition or Wolpe's reciprocal inhibition. Jones notes the danger of moving too rapidly and producing an effect the reverse of the one desired: for example, a fear response to food, rather than a favorable response (food-pleasantness) to the previously feared object. Jones in this article also notes the method of social imitation in which the stimulus of other children playing with and enjoying the feared object leads the subject to come in to active and pleasant contact with it. However, there is the possibility that a child who is not afraid may learn (imitate) the subject's fear, rather than the reverse.

Early instances of other techniques may be touched upon. While the Romans had a form of aversion treatment for alcoholism, that is, eels in the wine cup, we might cite Kantorovich (1929) for a conditioned aversion treatment of alcoholism, Max (1935) for an aversion treatment of an obsessional sexual difficulty, and Mowrer and Mowrer (1938) for the crucial article in the conditioned aversion treatment of enuresis. In all three of these articles we see the basic element of response contingency.

In three works Dunlap (1928, 1930, 1932) presented the method of what is called *negative practice* that has been found useful in the treatment of tics, stuttering, nail-biting, and, through Malleson (1959), some phobic and obsessive conditions. The undesirable behavior is practiced until, in Hullian terms, reactive inhibition builds up to the extent that not doing the behavior is a positively reinforcing experience (termination of the aversive condition of fatigue).

In line with Burnham's inhibition of the inhibitions as a forerunner of Wolpe's psychotherapy by reciprocal inhibition, we may cite two writers of the 1930's. The first is Hollingworth (1930) whose redintegration theory we have previously mentioned. Discussing stage-fright, Hollingworth (pp. 421–422) writes:

> On any of the three theories, the same therapy is indicated, the substitution of some other reaction for the disabling one, through re-education or new experience. If stage-fright is a direct fear phenomenon, the hopeful therapy is simply that of giving some other emotion

right of way by virtue of the frequency of its appearance. Elation, enthusiasm, confidence, must be connected with the appearance of an audience. If stage-fright is the conflict of two competing tendencies, the conflict can be resolved only by strengthening the emotion which competes with the disabling tendencies. And if stage-fright be an emotional red-integration, the only way of escape is by attaching new consequents to its typical stimulus.

A second writer during the 1930's who used the same language and concepts as we have in our psychological formulation of maladaptive behavior was Guthrie (1938, pp. 386–387):

> To break a habit it is first necessary to know the stimuli responsible for its release. It is then necessary to use whatever arts one has *to cause the person to do something else in this situation.* This is the full recipe. . . . The habit may be "sidetracked" by interrupting it in its very beginning and causing this beginning to be followed by some other action. Or the patient may, by having the action deprived of success in the sense that it removes the motivating stimulus, bring about by trial and error behavior his own substitution for the unwanted act. In all these cases we are merely insuring that a cue which was once followed by the undesirable action is *once* followed by something else. If practice of the substitution is required, this is because the undesired act had more than one cue and it is necessary to recondition all its cues.

Jersild and Holmes (1935) present material that was a by-product of work on children's fears. Central to this article were reports by parents on how they altered their children's fears. The techniques and their effectiveness are reported. In keeping with Jones' (1924b) findings, verbal explanation and reassurance, while the most frequent procedure, if unsupported by some other method, was relatively ineffective. This latter technique when combined with demonstration by an adult of the thing feared was somewhat more effective. A lack of repetition and technical skill might explain the relative failure of "positive but 'passive' conditioning" found by Jersild and Holmes. As with Jones, compelling the child through coercion and ridicule, removing the feared object (Jones' method of disuse), or ignoring the child's fear, were ineffective techniques. As we might have expected on the basis of our previous discussion and Jones' findings, active reconditioning was the most effective technique. This took two forms. The first form was called "graded presentation of the fear stimulus, introducing the child to it by degrees" and has been referred to as a technique of desensitization with real rather than visualized stimuli. It was infrequently used, but when it was used, it was "relatively very successful." Examples are of interest, especially because one is similar to Bentler's case (35) reprinted in this volume. Jersild and Holmes (p. 87) write: "Following are instances in which the method was used successfully: in dealing with a child who was afraid of the flow of water from faucets, the mother made it a policy to get him accustomed to a small flow of water, she then gradually increased the flow; to overcome fear of alarm clocks, the parents used a clock with a softer ring, and then later introduced the louder clock; mother herself begins to cut the child's hair in the barber shop . . . while he grows accustomed to the chair and the surroundings, and then the barber finishes the job; to cope with the fear of the dark, (the) child was first given a very dim light in his room and then subsequently this light was withdrawn." The second method of reconditioning was called "definite attempts to promote skill in dealing with the feared stimulus" and is consonant with techniques from Burnham (1924) to Lazarus and Abramovitch (36). Jersild and Holmes (pp. 88–90) give examples as follows: "One child was much afraid of an imaginary dog. . . . (The mother) entered into make-believe play with the child and brought the imaginary dog into the play. . . . One mother made a dark much-feared closet the center of games with her child, thereby leading the child to explore the closet, to incorporate it into her own activities. One mother encouraged her child's interest in doing small errands . . . by sending her occasionally on errands into a much feared room. . . . In many instances skills were first cultivated with a less intense stimulus: thus, the child is taught how to push the vacuum cleaner when it is silent, to operate the levers of a tractor when it is quiet." The elements of selecting the most effective rate of progress and the ability to formulate the procedure and stick to it for an adequate and effective period seem the major later contributions to these techniques by professional psychologists.

A summary of additional work accomplished prior to World War II may be found in Hilgard and Marquis (1940). The point we have emphasized in this review is that behavior modification had a considerable number of forerunners prior to the present surge of interest.

By the start of World War II, there was a considerable body of both theory and practice; yet there was a hiatus of a quarter of a century in a widespread use of these leads. There seem to be a number of possible explanations for this "cultural lag." A first possible explanation is that the majority of clinical psychologists working in a medical setting overlooked the writings of Burnham and Jersild and Holmes who worked in educational and research settings. Another possibility is that the limited time and energy of professional workers went into the diagnostic testing that from the time of the intelligence test was the psychologist's passport into clinical work.

Factors that led to renewed interest in the application of learning concepts and the direct modification of behavior were the increased number of clinical psychologists after World War II and, more importantly, the steadily increasing standards for doctoral research in clinical psychology. Clinical psychologists became increasingly well trained and interested in empirical problems. Among major influences at the graduate level were excellent new texts on learning and statistics. There was both an increasing transfer of skills and an increased questioning of traditional methods. In the area of psychodiagnostics, this trend was highlighted by Meehl's (1954) work on clinical versus statistical prediction. In the area of psychotherapy, perhaps the most provocative articles, both as stimulants and as reflections of the growing dissatisfaction with traditional modes of therapy were Eysenck's (1952) evaluation of the effectiveness of psychotherapy and Szasz's (1960, 1961a and b) articles on the myth of mental illness.

In this period of time there was increasing concern over the divergence between clinical and experimental psychology. Both to bridge the two disciplines of psychology and to meet the needs of a growing audience, a series of articles appeared (Dollard and Miller, 1950; Magaret, 1950; Mowrer, 1950; Shaw, 1948; Shoben, 1949) translating psychotherapeutic concepts into the language of learning theory. Unfortunately, these writings led to a new way of *talking* about therapy and not a new way of *doing* therapy.

Two crucial books represented the two overlapping schools within behavior modification. The first of these was B. F. Skinner's (1953) *Science and Human Behavior*.

The emphasis on frequency of behavior led to measurable, manipulatable objects of studies of a more molar and immediately interesting nature to clinical psychologists. A second crucial book was Wolpe's (1958) *Psychotherapy by Reciprocal Inhibition,* the first half of which included a summary of the laboratory work that led to his therapeutic regimen. Two particularly important review articles in this period were those by Eysenck (1959) and Bandura (1961). Eysenck's anthology (1960a) of writings on behavior therapy and the establishment of the *Behaviour Research and Therapy* journal (Rachman, 1963a) brought together much of the material and provided an outlet for authors interested in behavior modification. These writings reflected and supplemented the major factor in the marked increase in the use of behavior therapy, namely the direct use of research results. During the period of the 1950's, there was an increasing number of workers who turned their attention to studies of the change of behavior. Several anthologies (Bachrach, 1962; Berg and Bass, 1961; Biderman and Zimmer, 1961; Krasner and Ullmann, 1965) brought together a fair sampling of this material that includes studies of attitude change, group behavior, verbal behavior in interview situations, classical conditioning, sensory deprivation, drugs, hypnosis, physiological correlates of social stimuli, modeling, role-playing, and placebo response. Psychologists who were identified as research workers such as Azrin, Bachrach, Bijou, Ferster, Goldiamond, King, Lindsley, Patterson, and Staats turned their attention to clinical populations and problems so that the distinction between experimentalist and clinician became blurred. A psychology of social influence developed as an area that drew support from and made contributions to many other aspects of psychology. It was the development and application of a technology of behavior change, we think, that led to the increased effectiveness of behavior modification. The difference between the earlier formulations such as those of Shoben and Dollard and Miller, and the present direction in psychology represented by the cases in this book, is the application of research results as well as theory.

Ideas drawn from theory, as to the environmental conditions ("how") necessary to change behavior, were tested and refined. The procedures for implementing effectively the theoretical and programmatic views of Watson, Jones, and Burnham had to be developed and documented before consistent and effective techniques could be established. The first half of Wolpe's book (1958) and his later work (1962, 1963) are instructive examples.

In short, what was accomplished was a building from the ground up rather than a rationalization after the fact. While many clinical procedures were documented, many other clinical procedures were discarded as being irrelevant.

This discussion of experimental foundations is necessarily brief in the context of a collection of case histories. The points we wish to make are:

1. The practice is an application of experimental findings and theoretical formulations;
2. the laboratory work that spans theory and practice, developed in large measure during the decade of 1950–1959, and delineated the technique;
3. the laboratory findings, as will be seen in the next section, lead to new approaches and a broadening of the area of behavior modification;
4. classical (Pavlovian) conditioning, operant (Skinnerian) conditioning, hypnosis, role-

playing, sensory deprivation, and all techniques of attitude change from group pressure through total institutions and brainwashing, have a place in the foundations of behavior modification. The crucial variable is an operational and empirical approach.

Behavior Modification: Likely Future Directions

The future of behavior modification, just as its present status, depends upon psychological theory and research. Both of these bases are continually being elaborated, refined, and broadened. Because behavior modification is *not* a closed system it too will be elaborated, refined, and broadened. At this point, we will discuss some of the directions we think are likely to be pursued by behavior therapists in the near future.

In terms of *refinement,* the treatment of enuresis is an instructive example. Mowrer and Mowrer (1938) cite a number of early hospital observations on the favorable effects when forerunners of the Mowrer apparatus were used to signal a nurse to change the child. The Mowrers introduced improved equipment that led to improved training within a learning framework. They added the feature of having the child drink his normal amount of fluid before bedtime, and after he had been dry a week, having him take an extra glass of water to facilitate the occurrence of learning. Lovibond (1963a) introduced a twin-signal apparatus, which he predicted, on the basis of a theoretical analysis of the situation, would lead to more rapid teaching than previous devices, and in a well designed experiment, obtained significant confirmation of his point. In a second article Lovibond (1963b) addressed himself to the problem of relapse. On the basis of laboratory studies, he predicted that intermittent rather than continuous reinforcement would be more effective and offered some data to support his contention. Eysenck (1963b) also suggests intermittent rather than continuous reinforcement in the use of aversion therapies to reduce the frequency of relapse. In short, we may expect that improved theoretical analyses and more sophisticated application of research findings will lead to changes in treatment procedures. In similar fashion, we may expect application of concepts not presently used. One technique which seems particularly likely to be useful is that of time out from reinforcement as a mildly aversive, self-regulated response-contingent stimulus. Since removal from a positively reinforcing situation is aversive, whenever the subject behaves in a maladaptive manner, he is removed from the reinforcing situation for a brief period of time. In a situation known to one of the authors, table manners were taught by removing the plate for ten seconds whenever "slopping, stuffing, or grabbing" behavior took place. Improved behavior that followed the return of the dinner plate after the period of removal was then heavily reinforced with praise. Mild punishment is used to increase the likelihood that the next, hopefully more adaptive, behavior in the repertoire, will appear. The purpose of punishment is not to suppress a behavior permanently, but to increase the chance of obtaining a behavior that is incompatible with the maladaptive behavior. This alternative behavior is reinforced so that its likelihood of emission will become greater than that of the maladaptive behavior. An experimental situation that illustrates this concept is by Holz, Azrin, and Ayllon (1963) in which, again, the crucial element is that an alternative response was available for obtaining reinforcement.

In terms of *subjects* suitable for behavior modification, there is reason for great optimism. It seems to us, especially in the light of the work printed in this volume dealing with severely disturbed and brain injured children, that behavior modification may offer the opportunity for therapeutic intervention in many cases thought unsuitable for traditional psychotherapy. The work by the University of Washington group with retardates seems to us to be of particular value and social significance. Applications outside specific clinical situations, such as the nursery school, the home, and the factory, seem both feasible and important. On a very broad scale, Osgood's (1962) *An Alternative to War or Surrender* seems to be behavior modification writ most large.

Allied to the people or subjects suitable for behavior modification is the matter of *behaviors suitable for modification*. In work by Homme *et al.* (1963) and articles in this book by Azrin and Lindsley (43), and Madsen (37), as well as the work in nursery schools and summer camps, we see the beginnings of an effective and realistic program of preventive social psychology. Not only may maladaptive behavior be dealt with early, but adaptive behaviors may be selectively reinforced so that their frequency of occurrence decreases the likelihood of maladaptive behaviors. Behaviors such as cooperation, reciprocal reinforcement, interest, and responsibility may be fostered in the classroom and home. As we noted when we touched on the problem of values, the potential effectiveness of behavior influence procedures is such that ethical problems have arisen with pressing urgency. However, the best discussions of these problems still seem to be in novels such as Huxley's *Brave New World* (1932), Orwell's *1984* (1954), Skinner's *Walden Two* (1948), and Wolfe's *Limbo* (1952). This last book brings into the discussion the use of high speed computers as decision makers, a matter touched on by Norbert Weiner (1961) and already reaching some application in the researches of Colby (1963, 1965). In short, the range of social behavior that may be modified seems nearly unlimited and there is great potential for both good and ill.

In terms of *training* and the *role of the psychologist,* we foresee many possible changes. The first is the development of a profession of psychotechnicians trained in the application of behavior modification techniques. With an effective body of information and technique, the pressure for applied rather than research personnel will increase. We also see general public health implications in terms of the most fully trained persons devising programs for others to carry out. Finally, as we have noted before, teachers, nurses, parents, and other people usually either shunted to the background or cast as recipients of therapy, will now become actively involved in the treatment program.

In terms of new *techniques* we may predict that advances in laboratory work will lead to new procedures. Bachrach, Erwin, and Mohr's case (14) of anorexia, printed in this volume, suggests the use of environmental stimulation as a positive reinforcement, and Adams' case (15) points to the use of sensory deprivation as a technique to enhance later stimuli. Obtaining leverage, a worthwhile environmental contingency, is one of the problems of behavior modification, and we expect many new and ingenious techniques to be produced in this area.

One of the most interesting newer areas (Berger, 1961; Kanfer and Marston, 1963) is that of vicarious reinforcement, the learning from someone else's experience. It is conceivable that the same instructional media might be used with many subjects to prepare them for therapy or to increase their likelihood of emitting adaptive behaviors. Empirical substantiation of the feasibility of this procedure may be found in the articles by Kanfer (1965) and by Bandura (1965).

We think that one likely future development will be work with *larger units of behavior with increasingly general social application*. If behavior can be reliably categorized by observers and if subjects' responses can be generalized to physically dissimilar but functionally equivalent exemplars, then new and broader areas of behavior will become suitable foci for behavior modification techniques. Up to the present, relatively circumscribed operants and limited hierarchies have been the foci of modification. It seems possible that response classes that enter into many social situations may become the object of training and that this may lead to more rapid progress than the development of more restricted responses limited to specific acts in designated situations. For example, we think that an example of this is present in the changed attitudes of the students in the special Ranier school: concepts such as interest, enthusiasm, and attention are currently developed as by-products of successful experiences, and we entertain the notion that such attitudes might be fostered more directly and in turn be used to generate social success. We can conceive of training in accurate generalization of experience from one situation to another. At present, such generalization is usually haphazard and left up to the individual. Adaptive generalization of behavior might be increased through training. Other examples might be increasing the accuracy of social perceptions, role playing, and taking the other person's point of view to improve interpersonal skills and therefore the likelihood of social reinforcement in the extra-therapeutic environment.

In terms of techniques, that of *role playing* may well receive wider application. We mentioned briefly, in connection with assertion, Kelly's therapy by fixed-role constructs. In this technique, the individual is assigned a set of interrelated and internally consistent social behaviors. Through support, encouragement, and training by the therapist, and through the protection of an assumed identity, the individual is made capable of acting in a new manner. These new behaviors, if more adaptive, may be assumed to be more likely to receive reinforcement, and hence be increased in their likelihood of future emission. Other forms of role-taking and psychodrama may also be used to increase through practice and reinforcement the emission of adaptive behaviors. Further, as in emotive imagery as Lazarus and Abramovitz (36) use it in this volume, the stimulus may become associated with new and more favorable stimuli. Finally, to draw on the work of Sarbin (1965) there may be physiological correlates involved in playing the role, and there may be increased strength of reinforcement and personal involvement when the action is taken before an audience or increasing number of people. The concept of audience as a therapeutic device is a bridge between role-playing techniques and the use of groups which we will next discuss.

In Patterson's treatment (50) of a hyperactive child, the reader will note that part of the ingenuity with which the situation was set up involved the sharing with classmates of the reinforcing objects the subject earned through increased adaptive behavior. The social reinforcement of classmates was added to the intrinsic value of the immediate reinforcing stimuli. Further, the subject's adaptive behavior was reinforcing to his classmates, not only in itself, but as a source of candy or penny rewards. Bronfenbrenner (1962) has reviewed the Soviet use of the audience or collective as the recipient of reinforcement, and drawn American psychologists to the work of Makarenko (1936, 1953). Makarenko uses the collective or group, rather than the individual, as recipient of reinforcement. In this situation, to obtain reinforcement, the individual must improve the performance of his fellow member of the collective. This multiplies the number of people who are actively interested in and will differentially respond to any subject's behavior. In concepts of "therapeutic community," especially in the treatment of people whose major difficulty is socially disruptive behavior, such a technique seems very valuable. Rather than an ingroup of inmates opposed to guards or treatment staff, fellow inmates carry on the role of therapists by responding negatively to inappropriate behavior. The device of programing groups of meaningful people, the audience, to be actively interested in and support adaptive behavior seems likely to be widely used in the future.

We have mentioned training in accurate social perceptions. An article that illustrates this and uses *teaching machines* is that of Dailey (1963). The materials programed were life histories divided into segments or events. The subjects, normal adults, chose one of three alternatives of what would occur next and received immediate knowledge of results. Accuracy improved within cases and there was significant generalization of skill across cases. This article illustrates the teaching of interpersonal skills to nonclinical subjects. However, the technique might be used to aid individuals such as "schizophrenics" to improve their ability to correctly identify emotions from snapshots (Ekman, 1964a, 1964b), and stimuli such as the Sarbin-Hardyck Stick Figure Test (1955), or common associations to words or projective stimuli such as McReynolds' Concept Evaluation Technique (1954). The point is that teaching machines have been found useful in general academic situations and could be used to train severely disarticulated subjects to emit responses that will increase their likelihood of obtaining social reinforcement. Once a program has been built it may be used many times, and the cost in staff time or money per patient may be relatively low.

In terms of teaching machines and the concept of broader general responses, we foresee a *teaching of attitudes*. For example, in developing a program of self-control, whether in terms of eating (Ferster, Nurnberger, and Levitt, 1962) or indulgence in alcohol (Mertens, 1964a, 1964b), a first step is to gain knowledge of the aversive consequences of overeating or alcoholic indulgence. Mertens (1964b) presents teaching material that might well be programed and taught by machine. In more general terms, attitudes towards self may be changed. Rogers (1960) illustrates the use of verbal conditioning to do this, and Ellis (1962) presents arguments to combat maladaptive attitudes and false notions. This material might well be taught by programed instruction.

At the present time, the social influence variables that are the basis of the *placebo* response are being systematically investigated. The findings of this work will help strengthen other forms of behavior modification. It is also possible that placebo responses themselves may be used with increasing frequency as aids to taking healthy roles or as means to permit subjects, ready to do so, to change their behavior without losing face. There may well be an increasing use of *hypnosis*. Within behavior therapy, hypnosis is already used to deepen relaxation, decrease anxiety (compare Peterson and London, 33), and heighten images in systematic desensitization procedures. A strong case for the use of both direct and indirect suggestion is made by Platonov (1959) in *The Word as Physiological and Therapeutic Factor,* and we may expect that there will be an increased exploration of these techniques in the United States in the future.

Attitudes or expectancies may be changed to facilitate other forms of therapy. If the subject's attitudes and expectations are a major variable in his response to treatment (Goldstein, 1962) and if such attitudes and expectations have as great a therapeutic potential as work on placebos may lead us to believe (Frank, 1961; Shapiro, 1960), then, an effective behavior modification procedure might well lie in establishing therapeutic attitudes and expectations. Verbal conditioning has been effective in altering a variety of social attitudes (Ekman, 1958; Singer, 1961; Verplanck, 1955), and currently work is progressing (Krasner, Ullmann, and Fisher, 1964; Krasner, Knowles, and Ullmann, 1964) in which attitudes toward "medical science," the roles of research and therapy exemplified by the examiner, are influenced through verbal conditioning, and the effect is measured in terms of physical performance. The next step in this particular research program will be the enhancement of placebo responses. The point is that a possible future direction for behavior modification may be in systematically enhancing the therapist's reinforcing potentialities by modification of subject attitudes prior to treatment.

The final future direction we wish to mention is the use of the patient's own behavior as a stimulus. An example is Luria's treatment (1961) of certain brain injuries by using a verbal response to provide feedback. Another example is provided by Efron (1957) who discovered that a jasmine odor aborted a female's grand mal convulsions. He established a conditioned inhibition of fits by pairing the jasmine odor with viewing a silver bracelet so that the sight of the bracelet alone aborted the fit. Hefferline (1962) marshals experimental evidence to illustrate that awareness of bodily sensations can be taught. This area that probes the limits of man's control over his bodily environment may well be the basis of very exciting and important future clinical applications.

The foregoing crystal ball gazing has two purposes. First, it illustrates the potential application of the experimental work currently being done in psychological laboratories. Second, whether accurate in details of the future or not, it illustrates the growing, developing, integrating nature of behavior modification. Behavior modification is in its early stages and is very definitely not complete. We look forward to improvement of present techniques, development of new ones, and applications to new subjects and behaviors. Behavior modification is as strong as the research and theories on which it rests. The increasing quantity and quality of both is the best insurance of the future of behavior modification.

SECTION 1

SEVERELY DISTURBED BEHAVIORS

All the papers in this section deal with severely disturbed subjects who are labeled "schizophrenic." Disorganization of thinking, inappropriate affect, social withdrawal, and seemingly bizarre behavior are terms that are used to characterize this group. The present papers illustrate a direct approach to dealing with maladaptive behaviors. The frequency of such maladaptive behaviors must be reduced so that other socially more effective responses may have an increased opportunity to occur.

In the first paper Isaacs, Thomas, and Goldiamond (1) give an excellent illustration of shaping behavior. Their work also illustrates the problem of generalization, obtaining a specified, desired response in extra-therapeutic situations that are similar but not identical with the one in which the original treatment took place. It is important to gain control of the therapeutic environment so that the reinforcement schedule that maintained the maladaptive behavior does not become programed on an intermittent reinforcement schedule. This is illustrated in this article, "Other patients, visitors, and members of hospital-society-at-large continue . . . to interpret nonverbal requests and to reinforce them by obeying S."

This theme is elaborated by Ayllon (2) in his paper on eating difficulties, a common symptom, severely maladaptive, and seemingly self-defeating. Ayllon demonstrates that withdrawing the reinforcement that maintains the maladaptive behavior leads to a decrease in its emission. The third paper is also by Ayllon (3) and illustrates the use of three different techniques to obtain new responses to the stimulus situation. In this paper, in contrast to not eating, overeating had to be brought under control. This was done by making withdrawal from the situation contingent upon the first act in the sequence of food stealing. If an excessive amount of a reinforcer is available, that reinforcer loses its effectiveness to alter or maintain behavior. This technique of stimulus satiation was used to reduce the bizarre behavior of towel hoarding. Finally, to reduce the wearing of a bizarre amount of clothing, wearing less clothing became a behavior necessary to avoid the aversive stimulus of denial of entrance to the dining room. The patient ate while more appropriately dressed. Eating under such circumstances might either have further reduced anxiety (in Wolpean terms), or provided positive reinforcement in the new stimulus situation. A variety of symptoms and subjects are dealt with in Ayllon and Michael's article (4). Withdrawal of reinforcement, development of an incompatible behavior, positive reinforcement, aversive conditioning, and stimulus satiation are illustrated. Some of the points previously made are further illustrated: the need to gain control of the environment to avoid "bootleg" reinforcement, the fostering of generalization, the maintenance of more adaptive behavior by new reinforcement, and the instruction of ward personnel in therapeutic procedures based on the psychological model. In the Haughton and Ayllon paper (5) a bizarre "symptomatic" behavior is produced. This important paper, which ranks with Watson and Rayner's (1920) development of a phobia, illustrates that principles of learning are applicable to the develoment as well as the elimination of maladaptive behavior. The behavior in question was eliminated by extinction. However, as the authors note, it might have been shaped into sweeping behavior. This point is illustrated in a paper by Ayllon and Haughton (1962) in which once the self-feeding behavior had been instituted, it could be chained with responses such as the social behavior developed in normal children by Azrin and Lindsley (43) and in autistic children by Hingtgen et al. (11).

In the next four papers in this section, further illustrations of direct treatment are presented. King, Armitage, and Tilton (6) develop a therapeutic situation in the context of an experiment. To develop a requisite interest and appropriate response to the environment, a complex social situation was gradually developed. The procedure of starting with what the subject can do is both effective and rapid. The contrast between this method and "verbal therapy" in terms of improved verbalization is particularly impressive. Combining the work reprinted here and articles such as that by Mertens and Fuller (1963), and Blacker and Stone (1963), gives us not only some illustration of a *method* for treating schizophrenics, which is a major problem in the field of psychiatry, but also evidence that these people *can* be treated. Treatment failure can be attributed not to the subjects being stupid or unresponsive or afflicted with an incurable disease, but to the methods of training used by the professional staff. This hopeful approach will also be found in work with retardates.

In the two articles by Rickard et al. (7,8), verbal operant conditioning is used for a specific therapeutic purpose. Ayllon and Haughton (1964) have successfully used the verbal conditioning technique with the delusional speech of three subjects. Salzinger and Pisoni (1958, 1961) and Weiss, Krasner, and Ullmann (1963) have successfully increased the emotional expressiveness of hospitalized subjects through verbal operant conditioning. Sommer, Witney, and Osmond (1962) and Ullmann, Krasner, and Edinger (1964) have increased the emission of common associations (an approach to disorganization of thinking), and Ullmann, Weiss, and Krasner (1963) have worked with recognition of threatening stimuli (the "perceptual defense" which "constricts" the environment). The increase of speech behaviors such as illustrated by King et al. (6) may prepare the subject for verbal operant conditioning, which in turn can be used (Ullmann, Krasner, and Collins, 1961; Ullmann, Krasner, and Ekman, 1961) to facilitate performance in group therapy. Other articles that are germane to this area are by Dinoff et al. (1960a, 2) and Salzberg (1961). In a more general way, the approach illustrated by these articles owes much to Lindsley's (1956, 1960, 1963a, 1963b; Mednick and Lindsley, 1958) classic studies that presented both techniques and insights for the operational definition and alteration of severely maladaptive behavior.

In a final article dealing with adult hospitalized subjects, Cowden and Ford (9) use Wolpe's systematic desensitization procedure in the treatment of phobias exhibited by schizophrenics. This extension of procedures to new populations calls for careful work, but it offers great hope. Walton (1960b) treated the phobic responses of a schizophrenic by associating them with neutral rather than threatening content and obtained general as well as specific beneficial effects.

In the final group of papers in this section, we present four studies dealing with severely maladjusted children. In the first of these articles, Ferster and DeMyer (10) offer evidence that these children may be influenced by selective reinforcement and by gradual shaping of behavior and alteration of the reinforcement schedule. The children were able to work matching problems, material directly relevant to the treatment of deficits in thinking. In the next article, Hingtgen, Sanders, and DeMyer (11) repeat this procedure, this time focusing on a social response such as developed with normal children by Azrin and Lindsley (43) and by Ayllon and Haughton (1962) with hospitalized adults. The article by Wolf, Risley, and Mees (12) illustrates many techniques. Perhaps the most impressive are the development of a meaningful reinforcement contingency, the application of the method of dealing with temper tantrums developed by Williams (34) and the training of the parents to maintain and extend the therapeutic procedures initiated in the hospital when the child returned home. The final article by Davison (13) deals primarily with an integral but frequently overlooked aspect of treatment, that of training therapists. It also offers further evidence on the development of a necessary social response, that is, obeying. The development of rapport is made explicit rather than haphazard.

The major theme running throughout these first thirteen articles is the direct manipulation of behavior by response contingent reinforcement. There are problems of gaining control of the environment and discipline in following specified schedules of reinforcement. In terms of procedure, there is careful observation and recording of the emission of focal behaviors. And above all other considerations, there is a feeling of optimism and confidence that effective means for modifying severely maladaptive behavior are available.

1   APPLICATION OF OPERANT CONDITIONING
TO REINSTATE VERBAL BEHAVIOR IN PSYCHOTICS

Wayne Isaacs • James Thomas • Israel Goldiamond

In operant conditioning, behavior is controlled by explicitly arranging the consequences of the response, the explicit consequence being termed reinforcement. For example, a lever-press by a rat activates a mechanism which releases food. If the rat has been deprived of food, lever-pressing responses will increase in frequency. If this relationship between food and response holds only when a light is on, the organism may discriminate between light on and light off, that is, there will be no lever-pressing responses when the light is turned off, but turning it on will occasion such responses. From this simple case, extensions can be made to more complicated cases which may involve control of schedules of reinforcement. These procedures have recently been extended to the study of psychopharmacology (5), controlled production of stomach ulcers (4), obtaining psychophysical curves from pigeons (3), conditioning cooperative behavior in children (2), programming machines which teach academic subjects (11), analyzing the effects of noise on human behavior (1), and decreasing stuttering (7), to mention a few examples.

The following account is a preliminary report of the use of operant conditioning to reinstate verbal behavior in two hospitalized mute psychotics. Patient A, classified as a catatonic schizophrenic, 40, became completely mute almost immediately upon commitment 19 years ago. He was recorded as withdrawn and exhibiting little psychomotor activity. Patient B, classified as schizophrenic, mixed type, with catatonic features predomini-

The *Journal of Speech and Hearing Disorders*, 1960, **25**, 8–12.

nating, was 43, and was committed after a psychotic break in 1942, when he was combative. He completely stopped verbalizing 14 years ago. Each S was handled by a different E (experimenter). The E's were ignorant of each other's activities until pressed to report their cases. This study covers the period prior to such report.

CASE HISTORIES

Patient A —

The S was brought to a group therapy session with other chronic schizophrenics (who were verbal), but he sat in the position in which he was placed and continued the withdrawal behaviors which characterized him. He remained impassive and stared ahead even when cigarettes, which other members accepted, were offered to him and were waved before his face. At one session, when E removed cigarettes from his pocket, a package of chewing gum accidentally fell out. The S's eyes moved toward the gum and then returned to their usual position. This response was chosen by E as one with which he would start to work, using the method of successive approximation (9). (This method finds use where E desires to produce responses which are not present in the current repertoire of the organism and which are considerably removed from those which are available. The E then attempts to 'shape' the available behaviors into the desired form, capitalizing upon both the variability and regularity of successive behaviors. The shaping process involves the reinforcement of those parts of a selected response which are successively in the desired direction and the nonreinforcement of those which are not. For example, a pigeon may be initially reinforced when it moves its head. When this movement occurs regularly, only an upward movement may be reinforced, with downward movement not reinforced. The pigeon may now stretch its neck, with this movement reinforced. Eventually the pigeon may be trained to peck at a disc which was initially high above its head and at which it would normally never peck. In the case of the psychotic under discussion, the succession was eye movement, which brought into play occasional facial movements, including those of the mouth, lip movements, vocalizations, word utterance, and finally, verbal behavior.)

The *S* met individually with *E* three times a week. Group sessions also continued. The following sequence of procedures was introduced in the private sessions. Although the weeks are numbered consecutively, they did not follow at regular intervals since other duties kept *E* from seeing *S* every week.

Weeks 1, 2. A stick of gum was held before *S*'s face, and *E* waited until *S*'s eyes moved toward it. When this response occurred, *E* as a consequence gave him the gum. By the end of the second week, response probability in the presence of the gum was increased to such an extent that *S*'s eyes moved toward the gum as soon as it was held up.

Weeks 3, 4. The *E* now held the gum before *S*, waiting until he noticed movement in *S*'s lips before giving it to him. Toward the end of the first session of the third week, a lip movement spontaneously occurred, which *E* promptly reinforced. By the end of this week, both lip movement and eye movement occurred when the gum was held up. The *E* then withheld giving *S* the gum until *S* spontaneously made a vocalization, at which time *E* gave *S* the gum. By the end of this week, holding up the gum readily occasioned eye movement toward it, lip movement, and a vocalization resembling a croak.

Weeks 5, 6. The *E* held up the gum, and said, 'Say *gum, gum,*' repeating these words each time *S* vocalized. Giving *S* the gum was made contingent upon vocalizations increasingly approximating *gum*. At the sixth session (at the end of Week 6), when *E* said, 'Say *gum, gum,*' *S* suddenly said, 'Gum, please.' This response was accompanied by reinstatement of other responses of this class, that is, *S* answered questions regarding his name and age.

Thereafter, he responded to questions by *E* both in individual sessions and in group sessions, but answered no one else. Responses to the discriminative stimuli of the room generalized to *E* on the ward; he greeted *E* on two occasions in the group room. He read from signs in *E*'s office upon request by *E*.

Since the response now seemed to be under the strong stimulus control of *E, the person,* attempt was made to generalize the stimulus to other people. Accordingly, a nurse was brought into the private room; *S* smiled at her. After a month, he began answering her questions. Later, when he brought his coat to a volunteer worker on the ward, she interpreted the gesture as a desire to go outdoors and conducted him there. Upon informing *E* of the incident, she was instructed to obey *S* only as a consequence of explicit verbal requests by him. The *S* thereafter vocalized requests. These instructions have now been given to other hospital personnel, and *S* regularly initiates verbal requests when nonverbal requests have no reinforcing consequences. Upon being taken to the commissary, he said, 'Ping pong,' to the volunteer worker and played a game with her. Other patients, visitors, and members of hospital-society-at-large continue, however, to interpret nonverbal requests and to reinforce them by obeying *S*.

Patient B —

This patient, with a combative history prior to mutism, habitually lay on a bench in the day room in the same position, rising only for meals and for bed. Weekly visits were begun by *E* and an attendant. During these visits, *E* urged *S* to attend group therapy sessions which were being held elsewhere in the hospital. The *E* offered *S* chewing gum. This was not accepted during the first two visits, but was accepted on the third visit and thereafter. On the sixth visit, *E* made receipt of the gum contingent upon *S*'s going to the group room and so informed *S*. The *S* then altered his posture to look at *E* and accompanied him to the group room, where he seated himself in a chair and was given the gum. Thereafter, he came to this room when the attendants called for him.

Group Sessions 1–4. Gum reinforcement was provided for coming to the first two weekly sessions, but starting with the third, it was made contingent upon *S*'s participation in the announced group activity. The group (whose other members were verbal) was arranged in a semicircle. The *E* announced that each *S* would, when his turn came, give the name of an animal. The *E* immediately provided gum to each *S* who did so. The *S* did not respond and skipped his turn three times around. The same response occurred during the fourth session.

Group Session 5. The activity announced was drawing a person; *E* provided paper and colored chalk and visited each *S* in turn to examine the paper. The *S* had drawn a stick figure and was reinforced with gum. Two of the other patients, spontaneously and without prior prompting by *E*, asked to see the drawing and complimented *S*. Attendants reported that on the following day, *S*, when introduced to two ward visitors, smiled and said, 'I'm glad to see you.' The incident was followed by no particular explicit consequences.

Group Session 6. The announced activity was to give the name of a city or town in Illinois. The *S*, in his turn, said, 'Chicago.' He was reinforced by *E*, who gave him chewing gum, and again two members of the group congratulated him for responding. Thereafter, he responded whenever his turn came.

After the tenth session in the group, gum reinforcement was discontinued. The *S* has continued to respond vocally in the situations in which he was reinforced by *E* but not in others. He never initiates conversations, but he will answer various direct questions in the *group sessions*. He will not, however, respond vocally to questions asked *on the ward*, even when put by *E*.

DISCUSSION

Both *S*'s came from special therapy wards of patients selected because of depressed verbal behavior and long stay in the hospital; tranquilizing drugs were not used. The extent to which reinstatement of verbal behavior was related to the special treatment offered the patients in the special wards set up for them cannot readily be assayed. Among the special treatments accorded them were group therapy sessions. Nevertheless, the similarities between the pattern of reac-

quisition of verbal behavior by the patients and the patterns of learning encountered in laboratory studies suggest that the conditioning procedures themselves were involved in the reinstatement of verbal behavior.

In the case of Patient A, the speaking response itself was gradually shaped. The anatomical relation between the muscles of chewing and speaking probably had some part in *E*'s effectiveness. When a word was finally produced, the response was reinstated along with other response members of its class, which had not been reinforced. The economy of this process is apparent, since it eliminates the necessity of getting *S* to produce *every* desired response in order to increase his repertoire. In this case, *E* concentrated on one verbal response, and in reinstating it, reinstated verbal responses in general. On the stimulus side, when the response came under the stimulus control of *E*, the stimulus could be generalized to other members of *E*'s class of discriminative *stimuli*, namely, people. This may have relevance for the clinical inference of the importance for future interpersonal relations of prior identification with some person. In the case of Patient B, the stimulus control involved a *given setting*, the rooms where he had been reinforced. The discrimination of *E* in one case, and not in the other, may be explained in terms of the establishment of operant discrimination, which also involves extinction (9). Operant discrimination is established when a response in the presence of S^D, a discriminative stimulus, is reinforced, and a response in the presence of S^Δ, a stimulus other than S^D, is not. After some time, the response will occur when S^D is presented, but not when S^Δ is presented; the response discriminates S^D from S^Δ, it having been extinguished when S^Δ was presented. In the case of Patient A, *E* was with *S* on the ward, in the group room, and privately. Reinforcement occurred in all occasions. But *S* was on the ward (and other rooms) without *E*, and therefore without reinforcement for those responses which were occasioned by the ward and which only *E* reinforced. Hence, these responses would extinguish in the ward alone, but would continue in the presence of E, defining discrimination of E from other stimuli. In the case of Patient B, this process may have been delayed by the fact that E and the other patients reinforced only in a specific room. It will be recalled that attendants rather than E brought S to the group room.

Interestingly, in the group sessions, when Patient B emitted the responses which E reinforced, other psychotic patients also reinforced Patient B. They were thereby responding, on the occasion of S's responses (discriminative stimuli for them), in the same way that E did. The term *identification,* used as a label here, shares some behavioral referents with the term as used in the preceding paragraph and might be explained behaviorally in terms of the *generalized reinforcer (10).* These behaviors by the patients are similar to behaviors reported in client-centered group sessions, where clients increase in reflective behaviors as counseling progresses, and in psychoanalytic group sessions, where patients increasingly make analytic interpretations of each other. Here, the patients are also behaving like the therapist. While this parallel lends itself to the facetious thought that operant group sessions may produce operant conditioners, it does suggest that psychotics are behaving, with regard to responses by the major source of reinforcement in the group, according to the same laws which govern such group behaviors of nonhospitalized S's.

The various diagnostic labels applied to psychotics are based to a considerable extent upon differences between responses considered abnormal, for example, hallucinations, delusions of persecution, and the like. The therapeutic process is accordingly at times seen in terms of eliminating the abnormal behaviors or states. Experimental laboratory work indicates that it is often extremely difficult to *eliminate* behavior; extinction is extremely difficult where the schedule of reinforcement has been a variable interval schedule (6), that is, reinforcement has been irregular, as it is in most of our behaviors.

Such behaviors persist for considerable periods without reinforcement. Experimental laboratory work has provided us quite readily with procedures to *increase* responses. In the case of psychotics, this would suggest focusing attention on whatever *normal* behaviors S has; an appropriate operant, no matter how small or insignificant, even if it is confined to an eye movement, may possibly be raised to greater probability, and shaped to normal behavior (8). Stated otherwise, abnormal behaviors and normal behaviors can be viewed as reciprocally related, and psychotics as exhibiting considerable abnormal behavior, or little normal behavior. Normal behavior probability can be increased by decreasing probability of abnormal behaviors, or abnormal behaviors can be decreased by the controlled increase of normal behaviors. This preliminary report suggests that a plan of attack based upon the latter approach may be worth further investigation.

SUMMARY

Verbal behavior was reinstated in two psychotics, classified as schizophrenics, who had been mute for 19 and 14 years. The procedures utilized involved application of operant conditioning. The relationship of such procedures, based on controlled laboratory investigations with men and animals, to procedures based on clinical practice with human patients was discussed and was considered as directing our attention to shaping and increasing the probability of what normal behaviors the psychotic possesses.

ACKNOWLEDGMENTS

The authors wish to express their appreciation to Dr. Leonard Horecker, Clinical Director of Anna State Hospital, and to Dr. Robert C. Steck, Hospital Superintendent, for their encouragement and facilitation of the project. This investigation was supported in part by a grant from the Psychiatric Training and Research Fund of the Illinois Department of Public Welfare.

REFERENCES

1. AZRIN, N. H. Some effects of noise on human behavior. *J. exp. Anal. Behavior,* 1958, **1**, 183–200.

2. AZRIN, N. H., and LINDSLEY, O. R. The reinforcement of cooperation between children. *J. abnorm. (soc.) Psychol.,* 1956, **52**, 100–102.

3. BLOUGH, D. S. A method for obtaining psychophysical thresholds from the pigeon. *J. exp. Anal. Behavior,* 1958, **1**, 31–44.

4. BRADY, J. V. Ulcers in 'executive' monkeys. *Sci. Amer.,* 1958, **199**(4), 95–100.

5. DEWS, P. B. The effects of chlorpromazine and promazine on performance on a mixed schedule of reinforcement. *J. exp. Anal. Behavior,* 1958, **1**, 73–82.

6. FERSTER, C. B., and SKINNER, B. F. *Schedules of Reinforcement.* New York: Appleton-Century-Crofts, 1957.

7. FLANAGAN, B., GOLDIAMOND, I., and AZRIN, N. H. Operant stuttering: the control of stuttering behavior through response-contingent consequences. *J. exp. Anal. Behavior* 1958, **1**, 173–178.

8. GOLDIAMOND, I. Research which can be done in a mental hospital. Address delivered to Illinois State Mental Hospitals Conference, Giant City State Park, Illinois, 1958.

9. KELLER, F., and SCHOENFELD, W. *Principles of Psychology.* New York: Appleton-Century-Crofts, 1950.

10. SKINNER, B. F. *Science and Human Behavior.* New York: Macmillan, 1953.

11. SKINNER, B. F. Teaching machines. *Science,* 1958, **128**, 969–977.

2 SOME BEHAVIORAL PROBLEMS ASSOCIATED WITH EATING IN CHRONIC SCHIZOPHRENIC PATIENTS[1]

Teodoro Ayllon

In any mental hospital ward there are patients with behavior problems demanding much attention from the already overworked attendants and nurses. Behavior problems include such things as bothering staff and other patients with persistent requests or complaints, hoarding rubbish, staying secluded in a room or corner, behaving in a destructive or assaultive manner, and requiring extensive help with eating, dressing, bathing, etc. Such behaviors are generally attributed to the patient's psychosis, his lack of understanding, and not infrequently to stubbornness, or more professionally acceptable traits such as hostility, regression, etc.

Research carried out at the Saskatchewan Hospital shows that many of these behaviors are shaped and maintained primarily by the reaction of the aides and nurses, and can be changed within a few days to a few months by appropriate behavioral engineering techniques (Ayllon and Michael, 1959; Ayllon and Haughton, 1963). This report illustrates the treatment of two mental patients whose behavioral deficits were associated with eating.

[1] This report is based, in part, on a research project conducted by the author at the Saskatchewan Hospital, Weyburn, Sask., Canada, and supported by a grant from the Commonwealth Fund, N.Y. A portion of this paper was read at the meeting of the American Psychological Association, Chicago, 1960.

SUBJECTS

The subjects were two female patients in a mental hospital. Both patients had been classified as schizophrenic. Neither of these patients received medication or psychotherapy. Anne was 54 years old and had been in the hospital for 20 years. Emelda was 60 years old and had been in the hospital for 18 years.

BEHAVIORAL PROBLEM

Anne was a near mute catatonic who for the last 16 years would not eat unless a nurse led her to the dining room, gave her a tray, silverware, and food, and seated her at the table, then urged her to eat and occasionally spoonfed her.

PROCEDURE

A 14 day baseline of Anne's behavior associated with meals was obtained. Not once during this period did she go to the dining room on her own, nor did she help herself to food. This information suggested that her difficulty in both these behaviors was being maintained by the attention she received from the nurses as a function of this difficulty. The nurses were instructed not to take the patient to the dining room, but to help her as much as before once she entered the dining room.

During the 21st week of this program, it was decided to shape her behavior in the dining room so that the patient would go through the cafeteria line completely on her own, without the nurse's assistance (for four weeks previous to shaping, no records were taken once she had entered the dining room). The nurses were instructed not to help the patient in the dining room, but to reinforce her by dropping some candy on her tray, only after she had picked up a tray, silverware, and one edible item.

RESULTS

For four days the patient remained sitting in her chair during meal time thereby missing all her meals for those days. On the fifth day another patient took her to the dining room. A few meals thereafter she started going to the dining room entirely without help. This behavior change seemed to generalize to her behavior in the dining room. As can be seen in Figure 1 the percent

of taking tray-silverware-food unaided increased rapidly and stabilized at about 40%. Although the patient was going to the dining room unaided, it was clear that she was still being helped in the dining room. This was interpreted by a few nurses as evidence that, "you can lead a horse to water but you can't make him drink." It was at this point that all help was discontinued in the dining room.

It can be seen in Figure 1 that the patient's behavior changed quite quickly. This normal eating behavior was still displayed two years later.

DISCUSSION

Although candy had been used to reinforce the patient for helping herself to food in the dining room, the critical factor was that Anne found that she did not eat when she failed to help herself to food in the dining room. Therefore, when nurses discontinued helping her altogether the reinforcer became food itself. The quality of Anne's behavior during the treatment reveals the effectiveness of using food as a reinforcer.

After two days of the treatment (when she was no longer helped to go to the dining room) she was observed several times extending her hand towards a passing nurse right after meal call, and, on two occasions, she approached a nurse and stated, "I should go to dinner," and "I want to go." On the sixth day of the treatment program, the following observation was recorded: "Paid no attention to dinner call at first, then suddenly jumped up, walked a few steps, then ran the length of the corridor to the dining room, even pushing past some others." Her running to the dining room was still occurring one month after this observation.

The first few days under the program designed to extinguish her waiting to be given silverware and food tray she remained standing in line, but made no effort to help herself to food. Because no one helped her to obtain the food tray, she waited until the meal was over and, then, sauntered out of the dining room without eating. A few

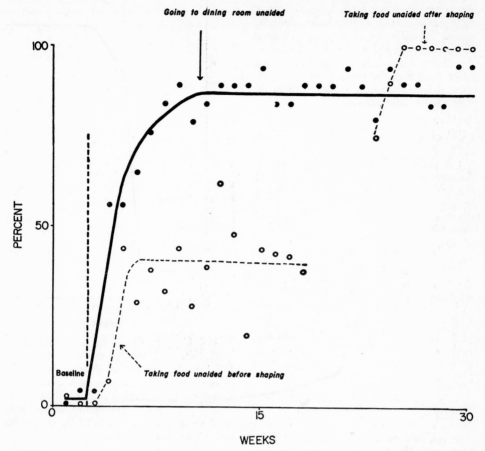

FIGURE I   This figure shows the percentage of two separate responses: "Going to the dining room unaided," and "taking food unaided." These behaviors were virtually absent during the pretreatment period (baseline), but each behavior increased from near zero to virtually 100% upon using a combination of extinction for the undesired behavior and reinforcement for the desired one.

meals later she proceeded to help herself just before the meal was over. What follows is a typical observation recorded during this period: ". . . was fourth person into dining room. Picked up tray and silverware. Then stood for a while and got pushed out of line (by a patient). Waited for a few minutes, then pushed her way back into line, and picked up all the food items."

During the four days that Anne fasted, she was observed drinking water regularly from the water fountain located in the dayroom. At no time during this period did she give signs of physical strain, as determined by body weight and other routine nursing procedures.

BEHAVIORAL PROBLEM

Emelda, a chronic schizophrenic patient, remained sitting in the dining room for so long after the meal was over that the nurses had to prompt her several times to leave the room. Two years prior to this investigation these verbal prompts increased in frequency so that the patient left the dining room only after the nurses had approached her from six to ten times per meal. Upon failure of these verbal prompts, the nurses led the patient forcefully out of the room. Because the patient appeared to be hallucinating in the dining room (gesticulating and talking while looking at the ceiling) the nurses attributed her failure to leave the room to the patient's psychotic behavior.

PROCEDURE

A 14 day baseline of Emelda's leaving the dining room was obtained. During this period, she left the dining room unaided (neither led nor verbally prompted) only about 10% of the time. This information suggested that the nurses' verbal prompts and leading her out of the dining room were reinforcing her staying in the dining room.

In order to bring the behavior of leaving the dining room under the control of positive reinforcement, it was decided to reinforce the patient when she left the dining room so long as there was at least one other patient in the room. Social attention and candy were used as reinforcers. In addition, the nurses were instructed not to prompt or lead her out of the room.

RESULTS

It can be seen from Figure 2 that upon withdrawal of social reinforcement for staying in the dining room and reinforcement for leaving it the frequency of leaving the dining room unaided rose from about 10% to virtually 100% in a matter of a few weeks.

The case of Emelda is a clear illustration of the effects of social reinforcement in strengthening the very behaviors that are considered undesirable. By taking Emelda out of the dining room, her behavior of staying there was increased in frequency. The success of the treatment program in this case also raises some questions. For example, Emelda's behavior of staying in the dining room after meals was eliminated but other symptomatic behaviors such as the "hallucinations" referred to previously (for example, looking at the ceiling, mumbling a few words and gesticulating) remained unaltered. It would seem that as long as the symptoms are com-

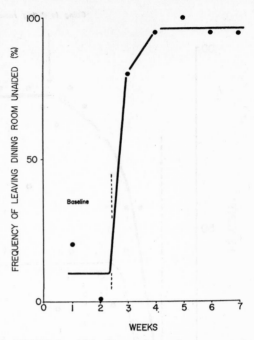

FIGURE 2   This figure shows the percentage of the response "leaving the room unaided." This behavior was seldom observed during the pretreatment period (baseline). A combination of extinction for "staying in the dining room" and candy and social reinforcement upon "leaving the room unaided" increased the desired behavior from near zero to virtually 100%.

patible with each other the elimination of one symptom does not insure equal elimination of associated symptoms. This also indicates that social reinforcement will not necessarily solve most behavior deficits.

DISCUSSION

In these two cases a combination of extinction for social attention and reinforcement contingent upon the desired unit of behavior brought about the desired behavioral changes. Two generalizations from this information appear possible. First, food appears to be the appropriate and most effective reinforcer to use to eliminate behavior deficits associated with eating. Many of the behavior difficulties patients display in the course of eating may be traced to the social reinforcement that attendants, unwittingly to be sure, shower upon such behaviors. Because the effectiveness of social reinforcement may be limited primarily by the severity of the patient's behavior disorder, there will be cases when the use of a powerful reinforcer such as food may warrant serious consideration.

REFERENCES

AYLLON, T. and J. MICHAEL. The psychiatric nurse as a behavioral engineer. *J. exp. Anal. Behav.*, 1959, **2**, 323–334.

AYLLON, T. and E. HAUGHTON. Control of the behavior of schizophrenic patients by food. *J. exp. Anal. Behav.*, 1962, **3**, 343–352.

3 INTENSIVE TREATMENT OF PSYCHOTIC BEHAVIOUR BY STIMULUS SATIATION AND FOOD REINFORCEMENT[1]

Teodoro Ayllon

Summary. This investigation demonstrates that extensive and effective behavioural modification is feasible without costly and lengthy psychotherapeutic treatment. In addition, the often heard notion that another undesirable type of behaviour will replace the original problem behaviour is not supported by the findings to date.

INTRODUCTION

Until recently, the effective control of behaviour was limited to the animal laboratory. The extension of this control to human behaviour was made when Lindsley successfully adapted the methodology of operant conditioning to the study of psychotic behaviour (Lindsley, 1956). Following Lindsley's point of departure other investigators have shown that, in its essentials, the behaviour of mental defective individuals (Orlando and Bijou, 1960), stutterers (Flanagan, Goldiamond and Azrin, 1958), mental patients (Hutchinson and Azrin, 1961), autistic (Ferster and DeMyer, 1961), and normal children (Bijou, 1961; Azrin and Lindsley, 1956) is subject to the same controls.

Despite the obvious implications of this research for applied settings there has been a conspicuous lag between the research findings and their application. The greatest limitation to the direct application of laboratory principles has been the absence of control over the subjects' environment. Recently, however, a series of applications in a regulated psychiatric setting has clearly demonstrated the possibilities of behavioural modification (Ayllon and Michael, 1959; Ayllon and Haughton, 1962). Some of the behaviour studied has included repetitive and highly stereotyped responses such as complaining, pacing, refusal to eat, hoarding and many others.

What follows is a demonstration of behaviour techniques for the intensive individual treatment of psychotic behaviour.

Behaviour Research and Therapy, 1963, **1**, 53–61.

[1] This report is based, in part, on a two-year research project (1959–1961), conducted by the author at the Saskatchewan Hospital, Weyburn, Saskatchewan, Canada, and supported by a grant from the Commonwealth Fund. Grateful acknowledgment is due to H. OSMOND and I. CLANCEY of the Saskatchewan Hospital. The author also thanks E. HAUGHTON who assisted in the conduct of this investigation, and N. AZRIN and W. HOLTZ for their critical reading of the manuscript.

Specific pathological behaviour patterns of a single patient were treated by manipulating the patient's environment.

The Experimental Ward and Control over the Reinforcement

This investigation was conducted in a mental hospital ward, the characteristics of which have been described elsewhere (Ayllon and Haughton, 1962). Briefly, this was a female ward to which only authorized personnel were allowed access. The ward staff was made up of psychiatric nurses and untrained aides who carried out the environmental manipulations under the direction of the experimenter. Using a time-sample technique, patients were observed daily every 30 minutes from 7:00 a.m. to 11:00 p.m.

The dining room was the only place where food was available and entrance to the dining room could be regulated. Water was freely available at a drinking fountain on the ward. None of the patients had ground passes or jobs outside the ward.

Subject

The patient was a 47-year-old female patient diagnosed as a chronic schizophrenic. The patient had been hospitalized for 9 years. Upon studying the patient's behaviour on the ward, it became apparent that the nursing staff[2] spent considerable time caring for her. In particular, there were three aspects of her behaviour which seemed to defy solution. The first was stealing food. The second was the hoarding of the ward's towels in her room. The third undesirable aspect of her behaviour consisted in her wearing excessive clothing, e.g. a half-dozen dresses, several pairs of stockings, sweaters, and so on.

In order to modify the patient's behaviour systematically, each of these three types of behaviour (stealing food, hoarding, and excessive dressing) was treated separately.

[2]As used in this paper, 'nurse' is a generic term including all those who actually work on the ward (attendants, aides, psychiatric and registered nurses).

EXPERIMENT I

Control of Stealing Food by Food Withdrawal

The patient had weighed over 250 pounds for many years. She ate the usual tray of food served to all patients, but, in addition, she stole food from the food counter and from other patients. Because the medical staff regarded her excessive weight as detrimental to her health, a special diet had been prescribed for her. However, the patient refused to diet and continued stealing food. In an effort to discourage the patient from stealing, the ward nurses had spent considerable time trying to persuade her to stop stealing food. As a last resort, the nurses would force her to return the stolen food.

To determine the extent of food stealing, nurses were instructed to record all behaviour associated with eating in the dining room. This record, taken for nearly a month, showed that the patient stole food during two thirds of all meals.

Procedure

The traditional methods previously used to stop the patient from stealing food were discontinued. No longer were persuasion, coaxing, or coercion used.

The patient was assigned to a table in the dining room, and no other patients were allowed to sit with her. Nurses removed the patient from the dining room when she approached a table other than her own, or when she picked up unauthorized food from the dining room counter. In effect, this procedure resulted in the patient missing a meal whenever she attempted to steal food.

Results

Figure 1 shows that when withdrawal of positive reinforcement (i.e. meal) was made dependent upon the patient's 'stealing', this response was eliminated in two weeks. Because the patient no longer stole food, she ate only the diet prescribed for her. The effective control of the stealing response is

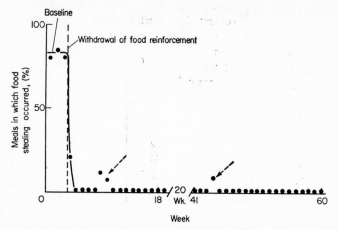

FIGURE I   A response, food stealing, is eliminated when it results in the withdrawal of food reinforcement. The dotted arrows indicate the rare occasions when food stealing occurred. For purposes of presentation a segment comprising 20 weeks during which no stealing occurred is not included.

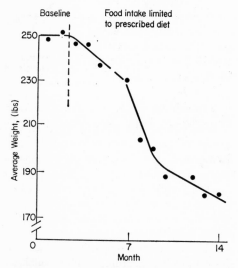

FIGURE 2   The effective control of food stealing results in a notable reduction in body weight. As the patient's food intake is limited to the prescribed diet her weight decreases gradually.

also indicated by the gradual reduction in the patient's body weight. At no time during the patient's 9 years of hospitalization had she weighed less than 230 pounds. Figure 2 shows that at the conclusion of this treatment her weight stabilized at 180 pounds or 17 per cent loss from her original weight. At

this time, the patient's physical condition was regarded as excellent.

Discussion

A principle used in the laboratory shows that the strength of a response may be weakened by the removal of positive reinforcement following the response (Ferster, 1958). In this case, the response was food-stealing and the reinforcer was access to meals. When the patient stole food she was removed from the dining room and missed her meal.

After one year of this treatment, two occasions of food stealing occurred. The first occasion, occurring after one year of not stealing food, took the nurses by surprise and, therefore the patient 'got away' with it. The second occasion occurred shortly thereafter. This time, however, the controlling consequences were in force. The patient missed that meal and did not steal again to the conclusion of this investigation.

Because the patient was not informed or warned of the consequences that followed stealing, the nurses regarded the procedure as unlikely to have much effect on the patient's behaviour. The implicit belief that verbal instructions are indispensable for learning is part of present day psychiatric lore. In keeping with this notion, prior to this behaviour treatment, the nurses had tried to persuade the patient to co-operate in dieting. Because there were strong medical reasons for her losing weight, the patient's refusal to follow a prescribed diet was regarded as further evidence of her mental illness.

EXPERIMENT II

Control of One Form of Hoarding Behaviour Through Stimulus Satiation

During the 9 years of hospitalization, the patient collected large numbers of towels and stored them in her room. Although many efforts had been made to discourage hoarding, this behaviour continued unaltered. The only recourse for the nursing staff was to take away the patient's towels about twice a week.

To determine the degree of hoarding behaviour, the towels in her room were counted three times a week, when the patient was not in her room. This count showed that the number of towels kept in her room ranged from 19 to 29 despite the fact that during this time the nurses continued recovering their towel supply from the patient's room.

Procedure

The routine removal of the towels from the patient's room was discontinued. Instead, a programme of stimulus satiation was carried out by the nurses. Intermittently, throughout the day, the nurses took a towel to the patient when she was in her room and simply handed it to her without any comment. The first week she was given an average of 7 towels daily, and by the third week this number was increased to 60.

Results

The technique of satiation eliminated the towel hoarding. Figure 3 shows the mean number of towels per count found in the patient's room. When the number of towels

kept in her room reached the 625 mark, she started taking a few of them out. Thereafter,

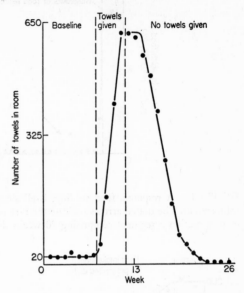

FIGURE 3   A response, towel hoarding, is eliminated when the patient is given towels in excess. When the number of towels reaches 625 the patient starts to discard them. She continues to do so until the number in her room averages 1.5 compared to the previous 20 towels per week.

no more towels were given to her. During the next 12 months the mean number of towels found in her room was 1·5 per week.

Discussion

The procedure used to reduce the amount of towel hoarding bears resemblance to satiation of a reinforcer. A reinforcer loses its effect when an excessive amount of that reinforcer is made available. Accordingly, the response maintained by that reinforcer is weakened. In this application, the towels constituted the reinforcing stimuli. When the number of towels in her room reached 625, continuing to give her towels seemed to make their collection aversive. The patient then proceeded to rid herself of the towels until she had virtually none.

During the first few weeks of **satiation**,

the patient was observed patting her cheeks with a few towels, apparently enjoying them. Later, the patient was observed spending much of her time folding and stacking the approximately 600 towels in her room. A variety of remarks were made by the patient regarding receipt of towels. All verbal statements made by the patient were recorded by the nurse. The following represent typical remarks made during this experiment. First week: As the nurse entered the patient's room carrying a towel, the patient would smile and say, "Oh, you found it for me, thank you." Second week: When the number of towels given to patient increased rapidly, she told the nurses, "Don't give me no more towels. I've got enough." Third week: "Take them towels away. . . . I can't sit here all night and fold towels." Fourth and fifth weeks: "Get these dirty towels out of here." Sixth week: After she had started taking the towels out of her room, she remarked to the nurse, "I can't drag any more of these towels, I just can't do it."

The quality of these remarks suggests that the initial effect of giving towels to the patient was reinforcing. However as the towels increased they ceased to be reinforcing, and presumably became aversive.

The ward nurses, who had undergone a three year training in psychiatric nursing, found it difficult to reconcile the procedure in this experiment with their psychiatric orientation. Most nurses subscribed to the popular psychiatric view which regards hoarding behaviour as a reflection of a deep 'need' for love and security. Presumably, no 'real' behavioural change was possible without meeting the patient's 'needs' first. Even after the patient discontinued hoarding towels in her room, some nurses predicted that the change would not last and that worse behaviour would replace it. Using a time-sampling technique the patient was under continuous observation for over a year after the termination of the satiation programme. Not once during this period did the patient return to hoarding towels. Furthermore, no other behaviour problem replaced hoarding.

EXPERIMENT III

Control of an Additional Form of Hoarding through Food Reinforcement

Shortly after the patient had been admitted to the hospital she wore an excessive amount of clothing which included several sweaters, shawls, dresses, undergarments and stockings. The clothing also included sheets and towels wrapped around her body, and a turban-like head-dress made up of several towels. In addition, the patient carried two to three cups on one hand while holding a bundle of miscellaneous clothing, and a large purse on the other.

To determine the amount of clothing worn by the patient, she was weighed before each meal over a period of two weeks. By subtracting her actual body weight from that recorded when she was dressed, the weight of her clothing was obtained.

Procedure

The response required for reinforcement was stepping on a scale and meeting a predetermined weight. The requirement for reinforcement consisted of meeting a single weight (i.e. her body weight plus a specified number of pounds of clothing). Initially she was given an allowance of 23 pounds over her current body weight. This allowance represented a 2 pound reduction from her usual clothing weight. When the patient exceeded the weight requirement, the nurse stated in a matter-of-fact manner, "Sorry, you weigh too much, you'll have to weigh less." Failure to meet the required weight resulted in the patient missing the meal at which she was being weighed. Sometimes, in an effort to meet the requirement, the patient discarded more clothing than she was required. When this occurred the requirement was adjusted at the next weighing-time to correspond to the limit set by the patient on the preceding occasion.

Results

When food reinforcement is made dependent upon the removal of superfluous clothing the response increases in frequency. Figure 4 shows that the patient gradually shed her clothing to meet the more demanding weight requirement until she dressed normally. At the conclusion of this experiment her clothes weighed 3 pounds compared to the 25 pounds she wore before this treatment.

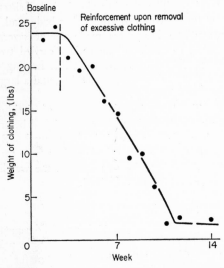

FIGURE 4 A response, excessive dressing, is eliminated when food reinforcement is made dependent upon removal of superfluous clothing. Once the weight of the clothing worn by the patient drops to 3 pounds it remains stable.

Some verbal shaping was done in order to encourage the patient to leave the cups and bundles she carried with her. Nurses stopped her at the dining room and said, "Sorry, no things are allowed in the dining room." No mention of clothing or specific items was made to avoid focusing undue attention upon them. Within a week, the patient typically stepped on the scale without her bundle and assorted objects. When her weight was over the limit, the patient was informed that she weighed "too much". She then proceeded to take off a few clothes, stepped on the scale again, and upon meeting the weight requirement, gained access to the dining room.

Discussion

According to the principle of reinforcement a class of responses is strengthened when it is followed by reinforcement. A reinforcer is such when it results in a response increase. In this application the removal of excessive clothing constituted the response and the reinforcer was food (i.e. access to meals). When the patient met the weight requirement she was reinforced by being given access to meals.

At the start of this experiment, the patient missed a few meals because she failed to meet the weight requirement, but soon thereafter she gradually discarded her superfluous clothing. First, she left behind odd items she had carried in her arms, such as bundles, cups and handbags. Next she took off the elaborate headgear and assorted "capes" or shawls she had worn over her shoulders. Although she had worn 18 pairs of stockings at one time, she eventually shed these also.

During the initial part of this experiment, the patient showed some emotional behaviour, e.g. crying, shouting and throwing chairs around. Because nurses were instructed to "ignore" this emotional behaviour, the patient obtained no sympathy or attention from them. The withholding of social reinforcement for emotional behaviour quickly led to its elimination.

At the conclusion of this behaviour treatment, the patient typically stepped on the scale wearing a dress, undergarments, a pair of stockings and a pair of light shoes. One of the behavioural changes concomitant with the current environmental manipulation was that as the patient began dressing normally she started to participate in small social events in the hospital. This was particularly new to the patient as she had previously remained seclusive spending most of the time in her room.

About this time the patient's parents came to visit her and insisted on taking her home for a visit. This was the first time during the patient's 9 years of hospitalization that her parents had asked to take her out. They remarked that previously they had not been interested in taking her out because the patient's excessive dressing in addition to her weight made her look like a "circus freak".

CONCLUSIONS

The research presented here was conducted under nearly ideal conditions. The variables manipulated (i.e. towels and food) were under full experimental control. Using a time-sample technique the patient was observed daily every 30 minutes from 7:00 a.m. to 11:00 p.m. Nurses and aides carried out these observations which were later analysed in terms of gross behaviour categories. These observations were in force for over a year during which time these three experiments were conducted. The results of these observations indicate that none of the three pathological behaviour patterns (i.e. food stealing, hoarding and excessive dressing) exhibited by the patient were replaced by any undesirable behaviour.

The patient displayed some emotional behaviour in each experiment, but each time it subsided when social reinforcement (i.e. attention) was not forthcoming. The patient did not become violent or seclusive as a consequence of these experiments. Instead, she became socially more accessible to patients and staff. She did not achieve a great deal of social success but she did begin to participate actively in social functions.

A frequent problem encountered in mental hospitals is overeating. In general this problem is solved by prescribing a reduction diet. Many patients, however, refuse to take a reduction diet and continue overeating. When confronted with this behaviour, psychiatric workers generally resort to two types of explanations.

One explanation of overeating points out that only with the active and sincere cooperation of the patient can weight reduction be accomplished. When the patient refuses to co-operate he is regarded as showing more signs of mental illness and all hopes of eliminating overeating come to an end.

Another type of explanation holds that overeating is not the behaviour to be concerned with. Instead, attention is focused on the psychological 'needs' of the patient. These 'needs' are said to be the cause of the observable behaviour, overeating. Therefore the emphasis is on the removal of the cause and not on the symptom or behaviour itself. Whatever theoretical merit these explanations may have, it is unfortunate that they fail to suggest practical ways of treating the behaviour itself. As a consequence, the patient continues to overeat often to the detriment of his health.

The current psychiatric emphasis on the resolution of the mental conflict that is presumably at the basis of the symptoms, is perhaps misplaced. What seems to have been forgotten is that behaviour problems such as those reported here, prevent the patient from being considered for discharge not only by the hospital personnel but also by the patient's relatives. Indeed, as far as the patient's relatives are concerned, the index of improvement or deterioration is the readily observable behaviour and not a detailed account of the mechanics of the mental apparatus.

Many individuals are admitted to mental hospitals because of one or more specific behaviour difficulties and not always because of a generalized 'mental' disturbance. For example, an individual may go into a mental hospital because he has refused to eat for several days, or because he talks to himself incessantly. If the goal of therapy were behavioural rehabilitation, these problems would be treated and normal eating and normal talking reinstated. However, the current emphasis in psychotherapy is on 'mental-conflict resolution' and little or no attention is given to dealing directly with the behavioural problems which prevent the patient from returning to the community.

REFERENCES

AYLLON, T. and MICHAEL, J. (1959) The psychiatric nurse as a behavioral engineer. *J. exp. anal. Behav.* **2**, 323–334.

AYLLON, T. and HAUGHTON, E. (1962) Control of the behavior of schizophrenic patients by food. *J. exp. anal. Behav.* **5,** 343–352.

AZRIN, N. and LINDSLEY, O. (1956) The reinforcement of cooperation between children. *J. abnorm. (soc.) Psychol.* **52,** 100–102.

BIJOU, S. (1961) Discrimination performance as a baseline for individual analysis of young children. *Child Develpm.* **32,** 163–160.

FERSTER, C. B. (1958) Control of behavior in chimpanzees and pigeons by time out from positive reinforcement. *Psychol. Monogr.* **72,** 1–38.

FERSTER, C. and DEMYER, M. (1961) The development of performances in autistic children in an automatically controlled environment. *J. chron. Dis.* **13,** 312–345.

FLANAGAN, B., GOLDIAMOND, I. and AZRIN, N. (1958) Operant stuttering: The control of stuttering behavior through response-contingent consequences. *J. exp. anal. Behav.* **56,** 49–56.

HUTCHINSON, R. R. and AZRIN, N. H. (1961) Conditioning of mental hospital patients to fixed-ratio schedules of reinforcement. *J. exp. anal. Behav.* **4,** 87–95.

LINDSLEY, O. R. (1956) Operant conditioning methods applied to research in chronic schizophrenia. *Psychiat. Res. Rep.* **5,** 118–139.

ORLANDO, R. and BIJOU, S. (1960) Single and multiple schedules of reinforcement in developmentally retarded children. *J. exp. anal. Behav.* **3,** 339–348.

4 THE PSYCHIATRIC NURSE AS A BEHAVIORAL ENGINEER[1]

Teodoro Ayllon • Jack Michael

The behavior which leads to a person's admission to a mental hospital often involves danger to himself or others, withdrawal from normal social functions, or a dramatic change from his usual mode of behaving. The professional staff of the psychiatric hospital directs its major efforts toward the discovery of the flaw in the patient's mental apparatus which presumably underlies his disturbing and dangerous behavior. Following the medical paradigm, it is presumed that once the basic disfunction has been properly identified the appropriate treatment will be undertaken and the various manifestations of the disfunction will disappear.

While diagnosis is being made and during subsequent treatment, the patient is under the daily care of the psychiatric nurses[2] in the ward. There, he often exhibits annoying and disrupting behavior which is usually regarded as a further manifestation of his basic difficulty. This behavior is sometimes identical with that which led to his admission; but at other times it seems to originate and develop within the hospital setting. Al-

Journal of the Experimental Analysis of Behavior, 1959, **2,** 323–334.

[1]This paper contains a portion of the data from a doctoral dissertation submitted to the Department of Psychology, University of Houston, in partial fulfillment of the requirements for the Ph.D. degree, in August, 1959. Grateful acknowledgment is due to the members of the doctoral committee for their help and encouragement, and also to Drs. H. Osmond and I. Clancey, Superintendent and Clinical Director of the Saskatchewan Hospital, for making research at this institution possible.

[2] As used in this paper, "psychiatric nurse" is a generic term including all those who actually work on the ward (aides, psychiatric nurses, and registered nurses).

though it is still regarded as a reflection of his basic problem, this disruptive behavior may become so persistent that it engages the full energies of the nurses, and postpones, sometimes permanently, any effort on their part to deal with the so-called basic problem.

Disrupting behaviors usually consist in the patient's failure to engage in activities which are considered normal and necessary; or his persistent engagement in activities that are harmful to himself or other patients, or disrupting in other ways. For example, failures to eat, dress, bathe, interact socially with other patients, and walk without being led are invariably disruptive. Hoarding various objects, hitting, pinching, spitting on other patients, constant attention-seeking actions with respect to the nurses, upsetting chairs in the dayroom, scraping paint from the walls, breaking windows, stuffing paper in the mouth and ears, walking on haunches or while in a squatting position are disruptive when they occur frequently and persistently.

At present, no systematic approach to such problems is available to the nurses. A psychodynamic interpretation is often given by psychiatrists and psychologists; and, for that matter, the nurses sometimes construct "depth" interpretations themselves. These interpretations seldom suggest any specific remedial actions to the nurses, who then have no other recourse than to act on the basis of common sense, or to take advantage of the physical therapy in vogue. From the point of view of modern behavior theory, such strong behaviors, or behavioral deficits, may be considered the result of events occurring in the patient's immediate or historical environment rather than the manifestations of his mental disorder. The present research represents an attempt to discover and manipulate some of these environmental variables for the purpose of modifying the problem behavior.

RESEARCH SETTING

The research was carried out at the Saskatchewan Hospital, Weyburn, Saskatch-ewan, Canada. It is a psychiatric hospital with approximately 1500 patients. Its most relevant features in terms of the present experiment are:

1. The nurses are trained as psychiatric nurses in a 3-year program.
2. They are responsible for the patients in their wards and enjoy a high degree of autonomy with respect to the treatment of a patient. The psychiatrists in the hospital function as advisers to the nursing staff. This means that psychiatrists do not give orders, but simply offer advice upon request from the psychiatric nurses.
3. The nurses administer incoming and outgoing mail for the patients, visitor traffic, ground passes, paroles, and even discharge, although the last is often carried out after consultation with a psychiatrist. The nurses also conduct group therapy under the supervision of the psychiatric staff.

The official position of the senior author, hereafter referred to as *E*, was that of a clinical psychologist, who designed and supervised operant-conditioning "therapy" as applied by the nurses. Once his advice had been accepted, the nurses were responsible for carrying out the procedures specified by *E*. It was the privilege of the nurses to discontinue any treatment when they believed it was no longer necessary, when they were unable to implement it because of lack of staff, or when other ward difficulties made the treatment impossible. Whenever termination became necessary, *E* was given appropriate notice.

SUBJECTS

The subjects used in this investigation were all patients in the hospital. Of the total 19 patients, 14 had been classified as schizophrenic and 5 as mentally defective. Except for one female patient who was resident for only 7 months, all patients had been hospitalized for several years. Each subject presented a persistent behavior problem for which he had been referred to *E* by the nursing staff. None of the *S*s was presently receiving psychotherapy, electroconvulsive therapy, or any kind of individual treatment.

The behaviors which were studied do not represent the most serious problems encountered in a typical psychiatric hospital. They were selected mainly because their persistence allowed them to survive several attempts at altering them.

PROCEDURE

Prior to a systematic observational study of the patient's behavior the nurses were asked about the kind and frequency of naturally occurring reinforcement obtained by the patient, the duration and frequency of the problem behavior, and the possibility of controlling the reinforcement. Next, a period of systematic observation of each patient was undertaken prior to treatment. This was done to obtain objective information on the frequency of the behavior that was a problem to the nurses, and to determine what other behaviors were emitted by the patient.

Depending on the type of behavior, two methods were used for recording it. If the behavior involved interaction with a nurse, it was recorded every time it occurred. Entering the nurses' office, and eating regular meals are examples of such behavior.

Behavior which did not naturally involve contact with the nurse was recorded by a time-sampling technique. The nurse who was in charge of the program was supplied with a mimeographed record form. She sought out the patient at regular intervals; and without interaction with him, she recorded the behavior taking place at that time. She did not actually describe the behavior occurring, but rather classified it in terms of a pre-established trichotomy: (a) the undesirable behavior; (b) incompatible behavior which could ultimately displace the undesirable behavior; and (c) incompatible behavior which was not considered shapeable, such as sleeping, eating, and dressing. (Although these latter acts are certainly susceptible to the influence of reinforcement, they were regarded as neutral behaviors in

the present research.) The period of observation varied from 1 to 3 minutes. After making an observation, the nurse resumed her regular ward activities until the next interval was reached, whereupon she again sought out the patient. Except for one patient, who was observed every 15 minutes, such observations were made every 30 minutes.

The relevant aspect of the data obtained by the time-check recording is the proportion of the total number of observations (excluding observations of neutral behavior) during which the patient was engaging in the behavior being altered. This will be called the relative frequency of the behavior. As an example, on the first day of the program of extinction for psychotic talk in the case of Helen (see below), 17 nonneutral behaviors were recorded. Of these, nine were classed as psychotic talk and eight as sensible talk; the relative frequency of psychotic talk was 0.53.

Although it would have been desirable, a long pretreatment period of observation was precluded by the newness of this approach and the necessity of obtaining the voluntary cooperation of the nurses.

After the pretreatment study had been completed, E instructed the ward nurses in the specific program that was to be carried out. In all cases the instruction was given at ward meetings and usually involved the cooperation of only two shifts, the 7 a.m. to 3 p.m., and 3 p.m. to 11 p.m., since the patients were usually asleep during the 11 p.m. to 7 a.m. shift.

The pretreatment studies indicated that what maintained undesirable behavior in most of the patients was the attention or social approval of the nurses toward that behavior. Therefore, the emphasis in instructing the nursing staff was on the operation of giving or withholding social reinforcement contingent upon a desired class of behavior. What follows illustrates the tenor of E's somewhat informal instructions to the nurses. "Reinforcement is something you do for or with a patient, for example, offering candy or a cigarette. Any way you convey attention to the patient is reinforcing. Patients may be reinforced if you answer their questions, talk to them, or let them know by your reaction that you are aware of their presence. The common-sense expression 'pay no attention' is perhaps closest to what must be done to discourage the patient's behavior. When we say 'do not reinforce a behavior,' we are actually saying 'ignore the behavior and act deaf and blind whenever it occurs.' "

When reinforcement was given on a fixed-interval basis, the nurse was instructed to observe the patient for about 1 to 3 minutes at regular intervals, just as in the pre-treatment observation period. If desirable behavior was occurring at the time of observation, she would reinforce it; if not, she would go on about her duties and check again after the next interval had passed. Strictly speaking, this is fixed interval with a limited-hold contingency (Ferster & Skinner, 1957). During a program of extinction the nurse checked as above; however, instead of reinforcing the patient when he exhibited the behavior being altered, she simply recorded it and continued her other work. Except for specific directions for two patients, the nurses were not given instructions on the operation of aversive control.

The programs requiring time-sample observations started after breakfast (around 9 a.m.) and ended at bedtime (around 9 p.m.), and were usually carried out by only one of the 6 to 12 nurses on each shift. Because of the daily shift changes, the monthly ward rotations, and a systematic effort to give everyone experience at this new duty, no patient's program was followed by any one nurse for any considerable length of time. Nineteen, as a minimum, different nurses were involved in carrying out each patient's program. Over 100 different nurses participated in the entire research project.

Most social ward activities took place in the dayroom, which was a large living room containing a television set, card tables, magazines, and games. It was here that reinforcement was given for social behaviors toward patients, and for nonsocial behaviors which were strengthened to complete with undesirable behaviors. The fact that the research was carried out in five wards distributed far

from each other in a four-floor building made it impossible for E to observe all the nurses involved in the research at any one time. Because of the constant change in nursing personnel, most of E's time was spent in instructing new people in the routines of the programs. In addition, since E did not train the nurses extensively, he observed them, often without their knowledge, and supervised them in record keeping, administering reinforcement, extinction, etc. That the nurses performed effectively when E was absent can be at least partially determined by the ultimate results.

RESULTS

The results will be summarized in terms of the type of behavior problem and the operations used in altering the behavior. In general, the time required to change a specific behavior ranged from 6 to 11 weeks. The operations were in force for 24 hours a day, 7 days a week.

Strong Behavior Treated by Extinction, or Extinction Combined with Reinforcement for Incompatible Behavior

In the five cases treated with this program, the reinforcer was the attention of the nurses; and the withholding of this reinforcer resulted in the expected decline in frequency. The changes occurring in three of the behavior problems, scrubbing the floor, spending too much time in the bathroom, and one of the two cases of entering the nurses' offices, were not complicated by uncontrollable variables. Lucille's case is presented in detail as representative of these three. The interpretation of the changes occurring in the other two behavior problems, entering the nurses' offices, and psychotic verbal behavior, is not so clearcut. Helen's case illustrates this point. For details concerning the cases not discussed in this paper, see Ayllon (1959).

Lucille. Lucille's frequent visits to the nurses' office interrupted and interfered with their work. She had been doing this for 2 years. During this time, she had been told that she was not expected to spend her time in the nurses' office. Frequently, she was taken by the hand or pushed back bodily into the ward. Because the patient was classified as mentally defective, the nurses had resigned themselves to tolerating her behavior. As one of the nurses put it, "It's difficult to tell her anything because she can't understand—she's too dumb."

The following instructions were given to the nurses: "During this program the patient must not be given reinforcement (attention) for entering the nurses' office. Tally every time she enters the office."

The pretreatment study indicated that she entered the office on an average of 16 times a day. As Fig. 1b shows, the average frequency was down to two entries per day by the seventh week of extinction, and the program was terminated. Fig. 1a shows the same data plotted cumulatively.

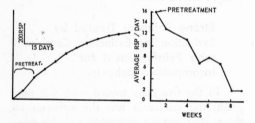

FIGURE I   Extinction of the response "entering the nurses' office;" (a) cumulative record, (b) conventional record.

Helen. This patient's psychotic talk had persisted for at least 3 years. It had become so annoying during the last 4 months prior to treatment that other patients had on several occasions beaten her in an effort to keep her quiet. She was described by one of the psychiatrists as a "delusional" patient who "feels she must push her troubles onto somebody else, and by doing this she feels she is free." Her conversation centered around her illegitimate child and the men she claimed were constantly pursuing her. It was the nurses' impression that the patient had "nothing else to talk about."

A 5-day pretreatment observation of the patient was made at 30-minute intervals to compare the relative frequencies of psychotic and sensible content in her talk. Some of the nurses reported that, previously, when the patient started her psychotic talk, they listened to her in an effort to get at the "roots of her problem." A few nurses stated that they did not listen to what she was saying but simply nodded and remarked, "Yes, I understand," or some such comment, the purpose of which was to steer the patient's conversation onto some other topic. These reports suggested that the psychotic talk was being maintained by the nurses' reaction to it. While it is recognized that a distinction between psychotic and normal talk is somewhat arbitrary, this case was included in the research because of its value as a problem involving primarily verbal behavior.

The following instructions were given to the nurses: "During this program the patient must not be given reinforcement (attention) for her psychotic talk (about her illegitimate child and the men chasing her). Check the patient every 30 minutes, and (a) tally for psychotic talk; and (b) reinforce (and tally) sensible talk. If another patient fights with her, avoid making an issue of it. Simply stop the other patient from hurting her, but do so with a matter-of-fact attitude."

The 5-day observation period resulted in a relative frequency of psychotic talk of 0.91. During treatment (Fig. 2), the relative frequency dropped to less than 0.25; but, later on, it rose to a value exceeded only by the pretreatment level. The sudden increase

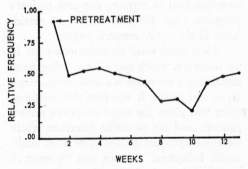

FIGURE 2   Extinction of psychotic talk.

in the patient's psychotic talk in the ninth week probably occurred because the patient had been talking to a social worker, who, unknown to the nurses, had been reinforcing her psychotic talk. The reinforcement obtained from the social worker appeared to generalize to her interaction with other patients and nurses. The patient herself told one of the nurses, "Well you're not listening to me. I'll have to go and see Miss ———— (the social worker) again, 'cause she told me that if she would listen to my past she could help me."

In addition to the reinforcement attributable to the social worker, two other instances of bootleg reinforcement came to light. One instance occurred when a hospital employee came to visit the ward, and, another, when volunteer ladies came to entertain the patients. These occasions were impossible to control, and indicate some of the difficulties of long-term control over verbal behavior.

It is of interest to note that since the reinforcement program began, the patient has not been attacked by the other patients and is only rarely abused verbally. These improvements were commented upon by the nurses, who were nevertheless somewhat disappointed. On the basis of the improvement shown in verbal behavior, the nurses had expected a dramatic over-all change which did not occur.

Strong Behavior Treated by Strengthening Incompatible Behavior

This case represented an attempt to control violent behavior by strengthening an incompatible class of responses, and to recondition normal social approaches while the violence was under control. The first phase was quite successful; but errors in strategy plagued the last half of the program, and it was terminated by the nurses because the patient became more violent.

The immediate reason for referral was that the patient, Dotty, had become increasingly violent over the last 5 years, and recently attacked several patients and hospital personnel without any apparent reason. Since admission and up the present, she had received many electroconvulsive-therapy treatments aimed at reducing this violence, with little or no success. In 1947, a physician recommended her as a good case for psychosurgery. In December of the same year, she attempted to strangle her mother who was visiting her at the time. In July 1948, the patient had a leucotomy. The situation had recently become so serious that at the least suspicious move on her part the nurses would put her in the seclusion room. She spent from 3 to 12 hours daily in that room.

A 5-day pretreatment study, at 15-minute intervals, indicated that one of the nonviolent behaviors exhibited fairly often was "being on the floor" in the dayroom. The response included lying, squatting, kneeling, and sitting on the floor. Strengthening this class of responses would control the violence and, at the same time, permit the emotional behavior of other patients and nurses toward her to extinguish. To strengthen the patient's own social behavior, her approaches to the nurses were to be reinforced. The response "approach to nurse" was defined as spontaneous requests, questions or comments made by the patient to the nurse. Ultimately, the plan was to discontinue reinforcing being on the floor once the patient-nurse social interaction appeared somewhat normal. Presumably, this would have further increased the probability of approach to the nurses.

For the duration of the program, continuous social reinforcement was to be available for her approach to the nurses. Social reinforcement was to be available for the first 4 weeks only, on a fixed interval of 15 minutes, contingent on the response being on the floor. For the last 4 weeks, social reinforcement was to be withheld for being on the floor.

The following instructions were given to the nurses for the first 4 weeks of the program: "Reinforce (and tally) her approaches to you every time they occur. Check the patient every 15 minutes, and reinforce (and tally) the behavior being on the floor."

From the fifth week on the instructions

were modified as follows: "Continue reinforcing (and tallying) her approaches to you every time they occur. Check the patient every 15 minutes, and tally but do not reinforce the behavior being on the floor."

During the period of reinforcement, as shown in Fig. 3, the relative frequency of the response being on the floor increased from the pretreatment level of less than 0.10 to a value of 0.21. During the succeeding 4 weeks of extinction, the frequency of being on the floor returned to the pretreatment level.

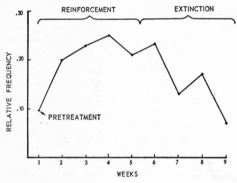

FIGURE 3   Reinforcement and subsequent extinction of the response "being on the floor."

It was clear that being on the floor was incompatible with the fighting behavior and that the latter could be controlled by reinforcing the former. During the period of reinforcement for being on the floor, she attacked a patient once; but during the period of extinction, she made eight attacks on others. Her approaches to nurses increased over-all during the 4 weeks of reinforcement, but they decreased during the last 4 weeks, even though they were still being reinforced. This decrease paralleled the decrease in being on the floor. While being on the floor was undergoing extinction, attacks on the patients and nurses increased in frequency, and the nurses decided to return to the practice of restraining the patient. The program was terminated at this point.

The patient's failure to make the transition from being on the floor to approaching the nurses suggests that the latter response was poorly chosen. It was relatively incompatible with being on the floor. This meant that a previously reinforced response would have to be extinguished before the transition was possible, and this, too, was poor strategy with a violent patient.

Weak Behavior Strengthened by Escape and Avoidance Conditioning

Two female patients generally refused to eat unless aided by the nurses. One, Janet, had to be forcefully taken to the dining room, where she would permit the nurses to spoon-feed her. The other patient, Mary, was spoon-fed in a room adjacent to the dining room. Both patients had little social contact with others and were reported to be relatively indifferent to attention by the nurses. Both were also reported to care only for the neat and clean appearance of their clothing. Mary had been at the hospital for 7 months, and Janet had been there for 28 years. These two patients were in different wards and apparently did not know each other.

The program involved a combination of escape and avoidance conditioning, with food spilling as the aversive stimulus. All spoonfeeding was to be accompanied by some food spilling which the patient could escape by feeding herself after the first spilling, or avoid by feeding herself the entire meal. Social reinforcement was to be given contingent on feeding herself.

It was hoped that once self-feeding began to occur with some regularity, it would come under the control of environmental variables which maintain this behavior in most people, such as convenience, social stimulation at meal time, etc. In both cases, the program ultimately resulted in complete self-feeding, which now has been maintained for over 10 months. Janet's behavior change was complicated by a history of religious fasting, and her change took a little longer. Mary's case will be given here in detail.

The following instructions were given to the nurses: "Continue spoonfeeding the patient; but from now on, do it in such a careless way that the patient will have a few drops of food fall on her dress. Be sure not to overdo the food dropping, since what we want to convey to the patient is that it is difficult to spoonfeed a grown-up person, and not that we are mean to her. What we expect is that the patient will find it difficult to depend on your skill to feed her. You will still be feeding her, but you will simply be less efficient in doing a good job of it. As the patient likes having her clothes clean, she will have to choose between feeding herself and keeping her clothes clean, or being fed by others and risking getting her clothes soiled. Whenever she eats on her own, be sure to stay with her for a while (3 minutes is enough), talking to her, or simply being seated with her. We do this to reinforce her eating on her own. In the experience of the patient, people become nicer when she eats on her own."

During the 8-day pretreatment study, the patient ate 5 meals on her own, was spoonfed 12, and refused to eat 7. Her weight at this time was 99 pounds. Her typical reaction to the schedule was as follows: the nurse would start spoonfeeding her; but after one or two "good" spoonfuls, the nurse would carelessly drop some food on her dress. This was continued until either the patient requested the spoon, or the nurse continued spoonfeeding her the entire meal. The behaviors the patient adopted included (a) reaching for the spoon after a few drops had fallen on her dress; (b) eating completely on her own; (c) closing her mouth so that spoonfeeding was terminated; or (d) being spoonfed the entire meal. Upon starting the schedule, the most frequent of all these alternatives was the first; but after a while, the patient ate on her own immediately. The relevant data are shown in Fig. 4. On the 12th day, the patient ate all three meals on her own for the first time. Four meals were refused out of the last 24: one meal was missed because she stated she didn't like "liver" and the other three because she said she was not hungry. Her weight when she left the hospital was 120 pounds, a gain of 21 pounds over her pretreatment weight.

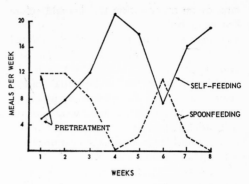

FIGURE 4   Escape and avoidance conditioning of self-feeding.

Mary's relapse in the fifth week, after she had been eating well for 2 weeks, was quite unexpected. No reasonable explanation is suggested by a study of her daily records; but, after she had been spoonfed several meals in a row, the rumor developed that someone had informed the patient that the food spilling was not accidental. In any event, the failure to feed herself lasted only about 5 days.

Since the patient's hospital admission had been based on her refusal to eat, accompanied by statements that the food was poisoned, the success of the program led to her discharge. It is to be noted that although nothing was done to deal directly with her claims that the food was poisoned, these statements dropped out of her repertoire as she began to eat on her own.

Strong Behavior Weakened through a Combination of Extinction for Social Attention and Stimulus Satiation

For 5 years, several mentally defective patients in the same ward, Harry, Joe, Tom, and Mac, had collected papers, rubbish, and magazines and carried these around with them inside their clothing next to their body. The most serious offender was Harry, whose hoarding resulted in skin rashes. He carried so much trash and so persistently that for the last 5 years the nurses routinely "dejunked" him several times during the day and before he went to bed.

An analysis of the situation indicated that the patient's hoarding behavior was probably maintained by the attention he derived because of it and by the actual scarcity of printed matter. There were few papers or magazines in the ward. Some were brought in occasionally; but since they were often torn up and quickly disappeared, the nurses did not bring them in very often.

It was expected that flooding the ward with magazines would decrease the hoarding behavior after the paradigm of satiation. Similarly, the availability of many magazines was expected to result in their being the major object of hoarding. The latter would facilitate an easier measurement of this behavior.

In addition, social reinforcement was to be withheld for hoarding magazines and rubbish. The results for all patients were essentially similar: a gradual decrease in hoarding. After 9 weeks of satiation and extinction, the program was terminated, since hoarding was no longer a problem. This improvement has been maintained for the last 6 months.

The following instructions were given to the nurses: "During this program the patients Harry, Mac, Joe, and Tom must not be given reinforcement (attention) for hoarding. There will be a full supply of magazines in the dayroom. Every night, after all patients have gone to bed, replenish the magazine supply in the dayroom. Every night while the patients are in bed, check their clothes to record the amount of hoarding. Do not, however, take their hoarding from them."

The original plan was to count the number of magazines in the patients' clothing after they had gone to bed. This is, in fact, the dependent variable shown in Fig. 5 for Joe, Tom, and Mac. The recording for Harry had to be changed, however; after 4 days of the program, he no longer carried the rubbish or magazines in his clothing. Instead, he kept a stack of magazines on his lap while he was sitting in the dayroom. The

number of magazines in his stack was counted when he left the dayroom for supper, and this is the dependent variable shown for Harry in Fig. 5. (Mac was out of the ward for 3 weeks because of illness.)

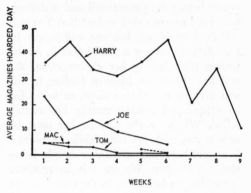

FIGURE 5   Satiation and extinction of two forms of magazine hoarding.

Prior to the program, one of the nurses questioned the possibility and even advisability of changing Harry's behavior. Her argument was that "behavior has its roots in the personality of the individual. The fact that he hoards so much indicates that Harry has a strong need for security. I don't see how we are going to change this need, and I also wonder if it is a good thing to do that." This was a point of view commonly encountered, especially regarding relatively nonverbal patients.

It would seem in this case that Harry transferred his security needs from hoarding rubbish and magazines to sitting in the dayroom and looking at magazines, especially during T.V. commercials. The transfer occurred with no apparent signs of discomfort on his part.

Other Cases

Combinations of extinction, reinforcement, and avoidance programs were set up for three patients; in two of these the problem behavior was eliminated in only a few weeks. The program of the third patient was followed for 20 days and then terminated since he had shown no changes by that time. An interpretation of the outcome of each of these programs is rendered questionable by the number of controlling variables involved and the nature of the changes.

The pretreatment study of four additional patients showed that the problem behavior of three of them did not occur often enough to justify carrying through a program; and in the fourth case, no easily controllable variables were available and, again, no program was undertaken.

DISCUSSION

On the basis of this work, further research along the same lines is now under way.[3] The present results are presented in this preliminary form in the hopes that they will provide encouragement to those who are in a position to conduct similar research. Therefore, it will be useful to mention a few other aspects of this work.

A major problem concerns the use of nurses as experimental assistants as well as substitutes for the recording and programming apparatus of the laboratory. There is no question as to the greater reliability of the ordinary laboratory component. In large part, however, the nurses' failures in carrying out E's instructions were unsystematic with respect to the results obtained, and although undesirable, they do not by any means render this kind of work uninterpretable. Systematic errors in observation can be reduced to some extent by dealing with response classes that are relatively easily identified. But, of course, this problem will become more serious as efforts are made to alter more subtle aspects of behavior. Perhaps the only solution is to be dissatisfied with one's techniques and principles until the behavioral changes are so obvious as to render statistical analysis superfluous.

Another question concerns the acceptability of this approach to the hospital staff.

[3] This new project is supported by a grant from the Commonwealth Fund, and is being conducted under the auspices of the Saskatchewan Hospital, Weyburn, Saskatchewan, Canada.

The nurses and psychiatrists who were familiar with the "reinforcement programs," as they were called, were given questionnaires and interviews to determine their attitudes toward this work. The results indicate a mildly favorable reception in general, with some enthusiastic support from both nurses and psychiatrists.

Regarding time actually spent in carrying out the programs, it might seem unreasonable to expect the already overworked nurse to devote 2 or 3 minutes every half-hour to observation and recording. However, this is only about 40 minutes of an 8-hour shift; and, besides, much of her work stems from patients' behavior problems, the elimination of which would make the 40 minutes an excellent investment of time.

Two sources of possible misunderstanding between E and nurses should be pointed out. First, when nurses were asked about the sort of problems they had in the ward, if no dramatic behaviors, such as attempts at suicide, or violent acts, had been recently reported, they often denied having any problems. Problems also went unrecognized because they were considered unsolvable. For example, since most nurses attributed the behavior of a patient to his diagnosis or age, little or no effort was made to discover and manipulate possibly relevant environmental variables.

Second, even after a behavior had been modified, it was not uncommon to hear nurses remark, "We've changed her behavior. So what? She's still psychotic." It seemed that once a persistent problem behavior was eliminated, its previous importance was forgotten and other undesirable aspects of the patient's repertoire were assumed to be the most important ones. In general, their specific expectations were unclear or unverbalized, and they tended to be somewhat dissatisfied with any change less than total "cure."

Finally, an objection often raised against this approach is that the behavior changes may be only temporary. However, permanent elimination of ward behavior problems requires a permanent elimination of the environmental variables that shape them up and maintain them. The clinical belief that a favorable behavioral change, if properly accomplished, will be permanent probably rests on a faulty evaluation of the role of environmental variables in controlling behavior. Certainly, it is not based on any actual accomplishments in the field of mental health.

REFERENCES

AYLLON, T.   The application of reinforcement theory to ward behavior problems. Unpublished doctoral dissertation, University of Houston, 1959.

FERSTER, C. B., and SKINNER, B. F.   *Schedules of reinforcement.* New York: Appleton-Century-Crofts, 1957.

5   PRODUCTION AND ELIMINATION OF SYMPTOMATIC BEHAVIOR

Eric Haughton • Teodoro Ayllon

This report deals with some environmental events that exercise control over behavior. The behaviors studied were those characterized by a high frequency and repetitive nature. A female patient in a psychiatric hospital in Weyburn, Saskatchewan[1] was studied. In this one case a repetitive response was developed and then eliminated.

Repetitive responses that resist modification and tend to be "purposeless" often come to the attention of the psychiatric or psychological clinician. A variety of interpretations are often made regarding the etiology and current factors maintaining the responses at a high level. In many instances responses that are repeated with exaggerated frequencies are given a poor therapeutic prognosis. Such behavior problems are often those "that need the notorious 'long' analyses . . . and great energy expended" (Fenichel, 1945, p. 310). Most clinicians learn to identify persistent and repetitive behavior patterns and attempt to deal with them using available techniques. Many current therapeutic approaches are based on psychoanalytic or psychodynamic theories. Skinner (1953) pointed out the potential contribution of a behavioral analysis to the treatment of abnormal behavior patterns. Recent laboratory findings involving the application of behavioral analysis and the experimental analysis of human behavior (Ayllon, 1963; Ayllon and Michael, 1959; Ayllon and Haughton, 1962; Lindsley, 1956, 1960; Barrett, 1962; Holz, Azrin, and Ayllon, 1963) suggest new techniques for the attenuation of some types of excessive behaviors.

ENVIRONMENTAL CONTROL

This investigation was part of a program of research on the applications of operant conditioning techniques in a psychiatric setting. A ward of about forty female schizophrenic patients was made available for this purpose. The ward was an independent and self-contained unit. Staff comprised equal numbers of female aides and graduate psychiatric nurses with three years training. A ratio of ten patients to one staff existed from 7:00 A.M. to 11:00 P.M. A physician

[1] This research was conducted in the Saskatchewan Hospital at Weyburn, Saskatchewan, and was partially supported by a grant from the Commonwealth Foundation, New York.

was available for consultation on problems involving patients' health. The ward was *off limits* to all hospital personnel including nursing staff, psychiatrists, social workers, and psychologists.

Only the ward's nursing staff had direct contact with patients. Staff made the observations and carried out all the instructions given them by the authors. Almost every facet of the life of the ward was under direct experimental control. Such events as eating, bathing, movies, walks, and the assignment of rooms was rigidly controlled to reduce the possibility of uncontrolled and unpredicted events occurring. Records of meals eaten, attendance at occupational therapy, walks, movies, and other events were taken continuously. Therefore, a continuous flow of objective information was available for each of the patients in the ward.

BEHAVIOR OBSERVATIONS

For over a year the patient was systematically observed at least every 30 minutes. This time sample technique was used in an earlier study and is reported in Ayllon and Michael (1959). Patient S (P S) was observed from 7:00 A.M. to 11:00 P.M. on the hour and half hour, while in addition, for 30 weeks she was also observed on the quarter hour. This observation every fifteen minutes produced 32 observations per day, rather than 16 in the 30 minute observation schedule. Ninety-five percent or more observations per patient per day were completed during the experiment, making a total of approximately 12,000 observations for P S. Patient was not under medication.

The observation was taken by the staff during a two minute interval at the hour, quarter or half hour. If an observation was taken outside of this time, staff were required to make a note of the exact time. In coding, though the staff were unaware of this practice, the two minute limitation was imposed. All observations occurring outside of this two minute interval were classed as "missed" and not counted in the data. Few observations were missed once the staff adapted to the observation time schedule.

Observations did not involve interaction between the staff and patient, and the behavior of the patient was recorded in a behavioral fashion. Not only was the exact behavior of the patient noted, but also the location was described through reference to an established numerical spatial system. For example, an observation might read "sitting in area 2, watching the television," or "walking in area 3, carrying a broom." The same record sheets were used for both the half hour and quarter hour observations. All observations were coded by the authors, who also carried out the necessary statistical and graphic analyses of these data.

Steps were taken to avoid observer bias. Half and quarter hour observations were taken by different personnel with each staff signing their observations. No cross checking between observations was allowed, nor did it tend to occur since promptness of taking observations was encouraged. A complex method of observing was established. Patients who were being observed were grouped. At the beginning of the shift a nurse was assigned a group for two hours. After taking four observations she changed groups with another nurse and took observations on the new group for the next two hours. This procedure continued throughout the shift so that no one person continued observing the same group more than twice a day.

As in most institutions staff rotated on the three available shifts. This was continued on the experimental ward so that only the supervisor and her assistant were continuously on the 7:00 A.M. to 3:00 P.M. shift; therefore, the majority of the staff saw the patients at different times of the day throughout the course of the experiment. To eliminate the possibility of the contaminating factor of knowing the results of the procedures, staff were given limited access to the data as it was collected. Without exception staff had experienced serious difficulty interpreting graphed data and no numerical data were presented to them.

EXPERIMENT I

Experimental "Symptom" Control

Subject. P S was a fifty-four-year-old schizophrenic patient who had been hospitalized for twenty-three years. According to ward reports the patient stayed in bed or lay on a couch most of the time. She was an "idle" patient who simply refused to do anything on the ward except smoke. These reports also indicated that she had consistently refused to work and participate in recreational or occupational activity for the preceding thirteen years.

Procedure. A daytime baseline of the behavior exhibited by P S was obtained by observing her every thirty minutes. During this period she was given only one cigarette at each meal to induce a level of deprivation with respect to cigarettes. The baseline data indicated that the patient spent sixty percent of her waking time lying in bed. She spent approximately twenty percent of her time sitting and walking. The rest of the time was accounted for in behaviors associated with meals, grooming, and elimination.

To develop a novel class of behavior in the repertory of the patient, an arbitrary response was selected and cigarettes were used as reinforcement. The objective response defined for the staff was "holding the broom while in an upright position." Figure 1 is a

FIGURE I

sketch of the stance of the patient in the reinforced position.

A period of response shaping was initiated during which a staff person gave the patient a broom and while she held it, another staff member approached the patient and gave her a cigarette. Intermittent reinforcement was later used to condition the behavior. Reinforcement was available on a mean-time interval (VI) in minutes when the patient exhibited the selected response, "holding the broom while in an upright position." In a matter of a few days, the patient developed a stereotyped behavior of pacing while holding the broom.

The VI schedule was designated to the staff by a list of times at which they could reinforce the patient contingent upon the appropriate behavior. During the early part of the study (phases I to II), the schedule was a VI *LH* with the mean time of five minutes and a limited hold of one minute.

During phase III a conditioned reinforcing stimulus in the form of a poker chip (token) was introduced. At this point the subject received a token (if responding) when a reinforcement time occurred on the staff's list and then exchanged it for a cigarette when the next reinforcement interval "set up." This segment of the experiment can be designated VI *LH* (50 percent) after Ferster and Skinner (1957). During this segment the VI schedules employed, ranged from 20 to 240 minutes. The terminal point in the schedule meant that optimally the patient could receive one token and exchange it for one cigarette during 8 hours. During the last phase of the experiment reinforcement was withdrawn.

Cigarette size was manipulated during the experiment. During shaping a whole cigarette was used, then from Phase I through VI a half cigarette was used while at Phase VII the full cigarette was reinstated.

Results. A response can be developed when reinforcement follows its occurrence. Figure 2 shows the effect of reinforcing the

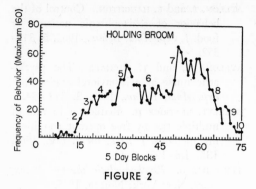

FIGURE 2

response of holding a broom while in a standing position. The stereotyped and repetitive response, "carrying broom," quickly developed. Once the response was well established, it was possible to maintain it through the use of a conditioned reinforcer or token.

The half cigarette was effective in increasing the frequency of the desired response, while the full cigarette also increased the frequency of the stereotyped response. When the intermittency of the reinforcement was lengthened to VI 240 (50 percent), the frequency of the reinforced response dropped markedly but was not eliminated. Extinction was introduced to insure the elimination of the reinforced behavior. At the conclusion of this experiment, the behavior of carrying the broom was no longer displayed by the patient. In a two year follow-up there has been no record of the response recurring.

Discussion. Upon the introduction of the token as a conditioned reinforcement, the patient threw the token away or misplaced it. When it was again time for reinforcement, the patient was asked if she had the token to exchange for a cigarette. When she failed to produce the token, she was told that a token was necessary to exchange for a cigarette. Within a few days, the patient's stereotyped response enlarged to include keeping the token and exchanging it for a cigarette while "holding the broom."

Several behaviors associated with the patient carrying a broom were observed in this experiment. For example, when other patients tried to use the broom and attempted to take it away from the patient, she resisted firmly and sometimes rather aggressively. The behavior of carrying the broom quickly became so stereotyped that there was no difficulty in recording the behavior. Her response seemed to bear many of the characteristics associated with behavior clinically described as "compulsive" behavior. In this respect it seemed useful to have other people evaluate the patient's behavior. Two psychiatrists were asked to observe and evaluate the patient from behind a one-way mirror. These two evaluations which were independently arrived at, help to put the experimentally established behavior into better clinical perspective.

Dr. A's evaluation of the patient's behavior was:

The broom represents to this patient some essential perceptual element in her field of consciousness. How it should have become so is uncertain; on Freudian grounds it could be interpreted symbolically, on behavioral grounds it could perhaps be interpreted as a habit which has become essential to her peace of mind. Whatever may be the case, it is certainly a stereotyped form of behavior such as is commonly seen in rather regressed schizophrenics and is rather analogous to the way small children or infants refuse to be parted from some favorite toy, piece of rag, etc.

Dr. B's evaluation of the patient's behavior follows:

Her constant and compulsive pacing holding a broom in the manner she does could be seen as a ritualistic procedure, a magical action. When regression conquers the associative process, primitive and archaic forms of thinking control the behavior. Symbolism is a predominant mode of expression of deep seated unfulfilled desires and instinctual impulses. By magic, she controls others, cosmic powers are at her disposal and inanimate objects become living creatures.

Her broom could be then:

1. a child that gives her love and she gives him in return her devotion;
2. a phallic symbol;
3. the sceptre of an omnipotent queen.

Her rhythmic and prearranged pacing in a certain space are not similar to the compulsions of a neurotic, but because this is a far more irrational, far more controlled behavior from a primitive thinking, this is a magical procedure in which the patient carries out her wishes, expressed in a way that is far beyond our solid, rational and conventional way of thinking and acting.

The apparent uselessness and irrelevance of the patient's behavior is indeed the hallmark of behavior often clinically described as "compulsive" or "psychotic." Yet, examination of some of the environmental conditions under which the response was developed, may make it easier to understand how similar classes of behavior are developed and maintained by environmental contingencies.

REFERENCES

AYLLON, T. Intensive treatment of psychotic behavior by stimulus satiation and food reinforcement. *Behav. Res. Ther.*, 1963, 1, 53–61.

AYLLON, T. and E. HAUGHTON. Control of the behavior of schizophrenic patients by food. *J. exp. Anal. Behav.*, 1962, 5, 343–352.

AYLLON, T., and J. MICHAEL. The psychiatric nurse as a behavioral engineer. *J. exp. Anal. Behav.*, 1959, 2, 323–334.

BARRETT, BEATRICE H. Reduction in rate of multiple tics by free operant conditioning methods. *J. nerv. ment. Dis.*, 1962, 135, 187–195.

FENICHEL, O. *Psychoanalytic theory of neuroses.* New York: Norton, 1945.

FERSTER, C. B. and B. F. SKINNER. *Schedules of reinforcement.* New York: Appleton, 1957.

HOLZ, W. C., N. H. AZRIN, and T. AYLLON. Elimination of behavior of mental patients by response-produced extinction. *J. exp. Anal. Behav.*, 1963, 6, 407–412.

LINDSLEY, O. R. Operant conditioning methods applied to research in chronic schizophrenia. *Psychiat. Res. Rep.*, 1956, 5, 118–139.

LINDSLEY, O. R. Characteristics of the behavior of chronic psychotics as revealed by free-operant conditioning methods. *Dis. Nerv. Sys.*, 1960, 21, 66–78.

SKINNER, B. F. *Science and human behavior.* New York: Macmillan, 1953.

6   A THERAPEUTIC APPROACH TO SCHIZOPHRENICS OF EXTREME PATHOLOGY:
An Operant-Interpersonal Method[1]

Gerald F. King • Stewart G. Armitage • John R. Tilton

One of the most severe forms of psychopathology is seen in cases culminating in a "vegetative" level of adjustment characterized by the patients being extremely withdrawn, anergic, and uncommunicative. Standard treatment procedures do not produce any appreciable benefits. It would seem that different, if not novel, therapeutic approaches need to be explored if changes are to be effected with this type of patient. This paper presents an evaluation of a therapeutic method that was devised for chronic schizophrenics with such extreme withdrawal symptoms.

Given the label "operant-interpersonal," the method of therapy that is proposed stems from recent work employing learning techniques with schizophrenics. Peters and Jenkins (1954) attempted to retrain chronic schizophrenics by using first simple psychomotor tasks and then increasing their complexity. To increase motivation, subcoma injections of insulin were given with fudge

Journal of Abnormal and Social Psychology, 1960, **61**, 276–286.

[1] The authors are indebted to the following individuals for assistance: Carl R. Brown, being largely responsible for the design and construction of the apparatus; Norman Graff and David W. Merrell, for collecting portions of the data; M. Ray Denny and Norman R. F. Maier, for their interest and suggestions; the late Edmund D. Barry, for conducting the recreational therapy group; Terrence M. Allen, for his statistical consultation; and Frank Restle, for his advice on the preparation of this manuscript. Grateful acknowledgement is also due John Berghost and other personnel of the Medical and Nursing Services for their extensive cooperation.

as a reward. Tilton (1956), employing instrumental motor and verbal techniques with even more debilitated patients, found that candy was an adequate reward in itself. His results revealed that mute patients responded better to the experimental sessions (mainly psychomotor in nature) than more verbal patients, while just the opposite trend was observed for "standard" verbal therapy, one of his control conditions. In a similar vein, Lindsley (1954) has discussed the possible extension of operant conditioning techniques to therapy.

OPERANT-INTERPERSONAL METHOD: RATIONALE

The therapeutic goal is to elicit more interest in the environment and to promote more appropriate response patterns. Assumptions about the underlying nature of schizophrenic behavior are not reflected in the therapeutic procedure, as virtually no attention is given to the patient's previous experiences or pathology. Thus, in light of the common tools associated with psychotherapy (Shoben, 1949), the operant-interpersonal method might be considered an unsophisticated therapeutic approach. Be that as it may, the following considerations are offered as the basis for developing the present therapeutic procedure with *highly withdrawn* patients:

1. The therapeutic sequence should be built on responses that are in the repertoire of the patient. Verbal communication is an inappropriate response medium because it has all

but been abandoned by many patients as part of the withdrawal pattern. Ward observations reveal that although such patients show little verbal activity, they still shuffle about the ward, manipulate eating utensils, smoke cigarettes, and so forth. In short, motor responses are more intact and, hence, more usable.

2. The course of therapy should allow an easy transition from the simple to the more complex. An increase in complexity refers to the addition of verbal and interpersonal components to the therapeutic structure.

3. In the role of "friendly leader," the therapist should provide guidance in a social atmosphere that is conducive to learning. The therapist should also function as a decision maker, continually evaluating the patient's behavior and judging whether or not the patient is ready to cope with more complex situations.

METHOD

Measurements

The following instruments constitute the principal measuring devices that were employed. Others of a minor nature will be described in the analysis of the data.

Indices of status. In earlier work with deteriorated, uncommunicative patients, two of the authors devised the Extreme Mental Illness Schedule (EMIS), an interview procedure for assessing low levels of adjustment. A similar scale, which was apparently developed at approximately the same time, has been reported by Farina, Arenberg, and Guskin (1957). The EMIS consists of 22 variables, which are rated in an interview setting on well defined four- or five-point scales. The first 10 variables involve ratings on what might be called "simple interpersonal tasks" (e.g., response to handshake, response to offer of a chair, response to offer of a cigarette). The remaining variables were assembled from other rating scales, the emphasis being on nonverbal behavior (e.g., posture, psychomotor tempo, peculiar gestures). The sum of the ratings on all the scales yields a morbidity score, with higher scores representing greater severity of neuropsychiatric illness.

Using two staff psychologists to make in-dependent EMIS ratings resulted in an interrater correlation of .95 ($N = 62$). With two different judges and different patients, a correlation of .92 was obtained for interrater reliability ($N = 50$). When the EMIS was readministered to 33 patients (all having achieved stable adjustments) after an interval of 8 weeks, the test-retest reliability was found to be .85. Several psychologists and psychiatrists were asked to rank small groups of patients on severity of illness. Converting the EMIS scores to ranks yielded validity coefficients (rho's) that ranged from .62 to .98. It was also possible to discriminate significantly between chronic schizophrenics with no privileges and chronic schizophrenics having limited privileges on the basis of EMIS morbidity scores.

Clinical status, as reflected by ward adjustment, was assessed with the Ward Observations Scale (WOS), the final 22 items of the Multidimensional Scale for Rating Psychiatric Patients (Lorr, 1953). In a pilot study, two attendants rated 20 chronic schizophrenics on the WOS, resulting in a correlation of .92 between the two independent morbidity scores. When a different attendant rated the same patients after an interval of 2 weeks, the test-retest correlation was .86.

A five-point scale for measuring amount of verbalization (AVS) was designed to be filled out at the end of the EMIS interview. The independent AVS ratings made by two staff psychologists correlated to the extent of .89 ($N = 62$). After 8 weeks, the test-retest reliability was .81 ($N = 31$).

Measures of clinical improvement. Difference scores obtained from successive ratings on the EMIS, WOS, and (to some extent) AVS provide measures of clinical improvement. In addition, the Clinical Improvement Scale (CIS) (King, Merrell, Lovinger, & Denny, 1957) was employed. The first section of the CIS consists of a simple five-point scale, in which the anchoring descriptions range from "has become worse" to "shows very marked improvement." In the event clinical improvement of any degree is indicated, the second section provides a check list which allows the rater to specify the nature of the behavioral changes. Previous studies (King, et al., 1957; Tilton, 1956) have indicated that ward personnel can make reliable assessments on the global scale of the CIS (first section). The following intercorrelations among the principal measures of clinical improvement were obtained ($N = 50$): EMIS vs. WOS, .51; EMIS vs. CIS, .62; and WOS vs. CIS, .45.

Subjects

Selection. All Ss were drawn from a large locked ward which housed approximately 300 long-term, male psychotics. The following criteria were used in soliciting possible Ss from the ward personnel: diagnosis of schizophrenia, under 45 years of age, low verbal and physical activity level, and no major change in behavior for at least two years. This procedure yielded 92 patients who were screened with interviews and then administered the EMIS and AVS. With the latter instrument, all patients were classified for level of verbalization using the following categories: mute or nearly mute, minimal verbalization, and below normal verbalization. Four groups of 12 Ss each were formed so that each group contained four Ss from each of the three verbalization levels. The Ss of the four groups were individually matched on severity of illness (EMIS) and length of hospitalization.

Characteristics. The ages of the final 48 Ss ranged from 25 to 42 years ($M = 33.8$, $SD = 4.4$), with length of hospitalization extending from 50 to 171 months ($M = 108.0$, $SD = 33.3$). Level of education was from 7 to 13 years ($M = 10.1$, $SD = 1.9$). The distribution of the schizophrenic subtypes was as follows: hebephrenic, 18; undifferentiated, 14; catatonic, 11; and paranoid, 5. No significant differences existed among the four groups for these variables. All 48 Ss had in the past undergone at least three of the following treatment procedures: electroshock therapy, insulin coma therapy, ataractic drug therapy, psychotherapy, and group therapy.

The Operant-Interpersonal Method

Apparatus. Section A of Figure 1 provides a diagram of the Multiple Operant Problem-Solving Apparatus (MOPSA), which was constructed to put the operant-interpersonal method into practice. A modification of the apparatus used by Skinner, Solomon, and Lindsley (1955–56), MOPSA was built into

an 8 by 8 ft. panel erected across the alcove of a large room. Projecting from the middle of the panel, 35 in. from the floor, were three wooden levers (6 in. in length) arranged in a row and spaced 5 in. apart. Below the outer levers were slots opening into trays, which were used for dispensing rewards of candy and cigarettes. A 14 by 14 in. screen for projecting slides was located above the middle lever protected by a Plexiglas cover. Each lever could be depressed 3 in. against a force of 3 lbs., as regulated by an extension spring. In order to obtain rewards (candy, pictures, cigarettes), it was necessary for S to depress the appropriate lever until there was a "click" followed by the ringing of a chime.

Lateral to each of the outer levers by 8 in. were two 11 by 13 in. aluminum plates, which could be concealed by covers. A cross, into which a lever could be inserted, had been cut in the center of each plate. Counterbalanced by just enough tension to return and maintain them at the cross intersections, the levers could be moved freely in the two planes of the crosses. If S moved the lever of either cross from the position of rest to the end of the correct crossarm, a green light at the end of the arm became lit. Through a system of relays, problems could be introduced requiring from one to four movements (lights), along with various patterns of the "right-left-up-down" sequence. Movements had to be executed in a prescribed order so that an error canceled any previously correct responses, requiring that the entire sequence be started again. In addition to the green lights at the crossarms, an amber light located at an upper corner of each plate flashed when a problem was solved. By changing the relay system, new problems could be introduced in a few seconds. As the two crosses could be operated independently or together, problems requiring cooperation between Ss could be employed.

Temporary screens enclosing an 8 by 10 ft. area were erected in front of MOPSA to reduce distraction and to restrict the movements of S. During the initial stages of therapy, the only furnishings in this area were two chairs. Behind the panel and not visible to S, a therapy-assistant operated the projector (scenic slides), released the candy (Hershey chocolate kisses), and cigarettes (Lucky Strikes), operated the relay system, and recorded the readings of the counters attached to the operant levers.

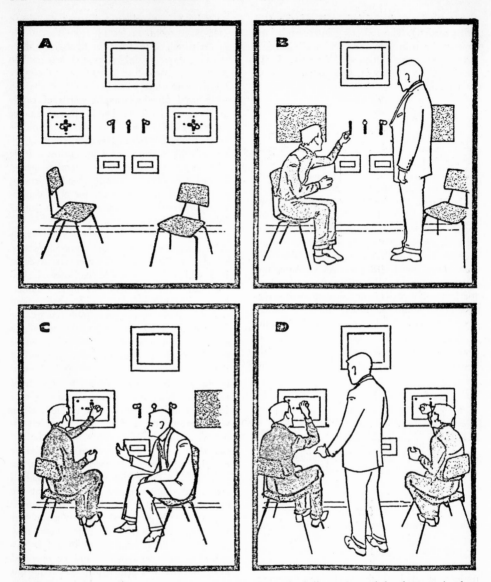

FIGURE I The operant-interpersonal method: apparatus and illustrations of the therapeutic phases. (A. Multiple Operant Problem-Solving Apparatus—MOPSA, B. Simple Operant Behavior—Phase I, C. Simple and Complex Problem-Solving—Phase II, D. Cooperative Problem-Solving—Phase III)

Therapeutic procedure. The 12 Ss undergoing operant-interpersonal therapy were seen three times a week for 3½ months (15 weeks). Therapeutic sessions lasted from 20 to 30 minutes. In adapting the operant-interpersonal method to the individual S, variations were bound to occur. However, the therapeutic procedure can be divided into the following three phases which applied to all Ss: Phase I, Simple Operant Behavior; Phase II, Simple and Complex Problem-Solving; and Phase III, Cooperative Problem-Solving.

At the beginning of Phase I, each S was led into the therapy room and seated in front of MOPSA. After directing S's attention to the three operant levers, the therapist briefly described their operation. The explanation was followed by a demonstration in which the therapist manipulated each of the levers, pausing to present the candy and cigarettes to S and to call his attention to the picture on the screen. The S was then urged to depress one of the levers. In a majority of the cases, it was necessary to repeat the demonstration. In a few cases, as a last resort, the therapist placed S's hand on the lever and then supplied the necessary force for depressing the lever. With one S, the therapist initially unwrapped the candy reward and placed it in the S's mouth. If S successfully manipulated a lever, his performance was greeted with a brief but definite acknowledgment (e.g., "good," "very good," "good work," etc.). Section B of Figure 1 gives an illustration of this simple operant behavior. Verbalization by the therapist was held to a minimum, and what was said was mainly directed toward the operation of MOPSA.

Although there was marked variability among Ss, all eventually began to respond voluntarily. When the individual S reached this point, frustration was introduced in the form of nonreinforced trials. When any of the Ss stopped pressing the levers (extinction) after nonrewarded trials, special attention (instructions and demonstrations) was given by the therapist until S was willing and able to respond to various conditions of nonreinforcement. Phase I lasted approximately 4 weeks.

In Phase II, one of the aluminum plates was uncovered, and a lever was inserted into the cross. Beginning with the simplest type of problem solving, the therapist demonstrated the one-light problem, which required the lever to be moved into a single crossarm. He showed that only one of the four possible movements turned on a green light (at the end of the crossarm) and subsequently the amber light (upper corner of the plate). After making the correct response on the cross, the therapist depressed one of the operant levers and called S's attention to the resulting reward. When S could satisfactorily solve a variety of one-light problems, he was gradually introduced to problems requiring more movements. Eventually all Ss reached at least the level of two-light problems, while five of the Ss consistently solved four-light problems.

This problem solving behavior is illustrated in Section C of Figure 1.

After approximately 3 weeks, verbalization was integrated into the problem-solving process. For example, S, after solving a two-light problem several times, might be stopped after making the first movement and asked, "Now where do you go next?" If the therapist failed to elicit a verbal response from a mute S, he would ask the S to point to the next movement. Another procedure was to ask S, after he had solved a problem and received a reward, to describe all the movements required in the problem. When S was confronted with a new problem, he might be asked, "What is going to be your first move?" At this time, the therapist also encouraged more verbal interaction at the beginning and close of sessions, with topics not directly related to MOPSA being discussed (e.g., "What did you have for breakfast this morning?"). Phase II lasted about 6 weeks.

The second cross was uncovered at the outset of Phase III, which was devoted to cooperative problem solving. Seated in front of the second cross, the therapist informed S that they would have to work as a team in order to obtain rewards. In a simple two-light problem, the therapist made the first movement and S the second, as well as vice versa. Quality of performance seemed to drop sharply in this interpersonal context, as most Ss experienced difficulty in coordinating their efforts with another individual. As progress did occur, the therapist and S proceeded to three- and four-light problems in which all possible therapist-subject orders of responding were required. As in the latter stages of Phase II, verbal interaction was emphasized.

When all Ss had considerable experience working with the therapist, two Ss functioned as a team. This feature of Phase III is shown in Section D of Figure 1. Then, two additional Ss entered the therapeutic situation, standing behind and observing the cooperating Ss before being called on to give either motor or verbal solutions. Stand-by chairs were pulled into the therapeutic area, and eventually as many as six Ss attended a single session. In this way, it was possible for every S to cooperate with every other S within a short period of time. Occasionally, the therapist again functioned with more advanced Ss and purposely made mistakes, placing the burden of making the corrections on the Ss. A by-product of this procedure was the introduction of some mild humor into this situation. Problems were also devised in which two Ss, after performing successfully, were required to communicate the solution to naive Ss (nonobservers). Phase III was terminated after about 5 weeks.

Control Groups

The following provides brief descriptions of the control groups which were conducted concurrently with the operant-interpersonal group.

Verbal therapy. The 12 Ss undergoing verbal therapy were given the same amount of time as the operant-interpersonal Ss, three sessions of 20 to 30 minutes per week. Therapy was adapted to the individual S. The therapist made every effort to establish verbal communication with them on whatever basis was possible. Depending on the S, a variety of topics were explored, ranging from routine daily events to S's feelings and concerns. With mute Ss, the sessions consisted of monologues by the therapist, punctuated by hopeful pauses. When operant-interpersonal therapy began using more than one S, a similar procedure was followed in verbal therapy. Hence, in the latter stages verbal therapy became group verbal therapy.

Recreational therapy. The 12 Ss in recreational therapy participated in a variety of activities, usually within a larger group of patients. Time spent in this form of therapy ranged from 3 to 5 hours per week.[2] The following indicates the nature of some of the activities: medicine ball manipulation, shuffleboard, rhythm band, singing, social games (e.g., hokey-pokey), dancing with volunteer workers. For the purpose of the present research, the Ss were given more individual attention than they ordinarily would have received.

No therapy. Although the 12 Ss in this group were not given any special treatment,

---

[2] The group receiving recreational therapy was a somewhat unusual control group. Due to a misunderstanding, this group was seen more than twice as much as the operant-interpersonal and verbal therapy groups.

they were allowed to continue to participate in the ward activity schedule (e.g., occupational therapy, corrective therapy), as did the other 36 Ss on a more limited basis. Heretofore, the program had produced no discernible change in the patients of the ward. Except when it was not possible (e.g., swimming), most of the Ss slept during the activities.

Procedure

All 48 Ss were transferred to a single dayroom in which they were the sole occupants. A specially selected attendant was transferred from night duty to function as an attendant-observer on the dayroom for several hours each day.

The Ss had been administered the EMIS and AVS by one of the authors prior to their being assigned to groups. Teams of attendants and nurses rated the Ss on the WOS. A staff psychologist not previously associated with the research readministered the EMIS and AVS at the end of the project (15 weeks later). The attendant-observer rated the Ss again on the WOS and filled out the CIS. Although the attendant-observer was aware that the Ss were participating in a special project, he was not acquainted with the nature of the various groups or their memberships.

The Ss of the operant-interpersonal and the verbal therapy groups were divided among two therapists (two of the authors) who were assigned six Ss from each group. Each of the four subgroups were represented by two Ss from each level of verbalization. The decision to use the two available therapists in this manner might be questioned since the same therapists saw the Ss in both the operant-interpersonal group and one of the control groups. Although the personality characteristics of the therapists would be held constant by this procedure, there was the possibility of differential effort or interest. To combat any possible bias, the therapists attempted to consider each S on an individual basis and to utilize all possible resources within the requirements of the research design. Detailed notes were kept for all therapeutic contacts. The therapists periodically monitored each other's sessions as hidden observers. The Ss receiving recreational therapy were assigned to an experienced activity-therapist who was particularly interested in chronic schizophrenics.

RESULTS

Since the Ss from the operant-interpersonal and verbal therapy groups were divided among two therapists, a preliminary analysis was concerned with any differences in the two groups attributable to the therapists. Improvement scores derived from the EMIS and WOS were each treated by analysis of variance. As none of the relevant F ratios were statistically significant at the .05 level, the null hypothesis was accepted, i.e., no differences produced by the therapists.

Differential Clinical Improvement

Table 1 gives the results of the analysis of variance for the EMIS improvement scores. As can be seen, a significant difference among the therapeutic groups was indicated by an F ratio of 7.313 ($p < .001$). Initial status (severity of illness and/or length of hospitalization) also produced a significant F ratio ($p < .05$) using T × I as the error

TABLE I   Analysis of Variance of EMIS Improvement Scores

Source	df	MS	F
Therapeutic Groups (T)	3	58.965	7.313**
Level of Verbalization (V)	2	22.312	1.057
Initial Status within V (I)	9	21.118	2.619*
T × V	6	3.924	0.487
T × I	27	8.063	
Total	47		

* $p < .05$.
** $p < .001$.

term, which is not entirely appropriate in this case. Contrary to Tilton's (1956) findings, no significant difference was found for level of verbalization, although it should be pointed out that only Ss relatively low in verbalization were used in the present research. The operant-interpersonal group showed the most EMIS improvement, with the control groups being in the following descending order: recreational therapy, no

therapy, verbal therapy. It was considered appropriate, and not a post hoc analysis, to compute t tests between the operant-interpersonal group and the means of each of the control groups. The results, using two-tailed tests, revealed that the operant-interpersonal group improved significantly more than the recreational therapy group at the .02 level and both the no therapy and verbal therapy groups at beyond the .01 level.

When the WOS improvement scores were treated by analysis of variance, only the difference among the therapeutic groups was significant ($F = 4.652$, $p < .01$). In fairly close agreement with the previous analysis, the descending order of the means of the groups on improvement was as follows: operant-interpersonal method, recreational therapy, verbal therapy, no therapy. While t tests revealed that the difference between the operant-interpersonal and recreational therapy groups was not statistically significant, the operant-interpersonal group showed a significantly higher level of improvement than the verbal therapy and no therapy groups, both at the .01 level. The full Lorr scale consists of 12 factors or dimensions derived from factor analysis, with

TABLE 2   Comparison of the Therapeutic Groups: Distribution of the Subjects on the Clinical Improvement Scale (CIS)

CIS[a] Ratings	Operant-Interpersonal	Verbal Therapy	Recreational Therapy	No Therapy
Has become worse	0	1	0	0
Essentially no change	4	10	8	10
Shows minor improvement	3	1	2	2
Shows considerable improvement	5	0	2	0

[a] The rating "shows very marked improvement" is not included in the table since no S was rated in this category.

TABLE 3   Comparison   of   the   Therapeutic Groups on Changes in Level of Verbalization

Changes in Level of Verbalization (AVS)	GROUPS[a]			
	Operant-Interpersonal	Verbal Therapy	Recreational Therapy	No Therapy
Decreased	0	6 (7)	2	1
Unchanged	5 (5)	6 (5)	8	9
Increased	7 (7)	0	2	2

[a] The numbers in parentheses for the operant-interpersonal and verbal therapy groups represent appraisals of changes in level of verbalization obtained from the notes kept by the therapists.

the WOS contributing at least three items to each of the following factors: activity level, compliance vs. resistiveness, submissiveness vs. belligerence, and withdrawal. Using scores based on each of the four factors, differences among the therapeutic groups were further explored with analysis of variance. Only improvement in the area of withdrawal yielded a significant difference ($F = 3.827$, $p < .05$).

Further support for the greater effectiveness of operant-interpersonal therapy can be found in Table 2, which presents a comparison of the therapeutic groups on the CIS. More Ss in the operant-interpersonal group (eight) exhibited some degree of clinical improvement than Ss in any of the control groups. Ranking the groups on amount of improvement from Table 2 results in the identical order as that obtained for the EMIS scores. The operant-interpersonal group was compared with each of the control groups with the Fisher exact test by using the dichotomy "improvement vs. no improvement" and constructing fourfold tables. With this analysis, the operant-interpersonal group was significantly better than the verbal therapy ($p = .009$) and no therapy ($p = .019$) groups; the trend in favor of the operant-interpersonal over the recrea-

tional therapy group was not significant ($p = .220$). Although nothing is known about its reliability, the CIS checklist (second section) provides information on the qualitative aspects of clinical improvement. An inspection of the checklist indicated that the nature of the clinical changes was quite similar for the improved Ss of the operant-interpersonal and control groups. The largest discrepancies occurred on the checklist items "improved verbal communication," where proportionately more improved Ss of the operant-interpersonal group were checked, and "less tension," where the incidence of controls was higher.

Changes in level of verbalization, as obtained from successive administrations of the AVS, are given in Table 3. The operant-interpersonal group was again superior. More Ss in this group showed an increase in verbalization, and it was the only group in which no S dropped in amount of verbalization. A striking feature revealed by Table 3 is that at least six Ss in the verbal therapy group showed a decrease in verbalization. When the dichotomy "increase vs. no increase" was used for the verbalization changes, the Fisher exact test revealed that the operant-interpersonal group was significantly different from the verbal therapy group ($p = .005$). The comparisons of the operant-interpersonal group with the recreational therapy and no therapy groups both approached significance ($p = .089$). These tests of significance are conservative ones, since the classification for change does not take into consideration decreases in verbalization.

During the last 3 weeks of the therapeutic sessions, one of the authors began attending as an observer the meetings of the ward personnel in which various patients were discussed and evaluated. At this time, patients were being considered for transfer to a small "privilege" section which had been opened on the ward. The observer recorded the names of all patients receiving favorable consideration for transfer. None of the ward personnel participating in the meetings knew what treatment procedures were being given the patients who were serving as Ss in the research. Listed according to group memberships, the number of Ss recommended for transfer was as follows: 5 (operant-interpersonal), 0 (verbal therapy), 2 (recreational therapy), 0 (no therapy). Actually, only one S, a member of the operant-interpersonal group, was transferred to the open section within 4 weeks after termination of the therapeutic sessions.

Subsequent evaluations. Some data on the status of the therapeutic groups were collected 6 months after the therapeutic sessions were discontinued. At this time, a team of ward personnel rated the Ss of the operant-interpersonal, verbal therapy, and no therapy groups on the WOS. The recreational therapy group was not included since it, as an exception, was still receiving therapeutic attention. Treatment of the WOS morbidity scores by analysis of variance yielded a significant difference among the three therapeutic groups ($F = 4.239, p < .05$), with the operant-interpersonal group having the least pathology. The operant-interpersonal group was the only one showing a significant improvement over the initial WOS rating ($t = 2.664, 11$ $df, p < .05$). The transferred S from the operant-interpersonal group was still functioning on the open section. However, no other Ss had been transferred during this time interval.

Other Comparative Data

When the screening interview was conducted, none of the Ss, as best as it could be determined, indicated any interest in leaving the ward for any purpose. During the thirteenth week of the therapeutic sessions, a staff psychologist not previously associated with the research briefly interviewed all Ss of the operant-interpersonal, verbal therapy, and no therapy groups. Each S was rated for motivation to leave the ward (either to an open ward or out of the hospital) on the following scale: 1—no interest, 2—some interest, 3—definite interest. It can be seen in

TABLE 4   Comparison of the Therapeutic Groups on Development of Motivation to Leave the Ward

Ratings on Motivation to Leave the Ward	GROUPS		
	Operant-Inter-personal	*Verbal Therapy*	*No Therapy*
No interest	4	10	10
Some interest	5	1	2
Definite interest	3	1	0

Table 4 that more Ss in the operant-interpersonal group displayed some degree of interest in leaving the ward than the Ss in the two control groups. When this measure of motivation was divided into "interest vs. no interest," the Fisher exact test indicated that these differences were significant ($p = .019$) when the operant-interpersonal group was compared with each of the control groups.

As was noted earlier, the Ss of the no therapy group continued to participate in the ward activity schedule. Although less time was available due to the various therapeutic procedures, the other Ss also attended these activities. The one activity in which all Ss participated was occupational therapy. At the close of the therapeutic sessions, the occupational therapist was given a list of all Ss and asked to indicate any who had displayed "increased interest or more constructive behavior" in occupational therapy during the preceding 2 months. The resulting distribution of Ss rated as showing some positive change was as follows: 4 (operant-interpersonal), 0 (verbal therapy), 1 (recreational therapy), 0 (no therapy).

In the initial evaluation of the Ss, it was found that each therapeutic group contained from one to three Ss classified as enuretic. At the close of the therapeutic sessions, only one S was designated as improved by the night attendants, and this S was a member of the operant-interpersonal group.

If the therapy notes compiled by the therapists are used, another comparison between the operant-interpersonal and verbal therapy groups can be made. The notes indicated that during the first 3 weeks two Ss from each group showed resistance, i.e., resistance to leaving the ward for the therapeutic sessions. No S from the operant-interpersonal group behaved in this manner during the last 3 weeks, but five from the verbal therapy group were described as resistant.

Clinical Observations

The progress shown by the Ss in the operant-interpersonal group was readily discernible to the authors and other daily observers. To give an example, there was the day during the eleventh week of therapy that a long-term mute S surprised the therapist by greeting him with, "Good morning. Got a match?" The authors were particularly impressed with the interest value that the therapeutic tasks held for the Ss. More than a month after therapy had been terminated, an apparently puzzled attendant contacted one of the authors to inquire about the "lights," as two former Ss were constantly asking him when they could resume this activity. Observations of the Ss in the verbal therapy group paralleled the formal analysis. A number of Ss in this group obviously became worse. Strong negativism toward the therapeutic sessions was common, and practically all of the eight verbal Ss responded less, several becoming mute.

Interrelationships among Subject, Therapeutic, and Outcome Variables

The interrelationships among the following types of variables were explored with the 12 Ss of the operant-interpersonal group: subject, therapeutic, and outcome. The subject variables were age, length of hospitalization, severity of illness, and level of prepsychotic adjustment. Severity of illness was indicated by a composite of the EMIS and the WOS. Using a scale derived partly from certain prognostic criteria (Kantor, Wallner,

& Winder, 1953; Phillips, 1953), one of the authors ranked the Ss on level of prepsychotic adjustment on the basis of case history information. Previous research (King, 1958) has shown a relatively high interrater reliability for ranking a similar dimension from case history material. The therapeutic notes were used by two of the authors who collaborated in ranking the Ss on the following therapeutic variables: operant rate, level of problem solving, and task improvement. Rate of operant response (number of responses) was based on performance during the first 4 weeks of therapy. Level of problem solving pertained to the ability of the Ss to solve the light-sequence problems of Phase II. Task improvement reflected the ranking of the Ss on overall improvement in coping with the task requirements throughout the course of therapy. Outcome was represented by the relative standings of the Ss on clinical improvement, as indicated by a composite of the improvement scores from the EMIS, WOS, and CIS.

The rank-order intercorrelations among the various subject, therapeutic, and outcome variables can be examined in Table 5. Of the subject variables, only severity of illness was related to any of the therapeutic variables, the rho's with operant rate and level of problem solving being significant at the .05 and .02 levels, respectively. The negative correlation between severity of illness and operant rate coincides with the results reported by Mednick and Lindsley (1958) with chronic patients. Although there was a trend for length of hospitalization to be negatively correlated with outcome ($p < .10$), the one subject variable significantly correlated with clinical improvement was level of prepsychotic adjustment ($p < .05$). Since it was negative, this latter correlation would appear to be inconsistent with previous findings which have shown that level of prepsychotic adjustment, as a reflection of more reactive than process characteristics, was positively related to prognosis. A possible explanation lies in viewing this finding in the light of an analysis presented by Zubin and

TABLE 5   Rank-Order Intercorrelations among Subject, Therapeutic, and Outcome Variables
(N = 12)

Variables	2	3	4	5	6	7	8
1. Age	.804****	−.139	.028	−.070	.028	−.244	−.434
2. Length of Hospitalization		.189	.140	−.301	−.322	−.378	−.545*
3. Severity of Illness			.105	−.601**	−.685***	−.566*	−.266
4. Level of Prepsychotic Adjustment				.119	.098	.091	−.580**
5. Operant Rate					.699***	.615**	.203
6. Level of Problem Solving						.769****	.294
7. Task Improvement							.594**
8. Clinical Improvement							

Values of p (two-tailed tests):

* $p < .10$.
** $p < .05$.
*** $p < .02$.
**** $p < .01$.

Windle (1954), who found that certain prognostic indices were positively related to favorable outcome in acute psychotics but negatively related for chronic psychotics (the status of the present Ss). All the therapeutic variables were positively intercorrelated at the .05 level or better, and each correlated positively with outcome. However, only the correlation between task improvement and clinical improvement was significant ($p < .05$). This correlation is compatible with the important assumption that therapeutic gains generalize to behavior outside of therapy. As in most post-mortem discussions, reasonable interpretations on the whole can be posited for the obtained correlations.

DISCUSSION

In giving fairly clear support for the therapeutic effectiveness of the operant-interpersonal method, the results concur with those reported by Peters and Jenkins (1954) and Tilton (1956) in their evaluations of similar therapeutic methods with chronic schizophrenics. There are few basic differences in the therapeutic orientations employed in these studies. While in the present study the analysis of therapeutic gains was based on measures tapping more facets of

clinical improvement, the principal difference between this and the previous studies seems to be that the patients selected for therapy, in addition to being more debilitated, represented a more homogeneous group. The selection of patients was guided by the notion that the operant-interpersonal method was especially applicable to extremely withdrawn schizophrenics. It appeared that restricting the patients to the aforesaid type sharpened the differences between the operant-interpersonal method and the control procedures. For example, evidence was obtained indicating that control patients undergoing verbal therapy actually experienced some adverse effects. This finding is compatible with one of the underlying assumptions of the operant-interpersonal method, expressible as follows: in conducting therapy with patients of this nature, verbal communication should not be emphasized, at least, as an initial procedure.

The present study does not throw any appreciable light on what processes or components, among the many in the operant-interpersonal method, are crucial ones in promoting clinical improvement. How much does the relationship that develops between therapist and patient contribute to success? Without getting into reinforcement theory, one might wonder about the operation of the rewards. For example, is the patient more responsive to social reinforcement ("good") or to more tangible rewards (e.g., candy)? Actually, the different features of the method pose some problems of more general interest, as attested by the following question: does the introduction of an interpersonal component result in a qualitative change in the therapeutic setting, or does it merely represent increased complexity? In regard to the latter issue, there is some evidence indicating that, instead of or in addition to increased complexity, interpersonal components represent a separate dimension of withdrawal, interpersonal-withdrawal as opposed to thing-withdrawal (King, 1956).

The practical aspects of the findings bring forward other matters of interpretation. The judgments of the ward administrators led to only one patient of the operant-interpersonal group being transferred to an open ward, not an imposing gain. It is not difficult to think of a reasonable defense for this finding. Since the patients were only seen for approximately 22 hours, there is the possibility of additional clinical improvement with a longer period of therapy. Further sessions could be devoted to extending the previous therapeutic pattern, i.e., increasing the complexity of the therapeutic environment. The therapeutic tasks would gradually require more complex discriminations and more conceptual solutions as the problems at the same time became more and more embedded in a verbal and interpersonal context.

On the other hand, there is the possibility that the obtained degree of improvement represents all that can be expected from the operant-interpersonal method. Such an outcome would be compatible with a commonly accepted orientation which implies that a necessary condition for significant gains in *functional* disorders is therapy that penetrates beneath symptoms. The authors are willing to entertain, are even inclined toward, the possibility of limited further improvement, but for different reasons. For one

thing, there is the question of whether the patients involved, instead of being clearly functional, do not have contributing organic factors (to be discussed in the next paragraph). In any event, if the results are accepted as they stand, the practical value of the operant-interpersonal method becomes less evident. No ready answer can be offered for the question "What comes next?" The authors resist the temptation to resort to the rationale so frequently associated with the newer psychopharmacological drugs: that the patients, while not "cured," are made accessible to psychotherapy. Whether or not organicity is a factor is one matter, but independently there are doubts about the extent to which psychotherapy can be applied. There is no convincing evidence that psychotherapy is a feasible method for *chronic* psychotics at any stage of illness.

The operant-interpersonal method might be given a final scrutiny in the light of the type of patients for which it was devised. In classifying such patients as being in the terminal stages of process schizophrenia, many clinicians tend to suspect, or even posit, the presence of organic factors either in their etiology or, at least, current functioning. Some evidence can be cited to support this notion (Brackbill, 1956). If this point of view is accepted for the sake of discussion, then psychological therapies for this class of patients would be peripheral approaches, ones that could only operate within certain "neurophysiological limits." Although beneficial results from purely psychological therapies would not be precluded, the implication is that therapeutic gains would be confined to symptomatic ones. Within the available limits, however, specificity of treatment might well be related to the amount of clinical improvement. According to this outlook, the operant-interpersonal method, by focusing on specific symptomatology (withdrawal behavior), becomes a reasonable *psychological* approach. This line of thought is similar to that offered by Jones (1956) in his discussion of therapeutic procedures for "constitutional" disorders.

SUMMARY

The operant-interpersonal method was developed as a therapeutic procedure for chronic schizophrenics with pronounced withdrawal symptomatology. In order to put the method into practice, the Multiple Operant Problem-Solving Apparatus was constructed. Emphasizing motor behavior, the operant-interpersonal method progressed from the simple to the complex. Initially, the patients undergoing this procedure on an individual basis made simple operant responses in the presence of a therapist for rewards of candy, cigarettes, and colored slides. More complex psychomotor, verbal, and interpersonal components were systematically incorporated into the procedure in accordance with the patient's progress. At its maximum complexity, the therapeutic environment required each patient to communicate with other patients and to enter into cooperative relationships in order to solve problems.

Operant-interpersonal therapy was given to 12 patients, while an equal number of patients concurrently underwent each of the following control conditions: verbal therapy, recreational therapy, no therapy. For the patients in the operant-interpersonal and verbal therapy groups, therapeutic sessions of 20 to 30 minutes were scheduled three times per week for 15 weeks.

The operant-interpersonal method was more effective than all the control methods in promoting clinical improvement, based both on ward observations and interview assessments. Comparisons on the following variables also yielded differences in favor of the operant-interpersonal method: level of verbalization, motivation to leave the ward, resistance to therapy, more interest in occupational therapy, decreased enuresis, and transfers to better wards. The patients undergoing verbal therapy actually became worse in some ways (e.g., verbal withdrawal). Some comparative data were also collected 6 months after the termination of the therapeutic procedures. Several frames of reference, both theoretical and practical, were used in interpreting the results.

REFERENCES

BRACKBILL, G. A. Studies of brain dysfunction in schizophrenia. *Psychol. Bull.,* 1956, **53**, 210–226.

FARINA, A., ARENBERG, D., & GUSKIN, S. A scale for measuring minimal social behavior. *J. consult. Psychol.,* 1957, **21**, 265–268.

JONES, H. G. The application of conditioning and learning techniques to the treatment of a psychiatric patient. *J. abnorm. soc. Psychol.,* 1956, **52**, 414–419.

KANTOR, R. E., WALLNER, J. M., & WINDER, C. L. Process and reactive schizophrenia. *J. consult. Psychol.,* 1953, **17**, 157–162.

KING, G. F. Withdrawal as a dimension of schizophrenia: An exploratory study. *J. clin. Psychol.,* 1956, **12**, 373–375.

KING, G. F. Differential autonomic responsiveness in the process-reactive classification of schizophrenia. *J. abnorm. soc. Psychol.,* 1958, **56**, 160–164.

KING, G. F., MERRELL, D. W., LOVINGER, E., & DENNY, M. R. Operant motor behavior in acute schizophrenics. *J. Pers.,* 1957, **25**, 317–326.

LINDSLEY, O. R. Discussant for B. F. Skinner, A new method for the experimental analysis of the behavior of psychotic patients. *J. nerv. ment. Dis.,* 1954, **120**, 403–406.

LORR, M. Multidimensional scale for rating psychiatric patients: Hospital form. *VA tech. Bull.,* 1953, No. 10-507.

MEDNICK, MARTHA T., & LINDSLEY, O. R. Some clinical correlates of operant behavior. *J. abnorm. soc. Psychol.,* 1958, **57**, 13–16.

PETERS, H. N., & JENKINS, R. L. Improvement of chronic schizophrenic patients with guided problem-solving, motivated by hunger. *Psychiat. Quart. Suppl.,* 1954, **28**, 84–101.

PHILLIPS, L. Case history data and prognosis in schizophrenia. *J. nerv. ment. Dis.,* 1953, **117**, 515–525.

SHOBEN, E. J., JR. Psychotherapy as a problem in learning theory. *Psychol. Bull.,* 1949, **46**, 366–392.

SKINNER, B. F., SOLOMON, H. C., & LINDSLEY, O. R. New techniques of analysis of psychotic behavior. *ONR tech. Rep.,* 1955–56, No. 3. (Contract N5-ori-07662)

TILTON, J. R. The use of instrumental motor and verbal learning techniques in the treatment of chronic schizophrenics. Unpublished doctoral dissertation, Michigan State Univer., 1956.

ZUBIN, J., & WINDLE, C. Psychological prognosis in mental disorders. *J. abnorm. soc. Psychol.,* 1954, **49**, 272–281.

7   VERBAL MANIPULATION IN A PSYCHOTHERAPEUTIC RELATIONSHIP[1]

Henry C. Rickard • Patrick J. Dignam • Robert F. Horner

PROBLEM

Numerous verbal conditioning studies have been reported in the literature and excellent reviews of the area are available.[2, 3] The writers have been unable to locate, however, a single study reporting verbal conditioning in an actual therapeutic treatment case. This paper reports the manipulation of verbal behavior in a 60 year old male who has been hospitalized continuously for over twenty years. The patient was verbose, expressing freely delusions of grandeur and persecution. It was decided that rational speech would be designated as the dependent variable to be increased while the verbalization of delusions would be ignored or mildly punished. In other words, a direct attempt was made to reduce a specific class of deviant verbal behavior; no attempt was made to cope with underlying attitudes, dynamics, or feelings.

PROCEDURE

Three different Es worked with the S in the experiments to be described. In Experiment I the patient was seen for 35 sessions each of which was 45 minutes in duration. Sixteen of the sessions were tape recorded and later timed by E 1 for minutes of rational speech. The delusional systems in the S were easily identified.[2] E 1 turned away from the S, gazed at the floor, looked out the window, etc., while the S's speech was delusional. This procedure was operationally defined as mild "punishment." E 1 reinforced all rational verbalizations at a rate of from six to ten reinforcements per minute. Reinforcement was grossly defined as a smile, nod, exclamation expressing interest, etc. Since resistance to extinction of the response class "rational verbalization" was desired, an attempt was made to place the response under a lower partial reinforcement schedule during the last 5 sessions. Reinforcement was cut in frequency from approximately 8 per minute to less than 1 per minute.

In Experiment II the same S was used and, again, rational verbalization was the class of behavior to be reinforced. At this point a second experimenter (E 2) saw the

Journal of Clinical Psychology, 1960, **16**, 364–367.

[1] Appreciation is extended to Dr. M. Dinoff and Dr. E. O. Timmons for critical readings of the manuscript.

[2] Examples of delusional speech were as follows: "I have a fractured head and a broken nose because of spinal pressure." "Stars have metal bottoms and exert a magnetic pressure on the earth."

patient once a week for approximately 6 additional months and followed the same conditioning procedure used in Experiment I. No attempt was made to record the data during this period. After 6 months, delusional material was still prominent in the patient's verbalizations, but contrary to earlier sessions it seemed evident that the delusional stream could be turned on and off by experimental manipulation. To test this hypothesis the patient was subjected to alternating 10 minute periods of "minimal reinforcement" and "maximal reinforcement." The former consisted of E 2 aperiodically directing his gaze toward the patient (who always maintained a steady flow of speech) at the rate of three times per minute, smiling, and saying "umhum." This "minimal reinforcement" was administered regardless of what the patient might be saying at the time and was designed to maintain rapport and keep the patient from becoming too uncomfortable. During "maximal" reinforcement, delusional verbalizations by the S were interrupted; the experimenter encouraged the expression of non-delusional material of known valence to the S. E 2 saw the S for four 30 minute sessions over a period of two weeks, during which the S was exposed to alternating periods of "minimal" and "maximal" reinforcement. After the fourth session E 3 was introduced to the S and the above procedure replicated.

RESULTS

In Experiment I the patient initially gave approximately two minutes of rational speech per 45 minute session. By the 21st session this had jumped to approximately 25 minutes of rational speech. The mean number of minutes of rational speech for the 21st through the 31st sessions was 30 minutes with a range from 8 to 44 minutes. It should be noted that during the period of time that Experiment I was being carried out, ward personnel were instructed to essentially ignore the patient when he was delusional on the ward, but to elicit and reinforce rational speech through questions,

smiles, etc. It was hoped that this procedure, which was very similar to that followed by E 1, would promote maximal generalization from psychotherapy to the ward environment. Generalization from the ward treatment back to the psychotherapy sessions is an equally tenable hypothesis. At the beginning of the 31st session the S was put on a lowered schedule of reinforcement. For the remaining 5 sessions a sharp, progressive decrement in amount of rational speech resulted; an average of only 7 minutes of rational speech occurred during the last two 45 minute sessions. The rapid drop in rational speech when a lower partial reinforcement schedule was attempted, the fluctuating nature of the dependent variable, and the fact that a full session of rational material was never achieved, demonstrates the tremendous resistance to the extinction of the delusional verbalizations.

TABLE I   Minutes of Rational Speech Emitted During Alternating 10-Minute Periods of Minimal and Maximal Reinforcement

10-Minute Periods		E 2	E 3
1st Session	1	1*	1*
	2	9	8
	3	8*	1*
2nd Session	1	9	10*
	2	5*	10
	3	9	5*
3rd Session	1	9*	10
	2	10	5*
	3	9*	10
4th Session	1	10	8*
	2	10*	10
	3	10	9*

* Represents minimal reinforcement periods.

The results of Experiment II are presented in Table 1. It is obvious that, initially, rational material was expressed at a very low level to the new experimenter (E 2), during periods of minimal reinforcement. Apparent also, is the fact that E 2 very quickly elicited a high percentage of rational speech during the maximal reinforcement period. The acquisition of rational verbalizations during periods of minimal reinforcement was less rapid. Table 1 also shows the second phase of Experiment II in which another experimenter (E 3) participated. It is apparent that both phases of Experiment II show similar trends. There is a suggestion that the dependent variable was expressed at a lower level to E 3 as compared to E 2 during the minimal reinforcement period.

DISCUSSION

The results of Experiment I strongly suggest that in a structured psychotherapeutic relationship a selected class of verbal behavior can be modified through reinforcement techniques. It is further indicated, however, that this modification may be quite tenuous, existing only under a high frequency of reinforcement. Attempts to place the dependent variable on a lower frequency of reinforcement and thus build a habit which would show substantial resistance to extinction[1] resulted in rational verbalizations dropping to a very low level.

At the time Experiment II was initiated it had become a simple matter to manipulate the dependent variable through elicitation and reinforcement. It was then demonstrated that the patient could be conditioned to increasing amounts of rational speech during reinforcement periods over a series of alternating periods of minimal and maximal reinforcement. The fact that the S tended to talk more rationally to E 2 than to E 3 can be viewed in different ways. Perhaps E 2 possessed more reinforcement value since he had previously seen the patient in a therapeutic relationship. On the other hand, it might simply be that E 2 could more easily initiate topics which would lead to rational speech since he had greater knowledge of the patient. The S's responses to both Es in Experiment II clearly show a progressive increment in the amount of rational speech for the 10 minute periods. In addition, learning in

the maximal reinforcement periods apparently generalized to the minimal reinforcement periods. It should be noted that when E 3 began working with the S the dependent variable dropped 90 per cent. Apparently the learned habit of rational responding to E 2 was disrupted by the radical "cue change" of a new experimenter.

A high level of rational speech was obtained in this patient through elicitation and reinforcement techniques. It is apparent, however, that the newly established behavior showed little resistance to extinction in either experiment. This is not too surprising since the incompatible habit, verbalization of delusional material, had been reinforced over a long period of time and under a wide range of stimulus conditions. Various other attempts could be made to build in the desired verbal behavior. For example, a series of experimenters could repeat the procedure followed by E 2 and E 3 in the expectation that generalization of the rational verbalizations to the stimulus class "other people" would eventually be enhanced.

SUMMARY

Rational verbalizations in a neuropsychiatric patient were chosen as the class of behavior to reinforce while an effort was made not to reinforce the incompatible class, delusional material. E 1 conditioned the dependent variable, rational speech, to a high level of occurrence under a high frequency of reinforcement, but the conditioned response dropped sharply when an attempt was made to lower the frequency of reinforcement. E 2 exposed the same S to alternating ten minute periods of "minimal" and "maximal" reinforcement and demonstrated conditioning of the same dependent variable. E 3 replicated the procedure which E 2 had followed and obtained similar results.

REFERENCES

1. JENKINS, W. O. and STANLEY, J. C. Partial reinforcement: a review and critique. *Psychol. Bull.*, 1950, **27**, 193–234.

2. KRASNER, L. Studies of the conditioning of verbal behavior. *Psychol. Bull.*, 1958, **55**, 148–170.

3. SALZINGER, K. Experimental manipulation of verbal behavior: a review. *J. gen. Psychol.*, 1959, **61**, 65–94.

8 A FOLLOW-UP NOTE ON "VERBAL MANIPULATION IN A PSYCHOTHERAPEUTIC RELATIONSHIP"

Henry C. Rickard • Michael Dinoff

This note is a 2-yr. follow-up on the manipulation of delusional verbalizations in a 62-yr.-old male (Rickard, Dignam, & Horner, 1960).[1] The original experiment consisted of two parts. (1) Using social reinforcement, E_1 conditioned rational speech from an extremely low to a high level of occurrence. Rational speech decreased sharply when a lower partial reinforcement schedule was attempted. (2) E_2 and E_3 exposed S to alternating 10-min. periods of "minimal" and "maximal" reinforcement. The former consisted of E's periodically directing his gaze toward the patient (who maintained a steady flow of speech) at the rate of 3 times a minute, smiling, and saying "um-hum" to reinforce talking behavior *per se*. During "maximal" reinforcement delusional verbalizations by S were interrupted; E actively elicited and reinforced the expression of rational speech.

In the follow-up study of two 30-min. sessions of alternating 10-min. periods of "minimal" and "maximal" reinforcement, E_2, who served in the original study, took notes on a clip-board and timed the procedure with a stop watch. Because of the

Psychological Reports, 1962, **11**, 506.

[1] At the beginning of the experimental contacts S was extremely delusional, emitting approximately 2 min. of rational speech during a 45-min. session. Examples of delusional speech were as follows: "I have a fractured hand and a broken nose because of spinal pressure." "Stars have metal bottoms and exert a magnetic pressure on the earth."

grossness of the dependent variable, rational speech, data were rounded to the nearest minute, as previously. During this study a second E behind a one-way screen obtained identical rounded measurements.

The patient emitted approximately 28 min. (93%) of rational speech during "minimal" reinforcement and 30 min. (100%) of rational speech during "maximal" reinforcement. This finding is almost identical with S's performance during Sessions 3 and 4 of "minimal" and "maximal" reinforcement carried out by E_2 2 yr. earlier (Rickard, *et al.*, 1960).

Contrary to the popular prediction that behavior resulting from direct conditioning procedures would quickly extinguish and/or lead to the adoption of compensatory symptoms, S continues to respond with predominately nondelusional speech to E and is reported to be emitting much less delusional speech in other hospital situations. This finding is in accord with other direct conditioning studies reported by Bandura (1961).

REFERENCES

BANDURA, A. Psychotherapy as a learning process. *Psychol. Bull.*, 1961, **58**, 143–159.

RICKARD, H. C., DIGNAM, P. J., & HORNER, R. F. Verbal manipulation in a psychotherapeutic relationship. *J. clin. Psychol.*, 1960, **16**, 364–367.

9 SYSTEMATIC DESENSITIZATION WITH PHOBIC SCHIZOPHRENICS

Richard C. Cowden • Leon I. Ford

"Psychotic patients do not respond to this treatment and of course receive it only if misdiagnosed as neurotic"(7). Thus is dismissed without a thorough investigation, a potentially useful therapeutic technique, systematic desensitization. As King(3) has shown, psychotic patients do respond to conditioning techniques and the benefits derived therefrom do generalize to other situations.

Although the paradigm of King differs considerably from that of Wolpe they both are essentially an attempt at treatment using learning principles. Certainly, there are many patients who are confined to a mental hospital because of one primary phobic or obsessional symptom. In some cases if this symptom can be removed the patient could return to society. Admittedly, the patient would have to be able to attend to the therapeutic situation and be able to recognize and communicate to the therapist what is an anxiety-arousing stimulus. As Reynolds (5) points out, the lack of similarity between a patient's verbal and overt behavior casts doubt on his ability to perform adequately any of the patient's duties in Wolpe's technique, such as arranging the hierarchy, guiding the relaxation training, or signalling the therapist when a high level of anxiety was reached. This verbal-behavioral discrepancy has been verified elsewhere(1).

Thus, there seem to be two major stumbling blocks in using this method with schizophrenics: 1) their unreliability in picking out anxiety stimuli, and 2) their inattentiveness and lack of concentration during therapy.

The authors, having demonstrated in a laboratory situation that schizophrenics do respond to systematic desensitization(2), felt it necessary to attempt to use the technique with actual clinical symptoms. Two long-term mental patients, with well structured and encapsulated phobic reactions, were chosen as experimental subjects. Both carried the diagnosis of paranoid schizophrenia. The methodology used was the same as used in a previous experiment(2) and, as described by Wolpe(7), and Lazovik and Lang(4). The results are presented in the form of a case report.

S1 was a 27-year-old, single, high school graduate who had served in the Marine Corps for 3 years. A survey of his clinical folder revealed that this patient began withdrawing and becoming more solitary toward the end of his military service. When he returned home he became very tense, restless, refused to work and drank excessively. He had frequent arguments with his parents. His mother became ill and was hospitalized and treated for a stroke and/or some mental disorder. The patient felt that the family blamed him for the mother's illness and as a result left home, toured the country, and, when he ran out of money, finally got a job in the midwest in electronics. Gradually he became quite hallucinated and deluded (delusions of reference, influence, persecution, etc.). Upon his return home the arguments with his family became more violent and he threatened to kill certain members.

He admitted himself to the hospital in 1956 and was diagnosed as schizophrenic reaction, paranoid type. He received a course of

The American Journal of Psychiatry, 1962, **119**, 241–245.

insulin coma treatments, with little sustained improvement, and has been treated with various tranquilizers since that time. He was seen in regular psychotherapy, off and on from 1957 to 1961, with little change shown on his part.

This patient was chosen for desensitization because he showed a clear-cut phobic reaction of being unable to talk to other people without becoming extremely panicky and frightened.

His movement in the usual type of psychotherapy had been very slow. Primarily, he appeared to be passively resistive and at times negativistic. Rarely did he speak freely for a whole interview, and this happened only when he was feeling at his best. Discussing such things as familial relations, anger, sex, *etc.,* was quite traumatic to him. He would tremble, chain smoke, become tearful or block completely and claim that his mind was blank.

The patient was asked to participate in this experiment and he agreed. The symptom to be removed was his marked fear of talking to other people. Experimental procedure began in October of 1960 and stopped with the eighteenth session in January of 1961. Some of the items from the hierarchy are talking freely:

2. About a movie you saw.
3. About your experience to an interested and sympathetic nurse.
6. About something extremely serious in a joking manner to nurse B.
7. To a patient in canteen who looks sloppy or revolting to you.
11. About current events to someone you consider less intelligent than you.
12. About current events to someone you consider more intelligent than you.
14. About your symptoms of mental illness to your therapist.
16. About your symptoms of mental illness to the ward nurse, Miss B. or Miss D.
17. About your personal difficulties to a pretty girl in a restaurant.
18. About your symptoms of mental illness and very personal difficulties to Dr. E.
19. About your very personal difficulties to your sister.
20. About your very personal difficulties such as hallucinations, delusions of persecution, racing thoughts, in group therapy.
22. About your very personal difficulties to your father.
24. To both your mother and father about your future plans or your lack of future plans.

The subject seemed to learn relaxation techniques quickly. However, his outside practice tended to be irregular. He preferred to practice while lying down, rather than while sitting. Invariably, he relaxed enough to fall asleep. Scores on Forms A and B of the Stanford Hypnotic Susceptibility Scale were both 11 out of a possible score of 12. He stated he was able to visualize the hierarchy scenes quite vividly. He refused to raise his hand if he felt disturbed; and he reported afterward that he thought he "would wait it out"—the second presentation of the scene was not as disturbing. Fortunately, this was reported in the first desensitization session, so thereafter, the experimenter watched for behavioral cues of disturbance (sharp intake of breath, tensing of body, rapid breathing, swallowing, *etc.*), and then stopped the visualization.

When about half way though the hierarchy, patient, ward personnel and others who worked with the patient, reported that he was more relaxed, friendly, and much more talkative. Auditory hallucinations had ceased before the experiment. However, there were other symptoms which bothered him and these began to decrease in severity. They ceased entirely within a month or two after the last experimental session. These were unusual thoughts, vivid dreams which disturbed his sleep, and ideas of reference. He began going home on passes again. He became regular in attendance and efficient in his work assignments. Cigarette smoking decreased. In regular therapy he talked freely and at length and was able to discuss things he had not mentioned in more than 3 years.

Patient reported that he still had some difficulty in talking in a very talkative group. For example, once while home on a weekend, many relatives were there and everyone seemed to be trying to talk at the same time.

Patient stated he felt overwhelmed and had to leave the room.

However, on a pass in early May he discussed with his mother and father the possibility of his coming home to live with them when discharged from the hospital. This was a very unusual bit of behavior for this patient. However, the parents refused to accept him at home. He stated that he felt very disappointed and was somewhat depressed afterwards. So far, no adverse effects have become manifest, and the patient continues to be relatively talkative. This case might well be considered a successful demonstration of the desensitization therapy with schizophrenic subjects.

S2 was a 42-year-old World War II Navy veteran. He was admitted to this hospital in 1955 with an admission diagnosis of paranoid schizophrenia, and has been hospitalized continuously since then. The symptoms present at admission were primarily ideas of reference and delusions revolving around financial matters. He felt that his wife, sister, minister, and friends were trying to take his property and money away from him.

He has been combative prior to and ever since admission. An assault upon his sister was the event that led to his present hospitalization. During the first 3 years of hospitalization he was continuously combative and was controlled in this matter only by EST. A symptom that he developed shortly after admission was difficulty in urination. This difficulty was manifested only when it was necessary for him to urinate in the presence of other people. If he was permitted to enter a booth the difficulty disappeared. He also expressed considerable concern over being sterile. He has had very little sexual experience other than with his wife, and even this has not occurred with much frequency. His records reveal that in 1958 he began to develop the symptom of being unable to leave a room without thoroughly checking to make sure he left nothing behind him. The primary thing he feared leaving behind was a letter. He told the experimenter that the worst thing he could leave behind was a letter dealing with financial matters. Also, the combativeness subsided considerably once this other symptom of checking on leaving something

behind him appeared. If the checking subsided then the combative behavior would begin to occur.

He was very anxious, extremely tense and had great difficulty in relaxing. Beyond the symptom of constantly checking for fear of leaving something behind him, the patient was rational and oriented. He was able to discuss various subjects and had some insight into his illness. He realized that the reason for his continued hospitalization was his inability to leave a room without the constant checking.

This patient seemed like an ideal candidate for the technique of systematic desensitization. His symptom was a marked obsessional reaction which appeared to be amenable to hierarchy development and gradual desensitization. This treatment technique was discussed with the patient, hypnosis was described to him and he was given the choice of participating in the experiment. He was quite enthusiastic about the therapy since he himself stated that ordinary psychotherapy had been of little benefit to him. Incidentally, this man had been exposed to continuous psychotherapy since admission to the hospital.

On the Stanford Hypnotic Susceptibility Scale he achieved a score of 8. Following this he was instructed in relaxation techniques and was told to practice as frequently as he could. This patient did very little practicing of relaxation on his own time. It may well be that this patient was unable to relax by himself because of his constant need to be alert against anyone taking anything which belonged to him. Another manifestation of this patient's symptoms was the need to collect large numbers of letters which had been written to him. At times there would be as many as 20 letters on his person. He would have them tucked in his belt, inside his shirt, and in all his pockets, even in his socks.

This subject was seen for 56 sessions. The usual technique was followed, in that there was a discussion of his fear of leaving things behind, then the development of the hierarchy followed by relaxation training.

The hierarchy is as follows, with the least anxiety creating situation as No. 1:

1. Entering a room.
2. Leaving yesterday's newspaper behind.
3. Leaving today's newspaper behind.
4. Leaving a book.
5. Leaving an advertisement received in the mail.
6. Leaving a bill received in the mail.
7. Leaving a pencil.
8. Leaving an office.
9. Leaving a picture of mother.
10. Leaving a picture of the wife.
11. Leaving the ward.
12. Leaving the day room.
13. Leaving a letter from his aunt.
14. Leaving a letter from a person he hadn't seen in 10 years.
15. Leaving a letter from a recent friend.
16. Leaving a letter from another aunt.
17. Leaving a letter from his mother.
18. Leaving a letter from his wife.
19. Leaving a letter from his guardian.

The hierarchy was constantly manipulated and changed to fit the therapeutic situation. As described before, the items had to be made extremely specific for the patient not to respond with anxiety. Starting with session 11, assertive responses were used with the relaxation technique. The patient was requested to leave a blank sheet of paper in the room when he left. Later it was necessary for the patient to sign his name on the sheet of paper and leave it behind him. Then this was followed by writing the name and address of his mother on a sheet of paper and leaving it in the room which was quite disturbing at first. Eventually, however, the patient got to the point where he could do this with considerable ease. Periodically, it was necessary to keep the patient hypnotized until he was out of the room because of the extreme tension and inability to make the voluntary move. Also, it was necessary at times to devote the entire session to relaxation and hypnosis because of the extreme tension and anxiety displayed by this patient.

Another unusual thing about this case is the fact that the patient was more disturbed when he had *no* letters on his person to check their presence. In other words, it appeared that the letters served as a "Jonah Rag" and were something upon which he could concentrate his anxiety. This may well fit in with the idea that the fear of leaving a letter behind him replaced the inability to urinate and the delusions about someone taking his money and property. So long as he could check on the letters, he felt the other two situations were handled. Also, the combative behavior increased when the checking decreased.

Following the 56th and last session, the patient had shown some improvement in that the combative behavior had decreased and the patient was able to leave a room when the therapist was present. However, this behavior did not generalize to other personnel. Upon completion of the experiment the patient was able to lay all his letters on the table and leave the room and walk out of the ward so long as the therapist was present.

The results with this patient were not nearly as successful as with S1. Whether this is a function of the patient's inability to pick out the anxiety stimuli and respond to it or whether it is due to his inattentiveness and lack of concentration it is difficult to say. However, from all appearances the patient was able to attend to the treatment situation and concentrate upon the scenes presented. One possibility in this case may be that the patient's symptoms serve as a terrific secondary gain to him in that it relieved him of anxiety involving other situations and concentrated it all in one area. Thus the removal of the symptom could have resulted in overwhelming, all-pervasive anxiety which would make the patient extremely uncomfortable.

Actually this symptom may not have been anxiety-creating—that is, leaving things behind; but rather the symptom was anxiety-relieving. Removal of this symptom may actually have increased the degree of anxiety which is converse to what is required of systematic desensitization.

The results of these two cases indicate that Wolpe's psychotherapy by reciprocal inhibition can be an effective therapeutic technique with schizophrenic subjects. However, due to the marked variability found in the schizophrenic population it can be effective only with certain specific cases. This is reasonable since the term schizophrenia does not define a homogeneous population. Therefore, one should not expect a particular therapy to be effective with the entire population.

It is possible that with S2, he was unable to identify the various anxiety-creating stimuli. Rather than using the verbal report which is frequently discrepant from the actual feeling or behavior of the schizophrenic subject as shown by Cowden, Reynolds and Ford(1) we should look for more objective measures of anxiety. What is needed is a more objective method of identifying stimuli which are anxiety producing for the individual schizophrenic. For example, peripherally recorded somatic responses may be able to serve this function of anxiety indicators. This would relieve the subject of the responsibility of indicating to the therapist what is anxiety-creating and what is anxiety-reducing.

CONCLUSION

Systematic desensitization is an effective therapeutic technique for some schizophrenic subjects. This neither refutes nor supports Wolpe's statement that psychosis is due to biochemical or physiological changes. It simply reaffirms that all learned behavior can be unlearned, even with schizophrenics.

BIBLIOGRAPHY

1. COWDEN, R. C., REYNOLDS, D. J., and FORD, L. I.: The Verbal-behavioral Discrepancy in Schizophrenia. J. Clin. Psychol., 1961.
2. COWDEN, R. C., and FORD, L. I.: Systematic Desensitization Using Schizophrenics. J. Abnorm. Soc. Psychol., 1961.
3. KING, G. F., ARMITAGE, S. G., and TILTON, J. R.: J. Abnorm. Soc. Psychol., 61 : 276, 1960.
4. LAZOVIK, A. D., and LANG, P. J.: J. Psychol. Studies, 11 : 232, 1960.
5. REYNOLDS, D. J.: Personal communication.
6. WOLPE, J.: Psychotherapy by Reciprocal Inhibition. Stanford: Stanford University Press, 1958.
7. WOLPE, J.: J. Nerv. Ment. Dis., 132 : 189, 1961.

10 A METHOD FOR THE EXPERIMENTAL ANALYSIS OF THE BEHAVIOR OF AUTISTIC CHILDREN[1]

Charles B. Ferster • Marian K. DeMyer

Behavior of severely disturbed autistic children was brought under the control of an arbitrary environment by techniques of operant reinforcement. It was possible to sustain substantial amounts of behavior, as well as to widen aspects of the children's behavioral repertoire. The experimental methods suggest objective techniques for controlling the current repertoire of the child, as well as means for developing new behaviors by which the child may deal with the environment.

A prominent feature of the autistic child's repertoire is a narrow range of activity and a small amount of behavior controlled by its effect on the environment. Whatever the causes or antecedent conditions of the narrow range of the autistic child's activities, it might be possible to deal with them experimentally by building a new behavioral repertoire beginning with activities already in the child's repertoire, finding a method of sustaining them, and then gradually widening

The American Journal of Orthopsychiatry, 1962, 32, 89–98. Copyright, the American Orthopsychiatric Association, Inc. Reproduced by permission.

[1] Presented at the 1960 Annual Meeting.

We are grateful to Smith, Kline & French, Inc., and The National Association for Mental Health, Inc., for financial support for this project.
We thank Drs. John I. Nurnberger, Professor of Psychiatry, Indiana University Medical Center, and Donald F. Moore, Medical Director, LaRue D. Carter Memorial Hospital, for their advice, encouragement, and assistance in obtaining the facilities required to carry out the experiment. We are also indebted to Mr. Robert Hudson who was the principal research technician in the conduct of the experiment.

their range. This paper describes such a method.

The general framework of the experiment is that of operant reinforcement (4, 8). The focus of the experimental method is on the consequence of the behavior as the factor which maintains it. Reinforcement is the major concept and refers to a technique for increasing the frequency of an activity by following it with a special consequence. The organism acts and the subsequent frequency of this activity increases because of the past effect on the environment. In this experiment simple performances of the autistic children are experimentally developed and maintained because of the specific effects they have on the child's environment. As a result, the behavior being studied is, at least potentially, under close and manipulative control by the experimenter. These methods have been in wide use in the study of animal behavior, where they have provided a behavioral technology in respect to phylogenetically general behavioral processes. Experiments using the techniques of operant reinforcement with normal and feebleminded and psychotic children have already demonstrated the feasibility of the technical application and the generality of some behavioral processes (1, 2, 3, 5, 6). In general, the paradigm of these experiments has been to select a simple response such as pressing an electrical switch (key) and sustaining it by arranging some consequence relevant to the particular organism's repertoire and its current level of deprivation. The reinforcers used have included trinkets with nursery school children (Bijou); pennies with grade school children (Azrin); and candy with feebleminded and psychotic children (Lindsley and Azrin). In many of these experiments, the authors report large satiation effects, inability to sustain the performance of every subject, necessity of using brief experimental sessions and frequently weak performances, all presumably arising from a reinforcer that is not sufficiently durable.

SUBJECTS

Three subjects have been studied in the experiment.

Thomas, aged 10 and hospitalized 3 years, has been studied for 12 months. He had a normal motor and speech development, speaking short sentences until he was 2½, when he developed severe rage reactions, wandering away from home, gradual loss of speech, an excessive reaction to changes in his daily routine, and withdrawing to a corner where he would remain for weeks.

The second child, Margie, 11 years old and hospitalized 4 years, has been studied for 6 months. Margie had a slower than normal motor development. The parents cannot recall with sureness any motor development milestones except her walking at 19 months. Her speech was definitely advanced, beginning before her first birthday and proceeding quickly to well-formed sentences with good diction. Speech began regressing when she was 3 years old, gradually dropping off until she was mute. When speech was regained, it was not used socially but as a means of entertaining herself. At 3 years she was cutting with scissors but lost this skill, lost bowel and bladder training, and control over her affect. She has never developed any peer relationships.

Patrick, the third child, aged 3½, was hospitalized 14 months. He has been studied for 4 months. In his first year he showed normal motor development but abnormal emotional development. He didn't like to be held by his mother, would not look her in the eye, would not respond to his name, and shunned the approaches of his sibling. Changes in routine brought rage reactions. He has never developed speech.

Each of these three children shows the common characteristics of an extremely narrow range of behavioral repertoire, disorders in speech ranging from muteness to atypical speech with reversal of pronouns and echolalia, lack of control or capricious control over affectual expression, and rage reactions with a change in routine. The boys have good physical development with no detectable neurological damage. Margie had a congenital breast tumor removed by radium shortly after birth and has a reduplicated left kidney and ureter. However, she has excellent fine neuromuscular coordination and a negative neurological examination. All three children have normal electroencephalograms. Tommy and Margie had severe emotional traumata in their first three years of life, living in homes where the mothers were depressed, the parents in extreme discord, and their handling of the children inconsistent. Patrick's home situation was much better.

All three children are part of a special therapeutic program for autistic children in a children's psychiatric hospital unit.

SPECIFIC FRAMEWORK OF THIS EXPERIMENT

The present experiment extends the work in this field by developing techniques for achieving a more durable reinforcer as well as methods for generating more complex activities. The two goals—developing a strong reinforcer and a complex repertoire—are closely interrelated. To develop complex forms of behavior it is necessary to have a durable reinforcer because of the intermittent reinforcement inevitably occurring whenever complex performances are developed. The ability of a given environmental consequence (reinforcer) to sustain an activity declines as the behavior is less and less frequently reinforced. As the reinforcement becomes more infrequent a durable reinforcer is necessary to continue to sustain the activity. A reinforcer able to sustain an activity when each response is reinforced might prove to be a very weak reinforcer when only occasional responses are reinforced. Such a weakening of behavior by infrequent reinforcement might occur when we attempt to bring a given activity under the control of a specific stimulus; for example, when we follow the key press of the child with food only in a green light and allow key presses to go unreinforced in the red light. During the early stages of training, before the colors come to control the child's behavior, the child emits many responses (in the red light) which go unreinforced and which may produce a cessation of responding.

In general, it is difficult to determine the durability of a reinforcer unless the behavior is maintained by intermittent reinforcement. Activities which have a high frequency of reinforcement will often be normally sustained even with weak reinforcers. Performances sustained under intermittent reinforcement, however, provide baselines which emphasize the frequency of occurrence of the activity as datum and give a continuous measurement of the strength of the behavior and the durability of the reinforcer. Under most conditions a response occurs less frequently as its frequency of reinforcement becomes less. An intermittently reinforced baseline also minimizes satiation effects, permitting longer sessions in which to experiment with the performances.

As a first stage in the experiment we therefore maintained performances of the children under intermittent reinforcement to provide a baseline for evaluating and developing durable reinforcers. If we could sustain the child's performance under intermittent reinforcement, then we would have achieved a reinforcer which could also maintain the child's activity during the development of complex behavior.

EXPERIMENTAL TECHNIQUE

The experimental room contains a large number of devices which when operated either by a coin or direct key provide some rewarding consequence for the child. These devices include: a pinball machine; a pigeon and trained monkey both trained to perform only when the animals' compartments are lighted; a color wheel giving a kaleidoscopic

effect; a television set; a phonograph; an electric train whose speed and direction the child can vary; an eight-column candy vending machine with a separate light and coin slot in each column so that the child can choose the particular candy; a second vending machine which can deliver small trinkets or small packages containing parts of the child's lunch (both the trinkets and the food were varied from day to day and from subject to subject depending upon the subject's preference); a telephone handset with music through the earpiece; an electric organ; and a 35 mm. slide viewer. Figure 1 is a schematized drawing of the experimental room. The room contains a one-way vision screen on the wall facing the experimental devices.

During the first phase of the experiment we measured the frequency with which the subject pressed a key. This activity was sustained because it delivered a coin (from an automatic coin dispenser) which, in turn, could be used to operate any of the reinforcing devices in the room. The major advantage of the generalized reinforcer, aside from the possibility of the summation of reinforcing effects, is the wide variety of devices contributing to the reinforcing effect of the coin to ensure that at least one of the reinforcing devices would be relevant to the current deprivation condition of the child. We do not know whether coins derive their reinforcing effect from a sum of the various uses of the coins or from the device currently relevant to the child's deprivation. The hospitalized subjects were deprived of all food between meals. One of the hospitalized patients, Tommy, received his lunch during the course of the experimental session (11:15 A.M. to 2:15 P.M.). The second subject's session was 90 minutes long, and the third subject's 60 minutes. In general the maximum length of the session was related to the level of deprivation and the rate of the child's satiation by the reinforcing devices in the room.

The entire experiment was programmed and recorded automatically through automatic vending machines, relays, electronic devices, and electrical recorders. Except dur-

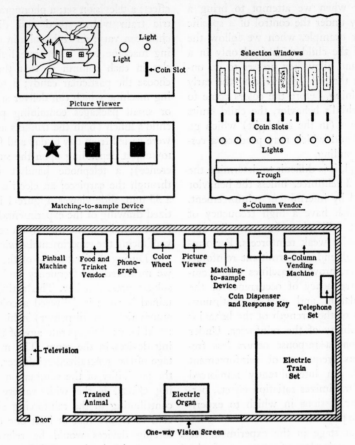

FIGURE I   Schematic diagram of the experimental room. Each device had a coin slot, coin light and light which was on whenever the device was operating. The detail of the picture viewer illustrates the typical arrangement. Also shown in detail are the matching-to-sample device and the coin slot, coin light arrangement on the 8-column vendor.

ing the first few days in the experiment, the child was alone in the experimental room during the entire experimental procedure. With few exceptions there were no interventions even during the most severe tantrums. There was an explicit attempt to minimize tantrums or other emotional upsets caused by sudden shifts in the frequency of reinforcement by arranging the changes of schedules of reinforcement as gradually as possible so that the child's behavior would be maintained strongly throughout. In gen-

eral the frequency of tantrums declined continuously during the course of the experiment.

THE EARLY DEVELOPMENT OF A PERFORMANCE

Food and candy appear to be the major reinforcers available, and candy was therefore the reinforcer used during the child's first introduction to the experimental procedures. Thereafter, the candy vending ma-

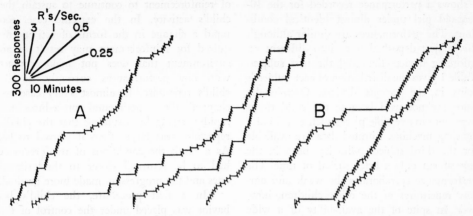

FIGURE 2   Graphic record of the subject's responses cumulated against time. The delivery of coins is indicated by the marks oblique to the curve and the scale is given by the grid. For more compact presentation, the records have been "collapsed" by removing the space between the excursions of the recording pen. Record A is for Thomas; Record B for Margie.

chine was supplemented by the gradual addition of the different reinforcing devices. Reinforcement conditions were manipulated during the early part of the experiment to give an estimate of how much activity might be controlled by the coin reinforcement and to demonstrate how much of the child's activity in the room was under the control of the specific parts of the environment that were manipulated.

When coins were delivered by pressing a simple key the pattern of emission of the child's behavior was like that normally occurring under similar reinforcement conditions in other species. Figure 2, Record A, shows a record of the performance of the boy when

every 15th operation of the key produced a coin (fixed-ratio schedule of reinforcement), and when most of the coin-operated reinforcing devices were already present in the room. Following the delivery of each coin (the oblique marks on the record) there is frequently a slight pause ranging from a few seconds to several minutes. Once responding begins, the boy presses the key rapidly (3 or 4 presses per second) and continues until the reinforcement. The boy is continuously active throughout the two hours of the experimental session, either pressing the key for coins or using the coins in the various devices. During the two-hour session, 208 coins were delivered. Record B of Figure

TABLE I   Summary of Distribution of Earned Coins in the Various Reinforcing Devices

		Total Coins	Candy Vendor	Rec. Player	White Vendor	Color Wheel	Organ	T.V.	Toy Car	35 mm. Viewer	Telephone	Monkey
FR 15	Tommy	208	161	12	17	8	0	0	0	4	4	0
	Margie	158	55	6	75	1	1	1	13	2	0	0
Matching	Tommy	257	175	12	18	8	6	6	4	4	12	5
	Margie	110	81	3	13	1	0	2	8	2	0	0

2 shows a performance recorded for the 10-year-old girl under almost identical conditions. The performances are similar although this subject deposited coins into different reinforcing devices than did the first subject. Table 1 gives the distribution of each subject's coins in the various devices. Occasionally coins are not used because the child drops them into inaccessible places such as behind a vending machine. Limited data are available for the third subject, who has been in the experiment only a brief period of time. His performance corroborates the weak and narrow repertoires of the other children, however. In spite of the availability of a wide variety of reinforcing devices, all of this child's activities are restricted to the food vendor. As more and more behavior occurs under the control of the reinforcements of the experimental room, it may be possible to begin to widen this child's repertoire.

DEVELOPMENT OF COMPLEX FORMS

Once it proved possible to sustain a simple activity for substantial periods of time and under conditions of infrequent reinforcement, we began to develop more complex forms of activity. The general plan here was to choose a variation in the child's activities in the direction of the desired repertoire and shift the reinforcement contingency in that direction. We attempted to choose slight variations so that reinforcement would not occur too infrequently. Once the child's performance changed to conform with the new contingencies of reinforcement, reinforcements were delivered only for further variations in the direction of the required performance. The same process was continued until the required performance was achieved, often over a period of many weeks. The rate at which the complex performance is developed cannot be predicted in advance, is tailored to the individual child, and depends upon how rapidly the child's performance conforms to the new conditions of reinforcement. Too rapid a development of the repertoire may result in too low a frequency of reinforcement to continue to sustain the child's activity. In the extreme case, too rapid a change in the forms of activity required for reinforcement may result in an environment that does not make contact with any performances currently in the child's repertoire. In almost every case we changed the experimental procedures too rapidly, erring by assuming that the child's repertoire was larger than it proved to be. As a result the conditions of reinforcement had to be returned closer to the original ones and the progression made more gradual.

In a first procedure, the child's behavior was placed under the control of the lights behind the plastic panel where the key was mounted, by delivering coins only when the panel was lighted. This control was developed without difficulty in all of the subjects with whom it was attempted. A second kind of stimulus control, developed by making the coin slots and associated lights inoperative whenever the coin slot was not lighted, was developed with more difficulty. This control was carried out by lighting the coin slots after the delivery of every nth (2nd to 5th) coin. Coins deposited as soon as they were received in unlighted coin slots would be wasted. The result was a "coin saving." The child worked at the key, accumulating coins, until the coin slots on the various devices were lighted, and then cashed in the accumulated coins. The development of this discriminative repertoire also made it possible to study how the reinforcing value of the coin depends on the number and kinds of machines in which the coin could be used. This could be done simply by turning off the appropriate coin lights. A second by-product of this technique was a sample of activity unaffected by the intercurrent eating or the use of the nonfood machines.

A further extension of the discriminative repertoire was provided by the 8-column vending machine containing a light and coin slot for each column. When a column became empty its coin light went out and further coins in that column were wasted. This arrangement permitted the coin to be exchanged for the particular kind of candy relevant to the child's current deprivation. The slow development of the control by the lights on the 8-column vendor illustrated the minimal perceptual repertoire of these children. Even though one child's behavior had come under almost perfect control of the coin lights during the previous coin-saving procedure, the more complex matrix of lights and slots of the 8-column vending machine totally disrupted the previously acquired repertoire. The control was re-established only by the addition of many procedures and some two months of training.

The further development of more complex repertoires was carried out by reinforcing "matching to sample" (7). Instead of a simple key, the child faced three windows (see Fig. 1), each producing an electrical connection when pushed. A device behind the windows programmed a strip of paper on which could be painted or pasted any kind of visual material. The subject was first trained to respond to the sample appearing in the center window. Touching the sample in the center window tended to force the child to attend to the stimulus and produced the second frame. The sample reappeared in the center window with a matching figure either to the left or to the right and a nonmatching figure in the remaining position. If the child touched the matching figure, a coin was delivered. If he touched a nonmatching window, the apparatus was disconnected electrically (time out) for a period variously ranging from 1 to 20 seconds. During the time out, the device was inoperative and no further coins could be earned. The matching procedure was established gradually by first giving the child a coin when he touched any window, and gradually approximating the final procedure over a period of several months. Once the child matched simple figures (for example, colored dots) the complexity of the material was gradually increased. Here again, introducing stimuli too rapidly would result in many mistakes, an increase in the amount of activity per reinforcement, and a low frequency of rein-

forcement. We have recorded several large changes in procedure precipitating severe tantrums. On the other hand, procedural changes sometimes of an unusual sort had little effect when they did not change the frequency or amount of activity per reinforcement.

Figure 3 contains performances recorded on the matching-to-sample procedure where the stimuli being matched were large bold drawings of a circle, star, rectangle, square, and a triangle. Each time the child matched correctly, the device moved to the next problem, but every incorrect match interrupted the procedure for 6 seconds by disconnecting all of the circuits. Every 2nd correct match delivered a coin. Figure 3, Record A-1, is a record for the boy of the correct matches during a typical 170-minute experimental session. The recording pen moves one step for each correct match and the delivery of coins is indicated by the oblique mark. As in the record shown in Figure 2 with simple key pressing, the boy is performing almost continuously during the entire experimental session with most of his behavior conforming to the requirements of the automatic environment. During this session 257 coins were delivered and used. The stimulus material is controlling the boy's performance closely with only 44 inappropriate responses out of a total of 1512 correct matching sequences. The incorrect matches are recorded on a separate recorder running concurrently. This record is shown in Record A-2 where the incorrect responses are emphasized by deflecting the pen obliquely as was done in the upper curve for reinforcements. Records B-1 and B-2 contain a similar performance for the girl for a 90-minute session. Again the performance is sustained almost continuously throughout the 90 minutes of the experimental session and the level of mistakes is about the same as for the previous subject, 6 mistakes out of 220 correct matching sequences. Table 1 also gives the distribution of coins in the various devices for the matching procedure.

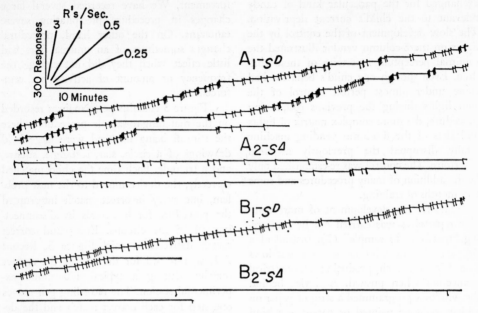

FIGURE 3   Graphic record of the matching procedure. Each matching sequence is recorded as a response and cumulated against time. Records A_1 and A_2 give the correct and incorrect matches respectively for Thomas. Both recorders ran concurrently. Each segment is a 1-hour portion. Records B_1 and B_2 give the records for Margie on the same procedures. The scale of the records is as in Figure 2.

DISCUSSION

The early results of this experiment, using the techniques of operant reinforcement to sustain and widen the repertoire of autistic children, show that it is possible to bring the behavior of these children under the close control of an artificial environment by means of a conditioned reinforcer possibly generalized. After sustaining simple performances it was possible to widen the behavioral patterns of the child by the normal processes by which behavior is sustained and altered in normal humans and in other species. While the behavioral repertoires developed in these children are still not nearly as complex as those involved in a normal social repertoire, they indicate at least the existence of normal processes at a very basic level. To date the results of these techniques do not suggest any basic deficit except in the rate at which these children acquire new types of behavioral control. Failures to develop normal performances as we get to more complex procedures will be difficult to interpret, however, because such failures might be due either to a basic deficit or to our inadequate development of behavioral techniques for affecting the children. It is difficult to equate the complexity of the various procedures to which the children are exposed, however.

We do not consider these techniques as attempts at rehabilitation but rather as experimental analyses of the actual and potential repertoires of these children. Perhaps these analyses can serve as guides for attempts to use the same processes of developing behavior in social situations where the performances sustained and altered would be activities in respect to other persons (social) and where the important consequences sustaining the activities would be the social effects of these performances. If it proves possible to develop and widen behavioral repertoires significantly in the experimental room, then this would seem to indicate the possibility that the same potential for behavioral change would exist in the social milieu if the proper conditions could be generated. In the same vein, systematic deficits in particular areas may indicate deficient areas of control which may be of use in determining techniques for handling these children.

It is not known, of course, to what extent the behavioral deficits observed in autistic children represent a basic constitutional or physiological deficit. The possibility of recording "lawful" activity in a situation where behavior of autistic children can be objectively recorded may open the way to techniques for evaluating the extent of focal physiological deficits, or whether in fact infantile autism represents a uniform condition. Once we can sustain the performance of the child and bring it under the control of arbitrary stimuli it should be possible to manipulate physiological conditions and record the effects on the behavioral baselines. Behavioral baselines could serve to evaluate the child's repertoire in terms of the performances ordinarily considered in intelligence tests, to test the effect of drugs, and to test the integrity of the central nervous system.

REFERENCES

1. AZRIN, N. H., and O. R. LINDSLEY. *The Reinforcement of Cooperation Between Children*. J. Abnorm. Soc. Psychol., **52:** 100–102, 1956.
2. BIJOU, S. W. *A Child Study Laboratory on Wheels*. Child Develpm., **29:** 425–427, 1958.
3. ———. *Operant Extinction After Fixed-Interval Reinforcement with Young Children*. J. Exp. Anal. Behav., **1:** 25–29, 1958.
4. FERSTER, C. B. *Reinforcement and Punishment in the Control of Human Behavior by Social Agencies*. Psychiat. Res. Rep., **10:** 101–118, 1958.
5. LINDSLEY, O. R. *Studies in Behavior Therapy, Metropolitan State Hospital, Waltham, Massachusetts*. Status Report III: 1954.
6. LONG, E. R., J. T. HAMMACK, F. MAY, and B. J. CAMPBELL. *Intermittent Reinforcement of Operant Behavior in Children*. J. Exp. Anal. Behav., **1:** 315–339, 1958.
7. SKINNER, B. F. *Are Theories of Learning Necessary?* Psychol. Rev., **57:** 193–216, 1950.
8. ———. *Science and Human Behavior*. New York: Macmillan, 1953.

11   SHAPING COOPERATIVE RESPONSES IN EARLY CHILDHOOD SCHIZOPHRENICS[1]

Joseph N. Hingtgen • Beverly J. Sanders • Marian K. DeMyer

Early childhood schizophrenics are characterized by an extremely narrow behavioral repertoire. A major deficiency in their range of activity is the lack of social interaction with their peers. They sometimes initiate social responses towards adults to obtain affection, food, water, or a favorite toy, etc. but little or no social behavior is observed among the children themselves.

Ferster and DeMyer (1961, 1962) have reported success in controlling and enriching the behavioral range of individual autistic children in a laboratory setting. Stable behavior was maintained and the entire repertoire was widened by the use of operant conditioning techniques. The application of these methods has also been taught to nurses, ward attendants, and parents so that control and maintenance of behavior could be extended over greater periods of time (Wolf, Mees, and Risley, 1963; DeMyer and Ferster, 1962).

It has been demonstrated that reinforcement techniques, which required no verbal instructions, were effective in shaping cooperative responses in normal children (Azrin and Lindsley, 1956). Ayllon and Haughton (1962) have also used these

[1] Supported by Research Grant MH 05154-02 of the NIMH, PHS.

We thank Drs. John I. Nurnberger, Professor of Psychiatry, Indiana University Medical Center, and Donald F. Moore, Medical Director, LaRue D. Carter Memorial Hospital, for their advice, encouragement, and assistance in obtaining the facilities required to carry out the experiment.

Presented at the Annual Meeting of the American Psychological Association, August, 1963.

methods in controlling social behavior in adult schizophrenics.

These studies suggest that social responses could be developed in early childhood schizophrenics by using operant conditioning techniques. One child could be led to interact with another if reinforcement were contingent upon that interaction. By gradually increasing the complexity of this interaction (method of successive approximation) (Ferster and Skinner, 1957) a form of social behavior could be obtained. The purpose of this study was to develop a method for shaping cooperative responses in early childhood schizophrenics by using reinforcement techniques in a controlled setting.

METHOD

Subjects

Six children, diagnosed as early childhood schizophrenics (autistic, autistic-symbiotic, or chronic undifferentiated), served as subjects for this study. The diagnosis was made according to DeMyer's (1963) categories of *schizophrenic disorders of childhood*. Autistic children are described as follows: characteristically ignore peers; may cooperate with an adult at the adult's request; often engage in some highly idiosyncratic repetitive activity such as twirling, patting, or tapping either themselves or other objects; do not speak for communication though they may play with words, hum, sing, recite lists or other verbal passages from rote, or make animal-like noises. Unusual motor patterns vary from child to child and include toe walking, tics, infantile arm waving, self-destructive activities, and body posturing. Eating habits are generally messy.

In addition to these characteristics, the

TABLE I   Subject Variables in Three Pairs of Early Childhood Schizophrenics

Subjects	PAIR I		PAIR II		PAIR III	
	P. K.	C. S.	N. R.	S. M.	T. M.	M. T.
Sex	M	F	F	M	M	M
Age	7–5	8–3	6–3	4–1	3–7	4–5
Communicative speech	some	none	none	none	none	some
Patient status †	in	day	in	day	day	in
Months of hospitalization	49	48	21	12	1½	1½
Months of previous experience in operant conditioning	36	2	2	6	1	1
diagnosis*	C U	A-S	A	A-S	A-S	C U

† in = inpatient   day = day care
* C U = Chronic undifferentiated   A-S = Autistic-symbiotic
A = Autistic

autistic-symbiotic child may have a few words to express immediate needs. He prefers to cling to adults for long periods of time, and may alternately cling to and reject adults.

The chronic undifferentiated child can use speech for communication though the other kinds of speech distortions are still present. They generally have extremely poor relationships with peers, but may respond to other children by rejecting them.

All subjects were patients in treatment at the Clinical Research Center for Early Childhood Schizophrenia in the Children's Service at LaRue D. Carter Memorial Hospital. Other than having the same general diagnosis, the children composed a very heterogeneous group. Table I describes the important differences between the children. Although they had different histories of operant conditioning, no two children had been in the experimental room together previous to this study. The subjects were paired on the basis of their length of hospitalization.

Apparatus

The experimental room, illuminated by eight 40-watt fluorescent lights, was fifteen feet long, eight feet wide, and nine feet high. A one-way window permitted continuous observation of the subjects during the daily sessions. Mounted on the walls of the room were many devices which could be operated by the use of coins, such as a color wheel, movie projector, electric organ, phonograph, etc.

During the course of this study, however, only a coin vendor, food vendor, and two-key response panel were operative. These were mounted on one wall at a height that made them easily accessible to all the children.

The coin vendor was a box with a toggle switch (coin lever) protruding from a translucent plastic panel which could be illuminated by a red or green light. Directly below this was a tray to catch the coins as they were delivered.

The two-key response panel had two keys (levers) mounted in translucent plastic panels. One panel could be illuminated by a red light, the other panel by a green light.

The food vendor was a modified six-column commercial vendor. Mounted below each column was a coin slot and an indicator light. Each of the columns was operated independently by putting a coin in the proper slot. When a column was empty the indicator light was no longer illuminated. A transparent plastic cover enclosed the columns so that the different foods could be seen by the children.

Automatic control and recording equipment was used throughout this experiment. Responses made by the subjects on both the coin lever and the two-key response panel were recorded on individual counters and cumulative recorders. A running time meter recorded the length of the session. Since the levers on the coin vendor and the two-key response panel could not discriminate between the two subjects of a pair, a remote control panel, mounted below the observation window, permitted the experimenter to change the color of the lights and to deliver or withhold reinforcement.

Procedure

Prior to shaping the cooperative response, all subjects received individual training in the experimental room on an FR 15 schedule of reinforcement. Under this schedule a coin was delivered by a vending machine when the coin lever was depressed fifteen times. This coin was then deposited in the vendor by the subject to obtain candy, crackers, or dry cereal. Each child worked daily for thirty minutes in the experimental room until a baseline of behavior was achieved. Both members of a pair were then placed in the room together for all following sessions, which had an average duration of twenty-five minutes. The children were seen five days a week (Monday through Friday), one session per day. During the other part of the day the children's time was spent in such varied activities as play therapy, psychotherapy, occupational therapy, music therapy, and so forth. The only control that was exercised over the children's other daily activities was the elimination of snacks between meals.

The actual shaping of the cooperative response was done in four steps. During the first step (free situation) no form of cooperative behavior was necessary for reinforcement. For the next three steps, however, reinforcement was contingent upon some type of cooperation. A single cooperative response involved two individual responses, that is, a response by S_1 (of a pair) permitting S_2 to operate the coin lever and a response by S_2 permitting S_1 to operate the coin lever. The complexity of the individual responses was increased with each step until the final form of cooperative behavior was obtained. As criterion (stable rates obtained for three consecutive sessions) was reached for each step (or condition), the next step was introduced. A description of the four steps used in the shaping procedure is given below.

Step 1—free situation—S_1 and S_2 of each pair were in the room together and were free to operate the coin lever (FR 15) at any time during the session. When S_1 operated the coin lever, a red light illuminated the panel behind the lever, whereas a green light illuminated the panel when S_2 operated the lever.

Step 2—alternation—S_1 was able to operate the coin lever only in the presence of the red light, and the coin lever could be operated by S_2 only in the presence of the green light. These lights were alternated so that after S_1 received a coin, the green light was presented, and after S_2 received a coin, the red light was presented. Whether the red or green light was presented at the beginning of the session varied from day to day.

Step 3—$R^D \rightarrow S^D$—A two-key response panel was introduced in another part of the experimental room. One lever (key) was illuminated by a red light and the other key by a green light. These lights alternated in the same way as the coin lever light in Step 2, that is, both lights on this panel were never on at the same time. No light illuminated the coin lever. S_1 was required to press the new lever (R^D) when the red light was on, which resulted in the red light (S^D) illuminating the coin lever permitting S_1 to get a coin (FR 15). S_2 was required to operate the new green-light lever (R^D) to get a green light (S^D) on the coin lever and get a coin.

Step 4—$R^D \rightarrow S^\Delta$—The procedure remained the same as in Step 3 with one variation. When S_1 pressed the key (R^D—red light), the coin lever was illuminated by the green light (S^Δ) permitting S_2 to receive a coin. A response by S_2 on the new green-light lever (R^D) gave S_1 the red light (S^Δ) on the coin lever, permitting S_1 to obtain a coin. This was the final form of the cooperative behavior in which S_1 and S_2 were working for each other by providing the appropriate coin lever lights.

During the entire shaping procedure of the experiment, no verbal instructions or demonstrations were given to the subjects.

RESULTS AND DISCUSSION

The mean rates of coin lever responses per session are given in Table 2. Individual rates are given for the conditions in which no cooperation was required for reinforcement. During the conditions requiring cooperation (alternation, $R^D \rightarrow S^D$, and $R^D \rightarrow S^\Delta$) the rates are given for pairs rather than individual subjects. Coins were obtained on an FR 15 schedule of reinforcement for all conditions.

The rates of the "alone" condition indicate the different levels of motivation for each subject. Although some rates are very low, they represent stable rates which were maintained for many sessions. Free situation rates point out the dominant partner of a pair. There is an obviously dominant subject in pairs I and II, whereas the subjects in pair III appear more equally matched for dominance. In the case of pair I, subject *P. K.* monopolized the coin lever for almost the complete length of the session.

The data for the alternation, $R^D \rightarrow S^D$, and $R^D \rightarrow S^A$ condition indicate that it was possible to shape the final cooperative response within an average of twenty-three sessions. The relationship between alterna-tion and $R^D \rightarrow S^D$ rates was different for each pair, but a decrease in rate going from $R^D \rightarrow S^D$ to $R^D \rightarrow S^A$ was found for all three pairs. After shaping of the cooperative behavior had been completed, a second alternation condition and finally an "alone" condition were given. A general increase in rates should be noted between the $R^D \rightarrow S^A$ and second alternation conditions. This increase suggests that the low $R^D \rightarrow S^A$ rates were the result of the long delay of reinforcement since R^D responses were followed by an S^A rather than an S^D.

Cumulative cooperative responses, rather than coin lever responses, are presented in Figures 1, 2, and 3. A cooperative response

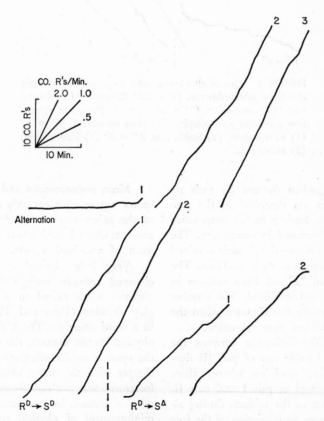

FIGURE 1   Cumulative cooperative responses of two early child-hood schizophrenics. (Pair I-P. K. and C. S.) Alternation (1) First session, (2) Stable rate, (3) Return to alternation condition after shaping has been completed. $R^D \rightarrow S^D$ (1) First session, (2) Stable rate. $R^D \rightarrow S^A$ (1) First session, (2) Stable rate.

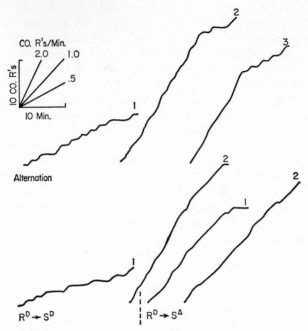

FIGURE 2 Cumulative cooperative responses of two early childhood schizophrenics. (Pair II-N. R. and S. M.) Alternation (1) First session. (2) Stable rate, (3) Return to alternation condition after shaping has been completed. $R^D \rightarrow S^D$ (1) First session, (2) Stable rate. $R^D \rightarrow S^\Delta$ (1) First session, (2) Stable rate.

was completed when S_1 and S_2 each received one coin. As described in the procedure, the steps leading to the cooperative response were increased in complexity. The curves that are numbered "1" were obtained from the first session of each condition. The curves numbered "2" are from sessions in which the rate had stabilized. The number "3" curve is a stable rate obtained when the alternation condition was reinstated.

There is little difference between the first session and stable rate of pair III during the alternation condition, whereas there are large differences in pair I and pair II. From observation of the subjects during alternation and from an inspection of the free situation coin lever rates, it appears that stable rates of cooperative responses during alternation are less rapidly attained in pairs that have a dominant subject.

Mean response rates and cumulative response curves represent only a small portion of the behavior observed during the daily sessions. Other behavior was recorded in the form of anecdotal reports.

Very little physical contact has been observed between early childhood schizophrenics when paired in a controlled toy play situation (Piers and Tilton, 1963) or in a ward situation. The high frequency of physical contact between the subjects during the operant conditioning sessions contrasted sharply with the above observations. Reinforcement was not directly contingent upon physical contact, but an example of indirect reinforcement of physical contact is given below.

Figure 4 presents the cumulative cooperative responses of pair II during an alternation session. In this particular ses-

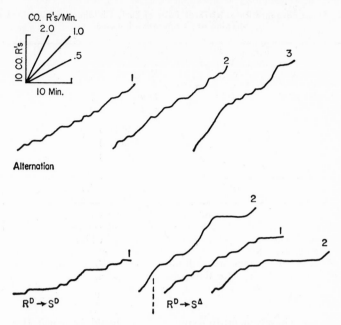

FIGURE 3   Cumulative cooperative responses of two early childhood schizophrenics. (Pair III-T. M. and M. T.) Alternation (1)
First session, (2) Stable rate, (3) Return to alternation condition
after shaping has been completed. $R^D \rightarrow S^D$ (1) First session, (2)
Stable rate. $R^D \rightarrow S^\Delta$ (1) First session, (2) Stable rate.

sion subject S. M. was responding at a very
low rate on the coin lever, often interrupt-
ing the FRs to engage in twirling behavior.
Since N. R. could not receive her coin until
S. M. received his, she began to pull him
over to the coin lever when he stopped to
twirl.

After one rather long pause in his responding, she slapped him (first arrow). An
increase in response rate followed and N. R.
continued to slap S. M. whenever his response rate lagged during successive FRs.
Following one of these slaps (second arrow),
S. M. began to cry and stopped responding
completely. After a long period of no responding, N. R. went over to S. M., hugged
him around the neck, and led him to the
coin lever. An increase in response rate followed and this hugging behavior was maintained for the remainder of the session. In
later sessions N. R. used both slapping and

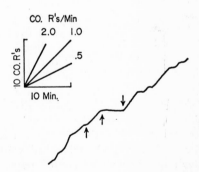

FIGURE 4   Cumulative cooperative
responses of pair II during one Alternation session.

hugging to increase S. M.'s response rate
when it fell too low.

Physical contact was observed in all
three pairs of early childhood schizophrenics
for virtually all sessions in which coopera-

TABLE 2   Mean Response Rates of Three Pairs of Early Childhood Schizophrenics During Shaping of Cooperative Behavior

	PAIR I		PAIR II		PAIR III	
Condition	P. K.	C. S.	N. R.	S. M.	T. M.	M. T.
Alone	37.3	30.4	11.9	7.1	9.2	2.1
Free Situation	42.2	2.1	12.4	4.5	13.0	9.1
Alternation	35.0 (14)		17.2 (12)		4.0 (7)	
$R^D \rightarrow S^D$	26.7 (5)		18.0 (8)		10.6 (6)	
$R^D \rightarrow S^\Delta$	15.4 (5)		12.6 (6)		4.3 (6)	
Alternation	34.8		14.8		17.4	
Alone	28.6	44.1	21.1	4.6	17.8	5.4

Note—Response rate = coin lever responses per minute. Rates were determined by dividing total coin lever responses per session by total session time. Each number in this table represents a stable rate—the mean of three consecutive sessions with rates that fall within a range of 3.5. The rates for the Alternation, $R^D \rightarrow S^D$, and $R^D \rightarrow S^\Delta$ conditions are the same for both subjects of a pair since the children alternated in obtaining coins under all three conditions. The number of sessions required to reach criterion (stable rates obtained for three consecutive sessions) is in the parentheses following the rate.

tion was required for reinforcement. In some sessions the frequency of physical contacts between subjects approached the frequency of the cooperative responses. This contact usually took the form of one subject leading the other to the correct lever. At times a subject operated the appropriate levers by manipulating the other subject's hand. At other times the physical contact consisted of one subject pulling another away from the lever or food vendor. All six subjects were observed to initiate physical contact during the sessions, but the dominant child initiated most of the physical contact within a pair. No subject was completely passive during a session, nor did one child manipulate another for an entire session. Most often each subject waited until the other had worked through his proper sequence of responses, and then began his own sequence.

In addition to physical contact, subjects P. K. and M. T. were observed directing verbal responses to their partners during shaping of the cooperative behavior, for example, "That's the red light," "That's enough," "Get the coin." All subjects made vocal responses and facial expressions (laughing, crying, smiling, etc.) that also appeared to be directed to their partners.

It should be noted that in this study, reinforcement was received so long as the reinforcement contingencies were fulfilled, for example, if S_1 was required to perform a particular response, that response would be completed as long as S_1's hand pressed the lever, in spite of the fact that S_2 may have been holding S_1's hand. The experimenter did not interfere in any of the interactions between the subjects unless there was danger of one child harming another. (This occurred only twice.) In addition, a subject was not prohibited from taking the candy or coins earned by another subject. The above situation usually produced a reduc- resulted in an extinction or suppression of "stealing" behavior.

The frequency of physical contact between subjects indicates that the children were able to modify their behavior rather effectively to obtain reinforcement. It should be remembered that physical contacts were not directly shaped and were the result of adapting to the experimental situation. When one subject's motivation was too low to work well with another child in the cooperative situation, the more highly motivated child increased the cooperative response rate by helping the other child make the proper response. This behavior suggests that the ability of these children to adapt to new situations is increased by the use of reinforcement techniques.

Since it was possible to shape cooperative responses in early childhood schizophrenics, it can be concluded that these children are potentially capable of fairly complex peer interaction in spite of the deficit in verbal behavior. Peer interaction and physical contact are not usually seen in the ward situation because no reinforcement is contingent upon this interaction. These children are not "aware" of their peers, as is tion of the cooperative response rate, which often stated, unless being "aware" will lead to reinforcement.

Although social interaction was effectively maintained during the operant conditioning sessions, there was little evidence of any continuation of this behavior on the ward. It would seem likely that peer interaction ceased because the reinforcement contingencies were not in effect beyond the experimental room. The next step in the development of social behavior in early childhood schizophrenics would be to reinforce social and cooperative behavior in a ward situation. This extended use of reinforcement techniques should lead to more permanent changes in social behavior.

SUMMARY

Six early childhood schizophrenics, who had been observed to initiate little or no social interaction with their peers, were trained to operate a lever to obtain coins on a fixed-ratio schedule of reinforcement (FR 15). These coins were used in vending machines to obtain candy, crackers, and cereal. Each child worked daily for thirty minutes in the experimental room until a baseline of behavior was achieved. The subjects were then paired on the basis of their length of hospitalization, and both members of a pair were placed together in the room for all following sessions.

Using nonverbal operant conditioning techniques, the cooperative response was shaped in succeeding sessions as follows:

1. S_1 and S_2 of each pair were free to operate the coin lever at any time during the session.
2. In order to obtain coins, S_1 and S_2 were required to alternate in using the coin lever.
3. In order to operate the coin lever, a new lever had to be operated first; S_1 and S_2 were required to alternate on this new lever.
4. S_1 was required to operate the new lever to enable S_2 to obtain coins and vice versa.

The results indicated that it was possible to shape cooperative responses in early childhood schizophrenics within an average of twenty-three sessions. The frequency of physical contacts between subjects, although not directly reinforced, was higher during shaping of the cooperative response than in a ward or toy play situation. The subjects were also observed to make vocal responses and facial expressions which appeared to be directed to their partners.

By making reinforcement (previously obtained in a nonsocial situation) contingent upon the emission of cooperative responses, these responses were obtained, and in addition, other forms of social interaction were observed to increase in frequency in the experimental room. While there was little evidence of any continuation of social interaction when the subjects were returned to the ward, it was suggested that an extension and a modification of the reinforcement contingencies in a ward situation might produce more permanent changes in behavior.

REFERENCES

AYLLON, T. and E. HAUGHTON. Control of the behavior of schizophrenic patients by food. *J. exper. Anal. Behav.*, 1962, **5**, 343–352.

AZRIN, N. H. and O. R. LINDSLEY. The reinforcement of cooperation between children. *J. abnorm. soc. Psychol.*, 1956, **52**, 100–102.

DEMYER, M. K. Personal communication. 1963.

DEMYER, M. K. and C. B. FERSTER. Teaching new social behavior to schizophrenic children. *J. Child Psychiat.,* 1962, **1,** 443–461.

FERSTER, C. B. and M. K. DEMYER. The development of performances in autistic children in an automatically controlled environment. *J. chron. Dis.,* 1961, **13,** 312–345.

FERSTER, C. B. and M. K. DEMYER. A method for the experimental analysis of the behavior of autistic children. *Amer. J. Orthopsychiat.,* 1962, **32,** 89–98.

FERSTER, C. B. and B. F. SKINNER. *Schedules of Reinforcement.* New York: Appleton, 1957.

PIERS, E. and J. TILTON. Personal communication. 1963.

WOLF, M., H. MEES and T. RISLEY. Application of operant conditioning procedures to the behavior problems of an autistic child. Western Psychological Association, 1963.

12   APPLICATION OF OPERANT CONDITIONING PROCEDURES TO THE BEHAVIOUR PROBLEMS OF AN AUTISTIC CHILD

Montrose Wolf • Todd Risley • Hayden Mees

Summary   An account is given of the treatment of a pre-school child who had serious behavioural and physical handicaps. In a sense this is a study involving both psychotherapy and rehabilitation. The treatment consisted of applying laboratory-developed techniques through the attendants and the parents over a seven-month period.

INTRODUCTION

During the past few decades an experimental analysis of behaviour has produced several powerful and reliable techniques for controlling behaviour (Holland and Skinner, 1961). Although these procedures were originally established with lower organisms, they are increasingly being applied in areas concerned with human behaviour (Ayllon and Michael, 1959; Baer, 1962; Bijou, 1963; Ferster, 1961; Isaacs, Thomas, and Goldia-

Behaviour Research and Therapy, 1964, **1,** 305–312.

mond, 1960; Lindsley, 1962; Williams, 1959; Zimmerman and Zimmerman, 1962). Even so, techniques developed for dealing with specific human anomalies are limited.

This case study is an example of the application of behaviour principles to psychopathology. We developed techniques for dealing with the behaviour problems of a hospitalized pre-school autistic boy. Each of the techniques was derived from procedures developed and studied in experimental laboratories, such as handshaping, extinction, food deprivation, time-out from positive reinforcement, and discrimination training.

Dicky, the subject, was 3½ years old when the study began. He is the son of middle socio-economic class parents and has one younger and two older apparently normal female siblings.

From hospital records it appears that Dicky progressed normally till his ninth month, when cataracts were discovered in the lenses of both eyes. At this time severe temper tantrums and sleeping problems began to develop. During his second year he had a series of eye operations which culminated with the removal of his occluded lenses. This made wearing of glasses necessary. For more than a year his parents tried, and failed, to make Dicky wear glasses. During this time Dicky was seen by a variety of specialists who diagnosed him, variously, as mentally retarded, diffuse and locally brain-damaged, and psychotic, with the possibility of such additional anomalies as phenylpyruvic oligophrenia and hyperthyroidism. One recommendation was that he be placed in an institution for the retarded since his prognosis was so poor.

Dicky did not eat normally and lacked normal social and verbal repertoires. His tantrums included self-destructive behaviours such as head-banging, face-slapping, hair-pulling and face-scratching. His mother reported that after a severe tantrum "he was a mess, all black and blue and bleeding". He would not sleep at night, forcing one or both parents to remain by his bed. Sedatives, tranquilizers, and restraints were tried, without success.

He was admitted to a children's mental hospital with the diagnosis of childhood schizophrenia at the age of three. After three months of hospitalization the terminal report stated that there was some improvement in his schizophrenic condition but no progress in the wearing of glasses. A few months later his ophthalmologist predicted that unless Dicky began wearing glasses within the next six months he would permanently lose his macular vision. At this point the authors were invited in as consultants by the hospital staff for the purpose of training Dicky to wear glasses.

After observing a 20 min interaction between Dicky and his mother, a period occupied by almost continuous tantrums, we recommended that he be readmitted to the hospital in order to separate him from his mother temporarily and to deal with his disruptive behaviours, while training him to wear glasses.

Our prescribed operations were carried out by the attendants and the parents both on the ward and in the home. In addition to general comments we carefully specified behaviours and environmental events to be recorded on Dicky's chart and in notes from the parents. As the specific events to be recorded were highly distinctive and co-operation by the attendants and parents was good, the data presented probably reflect actual events to a large but undetermined degree.

By manipulating the consequences of the behaviours, we concurrently developed techniques for dealing with Dicky's tantrums, sleeping and eating problems, for establishing the wearing of glasses, and appropriate verbal and social behaviour.

PROCEDURES, RESULTS AND DISCUSSION

Temper tantrums

There is some evidence that temper tantrums will succumb to extinction (Williams, 1959). However, under ward conditions, with personnel untrained in these procedures, it was far from certain that extinction would be reliably carried out. So the prescribed procedure was a combination of mild punishment and extinction. Dicky was placed in his room contingent upon each tantrum, the door remaining closed until the tantrum behaviour ceased. Each occurrence was to be noted on his chart.

Such a procedure, although initially involving social contacts and thus possible reinforcement at the onset of a tantrum, eliminated the possibility of continuous contact throughout the undesired behaviour. This procedure also provided for differential reinforcement of non-tantrum behaviour by the door being opened contingent upon such behaviour. Such a contingency, involving the removal of all social reinforcers for a period of time, resembles Ferster and Appel's (1961) use of a time-out from positive reinforcement as an aversive stimulus.

A cumulative record showing the frequency with which Dicky was placed in his room for tantrums and self-destructive behaviour is presented in the upper graph of Fig. 1. The curve is, however, partially artifactual. The record shows a constant rate of being placed in his room for tantrums during the first four months, indicating a lack of change in behaviour during this period which was contradictory to casual observation.

Several variables, each involving a sacrifice of experimental rigor, contributed to this discrepancy:

1. When Dicky was first admitted he whined, cried, slapped himself frequently. The attendant was therefore instructed to place him in his room only when he was engaging in two or more of these behaviours simultaneously. As Dicky's behaviour improved, the attendants lowered the original criterion finally to include any atavism. Since the authors believed this was to the distinct advantage of the child, the criterion change was encouraged.
2. During the first few weeks the attendants' records contained reports of elaborate explanations offered Dicky as he was escorted to his room, and of tender, practically tearful apologies and fondling after the door was reopened. This pattern evolved to a perfunctory trip to the room with the door simply being reopened at the end of the tantrum, presenting a ward going on much as before.
3. By the beginning of the third month, tantrums lasting less than five minutes began to occur frequently, creating the likelihood that the trip to the room would become a socially reinforcing event. A minimum time of ten minutes in the room was therefore imposed.
4. Dicky's contact with his family and home progressively increased during this time. The major changes are indicated in the tantrum curve.
At (a) Dicky's parents were permitted their first one-hour visit. Subsequently they made several scheduled visits a week, during which an attendant observed and instructed them in their handling of Dicky.
At (b) the father put Dicky to bed on the ward for the first time.
At (c) Dicky began wearing his glasses.
At (d) the mother put Dicky to bed on the ward for the first time.
Midway between (d) and (e) Dicky began

short home visits accompanied by the attendant.

At (e) Dicky spent his first night at home.

At (f) Dicky spent a second night at home.

After (f) he spent an average of three nights a week at home, increasing to five nights a week during the final month.

Some estimate of the decreasing severity of the tantrums is indicated in the middle cumulative record of Fig. 1. Each step represents a tantrum, either during the day or at bedtime, involving head-banging, hair-pulling, or face-scratching. Such severe self-destructive behaviour remained near zero after the first two and a half months. The remainder of the tantrum record consists of face-slapping, whining, and crying.

Conditions for handling tantrums at the home were made comparable to those on the ward. The attendants coached the parents to deal with Dicky's tantrums by putting him in his room both on the ward and at home. The descriptions of the parents' behaviour by the attendants and by the parents themselves indicated that this training was effective.

Bedtime problems

The bedtime problem was handled in a manner similar to the tantrums. Dicky was bathed at a regular hour each night, cuddled for a short time, put to bed, and left with the door open. If he got up, he was told to go back to bed or the door would be closed. If he remained up, the door was closed. The door was reopened after a short time, or if a tantrum occurred, after it subsided. He was told again to get in his bed. If he stayed in bed the door was left open. Each door-closing at bedtime was recorded.

The lower graph in Fig. 1 shows cumulative bedtime door-closings. The door was closed several times during the first five nights. The resulting tantrums were quite violent, one series totalling more than an hour. On the sixth night the attendant tucked Dicky in and said goodnight. Dicky

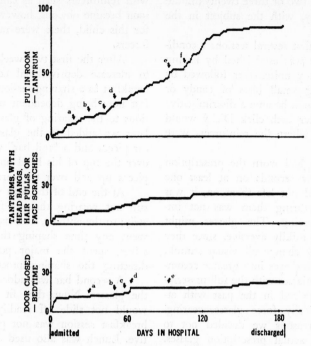

FIGURE I   Three cumulative records showing the effects of extinction and mild punishment (time-out from positive rein-forcement) upon the tantrums, severe self-destructive episodes, and bedtime problems of a hospitalized pre-school autistic boy.

remained in bed and soon went to sleep. Bedtime was seldom a problem again.

At (a) the father first put Dicky to bed on the ward.

At (b) the mother first put him to bed.

From (b) to (e) the parents put Dicky to bed once or twice a week.

At (c) and (d) the parents had to shut the door.

At (e) Dicky spent his first night at home. For a few weeks prior to this, he had been making short home visits accompanied by an attendant. Several days prior to (e) he was taken home in the evening, and after a few minutes of play, went through the routine of getting ready for bed with his siblings. The attendant then brought him back to the ward and put him to bed. Since this trial run was successful, he was sent home to spend the night several days later at (e). He was bathed and put in bed. After about thirty minutes he

was heard humming to himself. The mother started to go in to Dicky but the attendant dissuaded her. Fifteen minutes later, Dicky was asleep.

Over the next three months, until his release from the hospital, Dicky spent a progressively greater proportion of his nights at home. One night a week an attendant went along to observe both Dicky and his parents.

The four times the door had to be shut after point (e) all occurred at home. These may have been the result of a certain amount of reshaping by the parents during a period when Dicky had chronic diarrhoea.

Wearing glasses

Shaping (Skinner, 1953) was the basic procedure used to get Dicky to wear his glasses. Our shaper, an attendant, was instructed to spend two or three twenty-minute sessions each day, with the subject in the subject's room.

During the first several sessions a conditioned reinforcer was established by having the clicks of a toy noisemaker followed by Dicky's receiving small bites of candy or fruit. The click soon became a discriminative stimulus and after each click Dicky would go to the bowl where the reinforcers were placed.

Since Dicky had worn the prescription glasses for a few seconds on at least one occasion and had not left them on, it was assumed that wearing them was not immediately reinforcing. The glasses might even have been mildly aversive, since they would drastically change all visual stimuli, as well as force the eyes into greater accommodation. Also, glasses with the full prescription had been paired in the past with attempts to physically force glasses-wearing.

For these reasons we decided not to begin with the actual prescription glasses. Instead, several empty glasses frames were placed around the room and Dicky was reinforced for picking them up, holding them, and carrying them about. Slowly, by successive approximations, he was reinforced for bringing the frames closer to his eyes.

The original plan was, after he was wearing the lenseless frames, to introduce plain glass and then prescription lenses in three steps of progressing severity. This was not the actual sequence of events, however, since our shaper met with considerable difficulty in getting Dicky to wear the glassless frames in the proper manner, i.e. with the ear pieces over instead of under the ears and the eye openings in line with the eyes. Furthermore, it was impossible to help place the frames correctly since Dicky became upset when anyone touched any part of his head.

The slow progress was probably attributable to two factors. First, the attendant, although co-operative, was inexperienced and imprecise with the shaping procedure. Secondly, due to the reluctance of the ward staff to deprive the child of food we began with reinforcers such as candy and fruit. It soon became obvious, however, that, at least for this child, these were rather weak reinforcers.

After the first two weeks we attempted to increase deprivational control by using breakfast as a shaping session, bites of breakfast now being dependent upon approximations to the wearing of glasses. Two weeks later we added to the glasses larger adult ear pieces and a "roll bar" which would go over the top of his head and guide the ear pieces up and over the ears.

At the end of the fifth week Dicky was still not wearing the ear frames appropriately; so the authors, who had not previously spent any time shaping the subject themselves, spent the major portion of a day directing the shaping procedure.

A second bar was added to the back of the glasses. Now, they fit like a cap and would not slide off readily. As usual the breakfast session was not particularly effective. Lunch was also used as a session, but still there was no progress.

Later, at approximately two o'clock that afternoon, we had a third session. Dicky had received very little to eat all day, just a few pieces of dry cereal, and was most interested in the ice cream we brought to the session. We also decided to try the full prescription lenses. At the beginning of the session it was quite obvious that our reinforcers were much more powerful than earlier in the day. He carried the glasses at all times, often putting them up to his face, although not in the desired manner. However, since there was a great deal of the approximate kind of behaviour it was easy to differentially reinforce the two aspects of wearing we wanted, placing the ear pieces straight over the ears, and looking through the lenses. At the end of approximately thirty minutes Dicky was holding the ear pieces properly over his ears, and the nose piece at the tip of his nose. He was looking through the lenses at such objects as a ring, a clicker etc., that were displayed in the hopes of maintaining his looking behaviour.

After this, progress was rapid and he was soon wearing his glasses continuously during the meal sessions in his room.

After wearing the glasses was established in these sessions, it could be maintained with other, less manipulable reinforcers. For example, the attendant would tell Dicky, "Put your glasses on and let's go for a walk". Dicky was usually required to wear the glasses during meals, snacks, automobile rides, walks, outdoor play etc. If he removed the glasses, the activity was terminated.

The progress of glasses-wearing is presented cumulatively in the upper graph of Fig. 2. At the time of Dicky's release from the hospital he had worn the glasses for more than 600 hr and was wearing them about 12 hr a day.

Throwing of glasses

The lower cumulative record in Fig. 2 depicts the course of a problem that grew out of wearing glasses, namely, throwing the glasses. Wearing the glasses began at (a). Two weeks later Dicky threw his glasses for the first time. A week later he began throwing them approximately twice a day. Although this in itself was not a serious be-

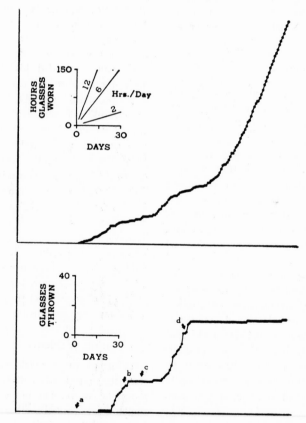

FIGURE 2   Two cumulative records showing the effects of positive reinforcement (bites of meals etc.) upon glasses-wearing and the effects of extinction and mild punishment (time-out from positive reinforcement) upon the glasses-throwng of a hospitalized pre-school autistic boy.

haviour problem, it was moderately expensive due to breakage, and there was the danger that, once home, it would be reinforced by the mother's ineffectual fussing and thereby increase the frequency of throwing to a degree incompatible with wearing the glasses. We therefore attempted to develop a technique to control it. Beginning at (b) Dicky was put in his room for ten minutes following each glasses-throw, or if a tantrum developed, until it ceased. Throwing the glasses decreased to zero in five days. At (c) the conditions were reversed: he was no longer to be put in his room for throws. After about three weeks the rate of throwing the glasses resumed its earlier high level. At (d) he was again put in his room for throwing his glasses, and six days later the rate reached and remained near zero.

Verbal behaviour

After the wearing of glasses was established we developed a technique for generating a verbal repertoire. The technique also aimed at maintaining the wearing of glasses and reinforcing visual attending. Like the glasses training, the verbal training consisted of sessions in which an attendant administered food reinforcers. Initially, we tried candy and fruit but these were unsuccessful. Only when we began using breakfast and lunch as training sessions did we have rapid and dramatic effects.

Dicky had no socially appropriate verbal behaviour and, according to his parents, neither his verbal nor non-verbal behaviour was under their verbal control. However, Dicky was far from mute. He had some long and complex verbal chains such as songs (*Chicago,* for example) and occasionally he would mimic quite clearly, but the mimicking could not be evoked under normal conditions.

Our training began with the attendant presenting, one at a time, five pictures (a Santa Claus, a cat etc.). The attendant would say, "This is a cat", "Now, say cat", and so on, until Dicky mimicked her, whereupon she would say, "Good", or "That's right" and give him a bite of his meal. After several more days of differential reinforcement the attendant gradually omitted saying the word first and Dicky would usually say the word in the presence of each picture without a prompt. In three weeks he did this in the presence of about ten pictures. We then progressed to picture books, common household objects, and finally to remote events, for example, "Where are you going tonight?", "What did you do outside?"

The more powerful food reinforcers were evidently necessary for initial strengthening, but weaker conditioned reinforcers, such as adult attention and approval, were effective for maintaining and expanding the original repertoire. The parents, although reluctant at first, were trained by the attendant to use the same technique at home. They have expanded his repertoire to include, for instance, the correct usage of personal pronouns, and Dicky now initiates requests and comments without adult prompting. However, his present verbal behaviour is by no means comparable to that of a normal five-year-old child.

Dicky's ability to mimic entire phrases and sentences was apparently crucial to the rapid progress in verbal training. The authors' current work with other children indicates that without this mimicking behaviour a long and arduous handshaping procedure would have been necessary to establish responses of the required topography (words, phrases, and sentences) prior to the discrimination training described above.

Eating problems

During those meals which Dicky ate with the rest of the children in the dining room, he would not use silverware, would snatch food from the other children's plates and would throw food around the room. We attempted to deal with these behaviours by having the attendant remove Dicky's plate for a few minutes whenever he ate with his fingers and, after a warning, remove Dicky from the dining room (and the remainder of his meal) whenever he would throw food or take food from other's plates. Dicky spent an average of 55 per cent of the mealtime inappropriately eating with his fingers. During one meal his plate was removed several times, and he was told to use his spoon. After this, and in all subsequent meals he used a spoon for all appropriate foods. It was only necessary to warn Dicky and send him from the dining room a few times to completely eliminate food-stealing and food-throwing.

Probably as the result of being consistently paired with the aversive consequence of being put in his room, such verbal stimuli as "No", "Stop that", or "If you do that again you'll have to go to your room", came to suppress much undesirable non-verbal behaviour. This type of control also seems important for normal child development.

According to a report from the mother six months after the child's return home, Dicky continues to wear his glasses, does not have tantrums, has no sleeping problems, is becoming increasingly verbal, and is a new source of joy to the members of his family.

Acknowledgments—This study was supported in part by a research grant (M-2232) from National Institutes of Health, United States Public Health Service. The authors are indebted to Sidney W. Bijou for his invaluable counsel throughout the course of this study. We were most fortunate in having the co-operation and encouragement of Jerman Rose, M.D., Clinical Director and Daniel Kelleher, Ph.D., Senior Clinical Psychologist of the Child Study and Treatment Center, Ft. Steilacoom, Washington.

Special appreciation is due to Dicky's attendants: Jim McCoy, Robbie Littles, Grant Schneider and particularly Betty Kazda, whose skill and co-operation were necessary conditions for the success of this study.

REFERENCES

AYLLON, T. and MICHAEL, J. (1959) The psychiatric nurse as a behavioral engineer. *J. exp. Anal. Behav.* **2**, 323–334.

BAER, D. M. (1962) Laboratory control of thumbsucking by withdrawal and re-presentation of reinforcement. *J. exp. Anal. Behav.* **5**, 525–528.

BIJOU, S. W. (1963) Theory and research in mental (developmental) retardation. *Psychol. Rec.* **13**, 95–110.

FERSTER, C. B. (1961) Positive reinforcement and behavioral defects of autistic children. *Child Develpm.* **32**, 437–456.

FERSTER, C. B. and APPEL, J. B. (1961) Punishment of S^Δ responding in match to sample by time out from positive reinforcement. *J. exp. Anal. Behav.* **4**, 45–56.

HOLLAND, J. G. and SKINNER, B. F. (1961) *The Analysis of Behavior*. McGraw-Hill, New York.

ISAACS, W., THOMAS, J. and GOLDIAMOND, I. (1960) Application of operant conditioning to reinstate verbal behavior in psychotics. *J. Speech Dis.* **25**, 8–12.

LINDSLEY, O. R. (1962) Operant conditioning methods in diagnosis, in *The First Hahnemann Symposium on Psychosomatic Medicine*. Lea and Febiger, New York.

SKINNER, B. F. (1953) *Science and Human Behavior*. Macmillan, New York.

WILLIAMS, C. D. (1959) The elimination of tantrum behavior by extinction procedures. *J. abnorm. (soc.) Psychol.* **59**, 269.

ZIMMERMAN, E. H. and ZIMMERMAN, J. (1962) The alteration of behavior in a special classroom situation. *J. exp. Anal. Behav.* **5**, 59–60.

13 THE TRAINING OF UNDERGRADUATES AS SOCIAL REINFORCERS FOR AUTISTIC CHILDREN

Gerald C. Davison

This is a report of a program for training nonprofessional personnel in a social learning therapy with autistic children. The importance of extending the work of investigators like Ferster and DeMyer (1961) to situations in which human beings are the agents of reinforcement is clear: children live among people, not machines; the range of behaviors that can be shaped by machines is limited; and most importantly, human therapists should be able to function as models for teaching complex patterns of social behavior more quickly than is possible with purely operant methods. The present paper reports a program that explored the possibility of programming undergraduates to function in this way.

The project was conducted at a private day-care center for autistic children.[1] The center was a very small, dilapidated house with five rooms and about an acre of land. Approximately fifteen children, ages three to fourteen, would be brought there weekdays by their parents, from 9:30 A.M. until 2:00 P.M., where volunteer workers, primarily housewives with college degrees, supervised their play-activities. The professional staff of the center, composed of a psychiatrist and a psychiatric social worker, described their own program as "milieu therapy," essentially nondirective play in a warm, nurturant atmosphere.

The feasibility of a social learning program in this setting was suggested by previous work of the author with a nine-year-old autistic boy. By using M&M candies as reinforcement for prosocial behaviors and withdrawal of reinforcement for antisocial behaviors, it was possible, within six two-hour sessions, to reduce noticeably the amount of tantrum and aggressive behavior and, in general, to increase the amount of behavior under control of the therapist.

THE TRAINING

Within the framework of an independent studies course at a university, four undergraduates were chosen from among several who were recommended by members of the psychology faculty.[2] The criteria for selection were dependability and ingenuity, judged on the basis of a short interview.

In a series of four weekly meetings, the author introduced them to the general area of behavior therapy, stressing the operant paradigm. Ferster's (1961) functional analysis of the syndrome of early infantile autism was examined at length to instill the "set" which would be necessary to carry out the proposed form of therapy; emphasis was laid on the instrumental nature of various deviant behaviors, and the implications for treatment were discussed. The case study of the nine-year-old boy was gone into in great detail. The author reconstructed many situations in which varied methods of behavioral modification were utilized. For example, rules were

[1] This program was conducted at the Peninsula Children's Center, Menlo Park, California. The author is grateful to Dr. Elmer F. North, Mr. Vern Drehmel, Mrs. Ian Mill, and Miss Aimee Siversten for their co-operation.

[2] Sincere thanks are rendered to Drs. Leonard Krasner and Albert Bandura and to Mr. David Rimm for their advice and encouragement. The student-therapists were Nancy Burns, Peter Henry, Gordon Hale, and Dana Smith.

set forth with respect to the alternatives available when the boy engaged in deviant behavior:

1. He was ignored unless;
2. he was likely to hurt himself or others, in which case,
3. he was distracted with the promise of candy for performing a simple motor response which was incompatible with the ongoing undesirable behavior.
4. If, after Step 1 the behavior ceased, he was reinforced immediately with a candy or another desired object.

It was explained how play-situations could be utilized for differentially reinforcing behaviors which complied with the commands of the therapist, namely, "Put these two tracks together, and I'll give you a candy." Modeling procedures could also be instituted, with the promise of a candy if the child imitated the therapist. The importance of accompanying candy-reinforcement with a smile and a suitable phrase was stressed, the aim being to reduce the frequency of primary reinforcement over time.

Readings from Bandura and Walters (1963) were discussed as well. At the end of the month of classroom-training, the writer felt that the students had acquired a sufficient understanding of the rationale for the treatment program and that further training could best be carried out with the children themselves.

Two therapist-teams were set up, a male and a female on each. Members of one team worked mornings with one child, the other team, afternoons with another child. In order to keep his partner and the writer informed of the progress of the treatment, each therapist wrote up a brief behavioral report of the day's session, namely, "Today we played with blocks for half an hour; there was only one outburst of screaming." These reports enabled the writer to monitor the treatment and provided case study material for evaluation.

Two 10-year-old boys were chosen in collaboration with the directors of the center. The criteria were fourfold:

1. that they not be in individual therapy;
2. that they have no known physiological damage;
3. that they not be on medication;
4. that they accept an M&M when offered.

In order not to interfere unduly with the center's program, it was agreed to work with each child for only eight of the forty hours he spent there each week.

An attempt at an "objective" evaluation was made. A list of simple commands was drawn up for the therapist to execute with the child prior to treatment; the percentage of items obeyed by the child was to be an index of the degree of therapist-control over the child's behavior. In practice this plan had to be abandoned because many destructive behaviors occurred with such frequency and intensity that the therapist *had* to intervene. Moreover, the list of commands turned out to be meaningless since the appropriateness of many of them depended on the outcome of the preceding ones, namely, "Hand me that top" was meaningless if the child would not stand up from the floor. Commands were, therefore, constructed on the scene, and it was possible in the postmeasurement to reconstruct to some degree the conditions which had prevailed during the premeasurement. Better procedures were not practicable in the setting.

Although inexperienced, all the workers adapted within one session to the bizarre behaviors of the children. While showing them around, the author used actual situations to demonstrate the mechanics of the treatment and, in general, to answer any remaining questions. By the end of the first session it was felt that each therapist would be able to carry on the program.

As mentioned above, reports were written to describe in behavioral terms the happenings of each session. Changes in the programed behavior of the therapists were made as necessary by the writer, and observations made towards the end of the four week program showed that the students were, in fact, behaving in a satisfactory way.

ASSESSMENT

The daily reports of the therapists, corroborated by observations of the center-staff, indicated that at least one team had acquired significantly more control over their child. The write-ups showed initially an increase in tantrums—to be expected if one is instituting a radically different set of reinforcement-contingencies. After two weeks, however, the child became more docile and had even learned to say "Push" in order to be pushed on a swing by the therapists. Reinforcement with candy became intermittent after several sessions, the child tending more and more to respond to generalized reinforcers, for example, "That's a good boy." The progress of the other team was less encouraging, but this was probably due, at least in part, to the fact that illnesses, both of the therapists and of the child, prevented the members from working regularly.

The results of the "objective" assessment procedure for the first team indicated a striking increase in commands obeyed for each therapist from pre to postmeasurement. With Therapist *A* the increase was from thirty-nine percent of commands obeyed to eighty-nine percent, and with Therapist *B* the increase was from fifty-five percent to ninety percent. It must be pointed out that the pre and postmeasurements were not analogous enough to warrant any conclu-

sions other than that the therapists *probably* were able to control the child better after the treatment.

CONCLUSION

The conditions at the center were not ideally suited for a social learning therapy. Less than fifteen percent of the child's waking hours were spent in the program. Inasmuch as learning theory looks to environmental contingencies for factors that shape and maintain behavior, the results were interpreted as good evidence for the fruitfulness of this general approach. More important, however, is the finding that intelligent, highly-motivated students can be trained in a very short time to execute a behavior-control program that requires the application of learning principles to the manipulation of psychotic behavior in children.

REFERENCES

BANDURA, A. and R. H. WALTERS. *Social learning and personality development.* New York: Holt, Rinehart and Winston, 1963.

FERSTER, C. B. Positive reinforcement and behavioral deficits in autistic children. *Child Develpm.,* 1961, **32**, 437–456.

FERSTER, C. B. and MARIAN K. DEMYER. The development of performances in autistic children in an automatically controlled environment. *J. chron. Dis.,* 1961, **13**, 312–345.

SECTION 2

CLASSIC NEUROTIC BEHAVIORS

In this section we will present ten cases that fall into the area that represents most common practice for therapists dealing with adults. Bachrach *et al.* (14), and Lang (22) deal with anorexia nervosa, a condition in which the subject has difficulty in swallowing and retaining food. As can be seen from the first case in this section, the maladaptive behavior is severe and can lead to death. The article illustrates the development of a reinforcing stimulus, the shaping of behavior, the development of a program (including instruction to parents to avoid reinforcing invalid behavior) to maintain adaptive behavior, and a continuing successful social adjustment without symptom substitution. In the case reported by Lang (22) the extent of maladaptive behavior was less, and the subject was treated on an outpatient basis by methods of systematic desensitization and the encouragement of assertive responses. As in the previous case, although underlying causes were not investigated, the general level of adaptation improved. Two other cases in this volume present treatment of maladaptive behaviors usually labeled as psychophysiological reactions, those by Peterson and London (33) and by Wolf, *et al.* (48) with children. Wolpe (1958, pp. 148–152) presents the treatment of a duodenal ulcer by systematic desensitization, and Haugen, Dixon, and Dickel (1958) present a case of hypertension by nonsystematic desensitization (relaxation practiced in increasingly complex extra-therapeutic situations without systematic pairing with specific stimuli). Jones (1960b) presents an instance of a urogenitary psychophysiological reaction treated by raising the threshold through monitored feedback. Walton (1960c) and Cooper (1964) present cases of bronchial asthma treated by behavior therapy, and Walton (1960d) presents a case of neurodermatitis. This case is particularly instructive because the symptom gained the patient attention that allowed her to compete with a sibling. Where medical treatment had failed during two prior years, programing the parents and fiance to pay no attention to the skin condition led to its becoming negligible in two months and its disappearance by the end of the third month. At follow-up, the patient had been happily married for three years, was employed, and no mention was made of symptom substitution. The point is that a variety of psychophysiological or psychosomatic reactions have been responsive to treatment within a psychological model.

In the second case, Adams (15) introduces the use of sensory deprivation to enhance and direct the patient to some immediate gain and greater future cooperation in his treatment. Among the points raised by Adams' presentation is the use of behavior influence techniques to facilitate more traditional forms of psychotherapy through manipulation of variables, such as strengthening the therapist as a reinforcing stimulus and changing the patient's attitudes, expectancies, and role behaviors.

149

The article by Brady and Lind (16) presents an excellent review of Skinnerian concepts and illustrates their use in the treatment of hysterical blindness. In a later section, we shall deal at length with tics and writer's cramp, two maladaptive behaviors frequently labeled conversion reaction or hysteria. Walton (1961a) presents a case of somnambulism (one of the classic Janet hysterias) in which every night for the previous six months the man had attempted to strangle his wife during his "nightmares." Investigation of the situation led to a formulation in which increasingly assertive responses toward the mother was suggested. The "treatment" consisted of a single interview followed by rapid reduction of the symptom and generally improved social adjustment on a two-year follow-up. In a case illustrative of the suggestive techniques used with shell shock cases in World War I, Brousseau (1923) eliminated maladaptive posture in a twenty-six-year-old mentally defective woman who had been lame for four years. A detailed illustration of the use of the demand characteristics (Orne, 1962) of the treatment situation is presented by Schreiber (1961) and a wide range of psychogenic disorders are treated by direct and indirect suggestion in Platonov's (1959) book. Bangs and Freidinger (1949, 1950) report the treatment of two cases of hysterical aphonia. In the first a thirteen-year-old girl who had been aphonic for seven years was extravagantly praised to motivate her to complete a series of tasks which went through breathing exercises, humming, consonants, reading and conversation. "The entire therapy covered a period of ten and one-half weeks. Follow-up interviews revealed no new conversion symptoms, and two years following discharge the patient was still maintaining vocalization." (Bangs and Freidinger, 1949, p. 317). The second case reported by Bangs and Freidinger (1950) was a thirty-two-year-old single woman who had been aphonic for five years. The case is of particular interest for the use of progressive relaxation for general (not systematic) tension reduction, the stricture of no talking for two weeks, and, after general speech exercises, the visiting by patient and therapist of commercial establishments in which the patient was required to speak with the clerks. Walton and Black (1959) also present the successful treatment of a case of hysterical aphonia. Aside from specifics of treatment, this case illustrates effective direct treatment in a case that had been unresponsive to intensive psychotherapy, hypnosis, insulin, ether and methedrine abreaction, narcoanalysis, and LSD treatments. That is, the chances of explaining the results as due to direct placebo reaction seem reduced. Second, the pattern of maladaptive behavior was a chronic one, the subject having been aphonic for seven years and completely mute during the last two. Finally, on follow-up, no evidence of symptom substitution was reported. The principal aspect of treatment involved asking the subject to read aloud material she found dull. If she did not read loudly enough additional time was added to her assignment. Avoiding the aversive situation reinforced increasing volume. In subsequent phases of treatment the number of people present and their participation were increased. Generalization to the ward situation was noted and described as follows: "She talked to patients and staff alike without fatigue and without any limits to the amounts she spoke." Follow-up of twenty months indicated that she was able to earn her own living and withstand two stressful situations. Additional material concerning maladaptive behavior called hysterical and treated within a psychological model may be found in Malmo, Davis, and Barza (1952), Hilgard and Marquis (1940, pp. 296–299), and Sears and Cohen (1933).

Four cases in this section, those by Wolpe (17), Kushner (18), Lang and Lazovik

(20), and Lazarus (21) deal with phobias and make use of Wolpe's technique of systematic desensitization. That other workers, scattered throughout the world, successfully use Wolpe's method is not sufficient evidence for validity, but certainly argues strongly for a necessary scientific requirement, reproducibility. Other workers who have reported successful use of the technique are Ashem (1963), Clark (1963a), Cooper (1963), Lazarus and Rachman (1957), Rachman (1959), and Paul (1964a, 1964b). Other illustrations of this procedure are Cowden and Ford's (9) use of the procedure with schizophrenics, Beech's (1960) use of the procedure in writer's cramp, Lazarus' (1963b) use of the method with frigidity, papers by Bond and Hutchison (26) and by Lazarus (25) on sexual difficulties, and Lazarus' (1959) use of the procedure with a nine-and-one-half-year-old girl. We have mentioned the use of nonspecific relaxation by Haugen, Dixon, and Dickel (1958) and Bangs and Freidinger (1950). We should also mention Pascal (1947) who used relaxation as a method to obtain crucial material rapidly. Of ten cases who were not transferred prior to completion of treatment, all ten benefited in an average of less than seven sessions. We are inclined to hypothesize that the aspect of therapy that led to this result was the coupling of the state of relaxation with the traumatic material presented by the patient rather than the recall of the traumatic material per se. Clark (1963b) also used relaxation in this manner.

In the present volume, Wolpe (17) attacks the problem of what is the specific active ingredient of therapy by eliminating variables that might confound the situation. Kushner's (18) case is important because it offers a replication of the treatment of the particular phobia. The articles by Lang and Lazovik (20) and by Lazarus (21) are experiments that rule out lapses of time, nonspecific relaxation effects, and the expectation of help through therapy. We have previously discussed Paul's (1964b) experiment in which no treatment, attention, insight, and systematic desensitization groups were compared. The four articles here presented, combined with Paul's experiment and the other reports in the literature, not only illustrate the procedure but form a core of evidence that there is indeed a specific useful effect.

As with the other areas reviewed in this volume, there are a variety of additional techniques within the psychological model that have been found to be useful. In our introduction we mentioned the progressive confrontation of the individual with situations likely to lead to maladaptive responses. Using either tranquilizers to inhibit fear responses or his own presence, the therapist can introduce the subject to objects of the class that are likely to lead to maladaptive responses. Examples of this procedure may be found in: Clark (1963b) who also used GSR apparatus to monitor signals of distress; Freeman and Kendrick (1960) who, to overcome a cat phobia, had the subject first feel different textured material from velvet to fur, then toy kittens, and finally raise a cat in her home from kittenhood; Meyer (1957); Walton (1960a); Walton and Mather (1963a, 1963b); and Meyer and Gelder (1963).

Aside from the material on assertion that we have discussed elsewhere in this volume, we might cite Herzberg (1941) who in the context of traditional psychoanalysis makes use of assigned tasks to increase contact with reality, reduce transference and "to remove the gains and . . . make the attacks of fear useless . . . as long as the symptoms yield sympathy and protection, they will not disappear and the repression will probably return."

Other examples of the use of tasks or assertive responses are discussed in Stevenson and Wolpe (1960), Salter (1961), Ellis (1964), Kelly (1955), Lazarus (1958), and Wolpe (1958).

Wolpe's anxiety-relief technique was discussed in the introductory material. Further examples of it may be found in Bevan (1960) as well as the case with a ten-year-old boy (Lazarus, 1959).

A technique which parallels the use of reactive inhibition developed in voluntary motor behavior by Yates (1958b) is Malleson's (1959) technique that was first used to treat a student suffering from acute panic over an imminent exam. In this procedure the subject is asked to investigate and experience the fear as fully as possible, the situation, the results of failure, and the like, until he is bored with the whole situation and cannot even think of it. The technique at first seems diametrically opposed to the use of systematic desensitization, but both have in common the development of new responses to the stimulus situation. Finally, we wish to mention the work of Saul, Rome, and Leuser (1946) with combat fatigue. The patients viewed combat films in small groups and with a therapist in whom they had confidence. The stimuli were limited and under the subjects' progressive control in terms of permission to leave at any time, the absence of sound effects at the start, an open door, and projection during the day with the lights on. After the men became bored with combat scenes, that had originally terrified them, they were shown movies of hand-to-hand combat. Marked success was reported with thirteen of fourteen subjects in an average of twelve fifteen minute showings.

In Sulzer's article (19) we see many different elements of behavior therapy: the programing of studying behavior so that stimulus control is gained, the use of friends as therapists, overt "suppression" of maladaptive impulses toward the wife in contradiction to psychoanalytic postulates, selective reinforcement of healthy behaviors and verbalizations, and coaching in adjustive behaviors. In short, a broad spectrum of techniques was applied by the therapist as he used his knowledge to shape more adjustive behavior in and out of the therapeutic setting.

In the final article in the section (23) we have selected an analysis of a more traditional therapy. This article may be contrasted with other articles by Murray (1956, 1962) on nondirective therapy and Rosen's direct analysis. There is considerable behavior influence in the therapy setting, and studies such as the one by Murray help to call attention to the need for therapists to take into account their own responses. For the future, such work points to studies of the process of psychotherapy as the influence of one person upon another. In this context we may cite the work of Adams, Butler, and Noblin (1962) on interpretation as a positive reinforcer. As in articles by Kanfer (1965), Heller, Myers, and Kline, (1963) and Krasner (1962a), the therapist can be viewed as a programed source of reinforcement and psychotherapy as a laboratory for the systematic study of meaningful interpersonal behavior.

14 THE CONTROL OF EATING BEHAVIOR IN AN ANOREXIC BY OPERANT CONDITIONING TECHNIQUES

Arthur J. Bachrach • William J. Erwin • Jay P. Mohr[1]

INTRODUCTION

The case to be reported in this paper is that of a patient diagnosed as anorexia nervosa on the basis of a disruption of normal eating behavior and a drop in weight over a period of several years from a customary approximate 120 pounds to a weight of 47 pounds.

Even though it is apparently rare for anorexia patients to perish (Nemiah, 1963, suggests only about 10 percent of the cases), the patient reported herein was definitely in danger of death and, for this reason, the most effective methods for restoring the eating behavior seemed critical. Thus, the basic questions were two: How do we get this patient to eat? and, to effect this, under what conditions will eating occur? The latter question was the basic methodological one, covering such basic data as those events that would be likely to increase the rate of eating behavior, and those events that would be likely to maintain increased eating rate. It might be noted that we talk of *restoring* eating behavior, a term based on the assumption that eating was once a part of the subject's behavioral repertoire, and not, therefore, a new response class to be shaped.

The material will be presented in the following general manner: first, the medical history and clinical course of the patient; then, a narrative account of the behavioral

methodologies used to restore and maintain increased eating rate; followed by a restatement of these behavioral methodologies in terms of an operant paradigm formulated as an experimental design before the experiment and modified during its course. Finally, there will be a general discussion, including the latest available data about the patient and some comments about these.

MEDICAL HISTORY AND CLINICAL COURSE

The patient, a divorced, childless, white female was admitted to the University of Virginia Hospital Medical Service on December 14, 1960 at the age of thirty-seven. Her chief complaint was "Why do I have this block about food?" The history of the present illness at the time of admission revealed that this woman's weight had been fairly stable at about 118 pounds between menarche at the age of eleven and marriage seven years later at eighteen. A photograph of her at eighteen is reproduced as Figure 1.

During the first six months of marriage her weight remained stable at 118 pounds. She began to lose weight in September of 1943 and by January 1944 she weighed 110 pounds. Her last menstrual period occurred in November 1944 and has not recurred to date (December 1963). By January 1945 she weighed approximately 95 pounds. Three years later her weight had dropped to 75 pounds. Food intake and body weight continued to diminish to such an extent that by the summer of 1949 she weighed 65 pounds. Between 1949 and the time of admission to the University of Virginia Hospital in De-

[1] When this case was worked with at the University of Virginia Hospital, Dr. Bachrach was Director of the Division of Behavioral Science at the University of Virginia School of Medicine, Dr. Erwin was a Resident on Neurology and Psychiatry at the Medical School, and Dr. Mohr was a medical student and research extern.

cember 1960, she had lost an additional 18 pounds. At that time she could stand only with assistance, was 5 feet 4 inches tall, and weighed 47 pounds. Photographs of her on admission are reproduced as Figures 2 and 3.

The physical examination revealed a creature so cachetic and shrunken about her skeleton as to give the appearance of a poorly preserved mummy suddenly struck with the breath of life. Her pasty white skin was mottled a purple hue over her feet and stretched like so much heavy spider webbing about the bony prominences of her face. Edematous ankles and feet ballooned out grotesquely from the margins of her slippers. Cavernous ulcers opened up over the right buttocks, pubis and back of the skull while smaller ulcers stood out over the knees, elbows and ankles. Delicate silky threads of hair hung lifelessly from her skull. Broken, gray teeth peered out between thin, white lips through which there weakly issued forth a high pitched distant voice, remarkable for its lack of pressing concern and alarm, which to the passing observer might have seemed a bit incongruous. Her blood pressure was 100/65. The liver and spleen were not palpable.

The pertinent past medical history probably dates back to 1935, when at 11 years of age she entered menarche with the not unusual problems of menorrhagia and metrorrhagia. At this time she described herself as "real chubby" weighing approximately 120 pounds. The family physician was consulted and advised the patient and her family that she had "glandular trouble," that she said plagued the maternal side of the family, and was the cause of heavy uterine bleeding and the tendency to be somewhat obese. For this reason she was admonished by the physician to never let her weight get out-of-hand. He prescribed for her one grain of crude thyroid extract daily. Her menstrual periods continued to be heavy and frequent, occurring at approximately two week intervals at the time of her marriage in 1943, but ceasing entirely in 1944. This patient experienced dyspareunia throughout her marriage

although she denied fear of sexual relations until after the initial painful experience. Prior to her marriage, the family physician had warned her that she was underdeveloped and that marriage would "make this worse or make it better." The only serious illness from which she has suffered is the present one. As a result of failure to eat, she has sustained numerous pathological fractures. In the past, she had been treated with general supportive measures, vitamins, injections that were said to be pituitary extract, Nilevar and tranquilizers, all to no avail. Prior to 1960 she had had a total of eight hospital admissions elsewhere with the primary diagnosis being either malnutrition or more commonly, anorexia nervosa. Such secondary diagnoses as hypoglycemic shock, osteoporosis, fractures, and anemia were frequently included. There was no history of prior formal psychiatric treatment.

The review of systems indicated a history of severe headaches, insomnia, pedal edema, decubitous ulcers, nausea, watery diarrhea, nocturia, dysuria, and amenorrhea, as well as episodes of crying and screaming.

It should be emphasized that no specific attempt was made to obtain a psychiatric history from the patient, nor was any psychotherapy engaged in. The reasons for this, as will be discussed later on, were simply that the authors considered the major goal to be that of restoring eating behavior, a critical goal in view of the very poor prognosis and the risk of death. Believing it possible that conditioning techniques might be successful in restoring eating behavior, the interaction was viewed as an experimental situation in which past history was relevant but beyond knowing with any degree of certainty, and that a more effective technique would be a current evaluation of those conditions under which eating could be brought under control.[2] During the course of the experiment,

[2] In keeping with this experimental control, no tranquilizers or other psychopharmacological agents were given the patient. The only drugs she received were in the form of daily multivitamins and an occasional hypnotic for sleep as needed at night.

FIGURE 1   Age 18; weight 120 lbs.

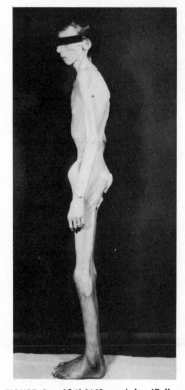

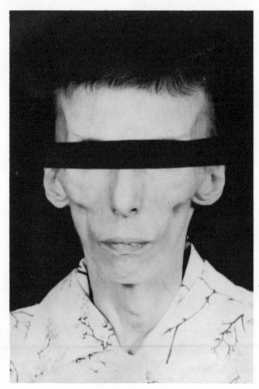

FIGURE 2   12/16/60; weight 47 lbs.   FIGURE 3   12/16/60; weight 47 lbs.

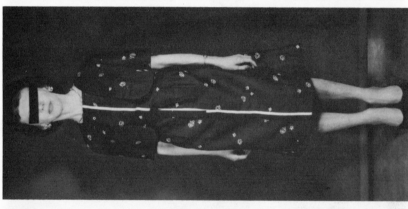

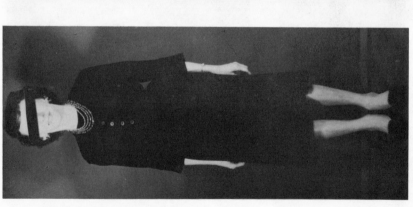

FIGURE 4   1/11/62; weight 74.5 lbs.   FIGURE 5   6/20/62; weight 88 lbs.   FIGURE 6   11/15/63; weight 76 lbs.

however, she spontaneously divulged certain aspects of her past life without reinforcement by the experimenter. She had always maintained a very close attachment to her mother, and during her marriage, was reported by the family to have been quite homesick, as evidenced by several cross-continent trips to Virginia, while living with her husband stationed in the military service in California. Her life in California was described as a lonely and unhappy one. Meals were taken in war-crowded, cheap restaurants because there were no facilities for cooking in their small apartment. With no attempt to elicit the information, the patient tearfully stated that her food intake while in California had been further reduced when a military physician whom she consulted suggested that she return home if she lost more weight.

A review of the family history indicates that there were two male siblings, both successful and well adjusted to their environment. The mother is an obese, pleasant woman with a history of cholecystitis and pancreatitis. At the time of the patient's admission in 1960, the mother was near complete exhaustion over her daughter's illness. The father, who might be described as a remarkably stoic man, had suffered a fairly recent myocardial infarction which left him without residual symptoms. No history of familial disease suggesting anorexia or cachexia could be elicited.

Following initial evaluation on the medical service, the differential diagnosis was felt to lie between anorexia nervosa and Simmond's disease or panhypopituitarism. Extensive laboratory tests were carried out in an attempt to further illuminate the problem, including ACTH stimulation of the adrenals with concomitant plasma corticoid measurements, urinary gonadatrophins, urinary 17 ketosteroids and urinary ketogenic steroids. Radioactive iodine uptake was carried out and a stool examination and d-xylose absorption studies were made. The results of all these tests were found to be within normal limits. The routine laboratory examinations only revealed abnormalities which reflected the secondary results of decreased food intake.

During the time she was being evaluated on the medical service, the patient was offered a diet which fitted her own specifications as well as three interval feedings of fruit ice and ginger ale. Six days after admission she was consuming an average of 1,451 calories daily and had gained 1.6 pounds in weight. Seventeen days after admission, on December 31, 1960, she was begun on 20 units of ACTH daily as a therapeutic and diagnostic trial. On January 10, 1961, this was increased to 20 units twice per

TABLE I

	DATE	WT.
1.	12/16/1960	47 lb.
2.	1/3/1961	50 lb.
3.	2/1/1961	53 lb.
4.	2/10/1961	59 lb.
5.	2/20/1961	61 lb.
6.	3/1/1961	60 lb.
7.	3/10/1961	63 lb.
8.	3/20/1961	64 lb.
9.	3/30/1961	64¼ lb.
10.	4/14/1961	63 lb.
11.	4/18/1961	64 lb.
12.	4/22/1961	65½ lb.
13.	5/6/1961	66 lb.
14.	5/10/1961	68½ lb.
15.	5/13/1961	67 lb.
16.	5/17/1961	70 lb.
17.	7/8/1961	70 lb.
18.	7/15/1961	71 lb.
19.	7/29/1961	72 lb.
20.	8/12/1961	71 lb.
21.	9/30/1961	72 lb.
22.	10/14/1961	75½ lb.
23.	11/11/1961	75¼ lb.
24.	11/25/1961	76½ lb.
25.	12/2/1961	76 lb.
26.	12/9/1961	77¼ lb.
27.	1/18/1962	74½ lb.
28.	1/27/1962	77 lb.
29.	2/3/1962	77½ lb.
30.	2/10/1962	77½ lb.
31.	3/31/1962	88 lb.
32.	4/21/1962	84 lb.
33.	5/14/1962	85 lb.
34.	5/21/1962	86½ lb.
35.	6/16/1962	85 lb.

day. It was then gradually reduced and finally discontinued on January 24, 1961. Her weight had stabilized at around 52.5 pounds and she was reported to be eating a high percentage of the food offered her. She denied regurgitation of ingested food at this time and throughout her hospital stay. By the end of January 1961, it had become apparent that much of the patient's weight gain was due to the fluid and electrolyte retention secondary to the administered ACTH.

An exhaustive medical and endocrinological evaluation had failed to reveal any specific lesion or disease process which could account for the patient's reduced food intake and state of severe malnutrition bordering on death. With the discontinuation of the ACTH and subsequent water diuresis, the patient weighed 50 pounds. At this time, just prior to her transfer to the psychiatry service on January 3, 1961, she was consuming between 1100 and 1400 calories each day.

BEHAVIORAL METHODOLOGIES: THE EXPERIMENTAL PLAN AND ITS EXECUTION

Inpatient course

When the patient was transferred from the Internal Medicine service to Psychiatry, she was assigned to one of the authors (WJE), then a Resident on Neurology and Psychiatry who got into contact with the other authors to formulate a plan for working with the patient. It was arranged for the junior author (JPM), then a medical student to be assigned to her on the wards. The three experimenters decided to approach the case from a standpoint of experimental manipulation of the relevant variables in order most effectively to restore eating behavior, as noted a critical problem of the moment. Assuming that behavior is largely under the control of its consequences and that it can be maintained and modified by manipulating consequences (among other variables) an analysis of the patient's immediate situation was the first task accomplished.

The patient was in an attractive hospital room, with pictures on the wall, flowers available and usually present, a lovely view of verdant grounds visible through the window. She had free access to visitors; a radio, books, records and a record player, television, and magazines were present, although she had considerable difficulty in reading because of her generalized debility (See Fig. 2). People would visit her and read to her as well as provide television control and record play. In discussion with her it was found that she enjoyed these activities and seemed to enjoy visitors as well. Because these activities apparently provided enjoyment for her and could thus be considered positively reinforcing to her behavior, she was removed from her pleasant hospital room and transferred to the psychiatric ward, to a private room from which all attractive accoutrements had been removed. The room was barren, furnished only with a bed, nightstand and chair. A sink was available at one end of the room. The view was of a hospital courtyard.

At this point, it must be emphasized that the full cooperation of the patient's family and the hospital administration was elicited and received. The family was told that the patient would be treated in an unusual fashion—she would not receive psychotherapy as it is usually conceived of but rather she would be placed on an experimental regimen in which her pleasures would essentially be denied her unless she ate. The procedure and goals were made quite clear and permission was received to try the design out in practice. She was then transferred to the barren experimental "box." At that stage, the cooperation of the nursing staff was solicited because all three experimenters believed that without the aid of the nurses, with whom patients have most contact, the plan would fail. The nurses, graduate and student staff, were consulted and a series of discussions took place in which the experimenters explained in detail the principles of behavioral modification to be applied and specifically what role the nurse would play in their implementation. The first re-action of "inhuman treatment" of the pa-tient, a natural feeling on the part of the nursing staff viewing the removal of those objects designed to make a patient more comfortable and happier, was avoided by a discussion of the realities of the patient's danger and the lack of success achieved so far in effecting meaningful change. The ex-perimenters felt it would be infinitely more inhuman to allow her to return home with a possible prognosis of death than to subject her to some methods which had proved suc-cessful in other situations and which might also be effective in her case. This feeling was transmitted to the others involved and a promise of cooperation was granted by the nurses and the psychiatric staff as well. No drugs were to be given (except, as noted above, multivitamins and occasional hyp-notics for sleep); no psychotherapy was at-tempted by residents or attending staff; medical students were not permitted to see her and no teaching sessions (usual with patients on the ward for didactic purposes with the third-year medical students) were scheduled. The patient was so debilitated at that stage that she could not move by her-self, so the injunction against visitors and personal contact was easy to effect with the cooperation of the ward personnel. The nurses, of course, had to go into her room to change linen and bring her water and meals, but they were careful not to reply to the patient's verbal inquiries or conversa-tional initiations with any response, other than a simple "good morning" uttered upon entering the room.

The patient was not told anything of the plan. She was told that she was to be transferred to another ward, on the psychi-atric service and that there would be three people working with her, the authors of the current paper. It was made clear who these people were, her resident, a medical school staff research psychologist supervising, and a medical student. She was told that each of these would eat one meal with her during the day, the resident (WJE) had breakfast

with her, the staff psychologist (AJB) had lunch with her and the medical student (JPM) had dinner with her. All of the meals were brought to her by a nurse and were consumed in her room. The experi-menters set up a reinforcement schedule, somewhat gross in its characteristics and difficult to achieve with exactness but never-theless attempted; this involved verbal rein-forcement of movements associated with eating. When the patient lifted her fork to move toward spearing a piece of food the experimenter would talk to her about some-thing in which she might have an interest. The required response was then successively raised to lifting the food toward her mouth, chewing, and so forth.

The same scheduled increase in required response was applied to the amount of food consumed. At first, any portion of the meal that was consumed would be a basis for a postprandial reinforcement (a radio, TV set, or phonograph would be brought in by the nurse at a signal from the experimenter); if she did not touch any of the food before her, nothing would be done by way of re-inforcement and she would be left until the next meal.[3] More and more of the meal had to be consumed in order to be rein-forced until she eventually was required to eat everything on the plate. The meals were slowly increased in caloric value, with the valued help and cooperation of the dieti-cians. Initially, she was presented with 2500 calories a day in increments ranging from 50 to 75 calories. Several attempts were made to adjust the caloric intake with the choice of menu left to the experimenters and dieti-cians. Later she was placed on a standard hospital menu of 2000 to 2500 calories a day with the menu her own choice from several alternative menus, as was true of all other patients on the ward. This self-choice of menu was provided later on as a rein-

[3] A consistent reinforcement available to her at all times, incidentally, was knitting, pro-vided to ease some of the potentially aversive qualities of very long waits without directly interfering with the control of eating behavior.

forcement for eating behavior, in generalizing reinforcements.

As her weight began to rise somewhat, there was a beginning of generalizing reinforcers from the social reinforcement of the experimenters eating with her (which we, at least, assumed to be reinforcing!) to a broader class of reinforcing events, such as having a patient of her own choice eat with her in her room or eating in the solarium with other patients, after her mobility improved. Later on, she was taken for walks around the university grounds by a student nurse or a patient of her choice. Her family and other visitors were also provided in increasing frequency as her eating and weight rose. All such reinforcements—visitors, walks, mail, hair care (such as setting and shampoos)—were postponed until after meal time so as to constitute a reinforcement for eating behavior. Later in her hospital stay she was permitted to go out to eat with family, friends or nurses, as she wished, in keeping with the goal of generalizing eating behavior to nonhospital situations.

At one point during her hospital stay she hit a plateau in which she did not gain any weight; from about March 10 to April 18 she ranged around the same weight, 63 pounds. Internists consulted said that this was understandable to a degree because she was laying down body constituents damaged in her previous noneating behavior. After a while, however, the weight gain could be expected to rise once again. When it did not, it was suggested that she might be vomiting the food she did take in because her caloric intake continued to be sufficient to produce weight gain. The suggestion was made that she was using the sink in her room to dispose of vomited food and someone cut off the water in the sink. The experimenters decided that control of her eating was not to be achieved through cutting off the sink water and so it was turned on again and the requirement for reinforcement was changed to weight gain and not simply eating. After this, any gain in weight, no matter how slight, was required for the walks, TV, and

other reinforcements. Eating alone was no longer sufficient. She was weighed every day at the same time, around 3:00 P.M. and the major class of reinforcements, walks and so forth, were made contingent upon her scale reading at 3:00 P.M.

Another question arose early in the experiment with regard to extra caloric intake to be provided by snacks and by such specific caloric light meals as Metrecal. The possibility of giving her between meal snacks was considered and rejected for the simple reason that the experimenters wished to have a clear stimulus situation delineated—mealtimes were for eating. We wished to avoid the problem of having her receive a snack at 4:00 P.M. and then excusing a lowered intake at dinner by claiming to be less hungry because of the snack. To keep the mealtimes as a temporal discriminative stimulus was critical in the initial stages; later on bedtime snacks were permitted.

Again, conversations were always about pleasant topics, never about her problems. Even when she spontaneously began to talk about some of her past history, as noted in the preceding section on medical history and clinical course, the experimenter present would not react but would politely allow her to talk without reinforcing the content, then go back to what the topic had been beforehand. This restraint on therapeutic intervention and interpretation was consistent with the experimental design.

Outpatient course

She was, as noted, admitted to the hospital December 14, 1960, and transferred to Psychiatry on January 3, 1961. The experiment was begun on February 1, 1961. She was discharged as an outpatient on March 25, 1961 weighing fourteen pounds more than she had when she had been transferred. The question now was one faced by every therapist—how to generalize the methods established under controlled conditions to the outside where such controls are lacking. The aid of the patient's family was enlisted in this regard; they were asked specifically:

1. to avoid any reinforcement of invalid behavior or complaints;
2. not to make an issue of eating (something that had been generally true of family and friends during her losing period before hospitalization);
3. to reinforce maintenance of her weight by verbal reinforcement, for example, as she began to fill out her clothes this was to be reinforced clearly but without over-reacting;
4. not to prepare any special diet for her;
5. to refrain from weighing her at home, inasmuch as weight was to be recorded only when she made periodic visits to see the resident (who was to be the only one of the experimenters to continue a direct personal relationship with her);
6. to discuss only pleasant topics at meal-times;
7. never to allow her to eat alone;
8. to follow a rigid schedule for meals, with an alarm clock to be present for each meal;
9. to use a purple tablecloth initially as a discriminative stimulus for mealtime table behavior, associated with eating, an idea borrowed from Ferster's work with obese patients (Ferster, et al., 1962); and, finally,
10. to encourage her to dine out with other people under enjoyable conditions.

She continued to return at regular intervals to talk to her resident. As an outpatient, she continued to respond favorably to the procedures, as indicated by the graph of weight gain in Table 1. At first, after her discharge, she was seen weekly, then bi-weekly, and finally, intermittently until her readmission to the hospital for further control in February 1962. During the period between March 1961 and February 1962 as an outpatient, the experimenters sought to generalize the reinforcements for maintained eating behavior as much as possible. She was active in church work and social events in the small town in which she lived. The visits to the resident were chats in which she told generally about what she had been doing. Some discussion of the ultimate rewarding and ultimate aversive consequences of her eating behavior took place and she received social verbal reinforcement for weight gain when she stepped on the scales. Her physical activity at that time began to be somewhat tiring as she reported it and she was enjoined against overdoing the social and church functions, if possible, while she was working on weight gain. This hyperactivity, as will be seen in later discussion, proved to be a critical variable.

One report she gave of a social situation in which social reinforcement seemed effective was an incident involving a woman's club of which she was a member. She recounted this experience with some glee. During the refreshment period, coffee and doughnuts were passed to the members and, as was the practice in her pre-hospital membership days, the woman passing the refreshments skipped the patient. She asked if she might have a doughnut and said that everyone turned to stare at her as she devoured a rather large doughnut. She reported that it was something like being in the zoo but that she derived a great deal of pleasure from the event even though it was a little disarming; not the least of the pleasure appeared to stem from the verbal reinforcement by the other members for her eating.

Another reinforcing event was the reappearance of healthy hair. During the severe physical distress caused by not eating, her hair had been brittle and easily cracked when it was touched. As her weight and health improved, her hair returned to a point where she could have it dressed, a reinforcing event. Photographs in later periods (see Figure 4, for example), show this improved hairdressing and a return to care for her hair. She also made her own clothes, as shown in Figures 4 and 5 in the series of photographs and took pleasure in finding attractive clothes to wear.

As noted, she was readmitted on February 18, 1962 to be seen again under controlled conditions. Essentially, the same regimen was applied as had been used on her previous admission and she gained an additional 7 pounds during the month she stayed; she was discharged once again on March 25, 1962 and was last seen on June 16, 1962 when her resident was preparing to leave for service in the Navy. At that time she weighed 88 pounds.

Behavior methodologies: the operant paradigm

It is apparent that the methodologies used in the restoration of eating behavior in this patient may be subsumed under a general operant conditioning approach. As Barrett (1962) observes, "The basic datum of the free operant method is the frequency of a specific and reliably defined response within a controlled experimental environment. The method is most readily applied, therefore, in cases where changes in the rate of a repeated movement are of primary concern." Certainly, eating as a response class is reliably defined and the desired result of the experiment was an increase in its rate.

Applications of operant conditioning methods to clinical problems have been varied; among the problems approached by the free operant method have been stuttering (Flanagan, Goldiamond, and Azrin, 1958), psychotic behavior (Lindsley, 1960) and autistic children (Ferster and DeMyer, 1961).

The present case was considered to be one in which operant conditioning techniques might be successful because of the specifiability of the response and the possibility of controlled environmental manipulation. The authors essentially used the operant paradigm as described by Goldiamond (1962) as a guide to formulating practices. The paradigm Goldiamond sketches is a summary statement of the general methodology of the free operant, and is as follows:

To modify Goldiamond's explanation of this paradigm somewhat, presenting a discriminative stimulus (S^D) in the presence of other constant stimuli (SS^C) will occasion a response (R); whether this response recurs is contingent upon the consequences (S^r) of that response (under these specific conditions) and the state variables (SV) usually referred to as "needs," "motivation," "deprivation," and the like which make the consequence of the response effective in controlling it. Assuming that behavior is governed by its consequences under specified conditions, discriminative behavior can be produced, maintained and altered if the constant stimuli, the discriminative stimuli, the response contingencies and the state variables are specified and controlled.

With respect to the present case, we visualized the variables within this operant paradigm to be as follows:

State Variables

(SV): essentially unknown; we could not evaluate with any degree of assurance those needs, motives or other inferred conditions that might have occasioned her drop in eating rate. The reinforcement history of any organism first studied is always an unknown; experimentally, the task is to manipulate deprivation states so that the past reinforcement history is less relevant and thereby bring the deprivation variables under experimental control. In the present case, the patient's past reinforcement history was inferred to have occasioned positively reinforcing values for such events as music, reading, social contact and the like and these could then be put on a deprivation schedule.

Controlling Stimuli

The discriminative stimuli to which we wished the patient to respond (S^Ds) were those which eventually were to exercise some

$$\text{Controlling stimuli:} \quad \left. \begin{array}{l} S^D - S^\Delta \text{ (discriminative)} \\ SS^C \text{ (constant)} \end{array} \right\} - R \text{ (response)} \longrightarrow S^r - S^o \text{ (differential reinforcement)}$$

$$\cdots\cdots\cdots\cdots\cdots SV \text{ (state variables)}$$

measure of control over her behavior, particularly eating behavior. Therefore, two S^D classes were considered, one for the inpatient controlled environment, the other for outpatient control. The Inpatient S^Ds included the experimenters as mealmates, the various utensils (plates, forks, knives, and so forth) and temporal S^Ds such as specific times for eating meals with no in-between eating. The Outpatient S^Ds included the alarm clock for mealtime, the purple tablecloth as an S^D for eating (particularly important if the table is used for other purposes such as sewing) and, again, temporal S^Ds in the form of specific mealtimes.

Constant Stimuli

(SS^C): in the hospital it would include the major stimulus class of the room itself and the various objects contained therein; the stimulus change from an attractive hospital room to a barren one is a shift in SS^C classes, limiting the number of S^Ds in the room by removing flowers, pictures, and similar stimuli. The SS^C as an outpatient would be more varied and less controlled but would include major stimulus situations such as the home and church.

Response

(R): clearly, the response to be manipulated was eating. Weight gain, which supplanted eating *per se* as a reinforced event, is obviously contingent upon eating, the major response.

Differential reinforcement

(S^r—S^o): in the hospital room, the reinforcements included social contact, television, radio, records, reading; the response of eating was reinforced by these events. Not eating (and no weight gain) occasioned lack of reinforcement (S^o) and, later, verbal disapproval, presumed aversive (S^a). As an inpatient, the S^rs were expanded to include walks around the grounds of the university, eating in restaurants, choosing her own menu and eating with other persons of her choice, as well as verbal approval as social reinforcement.

RECENT DATA REGARDING THE CASE PRESENTED

The data in Table 1 recording the weights over the period of the experiment stop at June 16, 1962. This was the last occasion on which the patient's weight was recorded in the hospital and the last time she had direct experimenter contact. As noted above, her resident left after this date, as did the research psychologist. She was interested in maintaining contact with the resident in particular as he entered the Navy and continued to write. On July 25, 1962 the patient wrote that she was taking a home study course in practical nursing and had passed her exam with a grade of 95, had received her cap and uniform, and was ready for practicum hospital training and her license. She was specialing a private case in her home town, a woman who was invalided by arthritis. The patient wrote that her patient had "an electric organ and I'm enjoying that especially, and play for her as she can not play now because of the arthritic condition in her back and neck. Also a fabulous collection of records. So we have a lot of mutual interests and are getting along fine together!" She also reported that she had hit the 90 mark in weight: "So it's a happy feeling to be out of the 80's!" This was her own self-reported weight. The reinforcements of music and social contact seemed to be available to her, as well as the reinforcing event of caring for someone else which became a major reinforcing class for her. It is also of interest to note that she did all the cooking for herself and her patient and reported good appetites.

At Christmas time, 1962, she wrote that she was working at the university hospital where she had been a patient, as a general practical nurse on a regular 8-hour shift. She had passed the physical required for such employment and reported that she enjoyed the work very much.

A letter dated June 16, 1963 indicated

that she had left her nursing work although she enjoyed it: "My hours became more demanding all the time. My schedule was so irregular, as I was relief nurse on all shifts. So often I'd work 3:00–11:30 P.M., then back on at 7:00 A.M. Consequently I was not getting an adequate amount of sleep. But I was so happy and completely wrapped up in my work, and lost weight before I realized. Even then I had an exceptionally good appetite. . . ." Her reported weight, as she wrote, was 78 pounds at that time, 12 pounds down from what she had indicated she weighed in July 1962 (see Figure 5, June 1962). Figure 6 shows her in January 1963 when she wrote she thought she weighed 76 pounds, as well as she could recall. (It should be noted that she indicates that she weighs herself before breakfast, instead of at the time (3:00 P.M.) at which the majority of the hospital records were made.) Her letter of June 1963 also indicated that she had put herself on a high caloric diet including "egg nog, ice cream, creamed soups, gobs and gobs of mashed potatoes, jello, and so forth, and have not lost 1 lb. through all this." "All this" referred to extensive dental surgery in which her lower jaw teeth had to be extracted on June 15, 1963; her dental problems were residua of the severe physical damage occasioned by the weight loss.

As of this writing, her last letter was dated December 17, 1963 in which she wrote that she was admitted as a student to a rehabilitation center; she was eligible for rehabilitation because of her spinal condition, kyphosis. This support freed her from requiring money from her family to go on with her goal of becoming a medical secretary and working in that role in a hospital situation. Again, she describes a full load:

I entered Business School Sept. 23, and am taking the General Clerical Course with Shorthand Optional. It is a very full course with classes everyday from 8:00 A.M. to 4:00 P.M. With extra activities. Was appointed Dormitory adviser for 25 girls, on my Dorm. So that involves a lot of nightly talks to solve their "petty problems," mostly boy friends, homesickness, etc. But am glad they feel I am capable of helping to solve their problems.

She complains sometimes of pain in her spine, particularly when she overworks and does something to "tax my strength." She wrote that her weight was around 72 pounds although she continues to eat. As she views it, when she works the way she wants to work she loses some weight but that the weight loss is apparently less disturbing than living what she calls a "sedentary life" which she says would be "an unpleasant one, because I've had too many years of idleness."

If it is true, as the patient suggests, that eating is maintained at a high rate and that lack of weight gain or actual weight loss (although nothing close to the dangerous level of before) results from overactivity or even following a routine that might be normal for a person not handicapped by the physical residua, the decision might be one of reinforcing a balance between activity and eating, reinforcing a steady rate of eating while reinforcing a lowered activity output, one that would be consonant with her physical capacities and yet also reinforcing her apparent social behavior manifest in counselling and nursing. Ideally, an accurate record of current weights and a direct manipulation of relevant behaviors should be continued. This is now being arranged with a research psychiatrist near her training center. On the positive side, certainly her current level of social interaction, her successful completion of one training program and entry into another, in addition to her ability (despite physical difficulties) to handle a responsible nursing position, both in special private nurse care and hospital nursing, reflect marked change, over and above the increase in weight over her level on admission to the hospital. Irreversible physical damage such as the kyphosis cannot be significantly improved but she did recover from the problems of insomnia, decubitus ulcers, edema and the other physical concomitants of severe weight loss. And, finally, the specific response manipulated—rate of eating behavior—has maintained itself at a high level.

DISCUSSION

The present case has been offered as an example of an operant conditioning approach to a clinical problem. The authors do not wish to suggest that the free operant method is inevitably the treatment of choice in such cases; we merely present this as an experiment in manipulating a specific response in a manner consonant with experimental analysis of behavior. The explanations for the drop in eating rate seen in patients diagnosed as anorexia nervosa have generally centered around symbolic conflicts. Nemiah (1963), for example, suggests than an anorexic may have a "conflict over sexuality," commenting that "Many patients with anorexia nervosa are thus beset by sexual conflicts expressed in an allied disturbance of eating." (p. 237). The fear of oral impregnation as a psychodynamic explanation of the disruption of eating behavior is the most frequent sexual conflict inferred. Nemiah also suggests that there may be a "conflict over aggression," observing that "avoidance of eating is related to the aggressive impulse; it represents a defense against the expression of it." (p. 237). This oral aggressive impulse and the reaction against it is a familiar psychodynamic explanation, also found in dynamic interpretations of speech disorders such as stuttering. It is not our purpose to review the literature on anorexia; the interested person may consult Nemiah (1950, 1958, 1963), Loeb (1960), and Wall (1959) as standard references.

It is certainly possible that Nemiah's inferences regarding the etiology of anorexia are valid, although they are essentially unproved. Valid or not, it would seem that the most important problem facing the therapist is how to get the patient to increase his rate of eating, to restore eating behavior somehow disrupted. Psychodynamic explanations always remain inferential, no matter how valid or logical they may appear. The specification of the response desired and the analysis of those variables relevant in producing and maintaining that response seem more effective enterprises.

REFERENCES

BACHRACH, A. J. Operant conditioning and behavior: some clinical applications. In H. Lief, V. F. Lief, and N. R. Lief (Eds.), *The psychological basis of medical practice*. New York: Hoeber, 1963. Pp. 94–108.

BARRETT, B. H. Reduction in rate of multiple tics by free operant conditioning methods. *J. nerv. ment. Dis.*, 1962, **135**, 187–195.

FERSTER, C. B. and M. K. DEMYER. The development of performances in autistic children in an automatically controlled environment. *J. chronic Dis.*, 1961, **13**, 312–345.

FERSTER, C. B., J. I. NURNBERGER, and E. B. LEVITT. The control of eating. *J. Mathetics*, 1962, **1**, 87–110.

FLANAGAN, B., I. GOLDIAMOND, and N. H. AZRIN. Operant stuttering: the control of stuttering behavior through response-contingent consequences. *J. exp. Anal. Behav.*, 1958, **1**, 173–177.

GOLDIAMOND, I. Perception. In A. J. Bachrach (Ed.), *Experimental foundations of clinical psychology*. New York: Basic Books, 1962, 280–340.

LINDSLEY, O. R. Characteristics of the behavior of chronic psychotics as revealed by free-operant conditioning methods. *Dis. nerv. Sys. Monogr. Suppl.* 1960, **21**, 66–78.

LOEB, L. Anorexia nervosa. *J. nerv. ment. Dis.*, 1960, **131**, 447.

NEMIAH, J. C. Anorexia nervosa. *Medicine*, 1950, **29**, 225–268.

NEMIAH, J. C. Anorexia nervosa: fact and theory. *Amer. J. Dig. Dis.*, 1958, **3**, 249–271.

NEMIAH, J. C. Emotions and gastrointestinal disease. In H. Lief, V. F. Lief, and N. R. Lief (Eds.), *The psychological basis of medical practice*. New York: Hoeber, 1963. Pp. 233–244.

WALL, J. H. Diagnosis, treatment and results in anorexia nervosa. *Amer. J. Psychiat.*, 1959, **115**, 997.

15   A CASE UTILIZING SENSORY DEPRIVATION PROCEDURES

Henry B. Adams

Although a substantial literature on the topic of sensory deprivation has appeared in recent years, relatively little attention has been given to the possibility of practical therapeutic applications. Most of the published studies have been concerned with the stressful and disruptive effects produced by prolonged exposure to extreme conditions involving drastic reduction in all forms of meaningfully patterned sensory stimuli. Under these extreme conditions, subjects have experienced hallucinations, delusions, thought disturbances, anxiety, personality disorganization, and other manifestations of impaired mental functioning (Fiske, 1961; Kubzansky, 1961; Wexler, Mendelson, Leiderman and Solomon, 1958).

The writer has been involved in an extensive research program investigating the effects of sensory deprivation procedures on psychiatric patients exposed to less drastic conditioning of shorter duration. The results which emerged show that these procedures can serve a useful therapeutic purpose. The major findings of this program of studies were that:

1. Disruptive phenomena rarely occurred during relatively short periods of mild sensory deprivation and social isolation;
2. unlike "normal" subjects, psychiatric patients as a group showed substantial positive changes following exposure to these conditions;
3. the greater the degree of personality disturbance in these patients prior to deprivation, the greater was the improvement observed afterward;
4. under conditions of reduced sensory input a generalized state of "stimulus hunger" gradually developed, in which patients became

more open and accessible to new sensory stimulation from any source; and
5. a standardized prerecorded tape message presented to individual patients during exposure to deprivation was more readily accepted and produced more positive changes in self-concept measures than the same message presented to a control group under non-deprivation conditions (Adams, Carrera, Cooper, Gibby and Tobey, 1960; Adams, Carrera and Gibby, 1960; Cooper, 1962; Cooper, Adams and Cohen, in press; Cooper, Adams and Gibby, 1962; Gibby, Adams and Carrera, 1960; Gibby and Adams, 1961).

Previous observations had already suggested that sensory deprivation methods were much more effective as facilitants for subsequent psychotherapeutic contacts than when used alone, and that additional modifications might augment these therapeutic effects even further. It was hypothesized that readiness for the acceptance of psychotherapy might be optimally facilitated by the use of individual stimulus messages specially prepared for presentation to patients during deprivation. After presentation of the individual message prepared for each patient arrangements could then be made for him to start immediately in psychotherapy. Each message would describe to the patient the unique patterns of maladaptive interpersonal behavior that had led up to his hospitalization and explain just how future contacts with a therapist might help him acquire new and more effective patterns.

The content of the individual messages was based on the theoretical rationale and the multilevel measurements of personality developed by Leary (1956, 1957). Leary and his associates at the Kaiser Foundation have devised an elaborate set of quantitative scoring procedures for assessing personality and measuring changes in the course of psychotherapy. He has also developed a comprehensive theoretical and conceptual framework that provides a basis for interpreting scores on the multilevel measure in ways that are concretely meaningful in terms of the immediate life experiences of patients. In a recent paper the writer has shown the universal applicability of the basic dimensions delineated in Leary's system for the description and classification of all interpersonal behavior (Adams, 1964). The multilevel system was particularly appropriate for the purposes of this study.

A group of twelve experimental subjects were presented individually prepared messages during sensory deprivation under the mild conditions of relatively brief sensory deprivation and social isolation described above. A full report of changes in this experimental group contrasted with two control groups has been presented elsewhere (Adams, Robertson and Cooper, 1963). The experimental group showed personality changes that differed significantly from the two control groups, along with generalized improvement, enhancement of insight, and increased realistic self-awareness. One control group received sensory deprivation but no message, while the other, which was a test-retest group, received no deprivation. The deprivation-only control group showed prepost changes significantly different from the test-retest group, reflecting the effects of deprivation alone. However, subjects in the experimental group receiving the individually prepared messages showed additional changes over and above those observed in the deprivation-only group.

This individual case study describes in more detail the procedures and results achieved with one of the twelve subjects in the experimental group. The changes were similar in nature to those observed in the group as a whole. The diagnosis, clinical symptom picture, and the profile of personality test scores were also representative,

except that this patient was a few years younger than the group average. Furthermore, his symptoms were much like those frequently encountered in hospitals, clinics, and other psychiatric settings all over the world. This very typical case thus illustrates the simplicity, economy, effectiveness, and wide therapeutic applicability of sensory deprivation techniques.

The procedures were intended to serve two aims. The first was to increase insight, self-awareness, and self-acceptance and to reduce overall symptomatology. Effectiveness in achieving the first aim could be assessed by an analysis of changes in test-taking behavior before and after. The second aim was to convince the patient of the advisability of more intensive individual psychotherapy on an outpatient basis. The degree of success in accomplishing the second aim could be determined quite easily by a later follow-up study inquiring whether the patient did in fact accept outpatient psychotherapy as a consequence of these procedures.

PROCEDURES

The patient was a hospitalized thirty-year-old white male veteran with the psychiatric diagnoses of (a) chronic anxiety reaction and (b) psychophysiological gastrointestinal reaction. He was selected in the same way as every other patient who acted as a subject. The selection criteria were that this patient was (1) white, (2) male, (3) between the ages of twenty and sixty, (4) carried a functional psychiatric diagnosis, (5) had no previous history or present evidence of organicity, and (6) was not receiving tranquilizing drugs, insulin, or electric shock treatment.

After the patient had been chosen, he was interviewed by the individual who was assigned to be his therapist and future arrangements for intensive individual psychotherapy were discussed. He was then administered the Minnesota Multiphasic Personality Inventory (MMPI) and the Interpersonal Check List (ICL), which were scored according to the multilevel system of interpersonal diagnosis (Leary, 1956).

On the basis of the MMPI and ICL scores and the multilevel interpersonal diagnosis, a written individual message was prepared for presentation during deprivation. The message included the following points which were interpreted according to Leary's rationale:

1. the patient's typical Level I overt behavior as predicted from his MMPI scores;
2. his Level II ICL conscious self-description;
3. his Level III covert or preconscious attitudes as inferred from MMPI scores;
4. his Level V description of the ideal person on the ICL; and
5. the discrepancies between levels and their psychological significance.

The message also included an explanation of the ultimate aims, goals, and purposes of therapy. After the message was written, the patient's therapist read it aloud into a microphone for recording on tape so that it could be played back later when the patient was placed in deprivation.

On the following day the patient received three hours of partial sensory deprivation and social isolation. He was placed on a bed in a quiet, comfortable, air-conditioned room, and his eyes were covered, his ears plugged with glycerine-soaked cotton, and his head wrapped in gauze. After two hours the prerecorded tape message was presented to him through a bone-conductivity speaker that had been placed in the gauze wrapped around his head. At the end of three hours he was removed and returned to the ward where he resumed his usual daily schedule of activities. Except for the individually prepared prerecorded message the experimental conditions were the same as those previously reported (Gibby and Adams, 1961).

On the third day the MMPI and ICL were readministered to evaluate changes. In accordance with the research design, the patient was not interviewed again by his future therapist until after all the posttesting had been completed.

The messages were deliberately made

repetitious in order to minimize any possible ambiguity. Previous experience had shown that there was less misinterpretation, distortion, or misunderstanding if the most important points were restated in different words several times in the course of the message. This seeming redundancy was intended to overcome resistances, to forestall confusion, and to help the patient understand clearly the ultimate purposes of psychotherapy.

The message presented to this patient began with an explanation of the aims, procedures, and rationale of psychotherapy as they applied to his particular case. The results obtained from the MMPI and ICL, which revealed considerable dissatisfaction with himself, were then discussed at some length. He was told that this dissatisfaction was an important motivating factor, making for a real desire to effect major changes in his patterns of interpersonal behavior. It was pointed out that an important initial step in therapy would be to acquire a clear understanding of his present patterns and an equally clear understanding of the directions in which he ultimately wished to change. After this initial step, subsequent therapy sessions could be concerned with ways and means of bringing about specific changes in the patient's attitudes, personality traits, and habitual patterns of overt behavior. He was cautioned not to expect immediate alterations in long-established patterns. He was frankly informed that it would require a sincere, sustained effort on his own part to achieve these changes in himself and to consolidate them anew as enduring habits of interpersonal behavior.

The message then gave a detailed description of his present personality make-up, as interpreted according to Leary's multilevel conceptual framework. The test results had indicated that in his overt behavior (Level I) the patient was characteristically meek, respectful, admiring, docile, submissive, and dependent, at least on initial acquaintance. His conscious description of himself (Level II) showed that he viewed himself in an unflattering light as weak, indecisive, passive, helpless, personally worthless, and lacking in self-confidence. But this description was somewhat inaccurate and unduly self-critical, since he failed to recognize that his meek, respectful behavior made him liked and accepted by others. He was then informed of the test results showing that he harbored covert, underlying attitudes (Level III) of skepticism and distrust, that these attitudes regularly appeared in all his significant interpersonal relationships, and that they would inevitably emerge during the course of therapy, making for potential resistances which could be anticipated, understood, and forestalled at the outset. Finally, there was a discussion of the significance of his description of the ideal person (Level V). The great discrepancy between his self-description and his description of the ideal person reflected intense dissatisfaction with his present personality make-up. The message concluded by encouraging the patient to feel hopeful and optimistic in the belief that he could in time gradually alter his own habitual behavior patterns in the course of therapy, so as to conform more closely to his own ideals.

RESULTS

The prerecorded tape message was aimed at reducing symptomatology and fostering realistic self-awareness. The changes in test scores provide an objective index of its effectiveness in achieving this aim.

In addition to the ten clinical scales and four validity scales, five special scales of the MMPI were also scored. These included the Welsh A (anxiety) and R (repression) scales, the Barron Es (ego-strength) scale, and Leary's Level I MMPI Dominance-Submission and Love-Hostility scales. Scores on nine of the ten clinical scales dropped on post-testing, indicating generalized improvement and reduction in the various kinds of pathology tapped by those scales. There were seven scales on which the scores decreased by one standard deviation or more on posttesting: the Hs, Hy, Pd, Pa, Pt, Sc, and K scales. The drop in scores on K and R indicated that the lowered scores on the clinical scales were not the result of increased repression, faking or defensiveness.

The ICL scores in Table 1 show the patient's conscious self-description, the traits he attributed to the ideal person, and the prepost changes on both sets of measures. The ICL was scored for eight component or octant scores, which were combined into two overall-dimension scores according to Leary's (1956) formulas. The two dimension scores provide summary points that indicate the

TABLE I   Description of Self and Ideal Person on ICL before and after Presentation of Message

	SELF-DESCRIPTION			IDEAL PERSON		
Octant Scores	Pre	Post	Change	Pre	Post	Change
			Raw Scores			
AP (Managerial-Autocratic)	4	3	−1	8	6	−2
BC (Competitive-Narcissistic)	4	1	−3	5	6	+1
DE (Aggressive-Sadistic)	4	3	−1	5	5	0
FG (Rebellious-Distrustful)	6	9	+3	1	1	0
HI (Self-Effacing-Masochistic)	10	9	−1	2	3	+1
JK (Docile-Dependent)	5	5	0	4	5	+1
LM (Cooperative-Overconventional)	5	5	0	13	11	−2
NO (Responsible-Hypernormal)	4	2	−2	9	9	0
Overall Dimension Scores			Standard Scores			
Dominance-Submission	43	36	−7	56	49	−7
Love-Hostility	49	48	−1	63	59	−4

patient's general picture of himself and of the ideal person. These scores reveal that he consciously viewed himself as a more passive, submissive person after hearing the message and that his description of the ideal person changed in the same direction. On both dimensions the self and ideal descriptions changed in the same directions but the amount of change on the Love-Hostility dimension was less than on the Dominance-Submission dimension.

To summarize, the test results showed generalized improvement after the message was presented to the patient. He had lower scores on all but one of the MMPI clinical scales when retested. These changes on the MMPI were accompanied by evidence of reduced defensiveness, faking, and repression. The multilevel measures revealed enhanced insight, more accurate self-perception, increased self-acceptance, and a reduction in the discrepancy between the patient's conscious ideals and his overt behavior. Covert preconscious attitudes of skepticism and distrust diminished, having been supplanted by a readiness to enter actively into a working relationship with a therapist. These changes on objectively scored tests could not have taken place unless presentation of the message under deprivation conditions had induced fundamental changes in the patient's basic attitudes and personality.

LONG RANGE FOLLOW-UP AND APPRAISAL

In addition to bringing about the personality changes described in the preceding section, the message presented to the patient was intended to serve a second aim. This was to foster understanding, readiness for, and acceptance of psychotherapy by providing him with a clear explanation of the rationale of psychotherapy and the goals he could expect to achieve.

In evaluating effectiveness in achieving the second aim, the patient's entire case history was reviewed thirty months after the date the message was presented. The case history indicated that as of the time of

follow-up he had been admitted to the hospital as an inpatient six times during the preceding ten years. He had been treated on the medical and psychiatric services for a psychophysiological gastrointestinal reaction and a chronic anxiety reaction. During three of those six admissions he had received a course of insulin therapy.

The patient was placed in sensory deprivation and presented with the message shortly before being discharged from his fifth admission. Since the patient had received only brief psychotherapy during previous admissions, plans were made for more intensive individual therapy on an outpatient basis. It was hoped that if he could be persuaded to begin a more intensive program of individual therapy contacts, he might be enabled to make a better adjustment outside the hospital and thereby have less future need for hospitalization. The entire program of research in therapeutic uses of sensory deprivation had been organized so as to permit coordination with other hospital treatment programs in cases such as this.

Immediately after posttesting on the day following presentation of the message, the patient had his first regularly scheduled therapy session. His reaction to the message revealed that it had indeed produced a great effect on him. He commented on it at length during the first session, telling his therapist that he had long known implicitly the things stated in the message, but that this was the first time he had ever had his own personality make-up and areas of conflict described to him in such graphic detail. Presentation of the message under sensory deprivation conditions which maximized his receptiveness had served to exclude irrelevant topics and to focus all his attention on the most important problem areas at the outset of therapy. One may readily appreciate the relative efficiency of this procedure compared with the customary passive techniques of psychotherapy, such as free association, nondirective Rogerian counseling, and orthodox Freudian psychoanalysis.

How effective were these novel procedures when judged in the light of the entire case history? According to the history the patient had been admitted to the hospital as an inpatient three times during a thirteen-month period immediately before the message was presented. This occurred just before he was discharged from the last of those three admissions (which was the fifth admission since his hospital record first began). After his discharge he continued in weekly outpatient psychotherapy sessions for a period of sixteen months. He was readmitted once again to the hospital for the last time a year later, following a recurrence of his previous symptoms of nausea and vomiting and subjective complaints of depression. When admitted for the last time he remained in the hospital about six weeks, still continuing psychotherapy with the same therapist while an inpatient. After discharge from his last admission he stayed in therapy as an outpatient for another two months, at which time he no longer felt the need for therapy. He then terminated by mutual agreement with his therapist after a total of sixteen months. When the case history was reviewed fourteen months after termination of therapy the patient had remained out of the hospital for the entire period since termination. By contrast, he had been admitted to the hospital as an inpatient three times in thirteen months before presentation of the message.

During previous admissions the patient had never received or indicated any particular interest in more than brief psychotherapy. But after he was placed in sensory deprivation and presented with the message individually prepared for him, he remained in psychotherapy for a full sixteen months. Whereas he had had three admissions during the thirteen months preceding this experience, he had only one admission in the entire thirty months afterward.

Obviously the patient could have been exposed to other influences that might have contributed to this reduced need for hospitalization. Any conclusion that this one experience could have contributed to keeping him in therapy and out of the hospital is of course a conjecture on the basis of the infor-

mation available. Nevertheless, it does not seem unreasonable to infer from the case history data and the objective psychological test results that the novel procedures used brought about lasting beneficial effects.

Since these procedures are simple, inexpensive, free of medical risks and hazards, and require little special equipment, staff, or hospital facilities for their use, there seem to be no significant contraindications to their use in facilitating therapeutic changes in any psychiatric setting. Widespread adoption of procedures like those described in this case study could result in great savings through facilitating the fundamental therapeutic processes of insight and self-awareness, while at the same time providing substantial benefits to patients. Their potential utility could be profitably considered in every case where any form of psychotherapy, counseling, or personal guidance seems called for.

REFERENCES

ADAMS, H. B. "Mental illness" or interpersonal behavior? *Amer. Psychologist,* in press.

ADAMS, H. B., R. N. CARRERA, G. D. COOPER, R. G. GIBBY, and H. R. TOBEY. Personality and intellectual changes in psychiatric patients following brief sensory deprivation. (Abstract) *Amer. Psychologist,* 1960, **15,** 448.

ADAMS, H. B., R. N. CARRERA, and R. G. GIBBY. *Behavioral reactions of psychiatric patients to brief sensory deprivation.* Cleveland: Convention Reports Duplication Services, 1960.

ADAMS, H. B., M. H. ROBERTSON, and G. D. COOPER. Facilitating therapeutic personality changes in psychiatric patients by sensory deprivation methods. Paper read at XVIIth International Congress of Psychology, Washington, August, 1963.

COOPER, G. D. Changes in ego strength following brief perceptual and social deprivation. Unpublished doctoral dissertation, Duke University, 1962.

COOPER, G. D., H. B. ADAMS, and L. D. COHEN. Changes in personality after sensory deprivation. *J. nerv. ment. Dis.,* in press.

COOPER, G. D., H. B. ADAMS, and R. G. GIBBY. Ego strength changes following perceptual deprivation. *Arch. gen. Psychiat.,* 1962, **7,** 213–217.

FISKE, D. W. Effects of monotonous and restricted stimulation. In D. W. Fiske and S. R. Maddi (Eds.) *Functions of varied experience.* Homewood: Dorsey Press, 1961, 106–144.

GIBBY, R. G., and H. B. ADAMS. Receptiveness of psychiatric patients to verbal communication. *Arch. gen. Psychiat.,* 1961, **5,** 366–370.

GIBBY, R. G., H. B. ADAMS, and R. N. CARRERA. Therapeutic changes in psychiatric patients following partial sensory deprivation. *Arch. gen. Psychiat.,* 1960, **3,** 33–42.

KUBZANSKY, P. E. The effects of reduced environmental stimulation on human behavior: a review. In A. D. Biderman and H. Zimmer (Eds.) *The Manipulation of Human Behavior.* New York: Wiley, 1961, 51–95.

LEARY, T. *Multilevel Measurement of Interpersonal Behavior.* Berkeley: Psychological Consultation Service, 1956.

LEARY, T. *Interpersonal Diagnosis of Personality.* New York: Ronald, 1957.

WEXLER, D., J. MENDELSON, P. H. LEIDERMAN, and P. SOLOMON. Sensory deprivation: a technique for studying psychiatric aspects of stress. *Arch. Neurol. Psychiat.,* 1958, **79,** 225–233.

16   EXPERIMENTAL ANALYSIS OF HYSTERICAL BLINDNESS

Operant Conditioning Techniques

John P. Brady • Detlev L. Lind

INTRODUCTION

The viewpoint adopted for experimental purposes in this study was that the behavior of an organism is generated and maintained chiefly by its consequences on the environment. Over a wide range of conditions, a hungry rat, placed in a so-called "Skinner box," will persist in pressing a bar if, as a consequence of this response, a pellet of food is delivered to it at least some of the time. This exemplifies the principle of reinforcement which is at the core of current

Archives of General Psychiatry, 1961, **4,** 331–339.

From the Institute of Psychiatric Research, Indiana University Medical Center.

This paper was read at the Irish Division Meetings of the Royal Medico-Psychological Association in Dublin, July 20, 1960.

behavior theory. Conditioning of this type is termed operant (instrumental) to distinguish it from respondent (classical Pavlovian) conditioning. The probability of a given response in relation to the conditions of reinforcement of that response has been the subject of much study by Skinner,[4] Ferster and Skinner,[2] and others. Recently, controlled experiments conducted with human subjects using cubicles analogous to the "Skinner box" have demonstrated the existence of these same relationships in human behavior and the feasibility of analyzing human behavior within this methodological framework.[3] However, the relationships between an organism's behavior, its environmental consequences, and the disposition or probability of the organism to repeat a particular response often are obscure in so complex a psychobiological unit as man. For example, when a man behaves in a given way, the most important consequence of his activity, from the standpoint of reinforcement, may be its effect on some part of his intricate social or intrapersonal environment. Further, the given behavior or its effect may be readily understood only in terms of its "symbolic meaning." Nevertheless, much of man's behavior, both normal and aberrant, can be analyzed in terms of these general principles and influenced by their systematic application.[5]

The present report concerns the application of operant conditioning methodology in the study of a patient with hysterical blindness. In the course of this study, the patient, who had been totally blind for 2 years, regained his sight. It is not the primary purpose of the present report to argue the utility of these techniques for the removal of hysterical symptoms or for psychiatric therapy generally. Rather, the intent is to demonstrate the unique advantages this methodological approach offers for the systematic analysis of symptomatic behavior within a controlled, experimental context. In the present instance, some of the variables of which the patient's seeing or not seeing were a function were studied by operant conditioning techniques. An attempt was made to influence his disposition to see by manipulating some of these variables in accordance with experimentally demonstrable principles. In the course of the study, note was taken of the patient's verbal and social behavior in addition to the operant response (pressing a button) being measured. Some of these clinical observations, elicited in part by the conditioning procedure, were quite understandable in terms of the conventional psychodynamic concept of hysteria.

REPORT OF CASE

The patient, now 40 years of age, was born on a farm in rural Indiana, the youngest of 4 children in a poor family. The father was described as an irresponsible man, who quit the family group entirely when the patient was 11, and has not been heard from since.

He depicts his mother as the strong and determining force in the family group especially with respect to him during his early years. It is of interest that the patient had 2 maternal aunts who were totally blind during their last years. He refers to them as "nice old ladies."

The patient was shy and retiring during his childhood and left school (the eighth grade) at the age of 16 because he "liked work better." He held a variety of jobs, chiefly unskilled, but never stayed at any more than a few months.

He was married in 1942, after a very brief courtship, to a woman who worked as a welder in the factory at which he also was employed. The patient describes her as "often nervous and upset," but it is clear that she makes the important decisions in the house and that he is greatly dependent on her. From his description of his married life, one gets the picture of almost constant harassment from his wife and mother-in-law. Nonetheless, he speaks of his wife only in the most endearing terms. They have 2 children, a boy 13 and a girl 17.

Shortly after his marriage, the patient, then 23, was drafted into the Army where he served for 3 years. He did not see active combat, but worked as a teletype operator and truck driver in the United States and England. One incident is of interest. While driving an Army truck in England, he had an accident with a civilian driving a sports car in which the civilian was seriously injured. He states that he can now recall nothing of the accident scene or the period of investigation by civilian and military authorities which immediately followed, although he himself was not injured in any way. This is one of several examples of the patient's ability to repress large areas of experience, visual and other, with remarkable facility. While still in the Army, the patient developed dendritic keratitis of the right eye, following a tonsillectomy. Corneal scarring resulted, and the visual acuity of the right eye was reduced to 20/80. Shortly after this, he was given a medical discharge from the Army and was awarded a small pension because of the loss of vision.

After release from service, the patient had a succession of semiskilled jobs, remaining at none for more than a year. He seemed to tolerate responsibility poorly and was very sensitive to criticism. During this period, there were 3 minor recurrences of his eye infection which were treated conservatively in the hospital. On each occasion, he requested an increase in his pension, but this was denied since the visual acuity of the affected eye had not decreased. Between his discharge from the Army in 1945 and the occurrence of his total blindness 12 years later, his general adjustment was poor. He depended greatly on public assistance and financial aid from relatives because of frequent periods of unemployment and poor planning in general.

Three days before Christmas in 1957, the patient, while shopping in a supermarket with his wife and mother-in-law, suddenly became totally blind in both eyes. He is able to recall few details of the episode, and no immediate precipitating event is apparent. It did occur at a time when his wife and mother-in-law were being more demanding than usual, requiring him to work nights and weekends at various chores under their foremanship. One immediate consequence of his blindness was, then, partial escape from this situation. The family group first interpreted the blindness in theurgic rather than medical terms and sought counsel from its Fundamentalist minister. Several days later, however, the patient was admitted to a veterans' hospital, where he remained for 2 weeks. Neurological and ophthalmological examinations were negative except for the small corneal scar in the right eye described previously. A diagnosis of total hysterical blindness was made. At the time, the patient did not seem greatly alarmed by his loss of sight, but instead had an attitude of patient forbearance. The obvious discrepancy between his report of total blindness and his ability to get about on the ward was apparent. He was not concerned with this, but felt hurt and unjustly accused when other patients pointed out this discrepancy to him. The nature of his illness was explained to him, and interviews under sodium pentothal were conducted in an effort to increase his vision. Blindness persisted, however. Immediately after release from the hospital, the patient applied for training for the blind through an appropriate public agency. Several months later, he was admitted to a veterans' diagnostic center, where several additional neurological and ophthalmological examinations were conducted with similar negative

results, and the diagnosis of hysterical blindness was confirmed. Although the blindness was not considered service-connected, a special pension was awarded because of his total disability. During the 18 months which intervened between his discharge from the diagnostic center and the beginning of the present treatment program, the patient was treated at an outpatient psychiatric clinic 2 hours weekly, without results. Various drugs were used as adjuvant treatments, as well as sodium pentothal interviews, but to no avail.

Because of the long history of generally poor adjustment, the fixity and duration of the symptoms, and the patient's resistance to psychotherapeutic intervention, a program of rehabilitation for the totally blind was recommended. His subsistence was derived from his government pension, financial aid from the local community to his underage children, some financial assistance from relatives, and other community resources on which he came to depend more and more. During these 18 months, he seldom left his house, but spent most of his time listening to radio or recorded reading supplied to him by an agency for the blind. Although he made some effort to learn Braille and to rehabilitate himself in other ways, he gradually came to depend on his wife more and more to meet his ordinary needs.

In summary, this is a man who developed total hysterical blindness which proved refractory to psychiatric intervention of various sorts for 2 years. Although the immediate precipitating cause of his blindness is not clear, one might conjecture, in dynamic terms, that somatically converted angry feelings toward a controlling wife upon whom he was greatly dependent were an important factor. Several items from the history could well support hysterical blindness as a symptom choice in this man: his exposure as a child to his 2 totally blind aunts; a recurrent eye infection which did leave him with some loss of vision and for which he was compensated financially; his immaturity, and his tendency to use amnesic repression as a means of adjustment. The long duration of the symptom despite psychiatric treatment may be accounted for, in part, by his passivity, the dependency needs which the symptom helped him satisfy, and the sizeable pension he was receiving for the disability.

BEHAVIORAL PRINCIPLES

A patient with total hysterical blindness is generally able to get around better than a patient with total blindness from an organic lesion. He states he can see nothing, yet is able to avoid large obstacles in walking, handle eating utensils, reach accurately for small objects, etc. This indicates that the hysterical patient does "see" in some sense. *Dynamically,* one would say that the patient reports being blind because he is consciously unaware of seeing. *Behaviorally,* one would say that the patient is not making full use of visual cues as evidenced by the fact that his behavior is not adequately under control. In order to study experimentally the effects of visual cues on the control of behavior, it is necessary first to generate some relatively stable behavior upon which the effect of visual stimuli can be measured. For this purpose, an operant conditioning situation was selected in which the behavioral requirement for reinforcement (reward) would be the spacing of responses (button-pressing) in a prescribed way. Specifically, the patient would be required to space his responses between 18 to 21 seconds. In other words, a response which followed the preceding response by less than 18 seconds or more than 21 seconds would not be reinforced, but would simply reset the apparatus for the start of another period. A response which followed the preceding response within the specified time interval (18 to 21 seconds) would be reinforced. Technically, such a schedule of reinforcement is termed a differential reinforcement of low rate (DRL) of 18 seconds, with a limited hold of 3 seconds.

It is convenient to study the performance of an individual on such a schedule by recording the actual intervals between responses (the inter-response times) over class intervals of 3 seconds each. The number of responses in each 3-second interval is recorded automatically and the number falling in the 18-to-21 second interval constitutes the patient's "score" for that session. After a stable distribution of inter-response times had been generated in this way, visual stimuli could be introduced to serve as cues for the correct spacing of responses. In other words, the patient can acquire more reinforcements (improve his score) by making use of visual cues. Hence, the effects of such cues on his operant performance and behavior in general can be systematically studied. One might wonder how so fixed a symptom as this man's blindness could be manipulated by simply differentially reinforcing responses that are contingent upon his making use of visual cues. However, use can be made of several behavioral principles demonstrable by the controlled study of operant behavior in lower animals.

Choice of Reinforcers

The potency of a reinforcer in maintaining behavior is a function of its importance to the organism. Rather than a single specific reinforcer, such as candy, multiple, generalized reinforcers were used. Use was made of the patient's great need for approval and sensitivity to criticism in bringing his behavior under experimental control. When he did well during testing, i.e., made a high score, he was given praise and approval. Conversely, when he did poorly, i.e., made a low score, disapproval and criticism were expressed toward him. These social reinforcers were supplemented by more tangible rewards and punishments, such as special privileges and trips to the hospital canteen, or withdrawal of these when he did poorly.

Immediacy of Reinforcement

The effectiveness of a reinforcer is a function also of the temporal proximity of the behavior and the reinforcing event. This is seen especially in the child who repeatedly eats green apples for the immediate pleasure it gives, although he knows they will give him a stomach-ache several hours later. Such behavior is characteristic also of the immature adult. Much of the present patient's financial and social difficulties are related to this. Hence, maximum use can be made of approval, praise, and other reinforcers by delivering them immediately after each testing session. The environmental consequences of his blindness which tend to favor its continuation are more remote in time.

Successive Approximation

This is the technique of developing complex responses in an organism by starting with some behavior in his present repertoire, and, by a series of small steps and the use of appropriate reinforcement, gradually approaching the desired behavior. Very complex responses involving difficult discriminations can be developed in lower animals by this technique. In the present study, the patient would be expected to show small but steady improvement in his score on successive sessions. His behavior first would come under the control of gross visual stimuli, and, later, after a series of small steps, under the control of finely discriminative stimuli.

Stimulus Generalization

After a stimulus has been conditioned to evoke a given response, similar stimuli tend to evoke the same response. In the present instance, it was anticipated that the control exerted over the patient's behavior by the visual stimuli in the experimental room would gradually generalize to visual stimuli produced in other situations (on the ward, home on visits, etc.). These visually cued responses then would be reinforced outside the testing room by the consequences of seeing which generally support this behavior in the community (e.g., enjoying television, ambulating easily, sight of a friend, etc.).

TESTING PROCEDURE

The present program was started 2 weeks after the patient entered the hospital for the fourth time since the onset of his blindness. At this time, he was complaining not of his blindness, but of a variety of minor gastrointestinal symptoms, without structure change. He was told that his digestive symptoms and blindness were related and that both would be treated by "reconditioning therapy." With no further explanation, the patient was started on a program of operant conditioning entailing two ½ hour sessions daily, 5 days a week.

At the start of each session, the patient was led into a small rectangular room and seated alone at a desk. His hand was placed on a small button mounted in a box. He was instructed to try to space his responses between 18 and 21 seconds as described earlier. For the remainder of the session, he was then left alone in the room. A correctly spaced response (18–21 seconds since the previous) caused a buzzer to sound, while an incorrectly spaced response (less than 18 or more than 21 seconds) caused no buzzer to sound but merely reset the apparatus for the start of another interval. After several practice sessions, visual stimuli of varying intensity and topography were introduced in the room in a manner described below. The entire experimental procedure was programmed automatically by appropriately designed switching circuits. This equipment, along with devices for recording the inter-response times (IRT's) automatically, was housed in an adjoining room.

RESULTS

It will be convenient to discuss the results of the study in 5 phases corresponding to 5 experimental conditions.

I. (Sessions 1 Through 6).

During Phase I, the illumination of the testing room was held constant, and there were no visual cues for the 18-to-21 second intervals.

After several days, the patient's performance became stable. Most responses fell within the correct interval, i.e., spaced 18-21 seconds apart, which rang the buzzer (reinforcement) and added to the patient's score for that day. Figure 1 shows the distribution of inter-response times (IRT's) for the sixth session. Note that in addition to the peak in the 18-to-21 second interval, a second peak appears in the first or 0-to-3 second interval. These first interval responses do not represent gross inaccuracies in the patient's effort to space his responses 18-21 seconds apart, but rather, "multiple" responses. On these occasions, the patient has pressed the button 2 or more times in rapid succession instead of making one discrete response. In some animal experiments, "multiple" responses on a schedule of this type (DRL) are considered to be related to the "emotionality" of the animal during testing. In the present study, they appeared to correlate with the patient's manifest anxiety. Indeed, the percentage of responses falling in this first interval may serve as an independent behavioral measure of the patient's affective state.

Clinically, the patient was moderately anxious during this phase of the study. The gastrointestinal symptoms which occasioned his admission to the hospital gradually disappeared, but there was no change in his blindness.

II. (Sessions 7 Through 16).

During this phase, a light bulb was present in the room located where it could not be seen directly by the seated patient. The voltage delivered to the bulb was reduced by means of a variable voltage transformer so that, when lit, the illumination in the room was increased by a barely perceptible amount. The light was programmed to go on after 18 seconds had elapsed since the last response and to go off again 3 seconds later. In other words, the appearance of the light corresponded exactly with the period during which a response would be reinforced (causing the buzzer to sound and adding to the patient's score for that session). The patient could greatly improve his score by

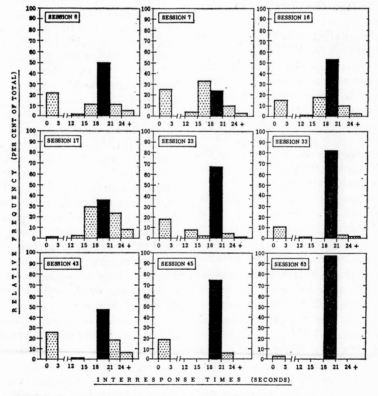

FIGURE I Relative frequency distributions of interresponse times (IRT'S) grouped into class intervals of 3 seconds each. Responses falling in the 18 to 21 second interval (black) are reinforced. IRT'S between 3 and 12 seconds (occurring only rarely) have been omitted.

making use of the visual cue thus provided.

Introducing this barely perceptible light had a profound influence on the patient's operant responding. Note the marked deterioration in the percentage of correct responses when the light was first introduced (Session 7 of Fig. 1). The introduction of this visual cue, then, was accompanied by deterioration rather than improvement in score. The greatest number of responses was made prematurely, in the 15-to-18 second interval. Premature responses reset the apparatus and hence postponed the appearance of the light. In other words, the approach of the crucial 18-to-21 second interval, now accompanied by a light, constituted a *preaversive situation*. By responding prematurely, the patient precluded the appearance of the light and thereby avoided an aversive experience. Note also the large number of responses in the first interval (multiple responses).

The *clinical* effect of introducing visual cues was equally dramatic. The patient came out of the seventh session trembling and perspiring and reported feeling "very frightened." He was unable to account for his marked distress, but reported simply that he suddenly became very afraid during the testing session. He gave no indication of being consciously aware of a light in the room. While still very apprehensive, at the end of the session, the patient made some spontaneous comments regarding his relationship with his wife. He recounted several episodes in which he became extremely angry at her.

With reassurance, the patient returned to the testing situation the next day, and his score gradually improved again in the sessions which followed. By the 12th session, the percentage of correct responses was back to the level obtained before the light was introduced (Phase I). There was also less anxiety. He then seemed to reach a plateau, with about 50% of his responses correctly spaced (as in Session 16, Fig. 1). In an effort to account for the patient's failure to improve his score beyond that obtained when no light was present (Phase I), he was observed

directly during Session 16. This was done without his knowledge by means of a peephole drilled in the wall of a closet in the room. He was observed to be resting his head on the table, his eyes covered by his forearm, during the entire session. In other words, he learned to avoid the now aversive and anxiety-provoking light by the simple expedient of covering his eyes. Since he was not told that a visual cue would be provided, and was not "consciously aware" of the light, this was acceptable and appropriate behavior in the situation.

III. (Sessions 17 Through 23).

It was decided to place the light at its full intensity (about 100 watts) in clear view in front of the patient and to tell him of its presence. He was told that the light would help him determine when to press the button and eventually enable him to make a perfect score and to see normally again. He expressed doubt about regaining his sight, but agreed to the new testing arrangements. Again, the light went on only during the 3-second interval during which a response would be reinforced.

Figure 1 shows the distribution of IRT's for the first session under these conditions (Session 17). Again, the number of correctly spaced responses fell (36% of total). The patient expressed concern over his poor performance and sought approval; he did not appear more anxious than usual, however. In the new situation making the presence of the visual cues known to the patient seemed to avoid the recurrence of anxiety, even though the performance was disrupted as before. The percentage of multiple (first-interval) responses was small, again in keeping with the level of overt anxiety present.

By making continued approval and acceptance contingent upon a continually improving score, the patient's percentage of correct responses gradually increased. In Session 23, 67% of his responses were correctly spaced (Fig. 1), but he was still unaware of seeing. He accounted for his high percentage of correctly spaced responses by reporting that he could feel the heat thrown off by the light bulb when it came on. This was clearly an unconscious rationalization for his use of visual cues, however, since the temperature changes were too small to be detected. There was some return of anxiety, again reflected in the percentage of 0–3 second IRT's.

IV. (Sessions 24 Through 45).

It was decided to decrease the intensity of the light by means of the variable voltage transformer in the circuit. The patient was told that this would be done gradually, so that he would switch over from feeling the heat of the bulb (which he admitted would become too small to be detected) to seeing it. As rewards continued to be delivered or withdrawn in accordance with his performance the patient's score continued to improve while the intensity of the light was reduced in small decrements. Eighty-two per cent of his responses were correctly spaced in Session 33 (Fig. 1).

The patient's score continued to improve in the sessions which followed.[1] His adjustment on the ward and his relationships with others also improved. He became less defensive about his blindness and less guarded in his behavior, entering into ward activities and aiding the nurses in various chores. Although he still reported seeing nothing, he used visual metaphors with increasing frequency, especially in the context of angry feelings toward his wife or mother-in-law. For example, he frequently spoke of not "seeing eye to eye" with his wife or having felt so angry toward her he "couldn't see straight."

The patient's operant behavior changed abruptly in Session 43 (Fig. 1). The percentage of responses during the correct interval

[1] During four of the sessions (No.'s 34, 40, 49, and 55) the interval that was reinforced, and the corresponding visual cues, was varied randomly among the 15-to-18, 18-to-21, and 21-to-24 second intervals to ascertain that the patient was not relying on the temporal cue of 18 seconds to guide his responses. Since the patient obtained a high score during these sessions also, reliance on a temporal cue was ruled out.

dropped to half its previous value (48%), and the number of multiple responses (first-interval) rose sharply. At the end of the session, the patient came out of the room exclaiming that he could see the light. He appeared both anxious and exhilarated, and sought praise and approval for his accomplishment. He accounted for his poor score during this session despite his awareness of visual cues by stating that he felt almost paralyzed by the light. His score improved rapidly over the next 2 sessions, however, and he became less anxious (Session 45, Fig. 1).

V. (Sessions 46 Through 63).

Now that the patient was able to make use of the visual cues provided by the 40-watt bulb on the desk in front of him, it was decided to introduce more difficult discriminative stimuli. At first, a stimulus board of 4 small lights mounted in a row was substituted for the single large bulb. This was programmed so that a change in pattern of the lights (the end two going off and the middle two coming on) signaled that 18 seconds had elapsed since the previous response. After this, a stimulus panel was used which consisted of a small pane of translucent glass on which various geometrical designs could be projected. With each change in experimental conditions, the correct spacing of responses was contingent upon making finer visual discriminations. With each new discriminative problem, the patient's performance was poorer for a few sessions and then gradually improved. Figure 1 shows the distribution of IRT's for the patient's last session (No. 63), in which a difficult visual discrimination was used. Except for a few multiple responses, all the presses were separated by 18–21 seconds, indicating a reinforcement on each occasion. The formal operant sessions were discontinued at this point.

During this phase of the study, the patient's clinical condition continued to improve. He used the visual modality (and was aware of seeing) more and more on the ward and at home during visits. After operant conditioning was discontinued, more conventional therapy was instituted. This consisted largely of support and efforts to rehabilitate him socially and vocationally.

COMMENT

In this study a chronic hysterical symptom has been analyzed and manipulated by operant conditioning techniques. The experimental program was such that the number of correctly spaced responses served as an index of the patient's use of visual cues and the number of multiple (first interval) responses a behavioral measure of his anxiety.

When visual cues were first introduced in the testing situation, profound effects were noted in the patient's clinical condition and operant behavior which are of interest from a psychodynamic point of view. Modern psychoanalytic theory would regard the patient's blindness as a manifestation of repression and his relative freedom from overt anxiety as an indication of the "success" of this repression. Put another way, anxiety maintains the repression, and any threat to this repressive defense would be accompanied by an increase of anxiety. In the present study, the patient was only moderately anxious in the testing situation when the spacing of responses was not cued by visual stimuli (Phase I). However, when such cuing was first introduced in Phase II, the responses were reinforced only in the presence of a visual stimulus, the coincidence of light and response simulated the visual *control* of his responses, and intense anxiety was observed. It may be argued that the patient's repression was weakened momentarily and anxiety was generated. As mentioned earlier, the aversive property of the light is evidenced by the shift in mode of the distribution of the IRT's to the earlier 15-to-18 second interval (Session 7 of Fig. 1). The patient's spontaneous remarks at this time suggested the areas of life experience and feelings which occasioned the development of the neurosis. This was confirmed by later clinical observations. These findings would seem to corrobo-

rate experimentally the dynamic view of hysterical blindness as a manifestation of repression, which, in turn, is maintained by anxiety.

In Phase III the patient was told that visual cues would be present. Again a disruption in performance was seen but little anxiety. It appears that alerting the patient to the presence of the light facilitated its repression and little anxiety was generated. In the sessions that followed the patient's behavior came more and more under control of visual cues; anxiety gradually mounted again and he defended himself for a time against conscious awareness of the cues by the rationalization that he could feel the bulb's heat. When he finally reported seeing, he was intensely anxious for a short time. After this it was possible to bring the patient's responding under finer and finer visual stimulus control until a high degree of visual acuity was demonstrated. This generalized to outside the testing situation.

The issue of therapy per se has been largely omitted by intention, but a few comments are in order. Eysenck[1] has recently reviewed the treatment of neurotic symptoms by techniques derived from learning theory, and Walton and Black [6, 7] have reported on the treatment of hysterical aphonia and other disorders by conditioning techniques, but within a different theoretical framework than the present essay. The treatment of psychiatric disorders by operant conditioning techniques is being studied at several centers in the United States. In the present study, it might be argued that the whole testing procedure constituted "psychotherapy" in the broad sense of the term, and that the specific conditioning procedures were incidental. This argument would be more persuasive, however, had the patient not proved so refractory to the many, but more usual, psychotherapeutic measures that were taken over a long period. Further, the systematic reappearance of anxiety, the occurrence of preaversive avoidance behavior, and the evolution of behavior clearly under the control of environmental cues support the authors' contention that return of visual function was specifically related to the events programmed in the testing procedure. Once visual function was regained by the process of successive approximation described earlier, the patient was amenable to more conventional rehabilitative techniques. For a time he worked at a community rehabilitation center during the day and stayed at the hospital at night. Seven months ago he was discharged from the hospital and returned to his own community.

He now returns to the hospital laboratory at monthly intervals for follow-up evaluation and general support; he is in on other treatment at this time. For several months his visual ability has been unchanged. On testing he is able to read small case newspaper print, to identify geometrical patterns, and to identify small objects. In a social situation, his performance is more variable. Sometimes he is slow to recognize the faces of persons who knew him when he was blind. Also, in the presence of these same persons, he walks with the awkward gait he exhibited when totally blind. Perhaps a more meaningful index of his present clinical condition, however, is his performance in the everyday business of living. He is gainfully employed in his community (as a switchboard operator), and is managing his family responsibilities and other affairs in a satisfactory manner. It is now 13 months since he first reported seeing.

SUMMARY

An experimental analysis of hysterical blindness by operant conditioning techniques is reported to illustrate the utility of this method for the study of psychiatric conditions. Clinical data, in part evoked by the conditioning procedure, also are reported. These are usually conceptualized within a "psychodynamic" framework. Some areas of *rapprochement* between concepts derived from dynamic theory and operant conditioning are suggested. Brief comments are made on some therapeutic aspects of the study.

REFERENCES

1. EYSENCK, H. J.: Learning Theory and Behaviour Therapy, J. Ment. Sci. 105: 61–75, 1959.
2. FERSTER, C. B., and SKINNER, B. F.: Schedules of Reinforcement, New York, Appleton-Century-Crofts, Inc., 1957.
3. LINDSLEY, O. R.: Characteristics of the Behavior of Chronic Psychotics As Revealed by Free-Operant Conditioning Methods, Dis. Nerv. Syst. 22: 66–78, 1960.
4. SKINNER, B. F.: The Behavior of Organisms, New York, Appleton-Century-Crofts, Inc., 1938.
5. SKINNER, B. F.: Science and Human Behavior, New York, The Macmillan Company, 1953.
6. WALTON, D., and BLACK, D. A.: The Application of Learning Theory to the Treatment of Stammering, J. Psychosom. Res. 3: 170–179, 1958.
7. WALTON, D., and BLACK, D. A.: The Application of Modern Learning Theory to the Treatment of Chronic Hysterical Aphonia, J. Psychosom. Res. 3:303–311, 1959.

17 ISOLATION OF A CONDITIONING PROCEDURE AS THE CRUCIAL PSYCHOTHERAPEUTIC FACTOR: A CASE STUDY

Joseph Wolpe

In a considerable number of publications (*e.g.*, 1-5, 7, 9, 11-13) it has been shown that methods based on principles of learning achieve strikingly good results in the treatment of human neuroses. Neuroses are usually characterized by persistent habits of anxiety response to stimulus situations in which there is no objective danger—for example, the mere presence of superiors, being watched working, seeing people quarrel, riding in an elevator. Since these habits of emotional response have been acquired by learning (10, 11) it is only to be expected that they would be overcome by appropriate procedures designed to bring about unlearning. Most of the procedures that have been used have depended upon inhibition of anxiety through the evocation of other responses physiologically incompatible with it (reciprocal inhibition); for each occasion of such inhibition diminishes to some extent the strength of the anxiety response habit (11).

When "dynamic" psychiatrists are confronted with the therapeutic successes of behavioristic therapy they discount them on the ground that the results are "really" due to the operation of "mechanisms" postulated by *their* theory: transference, insight, suggestion, or de-repression. Despite the fact that it is now manifest (14, 15) that the basic "mechanisms" of psychoanalysis have no scientifically acceptable factual foundations, their proponents can still content themselves with saying that the *possibility* of their operation has not been excluded. Resort to this kind of comfortable refuge would be

undermined if study of the therapeutic course of individual cases were to show *both* that there is a direct correlation between the use of conditioning procedures and recovery and that "dynamic mechanisms" are *not* so correlated, either because they cannot be inferred from the facts of the case or because even when they might be inferred they have no temporal relation to the emergence of change.

The case described below was made the subject of variation of several of the factors that are alleged from various standpoints to have therapeutic potency. A patient with a single severe phobia for automobiles was selected for the experiment because the presence of a single dimension of disturbance simplifies the estimation of change. It was found that a deconditioning technique—systematic desensitization (9, 11, 13)—alone was correlated with improvement, which was quantitatively related to the number of reinforcements given. At the same time, activities that might give any grounds for imputations of transference, insight, suggestion, and de-repression were omitted or manipulated in such a way as to render the operation of these "mechanisms" exceedingly implausible. Furthermore, the conduct of therapy in several series of interviews separated by long intervals had results incompatible with "spontaneous recovery"—a possibility that might have been entertained if improvement during the intervals had been as great as during the treatment periods; but in fact virtually no change occurred during the intervals.

This case incidentally illustrates how difficult it can be to find stimulus situations that evoke sufficiently low anxiety to enable

Journal of Nervous and Mental Disease, **134**, 316–329. Copyright ©, 1962. The Williams & Wilkins Co., Baltimore 2, Md. U.S.A.

commencement of desensitization, and how the details of procedure must be tailored to the needs of the case.

THE CASE OF MRS. C.

The patient, a 39-year-old woman, complained of fear reactions to traffic situations. Dr. Richard W. Garnett, Jr., a senior staff psychiatrist, had referred her to me after interviewing her a few times. I first saw the patient at the University Hospital on April 6, 1960. Briefly her story was that on February 3, 1958, while her husband was taking her to work by car, they entered an intersection on the green light. On the left she noticed two girls standing at the curb waiting for the light to change, and then, suddenly, became aware of a large truck that had disregarded the red signal, bearing down upon the car. She remembered the moment of impact, being flung out of the car, flying through the air, and then losing consciousness. Her next recollection was of waking in the ambulance, seeing her husband, and telling him that everything was all right. She felt quite calm and remained so during the rest of the journey to the hospital. There she was found to have injuries to her knee and neck, for the treatment of which she spent a week in the hospital.

On the way home, by car, she felt unaccountably frightened. She stayed at home for two weeks, quite happily, and then, resuming normal activities, noticed that, while in a car, though relatively comfortable on the open road, she was always disturbed by seeing any car approach *from either side,* but not at all by vehicles straight ahead. Along city streets she had continuous anxiety, which, at the sight of a laterally approaching car less than half a block away, would rise to panic. She could, however, avoid such a reaction by closing her eyes before reaching an intersection. She was also distressed in other situations that in any sense involved lateral approaches of cars. Reactions were extraordinarily severe in relation to making a left turn in the face of approaching traffic on the highway. Execution of the turn, of course, momentarily placed the approaching vehicle to the right of her car, and there was a considerable rise in tension even when the vehicle was a mile or more ahead. Left turns in the city disturbed her less because of slower speeds. The entry of other cars from side streets even as far as two blocks ahead into the road in which she was traveling also constituted a "lateral threat." Besides her reactions while in a car, she was anxious while walking across streets, even at intersections with the traffic light in her favor, and even if the nearest approaching car were more than a block away.

During the first few months of Mrs. C.'s neurosis, her panic at the sight of a car approaching from the side would cause her to grasp the driver by the arm. Her awareness of the annoyance this occasioned subsequently led her to control this behavior, for the most part successfully, but the fear was not diminished.

Questioned about previous related traumatic experiences, she recalled that ten years previously a tractor had crashed into the side of a car in which she was a passenger. Nobody had been hurt, the car had continued its journey, and she had been aware of no emotional sequel. No one close to her had ever been involved in a serious accident. Though she had worked in the Workmen's Compensation Claims office, dealing with cases of injury had not been disturbing to her. She found it incomprehensible that she should have developed this phobia; in London during World War II, she had accepted the dangers of the blitz calmly, without ever needing to use soporifics or sedatives.

She had received no previous treatment for her phobia. During the previous few days, she had told her story to Dr. Garnett; and then a medical student had seen her daily and discussed various aspects of her life, such as her childhood and her life with her husband—all of which she had felt to be irrelevant.

The plan of therapy was to confine subsequent interviews as far as possible to the procedures of *systematic desensitization,* and to omit any further history-taking, probing, and analyzing. Systematic desensitization (1, 3–5, 9–13) is a method of therapy that has its roots in the experimental laboratory. It has been shown experimentally (6, 8, 11) that persistent unadaptive habits of anxiety response may be eliminated by counteracting (and thus inhibiting) individual evocations of the response by means of the simultaneous evocation of an incompatible response (reciprocal inhibition). Each such inhibition leads to some degree of weakening of the anxiety response habit.

In systematic desensitization, the emotional effects of deep muscle relaxation are employed to counteract the anxiety evoked by phobic and allied stimulus situations presented to the patient's *imagination*. Stimulus situations on the theme of the patient's neurotic anxiety are listed and then ranked according to the intensity of anxiety they evoke. The patient, having been relaxed, sometimes under hypnosis, is asked to imagine the weakest of the disturbing stimuli, repeatedly, until it ceases to evoke any anxiety. Then increasingly "strong" stimuli are introduced in turn, and similarly treated, until eventually even the "strongest" fails to evoke anxiety. This desensitizing to imaginary situations has been found to be correlated with disappearance of anxiety in the presence of the actual situation.

In the second interview, training in relaxation and the construction of hierarchies were both initiated. To begin with, Mrs. C. was schooled in relaxation of the arms and the muscles of the forehead. Two hierarchies were constructed. The first related to traffic situations in open country. There was allegedly a minimal reaction if she was in a car driven by her husband and they were 200 yards from a crossroads and if, 400 yards away, at right angles, another car was approaching. Anxiety increased with increasing proximity. The second hierarchy related to lateral approaches of other cars while that in which she was traveling had stopped at a city traffic light. The first signs of anxiety supposedly appeared when the

other car was two blocks away. (This, as will be seen, was a gross understatement of the patient's reactions.) The interview concluded with an introductory desensitization session. Having hypnotized and relaxed Mrs. C., I presented to her imagination some presumably neutral stimuli. First she was asked to imagine herself walking across a baseball field and then that she was riding in a car in the country with no other cars in sight. Following this, she was presented with the allegedly weak phobic situation of being in a car 200 yards from an intersection and seeing another car 400 yards on the left. She afterwards reported no disturbances to any of the scenes.

The third interview was conducted in the presence of an audience of five physicians. The Willoughby Neuroticism Test gave a borderline score of 24. (Normal, for practical purposes, is under 20. About 80 per cent of patients have scores above 30 [11].) Instruction in relaxation of muscles of the shoulder was succeeded by a desensitization session in which the following scenes were presented:

1. The patient's car, driven by her husband, had stopped at an intersection, and another car was approaching at right angles two blocks away.
2. The highway scene of the previous session was suggested, except that now her car was 150 yards from the intersection and the other car 300 yards away. Because this produced a finger-raising (signaling felt anxiety), after a pause she was asked to imagine that she was 150 yards from the intersection and the other car 400 yards. Though she did not raise her finger at this, it was noticed that she moved her legs. (*It was subsequently found that these leg movements were a very sensitive indicator of emotional disturbance.*)

Consequently, at the fourth interview, I subjected Mrs. C. to further questioning about her reactions to automobiles, from which it emerged that she was continuously tense in cars but had not thought this worth reporting, so trifling was it beside the terror experienced at the lateral approach of a car. She now also stated that *all* the car scenes imagined during the sessions had aroused anxiety, but too little, she had felt, to deserve mention. While relaxed under hypnosis, Mrs. C. was asked to imagine that she was in a car about to be driven around an empty square. As there was no reaction to this, the next scene presented was being about to ride two blocks on a country road. This evoked considerable anxiety!

At the fifth interview, it was learned that even the thought of a journey raised Mrs. C.'s tension, so that if, for example, at 9 a.m. her husband were to say, "We are going out driving at 2 p.m.", she would be continuously apprehensive, and more so when actually in the car. During the desensitization session (fourth) at this interview, I asked her to imagine that she was at home expecting to go for a short drive in the country in four hours' time. This scene, presented five times, evoked anxiety that did not decrease on repetition. It was now obvious that scenes with the merest suspicion of exposure to traffic were producing more anxiety than could be mastered by Mrs. C.'s relaxation potential.

A new strategy therefore had to be devised. I introduced an artifice that lent itself to controlled manipulation. On a sheet of paper I drew an altogether imaginary completely enclosed square field, which was represented as being two blocks (200 yards) long (see Figure 1). At the southwest corner (lower left) I drew her car, facing north (upwards), in which she sat with her husband, and at the lower right corner another car, supposed to be Dr. Garnett's, which faced them at right angles. Dr. Garnett (hereafter "Dr. G.") was "used" because Mrs. C. regarded him as a trustworthy person.

This imaginary situation became the focus of the scenes presented in the sessions that followed. At the fifth desensitization session, Mrs. C. was asked to imagine Dr. G. announcing to her that he was going to drive his car a half-block towards her and then proceeding to do so while she sat in her parked car. As this elicited no reaction, she was next made to imagine him driving one block towards her, and then, as there was again no

reaction, one and a quarter blocks. On perceiving a reaction to this scene, I repeated it three times, but without effecting any decrement in the reaction. I then "retreated," asking her to imagine Dr. G. stopping after traveling one block and two paces towards her. This produced a slighter reaction, and *this decreased on repeating the scene, disappearing at the fourth presentation.* This was the first evidence of change, and afforded grounds for a confident prediction of successful therapy.

At the sixth session, the imagined distance between Dr. G.'s stopping point and Mrs. C.'s car was decreased by two or three paces at a time, and at the end of the session

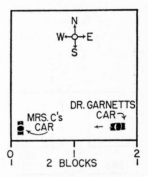

FIGURE I   Imaginary enclosed square where Doctor Garnett makes progressively closer advances to Mrs. C.'s car. (See text.)

he was able to stop seven-eighths of a block short of her (a total gain of about 10 paces). The following are the details of the progression. In parentheses is the number of presentations of each scene required to reduce the anxiety response to zero:

1. Dr. G. approaches four paces beyond one block (3).
2. Six paces beyond one block (3).
3. Nine paces beyond one block (2).
4. Twelve paces beyond one block, *i.e.,* one and one-eighth block (4).

At the seventh session, Mrs. C. was enabled to tolerate Dr. G.'s car reaching a point half a block short of her car without disturbance; at the eighth session, three-eighths of a block (about 37 yards); at the tenth, she was able to imagine him approaching within two yards of her without any reaction whatsoever.

The day after this, Mrs. C. reported that for the first time since her accident she had been able to walk across a street while an approaching car was in sight. The car was two blocks away but she was able to complete the crossing without quickening her pace. At this, the eleventh session, I began a new series of scenes in which Dr. G. drove in front of the car containing Mrs. C. instead of towards it, passing at first 30 yards ahead, and then gradually closer, cutting the distance eventually to about three yards. Desensitization to all this was rather rapidly achieved during this session. Thereupon, I drew two intersecting roads in the diagram of the field (Figure 2).

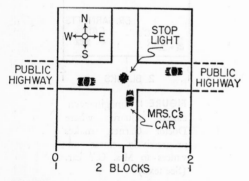

FIGURE 2 Imaginary enclosed square with crossroads and traffic light added. Other cars pass while Mrs. C.'s car has stopped at the red light. (See text.)

A traffic light was indicated in the middle, and the patient's car, as shown in the diagram, had "stopped" at the red signal. At first, Mrs. C. was asked to imagine Dr. G.'s car passing on the green light. As anticipated, she could at once accept this without anxiety; it was followed by Dr. G.'s car passing one way and a resident physician's car in the opposite direction. The slight anxiety this aroused was soon eliminated. In subsequent

scenes, the resident's car was followed by an increasing number of students' cars, each scene being repeated until its emotional effect declined to zero.

At the twelfth session, the roadway at right angles to Mrs. C.'s car was made continuous with the public highway system (as indicated by the dotted lines) and now, starting off again with Dr. G., we added the cars of the resident and the students, and subsequently those of strangers. Imagining two unknown cars passing the intersection produced a fair degree of anxiety and she required five presentations at this session and five more at the next before she could accept it entirely calmly. However, once this was accomplished, it was relatively easy gradually to introduce several cars passing from both sides.

We now began a new series of scenes in which, with the traffic light in her favor, she was stepping off the curb to cross a city street while a car was slowly approaching. At first, the car was imagined a block away, but during succeeding sessions the distance gradually decreased to ten yards.

At this point, to check upon transfer from the imaginary to real life, I took Mrs. C. to the Charlottesville business center and observed her crossing streets at an intersection controlled by a traffic light. She went across repeatedly with apparent ease and reported no anxiety. But in the car, on the way there and back, she showed marked anxiety whenever a car from a side street threatened to enter the street in which we drove.

Soon afterwards, the opportunity arose for an experiment relevant to the question of "transference." A medical student had been present as an observer during four or five sessions. Early in May I had to leave town for a week to attend a conference. I decided to let the student continue therapy in my absence. Accordingly, I asked him to conduct the fifteenth desensitization session under my supervision. I corrected his errors by silently passing him written notes. Since he eventually performed quite well, he agreed to carry on treatment during my absence, and conducted the eighteenth to the twenty-third sessions entirely without supervision. His efforts were directed to a new series of scenes in which, while Mrs. C. was being driven by her husband along a city street, Dr. G.'s car made a right turn into that street from a cross street on their left. At first, Dr. G. was imagined making this entry two blocks ahead, but after several intervening stages it became possible for her to accept it calmly only half a block ahead. The student therapist then introduced a modification in which a student instead of Dr. G. drove the other car. The car was first visualized as entering two blocks ahead and the distance then gradually reduced to a half-block in the course of three sessions, requiring 63 scene presentations, most of which were needed in a very laborious advance from three-quarters of a block.

At this stage, the therapist experimentally inserted a scene in which Mrs. C.'s car was making a left turn in the city while Dr. G.'s car approached from the opposite direction four blocks ahead. This produced such a violent reaction that the therapist became apprehensive about continuing treatment. However, I returned the next day. Meanwhile, the point had been established that a substitute therapist could make satisfactory progress. (Under the writer's guidance, but not in his presence, the student therapist went on to conduct two entirely successful sessions the following week.)

I now made a detailed analysis of Mrs. C.'s reaction to left turns on the highway in the face of oncoming traffic. She reported anxiety at doing a left turn *if an oncoming car was in sight.* Even if it was two miles away she could not allow her husband to turn left in front of it.

To treat this most sensitive reaction, I again re-introduced Dr. G. into the picture. I started by making Mrs. C. imagine (while hypnotized and relaxed) that Dr. G.'s car was a mile ahead when her car began the turn. But this was too disturbing and several repetitions of the scene brought no diminution in the magnitude of anxiety evoked. It seemed possible that there would be less anxiety if the patient's husband were not the driver of the car, since his presence at the time of the accident might have made him a

conditioned stimulus to anxiety. Thus I presented the scene with Mrs. C.'s *brother* as the driver of the car. With this altered feature, Dr. G.'s making a left turn a mile ahead evoked much less anxiety, and after four repetitions it declined to zero; we were gradually able to decrease the distance so that she could eventually imagine making the turn with Dr. G.'s car only about 150 yards away (see Table 1). Meanwhile, when she was able to "do" the turn with Dr. G. three-eighths of a mile away, I introduced two new left-turn series: a strange car approaching with her brother driving, and Dr. G. approaching with her husband driving—both a mile away initially. Work on all three series went on concurrently. When Mrs. C. could comfortably imagine her brother doing a left turn with the strange car five-eighths of a mile ahead, I resumed the original series in which her husband was the driver, starting with a left turn while the strange car was a mile ahead. This now evoked relatively little anxiety; progress could be predicted, and ensued. The interrelated decrements of reaction to this group of hierarchies are summarized in Figure 3.

Other series of related scenes were also subjected to desensitization. They are listed in Table 1, in order of commencement, but there was much overlapping of incidence. One comprised left turns *in the city* in front of oncoming cars. Since cars in the city move relatively slowly, she felt less "danger" at a given distance. At first, we dealt with left turns while an approaching car was about two blocks away, and in the course of several sessions gradually decreased the distance until Mrs. C. could comfortably "do" a left turn with the other car slowly moving 15 yards ahead. The series where Mrs. C. was crossing streets as a pedestrian was extended, and she was enabled in imagination to cross under all normal conditions. She reported complete transfer to the reality. A series that was started somewhat later involved driving down a through street with a car in a side street slowing to a stop. At first, the side street was "placed" two blocks ahead. The distance was gradually decreased as desensitization progressed, and eventually she could without anxiety drive past a car slowing to a stop. A series intercurrently employed to desensitize her in a general way to the feeling that a car was "bearing down upon her," was not part of any real situation. In our imaginary square field (Figure 1), I "placed" two parallel white lines, scaled to be about 20 feet long and 10 feet apart. During the session I said, "You are walking up and down along one white line and Dr. G. drives his car up to the other at one mile per hour. . . ." This was not disturbing; but at subsequent visualizings the speed was gradually increased and at an early stage the distance between the lines decreased to five feet. At four miles per hour there was some anxiety. This was soon eliminated, and several presentations of scenes from this series during each of 10 sessions made it possible for Mrs. C. calmly to imagine Dr. G. driving up to his white line at 18 miles per hour while she strolled along hers.

The total effect of desensitization to these interrelated series of stimulus situations was that Mrs. C. became completely at ease in all normal traffic situations—both in crossing streets as a pedestrian and riding in a car. Improvement in real situations took place in close relation with the improvements during sessions. A direct demonstration of the transfer of improvement with respect to crossing streets at traffic lights has been described above.

The patient's progress was slow but consistent. Because she lived about 100 miles away, her treatment took place episodically. At intervals of from four to six weeks she would come to Charlottesville for about two weeks and be seen almost every day. Noteworthy reduction in the range of real situations that could disturb her occurred in the course of each period of active treatment, and practically none during the intervals. She was instructed not to avoid exposing herself during these intervals to situations that might be expected to be only slightly disturbing: but if she anticipated being very disturbed to close her eyes, if feasible, for

she could thus "ward off" the situation. Every now and then, particular incidents stood out as landmarks in her progress. One day in late August, driving with her brother in a through street in her home town, she saw a car slowing down before a stop sign as they passed it. Though the car did not quite stop, she had no reaction at all, though gazing at it continuously. This incident demonstrated the transfer to life of the desensitization to the relevant hierarchy (No. 23) which had been concluded shortly before. Since then, similar experiences had been consistently free from disturbance.

At the conclusion of Mrs. C.'s treatment, she was perfectly comfortable making a pedestrian crossing even though the traffic was creeping up to her. Left turns on a highway were quite comfortable with fast traffic up to about 150 yards ahead. When the closest approaching car was somewhat nearer, her reaction was slight anxiety, and not panic, as in the past. In all other traffic situations her feeling was entirely normal. Another effect of the treatment was that she no longer had headaches due to emotional tension.

In all, 57 desensitization sessions were conducted. The number of scene presentations at a session generally ranged from 25 to 40. Table 1 records a total of 1491 scene presentations, which does not include a small number of test scenes that were not continued because they were too disturbing when presented. The last session took place on September 29, 1960. It was followed by the taking of Mrs. C.'s history, given below. It will be seen that it contains nothing to suggest that there were sexual problems underlying the automobile phobia.

When Mrs. C. was seen late in December, 1960, she was as well as she had been at the end of treatment. Her sexual relations with her husband were progressively improving. At a follow-up telephone call on June 6, 1961, she stated that she had fully maintained her recovery and had developed no new symptoms. Her relationship with her husband was excellent and sexually at least as satisfying as before the accident. A further call, on February 19, 1962, elicited the same report.

LIFE HISTORY

The patient was born in a small town in Virginia, the eldest of a family of five. Her father had died of heart disease in June, 1957. He had always been good to her as a child, and had never punished her. He had often embarrassed his family by getting drunk on weekends. The patient had felt very close to her mother, who was still living and had always been kind and loving, and punished the patient only occasionally. Mrs. C. had always got on well with her siblings. She could recall no traumatic childhood experiences. She had always been a good student and had liked school very much, participating in games and making friends easily. The only person whom she had especially disliked was a teacher who had once put a tape over her mouth for speaking in class. She graduated from high school at 17, spent two years in an office and then a year in college. In 1942, when 21, she had joined the U.S. Armed Forces and gone to England, where she had become engaged to an Air Force navigator who was later killed in action. She reiterated that during the blitz she had often been in danger, witnessed destruction and seen the dead and injured without any great distress. In December, 1945, returning to the United States, she had worked at an office job until 1957, when she had married.

Her first sexual feelings were experienced at the age of 12. She reported that she had never masturbated. From the age of 13 she had gone out in groups and at 17 begun individual dating. Her first serious attachment was to the airman who was killed, but she had seen little of him because of war conditions. After his death, she had lost interest for a time in forming other associations. On returning to the United States, she had resumed casual dating. Her next serious association was with her husband, whom she had met in 1955. They had married in May,

1957, about nine months before the accident. Until the accident, the marital relationship had been good. Sexual relations had been satisfactory, most often with both partners achieving orgasm. Since the accident, however, she had been negatively influenced by adverse comments that her husband had made about her disabilities, so that sexual behavior had diminished. Nevertheless, when coitus occurred, she still had orgasm more often than not.

DISCUSSION

Laboratory studies (6, 8, 11) have shown that experimental neuroses in animals are learned unadaptive habits characterized by anxiety that are remarkable for their persistence (resistance to the normal process of extinction). These neuroses can readily be eliminated through repeatedly inhibiting the neurotic responses by simultaneous evocations of incompatible responses (*i.e.,* by reciprocal inhibition of the neurotic responses) (6, 8, 11). The effectiveness of varied applications of this finding to human neuroses (*e.g.,* 1–5, 7–13) gives support to the view that human neuroses too are a particular category of habits acquired by learning.

In the systematic desensitization technique the effects of muscle relaxation are used to produce reciprocal inhibition of small evocations of anxiety and thereby build up conditioned inhibition of anxiety-responding to the particular stimulus combination. When (and only when) the evocations of anxiety are weakened by the counterposed relaxation does the anxiety response *habit* diminish. By systematic use of stimulus combinations whose anxiety-evoking potential is or has become weak, the habit strength of the whole neurotic theme is eliminated piecemeal.

The case of Mrs. C. illustrates with outstanding clarity how the course of change during systematic desensitization conforms to the expectations engendered by the reciprocal inhibition principle. Whenever a scene presented to the patient aroused a good deal of anxiety, that scene could be re-presented

TABLE I Summary of Data Concerning Hierarchies

No. of Hierarchy	Content of Hierarchy	No. of Presentations of Scenes from Each Hierarchy	Result
0	Baseball field (control scene)	1	No reaction
1	Approaching highway crossroads which another car approaches laterally (two distance variables—own distance and that of other car)	15	Nil
2	Stationary at city intersection while other cars approach (two blocks maximum)	2	Nil
3	About to be driven from country lodge—starting from distance of two blocks (temporal variable)	9	Nil
4	Approached by Dr. G.'s car on imaginary field (Fig. 1) starting two blocks away	41	+
5	As No. 4, but Dr. G. starts each advance from one block away	50	+
6	Dr. G. drives his car to pass in front of hers (decreasing passing distance, 30 yards to 3 yards)	10	+
7–8	Mrs. C. stopped by red in imaginary field (Fig. 2) and increasing variety and number of medical school cars pass on green	10	+
9–10	As No. 7 but the crossroad now continuous with public highway and increasing variety and number of strange cars pass (Fig. 2)	27	+
11	Walking across road at intersection while a car moves towards her (decreasing distances from 1½ blocks to 10 yards)	30	+
12	Goes through on green with increasing number of strange cars stationary at right and left	4	No disturbance from outset
13	As her car passes on green, Dr. G.'s car advances at side (decreasing distance from ½ block to 10 yards)	25	+
14	While Mrs. C.'s car moves slowly in town, Dr. G.'s car turns into her lane from side street (2 blocks to ¼ block) (Sessions by student, see text)	39	+
15	As No. 14, but strange car (2 blocks to ½ block) (Sessions by student, see text)	62	+
16	Dr. G.'s car makes left turn across path of her slowly moving car (2 blocks to ¾ block) (Sessions by student, see text)	22	+
17	As No. 16, but student's car (2 blocks to ¾ block) (Sessions by student, see text)	26	+
18	Mrs. C.'s car in city turns left while Dr. G. advances (Handled alternately by student and author) (6 blocks to 3¾ blocks)	22	+ with difficulty
19	On highway (Fig. 2) turns left in front of tractor moving 5 mph. (1 mile to ¼ block)	36	+
20	Turns left in car while at fixed distance of ½ block a car whose driver is instructed by Dr. G. is advancing. Its speed was gradually increased from 5 to 30 mph.	93	+

TABLE I—Continued

No. of Hierarchy	Content of Hierarchy	No. of Presentations of Scenes from Each Hierarchy	Result
21	Turns left while two strange cars advance a block ahead. Speed of the cars increased gradually from 15 mph. to 26 mph.	25	+
22	While driving in taxi in through street, sees a car moving very slowly to stop at intersection ahead. Distance decreased from 1 block to $\frac{5}{16}$ block	35	+
23	As No. 22, but the other car decelerates from normal speed. Distance gradually decreased from $\frac{1}{2}$ block to zero from line of intersection	102	+
24	Walking across intersection at green light, while car a block away approaches. Increasing speeds 10–20 mph.	5	+
25	Stepping off curb to cross at unguarded intersection while car on left approaches at 10 mph. Decreasing distance 1 block to $\frac{3}{8}$ block	137	+ very difficult progress from $\frac{1}{2}$ block on
26	Does left turn in city while a car approaches at 10 mph. Decreasing distance from $\frac{7}{8}$ to $\frac{5}{8}$ block	67	+ very difficult from $\frac{3}{4}$ block on
27	She walks back and forth in the imaginary enclosed field parallel to a white line up to which Dr. G. drives his car at 1 mph. Her distance from the line decreases from 10 yds. to $4\frac{1}{2}$ yds.	23	+
28	While she keeps constant parallel distance of 5 yds. from white line, Dr. G.'s speed increases from 1 to 18 mph.	68	+
29	Steps off curb at unguarded intersection while car on *right* approaches at 10 mph. Distances 1 block to $\frac{5}{8}$ block	14	+
30	On highway in car driven by brother, does left turn in face of approaching car driven by Dr. G. Distance between them decreases from 1 mile to 350 yards	70	+
31	As 30, but stranger drives other car. Distances from 1 mile to 150 yds.	126	+
32	As 30, but Mrs. C.'s husband drives her car. Distances from 1 mile to 175 yds.	117	+
33	As 30, but Mrs. C.'s husband drives her car and stranger drives the other. Distances from 1 mile to 150 yds.	100	+
34	In taxi that does U-turn while a car approaches in city. Distances 2 blocks to 1 block	6	+
35	Driven by husband does left turn in city in face of slowly oncoming car. Distances of $\frac{1}{2}$ block to 15 yds.	29	+
36	In sight of oncoming car, enters highway from side road after stopping. Distances $\frac{1}{4}$ to $\frac{1}{8}$ mile	43	+
	Total Scenes	1491	

a dozen times without diminution of the anxiety. On the other hand, if the initial level of anxiety was lower, decrements in its intensity were achieved by successive presentations. It is a reasonable presumption that, as long as evoked anxiety was too great to be inhibited by the patient's relaxation, *no change* could occur; but when the anxiety was weak enough to be inhibited, repeated presentations of the scene led to progressive increments of *conditioned inhibition* of the anxiety-response habit, manifested by ever-weakening anxiety-responding. At every stage, each "quantum" of progress in relation to the subject matter of the desensitization sessions corresponded in specific detail to a small step towards recovery in an aspect of the real life difficulty. The fact that change occurred in this precise way in itself almost justifies the elimination of various "alternative explanations."

Mrs. C. had a total of 60 interviews, at each of which, except the first two and the last, a desensitization session was conducted. Including the initial three which proved to be unusable, 36 hierarchies entered into the sessions. All of these, tabulated in Table 1, share the common theme of "car-approaching-from-the-side," but each has its own unique stimulus elements calling for separate desensitizing operations. The amount of attention a hierarchy needs is diminished by previous desensitization of other hierarchies that have elements in common with it. This is graphically illustrated in Figure 3. Hierarchies 30, 31, 32 and 33, each of which relates to turning left on the highway while another vehicle advances, differ, one from the next, in respect to a single stimulus condition and are in ascending order of anxiety arousal. Desensitization in overlapping sequences, starting with Hierarchy 30, shows parallel progressions. Now, desensitization of Hierarchy 33 was in fact first attempted before Hierarchy 30, from which it has three points of difference. At that time, presenting the approaching car at a distance of *one mile* evoked more anxiety than could be mastered by the patient's relaxation. But af-

ter Hierarchy 30 had been dealt with, and in Hierarchies 31 and 32, the "other car" could be tolerated at about one-half mile, it was possible to introduce Hierarchy 33 at three-quarters of a mile with very little anxiety. The increase in toleration was clearly attributable to desensitization to the stimulus elements that Hierarchy 33 *shared* with the three foregoing ones.

Figure 3 also illustrates the significant fact that *therapeutic change did not develop during the intervals when the patient was not receiving treatment,* and this was true even of reactions that were the main focus of treatment at the time. There is no drop, following the intervals, in the reactive level of any of the hierarchies represented. However, it is interesting to note that between July 2 and August 7 the reactive level of Hierarchy 31 has risen somewhat. This was not a "spontaneous" endogenously determined relapse, but due to the fact that, late in July, Mrs. C. had ridden in a taxi whose driver, despite her protests, had persisted in weaving among traffic at high speed. Immediately after this she was aware of increased reactivity. As can be seen, the lost ground was soon regained.

A question that may come to mind is this. What assurance did the therapist have of a correspondence between distances as imagined by Mrs. C. and objective measures of distance? The first, and most important answer is that only rough correspondence was necessary, since what was always at issue was *distance as conceived by the patient.* The second answer is that a firm anchoring referent was the agreement between patient and therapist that a city block in Charlottesville would be considered 100 yards in length. Similar considerations apply to Mrs. C.'s conceptions of speed.

Among other explanations that may be brought forward to account for the recovery, the only one that, even at face value, would seem to deserve serious consideration in this case is *suggestion.* We shall take this usually ill-defined term to mean the instigation of changes in the patient's behavior by means

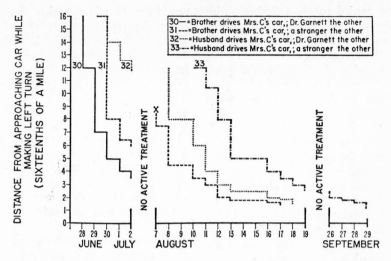

FIGURE 3   Temporal relations of "distances accomplished" in imagination in desensitization series 30, 31, 32 and 33. X: indicates some relapse in Hierarchy 31 following a taxi ride in which the driver insisted on exceeding the speed limit. The status of Hierarchy 32 was not tested before the relapse in 31 was overcome.

of verbal or nonverbal cues from the therapist. In all psychotherapy there is at least an implied suggestion of, "This will make you well." Getting well under the impulse of such a general suggestion would not be related to particular therapeutic maneuvers, as was the case with Mrs. C. Another kind of suggestion has the form, "You will get well if. . . ." In commencing Mrs. C.'s desensitization, the therapist was careful to say no more than, "I am going to use a treatment that may help you." He did not say under what conditions it would help. During the first few sessions (and also several times later) when the scenes presented aroused considerable anxiety, repetition brought about no decrement of reaction. Decrement was noted consistently when anxiety was less. To sustain a hypothesis that suggestion was behind this would require evidence of the very specific instruction—"You will have decreasing anxiety only to situations that produce little anxiety in the first place." In fact, no such instruction was in any form conveyed. The patient could only have become

aware *a posteriori* of the empirical relations of her changing reactions.

The relevance of the other "processes" —insight, de-repression, and transference— commonly invoked to explain away the effects of conditioning methods of therapy is negated by the absence of significant opportunity for such processes to have occurred. Any possible role of insight may be excluded by the fact that the only insight given to the patient was to tell her she was suffering from a conditioned fear reaction—and no change followed this disclosure. The possibility of de-repression may be ruled out by the nonemergence of forgotten material, and the de-emphasis of memory, even to the exclusion of the taking of a history during treatment —other than the history of the phobia's precipitation two years earlier and brief questioning about previous similar events, none of which had any effect on the neurosis.

The action of anything corresponding to "transference" is rendered implausible by the fact that interviews with the therapist led to improvement *only* when conditioning procedures were carried out in accordance with the requirements of reciprocal inhibition, and improvement was limited to the subject matter of the procedures of the time. Also, for a week, when the therapist was away, progress was effected by a medical student (20 years younger than the therapist) using the same conditioning techniques. In addition, the rather mechanical manner in which the sessions were conducted could hardly be said to favor the operation of transference effects; and certainly, the patient-therapist relationship was in no way ever analyzed. The third to the tenth interviews (and many others irregularly later) were conducted with the patient in full view of an unconcealed audience, without adverse effects on therapeutic progress.

The possibility of "spontaneous" recovery could be excluded with unusual confidence, since clinical improvement was a consequence of each of the periods of one to three weeks when the patient was being treated in Charlottesville, and was never noted during the four- to six-week intervals the patient spent at home.

"Secondary gain," so often invoked in explanations of post-traumatic neurotic reactions, can have no credence as a factor in this case, either as a maintaining force or as determining recovery by its removal, for the patient did not receive any financial benefit, came for treatment eight months before litigation, became well two months before litigation, and did not relapse after a disappointing decision by the court.

SUMMARY

The treatment by systematic desensitization is described of a severe case of phobia for laterally approaching automobiles. The initiation of desensitization required the introduction of imaginary situations in a fictitious setting in order to procure anxiety responses weak enough to be inhibited by the patient's relaxation. Recovery was gradual and at every stage directly correlated with the specific content of the desensitization

procedures. Certain operations that are usually performed in most systems of therapy were excluded or modified in order to remove any basis for arguing that the successful outcome was "really" due to insight, suggestion, de-repression, or transference.

REFERENCES

1. BOND, I. K. and HUTCHINSON, H. C. Application of reciprocal inhibition therapy to exhibitionism. Canad. Med. Assoc. J., 83: 23–25, 1960.
2. EYSENCK, H. J. *Behaviour Therapy and the Neuroses*. Pergamon Press, New York, 1960.
3. LAZARUS, A. A. New group techniques in the treatment of phobic conditions. J. Abnorm. Soc. Psychol. In press.
4. LAZARUS, A. A. and RACHMAN, S. The use of systematic desensitization in psychotherapy. S. Afr. Med. J., 31: 934–936, 1957.
5. LAZOVIK, A. D. and LANG, P. J. A laboratory demonstration of systematic desensitization psychotherapy. J. Psychol. Stud., 11: 238–247, 1960.
6. NAPALKOV, A. V. and KARAS, A. Y. Elimination of pathological conditioned reflex connections in experimental hypertensive states. Zh. Vyss. Nerv. Deiat. Pavlov., 7: 402–409, 1957.
7. RACHMAN, S. Sexual disorders and behavior therapy. Amer. J. Psychiat., 118: 235–240, 1961.
8. WOLPE, J. Experimental neuroses as learned behavior. Brit. J. Psychol., 43: 243–268, 1952.
9. WOLPE, J. Reciprocal inhibition as the main basis of psychotherapeutic effects. A. M. A. Arch. Neurol. Psychiat. 72: 205–226, 1954.
10. WOLPE, J. Learning versus lesions as the basis of neurotic behavior. Amer. J. Psychiat., 112: 923–927, 1956.
11. WOLPE, J. *Psychotherapy by Reciprocal Inhibition*. Stanford Univ. Press, Stanford, California, 1958.
12. WOLPE, J. Psychotherapy based on the

principle of reciprocal inhibition. In Burton, A. *Case Studies in Counseling and Psychotherapy*. Prentice-Hall, Englewood Cliffs, New Jersey, 1959.

13. WOLPE, J. The systematic desensitization treatment of neuroses. J. Nerv. Ment. Dis., **132,** 189–203, 1961.

14. WOLPE, J. The prognosis in unpsychoanalyzed recovery from neurosis. Amer. J. Psychiat., **118:** 35–39, 1961.

15. WOLPE, J. and RACHMAN, S. Psychoanalytic evidence: A critique based on Freud's case of Little Hans. J. Nerv. Ment. Dis., **131:** 135–148, 1960.

18 DESENSITIZATION OF A POST-TRAUMATIC PHOBIA

Malcolm Kushner

The patient was a seventeen-year-old youth whose automobile was struck at an intersection by a hit-and-run driver approximately one month prior to being seen. He was not physically injured beyond sustaining a bumped knee. Immediately following the accident the patient became very upset, tense, and anxious. His appetite was poor, he had considerable difficulty falling asleep, and had become obviously more grouchy and irritable. He was afraid to drive his car and while never a very good student, he began to do even more poorly. He complained of not being able to concentrate in school, being very much ill at ease, and his grades deteriorated so badly that just prior to coming for treatment he tried to enlist in the Air Force rather than be expelled from school. He failed to pass the Air Force mental examination, however.

When first seen the patient was very tense and quiet. Although his appearance and dress conformed to the usual stereotype of the "hot rodder" his behavior was quite reserved and polite. Being unable to drive a car presents a considerable difficulty for a young man today but for this patient it was even more of a problem inasmuch as he was a member of an organized drag-racing club, was an avid "hot rodder" and car tinkerer. Most of his energies, interests, and the object of his working after school had been

to support his car. To feel anxious around cars, uneasy when being driven by others, and to be unable to drive his own car was for this young man one of the most difficult situations imaginable and reflected the intensity of his fears. The patient had a prior history of being somewhat "wild" but he felt that he had settled down since meeting his girl friend whom he intended to marry. On first impression it was thought that there might be some ulterior motives contributing in part to the patient's reactions, that is, his talk of now leaving school in light of his poor prior performance and nonacademic interests and also considering the fact that his case was being handled by a lawyer. It was decided to utilize a systematic desensitization approach as a means of reducing this patient's high anxiety level and phobic reactions. As such, during the first session the patient was introduced to the concept of relaxation (Jacobson, 1938; Wolpe, 1958) and he was instructed briefly in some of the techniques involved. He was told to practice relaxation at home and to try to do this in varied settings as well. It was determined to see the patient three times a week.

The systematic desensitization approach as described by Wolpe (1958) consists of presenting to the patient a series of imaginary, graded situations representing his area of difficulty, beginning with one which is minimally anxiety-provoking, and gradually, step by step, approaching the situation which ordinarily evokes maximal anxiety in him. It is important that the increments be made in steps which at no time are overwhelmingly disturbing to the patient, or reinforcement of his fears is a possibility. An important element of procedure requires the patient to be completely relaxed as he imagines each situation. This is in recognition of Jacobson's findings (1938) that muscular relaxation inhibits anxiety thereby making its expression physiologically impossible. If the patient is completely relaxed and the situation elicits no anxiety, this, in effect, conditions him to tolerate the situation and enables him to proceed to the next step, and so forth, until he finally is able to visualize himself in the phobic situation without undue anxiety. Experience has shown that the nonanxious attitude in the imaginary situation transfers to the real life conditions eliminating the need to present the actual objects or situations. Exercises in deep relaxation are initially provided the patient to prepare him for this procedure. Wolpe and others (1958, 1960) utilize hypnosis or hypnoidal states as a means of inducing relaxation. As Wolpe noted, this writer has found that effective results may be obtained with subjects who are able to relax sufficiently without the need for hypnosis.

In the second session, three days later, the patient indicated feeling somewhat better. An effort was made to go into his background, particularly his schooling and aspirations, in somewhat more detail. He was not too bright and had just managed to get by in school prior to the accident. He now felt that he would not be able to pass the semester as a result of his problems and would probably have to drop out of school. He claimed that he could not concentrate in class, read magazines and, in general, was not attentive. A discussion with the patient's mother revealed essentially the same bits of historical information as reported by the patient. She also indicated that he appeared to be less anxious and fidgety and he appeared to her to be somewhat more relaxed since

initiating treatment. As a result of getting this additional information it was felt even more that secondary gains played an important role in the clinical picture. Nevertheless it was felt that the anxiety and the phobic condition could be diminished through relaxation and desensitization. Once again the relaxation procedures were described and practiced and the patient proved very adept at this. Because he was able to relax so readily the desensitization technique began at that session. Each imaginary situation was repeated once before proceeding to the next step. The initial instruction to the patient was to imagine himself looking at his car as it was prior to the accident. Since he did not report any feelings of tension or anxiety at this level, the next step was for him to imagine himself leaning against his car. From there the final situation for that session was for the patient to imagine himself sitting in his car without the ignition turned on. In each of these three imaginary situations the patient reported no feelings of tension or anxiety. Too rapid presentation of situations in the hierarchy was avoided to prevent the patient from being overwhelmed; hence this session was terminated after three steps in the series.

The third session was two days later and at the beginning the patient reported that he was able to fall asleep much more readily when he attempted to relax while in bed and that he felt much better, particularly in school. He stated that he had learned to relax before going into his classes and as a result had been able to take better notes. He reported getting a "C" on a quiz, which encouraged him considerably. Clinically he appeared to be more responsive and less agitated. The desensitization series continued, beginning this session with the last situation of the preceding meeting, that is, the patient sitting in his car with the ignition turned off. He then was asked to imagine himself sitting in his car and turning on the ignition, with the car stationary but the motor idling. He did not signal that he was upset by this thought and the next step was to have the patient imagine himself backing out of his driveway and turning the car so that he was in a position to drive off. Here, also, there was no signal of disturbance. The patient was then instructed to imagine himself driving the car around the block on which he lived and approaching an intersection on the way. At this point the patient showed some signs of growing tense although he did not signal this to the therapist. (Close observation of a patient will reveal changes in breathing rate, facial contortions, and so forth that are indicative of increased tension.) He was then told to "erase" the thought and relax. This same situation was repeated about one minute later and once more there was some evidence of disturbance although not as much as before. The desensitization was then stopped for the day.

On the first three visits the patient was accompanied by his mother who drove the car. On the fourth visit, which was ten days after first being seen, the patient drove through heavy downtown traffic accompanied by his girl friend. His face was much more relaxed, he smiled more frequently, was not irritable, and claimed that he was able to relax himself to sleep in five minutes or so. He also felt that he was able to concentrate in school. He no longer was thinking about quitting and, though worried about whether he would pass on his next report card, he felt that he could nevertheless get by the semester. The desensitization hierarchy of responses continued beginning this session with asking the patient to imagine himself driving along a straight road with no intersections. In the next step he was to imagine that he was approaching an intersection with no traffic appearing, and finally he was asked to imagine himself driving in the same situation but with another car nearing the intersection to his right at which there was a "Stop" sign. This was a reconstruction of the situation leading to his accident. At this point he reported only very little anxiety. The entire series was run through again and when the intersection situation was again presented the anxiety

was practically all gone. At this point the session was terminated. The next day the patient's mother spoke with the therapist and reported that his improvement was considerable, corroborating the patient's report.

In the fifth session, twelve days after first being seen, the patient indicated continued improvement. He reported feeling practically as well as before the accident. He stated that he had failed four subjects in school but he felt that he was now able to concentrate once more and confidently expected to pass the final six weeks. He appeared to be much more relaxed, was more spontaneous, and in general was responsive, alert, and happy. The desensitization program was resumed at this point, picking up with the patient imagining himself driving along a straight road with no traffic; following this, he was taken through various intersection situations none of which elicited anxiety. His progress was excellent in the office and he reported practically no difficulty while driving on the highway. It was decided to see him for one more session.

The sixth and final session was held two and one-half weeks following the first contact with the patient. At this time the patient considered himself ninety percent better. He had no trouble sleeping at night, his appetite was normal, he was no longer irritable, and his concentration in school had improved considerably. Relaxation techniques were reinforced at this last session and he was instructed in the various ways that he could bring these to bear and thus make his everyday activities more effective. The patient was discharged and a three-month follow-up revealed still further improvement with no exacerbation of his earlier symptoms.

It was felt that the rapid remission of his symptoms was mainly due to the quickness with which the patient adapted to the relaxation principles as well as to the acute nature of the problem. If, as was suggested above, secondary gain factors were involved in this case, they played no significant role in offsetting the effectiveness of the procedure used.

REFERENCES

JACOBSON, E. *Progressive relaxation.* Chicago: University of Chicago Press, 1938.

LAZARUS, A. A. and S. RACHMAN. The use of systematic desensitization in psychotherapy. *S. Afr. Med. J.,* 1957, **31**: 934–937.

WOLPE, J. *Psychotherapy by reciprocal inhibition.* Stanford, Calif.: Stanford University Press, 1958.

WOLPE, J. Reciprocal inhibition as the main basis of psychotherapeutic effects. In H. J. Eysenck (Ed.), *Behaviour therapy and the neuroses.* New York: Pergamon, 1960.

19 BEHAVIOR MODIFICATION IN ADULT PSYCHIATRIC PATIENTS[1]

Edward S. Sulzer

CASE NUMBER ONE

The patient was referred because of a long history of frequent alcoholic intoxication and the patient referred to himself as an "alcoholic." While being drunk frequently had aversive consequences and the patient would vow to stop drinking, no reduction in alcoholic intake had taken place. Traditional psychotherapy had been attempted briefly by another therapist without success.

The primary goal of therapy was a marked reduction or complete cessation of alcoholic beverage drinking behavior. As the patient rarely drank liquor alone, solitary drinking did not appear to be a serious problem. Aversive conditioning with emetine was proposed to the patient but he rejected this form of treatment because his job made him frequently enter taverns and cafes where alcoholic beverages were served. The patient did not wish to change his job or move to a "dry" community.

Further discussion with the patient suggested that he was concerned about losing the friendship of two men he had known throughout life who now found his frequent drunken states so objectionable that they avoided his company. While neither friend was a teetotaler, neither drank heavily. It appeared likely that the cooperation of the two friends might be enlisted to *create a situation in which social reinforcement for non-alcoholic drinking might be developed.*

The patient contacted his friends who agreed to the following plan. After working hours, they would meet in a conveniently located tavern where the three of them would drink for a time before going home. The patient could only order and drink soft beverages. If he ordered or drank hard liquor, the friends would leave immediately. However, the patient's friends might drink anything they wished. This plan was to continue on an at least once a week basis for an undetermined period of time. Also, the patient agreed to invite the friends to his home on all occasions that might call for alcoholic beverages to be served to guests and the friends agreed to come and remain only as long as the patient took no alcohol. His friends would also invite the patient to their

[1] The cases described in this paper were seen in the context of the form of psychotherapy described in: Sulzer, E. S. Reinforcement and the therapeutic contract. *J. counsel. Psychol.,* 1962, **9**, 271–276.

homes fairly frequently but would not serve him alcohol.

The first planned accompanied "drinking" occurred without incident and the patient reported that his initial discomfort quickly disappeared. The bartender, somewhat unexpectedly, served as an additional source of social reinforcement by acting more friendly than he had during the patient's previous visits. It appeared that the bartender also valued the patient's sobriety and sober behavior more than the selling of higher priced drinks, an impression subsequently confirmed by a discussion between the bartender and one of the patient's friends.

The following day, the patient, following the therapist's instructions, planned no business visits to taverns but restricted himself to other eating places not serving hard liquor. The day was without major incident although the patient reported drinking more coffee than usual. For business reasons, the patient had to visit taverns on the following several days and drank liquor again but less than his previous amounts. The last day of that week, the patient contacted his friends to meet him for a "drink" which they did. The patient was found to have already drunk several glasses of liquor when they arrived. The friends were uncertain as to whether they should stay but decided to remain with the patient while he drank other than hard liquor.

As he "sobered up," the patient reported that he felt quite comfortable and felt little desire to drink with his friends present. After almost two hours, the group broke up. That was the last day this patient has been known to drink any alcoholic beverage.

The patient continued his routine business visits to taverns and reported that bartenders generally seemed friendlier to him than they had been when he had come before and had a few drinks. The patient's friends continued to meet with him periodically for "drinks" but this soon ceased as they now tended to meet in places other than taverns.

During this period, the therapist met with the patient twice weekly. During these interviews, the therapist verbally and facially expressed approval of reported nondrinking behavior. Also during this time, the patient and his wife considered moving to a somewhat larger apartment in a different neighborhood. The therapist supported the proposed move because most of the patient's present neighbors responded to him and his family in a way that strained interpersonal relationships and made sobriety more difficult.

The move was made a little over a month after the beginning of therapy and appeared to have very favorable consequences. The patient continued his sober behavior and he made contacts with new neighbors whose response to him did not include the kinds of behaviors he had previously met in his old neighborhood where most people reportedly acted with mild disgust and open disapproval of him.

CASE NUMBER TWO

The patient came for help for a variety of problems including marked difficulty in studying, poor relations with a supervisor on the job, and a belief that he was a poor father to his child.

More specifically, the studying difficulty appeared to be the patient's inability to remain reading and note-taking for periods either long enough or frequent enough to maintain high grades in his graduate courses. The usual environment for studying was the young couple's living room. Here the student would generally sit in a comfortable chair with apparently sufficient illumination. A clip-board was used for note-taking. The patient reported that he could read and study this way for about twenty minutes to a half hour before he found that concentration was impaired and he would become restless. He would try to continue reading but usually found these attempts unsuccessful and would either go out, join his wife in watching television in their bedroom, or pick up some nonschool material to look at. Rarely did he return to his studying that day or evening.

A program was devised with the patient to change his location and way of studying. One of the reading rooms of the university's library was selected because of its relative quiet and absence of distracting visual stimuli. The schedule included going to the library daily for a week to read six pages of assigned material. The student was instructed to read no more or less than this amount of text material each day of the week. He was not to study at home and he had to arrange with an instructor to take an incomplete grade for one course because the material to be covered could not be handled in time for the final examination.

The average time per day spent the first week in reading was less than twenty minutes. The student reported no difficulty in performing the task. On the contrary, he indicated some difficulty in restraining himself from reading further. Also, he reported feeling guilty because he did so little studying. The therapist did not respond to these comments other than to insist that the student follow the planned program exactly.

The second week daily reading material was increased to eight pages. For each of the successive weeks, the number of pages to be read was increased by two until the amount was sixty pages daily. The time necessary to complete this number of pages generally ran between three and four hours a day. All this reading, however, was performed in the library and not at home and it was at home that the student wished to study.

After several discussions, it further appeared likely that the student's difficulty in studying at home was related to the problems he experienced with his wife. She worked part time to help support the family while he went to school. The patient's job was only part time and he earned less than necessary to maintain the family. His wife was not happy about this state of affairs as she felt it was the husband's function to support the family and she did not like working or scrimping to keep her husband in school. Occasionally, she would purchase something either frivolous or expensive that would burden their budget severely. The patient responded each time with anger followed by morose, sullen behavior that would ordinarily last several days. His wife, in turn, responded to him with anger followed by taunts regarding his inadequacy as a husband, father, and wage earner.

The atmosphere at home was, therefore, frequently quite unpleasant and under these circumstances the patient could not study adequately. Before a program for study at home could be planned, the following activity schedule was initiated. Each behavior performed by the wife which would ordinarily arouse anger in her husband, was *not* to be responded to with an overt action by the patient that would indicate anger or displeasure. Rather he was instructed to respond as much as possible without showing his feelings and direct the conversation into other, more palatable, subject areas. At first, the patient argued that this course of action was impossible and "unhealthy." He did not believe that he could do it or even if he could, that it would be desirable for him to do so. The therapist pointed out that if his goals were to be achieved, not only would his own behavior have to be modified but that those actions of his wife which were related to his behavior also had to be changed. With reluctance, he agreed to try. The therapist also instructed the patient to try to increase the social contacts he and his wife made with other, similarly situated couples.

For several weeks, there was little done by the wife to arouse the patient's displeasure. They initiated pleasant contacts with several graduate student couples. Unfortunately, their daughter became ill at this time, which led the mother to leave her job temporarily. The financial squeeze this created led to a great deal of complaining and critical behavior by the patient's wife. The patient reported being sorely tried, but he attempted not to respond in his old manner. Most of the time he apparently did not respond with anger. Along with an increased frequency of offering to assist his wife with the household chores and care of the sick child, this rather difficult period was passed with much less emotional upheaval in the home than the patient had expected on the basis of previous difficult times.

The patient continued his nonhostile response pattern to his wife's occasional critical and disturbing behaviors. Although no entirely adequate record could be made regarding the frequency of his wife's criticizing behavior, the therapist's records show a substantial drop in the frequency with which the patient reported such behavior a month after the initial instructions were given. The lower level of criticizing behavior remained throughout therapy, never disappearing altogether, but also never reaching anywhere near their frequency prior to the patient receiving the program of action.

Throughout therapy the patient's reports of his actions in following the plan were verbally approved by the therapist. Such statements as "That was wise" and "That showed restraint" were frequently used. Also, of course, the patient was progressing with the scheduled study pattern previously described. At times, he would deviate from it by reading too little, sometimes too much. The therapist would respond with mild disapproval and repeated instructions not to break the "rules of the game."

The patient's grades at the end of the first quarter were only fair, including the arranged incomplete mentioned earlier. The second quarter grades were somewhat higher. During the third quarter, the incomplete was erased by the patient taking an examination and getting an "A," only the second such grade he had received in graduate school. At this time, the patient suggested that he transfer his studying from the library to home. The therapist suggested doing this gradually by dividing the total number of pages between home and the library and doing most of the work at the library while increasing slowly the amount at home. He was reading sixty pages daily at this time and wanted to do most of it at home. The therapist disagreed with the plan but could not dissuade the patient from dividing the work equally. However, the patient agreed not to do more than half at home and the program continued with two page weekly increases but now about equally divided as to location. To the patient's delight, the plan worked out very well most of the time, and a desk and chair were now used instead of an upholstered armchair.

Many of the consultation sessions up to this time had included descriptions of various unpleasant interactions with the patient's supervisor on his part-time job as a bookkeeper. The supervisor was suspicious, nontrusting, and rather hostile towards the patient. These responses appeared to be somewhat independent of the patient's behavior and his supervisor appeared to act in this manner towards other people. After exploring the various alternatives open, it was decided that it might be best for the patient to change his job when another similar position became available. Unfortunately, it was several months before any other jobs became available and in each case the hours required would have interfered with his school work.

A job, however, of a slightly different kind became available to the student on the campus. Although it paid less, it was far more convenient and most of the patient's co-workers would be fellow students. For these reasons, the patient applied for and received a temporary appointment. The therapist directed the patient to avoid acting in certain ways that had in the past offended his fellow students. After the job began, each report by the patient of his engaging in the new behaviors would be responded to by the therapist with approval. The patient's reports of occasional discomfort with these new actions, would not be responded to by the therapist with any verbal behavior or change in expression or position. The reports of discomfort shortly became uncommon.

The patient had decided by now that he was not really a poor father to his daughter. After observing more families with children during the past several months, he felt he was not significantly different from most fathers and that his daughter could hold her own with her peers quite well. The child was to begin kindergarten in the autumn and his wife indicated that the patient was not very different from others as a father although at times she was critical of some of his actions towards their child. Descriptions

of his behavior to the therapist suggested little in the way of an unusual or a disturbing nature.

Therapy sessions ended at this time. This therapist makes no attempt to follow-up cases routinely. However, the university commencement program of the year following listed the patient as the recipient of a graduate degree.

20   EXPERIMENTAL DESENSITIZATION OF A PHOBIA[1]

Peter J. Lang • A. David Lazovik

24 snake phobic Ss participated in an experimental investigation of systematic desensitization therapy. Ss who experienced desensitization showed a greater reduction in phobic behavior (as measured by avoidance behavior in the presence of the phobic object and self-ratings) than did nonparticipating controls. Ss tended to hold or increase therapy gains at a 6-month follow-up evaluation, and gave no evidence of symptom substitution.

In recent years there has been increasing interest in the development of psychotherapeutic techniques based on learning theory models. These efforts are not limited to the translation of accepted psychotherapeutic practice into a laboratory language, in the manner of Shoben (1949) and Dollard and Miller (1950), but are attempts to extrapolate from laboratory findings to new methods of treatment. The most promising

Journal of Abnormal and Social Psychology, 1963, **66**, 519–525.

[1] This research is supported by Grant M-3880 from the National Institute of Mental Health, United States Public Health Service. The main content of this paper was presented by A. David Lazovik at the meeting of the American Psychological Association in New York, September 1961.

of these techniques with respect to clinical findings, is Wolpe's (1958) systematic desensitization therapy of phobic reactions. In a recent article Wolpe (1961) reported that desensitization was effective in the treatment of 35 of 39 phobic patients. Similar results have been reported by Lazarus (1961) utilizing group desensitization.

In a pilot project Lazovik and Lang (1960) demonstrated that desensitization could be successfully carried out under controlled laboratory conditions. This result opens the way not only to a more precise evaluation of treatment outcomes, but also makes it possible to test conflicting theories of the treatment process.

According to Wolpe (1958), desensitization is effective to the extent that subjects learn to make responses to phobic objects which reciprocally inhibit (are incompatible with) fear. Specifically, the treatment is designed to substitute muscular relaxation for anxiety. It is assumed that this process—not suggestion, "hello-goodbye" effects, or transference—is the agent of behavior change. It is further assumed that explorations with the patient of the genesis of the fear are not necessary to the elimination of a phobia. Wolpe proposes that the unlearning of a phobia follows the rules of what is generally called association learning theory. He therefore expects that therapy will be more difficult, the more generalized the anxiety response, but that "symptom substitution" is not a consequence of successful behavior therapy.

A very different set of predictions would be made by psychoanalytic therapists. This frame of reference expects little positive result unless the background of the phobia and its symbolic meaning, is elucidated and worked through with the subject. If this approach is not employed, only a temporary, "transference cure" may be anticipated. It is further assumed that the difficulty of the case is related to the importance of the symptom in the individual's "psychic economy," and that its temporary removal can only lead to the substitution of some new symptom.

The current experiment is designed to evaluate these two interpretations of desensitization therapy. The procedure developed previously (Lazovik & Lang, 1960), while it submits to the rigid control of the laboratory, is nevertheless sufficiently flexible that it can be employed in the treatment of actual phobic behavior. In this experiment snake phobic individuals served as subjects. This fear was chosen because it is frequent in a college population, approximately 3 in 100 students are to some degree snake phobic, and also because of the symbolic, sexual significance attributed to this fear by psychoanalytic theory (Fenichel, 1945, p. 49). The fact that snake phobias are held to reflect conflict in more fundamental systems of the personality, suggests that this is good ground for a stringent test of behavior therapy.

Specifically, the study is designed to: evaluate the changes in snake phobic behavior that occur over time, particularly the effects of repeated exposure to the phobic object; compare these changes with those that follow systematic desensitization therapy; determine the changes in behavior that are a direct function of the desensitization process, as opposed to the independent effects (when not part of desensitization) of hypnosis, training in deep muscle relaxation, and the estab-

lishment of a good patient-therapist relationship. In addition, an attempt is made to isolate factors which determine the success or failure of this method with individual subjects.

METHOD

Systematic Desensitization

The experimental treatment consists of two sequential parts, training and desensitization proper (Lazovik & Lang, 1960). The former procedure requires five sessions of about 45 minutes each. At this time an *anxiety hierarchy* is constructed. This is a series of 20 situations involving the phobic object, which each subject grades from most to least frightening. The actual items vary from subject to subject. However, the following scenes are typical: "writing the word snake," "snakes on display at the zoo (moving within a glass case)," "stepping on a dead snake accidentally."

The subject is then trained in deep muscle relaxation, following the method presented by Jacobson (1938). He is further instructed to practice relaxation 10–15 minutes per day at home. In the final phase of the training period the subject is introduced to hypnosis, and an effort is made to teach him to visualize vividly hypnotic scenes.

Following training, there are 11 45-minute sessions of systematic desensitization. In this, the subject learns to respond with relaxation to stimuli that originally evoked anxiety. At the beginning of the first session the subject is hypnotized and instructed to relax deeply. He is then told to imagine the hierarchy item which he previously rated as least distressing—the smallest "dose" of anxiety. If relaxation is undisturbed by this experience, the subsequent item is presented. Items which induce small amounts of anxiety are repeated, followed by deep relaxation, until the subject reports he is undisturbed by the scene. In this way successive items are presented from session to session. The goal of treatment is the presentation of the item originally ranked as most frightening without impairing the individual's calm state. At this point a new response (relaxation) has been attached to the imagined representative of the fear inducing stimulus, and clinicians working with the method assume that it will readily transfer to actual life situations.

In the experimental treatment described here, just these operations were carried out. No attempt was made to induce change through direct hypnotic suggestion, nor was an effort made to alter motivation. Subjects were informed that the experimenter was trying to evaluate a new method of treatment, and that he was much more interested in accurate findings than therapeutic successes. A majority of the therapist's actual verbalizations, as well as the step by step description of the training and desensitization procedures, was contained in a mimeographed program which guided the treatment of all subjects.

Subjects

A total of 24 subjects participated in this research. They were all college student volunteers, attending undergraduate psychology courses. The experimental groups included a total of four males and nine females. The control groups consisted of three males and eight females. None of these subjects presented evidence of a severe emotional disturbance on the basis of MMPI and interview data.

Subjects were selected on the basis of a classroom questionnaire which asked students to list their fears and rate them as mild, moderate, or intense. All subjects who participated in this experiment were afraid of nonpoisonous snakes, and rated this fear as "intense." Furthermore, the two authors interviewed all subjects who met this criterion. If despite the high self-rating on the screening questionnaire the subject's fear was judged to be weak, he was not asked to participate in the project. Subjects who formed the final experimental sample were characterized by most of the following behaviors: They reported somatic disturbance associated with the fear—"I feel sick to my stomach when I see one." "My palms get sweaty. I'm tense." They habitually avoided going anywhere near a live snake. They would not enter the reptile section of the zoo or walk through an open field. They became upset at seeing snakes at the motion pictures or on the television screen, and would leave, close their eyes, or turn off the set. Even pictures in magazines or artifacts such as a snake skin belt were capable of evoking discomfort in many of these subjects.

Measures of Phobic Behavior

All subjects filled out a Fear Survey Schedule (FSS) at the beginning and end of the experiment, and again at a 6-month follow-up evaluation. The FSS is a list of 50 phobias each of which is rated by the subjects on a 7-point scale. An estimate was thus obtained not only of the subject's snake phobia, but of other related and unrelated fears.

A direct estimate of the subject's avoidance behavior was obtained by confronting him with the phobic object. The subject was informed that a nonpoisonous snake was confined in a glass case in a nearby laboratory. He was persuaded to enter the room and describe his reactions. The snake was confined at a point 15 feet from the entrance to the room. On entering the room with the subject, the experimenter walked to the case and removed a wire grill that covered the top. The subject was assured that the snake was harmless. The experimenter then requested that the subject come over and look down at the snake as he was doing. If the subject refused, he was asked to come as close as he felt he could and the distance was recorded. If the subject was able to come all the way to the case, he was asked to touch the animal (a 5-foot black snake) after he had seen the experimenter do this. If the subject succeeded in this, the experimenter picked up the snake and invited the subject to hold it. After the avoidance test, the subject was asked to rate his anxiety on a 10-point "fear thermometer" (Walk, 1956). The subject's degree of anxiety was also rated on a 3-point scale by the experimenter.

In addition to the subjective scales and the avoidance test, all subjects were extensively interviewed concerning their fear. These interviews were tape recorded. The experimenter who conducted the interview and administered the avoidance test participated in no other phase of the project.[2]

Procedure

Following an initial interview and the administration of Form A of the Stanford Hypnotic Susceptibility Scale (SHSS; Weitzenhoffer & Hilgard, 1959), subjects were

[2] The authors would like to thank David Reynolds, who acted as interviewer and conducted the snake avoidance test.

placed in the experimental or control groups. Assignment was essentially random, although an effort was made to balance roughly these groups in terms of intensity of fear and motivation to participate in the experiment. All subjects were administered Form B of the SHSS when the experimental subjects completed the training period, and before desensitization began.

The basic plan of the study is described in Table 1. It consisted of two experimental and two control groups. The subgroups were created so that the effects of repeating the avoidance test, pretherapy training, and desensitization itself could be separately evaluated. Thus, the experimental groups E_1 and E_2 both experienced the laboratory analogue of desensitization therapy already described. However, subjects assigned to E_1 were administered the avoidance test before the training period, prior to desensitization, and again at the end of the experiment. E_2 subjects, on the other hand, were tested before desensitization and after, but did not participate in the initial evaluation. The control subjects did not participate in desensitization, but the C_1 and C_2 groups were evaluated at the same time as their opposite numbers in the experimental

TABLE 1   Design of the Experiment, Showing the Times at Which Subjects Were Evaluated (the Snake Avoidance Test, Experimenter's Rating, Fear Thermometer, and Taped Interview)

GROUP		EXPERIMENTAL PROCEDURES		
E_1	Test 1	Training	Test 2	Desensitiza- tion	Test 3
E_2		Training	Test 2	Desensitiza- tion	Test 3
C_1	Test 1	—	Test 2	—	Test 3
C_2		—	Test 2	—	Test 3

series. All available subjects were seen and evaluated 6 months after the termination of therapy.

Four replications of this experiment are reported here. They varied only in the therapists who were assigned to the experimental groups. Four experimental subjects and five controls participated in the first replication. The authors each saw two of the experimental subjects. In the second, third, and

fourth replications (which included three, four, and two experimental subjects and two, three, and one control subjects, respectively) three other therapists participated.[3] While two of these individuals are engaged in full-time private practice, they had never before attempted desensitization therapy. The third therapist was an advanced clinical graduate student, who also had his initial experience with the desensitization method in this project.

RESULTS

Avoidance Test

The results of this test were evaluated in two ways: an absolute criterion in which touching or holding the snake constituted a test pass, and scale scores based on the subject's distance in feet from the snake. Table 2 presents the number of subjects from the separate experimental and control groups who met the former criterion.

TABLE 2   Number of Subjects Who Held or Touched the Snake during the Avoidance Test

Group	N	Test 1	Test 2	Test 3
E_1	8	1	1	5
E_2	5	—	1	2
C_1	5	0	0	0
C_2	6	—	1	2
E_1 and E_2	13		2	7
C_1 and C_2	11		1	2

Note that the reliability of this test is high. The control subjects show no appreciable change, even with three exposures to the snake. Furthermore, the pretherapy training period does not affect the performance of the experimental subject: no more E_1 subjects pass at Test 2 than at Test 1. However, following therapy, the incidence of test passes goes up significantly in the experimental group. The percentage of increase from Test 2 to Test 3 yielded a t of 2.30,

[3] The authors would like to thank Robert Romano, Richard Miller, and James Geer, who participated as therapists in this project.

$p < .05$. A similar test of the control subjects was not significant.[4]

The above analysis does not, of course, measure subtle changes in behavior. In an attempt to increase the sensitivity of the avoidance test, subjects were assigned scores on a 19-point scale which roughly corresponded to their closest approach in feet to the phobic object. Holding the animal was equal to a scale score of 1; touching, 2; the 1-foot mark, 3; 2 feet, 4; and so on up to a score of 19 for subjects who refused to go to the testing room. The correlation between the first two presentations of the avoidance test $(N = 19)$ yielded an r of $+.63$.[5] Although this statistic suggests some degree of reliability, nothing is known about the relative distance between values at different places on the scale. The control sample employed in the experiment is too small to make an adequate analysis. Nevertheless, it is logical that the probability of a positive increase in approach lessens the closer the subject is to the phobic object, i.e., movement from a score of 15 to 12 is more likely or easier than movement from a scale score of 4 (2 feet away) to a score of 1 (holding a live snake). Thus, a simple difference score does not appear to be the best estimate of change.

The change score used in the following

[4] A live snake varies to some extent in activity, and this appears to be related to its effectiveness as a stimulus. In order to determine whether this factor influenced our results, the experimental assistant's ratings of the snake's activity during tests of the control and experimental subjects were subjected to a t test. No significant difference in snake activity for the two groups was found.

[5] The sample $(N = 19)$ used in estimating the reliability of the avoidance scale and the other fear measures includes the members of the control sample plus the eight subjects of the E_1 group. Although the training period does intervene between the first and second presentations of the fear measures for the E_1 group, it appears to have no appreciable effect on the phobia. The E_2 subjects could not, of course, be included in a reliability estimate, as actual therapy intervenes between their first and second fear evaluation.

analysis was the difference between pre- and posttherapy scale scores divided by the pretherapy score. For example, a subject who achieved a scale score of 12 on Test 2 and a score of 5 on Test 3 was assigned a change score of .58—the solution to the equation:

$$\text{change score} = \frac{12 - 5}{12}.$$

The mean change score for the first two avoidance tests $(N = 19)$ was only $+.03$. This suggests that the score has considerable stability, and tends to minimize chance fluctuations. The mean change scores for the experimental and control subjects from Test 2 to Test 3 may be found in Table 3. Note that the Mann-Whitney U test of the difference between groups is significant.

TABLE 3   Mean Snake Avoidance Scale Scores at Test 2 and 3, Mean Change scores, and the Mann-Whitney U Test

Group	Test 2	Test 3	Change score	U
Experimental	5.35	4.42	.34	34.5*
Control	6.51	7.73	−.19	

* $p < .05$.

Fear Thermometer and the FSS Snake Item

The correlation between the first two tests for the reliability sample $(N = 19)$ was $r = +.75$. The average difference score (obtained by subtracting the second fear thermometer score from the first) was only $+.63$. As in the case of the avoidance test, no significant change was associated with the pretherapy training period. The mean difference score for the E_1 group from Test 1 to Test 2 was $+.38$, less than the group mean cited above.

The difference between Test 2 and Test 3 scores for the experimental and control groups are presented at the top of Table 4.

TABLE 4   Mean Rating Scale Measures of Phobic Behavior before (Test 2) and after (Test 3) Desensitization Therapy

Group	Test 2	Test 3	Difference
	Fear thermometer		
Experimental	7.62	5.15	2.47
Control	6.45	5.45	1.00
	FSS-subject's rating of snake fear		
	Test 1ᵃ	Test 3	Difference
Experimental	6.69	5.31	1.38
Control	6.27	5.73	.54

ᵃ The FSS was not administered at Test 2. The difference score is between a pretherapy interview and Test 3.

While the therapy groups show a greater mean change than the control subjects, this difference did not attain statistical significance on the Mann-Whitney U test. The same trend and statistical findings were obtained for the snake item on the FSS. The experimenter's rating of the subject's level of anxiety during the avoidance test did not differentiate between experimental and control groups. In this case, the failure to discriminate may be attributed to the selection, prior to the experiment, of a 3-point rating scale. The experimenter reported that this measure was too gross for the behavior under observation.

Follow-Up Study

All subjects who were still available ($N = 20$) were re-evaluated approximately 6 months after the experiment was completed. This included 11 members of the original experimental group, 6 of whom touched or held the snake at the final avoidance test. Two of these subjects no longer met this criterion 6 months later. However, neither subject indicated an increase in self-rated fear and one actually showed improvement on this dimension. Furthermore, because of gains by others, the mean avoidance test change score for the entire experimental group indicates a slight reduction in phobic

behavior from Test 3 to the 6-month follow-up.

The therapy group showed even greater gains on the fear thermometer. The increase was sufficient that the difference between experimental and control subjects from Test 2 to the follow-up was statistically significant ($U = 16.5$, $p < .05$). Subjects who had experienced therapy also showed a significant reduction in their overall estimate of the intensity of their phobia as measured by the snake item of the FSS. The change in this score from pretherapy to the 6-month follow-up was significantly greater for experimental than control subjects ($U = 8.5$, $p < .02$).

Therapy Terminated and Unterminated

The design of the current experiment arbitrarily limited therapy to 11 sessions. This resulted in subjects being tested for change at varying points in the therapeutic process. Fortunately, in desensitization therapy it is possible to define a subject's degree of progress by referring to the number of hierarchy items successfully completed. It will be recalled that all subjects started with a 20-item hierarchy. This represented the combined efforts of the therapist and the subject to build an equal-interval scale, extending from a remote point where the subject felt little or no fear to a maximum fear involving close contact with the offending object. Normally, therapy would be terminated when the twentieth item had been passed. In the present experiment four subjects achieved this goal. Seven subjects completed 16 or more items and six subjects completed 14 or less items.

All subjects who completed their hierarchies touched or held the snake at the final avoidance test. Furthermore, subjects who completed over 15 items ($N = 7$) showed significant improvement on nearly all measures employed in this experiment: subjects who completed under 15 items differed little from controls. Table 5 presents the difference between the two therapy groups on the snake

TABLE 5 Avoidance Test Behavior Change from Test 2 to Test 3 for Therapy Subjects Who Completed More than 15 Hierarchy Items, for Those who Completed Less than 15, and for the Mann-Whitney **U** Test

Number of hierarchy items successfully completed	Test 2	Test 3	Change score	U
	Snake avoidance scale			
More than 15[a]	6.71	3.93	.49	5.0**
Less than 15[b]	4.17	5.00	−.07	
	Fear thermometer			
More than 15[a]	7.57	4.00	3.57	8.0*
Less than 15[b]	7.67	6.50	1.17	

Note—All scores are mean values.
[a] $N = 7$.
[b] $N = 6$.
* $p < .08$.
** $p < .03$.

TABLE 6 Changes in the Fear Survey Schedule (FSS) following Desensitization Therapy for Subjects Who Completed More than 15 Hierarchy Items, for Those Who Completed Less than 15, and for the Mann-Whitney **U** Test

Number of hierarchy items successfully completed	Pre-therapy	Post-therapy	Difference	U
	Fear survey schedule			
More than 15[a]	2.34	1.85	.49	4.5*
Less than 15[b]	3.21	3.20	.01	
	FSS-subject's rating of snake fear			
More than 15[a]	6.71	4.14	2.57	3.0**
Less than 15[b]	6.67	6.67	0.00	

Note—All scores are mean ranks or mean rank differences.
[a] $N = 7$.
[b] $N = 6$.
* $p < .02$.
** $p < .01$.

avoidance scale and the fear thermometer. Note that the improvement of the over 15 items group is significantly greater than that of subjects completing less than 15 items. Similar results were obtained for the FSS snake item and they are presented in Table 6. Note in this same table that the mean rank of the FSS also shows a significantly greater reduction in the over 15 items group, than in the group completing fewer items. This finding suggests that the elimination of snake phobic behavior does not initiate an increase in other fears, but in fact leads to a significant reduction in overall anxiety.

DISCUSSION

The results of the present experiment demonstrate that the experimental analogue of desensitization therapy effectively reduces phobic behavior. Both subjective rating of fear and overt avoidance behavior were modified, and gains were maintained or increased at the 6-month follow-up. The results of objective measures were in turn supported by extensive interview material. Close ques-

tioning could not persuade any of the experimental subjects that a desire to please the experimenter had been a significant factor in their change. Furthermore, in none of these interviews was there any evidence that other symptoms appeared to replace the phobic behavior.

The fact that no significant change was associated with the pretherapy training argues that hypnosis and general muscle relaxation were not in themselves vehicles of change.[6] Similarly, the basic suggestibility of the subjects must be excluded. The difference between the SHSS Form A scores of the experimental and control groups did not approach statistical significance $(U = 58)$.

[6] While these findings indicate that hypnotizing subjects or training them in muscle relaxation are not effective independent of desensitization, we do not yet know if they are a necessary part of the desensitization process, itself. Research currently underway, in which these procedures are included or omitted in different therapy groups, is designed to answer this important question.

Clearly, the responsibility for the reduction in phobic behavior must be assigned to the desensitization process itself. This is evidenced not only by the differences between experimental and control subjects but also by the relationship within the experimental groups between degree of change and the number of hierarchy items successfully completed.

One must still raise the question, however, why desensitization therapy could be accomplished in 11 sessions with some subjects and barely gotten underway with others. The intensity of the phobia is obviously not a relevant factor. The mean avoidance Test 2 score is actually higher for the experimental subjects who completed more than 15 items than for those who completed less (see Table 5). The base FSS snake item rank and the fear thermometer scores are almost exactly the same in both groups. On the other hand, a negative relationship ($r = -.58$) exists between the total FSS score at the first testing and the number of hierarchy items completed by individual members of the experimental group. The FSS is in turn positively related to the Taylor (1953) Manifest Anxiety (MA) scale ($r = +.80$ for the experimental group). Thus, the degree of progress attained in therapy in a constant period of time (11 sessions) appears to be a function of generalized anxiety, as measured by both the MA scale and FSS. These data suggest that desensitization therapy is more difficult, or at least slower, when many stimuli in the subject's environment are capable of eliciting anxiety responses. This is of course consistent with the clinical findings of Wolpe (1958) and the prediction of a learning theory model.

The present experiment also reveals an interesting connection between changes in overt avoidance behavior and the subject's verbal report. The relationship between these two dimensions is generally positive. However, even when precisely the same event is being evaluated, it is sometimes surprisingly low (Test 3 avoidance scale and fear thermometer $r = +.40$). Furthermore, initial changes in phobic behavior seem to occur in either one dimension or the other, rather than in both simultaneously. Most frequently subjective report lags behind overt behavior. Thus, avoidance test scores differentiated between experimental and control subjects immediately following the experiment, but it was not until the follow-up interview that the subjective scales yielded the same finding. It will be interesting to observe in future studies if this pattern continues, and to what extent it is characteristic of any reduction in phobic behavior, or simply a function of the desensitization technique.

The question of whether learning theory, specifically counterconditioning, best explains the desensitization process is not completely answerable by the present investigation. Certainly the theory is consistent with the results, and some of the other possible explanations have been eliminated. However, further research, particularly the direct measurement of changes in muscular tension during the presentation of hierarchy items, is necessary to an evaluation of theory.

But of the greatest immediate interest are the implications of the present research for traditional theories of clinical practice. The findings suggest the following important conclusions:

1. It is not necessary to explore with a subject the factors contributing to the learning of a phobia or its "unconscious meaning" in order to eliminate the fear behavior.
2. The form of treatment employed here does not lead to symptom substitution or create new disturbances of behavior.
3. In reducing phobic behavior it is not necessary to change basic attitudes, values, or attempt to modify the "personality as a whole." The unlearning of phobic behavior appears to be analogous to the elimination of other responses from a subject's behavior repertoire.

REFERENCES

DOLLARD, J., & MILLER, N. E. *Personality and psychotherapy: An analysis in terms of learning, thinking and culture.* New York: McGraw-Hill, 1950.

FENICHEL, O. *The psychoanalytic theory of neurosis.* New York: Norton, 1945.

JACOBSON, E. *Progressive relaxation.* Chicago: Univer. Chicago Press, 1938.

LAZARUS, A. A. Group therapy of phobic disorders by systematic desensitization. *J. abnorm. soc. Psychol.,* 1961, **63**, 504–510.

LAZOVIK, A. D., & LANG, P. J. A laboratory demonstration of systematic desensitization psychotherapy. *J. psychol. Stud.,* 1960, **11**, 238–247.

SHOBEN, E. J. Psychotherapy as a problem in learning theory. *Psychol. Bull.,* 1949, **46**, 366–392.

TAYLOR, JANET A. A personality scale of manifest anxiety. *J. abnorm. soc. Psychol.,* 1953, **48**, 285–290.

WALK, R. D. Self ratings of fear in a fear-invoking situation. *J. abnorm. soc. Psychol.,* 1956, **52**, 171–178.

WEITZENHOFFER, A. M., & HILGARD, E. R. *Stanford Hypnotic Susceptibility Scale.* Palo Alto, Calif.: Consulting Psychologists Press, 1959.

WOLPE, J. *Psychotherapy by reciprocal inhibition.* Stanford: Stanford Univer. Press, 1958.

WOLPE, J. The systematic desensitization treatment of neuroses. *J. nerv. ment. Dis.,* 1961, **132**, 189–203.

21   GROUP THERAPY OF PHOBIC DISORDERS BY SYSTEMATIC DESENSITIZATION[1]

Arnold A. Lazarus

The increasing demands for psychological and psychiatric services dictate the need for effective short-term therapeutic techniques and the extension of the existing services. Consequently, group techniques have grown in clinical stature, and the past decade has witnessed the development of numerous divergent procedures. A most promising variety of short-term therapy is Wolpe's (1958) system of "reciprocal inhibition," by which he achieved the recovery of 188 out of 210 neurotic cases in an average of 34.8 sessions.

A double economy can be achieved by combining the advantages of Wolpe's (1958) expedient clinical procedures with the additional time- and effort-saving properties of group therapy. This paper describes the adaptation of Wolpe's most important therapeutic procedure—the technique of systematic desensitization based on relaxation—to the group treatment of phobic disorders. In addition, the therapeutic effects of group desensitization were compared with more conventional forms of interpretive group psychotherapy on matched pairs of phobic subjects.

METHOD

General Procedure

The sample consisted of 35 middle-class urban white South Africans who were handicapped by phobic disorders.[2] Social class mem-

Journal of Abnormal and Social Psychology, 1961, **63**, 504–510.

[1] This paper is an outline of the experimental section of a thesis entitled "New Group Techniques in the Treatment of Phobic Conditions," which was accepted by the University of the Witwatersrand in December 1960, for the degree of Doctor of Philosophy.

[2] The sample was not drawn from psychiatric hospitals or institutions as it was felt that extraneous variables would be introduced. Since the rules of the South African Psychological Association forbid registered psychologists to advertise in the press, the patients were obtained with the generous aid of friends and colleagues who made announcements at lectures and contacted their own associates.

bership was defined in terms of education, vocation, and income. There were 7 university graduates, 16 matriculants, and 12 patients with at least 3 years of secondary schooling. Apart from 3 professional women, the majority of female patients were housewives whose husbands' average earnings were the equivalent of $550 a month. The mean income for the rest of the group was approximately $600 a month. In all, there were 12 men and 23 women, the mean age being 33.2 years with a standard deviation of 9.87.

The entire group included 11 acrophobics, 15 claustrophobics, 5 impotent men (treated as suffering from sexual phobia), and a mixed group of 4 phobic patients. The latter comprised a girl with a fear of sharp objects, a man with a fear of physical violence, a woman who was afraid to be a passenger in a moving vehicle, and a woman with a phobia for dogs.

The basic experimental design was to compare group desensitization therapy with more conventional methods of group treatment (or therapy based on "group dynamics"). The group desensitization technique consisted of systematically counterposing by relaxation graded lists of anxiety evoking stimuli which the separate groups of patients were asked to imagine.

The efficacy of group desensitization was first compared with group interpretation. The same therapist (the investigator) conducted all the therapeutic groups.

The initial comparison was made on a group of five acrophobic patients, two of whom received desensitization therapy, and three who were treated by interpretive group procedures.

Throughout the experiment, pairs of phobic patients were matched in terms of sex, age (within a 4-year range), and the nature and objective severity of the phobic disorders. A coin was tossed to decide whether a given member of each matched pair would be treated by desensitization therapy or by group interpretation. Extra (unmatched) individuals were always placed in the interpretive groups because it is generally agreed that these groups require a minimum of three members (Corsini, 1957).

When, after six sessions, treatment with the acrophobic groups was well underway, the next group (five impotent men) was selected and similarly subdivided into two additional groups, treated by desensitization and interpretation, respectively.

Three months later, the group of six claustrophobic patients was selected and equally subdivided to form a third separate desensitization-interpretation comparison.

Thus, at the end of 6 months, a total of seven patients had received group desensitization and nine had been treated by group interpretation.

Seven months later, additional acrophobic and claustrophobic patients were obtained in order to investigate the effects of relaxation per se. It was hypothesized that individuals who received training in relaxation at the end of each interpretive session would show a greater diminution of phobic reactions than those patients who had been treated solely by group interpretation. The suggestion that interpretation-plus-relaxation might be more effective than desensitization was also tested.

Accordingly, an additional six acrophobic patients were equally divided into two matched groups, the one receiving desensitization therapy and the other receiving interpretation-plus-relaxation. The latter group was trained in an accelerated version of Jacobson's (1938) progressive relaxation for about 15 minutes at the end of each interpretive therapeutic discussion.

A few weeks later, an additional nine claustrophobic patients were similarly subdivided. Group desensitization was administered to four patients and group interpretation-plus-relaxation was applied to five.

Finally, the mixed phobic group was treated by desensitization in order to determine whether desensitization could be successfully applied to a heterogeneous phobic group.

Thus, group desensitization was applied to 18 patients; group interpretation was applied to 9 patients, and 8 patients were treated by group interpretation-plus-relaxation.

Selection of Phobic Patients

Although there were numerous volunteers for inclusion in the investigation, only those people whose phobias imposed a severe limitation on their social mobility, jeopardized their interpersonal relationships, or hindered their constructive abilities were admitted to the therapeutic groups.

Several people who were greatly handicapped by phobic disorders were excluded because they had received previous psychiatric treatment, ranging from psychoanalysis to electroconvulsive therapy. These people were given individual treatment in order to avoid ambiguity concerning the effects of the therapeutic groups.

The character and severity of the phobias were assessed in the following manner: Patients reporting acrophobic symptoms were privately and individually required to climb a metal fire escape. The experimenter climbed the stairs directly behind the patients and urged them to see how high they could climb. Few of the patients were able to proceed higher than the first landing (approximately 15–20 feet from ground level). The patients who were admitted to the acrophobic groups were all able to achieve a pretherapeutic height of between 15 and 25 feet.

Similarly, patients with claustrophobic traits were admitted individually into a well-ventilated cubicle with large French windows which opened onto a balcony. The patient sat facing the open windows. To the left of the patient was a movable screen which could be pushed as far as the centre of the cubicle, thus, creating a sensation of space constriction. The patients were told that the experimenter would first shut the French windows and then proceed to push the screen towards the centre of the room. They were urged to remain in the cubicle for as long as possible and to reopen the windows only when they felt that the need for air had become unbearable. Most of the patients showed visible signs of discomfort as soon as the windows were shut, and no one was able to tolerate the screen at a distance of less than 20 inches.

Detailed information regarding the purpose of the investigation was withheld from the patients to avoid possible prejudice to the results. They were merely informed that the experimenter was conducting research into the alleviation of phobic disorders by group methods.

Apart from the initial screening procedures, individual contact with the patients was avoided in order to exclude the influence of any additional therapeutic factors. It is thought, for instance, that history taking and psychometric investigations may in themselves be therapeutic. In order to determine the value of group therapy per se, it was considered necessary to eliminate as many of these extraneous variables as possible. Attention was deliberately focused, therefore, on the specific techniques under investigation, avoiding the use of any supplementary measures which might facilitate therapeutic progress. For instance, in clinical practice it is customary to precede the application of systematic desensitization by a brief outline of the theoretical rationale behind the technique. Since it could be argued that this practice has a direct bearing on the results, the patients were directly desensitized without any preliminary explanation.

Group Desensitization

Anxiety hierarchies (graded lists of stimuli to which the patients reacted with unadaptive anxiety) were constructed (Wolpe, 1958). In preparing these hierarchies, the experimenter extracted common elements from remarks which individual patients wrote on the questionnaires they filled out, and a group hierarchy was constructed. It must be emphasized that the hierarchical situations were imaginary ones, listed on paper and presented only symbolically to the patients.

The acrophobic group hierarchy, for example, consisted of the following situations: looking down from a very high building, seeing films taken from an airplane, looking down from a height of 80–100 feet, looking down a well, sitting high up on a grandstand during a football game, looking down from a 60-foot balcony, sitting on a narrow ledge at a height of 60 feet with a safety net a few feet away, looking down from a height of about 55 feet, seeing someone jump from a 50-foot diving board, sitting on a wide ledge about 35 feet from the ground, looking down from a height of approximately 20 feet, looking down from a height of about 10 feet.

The claustrophobic group hierarchy consisted of 16 situations ranging from "sitting in a large and airy room with all the windows open," to "sitting in front of an open fire in a small room with the doors and windows shut." The group hierarchy applied to the impotent men contained 10 items referring to progressively intimate sexual situations requiring increasing amounts of initiative.

The first therapeutic session was devoted entirely to training the patients in intensive muscular relaxation. At the end of the session, the patients were instructed to practise specific relaxation exercises for about 15 minutes morning and night.

The second session was held 3 days later, when further training in relaxation was provided. Towards the end of this session, desensitization commenced with the presentation (in imagination) of the two weakest items of the relevant anxiety hierarchy. The acrophobic patients, for example, were first told to picture themselves looking out of a window about 10 feet from the level of the street. It was impressed upon them that if any scene proved upsetting or disturbing, they were to indicate this by raising their left hand. When any patient signaled in this manner, the scene was "withdrawn" immediately.

When the two least disturbing items in the relevant anxiety hierarchy had been presented, each of the patients was asked to report on the clarity of the imagined scenes and their accompanying levels of disturbance. The second session ended after the patients had been told to practice relaxation twice daily for periods of about 10 minutes.

The subsequent desensitization sessions followed a set pattern. The therapist named the various muscle groups to be relaxed. When a deep level of relaxation was reached, the patients were presented with successive items from the hierarchical series. The desensitization procedure was conducted at the pace of the "slowest" (i.e., most anxious) subject.

The third session was terminated only when all the patients were able to tolerate an exposure of about 10 seconds to the first three items on the hierarchy without signaling anxiety. Thereafter, new items were introduced only when a 10-second tolerance to the preceding item had been achieved. It took several sessions before the entire group was able to visualize a given item for as long as 10 seconds without one or another member's signaling some disturbance.

Apart from occasional restlessness in those who were ready for more "difficult" anxiety items but who were constantly re-exposed to stimuli which they had long since mastered, no harm seemed to ensue from proceeding at a pace that was obviously too slow for part of the group. On the other hand, experience has shown that too rapid a pace can prove extremely antitherapeutic and lead to increased levels of anxiety.

Therapy in the desensitization groups was terminated when the final item on the hierarchy was tolerated by the patients for 10 seconds without signaling. Patients often reported a marked amelioration of their phobic responses when the anxiety hierarchies were only half completed. It was insisted that each member would nevertheless have to undergo desensitization of the entire hierarchy in order to consolidate and reinforce their therapeutic gains.

The treatment of the claustrophobic groups was conducted out of doors. The patients in the mixed phobic group were handed the items of their relevant anxiety hierarchies on slips of paper. Here, the relaxation procedure adopted was as previously outlined, but instead of describing the items, the therapist handed a typewritten anxiety scene to each group member and instructed him to read the description of the scene, to close his eyes and to try to imagine the situation with tranquility. The patients were instructed to signal in the usual manner when a given situation became disturbing, and then immediately to stop imagining the scene and to continue relaxing. After about 10 seconds, all the patients were told to stop picturing the scene and remain relaxed. Those who had successfully imagined their item without undue disturbance were then handed a new anxiety situation. In this manner, each group member was able to proceed at his own pace. No more than two successive items were presented at any one session.

Group Interpretation

The approach used in the interpretive groups was a form of insight therapy with re-educative goals (Wolberg, 1954). Leadership was basically democratic, and the therapist's primary role was that of a participant observer. The groups passed through two phases: First, there was an introductory period during which the group situation was structured with the emphasis on a free and permissive emotional atmosphere. Feelings of initial tension and reticence were dealt with by open discussion, emphasizing group tolerance and acceptance and clarifying numerous misconceptions. Second, descriptions of phobic symptoms preceded intensive discussions which focused attention on emotions and on current interpersonal relationships. The emphasis shifted from a situational to a personal exploration. A considerable amount of historical data emerged and frequently provided abreactive and cathartic responses. The recall of forgotten memories was often accompanied by violent emotional reactions.

The group of impotent men displayed a high degree of empathy for one another, and frequently expressed feelings of hostility and resentment towards the therapist. These feelings were accepted by him and clarified for the patients; they were followed by discussions of the effects of frustration.

At the end of each session, the therapist provided a summary of the proceedings. He attempted not only to recapitulate the remarks of the subjects and to reflect back to the group the emotional significance of their statements, but also to suggest possible connections between their symptoms and their feelings. Interpretive remarks dealt mainly with possible motives behind the façade of manifest behavior. Premature interpretations were vigilantly avoided. Obvious rationalizations, as well as statements of overprotestation, were challenged by the therapist only when he sensed a readiness on the part of the group.

Both the interpretive groups and the desensitization sessions were usually conducted three times a week. The desensitization groups were disbanded when all the patients were able to tolerate the most severe anxiety producing stimulus in the hierarchy without undue disturbance.

Members of the interpretive groups were given the same number of sessions as the corresponding desensitization groups. Since very few patients recovered from their phobias by means of the interpretive procedures, the ones whose phobic symptoms persisted were provided with an opportunity of undergoing group desensitization. (There were too few desensitization failures to satisfy the minimum numerical requirements for comparable interpretive groups.) Although the main response was an immediate willingness to introduce the "different group technique," the group of impotent men decided to continue employing interpretive procedures a while longer. Group desensitization was then administered to those patients who were not rendered symptom-free by the interpretive methods.

RESULTS

Assessment of Recovery

One month after therapy had terminated, the acrophobic and claustrophobic patients who claimed to have recovered from their phobias were required to undergo additional stress tolerance tests.

The acrophobic subjects were required to climb to the third landing of a fire escape (a height of about 50 feet). From the third story, they were required to go by elevator with the experimenter to the roof garden, eight stories above street level, and then to count the number of passing cars for 2 minutes.

The claustrophobic subjects were required to remain in the cubicle with the French windows shut and the movable screen a few inches away. Those who were able to endure the situation with no apparent distress for 5 minutes were regarded as recoveries, provided that they were also able to present satisfactory evidence that they were no longer handicapped in their life situations. The tests were conducted individually in the presence of a witness.

With two exceptions, all the patients who stated that they had recovered from their phobias were able to face the tolerance tests with outward tranquility, although some of the acrophobic patients later admitted that they had felt "a trifle anxious" when looking down from the edge of the roof garden.

Neither the impotent men nor the members of the mixed phobic group were objectively tested.

The most rigorous criteria were used in assessing therapeutic results. For instance, only those patients who displayed an unambiguous posttherapeutic freedom from their respective phobic disorders were classified as recoveries. These criteria were, of course, essentially symptomatic. If a claustrophobic patient for instance, was still unable after therapy to visit the cinema for fear of suffocation, his treatment was considered a failure, regardless of any ex parte testimony to the contrary. Merely to enable a patient to "accept his neurosis" or to achieve a so-called "personality reintegration" without symptomatic relief was considered not good enough. Recovery from a phobic condition implies total neutrality or indifference to the formerly anxiety generating stimulus constellation. The present study made no provision for moderate or slight improvements. The latter were all classified as failures.

Statistical Analysis of the Results

Results are summarized in Table 1. As shown, there were 13 recoveries and 5 failures for desensitization, 2 recoveries and 15 failures for other forms of treatment. The resulting chi square is 10.69, which is highly significant ($p < .01$).

Additional statistical comparisons were computed for the matched pairs of acrophobic and claustrophobic patients who received group desensitization or group interpretation, respectively. There was a total of five matched pairs in these groups. Both members remained unimproved in one pair; in four, the desensitization patients recovered but the interpretation cases failed. There were no pairs in which both recovered or in which only interpretive methods succeeded. By applying the null hypothesis that the two methods are equally effective, the probability of obtaining this result is .0625.

In the case of the impotent men, no matching was carried out. Fisher's (1946, p. 97) exact test, which gave a probability of .1, was employed for testing significance. When the two probabilities, .0625 and .1, were combined (Fisher, 1946, p. 99), the resulting level of significance was .03, favoring desensitization.

It is interesting to note that when comparisons were made between the matched pairs of acrophobic and claustrophobic patients who received group desensitization as opposed to group interpretation-plus-relaxation, the level of significance in favor of desensitization was only 12.5%. There were three matched pairs in which desensitization proved successful and interpretation-plus-relaxation failed. There were no cases where group interpretation-plus relaxation succeeded while group desensitization failed. Both methods failed with three matched pairs and both methods succeeded with one matched pair.

Since a significance level of 12.5% falls outside the conventional limits, the obvious conclusion is that there is no evidence of differences between the desensitization and interpretation-plus-relaxation conditions. Of course, seven matched pairs provides one with little leverage and the statistical analysis of such a small number cannot be conclusive. It is worth noting, however, that of the six individuals who were initially unsuccessfully treated by interpretation-plus-relaxation, four later recovered from their phobias after a mean of 9.8 group desensitization sessions.

Of the total of 15 patients who had derived no apparent benefit from the interpretive procedures, 10 recovered from their phobias after a mean of 10.1 group desensitization sessions, as compared with the mean of 20.4 sessions which were necessary for effective group desensitization when only this procedure was employed.

TABLE I   Number of Patients Assigned to Each Condition and the Therapeutic Outcome

Patients	Treated by Desensitization	Recovered	Treated by Interpretation	Recovered	Treated by Interpretation and Relaxation	Recovered
Acrophobics	5	4	3	0	3	1
Claustrophobics	7	4	3	0	5	1
Impotence	2	2	3	0	—	—
Mixed group	4	3	—	—	—	—
Total	18	13	9	0	8	2

Follow-Up Studies

Follow-up studies were conducted by means of the following questionnaire:

1. Has your original phobic disorder returned?
2. If you have had a relapse, is it slight, moderate, or severe?
3. Since receiving treatment have you developed any new symptoms? (If so, please elaborate.)
4. Please underline all the following complaints which apply to you:
   Tension Depression Anxiety Palpitations
   Dizziness Insomnia Nightmares
   Headaches Tremors Sexual problems
   Fatigue Stomach trouble Other symptoms
   (Specify)
5. Please indicate whether any of the above complaints commenced *after* your participation in the therapeutic groups.
6. Are you still handicapped in any area of your daily living? (Specify.)
7. Have you consulted another therapist?

The duration of after-study history varied from group to group, and ranged from 15 months to 1.5 months with a mean of 9.05 months. All those subjects whose follow-up reports revealed even slight phobic recurrences were considered to have relapsed. Particular attention was devoted to the question of possible symptom substitution, but no evidence of this phenomenon was encountered.

When the follow-up evaluations were taken into account, 10 of the 13 patients who had recovered by means of group desensitization still maintained their freedom from phobic symptoms. Thus, 3 patients were regarded as having relapsed.

Of the 2 patients who had recovered after undergoing group interpretation-plus-relaxation, 1 maintained his recovery.

Eight of the 10 patients who recovered after undergoing postinterpretive group desensitization maintained recovery.

Summary of Findings

Group desensitization was applied to 18 patients of whom 13 initially recovered and 3 subsequently relapsed.

Group interpretation was applied to 9 patients. There were no recoveries in this group.

Group interpretation-plus-relaxation was applied to 8 patients of whom 2 recovered and 1 subsequently relapsed.

The 15 patients who had not benefited from the interpretive procedures were then treated by group desensitization. There were 10 recoveries of whom 2 subsequently relapsed.

DISCUSSION

Wolpe (1958) has expressed the basis of his "reciprocal inhibition" therapy as follows:

> If a response incompatible with anxiety can be made to occur in the presence of anxiety-evoking stimuli so that it is accompanied by a complete or partial suppression of the anxiety-responses, the bond between these stimuli and the anxiety-responses will be weakened.

His method of systematic desensitization based on relaxation incorporates Jacobson's (1938) finding that muscular relaxation inhibits anxiety and that their concurrent expression is physiologically impossible.

The deliberate use of the parasympathetic accompaniments of skeletal muscular relaxation to inhibit neurotic anxieties reciprocally may be termed "specific reciprocal inhibition." There is, however, a broad range of stimuli which have *nonspecific* properties for inhibiting neurotic responses reciprocally. The more usual clinical medium of verbal interchange, for instance, may in itself bring about the incidental or nonspecific reciprocal inhibition of neurotic responses. In other words, it is postulated that *interview situations* can sometimes evoke autonomic responses similar to those of deep muscle relaxation.

The fact that far fewer sessions were required to desensitize those subjects in the present sample who had previously received interpretive therapy may be explicable by the notion that interpretive group situations evoked appropriate emotional responses in most of the subjects to inhibit some of their anxieties. In other words, it is probable that some of the anxiety responses evoked by the group discussions underwent a measure of nonspecific reciprocal inhibition. Furthermore, those patients who received postinterpretive group desensitization had the advantage of having established a therapeutic relationship with the experimenter. It is postulated that "the therapeutic atmosphere of empathy and acceptance may in itself reciprocally inhibit neurotic anxieties" (Lazarus, 1959).

It should be mentioned that the interpretive groups apparently enabled many of the patients to achieve a constructive modification of their self-evaluation, often clarified their evaluation of others, and enhanced their potentialities of interpersonal integration. These gains, however, appeared to have little bearing on their phobic symptoms, which usually persisted until desensitization procedures were administered.

The comparatively high relapse rate in the present series is probably related to the fact that the treatment was rather narrowly confined to a single range of stimuli which could in some cases have been a small part of a broad constellation, other elements of which may have afforded additional and possibly more useful bases for desensitization. In a proper clinical setting, the group desensitization procedures would have been preceded by individual history taking and the compilation of detailed clinical information for use either individually or in the group situations. Consequently, the conditions for the application of desensitization therapy were far less than optimum, a point which suggests that the experimental outcomes are only minimally indicative of the utility of this therapeutic approach to phobic symptoms.

The concept of "experimenter bias" is a relevant consideration in any study of this kind. It is difficult to determine the extent to which the present results were influenced by the therapist's theoretical affiliations. In terms of subjective interest, however, it should be noted that the experimenter's preferences were decidedly in favor of the interpretive methods. Fortunately, the ennui which is generated while applying desensitization procedures is adequately offset by the gratifying results.

If another therapist had treated the interpretive groups, a significant difference in the results might merely have reflected the superiority of the individual therapist rather than the methods employed. The treatment of phobias by interpretive methods, however, is well known to be difficult. Curran and Partridge (1955), for instance, state that "phobic symptoms are notoriously resistant to treatment, and their complete removal is rarely achieved." Similar views are expressed by Maslow and Mittelmann (1951), Henderson and Gillespie (1955), and Mayer-Gross, Slater, and Roth (1955). By contrast, phobias respond to desensitization exceedingly well (Eysenck, 1960; Lazarus & Rachman, 1957; Wolpe, 1958). It is contended, therefore, that the superior results achieved by group desensitization are not a function of the therapist's disproportionate skills (or unconscious prejudices) but a reflection of the intrinsic value of desensitization per se in the treatment of phobic disorders.

The point may legitimately be raised as to whether desensitization achieves any result other than the elimination of the phobic symptom. Comments on the general repercussions of desensitization are not possible in the context of the present study. No attempt was made to study changes in personality or general adaptation. Many patients, however, made remarks which suggested that the elimination of a phobic symptom is not an isolated process, but has many diverse and positive implications. As Eysenck (1959) states:

The disappearance of the very annoying symptom promotes peace in the home, allays anxiety, and leads to an all-round improvement in character and behavior.

The extent to which desensitization is a method of *general* applicability (i.e., whether this method would benefit any neurotic patients other than those suffering from phobic disorders) is also worthy of mention. The value of desensitization is limited to those conditions wherein appropriate hierarchies can be constructed and where specific rather than pervasive anxiety is present. In other words, it is only where reasonably well-defined stimulus configurations can be identified that desensitization techniques should be applied. For example, patients whose interpersonal relationships are clouded by specific fears of rejection, hypersensitivity to criticism, clear-cut areas of self-consciousness, or similar specific anxiety evoking stimuli often derive benefit from desensitization procedures. By contrast, desensitization cannot readily be applied in such cases as character neuroses, hysterical disorders, and chronic inadequacy. A further prerequisite for the effective application of desensitization is the ability to conjure up reasonably vivid visual images which elicit emotional reactions comparable to the feelings evoked in the real situation.

While dealing with the limitations of desensitization procedures, one should not lose sight of the fact that systematic desensitization appears to be a most valuable technique in the alleviation of phobic disorders. The fact that this method can be effectively administered in *groups* suggests greater availability with little loss in economy or effectiveness for phobic sufferers.

SUMMARY

Wolpe's (1958) technique of systematic desensitization based on relaxation was adapted to the treatment of phobic disorders in groups. Of the 18 subjects who were treated by direct group desensitization, 13 recovered in a mean of 20.4 sessions. Follow-up inquiries after an average of 9.05 months revealed that 3 of the subjects had relapsed. With a more traditional form of interpretive group psychotherapy applied to 17 subjects, after a mean of 22 therapeutic meetings, it was found that only 2 patients were symp-

tom-free. Both these patients had attended groups in which relaxation was employed as an adjunct to the interpretive procedures. The 15 subjects who were not symptom-free after interpretive group therapy were then treated by group desensitization. After a mean of 10.1 sessions, 10 of them recovered. The very much shorter time required to effect a recovery by desensitization in those patients who had previously received interpretive therapy suggests that the therapeutic relationship and additional nonspecific factors may have facilitated the reciprocal inhibition of neurotic anxieties motivating the phobic symptoms. There is some basis for the idea that therapists of every persuasion could helpfully employ systematic desensitization as an adjunct to their traditional techniques in the management of phobic disorders.

REFERENCES

CORSINI, R. J. *Methods of group psychotherapy.* New York: McGraw-Hill, 1957.

CURRAN, D., & PARTRIDGE, M. *Psychological medicine.* Edinburgh & London: Livingstone, 1955.

EYSENCK, H. J. Learning theory and behavior therapy. *J. ment. Sci.,* 1959, **105,** 61–75.

EYSENCK, H. J. (Ed.) *Behaviour therapy and the neuroses.* Oxford: Pergamon, 1960.

FISHER, R. A. *Statistical methods for research workers.* Edinburgh: Oliver & Boyd, 1946.

HENDERSON, D., & GILLESPIE, R. D. *A textbook of psychiatry.* London: Oxford Univer. Press, 1955.

JACOBSON, E. *Progressive relaxation.* Chicago: Univer. Chicago Press, 1938.

LAZARUS, A. A. The elimination of children's phobias by deconditioning. *S. Afr. med. Proc.,* 1959, **5,** 261–265.

LAZARUS, A. A., & RACHMAN, S. The use of systematic desensitization in psychotherapy. *S. Afr. med. J.,* 1957, **31,** 934–937.

MASLOW, A. H., & MITTELMANN, B. *Principles of abnormal psychology*. New York: Harper, 1951.

MAYER-GROSS, W., SLATER, E., & ROTH, M. *Clinical psychiatry*. London: Cassel, 1955.

WOLBERG, L. R. *The technique of psychotherapy*. New York: Grune & Stratton, 1954.

WOLPE, J. *Psychotherapy by reciprocal inhibition*. Stanford: Stanford Univer. Press, 1958.

22   BEHAVIOR THERAPY WITH A CASE OF NERVOUS ANOREXIA

Peter J. Lang

This is a report of short term psychotherapy with an individual suffering from anxiety, loss of appetite and nervous vomiting.[1] The case was seen in connection with an experimental investigation of therapeutic methods derived from learning theory.[2] The therapy described here is wholly behavioral. No attempt is made to uncover early traumatic material or assist the client in gaining insight into unconscious motives. Neurotic behaviors are held to be unwanted responses of the organism, elicited by a determinable class of stimuli. They are removed by encouraging responses to these same stimuli that are incompatible with the unwanted behavior.

The client was a twenty-three-year-old registered nurse, working toward a university degree. She referred herself to the clinic after hearing a classroom announcement that treatment for students was available in the Psychology Department. N. told the intake worker that she was "not eating and vomiting." She reported that this occurred "whenever there is a new situation," or she does "anything opposed to someone's wishes." The previous six months had been quite difficult and she had lost twenty pounds. She was frightened about finding her way in the

city, anxious over the opinion of casual acquaintances, and how she looked and dressed. She felt nervous talking to people, insecure, "afraid of everything."

N. recalled that she had had a poor appetite from childhood, but that the vomiting dated from an out-of-state automobile trip she had taken as a high school student. At the time of the initial interview, riding in an automobile or bus made her anxious, and so ill that she had difficulty traveling except by train. She was unable to eat away from home, and thus avoided parties, dinners or other social activities. Examination by a physician revealed no organic pathology that could account for these symptoms.

A number of different techniques were employed in treating this client. The most direct was deep muscle relaxation, a procedure developed by Jacobson (1938). Training in relaxation was carried out during the first several therapy sessions. N. also practiced at home between fifteen and twenty minutes per day. Furthermore, she was instructed to take time out, if it were possible, and relax herself whenever she felt under stress.

During the therapy hours deep muscle relaxation was used to counter-condition specific anxiety responses. Wolpe (1958) has called this method systematic desensitization.

[1] A part of this material was presented to a colloquium at Temple University, May, 1962.

[2] NIH Grant M-3880.

It is assumed that anxiety cannot occur without an increase in muscular tension and general autonomic arousal; therefore, an effort is made to instigate muscle relaxation in the presence of the fear stimuli. As with M. C. Jones' (1924) method of treating children's fears, the patient starts with the least threatening material, and is then exposed to progressively greater increments of phobic stimulation. Jones was able to manipulate the feared objects themselves. However, in adult neuroses the relevant anxiety stimuli are seldom so easily controlled or readily available in the therapist's office. In systematic desensitization this difficulty is overcome by presenting the events as visualized scenes or hypnotic experiences.

During the initial interviews the stimuli that elicit the fear are defined, and then ordered into "anxiety hierarchies." These hierarchies are equal interval gradients, extending from the most frightening to the least frightening stimulus. Beginning with the latter, these events are then presented to the hypnotized client as scenes that she is actually experiencing. Each scene is presented a number of times, followed by instructions to relax deeply, until it no longer yields an anxiety response. Then the next item is taken up, and so on until the entire hierarchy is desensitized.

The success of desensitization depends on an accurate and complete detailing of the relevant anxiety stimuli. However, these are not always immediately apparent to the client, or readily discussed without discomfort. In behavior therapy, as in other approaches, goals must be clarified and anxiety about treatment worked through before good progress can be made. In the case of N., blocking appeared in the third session. While exploring some material for use in an anxiety hierarchy, she abruptly reported that she was unable to think of anything to say. The therapist expressed his understanding, his awareness of the pain it caused to describe the events under discussion. Prompted in this manner, N. was able to verbalize her initial feelings of discomfort with the therapists, her concern over being an ill person, and

her inability to solve things for herself. This was discussed, N. was reassured, and therapy then proceeded smoothly. Such blocking may occur from time to time, and must be dealt with before further work can be accomplished. However, if the behavior therapist does not waste time boxing with theoretical shadows, active treatment will not be greatly delayed.

During the first ten therapy sessions, N. described three general classes of anxiety stimuli: 1. *Travel.* She reported anxiety whenever she was called on to leave her apartment. The least anxiety was associated with brief journeys to familiar places. Fear increased regularly with an increase in distance or unfamiliarity with the destination. N.'s main travel hierarchy is presented in Figure 1. 2. *Disapproval by significant people.* An example of one of these criticism hierarchies is also included in Figure 1. 3. *Being the center of attention.* This fear is closely related to the second stimulus class. However, it proved convenient to consider it separately. Figure 1 contains a hierarchy of this type, concerned with classroom behavior.

N. was seen for seventy sessions, extending over an eleven month period.[3] During this time approximately seven hierarchies were used in desensitization. In each case, N.'s progress during the therapy sessions was matched by similar behavior changes in the life situation. This is well illustrated by the classroom hierarchy, the first one to be desensitized. When therapy was begun, N. was so distressed by new classes that she was unable to eat on these days. She always sat in the last row of the classroom, and avoided any discussion. She became acutely anxious if called on, even if only to acknowledge her attendance. By the time the classroom hierarchy was completed (at about the eighteenth therapy session) nearly all of these symptoms were eliminated. N. reported considerably less anxiety when the second term began. Classes did not interfere with eating. She now took her seat near the front of the room

[3] Dr. A. D. Lazovik was present and acted as co-therapist at most of the therapy sessions.

FIGURE   I   Anxiety   Hierarchies—Clinical   Case

TRAVEL

1. You take a streetcar to downtown Cleveland in order to shop.
2. You drive to the dressmaker's, accompanied by your sister, Florence.
3. You take the train to Columbus accompanied by friends, to attend a nurses' convention.
4. You travel by bus to Columbus accompanied by a friend.
5. You take the streetcar downtown for an appointment with the dentist (first appointment).

6. You take the streetcar to Parkside to attend the cinema (first time that you have gone to this theater).
7. You travel to a suburb of Cleveland alone on the bus.
8. You are driving alone from Stanton to Cleveland.
9. You drive alone to the dressmaker's house.
10. You are flying to Cincinnati with some friends.
11. Taking the train to Columbus to visit Bill.

CRITICISM

1. Your mother reminds you that you have not yet sent a thank you letter, to a relative from whom you received a gift.
2. Your Uncle wonders out loud why you don't visit him more often.
3. Your mother notes that you haven't been to church with her in quite a while.
4. Your mother comments that it has been a long time since you have visited your grandmother.
5. Your mother criticizes a friend: she just makes herself at home!
6. Your stepfather says that he can't understand how anyone could be so stupid as to be a Catholic.
7. You return an overdue book to the library. The librarian looks at you critically.

8. A physician making rounds discovers a baby in convulsions. He comments to a colleague: "You see what I mean about having to make rounds."
9. Bill looks over your shoulder as you are writing, and comments that it doesn't look very neat.
10. Bill comments that you are too heavy in the waist and should exercise.
11. Bill criticizes you for being quiet on a double date.
12. You are at a party given by one of Bill's friends. You mispronounce a word and Bill corrects you.
13. Your mother comes into a room and finds you smoking.

CENTER OF ATTENTION—
THE CLASSROOM

1. You enter a class that you have been attending regularly and take a seat at the back.
2. You enter a new class with a group of friends and take a seat in the back.
3. You enter a new class with a group of friends and take a seat in the first row.
4. You enter a new class alone and take a seat in the back.
5. You enter a class alone. You notice that the class is large, and you can't hear the instructor. You take a seat halfway from the front of the room.
6. You are asked a direct question by the instructor of a class that you have been attending regularly.

7. The instructor is calling the roll (he is about to start the "N"s). This is in a familiar class. He calls "L"s—starts "M"s—almost to your name—he calls it, you answer, he goes on to call the rest of the roll.
8. You are late for class. It is a large class. You enter and take a seat in the back.
9. You are asked to read a report in a class which you have been regularly attending. You give the report, standing at your seat.
10. You read a report from the front of a class. (This item is repeated, increasing the size of the class.)

and was able to participate actively in classroom discussion.

Not all the hierarchies were completed with such dispatch. The construction of the hierarchy is critical. If intervals between items are too long, the increment in anxiety great, progress cannot be made. The presentation of too potent stimuli is not only poor therapy, but it may actually increase the client's anxiety and interfere with future efforts at treatment.

In presenting these stimuli, the therapist must always be certain that a previous item is completely desensitized before another is begun. Occasionally he must deal with avoidance behavior on the part of the client, who "falls asleep" or does not see an item clearly. An equally difficult problem is the striving client who moves too rapidly, visualizing scenes of greater intensity than are called for by the therapist.

An attempt was also made to counter-condition directly feeding behavior. Candy was made available during therapy sessions, and N. was instructed to take some whenever she wanted. It was hoped that anxiety over eating in a social situation might be inhibited by the positive "comfort" responses associated with the therapeutic interaction. Some positive benefit may have been derived from this procedure. However, efforts to desensitize systematically feeding behavior to specific hierarchy items was not successful.[4] The therapists may have attempted to advance too quickly. An increment rather than a decrement in anxiety resulted, and the procedure had to be discontinued. As the other methods were more immediately successful, the feeding technique was not resumed.

It was apparent from the initial interview that the criticism and disapproval of others was a primary source of anxiety. When attacked verbally by another person,

[4] In this procedure N. took a candy coincident with visualization of the item. Thus, both the anxiety component associated with eating and that instigated by the hierarchy were simultaneously present. However, it was hoped that the combination of deep relaxation and the positive aspects of the alimentary response would be a sufficient inhibiting agent.

N. seldom retaliated. She would become anxious and tense, frequently nauseous and unable to eat. Both Salter (1950) and Wolpe (1958) have described the value of encouraging assertive behavior in such situations, as a method of counter-conditioning anxiety. This may be accomplished in part within the therapy hour, but the therapist and the client also plan out assertive behaviors that the client then executes in the life situation. For example, N. reported the holiday visits with her parents were extremely stressful. Conflicting demands on her time would be made by various relatives. Her dress, friends, and habits of work would be criticized. No social error went unnoticed. Because these interactions proved to have an almost ritual quality, it was possible for the therapist and client to plan assertive responses for nearly all the situations that would arise. Thus, on arrival at home N. announced unequivocally her plans for the subsequent few days— exactly when she would be with her parents, and when she would be occupied with her own errands or visiting friends. If her mother commented on the possible unsuitability of her dress, she replied that she had given it careful thought, and was convinced it was the best choice. Following this vacation, N. was able to report considerably less anxiety than during previous trips. Her success was, of course, reinforced with praise by the therapist. Prior to such sallies into the life situation, assertive behavior was practiced with the therapist. The latter would assume the role of some figure in N.'s life, and N. would practice assertive responses during the therapy hour. Furthermore, the therapist frequently manipulated the session in such a way that N. tended to behave more assertively. The client's rights were affirmed. Any assertive behavior during a session was pointed out by the therapist and approved.

Obviously, great care must be taken in employing these methods. Grave setbacks may be suffered if a powerful target is attacked too soon, and retaliation results. The context must be well understood and the behaviors well practiced in the therapy hour, before the client attempts these responses in the life situation. The general method of approach is the same as for desensitization—less threatening situations are broached first. Only after clear successes at this first level, can more anxiety evoking relationships be dealt with.

During the eleven months of therapy, N. made considerable progress. Her distress over travel was eliminated. She had purchased a car, drove freely around the city, and had successfully made a long vacation trip with friends. She gained back most of the weight that she had lost and only rarely had problems in eating. N. no longer had difficulty with school and was considering the pursuit of an advanced degree. Her improved command of social relationships proved to be an occupational asset. When seen at a one year follow-up interview, she reported that she was working in a major hospital, as head nurse on a large surgical ward.

Although there was considerable generalization of anxiety inhibition, situations that had been incompletely dealt with continued to be occasional sources of stress. The client's relationship with her fiance was a continual source of anxiety during therapy. The ambivalent character of her feelings made a systematic treatment of the problem difficult. Ultimately the engagement was broken, although problems with this relationship remained.

Despite the fact that this issue had not been resolved, N. elected to terminate therapy after slightly less than a year of treatment. She correctly argued that her improvement had been considerable; she hoped to solve the remaining problems by herself. At the one year follow-up, N. had maintained her gains and showed further amelioration of treated behaviors. However, she still had difficulty in her relationships with the opposite sex. It should also be pointed out that the consequences of overwhelming stress remained the same for this client, even after treatment. If sufficient pressure were brought to bear, the client's response of anxiety, nausea and avoidance could be elicited. The effect of therapy was to raise markedly the threshold of this response, and to reduce the range of stimuli that could call it up. This led directly to greater self confidence, a sense of well being, more pleasure in social relationships, and an increase in work efficiency. It thus became possible for the client to enjoy a reasonably full and active life.

REFERENCES

JACOBSON, E. *Progressive relaxation.* Chicago: University of Chicago Press, 1938.

JONES, MARY C. A laboratory study of fear: the case of Peter. *Ped. Sem.,* 1924, **31,** 308–315.

LANG, P. J. and A. D. LAZOVIK. The experimental desensitization of a phobia. *J. abnorm soc. Psychol.,* 1963, **66,** 519–525.

LAZOVIK, A. D. and P. J. LANG. A laboratory demonstration of systematic desensitization psychotherapy. *J. Psychol. Stud.,* 1960, **11,** 238–247.

SALTER, A. *Conditioned reflex therapy.* New York: Creative Age Press, Inc., 1950.

WOLPE, J. *Psychotherapy by reciprocal inhibition.* Stanford, Calif.: Stanford University Press, 1958.

23 A CASE STUDY IN A BEHAVIORAL ANALYSIS OF PSYCHOTHERAPY[1]

Edward J. Murray

Psychotherapy is of considerable interest to many psychologists today. This is partly because psychotherapy is the only rational approach to the treatment of neuroses and psychoses. It is also because psychotherapy is a unique source of data about some of the most important and elusive processes of human behavior. Yet, there is much we need to learn about psychotherapy. It is not clear why only some patients improve. Current research using measures before and after therapy, or comparing therapy with no-therapy, yields little useful information; such an approach establishes no relationship between what actually occurs during therapy and the outcome. Thus, there is no rationale for gradually improving tactics or understanding the changes in various kinds of patients. In spite of the general descriptions of therapy that are available, it is not clear just what happens between a therapist and his patient. To some extent this is due to the complexity and the number of the events in therapy. In addition, we have to contend with the subjectivity of the therapist's report. What is needed is an objective behavioral description of psychotherapy. Such a description must be comprehensive enough to capture the important events and yet simple enough to clarify the complexity of the events. With an adequate description of the events in psychotherapy, studies on the prediction of therapeutic progress from psycho-

Journal of Abnormal and Social Psychology, 1954, **49**, 305–310.

[1] This paper was presented at the 1952 meeting of the Eastern Psychological Association, Atlantic City, New Jersey.

logical tests, as well as studies on the evaluation of therapy using outside criteria, will take on new meaning and exert more influence on therapeutic conduct. The purpose of this paper is to describe a first step which was taken in the direction of an adequate description of psychotherapy.

Many events occur during psychotherapy. Those which are readily observable may be grouped as physiological, gross behavioral, and verbal. All three groups have been studied (e.g., 3, 10) and should be studied further. However, verbal behavior seems to be most critical from many points of view. There have been studies on the grammatical and formal properties of verbal behavior in therapy (e.g., 2), which are interesting in many ways but do not seem to be related to the major theories of personality in any determinate way. The content or meaning functions of verbalization seem much more relevant. The general method for studying such material is called content analysis. The research on psychotherapy done by the Rogers group (10) uses content analysis. However, in content analysis the categories which one selects are determined by theory. The theory guiding the Rogerian content analysis appears to be a vague preceptual schema. The content analysis which we are developing is guided by two other points of view: psychoanalytic theory and learning theory. In this context the most relevant categories are those concerned with motivation and defense. Thus, we propose to study the content of verbal behavior in psychotherapy with respect to underlying motives and defenses. This study illustrates this approach with one psychotherapy patient.

A CASE STUDY

The patient was seen for 17 hours in an outpatient clinic.[2] All hours except the thirteenth were phonographically recorded. The first hour was omitted because it consisted of history taking. The patient was referred by the medical clinic. His complaint was that "he has trouble getting to sleep at night— feels that if he falls asleep he may die. He is tremendously threatened but can't say what he is threatened by." At the time of the first interview the patient was described by the therapist as follows:

The patient is a well built, good looking young man of 24. His family was once well-to-do, he's a college graduate, and he's now working in a real estate firm. . . . His parents were divorced when he was eight after a protracted period of arguments which the patient remembers as painful to him. Apparently his mother was unfaithful and a good deal of the dispute was about this. The patient also remembers being taunted about his mother's behavior by one of his companions. Before the divorce the entire family moved about and finally lived with the maternal grandmother. He was surrounded by dominating and pampering females. He now relates this to a "complex" of going from person to person for aid. After the divorce he lived with his aunt. His mother remarried, had a child, who is now nine, and moved in with the patient and his aunt, which is the present home situation. His mother was harsh to him and he developed a distaste for her. He wanted to be different from her and rejected her "emotional" kind of living in favor of a "logical and rational approach." He adjusted to school and social relations with boys very easily. He tended, though, to be a teacher's pet in grammar school. He did well in science and math in high school and started out in biology at college. Upon his return to college after the war he changed to the social sciences taking his degree in history. His relations with girls were extremely innocent until he went

[2] The author wishes to thank Dr. Larry Hemmendinger of the Veterans Administration Regional Office, Bridgeport, Connecticut, for providing this case material.

in the army. He masturbated during adolescence in spite of guilt and fear about it. The army's attitude about masturbation enabled him to overcome a good deal of this guilt. While in the army he went out with a college girl without ever having intercourse, avoiding the kind of girls with whom he might have had sex and avoiding one situation with this girl which might have led to sex. While overseas he did have some sexual relationships. Generally he seems very cooperative and well motivated.

Therapy was mainly supportive but included interpretations about the defensive nature of his physical complaints and the hostility which arose when he became dependent. A permissive attitude toward the expression of hostility was maintained.

After a considerable period of trial and error, two main categories were selected for content analysis: *hostility* and *defense* statements. The hostility category was divided into six subcategories of hostility: (a) mother, (b) aunt, (c) other people, (d) general situations and groups, (e) the therapist, and (f) a vague "at home" (referring to one or more persons in his home). The defense category was composed of: (a) intellectual defensive statements which included the patient's views on philosophy, science, current events, etc., and (b) complaints about a wide variety of physical symptoms and discomforts. Everything else was considered irrelevant.

The unit scored was called a statement. This was either a simple sentence or the meaning phrases of a more complicated sentence. Each statement was judged as belonging to one of the several categories. The main measure was the number of statements in a given category for each hour. Relationships from hour to hour between categories, and between categories and the behavior of the therapist, were determined.

The record of each hour was played very slowly, and each statement was judged either as belonging to one of the eight categories or as irrelevant. A reliability study with three other judges scoring the same hour showed that the categories were defined in a way which was precise enough for teaching other people the method. The reliability was high when the eight categories were compared ($r = .86, .89,$ and $.91; p < .01$ in all cases), and even higher when the irrelevant category was added ($r = .94, .95,$ and $.98; p < .01$ in all cases).

HOSTILITY AND DEFENSES

Expressing hostility was a major problem for the patient. In the summary of the treatment, the therapist says, "his problems today seem centered around dependency and concomitant resentment." However, the therapist did feel that some progress was made in his ability to express his hostility as well as to see its relationship with his dependency. If the patient had trouble expressing hostility, then his hostility must have aroused anxiety. From the theory of conflict (1, 4) we would predict that if hostility is inhibited by anxiety, then, if anxiety is reduced by the permissive attitude of the therapist, the overt manifestations of hostility should increase while the overt manifestations of anxiety should decrease. In this study it is assumed that the hostility statements are the overt manifestation of hostility, and the defense statements the overt manifestation of anxiety. Figure 1 shows the hostility and defense statements throughout the course of psychotherapy. It can be seen that hostility increases and defenses decrease. Moreover,

the hour-to-hour fluctuations show a true reciprocal relationship which strengthens the conflict analysis. The crisscrossing from Hour 4 to Hour 8 takes place in between the part of the therapy when defenses were high and the later part when the expression of hostility was high. The correlation is negative and highly reliable ($r = -.73, p < .01$).

However, the objection might be raised that this is not a dynamic relationship between the two categories because the total number of statements is limited and when one category goes up the other must come down. This is not the case, because, with the exception of one hour, pooled hostility and defense statements never constituted more than 60 per cent of the total statements of one hour. An objection which can be made to this is that there may be nothing unique about the hostility-defense relationship if the residual or irrelevant statements also correlate with either hostility or defenses. This objection is ruled out by the fact that the residual is not correlated with hostility ($r = -.20$) or with defenses ($r = .19$). Another objection which might be raised is that, since the total number of statements varied from hour to hour because of differences in the patient's rate of speech, the length of pauses, and the number of therapist's remarks, the relationship is an artifact of the different totals. That this is not the case is shown in Fig. 2, where the percentage of the total number of hostility and defense state-

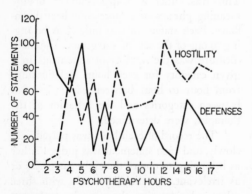

FIGURE 1   Frequency of hostility and defense statements throughout therapy.

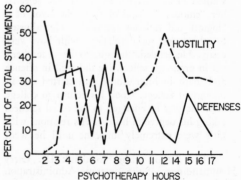

FIGURE 2   Percentage of hostility and defense statements throughout therapy.

ments is plotted.[3] In this form, hostility is still negatively and highly reliably correlated with defenses ($r = -.75$, $p < .01$). Hostility in percentage form correlates very highly with hostility in the frequency form in Fig. 1 ($r = .96$, $p < .01$). This is also true of defenses ($r = .94$, $p < .01$).

We feel that this result strongly suggests that the patient's anxiety about expressing hostility was decreased as a result of the therapist's activity and/or inactivity. However, this may be limited only to the therapeutic situation; outside observations are needed to demonstrate any more general conclusion. The verbal changes shown here may or may not be indicative of fundamental emotional change. Here again, other evidence is needed. It is also conceivable that this hostility was a defense against a more anxiety-arousing sexual problem. But in any event, the lawfulness of the change is encouraging for the usefulness of the method.

THE DISPLACEMENT OF HOSTILITY

An examination of the occurrence of statements in the subcategories of hostility from hour to hour reveals a sequence of persons toward whom hostility is directed rather than a global display on each hour. Figure 3 shows hostility to mother, aunt, and a combined "others" and "general." The sequence strongly suggests displacement. From a psychoanalytic point of view we would expect the mother to be the recipient of the most basic hostility. Mother, aunt, and others form a meaningful gradient of generalization. The patient's hostility to his mother gradually increased up to Hour 6. The therapist's summary of Hour 6 says, "he revealed that his mother had punished him for masturbating. She also forced food upon him and punished him for not eating promptly. He was 'too little to fight back' but did act in a spiteful way several times. He described other hostilities and retaliations with respect to his mother." The following hour showed

[3] The results presented in Figs. 3, 4, and 5 also show little change when plotted in percentage form.

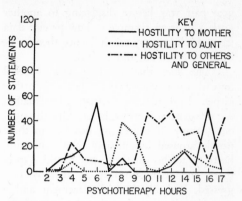

FIGURE 3   Hostility statements referring to mother, aunt, and others-general throughout therapy.

little hostility. Then for several hours he expressed hostility to his aunt. This is viewed as primarily a displacement from the mother, although the aunt elicited her own share of hostility. Following this there was a displacement to other people. We expected the sequence to reverse itself, i.e., after the hostility to others, hostility would be expressed first to the aunt again and finally to the mother again. However, a dramatic external event took place between Hours 15 and 16: his aunt was suddenly taken to the hospital for an emergency cancer operation. The therapist says that during Hour 16, "after considerable struggle he finally stated an ambivalency about the event." Furthermore, his hostility to his mother was increased because she had hinted that if the aunt died, *she* would take over the home.

It should be noted that the learning analysis of displacement (5), which has been confirmed in several animal experiments (6, 7, 9), does not predict sequences of hostility to various objects. Since it is desirable to make such predictions, we embarked on an extension of displacement theory (8) and an experimental investigation, in collaboration with Mr. Mitchell Berkun, of displacement with animals in a free-choice situation. Suffice it to say that if rats are both rewarded and punished at a given goal so as to establish a conflict, they will still approach that goal part way before displacing to another goal. This is an example of how precise data from psychotherapy can influence theories of behavior based on animal work.

The fact that hostility was directed toward people who were further and further displaced provides an alternative explanation for the general increase in hostility throughout therapy. If expressing hostility to these people aroused less anxiety than expressing hostility to his mother, we would expect more and more hostility as therapy progressed. Probably *both* displacement and a general reduction of anxiety because of the treatment operated to permit hostility to increase. The hostility expressed to the patient's mother in Hour 16 was much stronger and was concerned with much more recent events than was the hostility in Hour 6. Thus, there was a therapeutic effect. Indeed, expressing hostility to relatively unimportant people may be therapeutically valuable because it is less fearful. In learning theory terms, fear is extinguished in the displaced situation and these extinction effects are generalized back to the fear in the primary conflict situation. In the experiment mentioned above, the rats returned to the original goal after making unpunished goal responses in the displaced situation.

DEFENSES

The two defense categories seemed to operate as alternate members of a defensive armamentarium. In Fig. 4 it can be seen that the intellectual defense was high at the outset and decreased throughout the first part of therapy. This intellectual defense was never interpreted. The physical complaint defense increased as the intellectual defense decreased. After the major interpretation in Hour 5, the physical complaint defense dropped off sharply. In Hour 6 both defenses were low, and this hour proved to be especially fruitful, as was noted above. This expression of hostility also increased his anxiety, and the following hour was a dull one. Moreover, with the physical complaint de-

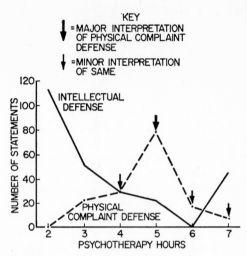

FIGURE 4   The interaction of intellectual and physical complaint defenses and the effects of interpretations during the first portion of therapy.

fense interpreted, the noninterpreted intellectual defense increased in a compensatory way in this subsequent hour. Both defenses decreased during the rest of psychotherapy and show no distinguishing features as far as the number of responses is concerned. The interpretation of the physical complaints may have functioned as a punishment, or may have established insight. Further indices are needed to distinguish between the two possibilities.

There is also a possibility that the two defenses had different functions. The intellectual defense was more assertive and self-aggrandizing. It may have been a way of telling the therapist that he was masculine or mature. On the other hand, the physical complaints had a pleading and ingratiating tone. This defense may have been motivated by feminine or dependent needs. However, both may be viewed as motivated by anxiety and both served the function of avoiding talk about conflict areas.

Fortunately, we examined another case which showed some striking similarities to this one. The general personality picture was the same as the present case. In addition, the two chief defenses were similar to the physical complaints and intellectualizations characterizing our present case. The second patient had physical complaints, although he had more insight into their psychogenesis. A category comprising physical complaints and more psychologically phrased feelings of tension, conflict, and blocking was defined. The intellectual defense was quite similar to the first case. Figure 5 shows the course of physical, etc. defensive statements and intellectual defensive statements throughout the eight hours of therapy. This second patient began with physical complaints which decreased from Hour 1 to Hour 3 without interpretation. As the physical complaints decreased, the intellectual defense increased. This was interpreted in a punitive way in Hour 2 and, less severely, in Hours 3 and 4. Both defenses were low in Hours 3 and 4 and it was in these hours, both in our opinion and in the unsolicited opinion of the therapist, that the most important hostile material came out. In Hour 5 it was the uninterpreted defense—physical complaints that showed the greatest increase. In this case, the therapist then proceeded to interpret the physical complaint defense on Hours 5 and 6. Both defenses were low for the last two hours.

This second case in a sense provides a

natural experimental control for the first case. In the first case intellectual defenses were highest at first and decreased without interpretation; in the second case this was true of physical complaints. In the first case physical complaints supplanted intellectual defenses; in the second case intellectual defenses supplanted physical complaints. In the first case the physical complaints met with the disapproval of the therapist; in the second case this was true of intellectualizations. In both cases the punitively interpreted defenses decreased. In both cases important hostile material emerged when both physical complaints and intellectualizations were low. In both cases the expression of hostility was followed by an upswing in the uninterpreted defense. These results strengthen our belief that the physical complaints and intellectualizations are alternate defenses against anxiety. They also tend to confirm the general conflict analysis we have made. The increase in defenses after the expression of hostility may be related to the "negative therapeutic effect" (1). We may also tentatively formulate the hypothesis that, with this kind of patient, uninterpreted (or unpunished) defenses have a greater probability of occurrence when anxiety is increased than interpreted (or punished) defenses. It is obvious that much more evidence is needed before making any definite conclusions.

SUMMARY AND CONCLUSIONS

In our present state of knowledge about psychotherapy, final conclusions should be avoided. Therefore, it is with trepidation that we approach the task of making a comprehensive summary statement about our illustrative case. This is true even though the therapy was brief and the changes were probably not fundamental. We might ask about the success of this case. The therapist does not sound optimistic in his summary: "The patient now has insight into his problems but can't extricate himself from them. Because of a general character weakness it is improbable that short term therapy will be of

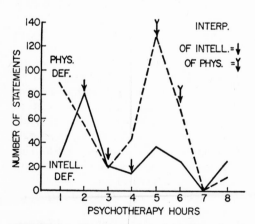

FIGURE 5 The interaction of intellectual and physical complaint defenses and the effects of interpretations throughout the therapy of a second patient.

much more value." But our feeling is that it is important to understand what has happened during these interviews, whether or not the therapy was eminently successful. We feel that our objective description aids in this. Here is a tentative recapitulation of the case in terms of the data presented in this study.

The patient began treatment with a good deal of anxiety and subsequent defensiveness. His defensiveness decreased as a result of a combination of permissiveness about hostility and punitiveness about defenses on the part of the therapist. As this occurred he expressed strong hostility to his mother. This expression of hostility led to an increase in anxiety and defensiveness. The defense which increased was the one not previously punished by the therapist. Subsequently, hostility was displaced further and further away from his mother. Hostility to displaced objects was stronger because it aroused less anxiety. It is possible that because of the unpunished expression of hostility to the displaced objects, the patient was able later in therapy, when environmental factors precipitated it, to express hostility about his mother much more strongly, at least in the therapeutic situation.

Although this integration involves several assumptions, we feel it is strongly supported by the data. It will be noted that the statements made in the summary concern motivational and defensive shifts. This is what the categories were set up to measure. Other events, such as the establishment of insight, require other kinds of categories. Thus, we offer no evidence to support the therapist's opinion that the patient understood the relationship between his hostility and his dependency at the end of therapy.

This preliminary study has been presented to illustrate the kinds of results which can be obtained by studying psychotherapy carefully and quantitatively. We feel that it also demonstrates the applicability of principles derived from animal and human experimentation to complex human behavior. On the other hand, it is only data as clear as these that will stimulate experimental work and modify existing theories. We also hope that this study has indicated some of the difficulties involved in a behavioral analysis of psychotherapy. Cases do not miraculously become comparable when studied quantitatively. New cases are expected to present as many problems as they solve. Nor do we feel that all of the important events in psychotherapy can be described by this method. Indeed, many important things in this case have been ignored. But, as this method becomes more refined, and as equally objective measures are added to it, we feel that our understanding of psychotherapy, and human behavior in general, will be furthered.

REFERENCES

1. DOLLARD, J., & MILLER, N. E. *Personality and psychotherapy.* New York: McGraw-Hill, 1950.
2. GRUMMON, D. L. An investigation into the use of grammatical and psychogrammatical categories of language for the study of personality and psychotherapy. Unpublished Ph.D. dissertation, Univer. of Chicago, 1950.
3. LASSWELL, H. D. Certain prognostic changes during trial (psychoanalytic) interviews. *Psychoanal. Rev.,* 1936, **23,** 241–247.
4. MILLER, N. E. Experimental studies of conflict. In J. McV. Hunt (Ed.), *Personality and the behavior disorders.* New York: Ronald, 1944. Pp. 431–465.
5. MILLER, N. E. Theory and experiment relating psychoanalytic displacement to stimulus response generalization. *J. abnorm. soc. Psychol.,* 1948, **43,** 155–178.
6. MILLER, N. E., & KRAELING, DORIS. Displacement: greater generalization of approach than avoidance in a generalized approach-avoidance conflict. *J. exp. Psychol.,* 1952, **43,** 217–221.
7. MILLER, N. E., & MURRAY, E. J. Displacement and conflict: learnable drive as a basis for the steeper gradient of avoidance than of approach. *J. exp. Psychol.,* 1952, **43,** 227–31.

8. MURRAY, E. J. Displacement in psychotherapy. Paper read at East. Psychol. Ass., Boston, 1953.

9. MURRAY, E. J., & MILLER, N. E. Displacement: steeper gradient of generalization of avoidance than of approach with age of habit controlled. *J. exp. Psychol.*, 1952, **43**, 222–226.

10. ROGERS, C. R. *Client-centered therapy*. Boston: Houghton Mifflin, 1951.

SECTION 3

OTHER DEVIANT ADULT BEHAVIORS:
SEX, TICS, STUTTERING

It is difficult to know if sexual difficulty is the cause or effect of other troubles, for if a person is shy, anxious, aggressive, self-centered, and hypochondriacal, it is not surprising that he might also have difficulty establishing warm interpersonal relations with the opposite sex.

In the first three cases reprinted in this section, we shall see a number of different techniques. In all the cases, however, the aim is a new response to stimuli that previously elicited maladaptive behavior. The maladaptive behavior in sexual difficulties may be conceptualized in two groups: behaviors that should be made are not, and behaviors that should not be made are. For the former, measures to increase adaptive responses, such as relaxation, are usually indicated, while for the latter, aversive stimuli, to decrease the frequency of the response, are likely to be used. However, the article by Bond and Hutchison (26) will cast doubt on this dichotomy by using a relaxation technique in the treatment of a behavior that is to be reduced.

In the first article in this section, Kushner (24) illustrates two methods. To reduce maladaptive behavior, fetishistic stimuli and fantasies were paired with an aversive stimulus, electric shock. After the overt maladaptive responses were reduced, the next step illustrated in Kushner's article was the increase of an adaptive pattern of behavior. In treating impotence, Kushner offers an illustration and confirmation of Wolpe's use of sexual responses to reciprocally inhibit anxiety responses. Kraines (1941) suggested a similar method based on clinical rather than experimental data: "In addition, in cases of impotence, if the patient is forbidden to have sex relations for a week (assuming as it were that his impotence will disappear) while indulging in much sex play, it will be found that freedom from the necessity of having sex relations combined with the stimulation from the sex play, will tend to make the patient so potent and eager as to make him disregard the command to wait for a week."

In the second article, Lazarus (25) not only gives illustrations of various behavior therapy techniques, but offers a dramatic example of a behavior therapist using his knowledge of people to make an inference. In the therapy proper Lazarus takes an active role in providing information and attacking unwarranted notions and attitudes. He makes use of the technique of reciprocal inhibition using sexual responses to help the patient achieve erections. A third form of treatment used in this article is systematic desensitization of four hierarchies dealing with areas that were directly and indirectly associated with difficulties in sexual functioning.

The article in this section by Bond and Hutchison (26) deals with exhibitionism and is particularly instructive for a number of reasons. As we mentioned above, a systematic desensitization rather than aversive conditioning procedure was used. Second, the case illustrates involuntary relaxation at one point, and at another, the use of an anxiety-relief response. Finally, while there was a considerable decrease in the frequency of the maladaptive behavior, particularly with the stimulus situation most likely to lead to it, the progress of the case indicated the need to desensitize further stimulus elements. As such, the material represents a partial success, and with the previous article by Lazarus, a healthy antidote to the notion expressed by Lazarus' patient that behavior therapy is always easy and rapid.

A clear exposition of a learning model formulation of exhibitionism, which might be applied to other forms of maladaptive behavior, was provided by Smith and Guthrie (1922) who noted the reinforcing aspects of gaining attention. In general, sexual release is an eminently reinforcing stimulus, and behavior that precedes it is likely to be increased. Maladaptive sexual behavior may be treated directly as any other learned behavior. Examples of aversive conditioning are provided by Blakemore et al. (1963a, 1963b), Clark (1963c), Freund (1960, 1963), Glynn and Harper (1961), James (1962), Lavin et al. (1961), Max (1935), Oswald (1962), Rachman (1961), Raymond (1956), Thorpe and Schmidt (1964), and Thorpe, Schmidt, and Castell (1963). In these cases an aversive stimulus such as an electric shock or nausea induced by apomorphine follows presentation of the stimulus. A variety of procedures may strengthen the effectiveness of the conditioning. For example, an intermittent reinforcement schedule may increase resistance to extinction. Pairing the stimulus with different aspects of the situation, such as different stages of female attire in a case of transvestism, may be helpful as are making aspects of the stimulus situation inescapable, such as recorded discussions of the fetish object by the subject that are played loudly as he vomits, or pictures of the fetish object in the emesis basin. Oswald's article raises the point that hypnosis or role-playing, along the lines used by Gordova and Kovaleve (1961) with alcoholism might be used in place of the physical techniques of producing aversive stimuli.

Greater detail on three examples will clarify the procedure. First, we wish to quote Max's (1935) abstract of his frequently cited paper:

> A homosexual neurosis in a young man was found upon analysis to be partially fetishistic, the homosexual behavior usually following upon the fetishistic stimulus. An attempt was made to disconnect the emotional aura from this stimulus by means of electric shock, applied in conjunction with the presentation of the stimulus under laboratory conditions. Low shock intensities had little effect but intensities considerably higher than those usually employed on human subjects in other studies, definitely diminished the emotional value of the stimulus for days after each experimental period. Though the subject reported some backsliding, the "desensitizing" effect over a three month period was cumulative. Four months after cessation of the experiment he wrote, "That terrible neurosis has lost its battle, not completely but 95 percent of the way."

Raymond (1956) reports the treatment of a thirty-three-year-old married man who had been referred for prefrontal leucotomy after he had attacked a perambulator. This was the twelfth such attack known to the police, but he had had impulses to damage handbags and perambulators since age ten and he estimated that he had made such attacks at a steady average of two or three a week. He had received many hours of analytical therapy, and had been able to trace back the history of his abnormality to see the significance of the events and the sexual symbolism of perambulators and handbags. However, the attacks had continued. The treatment was explained to the patient who was dubious of it but ready to try anything. A collection of handbags, perambulators, and colored illustrations was obtained and these were shown to the patient after he had received an injection of apomorphine and just before the nausea was produced. The treatment was given every two hours, day and night, and at night amphetamine was used to keep the patient awake. After a week, the patient was allowed to go home for eight days. He returned, and reported "jubilantly" that for the first time he had been able to have intercourse with his wife without using fantasies of handbags or perambulators. Treatment was recommenced. In addition, the patient was asked to write about the objects, which he did in great detail. After five days, he said that the mere sight of the objects made him sick. At this, he was confined to bed and handbags and perambulators were continually around him, the treatment being given at irregular intervals. On the ninth day, he broke down, and sobbed until the objects were removed. He handed over, on his own, a set of negatives of perambulators. He left the hospital and six months later he was readmitted for a booster course of treatment (which the patient did not feel he needed): a colored movie film was made of women carrying handbags and pushing prams. The film was started each time just before the onset of nausea. A follow-up nineteen months later showed that in addition to no overt behavior or trouble with police, the patient no longer required the fantasies for successful intercourse. He progressed on his job and no symptoms replacing the fetish were reported.

In a case reported by Lavin et al. (1961) a twenty-two-year-old married truck driver had a recurrent desire to dress in female clothing that had begun at age eight and from which he had derived erotic satisfaction from age fifteen. While transvestism had continued during service in the Royal Air Force and after marriage, his sexual relationships with his wife were good. Lavin et al. emphasize that the conditioned stimulus must be prepared so that it corresponds to the patient's perversion and does not include anything without significance to the behavior under modification. The patient was excited by dressing in female clothes and viewing himself in a mirror. Twelve 35-mm transparencies were taken of the patient in various stages of female dress. A tape recording was also made of the patient reading from a script describing his putting on various garments until all items of clothing in female dress were mentioned. This procedure was designed to strengthen the conditioned stimulus and to insure the presence of the stimulus even when the patient's eyes were closed during vomiting. It was also designed to make possible some generalization of what was learned. Aversion therapy was continued every two hours for six days and six nights. The unconditioned stimulus was nausea associated with apomorphine. As soon as the injection began to take effect, a slide was projected on to a screen and the tape recording played back. The stimulus was terminated after the patient started vomiting or reported relief. The patient and his wife were interviewed three times during the three months following treatment and each time they stated that recovery was complete. Six months after completion of therapy, the patient wrote reporting the continued absence of his symptoms. Finally, the authors note: "The prediction of symptom substitution inherent in the psychoanalytic theory has not so far been borne out."

As we pointed out in our general introduction, punishment is most useful when an alternative adaptive response is available. It is noteworthy that in the majority of articles we listed, the subjects were married and had a socially acceptable outlet available to them. Freund (1960) approached the problem of increasing the likelihood of the subject emitting adaptive sexual behavior by using hormones to increase approach tendencies and pairing heightened drive with pictures of appropriate sexual objects. Freund reports little success with patients sent by the police or suffering from unrequited homosexual love. However, out of thirty-eight subjects either sent by relatives or without obvious external pressure, twelve achieved heterosexual adaptation lasting several years, five achieved short-term heterosexual adaptation, four had insufficiently documented outcome, and seventeen showed no improvement. Considering the stringency of Freund's criteria of success, his remission rate compares very favorably with studies of other forms of treatment. However, Freund claims only speed as a special favorable consideration for his procedure.

In Bond and Hutchison's work (26), systematic desensitization is used to reduce maladaptive responses. A further illustration of this technique may be found in Wolpe's case of a man who equated violence, injury, and suffering with intercourse with a virgin and was therefore impotent (Wolpe, 1958, 8). Lazarus (1963c) reports on a series of sixteen women treated for frigidity by systematic desensitization. Of these cases, nine improved greatly by very stringent follow-up criteria (within an average of twenty-nine sessions, the longest being forty sessions) and the seven failures all terminated prior to fifteen interviews.

In connection with both Kushner's and Lazarus' articles we mentioned the use of reciprocal inhibition of anxiety by sexual responses. Further illustrations of the method may be found in cases presented by Wolpe (4 and 5 in 1958, and a new case, 10 in Eysenck, 1960a, pp. 110–111). A general approach of encouragement, suggestion, and advice may be successful and is used by Russian therapists (Apter, 1961; Platonov, 1959). Giving information and changing attitudes are illustrated in Lazarus' article and amplified by Ellis (1962) and Salter (1961).

An additional procedure, mentioned by Lazarus is that of assertion and the provision of tasks. Stevenson and Wolpe (1960) illustrate the use of assertion of legitimate rights in non-sexual areas to help develop a more successful masculine role. An example is that of a hairdresser who was encouraged to talk back to his female customers. Other examples of assertion, both general and in specific sexual situations may be found in Salter (1961).

In summary, sexual behavior is learned. Because it is an area of taboo, an area associated with a primary source of positive reinforcement, and involves a complicated interpersonal relationship, it is not surprising that it suffers particular vicissitudes in our society. Emphasis is continually placed on sexual success as a measure of personal worth and therefore, sexual difficulties may, by generalization, be associated with many other role behaviors. The point of the present section is that sexual difficulties may be treated directly by a variety of techniques.

Commonly associated with sexual difficulties are alcoholism and drug addiction. We have previously mentioned Gordova and Kovaleve's approach to alcoholism. Excellent reviews of the direct treatment of alcoholism have been prepared by Franks (1958) and Mertens (1964a). Mertens (1964b) and Narrol (1963) have developed a method for alcoholics similar to Ferster et al.'s treatment of overeating by self-control techniques. An early use of an aversive electrical stimulus in the treatment of alcoholism was by Kantorovich (1929). Voegtlin (1940), and Lemere, Voegtlin, Broz, O'Hallaren, and Tupper (1942) have presented major empirical results of aversive conditioning. In general, aversive conditioning would appear to be a rapid, inexpensive, and effective technique with approximately fifty percent of alcoholics. This percentage would probably be increased by use of intermittent reinforcement and booster courses prior to relapse.

Aside from alcoholism, aversion techniques may be used in the treatment of writer's cramp (Liversedge and Sylvester, 1955) as previously noted, and in the treatment of drug and cigarette addiction (Raymond, 1964). In terms of drug addiction, two very interesting cases using a nonaversive conditioning paradigm were reported by Rubinstein (1931). In short, it seems reasonable that the progress made in the area of sex will be reflected in other areas of so-called acting out or psychopathic behavior.

The next four articles in this section, like the previous three dealing with maladaptive sexual behaviors, represent the direct treatment of behavioral manifestations that have been classified under various diagnostic headings within disease models.

We have previously mentioned Flanagan, Goldiamond, and Azrin (1959) in connection with the demonstration of the instigation of stuttering in normally fluent individuals by making cessation of an aversive stimulus contingent upon stuttering. In the article reprinted in this section, these authors use an aversive stimulus, a blast of noise, to illustrate that stuttering is an operant behavior that may be brought under the control of environmental stimuli. In a recent article, Goldiamond (1965) presents the use of delayed auditory feedback in a thorough program of speech reeducation that grew out of studies such as the one presented in this book.

Rickard and Mundy's article (30) also treats stuttering as an operant behavior. The programing of nonprofessional people, the parents, is again illustrated. The use of shaping procedures and the careful extension of fluent speech into increasingly complex and difficult stimulus situations illustrates the way in which therapy may focus on adaptive behavior in the extra-therapy situation. In Rickard and Mundy's article, therapy, therapist, and extra-therapy situations are blended together.

The literature on stuttering is a very rich one. Makuen is generally credited (for example, Hollingworth, 1930, p. 433) with establishing the first speech deficit clinic in this country in Philadelphia, in 1914. Of the many medical model theories of stuttering (those relating stuttering to handedness or to respiratory, endocrine, and metabolic disorders) psychoanalytic theories are especially to be noted. Hollingworth (1930, pp. 439–440) describes concepts by Freud, Coriat, and Scripture in which the stuttering of words is related to psychic shocks, or conceals sexual and obscene thoughts, or is based on infantile oral eroticism (namely, sucking movements), or is a method of attaining desired isolation. To these might be added Fenichel's (1945) views: "Those functional disorders of speech that are more than simple inhibitions are typical examples of the group of pregenital conversion neuroses."

"The symptom of stuttering reveals more readily than other conversion symptoms that it is the result of a conflict between antagonistic tendencies; the patient shows that he wishes to say something and yet does not wish to. Since he consciously intends to speak, he must have some unconscious reason for not wanting to speak. . . ."

"Psychoanalysis of stutterers reveals the anal-sadistic universe of wishes as the basis of the symptom. For them, the function of speech regularly has an anal-sadistic significance. Speaking means, first, the utterance of obscene, especially anal, words and second, an aggressive act directed against the listener...."

"The same motives which in childhood were directed against pleasurable playing with feces make their appearance again in the form of inhibitions or prohibitions of the pleasure of playing with words. The expulsion and retention of words means the expulsion and retention of feces, and actually the retention of words, just as previously the retention of feces, may either be the reassurance against possible loss or a pleasurable autoerotic activity. One may speak, in stuttering, of a displacement upward of the functions of the anal sphincters...." Hollingworth writes (1930, p. 440): "Brill admits that in treatment by psychoanalysis 'my enthusiasm declined with the length of my experience.' He says that in eleven years he handled 600 cases, analyzed 69, and claims to have cured only 4. Reed tried psychoanalysis but gave it up finding no cases to which the notions applied. Scripture, also sympathetic to the methods of psychoanalysis, says one may 'get at the root of the fear by psychoanalysis (but) this alone is not adequate and no stutterer has ever been cured by it.'" The role of anxiety in stuttering, which is touched on by Flanagan, Goldiamond, and Azrin (27) in the article reprinted, is complicated. We might say that the person stutters because he is anxious or has a physiological disturbance, but we might just as easily say that he becomes anxious, ineffective, physiologically disturbed, or feels inferior *because* he stutters.

Aside from Hollingworth (1930) whom we have quoted at length, other stuttering reviews of interest are by Fletcher (1914, 1928) and Yates (1963). The major point is that, like maladaptive sexual behavior, stuttering is learned and (in the absence of definite physical disability) may be treated efficiently within a psychological model. Within such a psychological model, *a variety of techniques are available*. Examples of the use of both positive and negative reinforcing stimuli are given by Flanagan, Goldiamond, and Azrin (27) and by Rickard and Mundy (30). Another technique that fits closely is that represented by Sheehan (1951) who pointed out that there is a positive reinforcement following stuttering, namely the next fluently spoken word, that is, the ability to continue. Sheehan, in a well designed experiment, therefore had as his experimental condition the repetition of the stuttered word until it was properly spoken, thus interfering with the reinforcement of stuttering by "going on to the next word." Dunlap (1932) advocated negative practice, the repetition of the maladaptive behavior without reinforcement, possibly with an increased voluntary control over it, and a build-up of fatigue and boredom (for example, reactive inhibition). Lehner (1954) reviews negative practice with particular reference to speech difficulties. Case (1960) reports on thirty cases, ten of whom completed the course and were completely cured. Another fifteen of the cases ceased treatment either because of major improvement or the need to move away. Of particular interest in Case's work was the variety of techniques used. Among the methods presented were negative practice, graded social tasks or assertion, "pep talks," and manipulation of drive. The last mentioned technique is instructive (1960, 4, pp. 217–218). A freshman had had difficulty in speaking since age seven. There seemed a complete inability (as distinct from stuttering) to speak, particularly with girls; "He had a number of old-fashioned ideas about girls. He would not speak to those who smoked, wore short skirts or used slang, and as a result he spoke to very few." The subject was told to go two days without talking to anyone. Under this state of deprivation, when he returned to the clinic he was prepared to accept instructions to talk to designated people. These assignments were increased in difficulty and some counseling on matters pertaining to the opposite sex was given. Treatment lasted three months and a follow-up after a year indicated continued improvement in socialization. The deprivation was used to obtain reinforceable behavior, and once he had been trained in socially adaptive behavior, his blocking disappeared.

Another important technique used with stutterers is that of distraction. Action may be considered to be embedded in a nonthreatening context or distraction may be conceptualized as a method for reducing attention to stimuli that are likely to interfere with efficient performance. This concept is sharpened explicitly in the Cherry-Sayers technique in which feedback is a crucial element. Based on a series of laboratory studies that are a model of the experimental foundations leading to effective treatment (Cherry and Sayers, 1956), it is argued that stammering is a perceptual rather than a motor disturbance. By having the subject *shadow* speech he hears, that is, repeat *exactly* what he hears lagging behind the control by two syllables, the subject's attention is diverted from his own speech. Under these conditions, fluent speech is developed as a habit. Cherry and Sayers present ten cases, seven of which were successful. These cases illustrate the use of the technique with children as young as two-and-a-half years old, and with subjects who had been nonfluent over fifty years. After training in the procedure of shadowing, it is possible for the subject, when under environmental stress or falling back into poor habits, to practice by himself and shadow a tape recording of someone else reading. The Cherry-Sayers technique may be utilized within the context of therapy by reciprocal inhibition. Walton and Black (1958) report the case of a man whose stammer became markedly worse when he used a telephone. The treatment proceeded from reading two words behind the psychologist, shadowing over the telephone, relaying a message over the phone, talking to people known to him, and finally, talking over the telephone to people unknown to him. In another case (Walton and Mather, 1963a) a forty-year-old married male was symptom free in the therapy situation after use of the Cherry-Sayers method, but required systematic desensitization of a hierarchy of giving superiors precise information before he was free of stammering in the extra-therapeutic environment. In a further procedure to promote fluent speech in the extra-therapy situation, Meyer and Mair (1963) introduce a metronomic device similar in appearance to a hearing aid.

Nonfluent speech may be treated by: aversive stimuli, positive reinforcement for fluency, extinction, deprivation to increase the reinforcement of fluent speech, negative practice, distraction, embedding in positive contexts, disruption of feedback, systematic desensitization, and hierarchies of assertive behavior. In actual practice, it is not unusual that some combination of these techniques will be used.

The two other articles in the present section deal with tics, a behavior frequently called hysterical. Barrett's article (28) illustrates a Skinnerian approach to the problem in which tic-produced environmental consequences lead to noticeable improvement. Of particular methodological interest is the use of an own-control replicated design. Rafi's article (29) gives an excellent introduction to Yates' (1958b) technique that makes use of Dunlap's (1932) concept of negative practice in a sophisticated Hullian context. Jones (1960a) continued the work of Yates (1958b). Walton (1961b) and Ernest (reported in Jones, 1960a, p. 257) have found it useful with eleven and thirteen-year-old subjects respectively. Rafi's article illustrates not only successful treatment, but the modification of procedure when the objective measures, furnished in behavior therapy, indicated that therapy was not progressing satisfactorily. In terms of Rafi's revised method and the general view of direct treatment of maladaptive behavior, we quote a case from Hollingworth (1930, p. 249): "A boy who had previously shown slight tics of the facial muscles finally exhibited a persistent tic of the eyelids, which constantly blinked. Not only was this a conspicuous bit of behavior—it also definitely interfered with reading and with such simple acts as reading the scale beam in the grocery store where he worked. The tic was readily subjugated to voluntary control within the usual limits of winking, and when cured it did not break out elsewhere."

> The method was simple enough. The patient wore spectacles. Whenever he had occasion to sit quietly, as in reading, a lead pencil was laid across the frame of the spectacles so that it lightly came in contact with the upper surface of the eyelids. This constant stimulus or load adequately inhibited the wink so long as the pencil remained in position. The boy then practiced lifting the eyelids and closing them at will, thus moving the pencil up and down. Developing voluntary control of a muscle means establishing some subtle inner cue as its effective stimulus. As this occurred, the stimulus to the previous "automatic" movement lost its effectiveness and the tic disappeared. (Hollingsworth, 1930.)

Finally, we wish to mention another "hysterical symptom," writer's cramp. Liversedge and Sylvester (1955) report the development of equipment that delivers aversive electrical stimuli when the maladaptive behavior takes place. Conditions opposite to the positive reinforcement of getting out of a disagreeable situation are created. Sylvester and Liversedge (1960) report that twenty-nine of thirty-nine cases benefited markedly following three to six weeks treatment and twenty-four of the thirty-nine at follow-up of up to four-and-a-half years were employed and most engaged in writing from four to six hours a day. Quoting Glover's assertion that writer's cramp is a "typical case of conversion hysteria," the authors remark (p. 335), "We know of no evidence that any case of craft palsy has ever been relieved by psychoanalysis, but we have seen five cases where prolonged courses of psychoanalysis has failed to effect any improvement." The majority of failures in Liversedge and Sylvester's work are people who are highly anxious and in whom, it may be hypothesized, the situation of aversive conditioning is an overly difficult one. Beech (1960) relates four such instances, one of whom responded to negative practice and two others who were markedly improved following systematic desensitization of a hierarchy dealing with writing situations.

24 THE REDUCTION OF A LONG-STANDING FETISH BY MEANS OF AVERSIVE CONDITIONING

Malcolm Kushner

This is a case study of the successful treatment of a fetish of approximately twenty-one years' duration. The patient was a thirty-three-year-old male whose alcoholic father deserted the family when he was a child and who, from the age of about four or five, experienced a series of placements in relatives' homes, foster homes, orphanages, day camps, and so forth. He described his mother as probably being a schizophrenic who blamed the Communists for her difficulties and who felt everyone had a double, good and bad. He was the middle child of three boys. He places the onset of his fetishistic behavior at about twelve years of age. This consisted of his masturbating while wearing women's panties that he usually took from clotheslines. If these were not available, he masturbated when stimulated by pictures of scantily clad women or by fantasies of women wearing panties. He was a shy, retiring child and as he grew older he became more aware of the abnormal nature of his behavior, felt increasingly inadequate and unmasculine, and resorted to body-building and boxing as a means of proving his virility. After a brief period in the Marine Corps and two failures at attempted intercourse, wherein he found himself impotent, the patient consciously set forth to prove his virility by joining a tough gang, drinking, brawling, and earning the reputation of being a "cop fighter." As a result of assaulting a policeman he was sentenced to a reformatory for twenty-six months. A few years later, while slightly intoxicated and influenced by a friend of his from the reformatory, he broke into a hotel room, stole some luggage, was apprehended, and sentenced to six years in prison. While incarcerated he was re-moved from the exciting stimuli and the fetishistic attraction was considerably reduced. He rejected the overtures of the prison "wolves" but wondered why he was so often singled out as their homosexual target. Following this sentence he asked for treatment for his perversion. He recognized that while the fetishism did not directly get him involved with the law, it was nevertheless responsible for his antisocial behavior as a compensatory mechanism. When he began treatment he was tense, tormented and obsessed by the impulses, and increasingly guilt-ridden and self-depreciative following the act. He was bright and very well motivated for treatment. He had had no previous treatment.

A number of factors determined this particular choice of treatment, that is, the attempt to reduce symptoms through aversive conditioning. First, formal psychoanalytical treatment, the conventional treatment of choice for such a condition, was not available. Second, other methods appear to have been unsuccessful since there are only four cases in the entire psychiatric literature claiming a cure (Raymond, 1960) and, finally, the author had become particularly interested in the application of learning theory principles to clinical problems. The fetishistic behavior was conceptualized as being the product of maladaptive learning and it was proposed to extinguish the symptoms through aversive conditioning by means of electric shock.

It was recognized that a danger existed in possibly conditioning the patient adversively to normal sexual stimuli. As such, careful discriminations would have to be made in the procedure. It was also verbalized to the patient that masturbation per se was not being attacked, but rather the type of fantasies and the acting-out with which it was associated. The idea of "panties-woman" was also differentiated from "panties-masturbation" or "wearing panties." No efforts were made to deal with the patient's problems from the conventional "dynamic" point of view.

TREATMENT

The first two sessions were spent in obtaining a history. The patient recalled that the onset of the disturbing behavior occurred when he became curious and sexually excited watching girls sliding down a sliding-board with their panties exposed. It was at this same period in time that he was introduced to masturbation and he soon recognized experiencing similar sensations as when he watched the girls. His fantasies during masturbation quickly were centered about the girls and their panties and shortly this association was firmly made. This explanation for the development of such a fetish is certainly more parsimonious than the "dynamic" explanations involving castration threat, symbolism, and so forth. The above explanation for his behavior was briefly explained to the patient as well as the general approach and rationale that were to be used. He understood the method and was strongly motivated to undertake the treatment regimen.

On the third session, the patient was connected to a Grayson-Stadler PGR apparatus by means of two fingertip electrodes. A conditioning circuit was used to establish a baseline for this shock. Adjustments in the circuit had to be made that still did not deliver as strong a shock as desired, but since it was experienced as uncomfortable it was decided to proceed. Approximately three and one-half milliamperes were delivered.

At each session, anywhere from four to six different stimuli were presented, immediately followed by shock. The patient was instructed to tolerate the shock until it became so uncomfortable that he wanted it

stopped. He was then to signal for termination of the shock by saying "Stop." Twelve such stimuli were presented each session in random order. Approximately one minute elapsed between the sensation of the shock and the presentation of the next stimulus. The stimuli consisted of a magazine-size picture of the rear view of a woman from the middle of the back to the knees wearing panties; an actual pair of panties which was placed in his hand; and imaginal situations in which the patient was asked to imagine himself wearing panties, imagining a clothes-line with panties on it, and imagining himself standing in front of a lingerie shop window. The picture and the panties were always used, with the imaginal situations varying at each session depending upon his reports of particular areas of sensitivity. Discussion was limited as much as possible to the patient's response to the shock and his reaction to the fetish between visits. Each session lasted between twenty and thirty minutes. He was seen three times a week.

After forty-one shock sessions (fourteen weeks of treatment) conditioning was halted since the patient reported no longer being troubled by the fetish. Changes in the intensity of the fetishistic attraction and behavior were reported as early as the second shock session and progressed gradually with increases and decreases in the degree to which the patient was troubled by them. These fluctuations frequently reflected the degree of anxiety generated by extra-treatment conditions. Heightened anxiety often resulted in an increase in the fetishistic behavior that could conceivably be considered an important means by which the patient had learned to reduce the effects of tension and stress. As progress developed, the patient indicated that he had more and more difficulty in eliciting fetishistic fantasies during his masturbation. Soon, the nagging quality of the urges, the self-conflict and torment that accompanied his submission to these urges, and the self-depreciation that went along with it, were markedly reduced. Approximately one month following the termination of the shock sessions, spontaneous recovery of the fetishistic behavior occurred, but in a much milder form than the original. The patient was prepared for this in advance by the therapist and was not discouraged. It was decided to give him a reinforcement or booster session as suggested by Raymond (1960). About two days later when the patient appeared for the booster session he reported no longer being disturbed. Nevertheless, two successive reinforcement sessions were given for good measure.

By this time visits were spaced weekly and during the next phase of treatment the patient's impotence was dealt with. The desensitization approach reported by Wolpe (1958) was utilized and the impotence was relieved quickly to the extent that the patient is now leading a full and satisfactory heterosexual life. In brief, this approach considers the sexual difficulties to be related to high anxiety states that the patient associates with this activity. In order to reduce this anxiety he is instructed to engage in sex-play and stimulation with his partner but is told that he is under no circumstances to attempt to engage in intercourse. This immediately results in a lessening of anxiety since it precludes failure. After a few such contacts the patient is further relaxed and as a result is more sexually responsive. He is told that only when he has both a very strong erection and an overwhelming desire to have intercourse is he to do so and then he is to enter immediately and let himself go, disregarding efforts to prolong the act or to try to please his partner. If instructions are followed expressly success is readily achieved that allows for a continued development of satisfactory coital expression. As can be recognized, this approach requires the full cooperation and understanding of the female partner.

Three months following the reinforcement sessions, the patient was to appear in court for two driving offenses, one of which could possibly result in a jail sentence. He was naturally apprehensive and tense, and indicated that he had been thinking of the fetish again although he could readily dismiss it from his mind. It is possible that, due to the stress he was under, he resorted to his long-term method of seeking gratification and stress reduction, that is, through the fetish. One more reinforcement session was therefore given. The court hearing worked out satisfactorily and, after an eighteen-month follow-up, he no longer complained about the fetish.

At last report the patient is married and has a family and reports that he is doing well. He indicates that he has occasional fleeting thoughts of the fetish or is reminded of it when exposed at times to advertisements, and so forth, but he has no difficulty in thinking of other things and does not dwell upon it as in the past. He reports that occasionally when either fatigued or sexually unexcited he resorts to the fetishistic fantasies in order to attain a climax during intercourse. These instances are not the rule, however, and nevertheless would represent a substantial improvement over his former condition.

The Minnesota Multiphasic Personality Inventory was administered three times during the course of treatment: first, at the time of admission; second, fourteen weeks later at the point at which the aversive conditioning phase was terminated following the initial reduction in the fetishistic impulses; and third, as a follow-up measure six months later. The findings reflect no basic change in the personality make-up that is primarily of an obsessive, schizoid type. However, there was a notable reduction in the inner conflicts, together with a marked reduction in the aggressive acting-out components that were so evident in the first two records. Along with this, some of his suspicious and distrustful attitudes toward society were reduced. The Taylor Manifest Anxiety Scale taken from the three records also reflects a steady decrement in anxiety level. All in all, both behaviorally and psychometrically, the patient was less anxious, more relaxed, and there was considerably less conflict than when he was first seen.

This approach directly attacks the widely held and strongly entrenched position that symptoms serve a defensive purpose and/or are indicative of underlying disturbance. Such being the case they must not be removed without first substituting new defenses lest more serious decompensation occur or other disabling symptoms take their place. Prohibition against the removal of fetishistic objects has been raised by Freud (1928) and Stekel (1930) who believed that homosexuality would result. It was also felt that impotence or strong sadistic drives would result from their removal. In this particular case, homosexuality has not occurred. To the contrary, this man is no longer impotent and enjoys a very active heterosexual life and has so far no difficulty with acting-out aggressive impulses. Recent works by Raymond (1960), Eysenck (1960), Franks (1958), Sylvester and Liversedge (1960), and others strongly support the application of experimentally validated procedures based upon learning theory to clinical material and offer considerable evidence to refute objections such as those raised. Raymond (1960), in a case similar to this, successfully treated a fetishist by giving an emetic drug every two hours day and night for a week in conjunction with the fetishistic object. A nineteen-month follow-up revealed no recurrence of the perverted behavior.

In retrospect, it is felt that perhaps a stronger shock might have further reduced the time of treatment. An increase in the number of trials per session might likewise contribute to this end. Also, in the future, should the opportunity again present itself, partial reinforcement will be utilized with the expectation of greater prevention of extinction of the new response.

This case points up the efficacy of such an approach, rooted in a substantial body of experimentally validated material, on a condition heretofore highly refractory to psychotherapeutic intervention. Its promising application to disorders of a compulsive nature should be investigated further.

REFERENCES

EYSENCK, H. J. (Ed.) *Behaviour therapy and the neuroses*. New York: Pergamon, 1960.

FRANKS, C. M. Alcohol, alcoholism and conditioning: a review of the literature and some theoretical considerations. *J. ment. Sci.,* 1958, **104**, 14–33.

FRANKS, C. M. Conditioning and abnormal behavior. In H. J. Eysenck (Ed.), *Handbook of abnormal psychology*. New York: Basic Books, 1961, 457–487.

FREUD, S. Fetishism. *Int. J. Psycho-anal.,* 1928, **9**, 161–166.

RAYMOND, M. J. A case of fetishism treated by aversion therapy. In H. J. Eysenck (Ed.), *Behaviour therapy and the neuroses*. New York: Pergamon, 1960, 303–311.

STEKEL, W. *Sexual aberrations: the phenomena of fetishism in relation to sex*. New York: Liveright, 1930 (2 vols.).

SYLVESTER, J. D. and L. A. LIVERSEDGE. Conditioning and occupational cramps. In H. J. Eysenck (Ed.), *Behaviour therapy and the neuroses*. New York: Pergamon, 1960, 334–348.

WOLPE, J. *Psychotherapy by reciprocal inhibition*. Stanford, Stanford, Calif.: Stanford University Press, 1958.

25 THE TREATMENT OF A SEXUALLY INADEQUATE MAN

Arnold A. Lazarus

Where high degrees of anxiety produce an almost complete inhibition of sexual responsiveness, therapy must employ a broad range of anxiety-eliminating procedures. In the case outlined below the well-known virtues of a nonrejecting therapist furnished an interpersonal context in which several specific techniques were effectively administered.

Roy came for treatment at the beginning of May 1960. A thirty-three-year-old engineer with a lucrative business of his own, this talented, charming, well-read individual was nonetheless profoundly inadequate. His social facade was impenetrable. His feelings of panic and withdrawal sheltered behind a guise of aloofness and independence. What he recognized as crippling inhibition within himself, his friends termed "slight reticence," and women found that his "boyish shyness" tended to stimulate real or imaginary maternal needs in them.

Roy brought his well-practiced social graces into the therapeutic relationship and concealed his basic problems behind his habitual defenses. "I have come to you," he said, "in order to prove to myself that our social values are depraved." The first three sessions were taken up with impersonal topics that nevertheless revealed a common thread. With extraordinary articulation, Roy embroidered the proposition that the females of our culture blossom into maidenhood with "warped," "twisted," "attenuated," and "truncated" personalities due to their complete preoccupation with "marriage and propagation." The emerging personalities of young girls, he maintained, were irrevocably stunted by emotional strait jackets. They were insidiously brainwashed until the potential virtues of proper male-female friendship and comradeship were completely annihilated. He laboured the point that on innumerable occasions he had persistently endeavoured to establish a "proper friendship" with a woman but that the repercussions had always been mutually disastrous. "Their crippled perceptions are only capable of whittling men into two categories—eligible or ineligible marriage partners or lovers."

Roy dexterously avoided all attempts at meaningful therapeutic communication. Apart from what could be inferred from the above account, his most personal remark was that his acute awareness of the need for social reform frequently made him feel profoundly depressed.

He telephoned before his fourth appointment to ask the therapist whether further sessions were necessary. Roy maintained that he had gained some clarity of thought from the discussions and that in his opinion "therapy" should be terminated. Thereafter the conversation continued along the following lines:

> Therapist: But you haven't even come out with your real problem.
> Roy: How do you mean?
> Therapist: Why must you keep up this pretence?
> Roy: What pretence?
> Therapist: You know what I'm getting at.
> Roy: You psychologists think everyone's insane.
> Therapist: Things like anxiety and sexual problems have little, if anything, to do with insanity.
> (After a long pause) Roy: All right! I'll come in and see you tomorrow.

The fourth session was totally different from the three preceding discussions. In an affectless tone, Roy stated that he was utterly inadequate sexually. His most successful sexual attempt had occurred a year previously with a prostitute with whom he had managed to have an extra-vaginal orgasm and ejaculation with a completely flaccid penis. His life history revealed that his background provided a "breeding ground" for neurosis.

He was born in England and emigrated to South Africa with his parents and siblings after the outbreak of war. "I was an unwanted sixth child in an already overpopulated family consisting of two miscarriages and five daughters. My mother was a militant feminist and my father was an equally devout pacifist." Roy was expected to revere his sisters, to adore his mother and to tolerate his father. Actually, he feared his sisters, was terrified of his mother, and loved his father.

His attitude towards sex was obviously influenced by his mother's overzealous denunciations of promiscuity. An implicit belief in the virtues of chastity made the onus of protecting five daughters from the ravages of temptation a perpetual struggle. Roy and his sisters were constantly reminded that men inadvertently sought to undermine the moral fiber of the nation and that the women had to uphold the dignity of the human race, if there was to be hope for future generations. Roy was admonished to think of his sisters if ever faced with the temptation or opportunity to lead some misguided female astray.

Another influential factor in determining Roy's sexual inadequacies was a two-year period spent at a boarding school between the ages of fifteen–seventeen years. A favorite pastime of the senior boys in his dormitory was suddenly to pull the bedclothes off some unsuspecting victim and to penalize him if he was found to have an erection. Consequently, Roy taught himself to masturbate *without an erection*.

Now thirty-three years of age, Roy could not remember when last he had had a complete erection. He masturbated almost daily, occasionally obtaining a transient erection.

His fantasies during masturbation were exclusively heterosexual, usually involving "mature, persuasive and very seductive women." The reason for his complete refusal to reveal his sexual inadequacies when he first consulted the therapist was that he attributed his disabilities to his masturbatory indulgence, which he viewed with guilt and shame. (It was not out of character for his mother to have threatened him with insanity as the penality for what she regarded as "self-abuse.")

The first therapeutic objective was a concerted endeavour to correct Roy's misconceptions. His combination of genuine sophistication and worldiness was offset by remarkable areas of naïveté and widespread misinformation. One direct consequence of his mother's pejorative teachings was his social submissiveness and masculine ineptitude. This hinged largely on his confused and contradictory attitudes towards women. His ambivalence was exemplified by his tendency to fawn over women at the overt behavior level while inwardly mocking them. Numerous illogicalities between his thoughts, feelings, and actions were pointed out to him. This provoked definite feelings of antagonism in Roy that tentatively led to open hostility towards the therapist. At first, any expression of his own antagonism made him contrite and apologetic, but with practice (which the therapist encouraged both in and out of the therapeutic situation) Roy became less afraid of his own aggressive impulses. Therapy at this stage consisted largely of coaxing him into more and more assertive action tendencies. Although he became less reticent socially, he was still somewhat uncomfortable in feminine company.

Roy had been advised to masturbate to the point of orgasm only when he had a reasonable erection. After three months he reported that he usually awoke in the morning with an erection (which he claimed had last been present when he first entered boarding school) but close physical proximity with women still failed to evoke any reassuring signs of potential sexual adequacy.

At this stage Roy had undergone more

than twenty sessions spaced over approximately three and one-half months. He became increasingly despondent about his basic lack of progress. He began to express doubts about the therapist's competence on the grounds that other "behaviorists," often claimed to achieve dramatic results in less than twelve sessions. The therapist dealt with this impasse by accepting the patient's doubts while pointing out that they were largely based on subjective premises.

Apart from his specific sexual aberrations, Roy's chief failings centered around three main dimensions: *1.* An aversion to having personal altercations with women, typified by his complete inability to "stand up to" his mother or his sisters; *2.* a morbid dread of physical violence, and *3.* an exaggerated concern for public approval.

These areas together with Roy's sexual anxieties were concurrently treated by means of systematic desensitization. In essence, the desensitization procedure consisted of the following steps:

a. Training in progressive relaxation;
b. constructing anxiety hierarchies; (that is, graded lists of situations to which the patient responded with neurotic anxiety);
c. systematically presenting each item on the anxiety hierarchies to the imagination of the relaxed patient.

The four hierarchies constructed in Roy's case were as follows:

1. *A Sexual Hierarchy.* (There were eight items consisting of sexual situations requiring increasing initiative, that is, embracing, kissing, fondling, undressing. . . .)

2. *An Aggression-to-Females Hierarchy.* (There were twelve items such as expressing disapproval (*a*) to a strange woman, (*b*) to his sisters, (*c*) to his mother; refusing to accede to an unreasonable demand made (*a*) by his sisters, (*b*) by his mother; actually shouting at his sisters; and so forth.)
3. *A Physical Violence Hierarchy.* (There were six items ranging from a mild wrestling match between two young boys, to newspaper headlines dealing with violent riots in a foreign country.)
4. *A Rejection Hierarchy.* (There were six items consisting of the following type of situation: overhearing a mildly uncomplimentary remark passed about him; being called neurotic; a woman finds fault with his manners; and so on.)

Roy required fifty-seven desensitization sessions spaced over approximately eight months before he was able to picture the most exacting scenes in each hierarchy with comparative equanimity. Throughout this period, fluctuating changes accrued to his personality in an almost imperceptible but nontheless discernible manner. Roy's attitude towards the therapist constantly vascilated between antipathy and adulation.

About three months after the commencement of desensitization, Roy reported that he obtained an erection whenever he danced with a girl. After two months he successfully allowed himself to be seduced by "a notorious nymphomaniac." A few weeks later, Roy reported that he was having regular sexual relations with a woman at work.

At the time of writing, Roy is the adequate husband of a twenty-three-year-old ex-beauty queen and the father of a two-month-old daughter.

26 APPLICATION OF RECIPROCAL INHIBITION THERAPY TO EXHIBITIONISM

Ian K. Bond • Harry C. Hutchison

The therapeutic reconditioning techniques developed by Wolpe (2) and termed "reciprocal inhibition" therapy have been applied to a diversity of neurotic disorders. To our knowledge there are no reports of the use of these techniques with the sexual perversions of exhibitionism, overt homosexuality, or pedophilia. Explorations along these lines are being undertaken at the Forensic Clinic,[1] and this paper seeks to provide a detailed account of their use in a case of exhibitionism.

Psychoanalytic theory (1) considers the act of exposing the genitals a defence against the fear of castration. Experience with these patients reveals that exposure either follows some environmental stress which constituted a challenge to the patient's sense of adequacy, or is provoked by an encounter with a female of specified age and physical appearance (blonde hair, plump legs etc.). The exposure can be thought of as an instrumental act designed to reduce an anxiety response cued off by certain classes of stimuli, and as such, the systematic desensitization techniques described by Wolpe (2) would constitute an appropriate form of treatment.

The patient under consideration is a 25 year old, married, man of average intelligence (I.Q. 106). The elder of two boys, he recalls intense antagonism towards his brother dating from an early age. Ten years separated the two.

The parents are of Anglo-Saxon stock;

artisan class, and quite puritanical in outlook. The patient reports them as domineering. He recalls his mother's early admonition against childish sexual practices which she described as "evil" and "nasty," and her frequent injunctions that he conceal genitals from the view of females. An incident which increases his sexual guilt tremendously involved punishment by his mother for engaging in a contest with another boy to see how high up the side of a wall each could urinate. He recalls at this time feeling "hurt" by the observation that his friend's penis was the larger.

His first exposure occurred at 13 following sex play with a 10-year-old neighbour girl. He had felt a desire to perform coitus, but the girl appeared indifferent to his suggestion and had refused. Her indifference hurt him; this was followed by rage, then by the exposing of his erect penis to her. During an explanatory hypnotic interview he recalled having seen this same girl urinate some five years before this episode, and his experience of astonishment at the appearance of her genitals.

Throughout adolescence he suffered feelings of inadequacy and inferiority. His exhibitionism continued, and he indulged excessively in sexual daydreams and phallic auto-erotic practices. Mild asthma and peptic ulcer appeared at this time, but he has had no symptoms of these reaching adulthood.

At age 15 he developed a practice which served as substitute for exposing on occasions when he could not get out in the street. He would select single females from the telephone directory, call them, and attempt to engage them in lewd conversation. A period

The Canadian Medical Association Journal, 1960, **83**, 23–25.

[1] Forensic Clinic, Toronto Psychiatric Hospital. Supported by the Mental Health Division of the Ontario Department of Health.

of voyeurism occurred at this time, but disappeared after his first frank view of the adult female genitals. By the late teens and early twenties, his exhibitionism had reached bizarre proportions. Tension was constant and it was not unusual for him to expose several times during the day.

A frequent practice was to hide completely nude in a small wooded area in the centre of the town where he then lived and spring out and expose himself to the first woman who passed. Another was to hide himself in the cloakroom of a girls' school, exposing himself to the first girl to use the lavatory. If the door were latched, he would lie on the floor and thrust his erect penis under the door for the occupant's view. While driving a car, he would entertain exposure fantasies of such intensity that his driving was a public danger. These fantasies led to turning up a side street to get out of the car and expose. Passing an attractive female when driving led to exposure also.

The stimuli leading to exhibiting in this patient consisted of attractive young females of adolescent or early adult years. They were typically sophisticated and "sexy" but of respectable appearance. Particularly compelling were shapely legs and ankles, clad in sheer nylons worn with high-heeled shoes. Well-developed breasts, a trim waist and generous hips provided strong provocation also. Prostitutes or girls in bathing suits were inocuous stimuli. Fantasies of exposing to females with the appropriate attributes would lead to exhibiting.

The attack of exhibitionism was described by the patient as being preceded by a feeling of sexual excitement and dread. He would experience "a grim determination to expose, come what might." He would become tense and an erection would occur. At this time things would seem unreal, "as if watching myself do something in a dream." He would then expose to the female usually but not always, masturbating. When the girl registered shock, "the spell would be broken" and he would flee, trembling and remorseful. His wife, often present during such an attack, described his appearance as one of being

"paralyzed, with glazed eyes." On such occasions she could prevent his exhibiting only by forcefully dragging him away.

There was one interesting period of abstinence from acting out. At the age of 18 he became involved with a girl he hoped to marry and had sexual relations with her. He did not expose for six months, although his urges remained strong. Eventually he succumbed to his urges, was apprehended, and lost the girl. At the age of 23 when courting his wife he refrained from exhibiting for two months. His exposures occurred unabated just before marriage and immediately afterwards, however visits to prostitutes had no effect. He would frequently expose a short distance from the brothel he had just left.

The patient's police record indicated 24 charges of indecent exposure and 11 convictions with nine prison sentences of from four months to one year.

Previous treatment had included individual and group psychotherapy and CO2 abreaction therapy conducted over an 18-month period at a reformatory clinic. He had received a few weeks of individual psychotherapy and 10 months of group psychotherapy at the Forensic Clinic. During this period he wore a "chastity belt" which he decided to have made by a prosthetics manufacturer to prevent his exhibiting. His wife locked the belt in the morning and unlocked it at night. The treatment was interrupted by a conviction for indecent assault. While wearing the belt, the patient had attempted to grasp the legs and breasts of a young woman he saw in a crowd.

After his release from imprisonment for this offence, the patient sought help from a lay hypnotist. He attended four sessions, accompanied by his wife, and was given relaxation suggestions and moralistic exhortations. He found the latter useless and annoying, but he claimed some benefit from the relaxation suggestions. He renewed contact with the Forensic Clinic, and after consideration of the case, it was decided to attempt a form of reciprocal inhibition therapy. The treatment technique was discussed with the patient, who was willing to attempt anything that might help him, and it was arranged that he would attend four sessions per week, with the stipulation that his wife would continue to accompany him to avoid exposure, arrest and interruption of treatment.

In Wolpe's (2) description of systematic desensitization of anxiety patients, the therapist establishes, initially, a hierarchy of stimulus situations in terms of their anxiety-provoking potential. Training is given in relaxation of the skeletal musculature, and while hypnosis may be used to induce such relaxation, its use is unnecessary in one who can relax readily. In a deeply relaxed state, the patient is called upon to visualize a scene which incorporates the mildest of the anxiety-provoking situations. The deep relaxation, which is anxiety-inhibiting, is thus paired with the anxiety-provoking stimulus, and after a series of presentations, anxiety ceases to dominate as a response to that situation. The next most provoking stimulus situation is dealt with in a similar manner, and the next in turn as the former ceases to become effective in provoking anxiety.

From the content of the interview in this case, the therapist established a rough hierarchy of exposure-provoking stimuli in terms of type of female, her physical attributes, and place of exposure. It is interesting to note that when the patient returned to the scene of a previous exposure, this was sufficient to elicit strong exhibitionistic urges.

In the first sessions, the patient was relaxed by suggestions given while in a light hypnotic state. The therapist then described one of the milder situations conducive to exhibiting. A rapid mounting of tension was apparent at first. The procedure was repeated three times in the first session. After this session, the patient was instructed to practice relaxation at home, using the word "relax" as a cue for the appropriate postural adjustments. Subsequent sessions were similar to the first, with the exception that the more provoking situations were presented in progression.

After twelve sessions the patient was sent home with his wife by way of a nearby department store. These premises were re-plete with young women of the type to whom he usually could not resist exposing. When he arrived for the next session, he reported an involuntary relaxation when passing some of the women he had encountered. With two he did not relax involuntarily, and he used the word "relax" to initiate the process. With one woman he was unable to relax, but retained sufficient control to turn his back to her and this permitted him to recover.

The patient's wife was bedridden with duodenal ulcer for the eighth session, but he came along and returned home without event. During the next week he went out alone to seek employment. His quest was unsuccessful and this, coupled with his wife's illness, resulted in despondency. On passing a small park, he decided to enter it and expose. He unbuttoned his trousers and hid behind a clump of bushes. But when a girl approached he went into a state of involuntary relaxation and lost his erection. He then adjusted his clothing and continued on his way, "feeling foolish."

From this point, improvement was rapid. His exhibitionistic urges became weaker and less frequent and he felt quite confident of his ability to handle them. As his sexual fantasies diminished, exhibiting was involved in them to a much lesser degree. The patient was able to engage in mixed group activities without tension for the first time, and he astonished his wife attending a party and dancing with women attired in low-cut gowns. After the party, rather than experiencing tension and desires to expose, he felt "relaxed and at peace". Sexually he became more virile and he reported considerable enjoyment in his sex-relationship with his wife.

After 20 sessions, an unusual event occurred. He was at home, alone, and had an urge to telephone a female in order to engage her in prurient conversation, a practice he had given up four years previously. The urge was relatively weak, and he called his wife at work and indulged in amorous discussions. This behaviour did not alarm the patient, and he felt no urge to repeat this activity.

It was decided to terminate treatment after the 20th session. The patient continued practising relaxation at home. In following up contacts over the next month, thoughts of exposing were reported as occurring about once per week in very mild form. However, one day while walking through a department store he found himself stimulated by a young female. He followed her for a time; then another, and another, finding his excitement increasing. After three hours of following women shoppers through the store and masturbating through his trouser pocket, he arrived in the lingerie department. He then exposed in what was for him an uncharacteristic manner: he was unable to achieve an erection; he felt no urge to speak to the woman to whom he exposed; nor did he look to observe the effect he had upon her. He did not try to escape, and was arrested.

The court was lenient, and the patient was returned to the Clinic for treatment. This was resumed on a once-weekly basis by the second writer.

However, four sessions after this exposure, while walking up the street in broad daylight, he felt the uncontrollable urge to look up the skirts of a woman who was standing at a bus stop. He carried out the act and was promptly arrested. Once again the court returned the patient to the Clinic. Systematic desensitization to females was continued on a once-weekly basis for 5 months, and the patient, on reporting that he was free of symptoms, was terminated with a once-monthly follow-up arrangement. A total of 46 sessions had been completed at this time.

Following cessation of treatment, the patient was completely free of symptoms for a period of 13 months. He obtained heavy manual employment with a municipal agency, and, although slight of stature, earned a permanent staff position and promotion within six months. During the period of follow-up, he commented on how the lewd jokes told by his fellow-workmen had

no effect upon him, although they would have "set him off on a rampage before." Social and sexual adjustment was excellent.

Ten months after termination of treatment, he was called into the municipal office by the personnel officer, informed that the nature of his past offences was known, and was summarily dismissed from employment.

This experience was disheartening to him. He was unable to find employment, and within a month was under severe financial stress. The therapist suggested a resumption of treatment, but the patient expressed the wish to carry on without treatment to see whether his symptoms returned. Two months later, thirteen months after his last sexual offense, the patient was refused financial assistance in a welfare office. He left the building feeling depressed. He saw a woman on the street and found himself following her. She went into an office building and eventually to a washroom. The patient followed her inside, with urges to look under the door and perhaps expose as he had done in the past. The woman had heard him enter, and shouted in alarm, frightening the patient away. He felt that these urges were on the borderline of control, and he castigated himself for this episode. However, a week later, still in dire financial straits, as he passed by the door of an office building where he had exposed in the past, he felt an urge which he acted on again. He went in the building to a locker-room and exposed to a woman whose back was turned to him. He made good his escape without the woman knowing of his presence. The third incident in the series occurred when he was passing the building of the first incident on his way to the welfare office. He entered and went to the same washroom. As he entered a woman screamed. He ran, and was apprehended. When interviewed by the therapist regarding these three incidents, he observed that he was in no danger of exposing to women on the street or in department stores (the setting of the desensitization sessions) but that women's washrooms made him tense and excited, and that a woman in the washroom was a strong provocation.

The case presents certain interesting features. As noted at the outset, two broad classes of stimuli initiate the exhibitionistic response in the writers' experience with such cases: situations involving a threat to the adequacy of the individual; and females of specified age and appearance. There are of course individual differences in the matter of the relative strength of these two classes of stimuli.

In the case reported here, the stimulus of the female seemed the obvious point of attack, and the writers addressed their efforts to this hierarchy to exclusion of others. This was successful in that provocative females in public places as for example streets, parks, or department stores, ceased to be effective stimuli insofar as initiation of tension was concerned. Situations giving rise to feelings of inadequacy were ignored, and these were allowed to retain strength, as had weaker stimuli of washrooms which had been associated with the stimulus complex on previous instances of exposure. Under conditions which favoured the summation of these stimuli, the patient was rendered prone to exposure. A thorough application of Wolpe's technique would have consisted of establishing a complete inventory of the situations in which the patient had exposed or had experienced urges, followed by a progressive desensitization of all the stimulus hierarchies represented. This is being carried out at the time of writing.

While this case demonstrates the value of systematic desensitization technique in the treatment of exhibitionism of a nonpsychotic type, it should be noted that other forms of reciprocal inhibition therapy might be more suitable in a particular case. In a more recent and less severe case than reported here, although similarly resistive to group or individual therapy, exposure followed a slowly mounting tension which was initiated by situations giving rise to feelings of inadequacy. The second writer spent 26 sessions in teaching the patient to relax to a verbal cue whenever he felt his tension mounting. Over a 22 month follow-up, he has never been in danger of exposing.

While single case presentations of the type offered here are usually interesting and often instructive, what is required is an amassing of results with the technique over a wide range of severity of exhibitionistic conditions, coupled with appropriate comparisons of results with patients who have been treated by conventional methods. This may well prove reciprocal inhibition techniques the treatment of choice in exhibitionism.

REFERENCES

1. LORAND, A.S. and BALINT, M., eds.: Perversions: Psychodynamics and Therapy, Random House Inc., New York, 1956.
2. WOLPE, J.D.: A.M.A. Arch., Neurol. and Psychiat., **72**, 205, 1954.

27 OPERANT STUTTERING: THE CONTROL OF STUTTERING BEHAVIOR THROUGH RESPONSE-CONTINGENT CONSEQUENCES[1]

Bruce Flanagan • Israel Goldiamond • Nathan Azrin

The attempt to understand and control stuttering has received considerable attention in both clinic and laboratory. The concept of anxiety has played a major role in formulations in both areas; stuttering is considered "an anxiety-motivated avoidant response that becomes 'conditioned' to the cues or stimuli associated with its occurrence"(5).

This study reports a preliminary investigation designed to explore the extent to which stuttering can be brought under operant control.

Three male stutterers from the speech clinic, ages 15, 22, and 37, served as S's. The S read from loose printed pages; every time he stuttered, E pressed a microswitch which activated an Esterline-Angus recorder. A check was run by turning the microswitch over to another E, who had not been informed of the nature of the experiment, and instructing him to press upon each moment of stuttering. The E observed S through a one-way mirror in a room adjoining the experimental room, and heard him through a sound-amplification system.

When a curve of stuttering frequency considered smooth was obtained, E turned a switch which initiated a 30-minute period of response-contingent stimuli. After this period, S was observed for another 30 min-

Journal of the Experimental Analysis of Behavior, 1958, **1**, 173–178.

[1] The authors wish to express their appreciation to Dr. Chester J. Atkinson, of Southern Illinois University, for his assistance with equipment problems and active interest during the course of the study.

utes without such stimuli following each press of the microswitch. No specific S^D's were introduced to differentiate periods. A constant noise level of 60 decibels was present throughout the experiment.

Response-contingent periods were of two kinds. During the *aversive period*, every depression of the microswitch which activated the recorder also produced a 1-second blast of a 6000-cycle tone at 105 decibels in S's earphones. During the *escape period*, such a blast was constantly present; every depression of the microswitch shut off the tone for 5 seconds. Such use of noise as an aversive stimulus which was contingent upon responding or which could be escaped by responding followed a procedure used by Azrin (1).

Each S was run on two consecutive days. For S-1, the escape period was presented on the first day, and the aversive on the following day. For S-2 and S-3, the order was aversive-escape.

Record was kept not only of stuttering frequency, but also of elapsed time and number of pages of copy read. Data are presented in the accompanying figures. For all S's, the ordinate is cumulative words stuttered. For S-1, the abscissa is time, producing rate curves. For S-2 and S-3, however, the abscissa is number of pages read, and the curves depict stutters per page read.

Curves for sessions containing escape periods are presented in Fig. 1. For all S's, stuttering increases when escape from the tone is made contingent upon stuttering. When the tone is turned off, stuttering is no

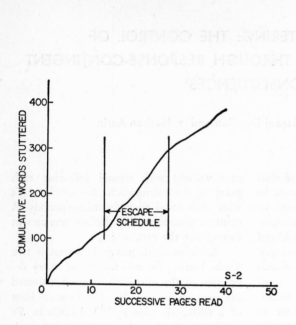

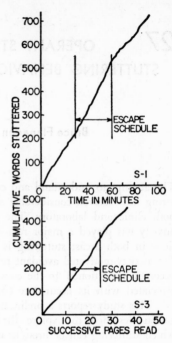

FIGURE I   Escape periods.

longer followed by such consequences, and the rate drops. All *S*'s display short interludes of diminished rate, characterized by irregularities in the curves. All sessions open with a high-burst stuttering activity. This concurs with findings of "adaptation" studies in stuttering (7).

Curves for sessions containing aversive periods for *S-1* and *S-3* are presented in Fig. 2. Making presentation of a blast contingent upon stuttering tends to depress the rate of stuttering during such a period in a marked manner; *S-1* seems to have been moving toward an asymptote of complete suppression. The compensatory rise previously noted (2, 8) following cessation of aversive consequences is pronounced in both *S*'s. The adaptation burst is again present.

The aversive-period session for *S-2* is presented in Fig. 3, which depicts total suppression of stuttering during the aversive period, and beyond. The period during which definition of stuttering was turned

over to another *E* is designated under the heading, Control *E*.[2] There is no discernible effect on response rate, arguing for the validity of the major *E*'s judgment of stuttering. The adaptation burst is again present.

Comparisons of the various figures tend to indicate that number of pages read can apparently be equated with time as a component of rate. Such an equation would follow if rate of reading itself, that is, pages per unit of time, were constant. For *S-2* and *S-3*, the mean reading times in minutes per page are:

	Base line	Escape	Final		Base line	Aversive	Final
S-2	2.20	2.12	2.07		2.28	2.10	2.30
S-3	2.48	2.30	2.42		2.50	2.65	2.75

[2] Both *E*'s are speech therapists. The major *E* is a stutterer who has had 7 years of experience as a speech therapist specializing in stuttering.

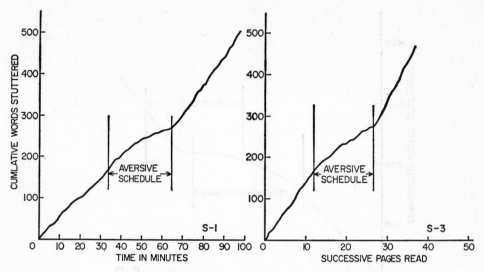

FIGURE 2   Aversive periods for S-1 and S-3.

The only safe conclusion seems to be that *S-3* reads more slowly than *S-2;* the apparent randomness of the data suggests constancy in reading rate.

The data presented suggest that the stuttering response is an operant which occurs in the context of another operant, namely, verbal behavior. Although one cannot stutter without talking, neither can one limp without walking, and limping can be controlled separately from walking. Reading rate was apparently not systematically affected by the response-contingent stimuli which controlled stuttering, hence the two are separable responses. The operant nature of reading has been discussed elsewhere (9); the way in which stuttering responses reacted to operant controls in this study can not be distinguished from reactions of other operant behaviors, and suggests that they are in this class of behaviors.

When termination of a noxious stimulus was made contingent upon stuttering, response rate rose. When onset of a noxious stimulus was made contingent upon stuttering, response suppression occurred, displaying compensation upon cessation of such consequences. For one *S*, the response was

completely suppressed, and this suppression continued beyond the termination of the aversive contingency. Where *S* avoids certain consequences by suppressing a response, the suppression will be maintained by absence of the consequences. Accordingly, elimination of the consequences by *E* will tend to maintain the suppression. The adaptation effects reported in the speech literature were found here. These consist of an initial burst of stuttering, which then "adapts out," that is, drops to a base-line rate. These curves have been considered similar to respondent extinction curves (10), although classical extinction is not obtained (cf. 7). Consideration of conditions related to the establishment of an operant base line would involve a stuttering response being occasioned by S^D's. Placing a stutterer in a speech clinic with instructions to speak is not a procedure calculated to diminish generalization of the S^D's to new stimuli present in the experimental session. The response rate should rise. As the experiment progresses, and no new consequences are applied to responses occasioned by the new S^D's, we are establishing conditions for discrimination of new from old S^D's; the new

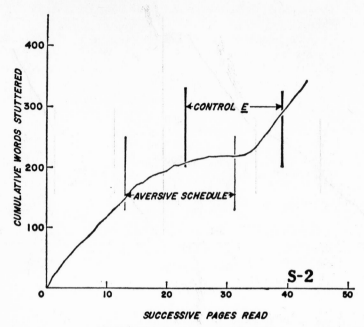

FIGURE 3 Aversive period for S-2.

stimuli lose their control; the situation is "perceived as familiar," or "perceived as non-threatening." Operant discrimination involves *operant* extinction of responses to S, the new S^D's.

Concerning the relationship of stuttering to anxiety, presumably of a respondent type, anxiety is associated with the suppression of operant behavior (3); stuttering behavior was both suppressed and intensified, and these changes are explainable on an operant basis. Since the stuttering response can be isolated from regular speech as a unit of response, we might speculate that such isolation would come about through differential consequences applied to breaks in speech, and smooth speech. Such differentiation might relate to the anxiety of the parent (rather than the child) upon hearing a stuttering response. She may reinforce the behavior by becoming attentive, and should she later decide to extinguish by ignoring, the usual burst of increased stuttering behavior during onset of extinction (4, 6) might increase *her* anxiety, lead to remorse, reinstate-

ment of reinforcement—and the establishment of a variable-interval schedule making extinction all the more difficult.

If further research supports the operant analysis presented here, then it would seem that controlled alteration of such behavior, that is, therapy, would involve application of procedures from the experimental analysis of operant behavior, notably of responses reinforced on a variable-interval schedule.

REFERENCES

1. AZRIN, N. Noise and human behavior. J. exp. anal. Behav., 1958, **2**, 183–200.
2. ESTES, W. K. An experimental study of punishment. Psychol. Monogr., 1944, **57**, No. 263.
3. ESTES, W. K., and SKINNER, B. F. Some quantitative properties of anxiety. J. exp. Psychol., 1941, **29**, 290–400.
4. FERSTER, C. B. Withdrawal of positive reinforcement as punishment. Science, 1957, **126**, 509.
5. JOHNSON, W. J. Stuttering in children

and adults. Minneapolis: University of Minnesota, 1955.

6. KELLER, F. S., and SCHOENFELD, W. N. Principles of psychology. New York: Appleton-Century-Crofts, 1950.

7. ROUSEY, C. L. Stuttering severity during prolonged spontaneous speech. J. speech and hearing Res., 1958, 1, 40–47.

8. SKINNER, B. F. The behavior of organ- isms. New York: Appleton Century Co., 1938.

9. SKINNER, B. F. Verbal behavior. New York: Appleton-Century-Crofts, 1958.

10. WISCHNER, G. J. Stuttering behavior and learning: a preliminary theoretical for- mulation. J. speech and hearing Dis., 1950, 15, 324–325.

28   REDUCTION IN RATE OF MULTIPLE TICS BY FREE OPERANT CONDITIONING METHODS

Beatrice H. Barrett[1]

The experimental investigation of neuro-muscular tics has probably been most limited by difficulties in developing sensitive and reliable behavioral measurement techniques. The closest approximation to an experimental study of tics, by Yates (18), was based on a patient's records of her ability to reproduce her tic symptoms. Yates did not attempt to obtain objective records or measurement of the patient's tics.

The method of free operant conditioning, originally developed by Skinner (15) to study animal behavior and later modified by Lindsley (9) to study the behavior of chronic psychotics, has provided precise techniques of behavioral measurement and con-trol. These techniques have been extended to the investigation of such pathological be-haviors as vocal hallucinatory episodes (10, 11, 12), pressure of speech (13), and stutter-ing (7). By the application of free operant techniques, Ferster (5) succeeded in expand-ing the very limited behavioral repertories of two autistic children, and Brady and Lind (3) performed an experimental analysis with therapeutic results in a patient with hysterical blindness.

The basic datum of the free operant method is the frequency of a specific and reliably defined response within a controlled experimental environment. The method is most readily applied, therefore, in cases where changes in the rate of a repeated movement are of primary concern. The present report describes an application of free operant methods to the control of multi-ple neuromuscular tics.

Journal of Nervous and Mental Disease, **135**, 187–195. Copyright © 1962. The Williams & Wilkins Co., Baltimore 2, Md. U.S.A.

[1] Ogden R. Lindsley, Ph.D., Director of the Laboratory, generously supplied the dia-grammatic sketch in Figure 1 and the control-ling and recording equipment. His advice and encouragement were invaluable in the conduct of this experiment. This research was supported by Research Training Grant 2M-7084 and Re-search Grant MY-2778 from the National In-stitute of Mental Health, U.S. Public Health Service.

METHOD

Patient

The patient in this experiment was a 38-year-old veteran, hospitalized in the Neurol-ogy Service of a local Veterans Administration hospital.[2] His extensive multiple tics started approximately 14 years ago, during his term of duty in the armed services. Although a medical discharge was available to him, the patient chose to continue in the service, eventually serving overseas, until regular discharge. Since then he has been employed as an accountant by a single firm.

An interview prior to the experiment revealed that the patient knew of no traumatic experience preceding the abrupt onset of tics. He told of awakening during the night with a choking sensation accompanied by a momentary inability to breathe or swallow. He recalled this as a frightening experience and was puzzled by the subsequent development of tics. Within a few months, spasmodic movements had developed in much of his body. At the time of this experiment, his major movements included contractions of neck, shoulder, chest, and abdominal muscles, head nodding, bilateral eye blinking, opening of the mouth, and other comparatively mild facial movements.[3] The patient complained of difficulty in swallowing, hence of slow ingestion. His clear, intelligent speech was marked only occasionally by barely noticeable hesitation.

In recent years the patient was not fully aware of the presence of his tics. On occasion, when he thought himself relatively free of them, his wife reported that there was no reduction in his twitching. The patient did feel, however, that his movements were reduced in frequency while he was playing his saxophone in a local band on weekends. His greatest concern was the extent to which his tics made him conspicuous to strangers and limited his business advancement. In general, little was known of the patient's personal history.

The patient had undergone psychological

counseling for a number of months and had received pharmacological treatment which included a variety of tranquilizing and muscle-relaxing drugs. Neither treatment had afforded symptomatic relief. The patient displayed no outstanding symptoms of psychopathology. His tics were considered symptomatic of an extrapyramidal system disturbance and untreatable by conventional methods.

Since he had experienced no success with other methods, the patient was highly motivated to participate in this experiment. Although he was soon discharged to return to work in a neighboring state, he voluntarily rehospitalized himself two months later for continuation of the experiment.

Arrangement of Apparatus

Patient's enclosure: A quiet, well ventilated room with observation facilities was equipped with a comfortable swivel-tilt armchair, an ashtray, a set of comfortable earphones which the patient wore throughout all experimental sessions, and a Grass EEG console (see Figure 1).

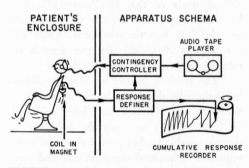

FIGURE I   Schema of apparatus used to pick up, automatically record, and program the contingent consequences of multiple tics.

Operandum: A large U-shaped magnet, securely attached to the outside of the chair back, served as a convenient device for summating multiple tics. Although the swivel arc of the chair was restricted and the chair's casters removed, its tilt was freely operative. An induction coil rested in a "nest" of electrical tape strung between the

[2] The author is grateful to Norman Geschwind, M.D., Department of Neurology, Boston VA Hospital, who suggested the experimental behavioral study of this patient and who arranged for space and the loan of various apparatus components.

[3] Some of the patient's movements were so strong that, when he was seated in a chair on casters, they caused slight rolling.

poles of the magnet.[4] Slack in the tape was adjusted so that when the patient was seated in the chair his most noticeable spasmodic movements, regardless of locus or amplitude, created a slight movement of the coil in the magnetic field.

Response definition and recording: The current induced in the moving coil was amplified by one channel of an EEG recorder to operate a sensitive relay. The operations of this relay were directly recorded as tics. The duration and amplitude of the recorded tics were determined by setting the amplifier gain so that each strong and obvious tic would operate the response relay and cumulative response recorder. After initial selection, this amplifier gain was held constant throughout the experiment.

Response-Contingent Events

In free operant conditioning, the frequency of a response is altered by programing particular consequences contingent upon the emission of that response. Generally this method has been used to generate steady rates of responding or to increase the frequency of a given response. When *reduction* in the frequency of a symptom is desired, the event contingent upon symptom occurrence may be 1) the removal of a positive stimulus or 2) the presentation of an aversive stimulus. In this experiment, both types of tic-contingent events were used.

By the use of a tape recorder, a positive stimulus (music) could be removed or an aversive stimulus (noise) presented when a tic occurred. Pulses from the response relay were transmitted through a timer to a circuit which controlled the tape recorder output to the patient's earphones (see schema in Figure 1). All recording and controlling equipment was located in a nearby room.[5]

[4] Michael J. Malone, M.D., offered the general idea of the "tic chair" and magnetic pickup.
[5] The cooperation, assistance, and patience of David Adkins and the staff of the EEG laboratory at the Boston VA Hospital made possible the occupancy of sufficient space to approximate good environmental control.

Music: In order to maximize the patient's interest, the music used in the experiment was selected by the patient himself from the hospital's music library. Boredom and satiation were minimized by using several selections with no repetitions.

The contingency arrangement was programed so that each tic produced a 1.5 second interruption of music. If the patient did not tic for at least 1.5 seconds, he could hear the music until it was automatically interrupted by the next tic. In effect, this schedule differentially reinforced time intervals between tics of 1.5 seconds or more.[6]

Noise: Azrin (1) found that responses could be eliminated by making the presentation of white noise contingent upon their occurrence; and Flanagan, Goldiamond and Azrin (7) successfully reduced chronic stuttering by presentation of a stutter-produced loud tone. In the present experiment a tape loop of white noise (60 db) was used as a tic produced aversive stimulus.

The contingency was arranged so that each tic produced 1.5 seconds of noise over the patient's earphones. When the patient was tic-free for at least 1.5 seconds, the noise was automatically interrupted and did not recur until the next tic.

Contingency Testing

As a control measure to test the effect of the contingencies described above, periods of continuous music and continuous noise were used. This amounted to removal of the contingency requirement which, in the case of music, more nearly approximated the conditions of music therapy.

Self-Control

The effects of music and noise were compared with the patient's own efforts to control his tics. A signal light (60 watt bulb) was introduced and the patient was instructed to control his tics by his most fre-

[6] In technical terms, this schedule is a time contingent crf drl of 1.5 seconds with an unlimited hold (6).

quently used methods for as long as the light was on.

Experimental Sessions

The patient was informed that we would be studying the effects of various conditions on his tic rate. He had selected a lasting supply of music tapes with the understanding that he would hear them at least some of the time during the experiment. He was instructed to make himself comfortable and to remain seated in the chair, with earphones on, throughout the sessions. Aside from previously mentioned instructions concerning the signal light, no further explanation was given. The experimental room was closed, and recording was begun. Experimental conditions were changed without interruption by adjusting the controlling equipment. The duration of sessions varied from two to three hours depending on meal schedules and other hospital routines. No attempt was made to set up predetermined time intervals for each experimental condition. With a few exceptions due to time limits, each condition was run long enough to show its maximal effect when compared with the normal tic rate or operant level.

RESULTS

Cumulative records of the first four sessions showing the effects of music and noise on tic rate are shown in Figure 2.[7] These sessions were conducted during a 48-hour period prior to the patient's discharge. The remaining sessions were held two months later when the patient voluntarily rehospitalized himself for continuation of the experiment.

To facilitate comparison of tic rates under the various experimental conditions,

[7] The cumulative response recorder feeds paper at a constant speed while each tic impulse moves the recording pen one step in a vertical direction. After 450 tics have been recorded, the pen automatically resets to the base and is ready to step up with the next tic (see Figure 1). Horizontal lines in the curves are periods when no tic impulses occurred.

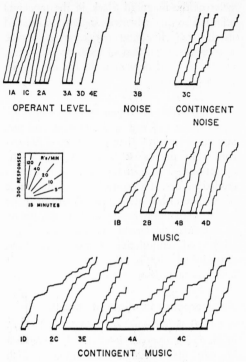

FIGURE 2 Cumulative response records of the first four experimental sessions showing changes in tic rate under conditions of tic-contingent noise and tic-contingent interruption of music and control runs of both noise and music without the contingency requirement. The experimental sessions are numbered and the sequence of conditions within each session identified by letters. Double bars connect all immediately successive curves under designated conditions. Breaks in double bars indicate a change of conditions.[8]

[8] For example, the first four pen excursions labeled 1A were continuously recorded tics during a 26-minute period at the start of the first session to get an operant level. Without interruption, the 1B curves follow, showing 27 minutes of tics under continuous music. The two curves labeled 1C record a return to the operant level for 10 minutes, followed immediately by the 1D period of 34 minutes with each tic producing interruption of the music. The 2A curves show operant level rates at the start of session 2, followed by 25 minutes of continuous music (2B), then 21 minutes of tic-contingent interruption of music (2C), and so on. The same identification system is used in Figure 4 for sessions 7 and 8.

the continuous records in all figures have been telescoped and grouped. The steeper the slope of the curves, the higher the tic rate. Rate estimates may be made by reference to the grid showing rates for representative slopes.

Operant level determinations: The patient's normal tic rate (operant level) ranged between 64 and 116 tics per minute (tpm), with some decrease in the short run at 4E during the last session in Figure 2. No diurnal variations in tic rate were noted. Although sessions were run during various hours of the day and evening to capitalize on limited time, neither fatigue nor hunger affected tic rate or response to experimental conditions.[9]

Effects of noise: There was a very slight increase in the tic rate during a brief seven-minute period when continuous white noise (60 db) was played ("noise" in Figure 2). However, when made tic-contingent, noise reduced the tic rate to about 40 tpm ("contingent noise" in Figure 2). The long tic-free intervals toward the end of the contingent noise period may have been due to dozing which the patient later reported. Because of its apparent soporific effect, noise was not used further.

Effects of music: Continuous music ("music" in Figure 2) reduced the tic rate about as much as did contingent noise (40 tpm). However, when each tic interrupted the music ("contingent music"), the rate was lowered to 15 to 30 tpm. During every period of contingent music, the effect of the contingency was an additional reduction of 40 to 50 per cent in tic rate. After the first session there was no overlap between the range of rates under continuous music and under tic-contingent interruption of music. The differential magnitude of these

---

[9] Sessions 2, 4, and 8 were run in the morning and terminated for the patient's lunch; sessions 1 and 3 occurred in the afternoon; sessions 5 and 7 were conducted in the evening.

effects on this patient thus requires no statistical test.

The fact that contingent music produced a greater reduction in rate of ticing than did continuous music appears to be the result of longer, more frequent tic-free periods when the contingency was in effect. The improbability of fatigue effects is indicated by a comparison of the 4A rate under contingent music obtained at the start of a morning session with the 1D, 2C, and 3E rates under this condition recorded at the end of the three previous sessions.

Effects of self-control: The tic-reducing effect of contingent music is compared with the patient's sustained efforts of self-control in Figure 3 (fifth session). In re-

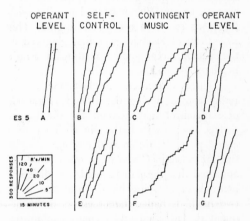

FIGURE 3   A continuous cumulative record of the fifth experimental session showing rate changes under sustained self-control compared with the greater reduction under tic-produced interruption of music. The sequence of conditions is indicated by letters.

sponse to instructions and a signal light, the patient reduced his tic rate to 50 to 60 per minute. This rate is only slightly higher than that previously obtained with contingent noise and non-contingent music. Under the condition of tic-contingent interruption of music, however, rates were considerably lower, ranging from 20 to 35 per minute.[10] Again there was no overlap between the range of rates under the three conditions (operant level, self-control, and contingent music). Note the initial rapid tic rate at the beginning of the C period of contingent music. This increase in rate following a period of self-control (B) parallels what clinicians have observed in tiqueurs (17). It appears that this effect was strong enough to counteract temporarily the effect of the contingent music (C).

In addition to the differential effects on tic rate of self-control and the music contingency condition, there was also a difference in the patient's general behavior topography. In the B period of self-control, the patient was observed to engage in head-holding and general prolonged contraction. In contrast, during the E period of self-control, he engaged in relaxed tapping with finger or foot and occasional singing. This new form of behavior was first observed as the patient accompanied contingent music in the C period.

These differences in behavior topography shown during the B and E periods of self-control may account for the longer tic-free intervals in E than in B. They may also explain the differential response to contingent music in C and F. In other words, it appeared that the patient used two different methods of reducing his tics and that these two methods had different effects on subsequent tic reduction under contingent music. During B, self-control was effected by a generalized rigid contraction which was followed in C by an initial increase in rate despite the availability of contingent music. In contrast, during E self-control was achieved through release methods with the subsequent rapid and marked rate reduction under contingent music (F).

Reliability of the effect of contingent music: The previously described data from six experimental sessions showed that tic-contingent interruption of music reduced the

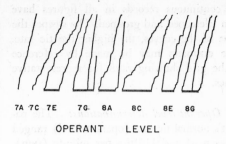

7A 7C 7E   7G. 8A   8C   8E 8G

OPERANT   LEVEL

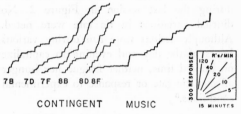

7B 7D 7F 8B   8D 8F

CONTINGENT   MUSIC

FIGURE 4   Records of sessions 7 and 8 demonstrating reproducibility of the marked tic-reducing effect of tic-contingent interruption of music in six replications. Letters designate the sequence of conditions within numbered sessions.

patient's tic rate far more than did non-contingent music, tic-produced white noise, or the patient's efforts at self-control. During those sessions, the patient had approximately six hours' exposure to contingent music. Following a two-month interruption of the experiment, the reliability of the tic-reducing effect of contingent music was subjected to empirical test by a series of replications on the same patient.[11] The result of alternating operant level control periods (7A, 7C, 7E, and 7G; and 8A, 8C, 8E, and 8G) with periods of tic-produced interruption of music (7B, 7D, and 7F; and 8B, 8D, and 8F) are shown in Figure 4. The effect of contingent music on tic-free intervals was dramatically and reliably demonstrated by reductions of from 55 to 85 per cent below the operant rate on each of these six replications.

The tic-reducing effect of contingent

[10] This differential effect was reproduced repeatedly in session 6, which is not shown here.

[11] Both Claude Bernard, in 1865 (2), and Murray Sidman, in 1961 (14), have pointed out that the most convincing test of reliability of an "effect" is the demonstration of its reproducibility in a series of replications.

music was more immediate and prolonged than in earlier sessions. Tic-free intervals were, for the most part, considerably longer and more frequent than previously, and only brief bursts of tics occurred with high local rate. The patient expressed irritation at the end of session 8 because he had wanted to hear the remainder of a jazz concert being played during 8F (the period with lowest tic rate: nine per minute). He commented that he was concentrating on the musical ideas and became annoyed when his brief bursts of tics interrupted it. During most of the 44-minute 8F period of contingent music he was observed to be almost motionless as he listened to the music.

The pattern of tic-free intervals followed by brief intervals of heightened local rate which developed in response to contingent music appeared to generalize to the operant ticing rate as early as session 4. If this was a true generalization, it may have therapeutic implications. On the other hand, it may simply represent a minor shift of unknown nature in the tic rate. Because of possible operandum unreliability (discussed below), the most valid comparisons should be limited to the differential effects of self-control, non-contingent music, and contingent music relative to the operant tic rate.

Intrasession decrease in operant level rate did appear with regularity during the last two sessions (Figure 4). Operant tic rates 7C, 7E, 8C, and 8E, which were recorded between periods of contingent music, showed somewhat longer tic-free intervals than those recorded at the beginning of these sessions (7A and 8A) or those recorded at the end of these sessions (7G and 8G). The reasons for this decrease are far from clear, but the decrease may have something to do with attention. The patient reported that during these sessions he was anticipating more music and knew he would not hear it if he had many tics.

DISCUSSION

The results of this experiment clearly demonstrate that non-contingent music and tic-contingent white noise reduced the tic rate to a level comparable with that produced by self-control. A far more powerful reduction was produced by tic-contingent interruption of music.

In evaluating the differential control of tic rate shown in these data and the possible extensions of the basic method to other symptoms for either therapeutic or research purposes, the most pertinent consideration is the design of the operandum, the device which permits the symptom to operate a switch (16). Two major requirements of a good operandum are the reliability of its operation and the specificity of the response class which actuates it.[12] The fragile tape arrangement of our crude operandum does not insure reliable operation for continued general application. It is not stable enough to maintain accurate calibration during repeated use. A more stable operandum might have permanently fixed pickups, preferably embedded in upholstery in different areas of a chair.

Although a chair operandum provided a relatively comfortable situation for the patient, it did restrict his motility more than might be desired. Moreover, it was not specific to tic movements alone. A more tic-specific operandum would be operated solely by tic movements. Improved specificity of tic measurement without restrictions on motility might be obtained by pickups placed at the loci of various tics which would be telemetered by transmitters worn on the patient's belt or in a pocket (8). The patient could then engage in routine daily activities while effects of interest are continuously recorded.

Once the operandum requirements have been refined, therapeutic effects can be more reliably evaluated. The use of tic-contingent

[12] Ferster (4) has discussed in some detail the general requirements of an accurate operandum (manipulandum). This device, which is manipulated by the subject's behavior, also defines the response being conditioned or attenuated. It is the point of contact between the subject and the automatic recording equipment. For these reasons its operating characteristics are of utmost importance.

interruption of music could be extended in time or otherwise modified. For example, the duration of the tic-free interval necessary to produce music could be progressively lengthened. With remote recording, the long term effects of an appropriate contingency arrangement could be evaluated by furnishing the patient with a portable contingency controller to plug into his home radio or television set for relief of his symptom. The contingencies for music and noise, already demonstrated to be effective, could be combined in a multiple contingency whereby each tic would bring 1.5 seconds of noise and pauses greater than 1.5 seconds would bring music, until the next tic impulse simultaneously interrupted the music and restored the white noise.

The observed behavior changes offered as possible explanations for differential tic rates recorded under self-control could be objectively measured to evaluate the interaction between symptomatic and non-symptomatic responses. For example, if operanda had been provided for simultaneously recording the patient's finger-tapping and singing, it might have been possible to show an inverse relationship between the rate of vocalizing and finger-drumming and the tic rate. In addition, experiments could be run to determine whether tic movements may be diminished or even eliminated by differentially reinforcing another more circumscribed and more socially acceptable motor response which serves the same discharge function as tics.

A free operant conditioning analogy to the negative practice technique used by Yates (18) could be readily investigated by positively reinforcing the patient for each tic. If this variation of the method is therapeutic, positive reinforcement of the symptom should be followed by reduction in the operant tic rate.

The general aspects of the pickup and continuous recording system described here provide a method for direct and objective behavioral measurement of motor symptom frequency which would be useful in studying the effects of drugs, the influence of attention, and variations in tic rate during diagnostic or therapeutic interviews.

SUMMARY

A method for continuous automatic recording of the rate of multiple tics has been used in a demonstration of differential control of tic rate by free operant conditioning procedures.

The results showed that the multiple tics of a neurological patient, previously refractory to pharmacological and psychological therapies, could be reduced in rate by self-control, by tic-produced white noise, and by continuous music. The most dramatic, rapid, and reliable reduction resulted from tic-produced interruption of music. The power of tic-contingent environmental consequences in controlling this patient's symptom was shown, and suggestions were offered for extending and refining the basic method for more definitive investigations of this and other motor disturbances.

REFERENCES

1. AZRIN, N. H. Some effects of noise on human behavior. J. Exp. Anal. Behav., 1: 183–200, 1958.
2. BERNARD, C. Introduction to the Study of Experimental Medicine. Paris, 1865, translated 1927. Dover Publications, New York, 1957.
3. BRADY, J. P. and LIND, D. L. Experimental analysis of hysterical blindness. A.M.A. Arch. Gen. Psychiat., 4: 331–339, 1961.
4. FERSTER, C. B. The use of the free operant in the analysis of behavior. Psychol. Bull., 50: 263–274, 1953.
5. FERSTER, C. B. The development of performances in autistic children in an automatically controlled environment. J. Chron. Dis., 13: 312–345, 1961.
6. FERSTER, C. B. and SKINNER, B. F. Schedules of Reinforcement. Appleton-Century-Crofts, New York, 1957.
7. FLANAGAN, B., GOLDIAMOND, I. and AZRIN, N. H. Operant stuttering: The control

of stuttering behavior through response-contingent consequences. J. Exp. Anal. Behav., 1: 173–177, 1958.

8. HEFFERLINE, R. F. Learning theory and clinical psychology—an eventual symbiosis? In Bachrach, A. J., ed. *Experimental Foundations of Clinical Psychology*. Basic Books, New York, 1962.

9. LINDSLEY, O. R. Operant conditioning methods applied to research in chronic schizophrenia. Psychiat. Res. Rep. Amer. Psychiat. Ass., 5: 118–139, 1956.

10. LINDSLEY, O. R. Reduction in rate of vocal psychotic symptoms by differential positive reinforcement. J. Exp. Anal. Behav., 2: 269, 1959.

11. LINDSLEY, O. R. Characteristics of the behavior of chronic psychotics as revealed by free-operant conditioning methods. Dis. Nerv. Syst. Monogr. Suppl., 21: 66–78, 1960.

12. LINDSLEY, O. R. Direct measurement and functional definition of vocal hallucinatory symptoms in chronic psychosis. Paper presented at Third World Congress of Psychiatry, Montreal, Canada, June, 1961.

13. SHEARN, D., SPRAGUE, R. L. and ROSENZWEIG, S. A method for the analysis and control of speech rate. J. Exp. Anal. Behav., 4: 197–201, 1961.

14. SIDMAN, M. *The Tactics of Scientific Research*. Basic Books, New York, 1961.

15. SKINNER, B. F. *The Behavior of Organisms*. Appleton-Century, New York, 1938.

16. SKINNER, B. F. Operandum. J. Exp. Anal. Behav., 5: 224, 1962.

17. WECHSLER, I. S. *Clinical Neurology*. Saunders, Philadelphia, 1952.

18. YATES, A. J. The application of modern learning theory to the treatment of tics. J. Abnorm. Soc. Psychol., 56: 175–182, 1958. Reprinted in Eysenck, H. J., ed. *Behaviour Therapy and the Neuroses*. Pergamon Press, New York, 1960.

29   LEARNING THEORY AND THE TREATMENT OF TICS

A. Abi Rafi[1]

Yates [1] reported a successful experiment on the extinction of four tics in a female psychiatric patient of high average intelligence. He based his method of treatment on a theoretical model treating the tic as a simple learned response which has attained its maximum habit strength. His general hypothesis was that massed practice in the tic leads to a significant decrement in the ability of the subject to respond voluntarily,

Journal of Psychosomatic Research, 1962, 6, 71–76.

[1] The author wishes to acknowledge his indebtedness to Dr. W. J. McCulley, Medical Superintendent, St. Andrew's Hospital, for permission to publish and for making it possible for the investigation to be carried out.

and eventually leads to extinction of the tic by the process of building up a negative habit of not performing it. His results confirmed this hypothesis, i.e., the number of repeated voluntary evocations of the tic per minute declined significantly, and there was an improvement in his patient's involuntary tics. As Yates was attempting to produce maximal conditioned inhibition ($_sI_R$), he varied the conditions of practice systematically but always used a "standard procedure", by which each tic was given five 1-min periods of massed practice with one minute's rest between each period, as a control. He describes several experiments in detail but the main outcome was that very prolonged periods of massed practice, followed by prolonged rest periods, produced the largest declines.

This paper reports the outcome of similar experiments on two psychiatric patients with tics. One was given the "standard procedure" of Yates and the other the procedure of prolonged massed practice followed by prolonged rest.

SUBJECTS

The two patients were referred to the psychology department with a view to treatment based on learning theory constructs. Before the experiments began, each patient underwent the usual neurological investigations and the possibility of an organic basis to the tics has been adequately excluded. Both patients were of high average intelligence (Wechsler Adult Intelligence Scale). One, a female, patient A, was 63 years old, and the other, a male, patient B, was 57 years old. The Maudsley Personality Inventory showed patient A to be very neurotic and slightly introverted, and patient B to be very extraverted but not neurotic.

Patient A suffered from a right foot tapping tic which appeared about two years before referral. The tapping, a see-saw-like movement of toe and heel, was continuous and forceful while she was standing up or sitting down. She was admitted to hospital on several occasions after the appearance of the tic complaining of depression and restlessness. She was treated with chlorpromazine and had modified electroconvulsive treatment. On every occasion she was discharged "relieved" but neither out-patient nor in-patient treatment, including ECT, had any influence on the tic. The tapping caused much annoyance to those who happened to be in her company. Her public life became considerably restricted because of the censure her tic evoked. She remained on chlorpromazine throughout the experiments.

Patient B was seen as an out-patient and remained one. His main complaint was a spasmodic movement of his head to the left. This began early in 1958, and gradually increased in conjunction with facial grimacing. He came to the out-patient clinic, had some physiotherapy, was given dexamphetamine and sodium amytal, also a series of pentothal abreactions, with no material progress. He continued on drugs but these were stopped with the consent of his psychiatrist after the fourth session of intensive practice.

METHOD

The tics were considered as symptoms which had developed originally as conditioned avoidance responses, became reinforced through satisfying temporary needs and thereafter existed as learned responses separated from the original circumstances which first occasioned them. The method of treatment by massed practice was adopted.

Both patients were treated separately. Patient A was given Yates' "standard procedure," two sessions a day, one in the morning and one in the afternoon under supervision. Patient B was given very prolonged massed practice sessions, each of two hours' continuous practice, followed by prolonged rest periods (one week). The instructions were the same for both subjects, namely, to produce the tic as accurately as possible, to repeat it without pause during the practice period, and to pay attention to the tic. No stress was laid on speed.

Each voluntary evocation of the tic was recorded by the author for about 70 per cent of the records of patient A, and for all the records of patient B. Patient A carried out about 30 per cent of the total number of sessions at her home. These were performed under the supervision of her husband who has been adequately trained by the author in the strict procedure to be followed. He also recorded the voluntary tics. An instructions form and record sheets were provided. Patient B attended regularly at the hospital once a week. A stop watch was used.

RESULTS

The score recorded was the number of tics per minute as counted from the record sheets.

Table 1 shows the results. In the case of patient A, the frequency of occurrence of

TABLE I   Changes in Mean Frequency of Two Tics Under Condition of Voluntary Evocation

	TAPPING						HEAD	
5 One-min. Sessions			5 Five-min. Sessions			Two-hour Sessions		
Sessions	M	σ	Sessions	M	σ	Sessions	M	σ
1–50	87·68	11·39	1–10	40·75	4·35	1–5	33·50	2·49
51–100	77·81	5·60	11–20	41·50	3·52	6–10	17·80	2·78
101–150	82·36	6·84	21–30	47·75	4·07	11–15	4·86	3·32
151–200	80·44	5·23	31–40	45·25	3·77	16–20	2·68	4·11
201–250	82·40	7·89	41–50	40·75	3·63	21–25	2·51	3·13
251–280	75·47	9·84						

the tic per minute (under test conditions) did not show any appreciable decline either within single sessions or between sets of 50 sessions. The mean score for any one set of 50 sessions is not significantly lower than the mean score for any other set of 50 sessions (the highest value of t was 1·16; the lowest, 0·46). The results of this experiment do not support the general theory propounded by Yates.

The "standard procedure" was discontinued after the 280th session and another introduced with sessions of five 5-min trials under conditions of massed practice, with one minute's rest between each period. Fifty such sessions were completed. The results of this experiment are reported in Table 1. Here again the mean score for any one set of 10 sessions is not significantly lower than the mean score for any other set of ten sessions. In neither of these two experiments was Yates' general hypothesis that massed practice leads to a significant decrement in the ability of the subject to respond voluntarily, confirmed.

Yates [2] suggests that very prolonged sessions of massed practice in terms of 6–7 hr continuous practice in one session followed by very prolonged rest, 2–3 weeks at least, could be very effective. Could it be that patient A has shown very little decline because of a simple lack of foot-pounds work? To test this, very prolonged massed practice in terms of 2 hr continuous practice in one session was introduced. Patient A was unable to tolerate this kind of stress and refused to

take another session. An apparatus was therefore devised (see Fig. 1)[2] with a foot treadle freely pivoted on two No. 12 screws. Under the foot treadle, at the front and back, are two bell push switches. Each time the foot treadle is pressed downwards, whether by toe or by heel, a buzzer is sounded. There is a 2/10 of an inch free play between the foot treadle and the bell push switches. Any slight pressure beyond that is enough to cause the buzzer to sound.

By the conditioned-response principle, it was hypothesized that a strong connection would be expected to develop between the stimulation arising from the desire to tap the foot and the response of hearing the buzzer and withholding the foot from tapping. Gradually this connection should become sufficiently well established to cause withholding of the foot from tapping in advance of the onset of the tapping, instead of afterwards. Patient A was given daily practice sessions each lasting one hour. She was instructed to sit comfortably, put her right foot on the foot treadle, pay attention to the buzzers and try to balance the foot treadle and not to cause the sounding of the buzzers. There were 70 sessions in all (see Fig. 2, curve 3). The results confirm the hypothesis. The frequency of occurrence of the tic almost invariably showed steady decline. A stage was reached where she was able to keep her foot still throughout any one practice session.

[2] Thanks are due to Mr. G. H. Tarlton, Chief Engineer, for building the apparatus to specifications.

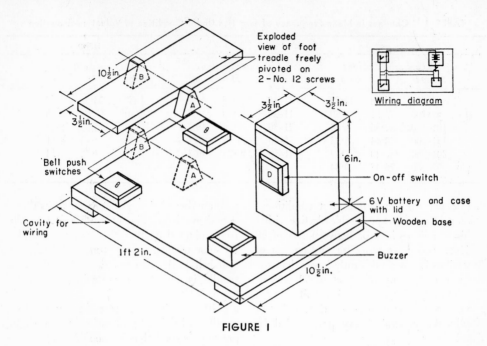

FIGURE I

At the termination of the experiment she felt much improved. The foot tapping became very faint and intermittent and ceased to be a source of annoyance to her or to those around her.

In the case of patient B, the procedure of intensive practice for 2-hr periods with one week's rest between sessions, led to significant decrement in his ability to respond voluntarily, (see Table 1). The frequency of occurrence of the tic per minute (under test conditions) showed a steady decline. The mean score for the second set of five sessions was significantly below that for the first set of five sessions ($t = 31.37$, $P = 0.001$). Similarly, the mean for sessions 11–15 was significantly lower than that for sessions 6–10 ($t = 18.81$, $P = 0.001$); the mean for sessions 16–20 was significantly lower than that for sessions 11–15 ($t = 3.10$, $P = 0.01$). The mean score for sessions 21–25 was not significantly below that for sessions 16–20 (value of t here was 0.37). The results of this experiment confirm to the general hypothesis of Yates.

The course of decline in the frequency of voluntary responding for each tic, using the different procedures, is shown in Fig. 2. Each point on curves 1 and 2, represents the average of five sessions (i.e., 25 1-min trials for curve 1; 5 five-min trials for curve 2). Each point on curve 3 represents the total number of tics (buzzes) of seven sessions (i.e., 7 one-hour trials). Each point on curve 4, represents the average of one session (i.e., one trial of 120-min).

CHANGES IN INVOLUNTARY TICS

Both patients reported improvement outside the test situation. Patient A felt more cheerful, started going out more frequently, and resumed her attendance at church which she stopped previously because of the annoyances her tapping caused to others; at one stage she used to put a cushion under her foot during church service, in order to make the continuous tapping inaudible. She reported total absence of the tic over three consecutive days, otherwise the frequency was sharply reduced, but complete cessation of involuntary tapping was not reported.

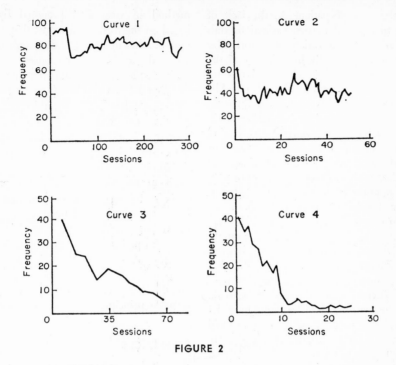

FIGURE 2

The condition of patient B did improve but not as dramatically as curve 4 appears to convey. The facial grimacings, which were very severely conspicuous in the early stages of treatment, completely vanished. He reported sleeping much better, whereas before treatment he used to lose a lot of sleep through the interference of the tic with any sleeping position he took. He feels much better generally, and although his head still has a tendency to move to the left, it is not so pronounced and so forceful as previously. He can now keep his head in a normal, facing-forward, position, for fairly long periods. The tic is much less frequent and very much less severe.

Towards the end of the experiment patient B was trained in the technique of systematic relaxation of muscles, with emphasis on the neck muscles. He was asked to maintain the relaxation exercises at home by devoting between fifteen and thirty minutes every day to this. He was also encouraged to try to cultivate the habit of general muscle relaxation whenever possible in the course of

his every day life. A follow-up after three months showed that he felt more relaxed and that he believed his tic had diminished.

DISCUSSION

The results outlined above suggest that the procedure of very prolonged massed practice which was applied to patient B supports the theory proposed by Yates [1] to explain the origin of certain tics. The other two procedures applied to patient A, did not support that theory. The data further suggest that the rate of decline was steady in that tic which received the largest amount of massed practice. There is no evidence in curve 4 (see Fig. 2) of a cessation of the rate of decline in the frequency of voluntary responding to the tic, or by an initial rise in frequency, following the very prolonged rest periods. This probably indicates that the growth of the negative habit of "not doing the tic" did actually proceed at a rapid rate and contributed towards the growth of conditioned inhibition ($_sI_R$) rather than $_sH_R$.

In the case of patient A, the lack of response to repeated massed extinction trials may be ascribed to a variety of factors. Her age may very materially have increased the difficulty of development of conditioned inhibition. Yates' patient was 25 years old. She was also receiving chlorpromazine throughout the experiments. Still another factor is her position on the introversion-extraversion continuum. However, she responded favourably to the alternative method of treatment, i.e., the strengthening of one incompatible response opposite to the one to be eliminated. The foot treadle exercises resulted in the inhibition of the muscular response, the tapping of the foot, by the progressive strengthening of the connection between the buzzer, the warning stimulus, and the withholding the foot from tapping, the response. Tapping responses become spontaneously inhibited on hearing the warning, and this inhibition, by a conditioning process, ultimately occurred spontaneously without the warning and without sounding the buzzer.

SUMMARY

An attempt was made to treat two psychiatric patients suffering from tics by the method of treatment, proposed by Yates, based on the theoretical model that some tics may be conceptualized as drive-reducing conditioned avoidance responses, originally evoked in a traumatic situation.

Three procedures of massed practice were applied in order to build up a negative habit of "not doing the tic." Yates' "standard procedure" and a modification of this, did not confirm the hypothesis that massed practice leads to a significant decrement in the ability to respond voluntarily. His procedure of very prolonged periods of massed practice followed by very prolonged rest, supported the validity of the theory.

The patient who failed to respond favourably to Yates' method, improved significantly by exercises on an apparatus built on the basis of the classical conditioned-response principle.

REFERENCES

1. YATES, A. J. (1958) The application of learning theory to the treatment of tics. *J. Abnorm. Soc. Psychol.* **56**, 175–182.
2. YATES, A. J. (1959) Personal communication.

30 DIRECT MANIPULATION OF STUTTERING BEHAVIOR AN EXPERIMENTAL-CLINICAL APPROACH

Henry C. Rickard • Martha B. Mundy[1]

Therapists are frequently reluctant to employ a direct conditioning approach to behavior modification. In direct conditioning, eliciting and reinforcing stimuli are applied to a selected dependent variable under specifiable conditions; no attempt is made to manipulate "underlying dynamics" or intervening variables. Caution in adopting this departure

[1] Miss Mundy served as the experimenter.

from usual psychotherapeutic techniques is commendable since in a given instance environmental circumstances might render a direct conditioning approach ineffective or even harmful. On the other hand too much fear of a direct conditioning approach could encourage neglect of effective, parsimonious treatment procedures. Over three decades ago Jones (1924), influenced by Watson, demonstrated that minor fears of childhood can be modified through direct conditioning. Bandura (1961), who has reviewed much of the literature concerned with the direct manipulation of "symptomatic" behavior, concludes that, "on the whole the evidence, while open to error, suggests that no matter what the origin of the maladaptive behavior might be, a change in behavior brought about through learning procedures may be all that is necessary for the alleviation of most forms of emotional disorder." In a somewhat different context behavior change, without recourse to the manipulation of intervening variables, has been repeatedly demonstrated in the operant and motor conditioning literature (Krasner, 1962).

Stuttering may be viewed as a circumscribed pattern of maladaptive behavior, acquired in the presence of certain cues, which is maintained through habit strength and/or reinforcement. The assumption that stuttering behavior is symptomatic of a core problem is an unproven position; it is more parsimonious to assume a reinforcement contingency. A portion of the reinforcement might come from the stutterer himself in the form of stuttering feedback. In addition, it is possible that stuttering continues to be reinforced on a low, aperiodic schedule by important environmental figures; and aperiodically reinforced habits are highly resistant to extinction (Jenkins and Stanley, 1950; Lewis, 1960). From a very simple, adynamic position, the problem becomes one of attaching new responses to old interpersonal stimuli— parents, teachers, siblings, and so forth. The S may be conditioned to emit nonstuttering behavior in the presence of E, and techniques employed to promote generalization of the new behavior.

STATEMENT OF PROBLEM

Overview

Stuttering behavior was defined by repetition errors per task unit; the tasks were verbal in nature and involved a series of increasingly difficult steps. The initial procedure was adapted from a verbal conditioning paradigm (Taffel, 1955). Later steps were taken on the basis of trial and error, and a program of increasingly difficult tasks evolved as the experiment progressed. At first, S was rewarded for nonstuttering responses with social reinforcements such as "good," "excellent," "that's fine," and so forth. Later, ice cream cones and points that could be acquired and later exchanged for yo-yos and other possessions were employed as reinforcers. Successful extinction of stuttering in the experimental setting would not guarantee transfer of the adaptive response to the home environment; consequently, conditions were provided under which S could emit nonstuttering behavior to the parents as stimuli. Three criterion levels were established. The first criterion level was near elimination of repetition errors on successively harder tasks within the experimental session; the second criterion level was fewer repetitions on a reading task; the third criterion level was improvement in everyday speech as reported by parents, teachers, and peers. The first two levels of behavior change were quite objective; the third involved more subjective observation and reporting.

SUBJECT

The S was a nine-year-old, well developed, white, male. He has an eight-year-old brother and a sister, five. His father is employed by the Federal Government and his mother is a housewife. The parents attended college for one and two years, respectively. The S was referred because of chronic stuttering behavior, characterized by repetition and blockage, which began at about four years of age. He had received speech therapy intermittently for two years prior to the experiment. The parents were more than willing to accept responsibility for the boy's stuttering behavior; the father, in particular, expressed concern over his tendency to be "harsh" when S was about four- or five-years-old. Although the birth of the youngest child coincides closely with S's initial stuttering, it was difficult to place the problem comfortably within the framework of sibling rivalry or rejection. The factors in the family situation that might have originally elicited and maintained stuttering behavior were no longer readily apparent; both parents would be rated above average for their culture in their knowledge of accepted child rearing practices including displays of affection toward the children. The S was administered the WISC and obtained a full scale IQ of 123. He grasped new situations readily and his thought processes appeared clear and coherent. He followed instruction with ease and expressed himself well in terms of content, although stuttering behavior was pronounced throughout the interviews. Academically, his record was good, and he related well to peers and authority figures. In short, the results of the psychological tests and interview data suggested that this individual was experiencing very mild psychological deficit other than his stuttering behavior. Several treatment plans were discussed, and the experimental approach reported in this paper was accepted on an exploratory basis by the parents and S.

Criterion Measures

Criteria of success were couched in terms of improvement at various levels. The first measure of success was S's performance on the conditioning tasks within the experimental setting. Tasks were divided into units of behavior of increasing difficulty and the number of repetition errors per unit were recorded. Reading behavior, the second level, was sampled through the use of standard paragraphs. Before, during, and after the experimental treatment, S, a fourth grade student, was asked to read excerpts from the third, fourth, and fifth grade levels of Gray's Oral Paragraph Readings. The third criterion level was a subjective report from the parents, teachers, and peers as to S's stuttering behavior outside the experimental setting.

The Dependent Variable

Stuttering behavior was defined by repetition errors per task unit ("g-g-g-going" as a one word task unit would yield a score of three repetition errors). Blocking, flushing, and other concomitants of stuttering were not recorded. The before, during and after paragraph readings were tape recorded; repetition errors were counted from the recordings

by two independent judges. Repetition errors, in the daily conditioning sessions, were counted by E.

Conditioning

Nonstuttering verbal behavior was elicited and reinforced in the experimental setting, and steps were taken to promote generalization of the nonstuttering response to the extra-experimental environment. The tasks were gradually increased from simple units (reading phrases) to a very complex unit of behavior (free conversation); nonstuttering responses were reinforced across the successively more difficult tasks.

PROCEDURE

Step I

Phrases Seventy cards with four pronouns (I, he, she, they) printed across the top and one past tense verb printed in the center were selected as the initial task unit. The S was instructed to select one of the four pronouns and pair it aloud with the various verbs for a total of seventy trials. He then chose a second, third, and fourth pronoun, pairing each with the seventy verbs. The S was reinforced with "good," "real good," "perfect," and so forth, when he read the pronoun and verb combination with fewer errors than his baseline. A new baseline was established at the beginning of each session by computing the mean number of repetition errors on twenty (nonreinforced) trials. During the first seven sessions improvement was negligible, but S insisted on continuing with the "exercises." At that point, ice cream was promised for a percentage of nonstuttering responses, and throughout the remainder of the experiment S worked for extrinsic, as well as intrinsic, reinforcement. Successively more perfect speech was required to obtain reinforcement; eventually S passed the stage of receiving reinforcement for a percentage of correct responses and began trying for 100 percent success with the two-word phrases.

Step II

Sentences Following the principle of successive approximations the next logical step appeared to be practice reading sentences.

To minimize transfer difficulties the sentences were constructed using verbs from the original seventy cards; S and E developed the sentences as a joint project. The S earned one point for each perfect sentence while working toward a collection of yo-yos. The sentences averaged approximately six words in length and were composed of words at the fourth grade level of difficulty. Fifty trials were given each day.

Step III

Paragraphs Thirty-one cards were typed, containing a variety of materials; short stories, poems, moron jokes, and fables. One point was earned for each card read without repetition errors.

Step IV

Conversation Spontaneous speech, which could be reinforced, was difficult to engineer in the experimental setting. During the search for appropriate tasks, S associated to the T.A.T. cards and repeated stories from memory. These procedures, and others which were tried, lacked spontaneity. The E then attempted to engage S in free conversation, rewarding him for each five minute period in which no stuttering errors were made, but S quickly exhausted his repertoire of topics. At that point, following an observer's suggestion,[2] a second E sounded a buzzer on an aperiodic schedule during free conversation, and S received extra points if he were talking when the buzzer sounded. A baseline of stuttering behavior was obtained for the first three (five minute) periods and, initially, S received five points for each five minute period containing fewer repetition errors than this baseline. After five sessions of free conversation a new reinforcement system was introduced. Cumulative bonus points, in addition to the usual five points, were awarded for each five minute period containing no repetition errors; for example, under the new scoring system the first five minute period containing no errors earned six points, the second error-free five minute period earned seven points and so forth.[3]

[2] Mrs. Jeanne Johnson made this valuable suggestion.
[3] Dr. George Passey suggested this technique of progressive reinforcement.

Step V

Generalization The mother was a silent participant in the conditioning sessions after the tenth session. A more intensive effort to promote generalization by involving both parents was made during the family vacation period. It was reasoned that the vacation cues would be different from the prior experimental setting and also different from the usual home environment, hopefully providing a transition step between the two. During this phase the parents became the experimenters and continued the procedure described in Step IV for nine sessions. Later the father, with the original E as a silent participant, became E for four additional sessions.

RESULTS

Figure 1 presents the percent of repetition errors on phrase reading for each of twenty-three sessions. On the first day S emitted repetition errors on sixty-four percent of the two hundred and eighty phrases. A marked reduction in repetition errors is evident over the twenty-three sessions of practice and reinforcement for nonstuttering responses. Figure 2 presents the percent of repetition errors for sentences, paragraphs, and stories. On the first sentence test day, thirty percent of the sentences contained repetition errors. By the fourth day, errors were reduced to zero for the fifty separate sentences. Only four days each were required to virtually eliminate errors on both paragraphs and stories.

The procedure of reinforcing talking behavior *per se,* in addition to rewarding nonstuttering responses, during the free conversation phase of the experiment proved successful. The S markedly increased his speech and was talking almost 100 percent of the time when the buzzer sounded. Although no count was made of total number of words per period, the S talked at a fairly steady rate, providing an approximately equal opportunity for repetition errors to occur across all sessions. Figure 3 shows S's performance over twenty-one free conversation periods. The data represent median repetition errors

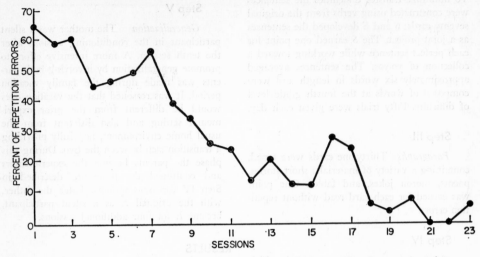

FIGURE 1   Percent of phrase reading trials on which repetition errors occurred.

per five minutes of free conversation within each thirty-minute period. The first eighteen periods represent S's performance with E in the original training setting. Considerable variability in performance is evident but a general decrease in repetition errors is apparent. The next nine periods represent S's performance during vacation when his parents assumed the responsibility of conducting the experimental sessions. For the first five periods the mother served as E, and a median score of zero repetition errors was made per five-minute period. During the last four periods the father served as E and the median number of repetition errors increased markedly. The last four periods in Figure 1 represent S's responses to the father in the original experimental setting; only two repetition errors were made during the last thirty minutes of free conversation.

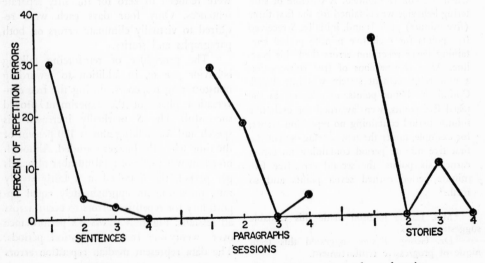

FIGURE 2   Percent repetition errors for sentences, paragraphs, and stories.

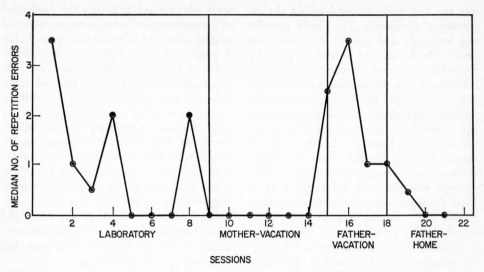

FIGURE 3   Median repetition errors per five minutes of free conversation for each 30-minute period.

These data indicate that S performed adequately on the tasks within the experimental setting. Repetition errors were eliminated or markedly reduced on successively more difficult conditioning tasks. Success, then is evident at the first criterion level—performance within the training sessions. Performance on the second criterion measure, paragraph readings, is reflected by the data presented in Table I. A very sharp reduction in repetition errors is noted during and after the experiment. The S also read new material at his grade level with few repetition errors, suggesting that the improvement was

TABLE I Gray's Oral Paragraph Readings (173 words)

	Judge A	Judge B	Mean
Pre-Test	120	136	128
After 35 Sessions	17	18	17.5
Post-Test* (after 21 additional 30-minute sessions)	0	0	0
Six month follow-up	16	16	16

* Training sessions extended over an eight-month period.

more than a reading adaptation effect. Success at the third criterion level, conversation in "real life," was less impressive. His parents reported "moderate" improvement while his teacher reported "marked" improvement. The S continued to stutter to some extent in free conversation—particularly under stress.

Follow-up

The S was seen for a follow-up interview approximately six months after the close of the experiment. He was again asked to read the selections from the Gray's Oral Paragraph Readings. The S emitted sixteen repetition errors on the first letter of the first word but made no errors on the remainder of the material. The subjective report on his verbal behavior elsewhere was less favorable. Much of his stuttering behavior had been reinstated in the home and school environment. He was again emitting repetition errors while reading at school and in conversation.

DISCUSSION

Although the reported procedures were based upon learning principles, the clinical role was frequently assumed within the experimental framework. The family complex was evaluated and clinical judgment was involved in the decision to treat the child by a conditioning method. Close contact was maintained with the parents, and their feelings and attitudes toward the experimental procedure were frequently discussed. Strenuous efforts were made to enlist the cooperation of S and to insure that he remain "motivated." Grading the task from the simple to the complex was accomplished on the basis of logic and the estimated progress of S. After the dependent variable was identified, in this case stuttering behavior, well established learning principles were followed: reinforcement of adaptive behavior, "shaping" the behavior through successive approximations, and stimulus generalization. The nonstuttering responses were reinforced while the stuttering behavior was ignored. The verbal task was gradually increased in difficulty and the parents became active in the stimulus situation, hopefully enhancing generalization. There were no purposeful attempts to deal with hostility, insecurity, or any other intervening variable or "dynamic factor." The S was given *no* clues as to how he might decrease his stuttering (such as slower speech or uniform breathing). The present approach was one of direct conditioning in which reinforcement was applied to a clinically selected bit of behavior possessing the characteristics of sensitivity, stability, and importance (Rickard, in press). Thus we have labeled our proceedings as an "experimental-clinical" approach.

SUMMARY

Stuttering behavior was identified as the dependent variable in a nine-year-old boy. Testing and case history material were obtained and it was found that S showed few deficits in other areas. Social reinforcement and points leading toward extrinsic rewards were administered following the production of nonstuttering behavior in the experimental setting; stuttering behavior was ignored. The S progressed successfully from very simple units of verbal behavior, phrases and sentences, to extremely complex units of verbal behavior, that is, free conversation with the parents serving as experimenters. The criteria of change were samples of verbal behavior on three levels: performance on the conditioning tasks, performance on a reading task, and verbal behavior in the home and school environment. The S showed marked improvement on the first two criteria. Initially, success generalized to the home and school situation but a six month follow-up indicated that the environmental gains had been only partially maintained.

REFERENCES

BANDURA, A. Psychotherapy as a learning process. *Psychol. Bull.,* 1961, **58**, 143–159.

JENKINS, W. O., and J. C. STANLEY, JR. Partial reinforcement: a review and critique. *Psychol. Bull.,* 1950, **47**, 193–234.

JONES, MARY C. The elimination of children's fears. *J. exp. Psychol.,* 1924, **7**, 382–390.

KRASNER, L. The therapist as a social reinforcement machine. In H. H. Strupp, and L. Luborsky (Eds.), *Research in Psychotherapy,* Washington, D.C.: American Psychological Association, 1962, vol. 2, 61–94.

LEWIS, D. J. Partial reinforcement: a selective review of the literature since 1950. *Psychol. Bull.,* 1960, **57**, 1–28.

RICKARD, H. C. Tailored criteria of success in psychotherapy. *J. gen. Psychol.,* in press.

TAFFEL, C. Anxiety and the conditioning of verbal behavior. *J. abnorm. soc. Psychol.,* 1955, **51**, 496–501.

SECTION 4

DEVIANT BEHAVIORS IN CHILDREN

Treatment of children has appeared previously in this book in terms of four articles with autistic children (10–13) and Rickard and Mundy's article (30) on the direct manipulation of stuttering behavior. In our introduction we cited material dealing with children from Watson and Rayner (1920), Jones (1924a, 1924b), Burnham (1924), Jersild and Holmes (1935), Mowrer and Mowrer (1938), and Lazarus (1959). In the remainder of this volume, the principle focus will be on children. First we shall present seven articles on typical clinic practice, next six articles on social behavior, and finally, in the fifth section, we will present seven cases with a focus on rehabilitation, particularly with retardates.

In the first article, Patterson (31) illustrates the reinforcement of responses that interfere with maladaptive behavior. Of particular interest is the role of the parent as co-therapist rather than recipient of expressive therapy. From Patterson's work we can hypothesize that parents can be helped to identify and reinforce adjustive behaviors.

Baer's article (32) on thumb sucking illustrates the degree of stimulus control that response contingent reinforcement may exert over a habit that is frequently the focus of clinical interest.

The article by Peterson and London (33) argues for larger units of behavior and the explicit giving of cues. Within this framework, the occurrence of an adaptive behavior is fostered and then strongly reinforced by the parents. Neale (1963) presents the successful treatment of three out of four cases of encopresis, lack of control of bowel movements. If the appropriate response is not made in response to the internal cues, control over the function is lost. The development of the operant response is through positive reinforcement and an avoidance of the all too typical stricture in our culture of holding back. That is, the desirable behavior is an appropriate response, not a lack of the response. In Madsen's (37) article we see these concepts applied before the development of maladaptive behavior and as a method of accelerating the training of a normal process. Finally, we may mention again work such as that of Jones (1960b), Mowrer and Mowrer (1938) and Lovibond (1963a, 1963b) on the treatment of enuresis through conditioning. In short, the eliminative processes that are so important in psychoanalytic formulations may be brought under control as matters of training in the development of adaptive responses.

The case by Williams (34) on the elimination of tantrum behavior has been referred to in other articles in this book (for example, Wolf, Risley, and Mees, 12). This procedure may be compared to that of Ayllon and Michael (4) with schizophrenics,

Walton (1960c, 1960d) with psychophysiological reactions, and Wolf and his co-workers (48) within the school setting.

Bentler (35) illustrates the use of a graded series of actual stimuli in overcoming a year old child's phobia. As we mentioned earlier, the article is a detailed illustration of the procedures briefly touched upon by Jersild and Holmes (1935).

Children's phobias may be dealt with in a variety of ways. One of the most interesting techniques is advanced by Lazarus and Abramovitz (36). Essentially, emotive imagery is a matter of reconditioning through the association of a context incompatible with the sort that leads to maladaptive responses. It is worth noting that the technique demands a great deal of active, skillful participation by the therapist.

The final article of these first seven cases is by Madsen (37). The extension of behavior modification techniques to develop adaptive responses that will prevent the development of maladaptive behavior is a most important and hopeful direction. As in other articles, Madsen's parents played an active therapeutic role. Phillips (1960) describes some of the ways in which the psychologist guides the parents:

5. The parent is given "common-sense" explanations of what the child's behavior means ("He's trying to get by with this and he probably thinks you won't stop him." "He's had luck with this approach before, so why won't he try it again?" "If you become more definite and consistent, this will help the child know where he stands with you.) . . ."

6. Stress is placed on "keeping structure," that is, on setting limits on behavior and specific aims for achievement. This allows the parent and the child to develop a success pattern in daily relationships rather than being bogged down with failures and impasses. . . .

8. Homework, household chores, and a fairly set (but *not* rigid) routine is emphasized. Children misbehave, it is hypothesized, largely out of having a too loose structure of requirements and relationships. If this structure is firmed up in sensible, fair, consistent ways, the child will usually improve. (Phillips, 1960, p. 196.)

Six articles are presented that deal with children in social situations. The first three articles represent applications of the same techniques to different behaviors. Allen *et al.* (38) on isolate behavior, Harris *et al.* (39) on regressed crawling, and Hart *et al.* (40) on operant crying, all illustrate the programing of nursery school teachers as social reinforcers, and the effect of selective reinforcement in altering the emission of maladaptive behavior. As illustrations of the psychological model of the development of maladaptive behavior, the combination of research and therapy, and the benefit to be derived from reinforcing adjustive rather than maladjustive behavior, these three articles have an important place in the literature of behavior modification. The preventive aspects of replacing maladaptive behavior with socially effective behavior as early as possible is of great importance. Maladaptive behavior need not wait until reaching critical importance or be allowed to continue during time in which a repertoire of adequate behaviors might be developed. Work such as that by Azrin and Lindsley (43) and Homme *et al.* (1963) further illustrate the development of behaviors such as cooperation and attention which will facilitate later schoolwork. Rickard and Dinoff (41) and Zimmerman and Zimmerman (42) extend this approach into the social settings of summer camps and grade school. Schwitzgebel and Kolb (1964) report a successful project involving utilizing operant conditioning procedures to induce behavior change among adolescent delinquents. A three-year follow-up of their "subjects" indicated a significant reduction in the frequency and severity of crime compared to a matched-pair control group.

Teaching machines (Skinner, 1958) facilitate the development of interest, individual pacing, rapid feedback, and maintained success. Aside from specific skills and backlog of information, they may be used to develop logical thinking (Bijou, 1965), creative and/or artistic ability (Skinner, 1948), and interpersonal sensitivity (Dailey, 1963). The point is to utilize fully the individual's abilities.

31   A LEARNING THEORY APPROACH TO THE
TREATMENT OF THE SCHOOL PHOBIC CHILD[1]

Gerald R. Patterson

Most attempts to apply learning theory to the practice of psychotherapy seem as much oriented to confirming the status of a particular learning theory as to changing the behavior of the patient. Within this tradition, Salter (1950) outlined procedures that fit within the model of classic conditioning; Eysenck (1960) within Hullian theory; and Wolpe (1958) made an unacknowledged application of Guthrie's theory. However admirable the faith that these writers have in the theories that they have espoused, it would seem more reasonable for the practicing clinician to select principles from any of these theories that fit the needs of the individual case. The present report outlines procedures for application of Guthrie's concept (1935) of interference and Skinner's concept (1953) of conditioning via approximations. Standard clinical procedures were modified to provide procedures for applying these principles to change the behavior of a "school phobic" child and the child's parents.

The term "school phobia" was introduced by Johnson, Falstein, Szurek, and Svendsen (1941) to describe an anxiety re-

[1] Part of this material was presented in a paper at the annual convention of the American Association for Mental Deficiency, 1961, Portland, Oregon. The research was carried out as part of USPH grant M-5429, which provides support for investigating the application of learning principles to the socialization of the child. The writer gratefully acknowledges the cooperation of Mrs. Becktolt, Director of Special Education, and her staff, who did much to make the approach successful. The writer also acknowledges the clinical labors of Ivan Ruly, J. Wishart, and F. Miles, who carried out much of the contact with the children.

action in children that results in their persistent absence from school. Most writers agree with Estes, Haylett, and Johnson (1956), who pointed out that the stimulus that elicits the anxiety reaction is not the school per se but rather any situation that represents separation from the parent. Although these writers very properly suggested the term "separation anxiety" as a label, the term school phobia remains in currency and will be used in this paper.

A general formulation for school phobic behavior would be as follows: separation from the parent functions as an eliciting stimulus (ES)$\longrightarrow$ anxiety reaction$\longrightarrow$ escape or avoidance behaviors. According to the interference concept (Guthrie, 1935), extinction will occur if new responses can be associated with the ES. If these new responses are incompatible with the anxiety reaction, the new associations will result in gradual extinction of the escape and avoidance responses and in a diminution of the anxiety reaction. This general formulation was anticipated by the now classic work of Jones (1924). In her study, the interfering responses, eating, when associated with the feared object resulted in extinction of the escape behaviors and a marked reduction in anxiety reactions.

In pairing the interfering responses with the ES, it was decided to strengthen this association by creating a contingency between these responses and a variety of reinforcing stimuli. To determine the kind of reinforcing stimulus appropriate for the patient, he was tested in a laboratory procedure described by Patterson, Littman, and Hinsey

(1963). It was found that in the early stage of treatment he was less responsive to social reinforcers dispensed by his therapist than were a hundred other children who had been reinforced by a variety of social agents. This nonresponsiveness to social reinforcers is in keeping with the findings by Levine and Simmons (1962), who showed that emotionally disturbed boys are less responsive to social reinforcers than are normal boys. For this reason, M&M candies were used in the present study as reinforcers in conjunction with social approval. It was assumed that this pairing of M&Ms and social reinforcers would increase the incentive value of social approval, resulting in a wider range of possibilities for behavior control.

In keeping with the suggestions by Jones (1924) and Wolpe (1962), the ES was presented on a graduate series so that initially only low intensity escape and anxiety reactions were evoked. As the trials progressed, the intensity of the ES was increased. In all situations, the ESs used in the conditioning trials matched as closely as possible situational cues from the child's environment.

Doll play, structured by the experimenter was the procedure used in the conditioning trials. These sessions occurred four days a week and lasted fifteen minutes; the sessions are described in detail below. Following each conditioning session, both the child and the parents were interviewed. During the early interviews, the procedure was explained in detail to the family. The nature of the specific interfering response being conditioned was discussed with particular emphasis upon the parents' being alert to its occurrence in the home. When these behaviors occurred, they were instructed to reinforce them immediately and then to describe them in the interview on the following day. Particular emphasis was placed upon reinforcing the appropriate behaviors and ignoring behaviors associated with reactions to separation anxiety. It is felt that these highly structured interviews with the parents are of particular importance in insuring generalization of conditioning effects from the laboratory to the home.

THE PATIENT

Karl was seven-years-old when referred to the University Clinic by the school nurse. In his first few days of attendance in the first grade, he had shown increasing reluctance to stay in school. In the second week of school, he would stay in the classroom only as long as one of his parents remained in the room with him.

Karl had similar difficulties in attending a nursery school during the previous year, even though the school was only a few blocks from his home. For the past few years, he found it necessary to play only in the immediate vicinity of his home. He would frequently interrupt his play to go into the house and "check" to see if his mother was still there. If the mother were going to the store, a short distance away, Karl would insist upon accompanying her. Attempts to use punishment, bribes, or cajoling had failed to keep him in school.

In the clinic, Karl was observed to be an attractive child, rather immature in his behavior and having a severe articulation defect. Testing at the end of treatment revealed a low reading readiness score and an above average intelligence quotient. Extensive intake interviewing with the parents revealed no marked pathology in the parents or in the family; this impression was in agreement with the essentially normal MMPI profiles of both parents.

Session 1

In his first appointment at the clinic, Karl refused to go to the playroom without his mother. Teeth chattering, he clenched one fist, while with the other he maintained a firm hold upon his mother's coat. Karl was seated at a table just inside the door of the playroom while the mother sat across from him in the doorway. The experimenter proceeded to set up a doll play situation in which a little boy, "Henry," was being taken by the mother to see a doctor. Karl divided his attention between the experimenter and his mother. The first reinforcing contingency was one M&M for each thirty-second interval during which Karl did not look at his mother. After five minutes, the mother left the room and sat outside the closed door.

The doll play was restructured so that Henry was inside the doctor's office. When Karl was asked where Henry's mother was, he replied, "Outside," and received one M&M. In the procedure that followed, the mother doll left the boy in the doctor's office for increasingly long periods of time; on each occasion Karl was queried as to how the boy felt and what he was going to do. If he replied that the boy was not afraid or that he would stay in the doctor's office, he received both praise and one M&M. Similar situations were structured in which the boy remained at home while the mother went shopping or the mother remained at home while the boy walked toward the school building.

In the interview with the mother that followed this session, she was encouraged to praise Karl for staying in the playroom without her. She was further instructed to keep track of Karl's "checking" behavior at home; if he stayed outside for longer than thirty minutes without coming inside, she was to make an announcement at the dinner table to the whole family. Karl seemed obviously pleased with his success on this first contact and listened very closely to the interchange between the mother and the experimenter.

Session 2

The mother seated herself in a chair outside the playroom. When Karl acquiesced to the experimenter's closing the door, he immediately received two M&Ms and praise from the experimenter. The doll play was repeated with the boy in the doctor's office and the mother's leaving him there for increasing periods of time. As in the previous session, if Karl said that the boy was not afraid or that the boy would stay in the situation, he was reinforced by both candy and social approval. At the end of this sequence of doll play, Karl was asked if he would, on the next visit, allow his mother to stay in the reception room rather than sitting outside the door of the playroom. He readily

agreed to this and was reinforced for his bravery with both praise and several M&Ms. For any given session, there were generally thirty or forty of these reinforcers dispensed by the experimenter.

The structured play relating to the school was again initiated; on this occasion, Karl specified the reaction of the boy to saying goodbye to the mother, getting upon his bicycle, walking into the school, sitting at the desk, and reading aloud from a book.

A third play theme was introduced in this session concerning Karl's anxiety about physical injury as being the outcome of playing with his peers. Doll play was initiated involving "Little Henry's" playing with his peers and receiving minor injuries; in each case Karl reported the boy was not afraid, did not return to the mother, and he showed how Little Henry would place a band aid upon his own leg.

In the interview with the father, he reported that Karl had actually stayed outside for an hour and that they had made an announcement at the dinner table. He was told about Karl's decision to allow his parents to remain in the reception room, and he responded with approval. He was encouraged to continue to reinforce Karl for independent behavior in the home and to be particularly careful not to overreact to small injuries that he might receive while playing. It was also suggested that they obtain some preprimers from the school and reinforce Karl whenever he indicated an interest in the books or in returning to school.

Sessions 3 through 9

Karl continued to allow his parents to remain in the reception room while he "worked" in the playroom. On each occasion he was reinforced for saying that he was not afraid; he began to boast that the parents would not have to remain in the clinic at all. Karl gave a brief report of his activities at the beginning of each conditioning session and was reinforced for reports indicating attempts to read, climbing trees without being afraid of injuring himself, playing some distance from home, and not checking on his mother. The structured play sessions were expanded to include two new areas. Karl expressed some further anxiety about being attacked by members of the peer group. In the play sessions he was reinforced for counteraggressing to such attacks and heavily reinforced for attempts to initiate play activity with the peer group. Karl was also reinforced for making discriminations between behaviors appropriate for Little Henry and those appropriate for a new and more mature "Big Henry." Both of these areas had been brought up in the interviews with the parents, and they had been encouraged to reinforce him for playing with children his own age and ignoring any expression of fear of the aggression of other children. The mother particularly had been instructed to label those aspects of Karl's behavior that were immature and to respond, if possible, only when he acted maturely. As before, the parents were required to bring examples of their attempts to reinforce Karl. Arrangements were also made for a visiting teacher to assist Karl in the development of reading skills.

Session 10

The material which follows is a brief excerpt from this session and illustrates in detail the procedures used throughout the sessions.

E: What shall we have Henry do today?

K: Well, we could have him go to school.

E: Yeah, I think that is a good idea, to have some work on going to school again today. That probably is the hardest thing for him to do. O.K., here he is (picking up the Henry doll). Where is mamma, oh here she is (sets up blocks and furniture). Ah, maybe we had better have Little Henry start off from home; when he does go to school, we won't have him go into the classroom today; he'll just run errands for the principal; no reading or writing this time. So Little Henry is talking to his mother and he says, "Mom, I think I'll go to school for a little while today." What does mom say?

K: O.K.

E: Is he afraid when he is right there talking to mamma?

K: No. (one M&M)

E: And so he gets on his bike and says byebye mamma. He stops half way to school. What does he think now that mamma is not there?

K: Ma-amma (laughs).

E: Yeah, but what does he do? Does he go back or go on to school?

K: Goes to school. (one M&M)

E: Yeah, that's right he goes to school; Little Henry would go back and look but Big Henry would go on to school . . . and he goes to the principal's office and says, "Hi, Mr. Principal. I thought I would come back to school for a little while. Can I run some errands for you . . . ?" Henry gives the note to the teacher, then he is coming back to the principal's office. He stops. What is he thinking about now?

K: Mamma is not there again.

E: Yeah, he is scaring himself again. Now, does he go back to the principal's office or does he go home?

K: He goes back to the office. (one M&M)

E: Yeah, that is right, he does. At least Big Henry would do that; Little Henry would get scareder and more scareder; but Big Henry feels pretty good. "I am back Mr. Principal." The principal says, "Why don't you go down to the cafeteria and get a glass of milk. I don't have any more errands for you to run right now." So he goes and is sitting here drinking his milk. What does he think about now? Every time he is alone he thinks about this.

K: Mamma again.

E: That's right, he always thinks about mamma. Does he go home?

K: No. (one M&M)

E: That's right, he doesn't. Big Henry doesn't go home.

K: (laughs) He sure is big.

—a few moments later—

E: . . . and he is lying there on the sleeping mat. What is he thinking about?

K: Mamma. No, I don't think so because he got a nice neighbor (child) next to him.

E: So, he is not thinking about mamma.

K: Nope. (E was too surprised to get reinforcement in on time.)

—about five minutes later—

E: Well, Karl what have you been doing at home like Big Henry?

K: Well, ah, yesterday I done some numbers (very excited) and I went up to a hundred. (one M&M)

E: You did! Good (with emphasis). What else did you do like Big Henry?

K: I made a cake . . .

E: Were you outside playing yesterday? Of course it was stormy yesterday.

K: Yes, I was outside playing.

E: Did you think about mamma when you were outside?

K: Uh-uh. I wasn't thinking about mamma. (one M&M) I'm not thinking about her now either. (one M&M)

In the past few sessions, several play sequences had been devoted to Little Henry's return to school for an hour or so with his visiting teacher. The possibility of Karl's actually doing this had also been discussed with him.

Sessions 11 through 23

Karl made his first trip to the school with the special teacher with him at all times. On the following day, he returned and the teacher left him alone in the room for a few minutes. On each of the days following this, the teacher left him for longer periods of time. This sequence at school was accompanied by conditioning sequences in the playroom and a good deal of praise and approval by his family. After a week of this, he announced at home that he would not be afraid to ride to school and stay by himself for one hour. He carried this out on the following day amid applause and acclaim for his singular act of bravery. He then announced that he would return to school full time within the week, which he did.

On the last week of the treatment program, Karl and the writer returned to the procedure for testing his reaction to social reinforcers. On this second trial, the reinforcers were effective in changing his position preference on the marble box game. Social reinforcers had no effect on a second disturbed boy tested at the same time as Karl but not receiving treatment. An important implication of this finding for Karl is that his behavior is now under the control of

social reinforcers dispensed by a wide variety of social agents.

On a follow-up of Karl's classroom adjustment three months after termination of treatment, the school reported dramatic improvement in his general adjustment as well as no further evidence of fearfulness. The Department of Special Education is continuing their program of remedial reading and speech.

DISCUSSION

At the cost of twenty bags of M&Ms and ten hours of staff time, Karl returned to school. This, of course, does not constitute a record for the "cure" of school phobia in the amount of time necessary for the return to school (Sperling, 1961), nor is it the first time that learning theories have been applied in treating this type of problem behavior (Lazarus, 1960). The implication is that the present modification of standard clinical practices is at least as effective as traditional procedures.

Since terminating the treatment program with Karl, the same procedures have been followed in conditioning a second child whose presenting symptoms were very similar to Karl's. The second case responded dramatically in less than six hours of staff time. These two cases are not offered as constituting confirmation for the efficacy of this procedure; however, the apparent success of the procedure has encouraged the author to apply a similar procedure to dealing with behavior problems that are ordinarily resistive to traditional clinical manipulations. In this third case, application of simple operant procedures was very successful in extinguishing hyperactive behaviors in the classroom setting (Patterson, 1963). Taken together, the successes strongly suggest that modifications of clinical procedures in accord with principles from learning theories will be a powerful tool in effecting behavior change in the clinical setting.

In retrospect, there is little doubt that one of the crucial variables involved in this procedure is the reinforcement contingencies being used by social agents other than the experimenter. Although it may very well be true that the same effect could be achieved by relying only upon the conditioning-play sessions, there is little doubt on both the theoretical and the practical levels that the parents and the teacher enhanced the generalization from behavior change in the playroom to behavior change in the natural setting. Although the clinician has been concerned traditionally with enhancing generalization from play therapy, the present procedure does not assume that the parents are emotionally disturbed but simply that they have been reinforcing the wrong behaviors. This being the case, it is not necessary for the parents to be involved in intensive psychotherapy, but it is necessary for the parents to be given specific instructions as to what to reinforce and how to reinforce child behaviors. In our extensive practice, with three cases, we have been impressed with the general lack of awareness displayed by these parents as to what it is that they are reinforcing and the effect of this reinforcement upon the behavior of the child. The procedure described here should be appropriate for a variety of child behavior problems and for parents who do not show obvious signs of pathology. This latter statement assumes of course that the reinforcing contingencies adopted by any particular parents are not necessarily determined by the intensity or kind of emotional conflict in the parents. It is hypothesized here that many parents have been conditioned rather than "driven" to adopt their idiosyncratic schedules of reinforcement.

The research by Levine & Simmons (1962), Patterson, Littman, and Hinsey (1963) agree in identifying the child with behavior problems as being unresponsive to social approval; the research by Patterson (1963) suggests that these children might be overly responsive to disapproval. Although satisfactory empirical evidence is lacking at the present time, it seems highly probable that the child with behavior problems is responsive to only a limited aspect of his social environment. In Karl's case, for ex-

ample, it seemed as if he was responsive only to the approval of his mother (and father perhaps). This restriction in responsiveness to one or two social agents would mean that his behavior was not being conditioned to the normal extent by other agents, such as the peer group or adults outside of the family circle. In such a situation, if the parental programing of reinforcers was not in accord with contingencies adopted by the remainder of the culture, it would not be surprising to observe that the child displayed some rather deviant behavior patterns.

If such a child were brought into the clinic, it would be predicted that much of his behavior would not be under the control of the therapist. One of the first functions of the therapist was to change the incentive value of social stimuli; once this was achieved, the therapist could potentially have some effect in changing the behavior of the child. It is of interest to note that Anna Freud strongly urged the pairing of such primary reinforcers as food with the presence of the therapist in order to create a "relationship" with the child (Freud, 1946). It is hypothesized here that whatever such pairing might do for the "relationship" the *effect* is to increase the status of the therapist as a secondary reinforcer as witnessed by Karl's increased responsiveness to social reinforcers at termination of treatment. This would suggest either that nonsocial reinforcers be used in the earlier phases of conditioning with these children or that the therapist make it a point to become associated with a wide range of pleasant stimuli before attempting any behavior manipulation.

SUMMARY

A procedure was described for applying the principles of interference and reinforcement to the treatment of a school phobic child. A series of twenty-three 20-minute conditioning sessions with the child followed by highly structured ten-minute interviews with the parents resulted in dramatic changes in behavior.

REFERENCES

ESTES, H. R., CLARICE H. HAYLETT, and ADELAIDE
M. JOHNSON. Separation anxiety. *Amer.
J. Orthopsychiat.,* 1956, **10**, 682–695.

EYSENCK, H. J. (Ed.) *Behavior therapy and
the neurosis.* New York: Pergamon,
1960.

FREUD, A. *The psycho-analytical treatment
of children.* New York: International
Universities, 1946.

GUTHRIE, E. R. *The psychology of learning.*
New York: Harper and Row, 1935.

JOHNSON, ADELAIDE M., E. J. FALSTEIN, S. A.
SZUREK, and MARGARET SVENDSEN. School
phobia. *Amer. J. Orthopsychiat.,* 1941, **11**,
702–711.

JONES, MARY C. The elimination of children's fears. *J. exp. Psychol.,* 1924, **7**,
382–390.

LAZARUS, A. A. The elimination of children's
phobias by deconditioning. In H. J.

Eysenck (Ed.), *Behavior therapy and
the neurosis.* New York: Pergamon,
1960. Pp. 116–119.

LEVINE, G. R. and J. T. SIMMONS. Response
to praise by emotionally disturbed boys.
Psychol. Rep., 1962, **11**, 10.

PATTERSON, G. R. Parents as dispensers of
aversive stimuli. Unpublished manuscript, 1963.

PATTERSON, G. R., R. LITTMAN, and C. HINSEY.
Parents as social stimuli. Unpublished
manuscript, 1963.

SALTER, A. *Conditioned reflex therapy.* New
York: Creative Age Press, Inc., 1950.

SKINNER, B. F. *Science and human behavior.*
New York: Macmillan, 1953.

SPERLING, MELITTA. Analytic first aid in
school phobias. *Psychoanal. Quart.,* 1961,
30, 504–518.

WOLPE, J. *Psychotherapy by reciprocal inhibition.* Stanford, Calif.: Stanford University Press, 1958.

32 LABORATORY CONTROL OF THUMBSUCKING BY WITHDRAWAL AND RE-PRESENTATION OF REINFORCEMENT

Donald M. Baer[1]

A 5-year-old boy was shown cartoons, and punished for thumbsucking during alternate cartoons by turning off the cartoons for as long as his thumb remained in his mouth. Thumbsucking weakened during such periods. During alternate periods of uninterrupted cartoons, thumbsucking promptly recovered, suggesting a quick discrimination process. Two other 5-year-old boys were shown the same cartoons; withdrawal of the cartoons was made contingent upon thumbsucking for one, and randomly yoked for the other. Then their roles were reversed. Contingent withdrawal and re-presentation of the cartoons controlled thumbsucking rate; yoked withdrawal and re-presentation did not.

Journal of the Experimental Analysis of Behavior, 1962, **5**, 525–528.

Positive reinforcement may be withdrawn from young children by showing them movie cartoons and programming interruptions of both picture and sound track. Making such withdrawal contingent upon a response effectively reduces its frequency (Baer, 1961); and the delay of such withdrawal by responding can set up stable avoidance behavior (Baer, 1960). In the present study, this withdrawal technique is used to produce temporary control of thumbsucking in three

[1] This study was supported by U. S. Public Health Service Grant M-2208. The author is grateful to Mrs. Anne Pilisdorf for her intelligent and reliable performance as A.

young children who are persistent thumb-suckers. The usual account of thumbsucking attributes it to inner tensions and conflicts (Spock, 1959, p. 211), to its selfreinforce-ment consequences (Fenichel, 1954, p. 63), or to a history of deprivation of sucking experience during infancy (Roberts, 1944). Palermo (1956) has summarized what experimental evidence exists, and argued that thumbsucking may be interpreted as a learned response which reduces anxiety. In this context, it would seem valuable to show to what extent thumbsucking may be modified by current environmental control, using explicit stimulus consequences of the response.

PROCEDURE

The first S was a 5-year-old boy from a local nursery school, who had seen the same three cartoons each session, for eight sessions separated from one another by 2 or 3 days. He showed great enjoyment, laughing and mumbling throughout, and also sucked his thumb virtually 100% of each 21-min session. During these eight preliminary sessions, the subject had seen the cartoons without interruption or any other experimental treatment. (A bar was located close to his right hand for collecting an extensive operant level; however, the operant level of bar pressing was zero throughout all of these sessions.) Thus, S was well adapted, but experimentally naive.

The general procedure was identical to that described in an earlier paper (Baer, 1960). The S was conducted to the experimental room by a young female adult, A, who seated him before a movie screen built into one wall of the room. She then sat behind a partition in a corner of the room. Cartoons were projected on the screen from the experimenter's control and observation room on the other side of the wall. During each of the eight preliminary sessions, three 7-min cartoons were shown without break or interruption. During each of the three experimental sessions reported here, S was shown the same three cartoons twice, with-

out any break between cartoons, in the sequence A, B, C, A, B, C. Thumbsucking was recorded on a Gerbrands cumulative recorder which stepped one response for every three cumulative seconds of thumbsucking. Observing through a one-way mirror, the experimenter held down a key on an otherwise automatic programmer whenever S's thumb was in his mouth. The programmer pulsed the recorder for every 3 sec the key was depressed. Under punishment conditions, the programmer turned off the projector lamp and opened the loudspeaker's voice coil as long as the key was depressed so that sight and sound of the cartoons were withdrawn.

During the experimental sessions, S was shown cartoon A without punishment; was punished for all thumbsucking during B (a Control period); allowed C as a Recovery period; punished again for all thumbsucking during the second (Control) showing of A; allowed the second showing of B as a Recovery period; and punished again for all thumbsucking during the second (Control) showing of C.

RESULTS AND DISCUSSION

Cumulative thumbsucking for the three experimental sessions is shown in Fig. 1 (a photographic reproduction of a tracing of the original record). The paper speed in the recorder was 22 in. per hr; thus, maximum slope was not steep. (Note the "maximum possible rate" in the figure.) During the first showing of A in each session (operant level), the rate of thumbsucking was very nearly maximal. For the first session, recovery during C was equal to the level established during A, but recovery during the second showing of B was less. However, during the second and third sessions, recovery was typically strong and prompt. The pattern was similar for responses under the Control conditions. During the first session, succeeding Control periods were progressively more effective in decreasing rate; during the second and third sessions, the rate was quite

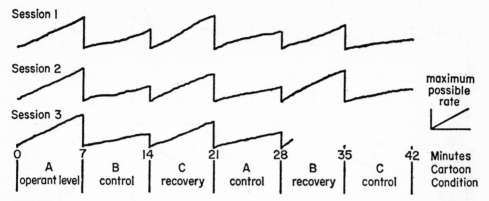

Session 1

Session 2

maximum
possible
rate

Session 3

| 0 | 7 | 14 | 21 | 28 | 35 | 42 | Minutes |

A
operant level

B
control

C
recovery

A
control

B
recovery

C
control

Cartoon
Condition

FIGURE 1   Cumulative thumbsucking curves of a single subject under alternating conditions of Control and Recovery.

uniformly and effectively lowered during all Control conditions.

The S left after seeing only four cartoons during the third session, saying he had "seen enough." This may be attributed to the periods of punishment undergone. On the other hand, it should be recalled that S had seen each cartoon a total of 13 times, at 2- or 3-day intervals: satiation is not unreasonable, punishment or not.

The prompt and strong recovery of thumbsucking during the Recovery periods of the second and third sessions, coupled with the immediate weakening of the response during Control periods, may suggest a rapid process of discrimination of the schedule components, rather than a generalized suppression of thumbsucking through punishment. At any rate, the response remained weak only during punishment, a typical enough result. Further experimental manipulation was frustrated by the "graduation" of S from nursery school 1 week later.

The procedure used to establish this temporary control of the thumbsucking response was a complex one. It involved withdrawal of reinforcement; re-presentation of reinforcement; and the contingency of withdrawal for thumbsucking and re-presentation for removal of the thumb from the mouth. In an attempt to show the role of the contingent use of these operations, compared with their random or noncontingent use,

two other 5-year-old boys were studied in a yoked situation.

In this situation, the two Ss sat side by side and watched the same cartoons projected on the screen before them. A small room-divider was placed between them so that they could not observe each other as they watched the cartoons. Two observers watched the Ss, each recording the thumbsucking of one S on separate cumulative recorders.[2] (The recorders were housed in boxes in a distant room, so that their clicking was inaudible to the Ss or Es.) The Ss were shown cartoons for a total of 30 min per session. No experimental procedures were used in the first three sessions, because the operant level of thumbsucking in this new situation was found to change steadily from uncharacteristically low values toward higher rates. By the end of the third session, both Ss showed stable rates of thumbsucking near 100%. Two experimental sessions, labelled Session 1 and Session 2 in Fig. 2, followed on successive days. In Session 1, S1 experienced alternating 5-min periods of continu-

[2] The reliability of the two observers in recording thumbsucking was checked by having both observers record the thumbsucking of a single S on separate recorders during the second of the three preliminary sessions. Their records, when superimposed, were virtually identical, implying near-100% reliability. This technique for assessing reliability was suggested by Goldiamond (1962).

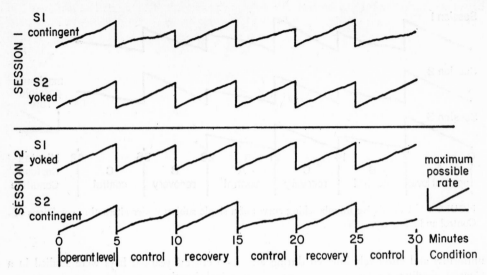

FIGURE 2   Cumulative thumbsucking curves of two subjects, one experiencing contingent withdrawal/re-presentation and the other yoked, under alternating conditions of Control and Recovery.

ous cartoons and contingent withdrawal/re-presentation of the cartoons. And S2, sitting beside him and watching the same screen, hence had a yoked withdrawal/re-presentation of the cartoons during the same alternate intervals. However, in his case, these operations had only a random contingency with his thumbsucking behavior. The next day, during Session 2, the roles of S1 and S2 were reversed: S2 experienced alternating periods of continuous cartoons and contingent withdrawal/re-presentation, while S1 experienced the yoked, noncontingent withdrawal/re-presentation operations during the same alternate periods.

Figure 2 shows the results. (The curves are slightly retouched in places where the pen left too fine a line for photographic reproduction.) In either session, the subject undergoing contingent withdrawal/re-presentation of the cartoons for thumbsucking came promptly under the control of this contingency. The subject who experienced yoked withdrawal/re-presentation under the same schedule at the same time, but only randomly associated with his thumbsucking, showed no obvious effect. However, the observer did note a transitory exception to this

pattern in S1 during Session 2. In the previous session, S1 had been subjected to contingent withdrawal/re-presentation for thumbsucking. When S1 was subjected to a random withdrawal/re-presentation of the cartoons (yoked to S2) during the first Control period of Session 2, he removed his thumb from his mouth quite frequently; but he replaced it almost immediately each time. This operation was closely correlated to the withdrawal operations (contingent upon the thumbsucking of S2). It did not appreciably reduce the amount of cumulative thumbsucking, and therefore is barely discernible in Fig. 2. During subsequent Control periods of Session 2, this pattern of response virtually disappeared.

Hence, contingent withdrawal/re-presentation of the cartoons appears to weaken the thumbsucking response during periods when it is in effect; but random withdrawal/re-presentation operations of the same frequency, extent, and timing do not appreciably affect a thumbsucking response occurring at the same time.

No claims are made about the generality of this effect. The Ss number three; all were boys; and all were chosen because of their unusually high rate of thumbsucking in nursery school settings. Hence, they are not a random sample of young thumbsuckers.

REFERENCES

BAER, D. M. Escape and avoidance responses of preschool children to two schedules of reinforcement withdrawal. *J. exp. anal. Behav.*, 1960, 3, 155–159.

BAER, D. M. The effect of withdrawal of positive reinforcement on an extinguishing response in young children. *Child Develpm.*, 1961, 32, 67–74.

FENICHEL, O. *The psychoanalytic theory of the neuroses.* New York: Norton, 1945.

GOLDIAMOND, I. The experimental analysis and control of fluent speech and stuttering. *J. Mathetics*, 1962, 1, 57–95.

PALERMO, D. S. Thumbsucking: a learned response. *Pediatr.*, 1956, 17, 392–399.

ROBERTS, E. Thumb and finger-sucking in relation to feeding in early infancy. *Am. J. Dis. Child.*, 1944, 68, 7–8.

SPOCK, B. *The common sense book of baby and child care.* New York: Duell, Sloan and Pierce, 1957.

33   A ROLE FOR COGNITION IN THE BEHAVIORAL TREATMENT OF A CHILD'S ELIMINATIVE DISTURBANCE[1]

Donald R. Peterson • Perry London

In its most common forms, behavior therapy is characterized not only by its allegedly effective outcome, but by certain idiosyncrasies of technique that result in the neglect of insight. The problems are behavioral, the procedures are behavior, and it is behavior change alone that the therapist seeks. Insight, it would appear, has nothing to do with either process or goal. This omission is most conspicuous in treatment systems that have grown from the work of Skinner and his associates, but it also holds for most other versions of behavior therapy. In the main, behavior therapists condition, extinguish, sensitize, desensitize, train and retrain their subjects in exclusive reference to behavioral functions. There is little or no emphasis on comprehension, understanding, hindsight,

[1] An earlier version of this article appears in the *Psychological Record* for October 1964 under the title "Neobehavioristic Psychotherapy: Quasihypnotic Suggestion and Multiple Reinforcement in the Treatment of a Case of Postinfantile Dyscopresis."

foresight, or insight in any of their work.

Exclusion of mental functions, however, is unnecessary and unwise in the framework of enlightened views of behavior. Suppose we define insight as reasonably accurate knowledge of the origins and consequences of one's own behavior. Insight, so defined, is more than an understanding of personal dynamics, and it goes beyond awareness of reinforcing contingencies. It is tantamount to cognition, circumscribed only in a topical way, as that knowledge which pertains to one's own behavior. Cognitive functions, of course, is a perfectly respectable area for scientific inquiry, and there is no reason for knowledge gained in the study of cognition to be ignored in therapeutic practice.

We do not propose that insight is essential to the learning of new behavior patterns or the unlearning of old ones. Pigeons can be taught, paramecia can be conditioned, and planaria can be trained through ingestion of their educated forebears—all without apparent benefit of awareness. But in human beings, it seems equally clear that insight, that is, cognition, can significantly facilitate the acquisition of adaptive skills. Insight may not be necessary, but it appears to be very helpful.

The recent flurry of research on learning and awareness seems to demonstrate nothing more clearly than that awareness is a very important determinant of learning (Greenspoon, 1955, 1962; Dulany, 1961, 1962; Farber, 1963; Krasner, 1958; Krasner and Ullmann, 1963; Salzinger, 1959; Eriksen, 1962). In a fairly typical experiment, Dulany (1961) reinforced plural nouns a la Greenspoon (1955). When he later asked subjects to describe what he had done that was significant in connection with the experiment, he found that those who said something like "I think you were trying to get me to use plural nouns" (aware subjects) were markedly superior in the production of plural nouns to those who reported no associative hypothesis. It might be interesting to see what changes would occur if subjects were instructed to use the word "we" as often as possible. Other investigators, using appropriately ambiguous tasks and asking sufficiently penetrating questions, have reported results that confirm those of Dulany and his colleagues (Kirman, 1958; Levin, 1959; Spielberger et al., 1962; Matarazzo et al., 1960). From myriad learning experiments, it is now apparent that if a subject (a) knows what he is supposed to do in a learning situation, and (b) wants to do it, then (c) he probably will.

Controversies have arisen over the precise role of awareness in the acquisition and performance of verbal and motor tasks. Whether, in the particular laboratory situations most popularly established for research in this area, learning can or cannot occur without awareness, is a matter of heated dispute. But all this is beside the point for the present argument. In human beings, awareness of a behavioral sequence, comprehension of a problem, knowledge of a situation, insight into one's own behavior and its repercussions, will facilitate learning dramatically.

This is one of the most fully documented facts in all psychology, and one of the most important. It probably explains the biological survival of the human species.

The deemphasis or denial of insight in modern behavior therapy has occurred, we believe, partly in reaction to the overemphasis on insight in traditional psychotherapy, and partly by way of historical accident. The fundamental principles on which behavior therapy is based have come almost entirely from learning laboratories. The investigators who worked in these laboratories—Pavlov, Hull, and those who followed—dealt principally with animals, where questions of awareness were seldom more than esoteric. Observations were focused on motor behavior. The classical studies of verbal conditioning were done by Thorndike, who proposed that learning could occur without awareness, and began to forge the structure of American Behaviorism. The latter became, at the hand of J. B. Watson, the ultimate negation of mind. A good deal of the later work has been inspired by B. F. Skinner, who worked with animals, dealt with motor behavior, and espoused a conception of man that left little place for insight or any function like it.

To restrict therapeutic attention to insight is ineffective and inefficient. To ignore insight is foolish. The therapeutic strategy we therefore recommend as a general paradigm involves the introduction of verbal and gestural stimuli, chosen by the therapist, to modify the client's cognitions regarding origins and/or consequences of his own characteristic mode of action in specified situations, along with the application of reinforcement and related techniques to shape adaptive behavior whenever it occurs. We presuppose that people who display disordered behavior are generally ignorant of or wrong about the meanings of their acts, both as to source and outcome, and that pertinent conceptual change will facilitate appropriate behavioral change. How best to encourage the conceptual shift is a matter for continuing investigation. It seems unlikely that client-centered reflection or occasional interpretation over the long course of psychoanalytic free association will turn out to be the most efficacious way to do this. From the general literature on cognition, it would seem more plausible to assume that vividness of presentation and clarity of form would be most strongly related to change, but that such parameters as the intellectual capacity, motivational state, and prior cognitive condition of the recipient would also be involved, in ways as yet largely unknown.

When cognitive learning occurs in a therapeutic situation, it may come about merely as a function of exposure. No reinforcement appears to be needed, and the concept of contiguity is irrelevant. Actually, no true association is formed. A client changes his mind about something. A concept is changed, and the fundamental way in which one person can generate change in the conceptual state of another may be nothing more nor less than exposure of the recipient to a new concept. The cognitive residuals of therapeutic experience, in the form of images or subvocal utterances, may then act as novel subjective components of the stimulus field whenever a patient encounters a situation in which he has previously experienced difficulty, and this may lead him to emit novel, more adaptive behavior. If the behavior is indeed more adaptive, reinforcement may intrinsically occur, and the behavioral tendency maintained or enhanced. In clinical treatment, however, it is frequently risky to depend on intrinsic reinforcement, and to the extent that extrinsic reinforcement patterns can be altered in a client's interest they clearly should be altered. But this is the burden of argument in most contemporary formulations of behavior therapy, and requires no further emphasis.

The approach is illustrated in the following case, which exemplifies general strategic principles and one possible set of tactical procedures.

THE CASE OF ROGER

The child's name is Roger, and at the time of treatment he was three years, four months old. He was the third of four children born to upper middle class parents in a small urban community. His father is a university professor and his mother holds a master's degree in Child Development in addition to two baccalaureate degrees. She has worked occasionally in her professional speciality but was not employed at the time the problem arose nor was she working when treatment was conducted. To all appearances, the members of the family are reasonably successful, content, and adapted to their lot. There has been some conflict between the parents over discipline, with the father tending toward leniency and the mother toward greater strictness, but this had never reached the point of open argument before the children, and had had no visible effect on Roger's emotional or social adjustment.

For his part, Roger had displayed no serious difficulties prior to his referral, aside from a certain accident proneness that seemed more a product of his exuberant energy than of any latent wish for self-destruction. As far as anyone could tell, he was loved by his parents, liked by his siblings, and enjoyed by most others with whom he came in contact.

Presenting Problem

The presenting problem, in brief, appeared circumscribed and limited to the fact that Roger did not defecate with either the frequency or aplomb that seemed meet in an otherwise normal and happy three-year-old. The interlude between eliminations was generally about five days, enough to concern the family pediatrician, and when they did occur, bowel movements were so painful that the child was reluctant to complete them. Eventually he would defecate, under increasing physical pressure, but he would hide under a bed (if indoors) or a bush (if outdoors) to perform the act. At the time of referral, he had not had a normal bowel movement in the usually appropriate location for more than three months.

Origin of the Problem

Toilet training had commenced, as with the older siblings, when Roger was about two-years-old. He had been placed on the toilet whenever he indicated by word or gesture that he "had to go," and effective performances were moderately praised. It seems the eliminative difficulty developed when Roger became so preoccupied in play, at times when the physical urge was present, that he did not ask to be taken to the toilet. His mother, in the adaptation that sometimes occurs with later children, had relaxed a good deal of her earlier watchfulness, and did not notice the change in routine until Roger had failed to defecate for three days. By that time, elimination was quite painful. Roger cried throughout the act and remained slightly upset for the rest of the day. When he was taken to the toilet the next day, he became very upset. He cried, struggled to get down, and refused to defecate. His mother did not insist, but she took Roger back to the bathroom two or three more times that same day, and offered him additional opportunities over the days that followed. The patient did not eliminate again for six days, and the experience at that time was even more painful than before.

The mother called her pediatrician, who prescribed laxatives, but these had no effect, and after three months of increasing urgency and distress on the part of parents and child alike, Roger was referred, with the concurrence of the pediatrician, to the agency in which the writers were employed.

Strategy of Treatment

Although the origin of the symptom was partly obscure, it seemed plain enough that there were two separate components involved in its retention (so to speak): (1) Whenever the urge to defecate occurred, Roger experienced a primary negative reinforcement for responding to it, that is, the initiation of a downward peristalsis towards the anal sphincter was immediately followed by pain, and (2) whatever primary drive may have initiated the sequence in the first place, was of insufficient strength to sustain it against the combined presence of pain and absence of any secondarily reinforced positive motivation. The only secondary motive of

any consequence was the concern and displeasure that his parents manifested in connection with his symptom, and though Roger was uncomfortable with the parental pressure he experienced, the alternative of succumbing to fecal pressure seemed even less desirable.

The therapeutic strategy that was planned on the basis of the foregoing analysis consisted of (1) generation of insight (cognitive stimulation) to facilitate the initiation of the eliminative sequence, and (2) reinforcement of the adaptive, that is, "target" behavior, upon its occurrence.

(1) Generation of insight consisted in part of communicating to the child verbally that the issue of therapy was his eliminative reticence and that it would be "good" for him, and would feel good, to move his bowels. It was assumed that recognition of positive value in the behavior would interact with need for social approval and primary drive in a way that would make Roger desire, at least at a cognitive level, to undertake the behavior.

Hypnotic suggestion was elected as the means of changing expectancies regarding the pain of sphincter pressure and the act of elimination itself. Hypnosis has been used successfully for the relief of pain in a variety of clinical settings, and in the present instance, where skeletal and other muscle tension contributed much of the painful sensation, the generally relaxing character of hypnosis might be even more than usually effective.

In this case, the technique consisted largely in the delivery of a post-hypnotic kind of suggestion to the general effect that well-timed defecation would not hurt. As it turned out, Roger did not satisfy *any* standard criteria for hypnotic behavior though the therapist conducted himself as if the child were hypnotized.

(2) The importance of selecting effective and immediate positive reinforcements is apparent when one considers the immediacy and potency of the negative reinforcement that generally applied in this case. Both verbal and nonverbal reinforcements

were used here; the former consisted of parental praise (P_1), and the latter of the administration of popsicles (P_2). The efficacy of verbal reinforcement has, of course, been widely studied, though often with ambiguous or contradictory results (London & Rosenhan, 1964). It is, at all events, only a secondary reinforcement. Popsicles, on the other hand, have both primary and secondary reinforcing characteristics. Though little laboratory research has reported their use as reinforcers, indications of their popularity, particularly with children high in hypnotic susceptibility, have been reported by London (1962).

Course of Treatment

Roger was seen for three therapy sessions; the first (7/30/62) lasted for about twenty minutes, the second (8/1/62) for ten minutes, and the third (8/6/62) for about fifteen minutes. The entire course of treatment transpired over an eight-day period.

The first session began in a play therapy room. After about five minutes, in which Roger played quite happily with the therapist, he was escorted to the therapist's office. Seated there, he was first asked to draw a picture, which he willingly did. He was then presented with a Chevreul pendulum and a formal hypnotic induction was attempted by means of the procedures of the *Children's Hypnotic Susceptibility Scale* (London, 1963). This was totally unsuccessful because Roger became quickly bored. Therapist (T) then insisted that he lie down on the couch and, abandoning more formal procedure, began stroking his forehead, at the same time softly and monotonously talking to him about how T knew that Roger did not like to "go potty," that Mommy and Daddy wanted him to, and so forth. This gradually evolved into a soft hypnoidal chant, as follows:

> Mommy and Daddy want Roger to go potty all the time, but he doesn't like to, Roger doesn't like to. Everybody wants for Roger to go potty, Roger to go potty, Roger's going potty. Everybody likes Roger to go potty, 'cause then he'll feel real good.

After about ten minutes of this, Roger quietly said, "Can I wake up now?" T agreed to this, and Roger said he wanted to go home. They returned to the waiting room, where his mother was waiting. His only comment on the session was that he had played. Another appointment was scheduled for two days later.

When he arrived home with his mother, Roger immediately went to the bathroom and defecated. Mother lavished praise on him (P_1) and gave him a popsicle (P_2). This did not recur the next day.

The second session occurred as scheduled. Roger did not wish to lie down this time, however, or to go to the therapist's office. He did go to the playroom, and while playing there, listened quietly to the therapist's hypnotic-like suggestions that it would not hurt when he went to the potty, that it would feel very good, and that Mommy and Daddy would be very happy. After ten minutes, he was returned to Mother, who took him home immediately. As before, there was no discussion of the session or other symptom relevant material, but on arrival at home, Roger again went to the bathroom and moved his bowels, again followed immediately by P_1P_2. There was no further discussion of the matter, but for each of the next four days, Roger moved his bowels once daily with P_1P_2. (No inquiry was ever conducted to ascertain the extent to which he was aware of the reinforcement contingencies, since this was not important to the therapeutic procedure. Both parents and therapist, however, are of the opinion that there was some cognizance of them, both with respect to P_1 and P_2.)

The final therapy session came five days later. After a few minutes in the playroom, Roger again agreed to go to T's office. He was congratulated on his recent successes, asked if it felt good when he "went," and when he responded affirmatively, asked if he intended "to go" regularly and would never have any trouble again. He affirmed all these suggestive queries, which were then repeated at length by the therapist in a hypnotic fashion, accompanied by glowing descriptions of the joy in Roger's household at his good behavior and the plethora of praise and popsicles which would subsequently result. Roger was visibly pleased by this imagined scene, and after about five minutes of its reptition, the session was terminated and he was remanded to his mother. As in the previous session, no formal hypnotic induction was employed. Therapy was discontinued at this point by mutual agreement for though formal hypnosis plainly had not worked, the treatment apparently had.

Follow-up

At this writing, exactly one year after the termination of treatment, Roger's remission is still complete. For some 75 days after treatment, P_1P_2 was administered directly in response to completion of bowel movements, which occurred approximately once each day. One day, at the end of that period, a movement occurred under circumstances where P_2 was not available. Roger did not seem to notice its absence, however, and continued the behavior pattern established during the previous three months. Approximately 290 trials have been successfully completed since that time with no visible signs of extinction and no new symptoms have replaced the original ones. It may be safely concluded at this point that the desired behavior is habituated and the child cured.

DISCUSSION

Interpretations may differ as to the reasons for maintenance of the new pattern in the absence of continued primary reinforcement. Freudians might sense a symbolic libidinous gratification in the placement of a cylindrical shape in the hole of a plumbing fixture. Some might argue functional autonomy (Allport, 1937). We believe the most parsimonious explanation is that, in the relative absence of pain, other reinforcements (primary satisfaction of the eliminative drive, and secondary reinforcement mainly through

parental approval) have sufficed to sustain the behavior. Reinforcement, furthermore, probably served to sustain and enhance the cognitions initially established in treatment. For Roger, an implicative contingency was established. "If you go potty when your first feel you have to, it won't hurt, and it will feel good." This, in fact, must have been the case, and once experience had confirmed the expectancy verbally initiated by the therapist, Roger continued to act as if it were valid. Indeed we propose that the general relation between reinforcement, the principal agent in behavior therapy, and the induction of cognitive behavior contingencies, the principal element in insight therapy, is one of mutual enhancement. To the extent that a therapist can show a patient that the latter's previous cognitions were inaccurate, and that some alternative recollections and expectancies square more truly with the facts of life, and to the extent that the satisfactions and displeasures of daily living actually occur as the therapist said they would, just to that extent will the patient modify his behavior, and continue in his revised adaptation until new cognitive disparities or new displeasures arise.

REFERENCES

ALLPORT, G. W. *Personality.* New York: Holt, Rinehart and Winston, Inc., 1937.

DULANY, D. E. Hypotheses and habits in verbal "operant conditioning." *J. abnorm. soc. Psychol.,* 1961, **63**, 251–263.

DULANY, D. E. The place of hypotheses and intentions: an analysis of verbal control in verbal conditioning. *J. Pers.,* 1962, **30**, 102–129.

ERIKSEN, C. W. (Ed.) *Behavior and awareness: a symposium of research and interpretation.* Durham, N.C.: Duke University Press, 1962.

FARBER, I. E. The things people say to themselves. *Amer. Psychologist.,* 1963, **18**, 185–197.

GREENSPOON, J. The reinforcing effect of two spoken sounds on the frequency of two responses. *Amer. J. Psychol.*, 1955, **68**, 509–516.

GREENSPOON, J. Verbal conditioning and clinical psychology. In A. J. Bachrach (Ed.), *Experimental foundations of clinical psychology*. New York: Basic Books, 1962, 510–553.

KIRMAN, W. J. The relationship of learning, with and without awareness, to personality needs. *Dissertation Abstracts*, 1958, **19**, 362.

KRASNER, L. Studies of the conditioning of verbal behavior. *Psychol. Bull.*, 1958, **55**, 148–170.

KRASNER, L. and L. P. ULLMANN. Variables affecting report of awareness in verbal conditioning. *J. Psychol.*, 1963, **56**, 193–202.

LEVIN, S. The effect of awareness on verbal conditioning. *Dissertation Abstracts*, 1959, **20**, 3835.

LONDON, P. Hypnosis in children: an ex-perimental approach. *Int. J. clin. exp. Hypnosis*, 1962, **18**, 79–91.

LONDON, P. *The Children's Hypnotic Susceptibility Scale*. Palo Alto, Calif.: Consulting Psychologists Press, 1963.

LONDON, P., and D. L. ROSENHAN. Personality dynamics. In P. R. Farnsworth (Ed.), *Annual Review of Psychology*, 1964, **15**, 447–492.

MATARAZZO, J. D., G. SASLOW, and E. N. PAREIS. Verbal conditioning of two response classes: some methodological considerations. *J. abnorm. soc. Psychol.*, 1960, **61**, 190–206.

SALZINGER, K. Experimental manipulation of verbal behavior: a review. *J. gen. Psychol.*, 1959, **61**, 65–94.

SPIELBERGER, C. D., S. M. LEVIN, and MARY SHEPARD. The effects of awareness and attitude toward the reinforcement on the operant conditioning of verbal behavior. *J. Pers.*, 1962, **30**, 106–121.

34 THE ELIMINATION OF TANTRUM BEHAVIOR BY EXTINCTION PROCEDURES

Carl D. Williams

This paper reports the successful treatment of tyrant-like tantrum behavior in a male child by the removal of reinforcement. The subject (S) was approximately 21 months old. He had been seriously ill much of the first 18 months of his life. His health then improved considerably, and he gained weight and vigor.

S now demanded the special care and attention that had been given him over the many critical months. He enforced some of his wishes, especially at bedtime, by unleashing tantrum behavior to control the actions of his parents.

Journal of Abnormal and Social Psychology, 1959, **59**, 269.

The parents and an aunt took turns in putting him to bed both at night and for S's afternoon nap. If the parent left the bedroom after putting S in his bed, S would scream and fuss until the parent returned to the room. As a result, the parent was unable to leave the bedroom until after S went to sleep. If the parent began to read while in the bedroom, S would cry until the reading material was put down. The parents felt that S enjoyed his control over them and that he fought off going to sleep as long as he could. In any event, a parent was spending from one-half to two hours each bedtime just waiting in the bedroom until S went to sleep.

Following medical reassurance regarding

S's physical condition, it was decided to remove the reinforcement of this tyrant-like tantrum behavior. Consistent with the learning principle that, in general, behavior that is not reinforced will be extinguished, a parent or the aunt put S to bed in a leisurely and relaxed fashion. After bedtime pleasantries, the parent left the bedroom and closed the door. S screamed and raged, but the parent did not re-enter the room. The duration of screaming and crying was obtained from the time the door was closed.

The results are shown in Fig. 1. It can be seen that S continued screaming for 45 min. the first time he was put to bed in the first extinction series. S did not cry at all the second time he was put to bed. This is perhaps attributable to his fatigue from the crying of Occasion 1. By the tenth occasion, S no longer whimpered, fussed, or cried when the parent left the room. Rather, he smiled as they left. The parents felt he made happy sounds until he dropped off to sleep.

About a week later, S screamed and fussed after the aunt put him to bed, probably reflecting spontaneous recovery of the tantrum behavior. The aunt then reinforced the tantrum behavior by returning to S's bedroom and remaining there until he went to sleep. It was then necessary to extinguish this behavior a second time.

Figure 1 shows that the second extinction curve is similar to the first. Both curves are generally similar to extinction curves ob-

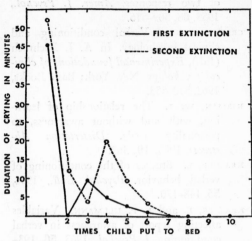

FIGURE 1   Length of crying in two extinction series as a function of successive occasions of being put to bed.

tained with subhuman subjects. The second extinction series reached zero by the ninth occasion. No further tantrums at bedtime were reported during the next two years.

It should be emphasized that the treatment in this case did not involve aversive punishment. All that was done was to remove the reinforcement. Extinction of the tyrant-like tantrum behavior then occurred.

No unfortunate side- or aftereffects of this treatment were observed. At three and three-quarters years of age, S appeared to be a friendly, expressive, outgoing child.

35 AN INFANT'S PHOBIA TREATED WITH RECIPROCAL INHIBITION THERAPY[1]

Peter M. Bentler

Phobias which are complex to unravel often have simple beginnings as conditioned emotional reactions. This paper reports a successful attempt to apply reciprocal inhibition psychotherapy to a female infant child whose primary phobia consisted of a fear of water.

According to some recent interpretations of the origins of phobias, a traumatic fear-producing event occurring temporally and spatially with neutral stimuli may suffice to initiate phobic reactions to these stimuli. In this view, a phobia is a learned response, following the same laws of learning and unlearning as other responses (Wolpe, 1958). This etiological explanation is used for adults, and applies to children as well (Rachman and Costello, 1961).

Psychotherapy aimed at treating phobias should, therefore, be consistent with principles of learning theory relevant to the unlearning of responses. The theory upon which reciprocal inhibition therapy is based states that conditioned fear or anxiety is the central constituent of neurotic behaviour, such as is evident in phobic reactions. Since conditioned fear is the product of learning, removing the fear through extinction or counter-conditioning procedures consistent with learning theory should remove the

Journal of Child Psychology and Psychiatry, 1962, **3**, 185–189.

[1] This investigation was supported in part by a Public Health Service fellowship number MPM-15,840 from the National Institute of Mental Health, U.S. Public Health Service. I am indebted to Martha F. Newman and Professors Albert Bandura and Ernest R. Hilgard for their advice in relation to a critical reading of the manuscript.

phobia (Wolpe, 1961). The fear is removed on the principle that a response inhibitory to anxiety or fear occurring in the presence of anxiety-provoking stimuli weakens the bond between the stimuli and the anxiety response.

A variety of procedures have been developed for treating phobias with reciprocal inhibition therapy. The most extensive application of reciprocal inhibition has been to adult neuroses, where hypnotically induced relaxation is usually used to counteract the anxiety created by having the patient imagine phobic objects. Treating children's phobias has not been as popular, though the earliest work had been with children. M. C. Jones (1924), in her classic study directly foreshadowing current emphasis in this area, successfully treated a 34-months-old boy for fear of a white rat, rabbit, and other furry objects by presenting food and the fear-object simultaneously. Jones also mentioned other techniques which appear to be practicable with children and at the same time to be in accord with current learning theory—social imitation and systematic distraction. Lazarus (1960) has reported cases of children treated with systematic desensitization based on relaxation, deconditioning aided by the use of drug-induced sedation, and deconditioning obtained by conditioned avoidance responses. Rachman and Costello (1961) point out that assertive responses and pleasant responses in the life situation can also serve, among others, to aid treatment of children's phobias.

Many of these techniques are not feasible with very young children or infants. It is difficult to arrange therapy in such a way that social imitation of approach responses occurs when desired. While distraction aimed at offering the infant a substitute activity will lead to non-practice of the phobic reaction, the necessary reciprocal inhibition of anxiety may not occur. Getting a small child to cooperate sufficiently for the use of relaxation with imagined phobic scenes also presents a problem. Conditioned avoidance responses in conjunction with deconditioning present a situation potentially useful with infants, but this procedure generally requires a stationary, non-active, and cooperating child. Such a child may be difficult to obtain.

The use of drugs for the purpose of relaxation along with the gradual introduction of fear-producing stimuli, as described by Lazarus, should be possible with infants. This method presents an advantage over treatment of adult patients with imagined scenes in that the real objects of fear can be presented instead of such imagined scenes. The feeding situation represents a more easily manipulable situation. Fear-object and food can be presented simultaneously, with the food serving to inhibit anxiety created by the phobic object. The recent work of Harlow (Harlow and Zimmerman, 1959) demonstrating the importance of a soft and cuddly terry-cloth monkey mother in allaying infant monkeys' fear, such as that produced by a strange environment, would lead one to expect that body-contact with a warm mother can serve to inhibit phobic reactions in human infants. In addition to any innate reciprocally-inhibiting effects stemming from body-contact, the association of mother and child in the feeding situation should result in learned fear inhibition with contact, if the mother-child relationship has been normal. These secondary rewarding and fear-reducing responses should, with time, become associated not only with the contact, but also with the sight and sound of the mother. Another method of inducing reciprocal inhibition in infants would be the simultaneous presentation of attractive toys and the phobic object, since these toys could evoke positive affective responses which may be inhibitory to anxiety.

In the case reported in this paper, distraction, affective responses towards attractive toys, and body-contact with the mother as well as other mother-related stimuli, were used to elicit responses incompatible with anxiety. This year-old infant represents the youngest reported case treated with the method of reciprocal inhibition.

CASE HISTORY

Description

At approximately 11½ months of age Margaret gleefully waded in a small swimming pool, bathed with evident delight, and never objected to being washed when her diaper was changed. At this time she was placed with a baby-sitter for daily care while her mother went to work for several days. At the end of this time, Margaret's mother attempted to bathe her again in the bathroom. During the first few moments of the bath, Margaret was happy. She tried to stand up in the bathtub, slipped, and began screaming. She refused further bathing with violent screams and had to be removed from the tub.

Testing during the next few days indicated that Margaret reacted with violent emotion not only to the bathtub, the faucet, and water in the tub, but also to being washed in the handbasin, to faucets or water at any part of the house, and to the wading pool. It is clear that slipping in the tub plus other possible unknown prior circumstances (e.g. at the baby-sitter's) or concomitant events (e.g. soap in the face) caused a great change in Margaret's emotional responsiveness to a wide range of situations.

During the next week it became apparent that Margaret would continue this behaviour unless systematic steps were taken to overcome her fear. Being cleaned in the washbasin brought only further screams and Margaret refused to play with water.

Interpretation

Here were the beginning stages of a phobia. The initiating traumatic event was in view. Generalization had already occurred, since Margaret was now afraid of water, not only in the bathtub, but anywhere around the house, as described above. Defence mechanisms were still clearly limited to physical avoidance of the traumatic situation and its generalized stimuli. The problem appeared to be one of eliminating or extinguishing a conditioned fear or phobia, so the technique of reciprocal inhibition was applied.

Treatment

As mentioned above, distraction, affective responses toward toys, body-contact, and other mother-related stimuli were used to elicit responses incompatible with anxiety. Since the author was not an expert in reciprocal inhibition therapy, use of the feeding situation to inhibit fear was considered inadvisable, since inappropriate handling of the case could result in the transfer of the fear to feeding rather than transfer of pleasant emotional responses to the phobic object. No specific schedule was followed; the mother was instructed in the course of treatment, but could be lax about applying it. The basic rule was that Margaret should be exposed only to small amounts of anxiety.

Treatment consisted of four parts and lasted approximately a month. First, toys were placed in the empty bathtub and Margaret was given free access to the bathroom and the toys. She would enter the bathroom and remove a toy from the tub occasionally, but she did not stay near the tub and refused to play with the toys while leaning over the tub. She continued to scream if any washing was attempted, but became less emotional toward the tub. Free access of this type was allowed throughout the duration of treatment. Second, Margaret was twice placed on the kitchen tables surrounding the sink while the sink was filled with water and toys were floating in it. At first Margaret screamed when near the water. She started to play with the toys on the table, but these toys were gradually moved towards and into the water, so that

she had to move towards it in order to play. She refused to enter the water. All toys were then placed on the other side of the basin, and onto a ledge above it so that Margaret would have to walk through the basin in order to reach them. After several vacillations, Margaret entered the water reluctantly. Some minor crying resulted from wetting her buttocks, but the kitchen sink helped desensitize Margaret to water. The third step consisted of washing Margaret, at diaper-changing time, in the bathroom sink. She was generally given a favourite toy to play with, but the mirror hanging over the sink proved more interesting, and initial crying soon turned to happy squeals. Margaret also started playing with the water, and during this time she again learned to play with the sprinkler in the yard. The fourth and final step was washing Margaret at diaper-change time in the tub, with water running. To this she objected at first, with screams, but parental hugging and firmness caused her to stop crying after two days.

Behavioural changes resulting from treatment

At age 12¾ months Margaret was thoroughly recovered and played normally though cautiously in the tub while taking baths. She had no more fear of faucets, tubs, or water anywhere around the house. Her behaviour had undergone extensive changes. At 13 months she was not only willing to take baths or to be washed, but she gleefully initiated approach responses to water. On warm days Margaret would rush madly towards the wading pool in the backyard, enter it, and splash about joyously while playing. A follow-up study conducted at age 18 months indicated that these changes were quite permanent. She gladly played in the bathtub and showed no aversive reactions to water anywhere in or near the house.[2]

[2] An additional follow-up conducted when Margaret was 42-months-old indicated that recovery from the phobia was still complete. No "symptom substitution" has been observed to date.

DISCUSSION

While treatment of Margaret's case appears to be successful, it is also evident that several procedures could have accelerated the treatment process. More careful sequencing of anxiety-related cues should have been advantageous. For example, a play session with toys floating in a small pail far removed from the bathroom might have been a good first step to be followed by playing with toys floating in larger quantities of water. The play scene could have gradually been moved closer and closer to the bathroom until it was finally inside the tub itself. This routine should be executed regularly and not as laxly as the parents applied the methods in this case. Furthermore, the addition of attractive food would seem to be a most important therapeutic tool in reducing the anxiety and treating the phobia.

SUMMARY

A year-old female child acquired phobic reactions to water when slipping in a bathtub. She was treated with reciprocal inhibition psychotherapy. Attraction toward toys and body-contact with the mother were used to elicit responses which were presumed to be incompatible with anxiety. One and a half months after the traumatic incident the infant gleefully initiated approach responses toward the formerly phobic object. A follow-up study conducted at age 18 months indicated these changes were quite permanent.

REFERENCES

HARLOW, H. F. and ZIMMERMAN, R. R. (1959) Affectional responses in the infant monkey. *Science* **130**, 421–432.

JONES, M. C. (1924) A laboratory study of fear: the case of Peter. *Pedagog. Sem.* **31**, 308–315.

LAZARUS, A. A. (1960) The elimination of children's phobias by deconditioning. In *Behaviour therapy and the neuroses.* (Ed. by H. J. Eysenck.) Pergamon Press, New York. Pp. 114–122.

RACHMAN, S. and COSTELLO, C. G. (1961) The aetiology and treatment of children's phobias: a review. *Amer. J. Psychiat.* **118**, 97–105.

WOLPE, J. (1958) *Psychotherapy by reciprocal inhibition.* Stanford University Press, California.

WOLPE, J. (1961) The systematic desensitization treatment of neuroses. *J. Nerv. Ment. Dis.* **132**, 189–203.

36 THE USE OF "EMOTIVE IMAGERY" IN THE TREATMENT OF CHILDREN'S PHOBIAS

Arnold A. Lazarus • Arnold Abramovitz

Some of the earliest objective approaches to the removal of specific anxieties and fears in children were based on the fact that neurotic (learned, unadaptive) responses can be eliminated by the repeated and simultaneous evo-

Journal of Mental Science, 1962, **108**, 191–195.

cation of stronger incompatible responses. An early and well-known example of this approach was the experiment of Jones (1) in which a child's fear of rabbits was gradually eliminated by introducing a "pleasant stimulus" i.e., *food* (thus evoking the anxiety-inhibiting response of eating) in the presence of the rabbit. The general method of "gradual habituation" was advocated by Jersild and Holmes (2) as being superior to all others in the elimination of children's fears. This rationale was crystallized in Wolpe's (3) formulation of the Reciprocal Inhibition Principle, which deserves the closest possible study:

> If a response antagonistic to anxiety can be made to occur in the presence of anxiety-evoking stimuli so that it is accompanied by a complete or partial suppression of the anxiety responses, the bond between these stimuli and the anxiety responses will be weakened.

A crucial issue in the application of this principle is the choice of a clinically suitable anxiety-inhibiting response. The most widely-used method has been that of "systematic desensitization" (Wolpe, 4) which may be described as gradual habituation to the imagined stimulus through the anxiety-inhibiting response of *relaxation*. Lazarus (5) reported several successful paediatric applications of this procedure, using both feeding and relaxation. It was subsequently found, however, that neither feeding nor relaxation was feasible in certain cases. Feeding has obvious disadvantages in routine therapy, while training in relaxation is often both time-consuming and difficult or impossible to achieve with certain children. The possibility of inducing anxiety-inhibiting *emotive* images, without specific training in relaxation, was then explored, and the results of our preliminary investigation form the subject of this paper.

Our use of the term "emotive imagery" requires clarification. In the present clinical context, it refers to those classes of imagery which are assumed to arouse feelings of self-assertion, pride, affection, mirth, and similar anxiety-inhibiting responses.

The technique which was finally evolved can be described in the following steps:

(a) As in the usual method of systematic desensitization, the range, intensity, and circumstances of the patient's fears are ascertained, and a graduated hierarchy is drawn up, from the most feared to the least feared situation.

(b) By sympathetic conversation and enquiry, the clinician establishes the nature of the child's hero-images—usually derived from radio, cinema, fiction, or his own imagination—and the wish-fulfilments and identifications which accompany them.

(c) The child is then asked to close his eyes and told to imagine a sequence of events which is close enough to his everyday life to be credible, but within which is woven a story concerning his favourite hero or *alter ego*.

(d) If this is done with reasonable skill and empathy, it is possible to arouse to the necessary pitch the child's affective reactions. (In some cases this may be recognized by small changes in facial expression, breathing, muscle tension, etc.).

(e) When the clinician judges that these emotions have been maximally aroused, he introduces, as a natural part of the narrative, the lowest item in the hierarchy. Immediately afterwards he says: "if you feel afraid (or unhappy, or uncomfortable) just raise your finger." If anxiety is indicated, the phobic stimulus is "withdrawn" from the narrative and the child's anxiety-inhibiting emotions are again aroused. The procedure is then repeated as in ordinary systematic desensitization, until the highest item in the hierarchy is tolerated without distress.

The use of this procedure is illustrated in the following cases:

Case 1

Stanley M., aged 14, suffered from an intense fear of dogs, of 2½-3 years duration. He would take two buses on a roundabout route to school rather than risk exposure to dogs on a direct 300-yard walk. He was a rather dull (I.Q. 93), sluggish person, very large for his age, trying to be co-operative, but sadly unresponsive—especially to attempts at training in relaxation. In his desire to please, he would state that he had been perfectly relaxed even though he had betrayed himself by his intense fidgetiness. Training in relaxation was eventually abandoned, and an attempt was made to establish the nature of his aspirations and goals. By dint of much questioning and after following many false trails because of his in-articulateness, a topic was eventually tracked down that was absorbing enough to form the subject of his fantasies, namely racing motor-cars. He had a burning ambition to own a certain Alfa Romeo sports car and race it at the Indianapolis "500" event. Emotive imagery was induced as follows: "Close your eyes. I want you to imagine, clearly and vividly, that your wish has come true. The Alfa Romeo is now in your possession. It is your car. It is standing in the street outside your block. You are looking at it now. Notice the beautiful, sleek lines. You decide to go for a drive with some friends of yours. You sit down at the wheel, and you feel a thrill of pride as you realize that you own this magnificent ma-chine. You start up and listen to the wonder-ful roar of the exhaust. You let the clutch in and the car streaks off. . . . You are out in a clear open road now; the car is performing like a pedigree; the speedometer is climbing into the nineties; you have a wonderful feel-ing of being in perfect control; you look at the trees whizzing by and you see a little dog standing next to one of them—if you feel any anxiety, just raise your finger. Etc., etc." An item fairly high up on the hierarchy: "You stop at a café in a little town and dozens of people crowd around to look enviously at this magnificent car and its lucky owner; you swell with pride; and at this moment a large boxer comes up and sniffs at your heels—If you feel any anxiety, etc., etc."

After three sessions using this method he reported a marked improvement in his reaction to dogs. He was given a few field assignments during the next two sessions, after which therapy was terminated. Twelve months later, reports both from the patient and his relatives indicated that there was no longer any trace of his former phobia.

Case 2

A 10-year-old boy was referred for treat-ment because his excessive fear of the dark exposed him to ridicule from his 12-year-old brother and imposed severe restrictions on his parents' social activities. The lad became acutely anxious whenever his parents went visiting at night and even when they remained at home he refused to enter any darkened room unaccompanied. He insisted on sharing a room with his brother and made constant use of a night light next to his bed. He was especially afraid of remaining alone in the bathroom and only used it if a member of the household stayed there with him. On ques-tioning, the child stated that he was not anxious during the day but that he invariably became tense and afraid towards sunset.

His fears seemed to have originated a year or so previously when he saw a frighten-ing film, and shortly thereafter was warned by his maternal grandmother (who lived with the family) to keep away from all doors and windows at night as burglars and kidnappers were on the prowl.

A previous therapist had embarked on a programme of counselling with the parents and play-therapy with the child. While some important areas of interpersonal friction were apparently ameliorated, the child's phobic re-sponses remained unchanged. Training in "emotive imagery" eliminated his repertoire of fears in three sessions.

The initial interview (90 minutes) was devoted to psychometric testing and the de-velopment of rapport. The test revealed a superior level of intelligence (I.Q. 135) with definite evidence of anxiety and insecurity. He responded well to praise and encourage-ment throughout the test situation. Approxi-mately 30 minutes were devoted to a general discussion of the child's interests and activities, which was also calculated to win his con-fidence. Towards the end of this interview, the child's passion for two radio serials, "Su-perman" and "Captain Silver" had emerged.

A week later, the child was seen again. In addition to his usual fears he had been troubled by nightmares. Also, a quarterly school report had commented on a deteriora-tion in his schoolwork. Emotive imagery was then introduced. The child was asked to imagine that Superman and Captain Silver had joined forces and had appointed him their agent. After a brief discussion concern-ing the topography of his house he was given his first assignment. The therapist said, "Now I want you to close your eyes and imagine that you are sitting in the dining-room with your mother and father. It is night time. Suddenly, you receive a signal on the wrist radio that Superman has given you. You quickly run into the lounge because your mission must be kept a secret. There is only a little light coming into the lounge from the passage. Now pretend that you are all alone in the lounge waiting for Superman and Captain Silver to visit you. Think about this very clearly. If the idea makes you feel afraid, lift up your right hand."

An ongoing scene was terminated as soon as any anxiety was indicated. When an image aroused anxiety, it would either be re-presented in a more challengingly assertive manner, or it would be altered slightly so as to prove less objectively threatening.

At the end of the third session, the child was able to picture himself alone in his bath-room with all the lights turned off, awaiting a communication from Superman.

Apart from ridding the child of his specific phobia, the effect of this treatment appeared to have diverse and positive implica-tions on many facets of his personality. His school-work improved immeasurably and many former manifestations of insecurity were no longer apparent. A follow-up after eleven months revealed that he had maintained his gains and was, to quote his mother, "a com-pletely different child."

Case 3

An eight-year-old girl was referred for treatment because of persistent noctural enuresis and a fear of going to school. Her fear of the school situation was apparently engendered by a series of emotional upsets in class. In order to avoid going to school, the child resorted to a variety of devices in-cluding temper tantrums, alleged pains and illnesses, and on one occasion she was caught playing truant and intemperately upbraided by her father. Professional assistance was finally sought when it was found that her younger sister was evincing the same behav-iour.

When the routine psychological investiga-tions had been completed, emotive imagery was introduced with the aid of an Enid Bly-ton character, Noddy, who provided a hier-archy of assertive challenges centred around the school situation. The essence of this pro-cedure was to create imagined situations where Noddy played the role of a truant and responded fearfully to the school setting. The patient would then protect him, either by active reassurance or by "setting a good ex-ample."

Only four sessions were required to eliminate her school-going phobia. Her enu-resis, which had received no specific thera-peutic attention, was far less frequent and disappeared entirely within two months. The child has continued to improve despite some additional upsets at the hands of an unsym-pathetic teacher.

DISCUSSION

The technique of "emotive imagery" has been applied to nine phobic children whose ages ranged from 7 to 14 years. Seven chil-dren recovered in a mean of only 3·3 ses-sions. The method failed with one child who refused to co-operate and later revealed wide-spread areas of disturbance, which required broader therapeutic handling. The other failure was a phobic child with a history of encephalitis. He was unable to concentrate on the emotive images and could not enter into the spirit of the "game."

Of the seven patients who recovered, two had previously undergone treatment at the hands of different therapists. Two others had been treated by the same therapist (A.A.L.) using reassurance, relaxation and "environmental manipulation." In none of these four cases was there any appreciable remission of the phobic symptoms until the present methods were applied. In every instance where the method was used, im-provement occurred contemporaneously with treatment.

Follow-up enquiries were usually con-ducted by means of home-visits, interviews and telephone conversations both with the child and his immediate associates. These revealed that in no case was there symptom substitution of any obvious kind and that in fact, favourable response generalization had occurred in some instances.

It has been suggested that these results may be due to the therapist's enthusiasm for the method. (Does this imply that other therapists are unenthusiastic about *their* methods?) Certainly, the nature of the pro-cedure is such that it cannot be coldly and dispassionately applied. A warm rapport with the child and a close understanding of his wish-fulfilments and identifications are essential. But our claim is that although warmth and acceptance are necessary in any psychotherapeutic undertaking, they are usually not *sufficient*. Over and above such non-specific anxiety-inhibiting factors, this technique, in common with other reciprocal inhibition methods, provides a clearly defined therapeutic tool which is claimed to have *specific* effects.

Encouraging as these preliminary experiences have been, it is not claimed that they are, as yet, anything more than suggestive evidence of the efficacy of the method. Until properly controlled studies are performed, no general inference can be drawn. It is evident, too, that our loose *ad hoc* term "emotive imagery", reflects a basic lack of theoretical systematization in the field of the emotions. In her review of experimental data on autonomic functions, Martin (6) deplores the paucity of replicated studies, the unreliability of the measures used, and the lack of operational definitions of qualitatively labelled emotions. The varieties of emotion we have included under the blanket term "emotive imagery" and our simple conjecture of anxiety-inhibiting properties for all of them is an example of the *a priori* assumptions one is forced to make in view of the absence of firm empirical data and adequately formulated theory. It is hoped that our demonstration of the clinical value of these techniques will help to focus attention on an unaccountably neglected area of study, but one which lies at the core of experimental clinical psychology.

SUMMARY

A Reciprocal Inhibition (3) technique for the treatment of children's phobias is presented which consists essentially of an adaptation of Wolpe's method of "systematic desensitization" (4). Instead of inducing muscular relaxation as the anxiety-inhibiting response, certain emotion-arousing situations are presented to the child's imagination. The emotions induced are assumed, like relaxation, to have autonomic effects which are incompatible with anxiety. This technique, which the authors have provisionally labelled "emotive imagery" was applied to nine phobic children whose ages ranged from 7 to 14 years. Seven children recovered in a mean of 3·3 sessions and follow-up enquiries up to 12 months later revealed no relapses or symptom substitution. An outstanding feature of this paediatric technique is the extraordinary rapidity with which remission occurs.

REFERENCES

1. JONES, M. C., "Elimination of children's fears", *J. Exp. Psychol.*, 1924, **7**, 382–390.
2. JERSILD, A. T., and HOLMES, F. B., "Methods of overcoming children's fears", *J. Psychol.*, 1935, **1**, 75–104.
3. WOLPE, J., *Psychotherapy by Reciprocal Inhibition*, 1958. Stanford Univ. Press and Witwatersrand Univ. Press.
4. *Idem*, "The Systematic Desensitization Treatment of Neuroses", *J. Nerv. and Mental Disease*, 1961, **132**, 189–203.
5. LAZARUS, A. A., "The Elimination of Children's Phobias by Deconditioning", In *Behaviour Therapy and the Neuroses*, ed. H. J. Eysenck, 1960. Oxford: Pergamon Press.
6. MARTIN, I., "Somatic Reactivity". In *Handbook of Abnormal Psychology*, ed. H. J. Eysenck, 1960. London: Pitman Medical Publishing Co. Ltd.

37 POSITIVE REINFORCEMENT IN THE TOILET TRAINING OF A NORMAL CHILD: A CASE REPORT

Charles H. Madsen, Jr.

While the greatest interest in application of learning principles has been in the modification of maladaptive performances, positive reinforcement may also be used to increase the rate of desirable behavior in normal individuals. Examples of this approach may be found in Azrin and Lindsley's article (1956) on cooperation in children, Birnbrauer *et al.*'s (47) use of reinforcement to increase the attention span and motivation of mentally defective children, and, in particular, Homme *et al.*'s use (1963) of the Premack principle in controlling the behavior of nursery school children. When dealing with the problem of toilet training, it is typical in our culture to stress the aspects of withholding rather than, as Neale (1963) has pointed out, the muscle contractions necessary for performance of the act at the proper time and place. In dealing with a case in which a maladaptive pattern had occurred, Peterson and London (33) illustrated (1) the reduction of tension that may develop around bowel movements, and (2) the use of positive reinforcement, praise and popsicles, in the reinforcement of an adaptive response.

In short, it may be hypothesized that toilet training can be made more rapid and less stressful if principles of reinforcement learning are used. In fact, not to use such reinforcement seems at times to reflect parental prejudices centering around a normal biological function.

The present case was brought to the author's attention when the child's family planned an extended trip by automobile within a month. The child's mother consulted the author as to the best method to train the child in the shortest possible time. It was of the utmost importance to the mother that the child be trained prior to the trip.

The child was a nineteen-month-old girl, the only child of parents who were both college graduates. The child was not suffering from any behavior problems, was normal to above average in development (Cattell Infant Scale, DQ 143, at 18 months), and appeared to have been disciplined with relative consistency by parents who were in marked agreement on child-rearing practices. It was further ascertained that the mother had recently purchased a small toilet, had removed all restraining devices, and allowed the child to sit on the toilet whenever she so desired. While at the time of consultation the mother was placing the child on the toilet and remaining with her, there had been no successful eliminations. Despite a regular eight-ounce glass of orange juice at both nap-time and bedtime, the child had remained dry on a number of occasions. The frequency of "dry diapers after bed" was noticeably on the increase. However, while there was evidence of physiological readiness and a relatively permissive approach to the situation, the mother did mention that the child was beginning to react with crying and tears after two days of placing her on the toilet about four times a day. The mother, in discussing the situation, was noticeably anxious and was anticipating nothing but unpleasant experiences until the child was trained.

It was decided that the most efficient method of training would be to give the child a candy reward whenever there was successful elimination. It was recommended that immediately after a dry diaper in the morning or after a nap the mother should place the child on the toilet, read to her or entertain her in some way, and allow her to leave the toilet when she so desired. During this time on the toilet, the mother or father was to tell the child that she would receive candy if she "went" on the toilet. Candy was withheld after failures, although the parents occasionally gave the child candy after meals and other times during the day, but always without any connotations of reward.

The program was started when the child was eighteen months, twenty-nine days old, and thirty days before the scheduled trip. The second training session on the toilet ended in success. On that occasion and thereafter, the child was 1. given a brand of candy especially desired (Kraft Caramels) immediately upon completion of urination or defecation and before she was removed from the toilet; 2. lavishly praised by one or both of the parents present; 3. told that when she "went" in the toilet candy would be forthcoming, and 4. told that it would be very nice if she told her daddy or mommy when she had "to go." The fourth day the child made the comment, "Urinate a toto, get candy." The fifth day the child was allowed to ask her parents to take her to the toilet when she wanted (instead of being placed on the toilet by the parents) and there were two successful performances. The frequency of independent action increased, until on the twelfth day after the start of the program, the parents were satisfied that the child was trained. After the fifteenth day, the reinforcements were given only if requested by the child. The trip occurred on schedule and although there were five days of driving at least eight hours a day in the car, there were no (toilet) accidents and the child made consistent use of a portable toilet. Sixty days after the start of the program the child's requests for candy had dropped to zero and she was using the bathroom on her own. On a follow-up after six months, it was found that only during an illness lasting one week, at age twenty-two months

had there been any relapses. This setback had been minor and affected only defecation. The mother reinstituted the reinforcement procedure and promised the child a candy reward upon successful elimination in the proper place. During the week of retraining the reward was given only when specifically requested by the child. This procedure was successful and there were few problems during the week of retraining, after which the program ceased.

While physiological readiness is a necessary condition for success in toilet training, and a case history does not replace an experimental study, the present experience illustrates how the principles of reinforcement learning may be used to help foster adaptive patterns of behavior. In the present situation prior to the program, despite the most favorable current child-rearing practices, some evidences of mother-child conflict were appearing. The use of reinforcement not only led to a rapid training period of twelve days, but also permitted the mother to assume a role which in addition to being more efficient was also more comfortable. The spontaneous decrease and eventual cessation of requests for the reinforcement argue against the continued need for reinforcement which might have been expected on an "arm-chair" basis. Rather, it seems that being mature, grown-up, and behaving like the adult models is adequate reinforcement to maintain an adult adaptive behavior. Rather than being hindered, self-control is fostered by a training program such as this. Before there can be self-control, there must be the development of the performance, that is, the capability to act successfully. After this has been done, it is possible on the one hand for the reinforcement schedule to be changed, and on the other, for the child to experience feelings of mastery, maturity, and bodily and social self-control which are reinforcing in themselves.

REFERENCES

AZRIN, N. H., and O. R. LINDSLEY. The reinforcement of cooperation between children. *J. abnorm. soc. Psychol.*, 1956, **52,** 100–102.

BIRNBRAUER, J. S., S. W. BIJOU, M. WOLF, and J. D. KIDDER. Programmed instruction in the classroom. (47 in this volume.)

HOMME, L. E., P. C. DEBACA, J. V. DEVINE, R. STEINHORST, and E. J. RICKERT. Use of the Premack principle in controlling the behavior of nursery school children. *J. exp. Anal. Behav.*, 1963, **6,** 544.

NEALE, D. H. Behaviour therapy and encopresis in children. *Behav. Res. Ther.*, 1963, **1,** 139–149.

PETERSON, D. R., and P. LONDON. A role for cognition in the behavioral treatment of a child's eliminative disturbance. (33 in this volume.)

38 EFFECTS OF SOCIAL REINFORCEMENT ON ISOLATE BEHAVIOR OF A NURSERY SCHOOL CHILD[1]

K. Eileen Allen • Betty M. Hart • Joan S. Buell • Florence R. Harris • Montrose M. Wolf

This report presents an application of reinforcement principles to guidance in a preschool. Teachers used systematic presentation of positive social reinforcement (adult attention) to help a child showing persistent and marked isolate behavior to achieve and maintain more play relationships with her peers. Adult attention was defined as: a teacher's going to, talking to, smiling to, touching, offering and/or giving assistance to the child. Play relationships were defined as interactions between the subject and one or more children; such as conversing, looking or smiling toward each other, touching, helping, or working with each other on a project.

Reinforcement principles have been established in experiments with several subhuman species, and some applications have been made to human problems. Wolf, Risley, and Mees (7) and Ferster and DeMyer (4) have applied them to the treatment of autism in children; Brady and Lind (3) to functional blindness; Ayllon and Michael (1) and Ayllon and Haughton (2) to psychotic behavior; Harris, Johnston, Kelley, and Wolf (5) to regressed motor behavior of a preschool child; and Hart, Allen, Buell, Harris, and Wolf (6) to operant crying. In each instance systematic improvement in behavior was achieved.

Child Development, 1964, **35,** 511–518.

[1] Of inestimable value in planning and carrying out this study were the counsel and steady support of Sidney W. Bijou, Donald M. Baer, and Jay S. Birnbrauer. Refinement of observation techniques depended heavily on the collaboration of Robert G. Wahler, who is currently exploring and developing methods for recording behavior in the child clinical situation. This investigation was supported in part by Public Health Service Research Grants MH–02232 and MH–02208, from the National Institute of Mental Health.

METHOD

Subject

Ann was 4.3 years old at the start of the study. She was enrolled at the Laboratory Preschool of the University of Washington in a group of 8 boys and 8 girls, homogeneous in terms of age (4–4.5 years), intelligence levels (higher than average), and family background (upper middle class).

During the first days of school, Ann interacted freely with adults but seldom initiated contact with children or responded to their attempts to play with her. She did not seem severely withdrawn or frightened; instead she revealed a varied repertoire of unusually well-developed physical and mental skills that drew the interested attention of adults but failed to gain the companionship of children. Teachers gave warm recognition to her skilled climbing, jumping, and riding; her creative use of paints and clay; her original songs and rhythmic interpretations of musical selections; her collections of nature objects; her perceptive and mature verbalizations; and her willing and thorough help-with-cleanup behaviors.

With passing days she complained at length about minute or invisible bumps and abrasions. She often spoke in breathy tones at levels so low that it was difficult to understand what she said. Her innumerable, bulky collections of rocks or leaves seemed to serve as "conversation pieces" valued only so long as they drew adult comments. She spent increasing time simply standing and looking. Frequently she retired to a make-believe bed in a packing box in the play yard to "sleep" for several minutes. Mild, tic-like behaviors such as picking her lower lip, pulling a strand of hair, or fingering her cheek were apparent.

After six weeks of school, a period considered ample for adjustment to the nursery school situation, the teachers made a formal inventory of Ann's behaviors and appraised the time she spent with children, with adults, and by herself. The evaluation revealed that Ann's behavior consisted of isolating herself from children and indulging in many and varied techniques for gaining and prolonging the attention of adults. Close scrutiny further revealed that most of the adult attention given to her was contingent upon behaviors incompatible with play behavior with peers.

A plan was instituted to give Ann maximum adult attention contingent on play with another child, and minimum attention upon isolate behavior or upon interactions with an adult when alone. Approximately the same total amount of adult attention was to be available to Ann each day provided she met the criteria for obtaining such behavior from the teachers.

Effort was made to hold all variables other than adult social reinforcement constant throughout the study: no changes were to be made in the regular nursery school program or in supervisional assignments of the three teachers. Teachers were to continue to be physically present, as usual. The only change instituted was in the conditions under which they were to give Ann attention, and this was governed by the schedule of reinforcement in effect at a given phase of the study.

Recording

In order to make assessments of changes in Ann's behavior, objective data were obtained each morning by two observers, the same throughout the study. Each observer worked half the morning. To ascertain rater reliability they recorded jointly for two mornings. Their records showed 81 and 91 percent agreement.

Proximity and interaction with adults and with children were recorded at ten-second intervals. An example of the form and recording technique is given below.

a = adults
c = children
$/$ = Proximity—physical closeness to adult or child (within 3 feet).
X = Interaction—conversing, smiling, touching, helping, making eye contact with adult or child.

The above line from a data sheet shows 5 minutes of behaviors recorded in 10-second intervals. In the top row (a), the single strokes indicate 4 intervals of proximity to adults; the x's indicate 7 intervals of interaction with adults. In the bottom row (c), single strokes indicate 8 intervals of proximity to children; x's indicate 7 intervals of interaction with children. Blank squares indicate intervals when Ann was neither in proximity to nor interacting with an adult (upper row) or a child (bottom row). A behavioral account might read as follows: Ann stood near a child when a teacher drew near (A). Ann talked to the child, and the teacher at once smiled at her and spoke to both children. Ann turned all her attention to the teacher, following her as she moved away. The teacher busied herself exclusively with some other children, and Ann turned and walked to a gravel area where she started to gather pebbles alone. She moved near some children and a teacher (B), where she stayed for half a minute without interacting with them. Shortly after the teacher left the group, Ann moved away, continuing to gather pebbles by herself. A child approached her (C) and joined her in picking up pebbles. They smiled at each other. A teacher at once came and talked to both children. The teacher left after half a minute. Ann continued to play with the child for 20 seconds. After the child left, Ann continued picking up pebbles alone.

Behavior during a daily scheduled group activity which averaged about 15 minutes was excluded from the data. During this part of the nursery school program the children were expected to sit in close proximity to each other and to the teacher.

Procedures

Before reinforcement procedures were initiated, an objective record was obtained of the actual amounts of time Ann was spending with children, adults, and alone.

After 5 days of baseline data had been secured, teachers were instructed to give attention to Ann whenever and only when she interacted with children. To begin with, any approximations to social interaction, such as standing near another child or playing beside another in the sandbox or at a table, were followed by teacher attention. As soon as Ann interacted with a child, an adult immediately gave her direct individual attention. A sample interaction was, "Ann, you are making dinner for the whole family." When she played alone, Ann was not given attention, and when she contacted an adult she was given minimum attention unless she was with another child.

It was immediately apparent that a direct approach to Ann tended to draw her away from play with children and into interaction with the adult. Original procedures were amended as follows: the teacher made comments and directed other attending behaviors to Ann, not individually, but as a participant in the ongoing group play; whenever possible, the adult approached the group prepared to give Ann an appropriate material or toy to add to the joint play project. A sample amended operation was, "You three girls have a cozy house! Here are some more cups, Ann, for your tea party." Whenever Ann began to leave the group, the teacher turned away from her and became occupied with some other child or with equipment. This procedure, which extended over 6 days, seemed to bring Ann into interaction with other children more frequently and for longer periods.

In order to substantiate whether the behavior changes effected by the above procedures had indeed been produced by the application of reinforcement principles, procedures were reversed for 5 days. Solitary pursuits and contacts made solely with an adult were once more made discriminative stimuli for adult attention. Ann was disregarded by adults whenever she interacted with children, and given only an unavoidable minimum of attention when she, in the company of another child, contacted them.

After this reversal, the previous contingencies were reinstated. For the next 9 days teachers again gave (1) a maximum of attention for all play with children, (2) no attention when Ann was alone, and (3) a minimum of attention when she contacted adults, unless she was with a child. When she began spending longer periods in continuous interaction with children, adult reinforcement of interaction was gradually made more intermittent until she received adult attention in an amount normal for the group.

Following the last day of systematic reinforcement of interaction, the observers recorded Ann's behaviors on four days spaced at irregular intervals (see Fig. 1, Post Checks) during the last month of school. The data showed that Ann's play with peers was being consistently maintained.

RESULTS

The data on interactions with adults and with children are shown in Figure 1. Since the total observation time each morning varied slightly (average of 114 minutes, with a range from 100 to 130 minutes), each dot on the graph represents the percent of a morning Ann spent in interaction (1) with adults and (2) with children. Open dots represent periods in which baseline and reversal procedures were carried out. Closed dots represent periods in which interactions with children were reinforced by the teachers. The percentage of interactions on a given day sometimes total more than 100%, since Ann often interacted with both an adult and a child in the same 10-second interval (see C on the example of the form used to record behavior).

As can be seen in Figure 1, the baseline data collected over five days showed that Ann was spending little more than 10% of the time interacting with children and 40% with adults. For at least half the time she was essentially solitary. Analysis of the data indicated that her isolate behavior was being maintained and probably strengthened inadvertently by adult social reinforcement. Using traditional nursery school guidance techniques, the teachers responded warmly to Ann whenever she contacted them and remained in conversation with her for as long as she desired. When she stood about alone, they usually went to her and tried to get her into play with children. If they suc-

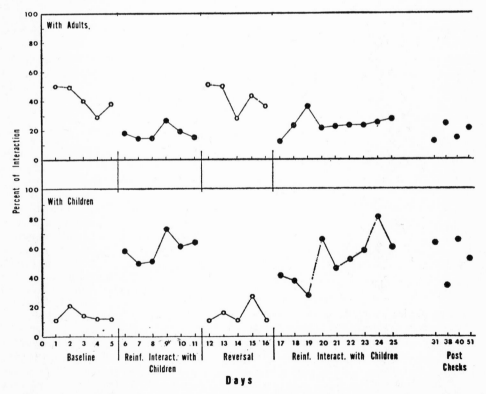

FIGURE I   Percentages of time spent in social interaction during approximately two hours of each morning session.

ceeded, they left shortly, to allow Ann to play freely with other children. All too frequently Ann was "out" again as soon as the teacher left, standing on the periphery, soliciting teacher attention, or playing alone.

On day 6, when Ann was first given teacher attention only when she was near children or interacting with them, an immediate change in her behavior took place. She spent almost 60% of that morning, first in approximations to interaction, and then in active play with children. Adult-child interaction, which was not followed by attention, dropped to less than 20%. These levels of interactions varied little throughout the six-day period of continuous reinforcement of child-child interaction. Over the period, Ann spent increasing time in play with other children.

When procedures were reversed (12th day), Ann's previous patterns of behavior immediately reappeared. She spent the first few minutes after her arrival in close one-to-one interaction with a teacher, which was, of course, continuously reinforced. With this beginning, she spent the remainder of the morning much as she did during the baseline days. Over the five days of reversal she averaged less than 20% of mornings in interaction with children and about 40% in interaction with adults. She repeatedly ignored the contacts of other children and remained in some solitary activity where a teacher could attend to her. When she did enter play with children, she nearly always broke away after a few minutes to contact and remain with a teacher.

On the 17th day the final shift in contingencies was initiated and Ann was given adult attention only when she interacted with children. An immediate change in her behaviors again occurred. Less than 20% of that morning was spent interacting with adults and 40% interacting with children. Interaction with adults was for the most part adult-initiated, as when the teacher reinforced her play or gave routine instructions. Over the ensuing eight days of the study her interactions with adults stabilized at about 25% of mornings; interactions with

children rose to the previous level of about 60%. During the last days of this reinforcement period, teachers gave increasingly intermittent (nonsystematic) attention for interaction with children. The schedule of non-reinforcement of adult contacts was similarly relaxed.

Six school days after the last day of reinforcement (25th day), the first post-check of Ann's interactions with children and adults was made (Fig. 1, 31st day, Post Checks). The data showed Ann to be spending more than 60% of the morning in interaction with children, and only 12% in interaction with adults. Further checks taken on the 13th, 15th, and 26th days subsequent to the last reinforcement day (25th day) indicated that Ann was maintaining an average interaction rate with other children of about 54% per morning. Interaction with adults on these days averaged about 18% per morning. On day 38, Ann's mother was present during school hours. Her presence seemed to influence Ann's behavior in the direction of less interaction with children, although the rate was higher than during either the baseline or the reversal periods.

DISCUSSION

Within the first half hour of the first morning of reinforcing interaction with children, Ann seemed to react to the contingencies for getting teacher attention. The immediate change may be attributed to the fact that she already had a repertory of skills readily adapted to play with peers. Similar studies in progress show that the development of adequate play behavior is not always so rapid as in Ann's case. Other children who tend to be off to themselves have taken several weeks to achieve similar levels of social play. During the six days of increasing interaction with children other changes were noticed. Her speech rose in volume, tempo, and pitch, and complaints about abrasions and bumps dropped out entirely. She appeared to enjoy her play contacts, and the other children responded well to her.

When baseline procedures were again

instituted, it immediately became apparent from the decrease in percentage that Ann's play with children was not yet so reinforcing as interaction with adults. Concurrently, her speech again became slow, drawling, and frequently almost inaudible. She again sought adult attention for various minor ills.

During the final period of reinforcing interaction with children, the inappropriate vocal and complaining behaviors quickly disappeared. At times Ann even took and held a strong, give-and-take role in play with five or six other children. Occasionally she defended herself vigorously. In general, her behavior indicated she had become a happy, confident member of the school group.

During the final period of the study teachers had further evidence of the care they must continue to exercise in judging how and under what circumstances to give adult social reinforcement to Ann: On the 19th day (see Fig. 1) the children, with the help of a teacher, were making Easter baskets and dyeing eggs. Ann was in almost continuous proximity to both children and the teacher. But most of her interaction was with the adult, as can be seen from the sharp rise in child-adult interaction on this day. This tendency for Ann to gravitate readily to exclusive interaction with the reinforcing adult had been noted early in the study. Teachers had been trained to give attention and approval to Ann as a member of the group by commenting to the group on her contribution, offering some item which Ann could add to the group's play, or approving the group activity as a unit. Such close pairing of adult reinforcement with children seemed effective in increasing the positive reinforcement values of Ann's peers.

Systematic application of reinforcement principles as a nursery school guidance technique seems to be an important advance toward more effective analysis and use of existing knowledge about child behavior and development. Guidance measures such as, "Encourage him to play with other children," are familiar to every parent and teacher. They imply that adults are to give attention to the child. Reinforcement prin-

ciples offer a clear, objective guide for precisely discriminating occasions for giving and for withholding adult attention, a positive reinforcer for most young children. The only aspect of reinforcement principles that seems relatively new in nursery school guidance can be subsumed under the word *systematic*.

It seems noteworthy that this study was conducted by teachers in the course of their regular professional work with children. As they helped a child needing special guidance, they examined a guidance technique. Such a combination of the functions of research and service seems both practical and desirable.

REFERENCES

1. AYLLON, T. and MICHAEL, J. The psychiatric nurse as a behavioral engineer. *J. exp. Anal. Behav.,* 1959, **2**, 323–334.

2. AYLLON, T. and HAUGHTON, E. Control of the behavior of schizophrenic patients by food. *J. exp. Anal. Behav.,* 1962, **5**, 343–352.

3. BRADY, J. P. and LIND, D. L. Experimental analysis of hysterical blindness. *Arch. gen. Psychiat.,* 1961, **4**, 331–339.

4. FERSTER, C. B. and DEMYER, MARIAN K. The development of performance in autistic children in an automatically controlled environment. *J. chronic Dis.,* 1961, **13**, 312–345.

5. HARRIS, FLORENCE R., JOHNSTON, MARGARET K., KELLEY, C. SUSAN, and WOLF, M. M. Effects of positive social reinforcement on regressed crawling of a nursery school child. *J. Ed. Psychol.,* 1964, **55**, 35–41.

6. HART, BETTY M., ALLEN, K. EILEEN, BUELL, JOAN S., HARRIS, FLORENCE R., and WOLF, M. M. Effects of social reinforcement on operant crying. *J. exp. child Psychol.,* 1964, **1**, 145–153.

7. WOLF, M., RISLEY, T. R., and MEES, H. L. Application of operant conditioning procedures to the behavior problems of an autistic child. *Behav. Res. Ther.,* 1964, **1**, 305–312.

39 EFFECTS OF POSITIVE SOCIAL REINFORCEMENT ON REGRESSED CRAWLING OF A NURSERY SCHOOL CHILD[1]

Florence R. Harris • Margaret K. Johnston • C. Susan Kelley • Montrose M. Wolf

INTRODUCTION

This paper reports a use of positive social reinforcement procedures to help a nursery school child to substitute well-developed walking behavior for recently reacquired crawling behavior. Principles of reinforcement have long been established through experimental research with infra-human subjects. Recently, many of these principles have also been demonstrated with human beings and have been successfully applied to practical problems. Examples of the latter include Ferster's study of autistic children (Ferster, 1961), Brady's treatment of functional blindness (Brady and Lind, 1961) and Ayllon's work with psychotic patients (Ayllon and Haughton, 1962). Ferster and Brady applied the principles in a controlled laboratory situation. Ayllon, however, made applications in a "natural" situation, comparable to the setting in the present study.

Application of reinforcement principles to nursery school children may be an important step in the process of learning more about child behavior and its relation to guidance practices. Such knowledge relates directly not only to teacher guidance at school

Journal of Educational Psychology, 1964, **55,** 35–41.

[1] The authors gratefully acknowledge indebtedness to Sidney W. Bijou, Donald M. Baer, and Jay S. Birnbrauer, without whose counsel and encouragement this study would not have been possible. Robert G. Wahler also contributed generously to development of observation techniques. This investigation was supported in part by Public Health Service Research Grants MH–02232 and MH–02208, from the National Institute of Mental Health.

but also to parent guidance of children in the home.

The main concern of the study was to see (1) whether presentation of positive social reinforcement by teachers could be used to help a three-year-old use more frequently her already well-established walking behavior; (2) if this occurred, whether withdrawing such reinforcement weakened the behavior; and (3) whether reinstating social reinforcement practices reestablished walking behavior. The reason for the second and third objectives was, of course, to attempt to demonstrate that the positive reinforcing stimuli used were in fact the determining conditions in such behavior change. Conclusive data were essential to effective guidance of the child at school, as well as to subsequent counseling with the child's parents.

SUBJECT

The subject was a girl three years and five months old who had just enrolled in a university nursery school. She will hereafter be referred to as Dee. Dee was the oldest child in her family, having two younger brothers, one eighteen months old and one eight months old. The parents were a pleasant and likable young couple. Both held college degrees, the father also having an advanced degree. He was well launched upon a professional career. The mother seemed a warm and responsive person whose primary interest was her family.

Dee was one of twelve children in the nursery school group of six boys and six girls. Ages ranged from three years to three years and six months. Two teachers supervised the group, which attended school mornings for two and a half hours five days a week.

On the first day of school Dee showed unusually strong withdrawal behavior. That is, she crouched on the floor most of the time, turning her head away or hiding her face in her arms whenever an adult or a child approached. She did not attempt to remain close to her mother, who sat in one corner of the room or of the play yard. Dee spoke to no one, and crawled from indoors to outdoors and from place to place as school activities shifted.

Dee continued to show little reaction to her mother's presence during subsequent days at school. On the seventh day of school her mother was leaving a few minutes after bringing her and coming back to get her two hours later (the same as most of the other mothers), with Dee seemingly indifferent to her presence or absence.

Typically, Dee removed and put on her wraps while sitting on the floor in the locker area, and then either left them on the floor or crawled to her locker and stuffed them in. Sometimes she pulled herself to her feet with her hands on the locker edges and hung her wraps on the appropriate hooks. Then, dropping to hands and knees, she crawled to an out-of-the-way spot and sat or crouched. She crawled into the bathroom beside other children before snack time and occasionally pulled herself to a standing position beside a sink to rinse her hands. She did not use a toilet at school but remained dry. From the sink she usually crawled to a group gathered for snacks and sat near a teacher and some children. She usually accepted and ate a snack, but remained impassive, somber, silent. The rest of the group talked, laughed, and in general responded freely to both the teachers and to other children. The usual teacher approaches to Dee (friendly, warm, solicitous) resulted in strong withdrawal behavior as described.

Her mother reported that the same behavior was strongly evident when visitors came to her home or when Dee was taken on visits. Otherwise Dee was described as "gentle, sweet, and cooperative." The mother was, of course, greatly concerned over her child's withdrawal behavior. It was this concern which had, at least in part, prompted her to enroll Dee in a nursery school.

By the end of the second week of school Dee was avoiding all contacts with children or adults and avoiding use of most material and equipment. A half-hour record written at this time showed Dee in a standing position for only 6.7% of the time, once at her locker and once at a bathroom sink. For 93.3% of the observation period she sat, or crouched on hands and knees. She had spoken only a few words during these weeks. She had spoken only to teachers. The words had consisted of a soft "no" or "yes" at snack time. In staff discussion, teachers gave a conservative estimate that at least 75% of her time at school, exclusive of group times when everyone was normally seated, Dee was in off-feet positions. Since this behavior prevented her participation in the broad range of available learning activities, and since the behavior was such as to be readily observable by students and by staff, the staff decided to help the child by applying reinforcement principles.

INITIAL REINFORCEMENT PROCEDURES

It was decided that the teachers should attempt to weaken Dee's off-feet behavior by withholding attention when Dee was off her feet. An exception to this might occur at group times, when attention was to be a minimum consonant with courtesy. The withdrawal-of-attention procedure was to be casually implemented by a teacher's simply becoming fully occupied with any one of the many immediate requirements always confronting nursery school teachers. In other words, teacher-attention was to show no obvious relationship to Dee's off-feet behavior. Teachers were also to avoid displaying any behavior that might suggest anger, disappointment, disgust, shame or dislike. There was to be nothing punitive about their behavior.

Concurrent with the above procedure, on-feet behavior was immediately to be positively reinforced. That is, Dee was to be given attention whenever she displayed standing behavior. Since she stood up so infrequently, and so briefly, the behaviors closely approximating standing were also to be reinforced during initial days. That is, when she rose even partially to her feet, as well as when she stood, a teacher was to give her attention. Such attention was to consist of going immediately to her and making appropriate interested comments about what she was doing. Sample comments might be, "You hung that up all by yourself. You know just where it goes," and "It's fun to let water slide over your fingers. It feels nice and warm, doesn't it?" A teacher's attention behavior was to convey to Dee that she was liked, appreciated, and considered capable.

In order for a reinforcer to be most effective, it must immediately follow the behavior to be changed. Therefore, to insure that Dee received immediate positive reinforcement for standing positions, one teacher was assigned to remain within range of her at all times, carrying major responsibility for this aspect of the guidance program. The other teacher was to carry major responsibility for the program of the rest of the children in the group. The teacher assigned the role of giving positive reinforcement every time Dee got on her feet was selected because she seemed to have a good relationship with the child. For example, Dee usually crawled to her group at snack time.

RECORDING BEHAVIOR CHANGES

No special plans beyond teacher observations were made, at first, for recording behavior changes and the incidence of reinforcement. A staff member recorded the previously-mentioned half-hour observation. Teachers, of course, observed Dee's behavior from the first day and recorded the kinds of incident notes that they took on behavior of each child in the group. Teachers' subjective estimates based on their daily observations were also used. In addition, subjective estimates by students in an observation course were considered. These students first observed Dee's group during the second week of school. All noted her behavior at once, although no reference had been made to it in class, and discussed it at the next class meeting.

Two weeks after reinforcement procedures were begun, several students volunteered to procure more adequate recordings of Dee's behavior for purposes of making a more systematic study and to satisfy their own interest. Most of the data presented in curves 2 and 3 in Figure 1 were secured by these students, each recording for an hour. Their efforts could provide only about four hours of data. The remainder (about two and a half hours) were recorded by a staff member.

RESULTS OF INITIAL PROCEDURES

The intensive recording of Dee's behavior by students and staff was stimulated by dramatic results of application of the planned procedures. Within one week from the start of reinforcing on-feet positions and ignoring off-feet behavior, Dee was on her feet a large proportion of time. Percentages of time on-feet and time off-feet seemed to have reversed. By the end of two weeks (one month after she entered school) Dee's behavior was indistinguishable from that of the rest of the children. She talked readily, often with smiling animation, to the teacher administering the planned schedule of social reinforcement. She used all of the outdoor equipment with vigor and enthusiasm. She worked with obvious enjoyment at the easels, with housekeeping-play facilities, and with such materials as clay.

However, Dee was not making direct responses to children, although she engaged in much parallel activity; nor did she initiate contacts with children or with the other teacher, ignoring them for the most part. But she accepted without position changes any approach or suggestion made by the other teacher or a staff member, and on the whole made use of available learning experiences as effectively as most of the other children in the group. She could no longer be considered severely withdrawn at school. Her mother also reported a remarkable improvement in her social behavior at home.

REVERSING REINFORCEMENT PROCEDURES

In order to be sure that the reinforcement procedures applied had been the significant causative factor in Dee's change in behavior, the teaching staff were obliged to pursue their study through two more processes: (1) reinstate off-feet behavior, and then (2) once again establish appropriate on-feet behaviors. In addition to personal reluctance to institute these processes, the staff at this point seriously questioned their ability to succeed in getting Dee again into off-feet behavior. She appeared to be getting strong reinforcement from her vigorous and exploratory activities, from exchange of speech with adults, and from parallel activities with children. It seemed unlikely that manipulation of adult social reinforcers could now have an effect strong enough to compete with these newly-experienced reinforcement. Partly because of this doubt, and partly because of the necessity to be certain that adult social reinforcement had been the critical independent variable, the staff agreed to attempt to reinstate Dee's off-feet behavior.

The teachers' procedure in extinguishing on-feet behavior was to reverse their previous reinforcement contingencies; that is (1) give no attention when Dee was on-feet, and (2) give continuous attention when she was off-feet. The staff agreed that any evidence of detrimental effects, such as loss of speech, crying or other emotional behavior, would be sufficient cause for terminating the plan.

At this phase of the study students as-

sisted in getting more detailed and extensive records.

RESULTS OF REVERSE PROCEDURES

During the first morning of giving Dee attention (reinforcement) during off-feet but not during on-feet behavior, a two-hour record was kept. Each 30-second period of these two hours was then arbitrarily considered as a discrete unit of behavior. Units of time off-feet were then plotted in a cumulative graph, the horizontal axis showing time and the vertical axis showing number of off-feet units. (See Figure 1, curve 1.) Rises on the graph indicate periods of time off-feet, while plateaus indicate periods on-feet. Exclusive of a group time of 12 minutes, during which children were expected to be seated together, Dee spent 75.7% of the morning off her feet. On the following day, which was similarly recorded and graphed, she spent 81.9% of the morning off her feet. (See Figure 1, curve 2.) There were no signs on either day of detrimental effects on Dee other than those associated with behaving from a crawling position.

With nearly 82% of her time spent off her feet, clearly Dee had returned to her old behavior pattern. The staff therefore decided at that point to reinstate on-feet behavior.

SECOND REVERSAL OF PROCEDURES

Reinforcement procedures were again reversed, that is, teachers gave steady attention whenever Dee got to her feet and gave no attention when she was off her feet. Figure 1, curve 3, graphs her off-feet behavior for the first hour of the third subsequent day. During the observation, Dee spent 75.9% of the time off her feet and only 24.1% on-feet. Teachers reported, however, that during the last half of the morning, for which a written record was not secured, Dee spent most of the time in vigorous activity on her feet. Figure 1, curve 4, graphs the first hour of the following day. Dee spent 37.8% of the hour off-feet and 62.2% on-feet. Again, the second hour she was reported

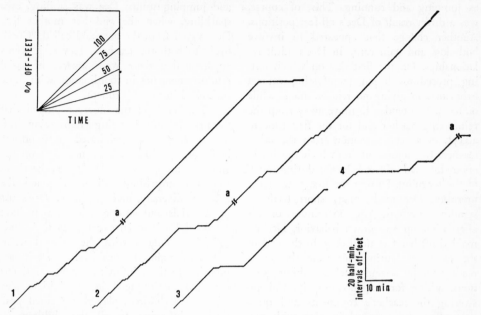

FIGURE 1   Subject's off-feet behavior on four different mornings: the first (Curve 1) and second (Curve 2) mornings of giving attention during off-feet and ignoring on-feet behavior, and the third (Curve 3) and fourth (Curve 4) mornings of giving attention during on-feet and ignoring off-feet behavior. Breaks at *a* indicate snack times averaging 12 minutes duration, which were not included in the data.

to have spent on her feet almost steadily. From this day on, Dee's behavior was in every way adequate and she seemed happily occupied.

DISCUSSION

The data strongly indicate that adult attention changed Dee's behavior in the desired direction (was the significant independent variable), and that for Dee adults were very powerful reinforcers. It also seems that social reinforcement principles, carefully delineated and applied, can provide effective and efficient guidance tools for teachers and parents of young children.

Although the graphs show only the time Dee spent in the positional behaviors being specifically controlled, other interesting behavioral changes occurred during the study. These changes seemed to be largely salutary and to develop with unusual rapidity. Some

changes seemed causally linked to the fact that reinforcement contingencies were reversed twice, a possibility that merits further study.

Much of the normal behavior, in addition to positional changes, resulted from the initial process of reinforcing only on-feet behaviors. This normal behavior included (1) ready verbalization with one adult (the assistant teacher), (2) adequate verbalization in response to questions from other adults but little if any initiation of contacts with them, (3) parallel activities with other children but little if any verbalization to them, (4) play using a wide range of materials and equipment. These changes occurred within two weeks of instituting the reinforcement procedures.

When a shift was made from reinforcement of on-feet to reinforcement of off-feet behavior, some loss was observed, but significant gains appeared as well. The major loss appeared to be vigorous motor activities such as jumping and running. This, of course, was a direct result of Dee's off-feet positions. Another change that appeared to involve both loss and gain came in Dee's adult relationships. On the first day on which testing procedures began (reinforcing off-feet behavior and giving no reinforcement while on-feet), Dee tended to move away from the reinforcing teacher and for the first time to accept, even seek, attention from the other teacher. Reinforcement from both the teachers maintained off-feet behavior during much of the morning. During the first part of the morning, Dee made many short trials of standing positions. After 35 minutes of this alternating up and down behavior, Dee remained off her feet until close to the end of the morning. During this time she spoke readily to the second teacher, asking questions, asking for help occasionally, and answering the teacher's comments and questions. She also engaged in play with materials, near other children. Occasionally she exchanged words with the latter, a new aspect of behavior for Dee. Part of her activity consisted of going upright on her knees from one play situation to another. At the doll-corner table where two other children were making cookies with dough and utensils, Dee insisted on staying on her knees beside the table although the teacher pointed out that there was an empty chair beside her and that the other children were seated. Dee's response was, "I *want* to be on the floor doing it."

Near the close of that morning (reinforcement of off-feet positions) Dee went outdoors again. She got to her feet at the door, ran across the yard to where another child played on packing boxes and boards, and joined the other in vigorous running and jumping. This play was at a distance from both teachers, and of course neither teacher approached. The play continued with much laughter, shouts, and some talking. It drew two more children. Dee's mother arrived shortly. She showed great pleasure in finding Dee in joyous active play with other children. She stood near, smiling and commending Dee's and her friends' balancing and jumping stunts. Dee was smiling, eyes sparkling, when she and her mother left. Dee waved from the gate and called "Goodbye!" to both the teachers. Hence, it seems apparent that there were sources of social reinforcement not in coordination with those controlled in the experiment.

Teachers and the observer judged that the first day of reinstating (reinforcing) off-feet positions (1) precipitated much off-feet behavior, (2) had little or no effect on the amount and quality of Dee's verbalizations, (3) had surprisingly slight effect on the amount, diversity, and quality of Dee's use of materials and equipment, (4) may have extended Dee's social experiences to include satisfying contacts with the other teacher, (5) had reduced considerably Dee's approaches to the reinforcing teacher, and (6) may have encouraged her to initiate play with other children, play that seemed positively reinforcing to all the children involved. In other words, the positive effects of reversing reinforcement contingencies seemed to outweigh by far the momentary negative results.

During the second day of reinforcement of off-feet behavior, the first two-thirds of the session was punctuated by tentative bursts of standing. During two of the longer bursts, Dee moved about the yard pushing over the movable upright equipment. Teachers presented no reinforcement. Periods of standing dwindled to steady off-feet behavior. Even the arrival of Dee's mother at the end of the morning did not draw Dee to her feet. Mother walked across to her and somewhat impatiently pulled her to her feet and took her away. Although Dee seemed to lose only those vigorous behaviors for which standing postures were essential, the investigators judged that her behavior for the two days gave sufficient demonstration of the power of adult social reinforcement in changing her behavior. Rather than risk possible loss in the areas of verbal or child-child social behavior, they decided to terminate the study by again reinforcing on-feet behavior. In addition, they decided to reinforce all verbal behavior, regardless of Dee's position. Another influential aspect in terminating the "test" procedure was that it was distasteful to the investigators and therefore made them apprehensive about its effects on Dee. Further, no observer besides the teachers could be available during the following two days of school.

During approximately one hour of the third day of again reinforcing on-feet behavior, plus positive reinforcement of all verbal behavior, a record was taken during the first half of the morning. Teachers reported that during most of the latter half of the morning Dee played vigorously on her feet on climbing equipment with other children, with apparent pleasure and with much reinforcement from adults and children. The behavior of pushing over equipment, which was at no time followed by presentation of either positive or negative reinforcement, had dropped out entirely. On the fourth day of reinstating on-feet behavior, Dee spent better than 60% of the recorded hour on her feet, a proportion of time which made her positional behavior indistinguishable from that of the group. Teachers noted that some of her standing behavior at this time was sufficiently different from the group mode to be classed as "stunting on equipment." She stood up to swing and also to propel the long rocking-board, two activities usually pursued by the threes in a sitting position. The latter part of the morning, Dee played vigorously with children, usually on her feet.

By the end of a week of reinforcing on-feet positions, Dee showed positional behavior that was normal in the group. In addition, she was readily initiating and accepting social contacts with all of the adult staff as well as with several of the children in the group. Within a five-week period of school attendance, Dee's behavior showed a degree of progress that would have been expected within not less than five or six months under previous guidance techniques. Her parents were as pleased as the staff over her progress, as well as over their fresh understandings of their roles in helping her develop appropriate social behaviors.

SUMMARY

Use of social reinforcement as a guidance procedure with young children was studied in a university laboratory nursery school, the subject being a three-year-old girl who exhibited strong withdrawal behavior. Results of the study seemed to indicate that (1) adult attention had strong reinforcement values for this child, (2) reversal of the initial reinforcement procedures had distinct positive effects on the child, apparently through helping her quickly to seek relationships with all adults and many of the children in the school situation, and (3) use of reinforcement principles brought about much more rapid changes in the child's behavior than would have been expected under previous guidance techniques.

It would seem that the systematic application of reinforcement principles to guidance of young children shows considerable promise for facilitating the learning behaviors of children and the teaching tasks of adults, both teachers and parents.

REFERENCES

AYLLON, T. and HAUGHTON, E. Control of the behavior of schizophrenic patients by food. *J. exp. anal. Behav.,* 1962, **5,** 343–352.

BRADY, J. P. and LIND, D. L. Experimental analysis of hysterical blindness. *Arch. gen. Psychiat.,* 1961, **4,** 331–339.

FERSTER, C. B. and DEMYER, MARIAN K. The development of performance in autistic children in an automatically controlled environment. *J. chronic Dis.,* 1961, **13,** 312–345.

EFFECTS OF SOCIAL REINFORCEMENT
ON OPERANT CRYING[1]

Betty M. Hart • K. Eileen Allen • Joan S. Buell • Florence R. Harris
Montrose M. Wolf

The application of reinforcement principles as a preschool guidance technique under field conditions has recently come under study (Allen *et al.*, 1964; Harris *et al.*, 1964; Johnston *et al.*, 1963). Other applications made under field conditions in hospital situations include Wolf's treatment of autism in a child (Wolf *et al.*, 1964) and Ayllon's work with psychotic patients (Ayllon and Haughton, 1962). The present paper deals with the application of reinforcement principles to two cases of "operant crying."

Two classes of crying behavior seem readily discriminable on an "intuitive" basis by almost every teacher and parent: respondent crying and operant crying. Criteria for each class can be defined in terms of its independent variables. Respondent crying occurs in response to a sudden unexpected and/or painful stimulus event. In general, preschool teachers assume crying to be respondent if the child has a hard or sudden fall; if he falls in an awkward position or is caught in equipment; if he is forced down and pummeled by a larger child; or if he has just faced a dire, unexpected event, such as a near accident. Teachers attend at once to respondent crying. Operant crying, on the

other hand, is emitted and/or maintained depending upon its effects on the social environment. In general, the most clear-cut indication that a crying episode is operant rather than respondent is that the child looks around momentarily and makes eye-contact with an adult before he begins to cry. An increase in the volume and intensity of the child's cry when an adult fails to attend immediately, together with the child's neither calling nor coming for help, provides other criteria for operant crying. Obviously, crying that is initially respondent may readily become operant.

Since by three years of age children vary widely in their patterns of response to pain-fear situations, any reasonably exact discrimination between respondent and operant crying of an individual child can be made only on the basis of close daily observation of his crying behavior.

This paper presents two studies of the systematic use of positive social reinforcement to help children showing a high rate of operant crying to acquire more effective behavior in mildly distressful situations. Although the studies were conducted at different times, procedures and recording methods were the same in each.

Journal of Experimental Child Psychology, 1964, **1**, 145–153, and Academic Press, Inc.

[1] The authors acknowledge their indebtedness to Sidney W. Bijou, Donald M. Baer, and Jay S. Birnbrauer for frequent consultation and ready assistance with technical and procedural problems. This investigation was supported in part by Public Health Research Grants MH–02232 and MH–02208, from the National Institute of Mental Health.

METHOD

Subjects

Both subjects were enrolled in the Laboratory Preschool at the University of Washington. Both were in the same group, which included eight boys and eight girls of similar age (4–4½), socioeconomic level (upper middle class), and intelligence (above average). All children attended school five mornings a week for approximately two and one-half hours.

Subject 1. The first subject, Bill, was four years and one month old when he entered school. He was a tall, healthy, handsome child with well-developed verbal, social, and motor skills. Outdoors he ran, climbed, and rode a tricycle with energy and agility; indoors, he made use of all the available materials, though he appeared to prefer construction materials such as blocks, or imaginative play in the housekeeping corner, to activities such as painting or working with clay. His verbalizations to both teachers and children were characterized by persuasive and accurate use of vocabulary, and frequently demonstrated unusually sophisticated conceptualizations. He and many of the other children who entered nursery school at the same time had been together in a group situation the previous year and were thus fairly well acquainted. His former teachers had described Bill as a child eagerly sought by other children as a playmate. His capability and desirability as a playmate were immediately evident at the beginning of the second year. He moved almost directly into play with two other boys, and with his many good ideas structured one play situation after another with them, situations which often lasted an entire morning. Bill was frequently observed arbitrating differences of opinion between his playmates, insisting on his own way of doing things, or defending his own rights and ideas; nearly always, he did so verbally rather than physically.

In the first few days of school, teachers noted that in spite of Bill's sophisticated techniques for dealing with children, he cried more often during the morning than any other child in school. If he stubbed his toe while running or bumped his elbow on a piece of furniture, he cried until a teacher went to him. If he fell down, or if he was frustrated or threatened with any kind of physical attack by another child, he screamed and cried; all play, his and his companions, stopped until Bill had had several minutes of comfort from a teacher. In view of his advanced verbal and social skills, teachers questioned whether his crying was due to actual injury or maintained by adult attention.

Subject 2. The second subject, Alan, lacked two weeks of being four years old when he entered the Preschool. He was enrolled in the same four-year-old group as Bill. Unlike Bill, however, Alan was new to the group and therefore had had no previous acquaintance with any of the children. He spent most of the first month of school exploring with vigor all the equipment, materials, and social situations the school had to offer. He climbed, rode trikes, swung and dug, with skill and application. His use of creative materials was free and imaginative; his block-buildings were complex, intricately balanced structures. With children and adults he spoke confidently and assertively, often demanding that they listen to a lengthy story or fulfill his requests immediately. He defended himself both verbally and physically, holding on tenaciously to a possession or saying, "Don't!" over and over. Sometimes he forcibly appropriated an object from another child, calling names when the child resisted; but though he was the physical equal or superior of most of the others, he rarely attacked another child. He was attractive and vivacious as well as skillful. By the end of the first six weeks of school he was playing as an integral member of one or more groups of children every morning.

Though he did not cry quite as often as Bill, Alan cried equally as hard over much the same kinds of bumps and falls. Like Bill, he screamed and cried whenever another child succeeded in appropriating an object in his possession. He was observed to endure shoving and even hitting by a child smaller than he but to cry vociferously at a push by a child equal to him in size and strength. Though Alan's crying was noted from the beginning of school, the staff thought that Alan should fully adapt to the school situation and develop in play skills before any procedures were undertaken to deal directly with his crying behavior.

In dealing with both Alan and Bill, a distinction was made between respondent and operant crying. Teachers had observed that both could defend themselves, both were physically strong and large in the group, neither was unjustifiably aggressive, and both had better than average physical, verbal, and social skills. Neither had injured himself or been injured by another child in the group. Both were often observed to make momentary eye-contact with a teacher before beginning to cry, and the cries of both rapidly increased in volume until a teacher attended to them. Teachers agreed that both children would benefit if the frequency of crying episodes could be decreased and if more appropriate responses to mild pain and frustration could be developed.

Recording of Crying Episodes

In both cases the operant crying behavior was recorded by a teacher using a pocket counter. She depressed the lever on the counter once for each crying episode. A crying episode was defined as a cry (a) loud enough to be heard at least 50 feet away and (b) of 5 seconds or more duration. At the end of the day the total number of crying episodes was recorded and plotted on a cumulative graph.

Procedures for Presenting and Withdrawing Reinforcers

For ten days before initiating reinforcement-extinction procedures, the number of Bill's operant crying episodes per morning was to be recorded in order to obtain a baseline record of the operant level of the behavior. This was done at the end of his first month of school. A baseline record of Alan's daily crying episodes was similarly planned several months later, after Alan had attended school for three months.

Immediately after this data had been secured, in the case of each child, extinction of operant crying was to be instituted. Teachers were to ignore each child's operant cries, neither going to him, speaking to him, nor looking at him while he was crying, except for an initial glance in order to assess the situation. If he was in close proximity to a teacher when he began to cry, she was to turn her back or walk away to be busy with another child. However, every time that either child responded in a more appropriate manner after a fall, scrape, push, or dispossession, however minor, he was immediately to be given much teacher attention and approval.

In order to substantiate that the operant crying of these children was truly a function of adult reinforcement, it was judged necessary, if the extinction process was successful, to reinstate the behavior. At first teachers

were to give attention to every approximation to a cry, such as whimpering and sulking; then, if and when the behavior was re-established in strength, they were to go to the child immediately every time he began to cry and give him solicitous attention for several minutes.

If and when operant crying had again reached a level similar to that of the baseline period, it was again to be extinguished. The procedures of the first extinction period were to be re-instituted, teachers ignoring all operant cries by turning away or focusing their attention elsewhere. At the same time, they were to reinforce the boys for all verbal responses emitted during mild pain or frustration. As the second extinction progressed, teachers were gradually to refine the criteria for reinforcement to "appropriate" verbal responses, and differentially reinforce more socially acceptable verbal behavior evoked by minor injuries and frustrations. Threats and name-calling were to be ignored, and attention given only for such verbalizations as "Stop that," "That hurts," "Ouch!" or explanation of prior possession.

RESULTS

Subject 1. As can be seen in the baseline period for Bill (see Fig. 1), at the beginning of the study he was crying 5–10 times every morning at school. Within five

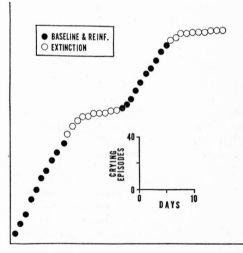

FIGURE I

days after introduction of extinction procedures his operant crying decreased to between 0 and 2 episodes per day. When continuous adult attention was again given to all operant cries and approximations to cries, the baseline rate of crying episodes was soon re-established. Then, four days after re-introduction of extinction for operant crying, the behavior was practically eliminated.

Subject 2. Alan's rate of operant crying during the baseline period (see Fig. 2) averaged about 5 episodes per morning. As with Bill, Alan's crying episodes decreased to 2 or fewer per day within five days after the introduction of extinction procedures. The behavior again reached a level nearly as high as baseline four days after reinforcement of operant crying was re-instituted, and maintained approximately this level for six days. On the eleventh day of reinstatement of operant crying, the behavior suddenly decreased to one or fewer episodes per day (28th day, Fig. 2). After continuing reinforcement procedures for seven more days, teachers decided that, though their attention may have initially reinstated the behavior, other uncontrolled factors in the environment had apparently led to its cessation. Therefore systematic reinforcement techniques were discontinued (after day 35 on

Fig. 2). However, very soon the behavior reappeared and gradually increased in frequency until on the 50th day it had reached a frequency almost double that of the baseline period. Extinction procedures were again introduced (on day 51, Fig. 2). The rate of operant crying dropped much more gradually this time than had Bill's; there was a burst on the 56th day, and it was not until ten days later that operant crying episodes stabilized at one or fewer per day.

DISCUSSION

During the extinction periods for both Bill and Alan, teachers noticed no unexpected side-effects. They had anticipated that play would become more rewarding to both children once the frequent interruptions for crying episodes were eliminated. Each of the children, during the extinction periods, sustained a cooperative, sometimes directing role in play. Each appeared to become more constructively absorbed in such play, often to the point of appearing oblivious to the people outside the realm of the imaginative play situation.

Subject 1. After Bill's operant crying was reinstated and his play was again being

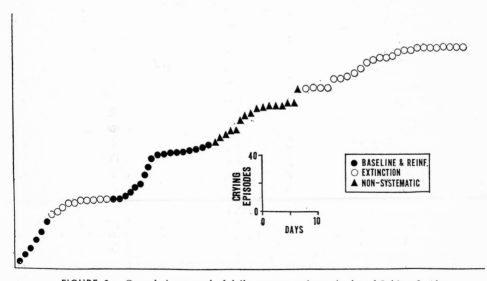

FIGURE 2   Cumulative record of daily operant crying episodes of Subject 2, Alan.

interrupted six or seven times a morning for operant crying episodes, teachers began to notice occasional signs of impatience on his part. Even as teachers comforted him and he continued to shriek, he sometimes turned away from their comfort, though he did not leave. Also, the extent of the interruption of his play seemed more noticeable than it had during the baseline period. At that time his companions had often ignored, or retreated from, his crying episodes. During the reinstatement period they usually remained near Bill, watching him throughout the episode. Teachers thought that the powerful reinforcement that Bill obtained from play with his companions greatly contributed to the rapidity of the second extinction process.

Subject 2. After Alan's operant crying had risen during the reinstatement period to a rate equal to that of the baseline period, the sudden disappearance of the behavior was completely unexpected. Teachers continued to reinforce all cries and approximations to cries for seven more days before deciding that some other factor in the environment had apparently decreased Alan's operant crying. Only after reinforcement procedures had been discontinued and the behavior had begun to reappear did teachers reflect on the possible significance of particular behaviors they had observed during the reinstatement period. At that time they had noticed that Alan often screwed up his face as though about to emit a loud cry when he was in close proximity to them. In accordance with the reinforcement procedures in effect, they immediately offered him comfort, and frequently he did not actually cry (only audible cries were counted in the data). One day, for example, Alan was climbing on an iron frame, a teacher watching him. As he climbed down from the frame he screwed up his face and clutched his ankle. The teacher approached at once, asked what had happened and comforted him. Alan explained that he had bumped his ankle, and then said, "I'm going to do that (climb the frame) again." As he descended the frame a

second time, Alan bumped his leg and, looking at the teacher, emitted a low whimper. The teacher immediately comforted him, whereupon he again climbed the frame, and again bumped himself descending. On none of these occasions did Alan actually cry. It appeared, upon subsequent reflection, that Alan did not need to cry; he had apparently effectively "shaped up" a teacher to give him comfort and attention whenever he merely looked as if he were about to cry.

When systematic reinforcement procedures were discontinued and Alan's "looking as if he were about to cry" was no longer given immediate adult attention and comfort, full-scale operant crying reappeared and was apparently reinforced in the period that followed, on some sort of unsystematic intermittent schedule. The rate of operant crying increased irregularly; the decline in rate after several days of a rise in rate might possibly be correlated (a) with teachers' having inadvertently put the behavior on extinction for a time after it became aversive to them and (b) with such frequent interruptions in Alan's play that his playmates moved away from him and into other activities. These intervals of extinction, if such they were, were not, however, planned procedures.

After systematic extinction procedures were reinstated, Alan's operant crying behavior extinguished much more gradually than had Bill's. A possible cause was the preceding unsystematic intermittent schedule of reinforcement in Alan's case. In the literature (e.g., Ferster & Skinner, 1957) it has been well demonstrated that extinction after a continuous schedule of reinforcement is more rapid than after an intermittent schedule.

Though many of the findings concerning Alan's operant crying are still conjectural, the data from the studies seem to demonstrate that frequent crying may be largely a function of social reinforcement. The implications for parents and teachers in helping children to behave more appropriately appear evident.

SUMMARY

Two preschool boys who showed a high frequency of operant crying were helped to develop more effective responses to mild frustrations. Teachers systematically applied reinforcement procedures: gave no attention to outcries, unless the child was actually hurt, and gave immediate approving attention to every more appropriate response to mildly distressful situations. Within a week, operant crying had practically disappeared in each case.

Reversal of procedures reinstated operant crying responses in Subject 1. Return to original procedures quickly reduced operant crying to a very low level, which was maintained during the rest of the year. With Subject 2, reversal of procedures raised the operant crying level for a few days. Then suddenly the crying dropped out. When the crying rate remained at practically zero for several more days, all procedures were dropped. Shortly, operant crying again rose. The original procedures were again applied. Operant crying quickly dropped and remained negligible during the rest of the school year.

The studies indicated that frequent crying may be largely a function of adult attention.

REFERENCES

ALLEN, K. EILEEN, HART, BETTY M., HARRIS, FLORENCE R., and WOLF, M. M. Effects of social reinforcement on isolate behavior of a preschool child. *Child develpm.,* 1964, **65**, 511–518.

AYLLON, T. and HAUGHTON, E. Control of the behavior of schizophrenic patients by food. *J. exp. Anal. Behav.,* 1962, **5**, 343–352.

FERSTER, C. B. and SKINNER, B. F. *Schedules of reinforcement.* New York: Appleton-Century-Crofts, 1957.

HARRIS, FLORENCE R., JOHNSTON, MARGARET S., KELLEY, C. SUSAN, and WOLF, M. M. Effects of positive social reinforcement on regressed crawling in a preschool child. *J. educ. Psychol.,* 1964, **55**, 35–41.

JOHNSTON, MARGARET S., KELLEY, C. SUSAN, BUELL, JOAN S., HARRIS, FLORENCE R., and WOLF, M. M. Effects of positive social reinforcement on isolate behavior of a nursery school child. Unpublished manuscript, 1963.

WOLF, M. M., RISLEY, T., and MEES, H. Application of operant conditioning procedures to the behavior problems of an autistic child. *Behav. Res. Ther.,* 1964, **2**, 305–312.

41 SHAPING ADAPTIVE BEHAVIOR IN A THERAPEUTIC SUMMER CAMP

Henry C. Rickard • Michael Dinoff

The concept of therapeutic summer camping has recently received considerable attention. An entire issue of the *Journal of Social Issues,* (1957), for example, was devoted to the subject of therapeutic camping. The program, briefly commented upon in this note is thought of as a therapeutic summer community whose orientation is rooted within the framework of learning principles.

During the 1963 summer season eleven boys, exhibiting problems in their school work and interpersonal relations, attended a specialized 8-week camping program. The campers ranged in ages from 8 to 14 and were average or above in personal appearance. None manifested obvious physical handicaps, although two boys possessed slight speech impediments and two exhibited below average muscular coordination. The median I.Q. score obtained by the campers was 119 with a range from 100 to 147, demonstrating an exceptionally bright camper population. During the camping season each boy received considerable formal psychotherapy but, more important, he was treated as an individual toward whom the entire staff directed common attitudes and behaviors. Staff decisions were made as to what classes of behaviors would be rewarded and what limitations would be imposed upon each child. The camping program was directed by two clinical psychologists, staffed by three male counselors, a psychiatric nurse, and a female school teacher, and enriched by consultants in psychiatry, social work, speech therapy, and psychology.

Deviant behavior patterns were identified for each camper individually and situations were devised in which desired, incompatible behaviors would likely emerge. Staff members were alerted to administer immediate reinforcement as the adaptive behavior patterns occurred. Behaviors were not uniformly easy to identify and selecting appropriate reinforcers often presented problems. Furthermore, many of the benefits of the camping program were probably derived from a kind of natural therapy intrinsic to camping rather than planned reinforcement contingencies. However, the staff operated within a learning principle framework and remained alert to reinforcement opportunities.

It is obvious that the ability to reinforce is partially dependent upon personality characteristics of the reinforcer. He may "inherit" reinforcement value based upon cues he generates that are similar to cues provided by important figures in the camper's life. He may also present a complex of cues that cause him to emerge as a beneficient cultural stereotype, capable of emitting "goods" or

similar social reinforcements that will affect behavior. In the main, however, a counselor in a therapeutic camp community must develop his individual reinforcement value. Consequently, reflections of feelings, interpretations of ongoing behavior, and other verbal and nonverbal efforts to make the camper feel understood were employed frequently. The very high staff to camper ratio (seven staff to eleven campers) permitted regular counselor-camper talks, mutual activities, and the expenditure of a great deal of time together. Perhaps most critical of all in the development of reinforcement value is the fact that an individual who reinforces subsequently becomes part of a stimulus complex which in itself elicits desired behavior. It is presumed that each time a counselor was successful in the reinforcement of a desirable behavior, his personal reinforcement value was enhanced.

The case of Bill Adams: The following case illustrates the selection and reinforcement of behavior patterns. Bill Adams was a thirteen-year-old boy who was referred to the camp jointly by a psychiatrist and a speech therapist. Earlier Bill had removed himself from school because he was having difficulties with his peers and because he was failing academically. Bill had a tested I.Q. of 132, and hence there was no question about his potential scholastic ability. He had completely disrupted the family living pattern by staying up all night, sleeping all day, and refusing to comply with ordinary routine. Bill was referred to the camp with the hope that he would learn to respond to routine and develop more adaptive ways of interacting with his peers and authority figures. It should be noted that his parents were considering some sort of residential treatment for this boy.

The first staff efforts were directed toward lowering stress in the camper and establishing themselves as individuals with reinforcement value. Much time was spent with Bill quietly accepting his verbal and nonverbal behavior. Attempts were made to demonstrate through reflections, interpretations, questions, and so forth, that his communications both verbal and nonverbal were understood. The staff was very much alert to minute positive responses and administered immediate social reinforcement. By the fourth week of camp the reinforcement value of several staff members was judged quite high.

The specific behavior selected for modification had to do with Bill's acceptance of routine procedures and his response to authority figures. Initially he refused to go to bed at the proper time, refused to get up in the morning, refused to take part in camping activities, and refused to carry out work assignments. These various "bits of behavior" that had generalized from the home situation, could be lumped together and labeled rebellious behavior. However, in establishing reinforcement contingencies it is difficult to identify and reinforce responses incompatible with "rebellious behavior." On the other hand it is relatively simple to reinforce behavior incompatible with not going to bed, not getting up, not taking part in activities, and so forth. Whenever possible, then, specific observable behavior was identified as the dependent variable.

Efforts were made to help Bill move into activities by small steps. For example, it was discovered that while Bill did not like baseball he was intrigued with cameras and readily agreed to go to the ball field to take pictures. As Bill stood on the edge of the field a counselor might toss him a ball. On other occasions the necessary skills and rules of the game were discussed with him. Somewhat later Bill agreed to play a position on one of the teams.

Throughout the season the entire staff maintained the expectancy that Bill would take part in activities and that adaptive behavior would occur. Thus the verbal and nonverbal behavior of the staff presumably set the stage for adaptive behavior to emerge. Perhaps the prime technique used in eliciting adaptive behavior from Bill was an emphasis upon the "terms of the contract." Whenever Bill refused to take part in activities or to comply with camp regulations, al-

ternate channels were pointed out to him and the expected behavior was clearly labeled in a nonpunitive, nonjudgment manner.

Athletic skill as such was entirely deemphasized, and the staff issued commendations for performance in a group activity regardless of its expertness. The important reinforcement parameter of immediacy was invoked; whenever possible adaptive behavior was followed by immediate reinforcement. The search for reinforcement is frequently an empirical one and such was the case with the campers. It was discovered that Bill responded particularly well to an arm on the shoulder and other similar nonverbal reinforcements. It might be noted that Bill often "saw through" traditional verbal reinforcement.

By the fifth week of camp Bill was taking part in all activities and responding well to demands from authority figures. He had established communication with the four other boys in his cabin and was developing a fairly close friendship with one of the boys. Only on two brief occasions did he again display former resistive behavior. At the end of the camping season, his parents reported their observation that he had made marked gains during the camping season. On three occasions counseling sessions were held with the parents in an effort to promote generalization of adaptive behavior.

A follow-up interview with the parents, three months after camp closed, indicated that Bill was relating much more adequately with his peers and authority figures. He has been enrolled in a private school and his progress there is judged adequate. The parents report deep satisfaction with Bill's more adaptive behavior which they attribute, in a large measure, to his camp experience.

In summary, the authors believe that a therapeutic summer community provides a unique framework for the shaping of adaptive behavior. Efforts to modify selected patterns of behavior in campers through elicitation and reinforcement procedures show promise, but it must be emphasized that the entire camping program cannot be easily encompassed in a reinforcement framework at this time. As more information concerning the efficacy of direct behavior modification accumulates more staff time may properly be consumed in specific behavior manipulation tasks. In the meanwhile, learning principles, and particularly the operant conditioning paradigm, provide a very useful framework for the modification of "bits of behavior."

REFERENCES

SOCIETY FOR THE PSYCHOLOGICAL STUDY OF SOCIAL ISSUES.   Therapeutic camping for disturbed youth. *J. soc. Issues*, 1957, **13**, 1–62.

42   THE ALTERATION OF BEHAVIOR IN A SPECIAL CLASSROOM SITUATION

Elaine H. Zimmerman • Joseph Zimmerman

Unproductive classroom behavior was eliminated in two emotionally disturbed boys by removing social consequences of the behavior. Behavior which was more adequate and efficient with respect to social and scholastic adjustment was shaped and maintained with social reinforcers.

The classroom behavior of two emotionally disturbed boys was altered by arranging and manipulating its consequences.

The boys, in-patients in a residential treatment center (LaRue D. Carter Memorial Hospital), attended the first author's English class daily for 1 hr as part of an educational therapy program. There were three boys in the class, each receiving individual attention.

CASE I

Subject 1 (S-1) was 11 years old. He appeared to have no organic disorder and was of normal intelligence. In early class sessions, whenever S-1 was called upon to spell a word which had previously been studied and drilled, he would pause for several sec-

Journal of Experimental Analysis of Behavior, 1962, **5**, 59–60.

onds, screw up his face, and mutter letters unrelated to the word. Following this, the instructor (E) consistently asked him to sound out the word, often giving him the first letter and other cues, encouraging him to spell the word correctly. Only after E had spent considerable time and attention would the boy emit a correct response. The procedure was inefficient and profitless for improving the boy's spelling behavior. In fact, it may have been maintaining the undesirable pattern, since over the first 10 or 15 class sessions, consistently more time and attention were required of E to obtain a correct spelling response.

While "studying" in class, S-1 would obtain sheets of paper, wrinkle them, and throw them away, laughing as he caught E's eye or that of one of the other students.

The Change in Approach

After several weeks in class, S-1 was quizzed via paper-and-pencil test on a lesson based on 10 spelling words, with time allotted for study and review. He handed in a paper with a muddled combination of barely legible letters. Immediately, E asked him to go to the blackboard. Her instructions were simply: "We will now have a quiz. I will read a word and you will spell it correctly on the board." She read the first word, and the subject misspelled it 10 or more times on the board. During this time, E sat at her desk, ignoring S-1, apparently busy reading or writing. Each time S-1 misspelled the word, he glanced at E; but she did not respond. The boy erased the word and tried again, several times repeating "I can't spell it," or "I can't remember how," etc. Although ignored, the boy made no effort to sit down or leave the room. After approximately 10 min, he spelled the word correctly; E looked up at him immediately, smiled, and said, "Good, now we can go on." She read a second word; and after a similar series of errors and verbal responses, S-1 spelled the word correctly. With each successive word (through 10 words), the number of inappropriate (unreinforced) responses decreased, as did the latency of the correct response. At the end of the quiz, E took the boy's spelling chart, wrote an "A" on it, and praised him. She then asked the subject to help her color some Easter baskets. They sat down together, and chatted and worked.

Thereafter, attention in the form of smiling, chatting, and physical proximity was given only immediately after the emission of desired classroom behavior or some approximation of it in the desired direction. Undesirable behavior was consistently ignored. As a result of a month of this treatment, the frequency of bizarre spelling responses and other undesirable responses declined to a level close to zero per class session. At the conclusion of this study, the boy was working more efficiently, and was making adequate academic progress.

CASE II

Subject S-2 was an 11-year-old boy, who, like S-1, had no apparent organic disorder and was also of normal intelligence. In initial class Sessions, S-2 emitted behavior considered undesirable in the classroom context with high frequency. He displayed temper tantrums (kicking, screaming, etc.), spoke

baby-talk, and incessantly made irrelevant comments or posed irrelevant questions.

Several times a week, attendants dragged this boy down the hall to one of his classes as the boy screamed and buckled his knees. On several of these occasions, the boy threw himself on the floor in front of a classroom door. A crowd of staff members inevitably gathered around him. The group usually watched and commented as the boy sat or lay on the floor, kicking and screaming. Some members of the group hypothesized that such behavior seemed to appear after the boy was teased or frustrated in some way. However, the only observable in the situation was the consistent consequence of the behavior in terms of the formation of a group of staff members around the boy.

Observing one such situation which occurred before E's class, E asked the attendant to put the boy in the classroom at his desk and to leave the room. Then E closed the door. The boy sat at his desk, kicking and screaming; E proceeded to her desk and worked there, ignoring S-2. After 2 or 3 min, the boy, crying softly, looked up at E. Then E announced that she would be ready to work with him as soon as he indicated that he was ready to work. He continued to cry and scream with diminishing loudness for the next 4 or 5 min. Finally, he lifted his head and stated that he was ready. Immediately, E looked up at him, smiled, went to his desk, and said, "Good, now let's get to work." The boy worked quietly and cooperatively with E for the remainder of the class period.

The Handling of Tantrums, Irrelevant Verbal Behavior, and Baby-talk

Each time a tantrum occurred, E consistently ignored S-2. When tantrum behavior was terminated, E conversed with the boy, placed herself in his proximity, or initiated an activity which was appealing to him. After several weeks, class tantrums disappeared entirely. Because the consequence of tantrum behavior varied in other situations, no generalization to situations outside the classroom has been observed.

Furthermore the frequency of irrelevant verbal behavior and of baby-talk declined almost to the point of elimination following the procedure of withholding attention after the emission of such behavior. On the other hand, when S-2 worked quietly or emitted desirable classroom behavior, E addressed him cordially and permitted some verbal interchange for several seconds. When a lesson was being presented to the class at large and S-2 listened attentively, E reinforced him by asking him a question he could answer or by looking at him, smiling at him, etc. The reinforcement was delivered intermittently rather than continuously because: (a) reinforcing every desired response of one student was impossible since E's time was parcelled out among several students; and (b) intermittent reinforcement would probably be more effective than continuous reinforcement in terms of later resistance of the desired behavior to extinction. Like S-1, at the conclusion of the study this boy was working more efficiently in class and was making good progress. His speech was more generally characterized by relevancy and maturity.

43   THE REINFORCEMENT OF COOPERATION BETWEEN CHILDREN[1]

Nathan H. Azrin • Ogden R. Lindsley

Most methods for the development and experimental analysis of cooperation between humans require specific instructions concerning the cooperative relationship between the individual responses. Peters and Murphree have developed one of the most recent of these methods (1). Skinner has suggested (2), and shown with lower organisms (3), that cooperation between individuals can be developed, maintained, and eliminated solely by manipulating the contingency between reinforcing stimuli and the cooperative response.

The advantages of eliminating instructions concerning cooperation are that (a) the initial acquisition of cooperation can be studied, (b) subjects (Ss) that learn by demonstration and instruction with difficulty (i.e., infants, certain classes of psychotics, and lower organisms) can be studied, and (c) no problems involving the effects of instructions upon the behavior of the Ss are involved.

Some more general advantages of operant conditioning techniques are (a) a more continuous record of the cooperative process is obtained, (b) extraneous environmental variables are minimized, and (c) relatively long periods of experimental observation are possible.

PROBLEM

Can cooperation between children be developed, maintained, and eliminated solely by the presentation or nonpresentation of a single reinforcing stimulus, available to each member of the cooperative team, following each cooperative response?

Cooperative Teams

Twenty children, seven to twelve years of age, were formed into ten cooperative teams of two children. The children in each

Journal of Abnormal and Social Psychology, 1956, **52**, 100–102.

[1] This paper was read at a meeting of the Eastern Psychological Association on April 10, 1954, New York City.

team were matched as to age and sex. Seven teams were boys and three were girls.[2] Selection was made via the request, "Who wants to play a game?" The first two volunteers of the same age and sex were chosen for each team. The age given by the children was verified against available community center records. No information concerning the game was given during the selection. No teams were rejected.

Cooperative Response

Cooperation was assured by designing an apparatus that (*a*) could not be operated by one individual alone (assuring group behavior), and (*b*) demanded that one individual respond to the behavior of the other individual in order to produce reinforcement (assuring cooperation).

Procedure

The two children of each cooperative team were placed at opposite sides of a table with three holes and a stylus in front of each child (see Fig. 1). A wire screen down the center of the table prevented each child from manipulating the other child's stylus, which was on the other side of the table.

FIGURE I   Apparatus used for the reinforcement of cooperation between children.

The following instructions were given: "This is a game. You can play the game any way you want to or do anything else that you

[2] We wish to thank the Harriet Tubman House and the South Bay Union of Boston, Mass., for providing the subjects and the use of their facilities.

want to do. This is how the game works: Put both sticks (styli) into all three of the holes." (This sentence was repeated until both styli had been placed in the three available holes.) "While you are in this room some of these" (the experimenter (*E*) held out several jelly beans) "will drop into this cup. You can eat them here if you want to or you can take them home with you." The instructions were then repeated without reply to any questions, after which *E* said: "I am leaving the room now; you can play any game that you want to while I am gone." Then *E* left the room until the end of the experimental session.

If the styli were placed in opposite holes within 0.04 seconds of each other (a cooperative response), a red light flashed on the table (conditioned reinforcing stimulus) and a single jelly bean (reinforcing stimulus) fell into the cup that was accessible to both children.[3] Cooperative responses were recorded on counters and a cumulative response recorder in an adjoining room.

Experimental Design

Each team was studied for one continuous experimental session divided into the following three consecutive periods without experimental interruption:

1. First reinforcement period. Every cooperative response was reinforced for over 15 min. If the rate of response was not steady at this time, the reinforcement was continued until five minutes passed with no noticeable change in the rate of cooperation.

2. Extinction period. The cooperative responses were not reinforced for a period of at least 15 minutes and until a steady rate of response for at least five minutes was observed.

3. Second reinforcement period. The cooperative responses were again reinforced until at least three minutes of a stable rate occurred. This was done to determine whether a reduction in rate during the extinction period was due to extinction, satiation, or fatigue.

RESULTS

All teams learned to cooperate without specific instructions in the first 10 min. of

[3] Skinner (3) presented two reinforcing stimuli (one to each pigeon) following each cooperative response.

experimentation. Observation through a one-way vision screen disclosed that leader-follower relationships were developed and maintained in most cases. Almost immediately eight teams divided the candy in some manner. With two teams, one member at first took all the candy until the other member refused to cooperate. When verbal agreement was reached in these two teams, the members then cooperated and divided the candy. Most vocalization occurred during the initial acquisition period and throughout the extinction period. This vocalization was correlated with a higher variability in rate during these periods. (See below.)

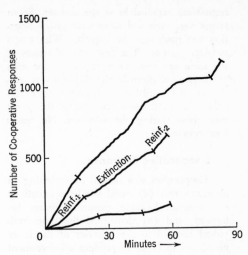

FIGURE 2 Cumulative response records for the teams with the highest, median, and lowest rates of cooperation.

TABLE I The Median and Range of the Number of Cooperative Responses per Minute for the Critical Experimental Periods

N 10	NUMBER OF COOPERATIVE RESPONSES PER MINUTE			
	First three mins. of first reinf. period	*Last three mins. of first reinf. period*	*Last three mins. of extinction period*	*Last three mins. of second reinf. period*
Median	5.5	17.5	1.5	17.5
Range	1–26	6–26	0–7	6–27

Figure 2 contains cumulative records of the cooperative responses of the three teams with the highest, the median, and the lowest number of cooperative responses for the experimental session. These curves show a large difference in the rate of acquisition of cooperation. One team took almost 10 minutes to acquire a high cooperative response rate. Stable rates of cooperation can be observed during the latter parts of the first reinforcement period. The gradual, rather than immediate, decline in cooperation during extinction suggests an orderly extinction of cooperative behavior as is found with individual extinction curves. In all cases the variability of rate was greater during extinction than during reinforcement. Skinner has

found this increased variability in rate during extinction with lower organisms and has described it as emotional behavior (2, p. 69). The high rate of response following the first reinforcement of the second reinforcement period shows that reacquisition is almost immediate.

Table 1 contains a quantification of the records for statistical analysis. The median and range of the number of cooperative responses per minute for all 10 teams during the critical periods of the experiment are given. The number of cooperative responses per minute for the first three minutes of the first reinforcement period was significantly lower than the rate during the last three minutes of the first reinforcement period ($p < .02$).[4] This shows that the rate of cooperation was significantly lower during initial acquisition than during maintenance of cooperation. The number of cooperative responses per minute during the last three minutes of extinction was significantly lower than the rate during the last three minutes of the first reinforcement period ($p < .001$). This shows that the removal of reinforce-

_____
[4] Wilcoxon's nonparametric T for paired associates was used in all statistical treatments (4).

ment during extinction significantly lowered the rate of cooperation between these children.

The number of cooperative responses per minute during the last three minutes of the second reinforcement period was significantly above the rate during the last three minutes of the extinction period ($p < .001$). This shows that the rate of cooperation was significantly increased during the second reinforcement period and that the drop in rate during extinction was due to the absence of the reinforcing stimulus rather than satiation or fatigue. The rates of cooperation during the second reinforcement period and the last three minutes of the first reinforcement period were not significantly different and show that the rate was almost immediately restored to its pre-extinction value upon the presentation of reinforcement for the second time. The rate of cooperative responding during the first three minutes of the second reinforcement period was significantly higher than during the first three minutes of the first reinforcement period ($p < .02$). This again shows that the reacquisition of cooperation was not gradual, as was initial acquisition, but occurred almost immediately.

CONCLUSIONS

Operant conditioning techniques can be used to develop, maintain, and eliminate cooperation between children without the use of specific instructions concerning cooperation. The rate of a cooperative response changes in much the same way as a function of single reinforcements as does an individual response. In the reinforcement of cooperative responses, a reinforcing stimulus need not be delivered to each member of the cooperative team following each cooperative response. The presentation of a single reinforcing stimulus, available to each member of the cooperative team, is sufficient to increase the rate of cooperation. The cooperative response gradually increases in frequency when reinforced and gradually decreases in frequency when no longer reinforced (extinction). Cooperative responses are maintained at a stable rate during reinforcement but occur in sporadic bursts during extinction. Reinforcement following extinction results in an almost immediate restoration of the rate of cooperation to its pre-extinction value.

REFERENCES

1. PETERS, H. N., and MURPHREE, O. D.   A cooperative multiple-choice apparatus. *Science,* 1954, **119,** 189–191.
2. SKINNER, B. F.   *Science and human behavior.* New York: Macmillan, 1953.
3. SKINNER, B. F.   Classroom demonstration Personal communication, 1952.
4. WILCOXON, F.   *Some rapid approximate statistical procedures.* New York: American Cyanamid Co., 1949.

SECTION 5

MENTAL DEFICIENCY

Perhaps the most exciting work in the area of behavior modification is reflected in the series of cases in this section. These cases deal with people who have usually not been considered within the province of psychological treatment. While writers such as Kirk (1962) have detailed what might be accomplished with programs of re-education, the general trend has been one of pessimism.

A major challenge is to program an environment to offer the child adequate opportunity to establish a response that he might not ordinarily achieve when going at too rapid a rate and to shape behavior to build responses that other children learn incidentally. Bijou (1963) marshals arguments to suggest that what has been labeled as mental deficiency may not be an impairment of the brain, but may be fruitfully viewed as a failure of coordination of stimulus and response functions. The task then is to discover the conditions that will lead to emission and development of the appropriate responses. In a more theoretical context, Hayes (1962) makes the same point. This viewpoint results in a very hopeful and challenging orientation.

The first article in this section, by Fuller (44), is, as far as we know, the first report of a deliberate application of the operant conditioning technique to a clinical situation. In illustrating the applicability of the method to a vegetative idiot Fuller points up the potential for training of all human organisms. The next two articles, by Bijou and Orlando (45) and by Barrett and Lindsley (46) illustrate the growing literature of laboratory techniques on which clinical and classroom procedures may be based (Bijou and Orlando, 1961; Bijou and Oblinger, 1960; Barnett et al., 1959; Ellis and Pryer, 1958; Ellis, 1962; Ellis, Barnett, and Pryer, 1960; Orlando et al., 1960). That is, treatment of retardates by these procedures are examples of the development in the laboratory of techniques that have direct clinical value in the manner described in the last section of our introduction. The article by Birnbrauer et al. (47) illustrates both the application of a variety of procedures and the heartening results obtained. Of particular interest is the use of reinforcement to make performances meaningful and the development of study habits as well as specific academic accomplishments.

We have previously mentioned the article by Wolf et al. (48) on the extinction of vomiting behavior as an example of the treatment of a psychophysiological reaction. We may note again that just as no dichotomy exists between "healthy" and "sick" behavior, so maladaptive behavior manifested by a retardate is treated in the same manner as that behavior would be treated if manifested by a normal child.

As Birnbrauer et al. (47) note when they make an explicit reinforcement contingent upon giving the correct answer, a crucial aspect of treatment is not permitting errors or indifference to become a matter of course. To quote Rotter (1964) "It is probably true that in many cases there has been underemphasis on what a particular feebleminded person could learn with optimal training and overemphasis on what he cannot learn because of his condition. R. Cromwell and his associates have shown in numerous studies that because of the feebleminded individual's inability to learn what others expect of him, he tends to become discouraged and so learn less than he can. Studies of prolonged institutionalization indicate that the absence of intellectual stimulation, with no real attempt at training, results in a continuous loss of ability." It is to the task of optimum training, making use of laboratory findings, that behavior therapists have turned with results that leave them very optimistic.

The article by Kerr, Meyerson, and Michael (49) illustrates the application of operant techniques in a rehabilitation setting. As in the Bachrach's et al. paper (14) lack of information about etiology is not an obstacle to treatment. Rather, the object of treatment, the performance to be developed, is specified, and a program to overcome the deficit is instituted.

While we present one example in terms of Kerr et al., we might well quote from a Michael (1963) speech: "It seemed to me on first contact with the rehabilitation field that it was surprising that anybody did anything, that patients did much activity, because the reinforcements were often absent, taken for granted, presented in poor temporal relation to the behavior that was involved, and, unfortunately, often presented for the wrong behavior." Michael cites work with two brain injured girls who supposedly had short attention spans and were irresponsible and hyperactive in the classroom. The student working with the children made attention to the child contingent upon folding papers and placing them in envelopes. An hour of envelope filling behavior was obtained on this first session. The next two times the usual or "traditional" technique of urging the child when there was a lag in productivity was used, and approximately 10 minutes of productive behavior was obtained. The next two sessions used reinforcement contingent upon the desired response, and a full hour of work was obtained each time. Michael also describes a program in use with cerebral palsied and other brain injured children in a rehabilitation setting. He started with a pre-training situation in which the children were rewarded for putting together nuts, bolts and washers in a little factory assembly system. The aim of developing tokens, exchangeable for toys, as reinforcers, was successfully attained. These tokens were then used successfully to reinforce desirable rehabilitative behaviors such as standing, walking, and falling. The major point to be made is that reinforcement must be prompt, appropriate to the behavior to be increased, and, at least in the beginning of a treatment program, frequent. In a broader context, the goal is to make behavior meaningful, avoid plateaus, and permit full utilization of the person's endowment by providing him with an environment that will foster his growth at his own rate.

The final case in this section is by Patterson (50) and illustrates the application of operant techniques to a brain injured child. Of particular interest is the use of the child's classmates. The situation was set-up so that the peers shared in the reward and had a strong interest in the child's improving performance. Another aspect of this article is the development of accurate labeling of maladaptive behavior. This case, the last in this volume, may act as a summary because it illustrates the use of a variety of techniques, the locale of treatment in a classroom rather than a professional office, and the generally encouraging results with a problem considered inappropriate for traditional psychotherapy.

44 OPERANT CONDITIONING OF A VEGETATIVE HUMAN ORGANISM

Paul R. Fuller

While it is maintained that a large part of human behavior is operant in nature,[1] the majority of experiments in operant conditioning have been performed with infrahuman organisms. Classical conditioning experiments, however, have been conducted with both normal and subnormal human Ss.

Razran reports experiments in classical conditioning with some feebleminded Ss.[2] Osipova found that subnormal children formed conditioned responses to shock faster than normal children.[3] Segal, working in Lenz's laboratory, attempted to condition a salivary response in an 18-yr.-old idiot but had little success, probably due in part to S's reluctance to have the saliometer attached.[4] Shastin was able to establish a conditioned response in a 15-yr.-old cretin.[5] Wolowick established a conditioned response in a sickly, retarded 6-yr.-old.[6] On the whole,

American Journal of Psychology, 1949, 62, 587–590.

[1] E. R. Hilgard, Theories of Learning, 1948, 117.

[2] G. H. S. Razran, Conditioned responses in children, Arch. Psychol., 23, 1933, (No. 148), 33–81.

[3] V. N. Osipova, Speed of formation of the associated reflex in school children, Novoye v Reflexologii i Fiziologii Nervnoy Systemy, 2, 1926, 218–234.

[4] I. X. Segal, Materials for the study of conditioned salivary reflexes in oligophrenics, Zhurnal Nevropatologii, 22, 1929, 625–632.

[5] N. R. Shastin, Unconditioned and conditioned reflexes in Myxedema, Medico Biologichesky Zhurnal, 6, 1930, 470–482.

[6] A. B. Wolowick, Materials to the study of conditioned reflex activity in children with weak excitatory and inhibitory processes, Medico-Biologichesky Zhurnal, 1, 1929, 110–119.

however, few experiments have been done in conditioning feeble-minded Ss.

Recently an opportunity was offered us to conduct an operant conditioning experiment on an 18-yr.-old inmate of a feeble-minded institution, whose behavior was that of a 'vegetative idiot.' The term 'vegetative' describes well his condition. He lay on his back and could not roll over; he could, however, open his mouth, blink, and move his arms, head and shoulders, to a slight extent. He never moved his trunk or legs. The attendant reported that he never made any sounds; but in the course of the experiment vocalizations were heard. He had some teeth but did not chew. He had been fed liquids and semi-solids all his life. While being fed, he sometimes choked and would cough vigorously.

According to his medical record he had a clonic seizure shortly after birth, and these seizures had continued at irregular intervals throughout his life. No other pertinent information could be obtained from the records or from the institution's physician. S had been in the institution for almost a year and had increased in weight from 30 to 50 lb. during his stay. His activity had also increased slightly.

The conditioning apparatus consisted of a syringe filled with warm sugar-milk solution—the reinforcing stimulus. The response selected to condition was a movement of S's right arm to a vertical or nearly vertical position. This arm was selected because we observed that he moved it about a third as frequently as his left arm.

S was deprived of food for 15 hr. Then, when he moved his right arm, a small amount of the sugar-milk solution was injected into his mouth. Two experiments were conducted. In the first, an assistant recorded the responses and time. In the second, a polygraph was so arranged that movements with either arm and head were recorded.

The first experiment was conducted early in June, 1948. There was one session of 20 min. each day. During the first session the rate of response was 0.67 per min. During the fourth session the rate increased to 1.67 per min. Since we lacked adequate apparatus to record the responses, the experiment was discontinued at that time to be repeated later in June.

During the interim between experiments, S was fed as usual by the attendant who stuffed food into S's mouth when he was still. S was being reinforced for not moving during the regular feeding situation while during the experiment the reinforcing stimulus followed the movement of the right arm. It could be expected, therefore, that the rate of response at the beginning of the second experiment would be less than the rate at the end of the first. This was true; the rate of response was low, less than 1 per min. During the first 10 min. of the first session of the second experiment, S was merely observed and his movements recorded. During the next 10 min., the tube with milk in it was held in position close to S's mouth. A slight increase in the rate of his right arm movements was observed but it could hardly be termed significant. The rate for the whole 20 min. was less than 1 per min.

Conditioning was then begun. Every time the right arm was raised to a vertical position, the milk was injected into S's mouth. There were movements in which the arm was not raised to a vertical position, and at the other extreme, there were times when not only the arm, but the head and shoulders also were moved. These were not reinforced because the attempt was to condition a discrete movement rather than a gross, generalized one. No appreciable increase in rate was observed during the first session.

The next morning, in a 40-min. session, a total of 45 reinforcements were given S

as compared with 24 the previous day. The rate of his responses rose to 1.12 per min. If we had counted the responses in which the shoulders as well as the right arm were raised, the rate would have been 1.8 per min. A brief experimental session was held that evening after only a 5-hr. food-deprivation. After 19 responses in 16 min., S fell asleep.

The fourth and final session took place the next morning. S made definite and discrete responses at the rate of 3 per min. He would life his arm and open his mouth immediately. In the beginning of the experiment this sequence of movements had not been observed. This looked like anticipation of the reinforcing stimulus. The rate of three responses per min. allowed just enough time for the milk to be injected into S's mouth and be swallowed. The rate of responding during the fourth session was more than three times as great as during the first.

During the first sessions there was an increase in movements of the left as well as the right arm, but in the last two sessions of the second experiment these unreinforced movements dropped out almost completely, as did the gross movements in which S raised his arm, head and shoulders. The response was well differentiated during the final period.

Immediately following the 30 min. conditioning, during which S's responses averaged 3 per min., an extinction period was begun. For the first 30 min. of extinction, the rate of S's responses was maintained at almost as high a level as during conditioning. Then the rate decreased until by the seventieth minute of extinction it approached zero. After the seventy-second minute, no more responses were observed. The shape of the extinction curve is similar to what is considered a 'typical' extinction curve following continuous reinforcement during operant conditioning. During extinction, S's movements gradually became more generalized; the left arm, which had moved very little in the last two sessions, moved more frequently after the rate of movement of the right arm noticeably decreased.

An interesting feature of this study is

the example it affords of phylogenetic overlap. While of normal human parentage, this organism was, behaviorally speaking, considerably lower in the scale than the majority of infra-human organisms used in conditioning experiments—dogs, rats, cats.

The attending physicians of the institute in which S was an inmate thought it was impossible for him to learn anything—according to them, he had not learned anything in the 18 years of his life—yet in four experimental sessions, by using the operant conditioning technique, an addition was

made to his behavior which, at his level, could be termed appreciable. Those who participated in or observed the experiment are of the opinion that if time permitted, other responses could be conditioned and discriminations learned. For years many psychologists have experimented exclusively with infra-human Ss, and they have expressed a preference for the simple, less variable behavior of the lower organisms in the laboratory. Perhaps by beginning at the bottom of the human scale the transfer from rat to man can be effected.

45   RAPID DEVELOPMENT OF MULTIPLE-SCHEDULE PERFORMANCES WITH RETARDED CHILDREN[1, 2]

Sidney W. Bijou • Robert Orlando

Problems encountered in the process of modifying simple operant behavior of a retarded S from what is observed at the beginning of a study to that required by a multiple schedule have two major implications. One bears on an experimental analysis of individual differences; the other, on the development of techniques for the efficient establishment of complex-schedule performances.

When a child enters an experimental situation, receives instructions, and sets about to perform the task, the behavior displayed is, of course, a function of the current situation and interactions with similar situations in the S's history. The influences of such

Journal of the Experimental Analysis of Behavior, 1961, **4**, 7–16.

[1] This investigation was supported by a research grant (M-2232) from the National Institute of Mental Health, Public Health Service.
[2] The authors are grateful to Russell M. Tyler and David A. Marshall, Research Assistants, for their fine work in conducting many of the individual sessions.

antecedents may be conceptualized as effects of independent variables (e.g., kinds of reinforcers received, typical schedules, and frequency of punishment contingencies), and of differences in behavioral processes (e.g., rate of change in operant conditioning) (Skinner, 1953). Such effects may be quantified by psychometric devices such as inventories of traits and abilities, or by experimental procedures. The latter, which involve observation of the successive changes in behavior required to perform an experimental task to criterion, may be approached in two ways. One consists of presenting the task and recording time (and "errors"). This procedure is often abortive. If the task is complex, even slightly so, learning may take an unreasonable length of time, or may not be achieved at all. The other approach involves presenting S with a series of graded tasks and reinforcing responses that approximate more and more the final performance required. The procedure is designed so that the S sets the pace; that is, each response class is strengthened to criterion before the next task is introduced.

This alternative has several advantages. Most important, it yields not only measures in terms of time, but also an account of the strengthening and weakening operations necessary to arrive at final performance. Experimental studies of retarded children in which the second procedure is being used are currently in progress.

Studying initial behavior is especially pertinent from a technique point of view, particularly for investigations on human Ss using individual base lines. At the current stage of our knowledge of operant procedures with humans, many Es spend considerable time and effort exploring ways of establishing a schedule or multiple schedules. The objective of this paper is to describe and illustrate a method that has proven satisfactory for the rapid establishment of multiple-schedule performance in a single-response, free-operant, experimental situation with retarded subjects. A multiple schedule has been described as one ". . . in which reinforcement is programmed by two or more schedules alternating, usually at random. Each schedule is accompanied by a different stimulus, which is present as long as the schedule is in force." (Ferster & Skinner, 1957, p. 7). The multiple schedules discussed here have *two* components (one always involving extinction), with the accompanying discriminative stimuli presented in *regular* alternation.

Initial attempts in this laboratory to establish discriminated-operant base lines in children (Bijou, 1961) started with principles outlined for infrahuman Ss (Keller & Schoenfeld, 1950) and "hand-shaping" techniques popular as classroom demonstrations and developed most fully in animal training (Breland & Breland, 1951). Satisfactory two-component base-line performances were obtained, but only after an investment of seven or more weekly sessions. The technique reported here is the result of subsequent studies in which progressively refined procedures were explored on retarded children. Data to be presented are illustrations of the technique.

The steps in training to a multiple schedule are described in detail, not because they are expected to be followed as given, but because this is a convenient way of giving an account of the technique. Investigators probably will find it necessary to modify the steps in accordance with the nature of their subjects, the type of multiple schedules desired, and variations in the experimental situation.

THE LABORATORY SITUATION

The experimental setting is a well-illuminated room, 10 by 8 feet, with a standard table and two chairs. A wooden box approximately 12 by 12 by 16 inches is on the table. A wooden chute with tray attached for presenting reinforcers is at the left of the box. The upper end of the chute extends through an opening in the wall separating the experimental and control rooms. On the front panel of the box are a red jewel light in the upper left-hand side, a blue jewel light in the upper right-hand side, and a sturdy metal lever (a handle grip for the squeezer of an O'Cedar sponge mop) protruding from a rectangular opening in the center. Pressing the lever down is always accompanied by a relay click and occasionally by a reinforcer dispensed by a Gerbrands Universal Feeder in the control room. Reinforcers are: M & M's, Hersheyettes, candy corn, Payroll mint coins, and Sixlets. These candies were selected because they are readily consumed, easily dispensed, and are not sticky (Bijou & Sturges, 1959).

Control and recording equipment similar to devices used with infrahuman Ss (Ferster & Skinner, 1957; Skinner, 1957; Verhave, 1959) are located in the adjoining room. They consist of timers, tape-programmers, and relay circuits for scheduling stimulus events and reinforcements. Impulse counters and a Gerbrands cumulative recorder are used to record responses on the lever. The cumulative recorder also indicates reinforcements and the type and duration of discriminative stimuli. "Blips" on the cumulative curve indicate reinforcements, while the event-pen base line under each curve records which of the two discriminative stimuli is present.

SUBJECTS

The 46 subjects are residents at the Rainier School, Buckley, Washington. The 25 girls and 21 boys ranged in age from 9 to 21 with a median of 16 years, and in IQ from 23 to 64 with a median of 42. Length of residence was from 1 to 14 years with a median of 6 years. Their clinical diagnoses spread over most categories. Since all were ambulatory, they came on request to the reception room of the laboratory from their residence halls, classrooms, or work assignments.

INSTRUCTIONS

Instructions are treated as drive operations, considered to be verbal and nonverbal procedures which may affect Ss' rates and patterns of responding. The instructions described here, deliberately simple and brief, were designed to get lever-pressing behavior emitted at a moderate rate. Uncomplicated instructions such as these may be applied without modification to a wide range of Ss (e.g., those with physical immaturities, sensory defects, and emotional disturbances, as well as normal children), and are less likely to contain discriminative and conditioned stimuli which may successfully compete with shaping the experimental operant (Azrin & Lindsley, 1956; Bijou & Sturges, 1959).

1. Instructions to a new S begin when E enters the reception room and says, "Hello, now it's your turn to get some of these." (He shows a handful of reinforcers.) "Come with me." (The E ushers S into the experimental room, closes the door, and points to the chair in front of the response box.) "Sit here."

2A. If S pulls his chair up to the table and works the lever up and down five times, a piece of candy comes down the chute. If S notices the candy and continues to respond, no instructions on performing the experimental task are given. Then E says,

"I'll be back when it is time for you to go," and leaves the room. He goes into the control room, where he observes S through a one-way screen and monitors the controls for the next 60 seconds in accordance with the next step in the procedure.

2B. If S sits in the chair and waits for instructions, E says, as he places his *own* hand on the lever, "Now watch me; I'll show you how to get candy." (Then E responds at the rate of approximately two per second for five responses.) "Look. Here is some candy. It is yours. You may eat it if you wish. Now you do it. Go ahead and get some candy." If S responds as instructed (a reinforcement is delivered after 5 responses), E says, "I'll be back when the time is up for you to go," and leaves the room. As in 2A, E enters the control room and observes S's behavior for the next 60 seconds. If S stops responding during the 60-second period, E returns and repeats the instructions beginning with, "Now watch me." If S repeatedly presses the lever in response to this repetition, but again stops during the 60-second period following instructions, E returns and terminates the session. (If S is needed for the study, he is brought back on another day and given training to abolish this discriminative behavior.)

2C. Some Ss do not respond to the lever after the first set of instructions. Under these circumstances, E repeats the instructions beginning with "Now watch me." If S does not work the lever after repetition, E repeats the instruction a third time. This time, however, he takes S's hand and puts him through the motions of responding and handling the reinforcers. If S does not work the lever with this assistance, the session is terminated. (He is eliminated if a substitute S is available. If not, he is brought back another day, and an attempt is made to shape his behavior toward the lever response in gradual stages.)

3. When it is time to end the session, E returns and says, "That's all for today. Go and sit in the waiting room." (If necessary, E gives S a waxed-paper sack for his candy.)

4. On subsequent sessions, E goes to the reception room and tells S it is his turn to go to the experimental room. After S is seated, E says, "Go ahead and get some candy. I'll be back when it is time for you to go." At

the end of the session, E terminates in the standard manner: "That's all for today. You may go and sit in the waiting room."

PROCEDURE

The procedure has four phases: (1) rate evaluation and strengthening, (2) pause building, (3) rate-recovery evaluation, and (4) final multiple-schedule training. To simplify the description of the procedure, the *blue* light will be referred to as the discriminative stimulus for pause building and nonreinforcement, and the *red* light as the discriminative stimulus for reinforcement.

Rate Evaluation and Strengthening

The purpose of evaluating S's initial rate of responding is to arrive at a workable rate for training S to increase, for longer and longer periods, the intervals between responses in the presence of the blue light. If training on low rates of responding is undertaken when the initial rate is low or is weakened by the schedule in force, extinction may develop. Hence, this stage includes operations designed to strengthen rate when required. On the other hand, if pause training is attempted when the initial rate is very high, pausing may require an excessive amount of time to develop and stabilize. The second function of the evaluation procedure, therefore, is to detect high rates as early as possible to avoid dispensing any more reinforcers than necessary.

The S begins (with the red light on) on a schedule in which he is reinforced every 15 seconds (FI 15 seconds). This continues for 1 minute. If S makes at least 20 responses and receives at least one reinforcement during this minute, the red light goes off, the blue comes on, and the next stage of training (pause building) begins. If S makes fewer than 20 responses but shows an acceleration in rate during the latter part of the period, the red light remains on and the schedule remains in force for an additional minute. If 40 responses or more are made in the 2 minutes, the red light goes off, the blue comes on, and pause training begins.

If S gives fewer than 20 responses in the first minute and does not show acceleration in rate, or does not make 40 responses in 2 minutes, the red light stays on but the schedule is changed from FI 15 seconds to an "increasing ratio." In this schedule, the ratio is gradually increased from 1:1 to 1:5 by successively requiring more responses between reinforcements. The schedule used here reinforces response numbers 1, 2, 4, 6, 9, 12, 16, 20, 25, and 30. If the rate has increased by the end of this increasing-ratio regime, S is again given the FI 15-second schedule and re-evaluated, i.e., observed to determine whether he will make 20 responses in 1 minute or 40 in 2. If he does not perform at the rate-level required, the session is terminated. Like those terminated in the other stages, S is eliminated or requested to return for further training depending on the needs of the study.

Pause Building

The purpose of pause training is to strengthen response "withholding" for increasing periods while the blue light is present, and, at the same time, maintain prompt responding with the onset of the red light. To do this, pausing is differentially reinforced in gradually more demanding stages.

The procedure is:

1. After S has demonstrated a rate of responding at or above the minimum required, the red light goes off and the blue light comes on.
2. When S pauses for a predetermined number of seconds (IRT x seconds), the blue light goes off and the red comes on. The time unit (x) selected depends, in part, upon S's performance during the rate-evaluation phase.
3. The first response (with red on) is reinforced, and the red light is replaced by the blue. The blue remains on until S *again* pauses for x seconds.
4. This sequence is repeated until S pauses for x seconds, y times.
5. The length of the pause is then increased by an amount z, and the conditions alternated as previously described until S pauses x + z seconds for y' times.

6. The procedure in Step 5 is repeated with a further extension of time, and the whole process is continued until the duration of pausing with blue light on meets specifications.

The following is an example of pause building with three repetitions at 5, 10, 15, and 30 seconds of pause ($x = 5$, $x + z = 10$, $x + 2z = 15$, etc.).

1. When rate evaluation is completed, the red light is replaced by the blue.
2. The *first* time S gives an inter-response time of 5 seconds, the blue light goes off and the red comes on. The first response is reinforced and the red light is replaced by the blue.
3. Immediately after the *second* 5-second inter-response time, the red light replaces the blue. The first response is reinforced and the blue replaces the red light.
4. Immediately after the *third* 5-second inter-response time, the red light replaces the blue. The first response is reinforced and the blue light replaces the red.
5. When S delays responding for 10 seconds, the blue light goes off, the red comes on, and the first response is reinforced.
6. The procedure in Step 5 is repeated twice more, and then a 15-second pause is required.
7. After three successful 15-second pauses on blue, a delay of 30 seconds is required.
8. After three successive 30-second pauses on blue (and reinforcements on red), the next stage of training begins. This involves lengthening the time on the red light or on both the red and blue lights, and changing from a continuous to an intermittent schedule.

As is apparent, the objective of pause training is not only to increase the delays between responses in the presence of the blue light, but also to maintain prompt responding with the onset of the red light. There are two clear-cut indications if this stage is proceeding too rapidly: long periods of failure to pause, and/or increased latency to the red light. In both instances, completion of a sequence will be delayed and additional training may be required before pauses can be longer. The following procedure has been shown to be serviceable. When a given y series has not been completed in 5 minutes,

the entire series is repeated before training on a longer pause is begun. For example, if S required more than 5 minutes to make three successive 5-second pauses, training is given in making three more 5-second pauses (total of 6) prior to training on 10-second pausing. Similarly, if more than 5 minutes is required to complete three 10-second pauses, three more 10-second pauses are programmed before 15-second pauses are begun.

Rate-recovery Evaluation

The objective in this phase is to assess the S's reaction to lengthening the duration of the red light and to change from a continuous to an intermittent schedule. After the last pause in the final series under blue light, the red light comes on and S is given 1 minute on a 15-second, fixed-interval schedule. If he makes more than 20 responses, he is moved to the next (multiple-schedule) phase. If he makes fewer than 20 responses, the schedule is changed to increasing ratio (the one used for strengthening rate in phase one). This training continues until the rate reaches 20 responses for a 60-second period.

Final Phase: Multiple-schedule Training

The Ss who meet the criterion of rate in the previous stage are moved to the final multiple-schedule stage, provided the times of the discriminative stimuli are not over approximately 3 minutes each and the intermittency of reinforcement is not greater than a ratio of 50 or any interval of 1 minute. If discriminative-stimuli duration or schedules are greater than these values, it is suggested that changes take place in graduated steps.

DATA AND DISCUSSION

The performances of eight Ss in two experimental sessions each are presented as representative illustrations of the data. These Ss show a variety of behavioral effects and demonstrate a range of schedules and procedures. The clinical diagnosis is included in the brief descriptions of each S for whatever value it might have. However, because this study was not concerned with the relationship between diagnoses and operant behavior, implications of such relationships from these data are not intended. To facilitate identification of the figures, each record is identified by S (e.g., EMN), session number (e.g., S-1, S-2), and the schedule during the final phase (e.g., mult VR 25 ext).

The first four Ss shown in Fig. 1 illustrate the procedure, with particular emphasis on variations in development rather than in the final schedule. The last four Ss, presented in Fig. 2, show some of the range of final schedules established with the procedure.

The top two records in Fig. 1 show the first and second sessions of EMN, a 16-year-old girl with an MA of 5 years 3 months and an IQ of 42. She has been living at the institution for 4 years and is diagnosed as undifferentiated. In these records, as well as in the others, the horizontal line under the cumulative-response curve indicates the discriminative stimulus in force. When the line is elevated, the blue light was on; and when depressed, the red light was on. The colored light serving as S^D can be inferred from the reinforcement marks in the cumulative curve.

Since EMN's initial rate was high, rate strengthening was omitted. Pause building proceeded slowly and steadily. When shifted to mult VR 25 ext with fixed 1-minute alternation of lights, she performed at a steady rate under VR 25 and showed some anticipatory responses during S^Δ. The Session 2 (S-2) performance on mult VR 25 ext with 2-minute alternation is orderly, with some tendency to respond during S^Δ.

The second S (FJL) is a 14-year-old mongoloid girl with an MA of 3 years 1 month and an IQ of 32. She has lived in the institution for 4 years. The initial reaction to pause building in Session 1 consisted of a rate increase. After pause building, a rate-recovery interval showed that rate strengthening was not necessary, and she was shifted immediately to mult VR 25 ext with fixed 2-minute alternation of S^D and S^Δ. Evidence

of a discrimination is shown during the middle part of the session. Performance is good, but rate drops toward the end. This extinction trend was continued during the second session, S-2 (not shown), in which only 2 responses were made. In the third session (S-3), the increasing-ratio schedule recovered the rate, and discriminative performance on mult VR 25 ext with variable 2-minute alternation followed.

The third S in Fig. 1 (GJB) is a 21-year-old mongoloid girl with an MA of 3 years 5 months and an IQ of 30. She has lived at the institution for 11 years. She began Session 1 with a high rate; and although pause building progressed well, she responded to the onset of S^D with "runs" of responses. Rate recovery was good; and when shifted to mult VR 25 ext with fixed 2-minute alternation, discrimination was only fair because of the large numbers of responses during S^Δ shown in the middle of the session.

Session 2 for GJB is not shown. The performance was almost continuous responding, very much as in the initial part of Session 3. In Session 3 the schedule was mult VR 25 ext, with variable 2-minute alternation of the stimulus condition.

The final S in Fig. 1 (HMV) is a 21-year-old mongoloid boy with an MA of 4 years 9 months and an IQ of 32. He has been institutionalized for only 3 years. His initial high rate and virtually continuous responding during pause building quite suddenly gave way to rapid learning to pause. The pause series was terminated at the end of five 10-second pauses, and rate recovery showed no necessity for strengthening. Performance on mult VR 25 ext with fixed 2-minute alternation was nearly perfect, and this high level of discrimination was continued in Session 2 on mult VR 25 ext with variable 2-minute alternation.

The first S in Fig. 2 is ADP, an 11-year-old boy with an MA of 3 years 2 months and an IQ of 46. He has been at the institution for 5 years and is classified as cerebral birth trauma. Subject ADP maintained a high steady rate for more than 2000 re-

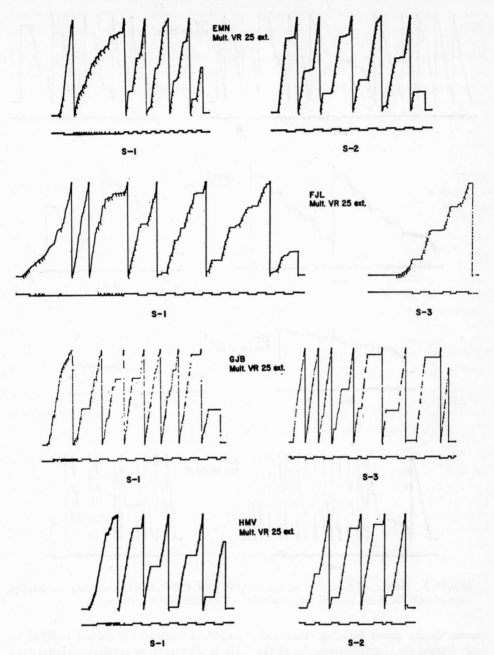

FIGURE I   Records of two sessions each for Ss EMN, FJL, GJB, and HMV showing the development of mult VR 25 ext.

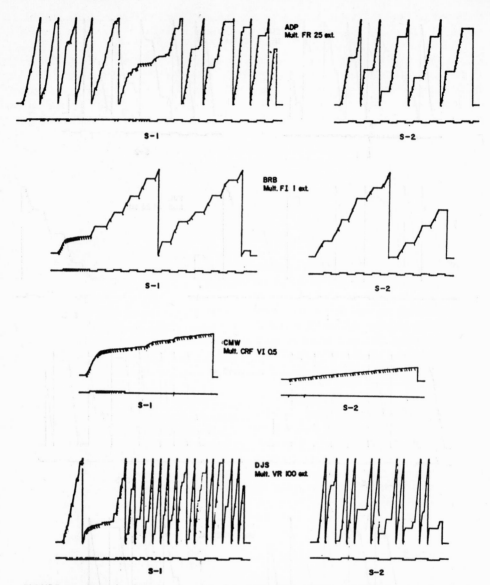

FIGURE 2   Records of Session 1 and 2 of Ss ADP, BRB, CMW, and DJS showing the development of mult FR 25 ext, mult FI 1 ext, mult CRF VI 0.5, and mult VR 100 ext.

sponses during pause building, then suddenly learned the discrimination. All of the series of 20-second pauses were nearly perfect. Performance on mult FR 25 ext with fixed 2-minute alternation shows good stimulus control, and regular postreinforcement pauses appear in Session 2.

Subject BRB is an 18-year-old boy with

an MA of 6 years 6 months and an IQ of 43. He is diagnosed as familial, and has been in the institution for 12 years. Pause control was quickly established; and although no rate recovery was given, an adequate rate was immediately obtained and performance on mult FI 1 ext with fixed 2-minute alternation was at a high level. This performance continued in Session 2, with some suggestions of FI scallops.

Subject CMW is a 17-year-old boy with an MA of 3 years 7 months and an IQ of 43. He has been institutionalized for 11 years and is diagnosed as cranial anomaly. His initial high rate in Session 1 was rapidly replaced by pause control. After pause building, both lights were turned off, and a buzzer was introduced as the cue in a mult CRF VI 0.5 schedule. Generalization is shown by continued low rate and few responses in the absence of the buzzer. Close-to-perfect performance is shown in Session 2, where he responded immediately to cue onset and refrained from responding in the absence of the cue.

Subject DJS is a 19-year-old girl with an MA of 4 years 8 months and an IQ of 36. She has been in the institution for 8 years and is classified as undifferentiated. Very rapid learning to pause followed a period of steady responding. She was shifted in gradual stages to a final schedule of mult VR 100 ext with fixed 3-minute alternation of lights. Successively, the stages were 4 minutes on mult VR 25 ext (fixed 0.5 alternation), 10 minutes on mult VR 25 ext (fixed 1-minute alternation), and 8 minutes on mult VR 50 ext (fixed 2-minute alternation). This progression is shown by changes in segment lengths in the event line. Stimulus control is evident, but a strong tendency to make responses in the presence of the S^Δ persisted. During Session 2, discrimination increased gradually but did not reach a high level.

SUMMARY

This paper deals with modifying simple operant behavior of institutionalized retarded children which is observed at the beginning of a study of the behavior required for a multiple schedule. A study of such procedures has promise both for an experimental analysis of individual differences, and for the development of techniques for the rapid acquisition of discrimination relative to multiple schedules. Concern here is with multiple schedules. The technique, which is designed to allow S to set the pace, is outlined in detail. All the multiple schedules described consist of two components which alternate in some fashion. Sample data are presented on eight Ss illustrating some of the phases and some of the final performances.

REFERENCES

AZRIN, N. H., and LINDSLEY, O. R. The reinforcement of cooperation between children. *J. abnorm. soc. Psychol.*, 1956, **52**, 100–102.

BIJOU, S. W., and STURGES, PERSIS T. Positive reinforcers for experimental studies with children—consumables and manipulatables. *Child Develpm.*, 1959, **30**, 151–170.

BIJOU, S. W. Discrimination performance as a baseline for individual analysis of young children. *Child Develpm.*, 1961, **32**, 163–170.

BRELAND, K., and BRELAND, MARION. A field of applied animal psychology. *Amer. Psychol.*, 1951, **6**, 202–204.

FERSTER, C. B., and SKINNER, B. F. *Schedules of reinforcement.* New York: Appleton-Century-Crofts, 1957.

KELLER, F. S., and SCHOENFELD, W. N. *Principles of psychology.* New York: Appleton-Century-Crofts, 1950.

SKINNER, B. F. *Science and human behavior.* New York: Macmillan, 1953.

SKINNER, B. F. The experimental analysis of behavior. *Amer. Scientist*, 1957, **45**, 343–371.

VERHAVE, T. Recent developments in the experimental analysis of behavior. *Proceed. Eleventh Res. Conf., Amer. Meat Inst. Found. of the Univer. of Chicago*, 1959.

46   DEFICITS IN ACQUISITION
OF OPERANT DISCRIMINATION AND DIFFERENTIATION
SHOWN BY INSTITUTIONALIZED RETARDED CHILDREN[1]

Beatrice H. Barrett • Ogden R. Lindsley[2]

This research was undertaken to explore the discrimination abilities of retarded children using controlled laboratory methods with automatic programing and recording devices. The primary goal was the location, automatic measurement, and functional definition of behavioral deficits which are relevant in both clinical and educational diagnosis.

Response differentiation (i.e. making one response instead of another) and stimulus discrimination (i.e. responding to one stimulus instead of another) are two basic component behaviors demanded by complex tasks. To assure a broad range of sensitivity in measuring devices and to conserve valuable experimental time, identification of deficits in differentiation and discrimination should precede investigation of more complicated components.

While there are numerous clinical psychological tests purporting to detect deficits which affect the response of retarded children to the usual formal educational methods, such tests have repeatedly shown themselves to be nonspecific; they do not clearly delineate defects. Furthermore, because of their culture-bound content, they frequently put the child from a deprived environment at

American Journal of Mental Deficiency, 1962, **67,** 424–436.

[1] This research was supported by Research Training Grant 2M–7084 and Research Grant MY–5054 from the National Institute of Mental Health, U.S. Public Health Service.
[2] The first author was solely responsible for conducting the experiments and writing this paper. The second author designed the apparatus and provided the laboratory space.

an immediate disadvantage. For the severely retarded nonverbal child, they afford only rough estimates which depend upon the judgment and experience of the clinician who administers and interprets the tests. In all cases, they represent poorly controlled testing situations in which observer bias and the interaction of the examiner with the child can have remarkable effects on the test scores. Perhaps most important from a research point of view is the progressive loss of sensitivity of clinical tests with repeated administration.

Educational technology is now in a period of rapid advance in the use of automated methods (Skinner, 1961). Development of these methods is based on principles of behavior generated from laboratory study of the interaction of lower animals with a highly controlled environment. Modifications of the basic methods of free operant conditioning have been used recently to study the behavior of mentally retarded children by Bijou and Orlando (1961), Orlando (1961a, 1961b), Orlando and Bijou (1960), Ellis, Barnett, and Pryer (1960), and Zeaman (1957, 1960). All have shown that the method can be used to obtain fruitful data on retarded behavior. With full environmental control, automatic programing techniques, and adequate reinforcing agents, these investigations have demonstrated that the behavior of retarded children may be rapidly brought under stimulus control. Sensitively arranged changes in the programing of discriminative and reinforcing stimuli may readily speed up acquisition of discriminations, and the nature of the stimuli supporting the discriminative behavior may be analyzed within experimental sessions.

While the above findings demonstrate the efficacy of the free operant method for therapeutic and prosthetic purposes in producing apparently "normal" uniformity in a group of retarded children, none has been oriented toward development of devices which automatically measure *behavior deficits*. To date, the only systematic application of free operant conditioning in the area of diagnostic measurement is that of Lindsley (1960, 1962). In his experimental analysis of the behavior of chronic psychotics, Lindsley has clearly shown that some of the most clinically relevant data are produced only through long-term, continuous, controlled observation. To the clinician this is not surprising, for there are obvious parallels in his own training. If he decides, for example, to use a new clinical tool for detecting behavior deviations, he may spend many years using the instrument before he is certain of its value for his purpose.

This report presents some of the findings which emerged during a year of exploratory research with a measurement device never before applied to the study of mentally retarded children.

METHOD

Subjects

Twenty-five institutionalized mentally retarded children, ranging in age from 7 to 20 years and in Stanford-Binet IQ from 33 to 72, were selected from the Walter E. Fernald State School[3] without regard to diagnosis. These children were studied for periods of time varying from 1 to 40 hours. The initial group of seven children, all considered educable, were attending classes regularly. Two

children were selected from the extremes of a group on whom there were objective data from a matching to sample automated instructional program on coin recognition.[4] One of these children had little difficulty with the program; the other persisted in random responding irrespective of the stimulus material presented to him. Gradually other children were added for purposes of following leads suggested in the data from the original core group. Seven children were selected because they had a history of seizures. Two children who were incapable of verbal communication and were not attending classes within the institution were added. Sibling groups representing both sociocultural retardation and congenital defects were also included. Since the sensitivity of the laboratory device to varying degrees and types of retardation was considered important, a representative sample was preferred to a "homogeneous" one.

Subject's Enclosure

Each subject was taken to a small room containing only a chair and a sloping wall-mounted panel on which were two lights, each located above a plunger manipulandum.[5] The child could pull these manipulanda either separately or simultaneously, and he could retrieve reinforcements from a tray inset on the right of the panel.

Experimental Design

All children were started on a program designed by Lindsley to locate behavior deficits in psychotic patients (1958a, 1958b, 1962). The design is diagrammed in Figure 1. Each light configuration was presented for one minute (C1 or C2) on a regularly alternating schedule, and either or both manipulanda (M1, M2) could be operated at any time. Thus there were four possible response conditions or reflexes. Pulling the left manipulandum with the left light on (C1M1) was reinforced on a fixed-ratio 10 schedule (every tenth response reinforced) with a penny or

[3] The assistance of Malcolm J. Farrell, M.D., Superintendent, Clemens Benda, M.D., and Benjamin Matzilevich, M.D., of Walter E. Fernald State School is gratefully acknowledged. Without the excellent cooperation of the Fernald School staff and, most importantly, the children themselves, this research would not have been possible.

[4] Personal communication from J. G. Holland, 1961.

[5] This experimental room was described in greater detail by Lindsley (1958b). The conditioning panel is commercially available from Robert C. Dalrymple, 20 Fletcher Ave., Lexington, Mass.

EXPERIMENTAL DESIGN FOR DIFFERENTIATION AND DISCRIMINATION ANALYSIS

DURATION OF EXPERIMENTAL SESSION	ONE HOUR			
	30 MINUTES		30 MINUTES	
STIMULI ALTERNATE EVERY MINUTE	C1		C2	
RESPONSES EITHER OR BOTH POSSIBLE AT ALL TIMES	M1	M2	M1	M2
CUMULATIVE RESPONSE RECORDS	C1 M1	C1 M2	C2 M1	C2 M2
		M1 M2		
REINFORCEMENT CANDY AND PENNIES	FR 10	NONE	NONE	NONE

FIGURE 1 Schematic diagram of experimental design for analysis of response differentiation and stimulus discrimination.

piece of candy. The penny to candy ratio was approximately 1:6. Pulling the right manipulandum with the left light on (C1M2), the left manipulandum with the right light on (C2M1), or the right manipulandum with the right light on (C2M2) was never reinforced. Each of these four reflexes was separately recorded on counters and cumulative response recorders. A fifth recorder continuously recorded simultaneous responses (within 125 ms. of each other) on both manipulanda. All programing and recording was controlled by relay circuitry located in a separate room from which one-way observation of the child was possible.

The design permitted independent measurement, within a single subject in a single session, of the three behavior processes which are schematically represented in Figure 2. A

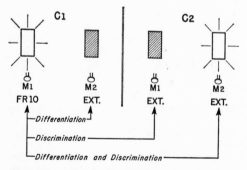

FIGURE 2 Schematic diagram for the functional description of differentiation and discrimination.

significant reduction in the rate of C1M2 reflexes below the rate of the reinforced reflex (C1M1) indicated the formation of response differentiation (making one response instead of another). Reduction in the rate of C2M1 reflexes relative to the C1M1 rate indicated stimulus discrimination (responding to one stimulus and not to another). Reduction in the C2M2 rate below the C1M1 rate indicated formation of both differentiation and discrimination. Maintenance of high rate on C2M2 with concurrent reduction of the C1M2 and C2M1 rates indicated overgeneralization or defective reality testing. The general motivational level of the subject was indicated by the total number of responses per session.

Procedure

Each child was brought from his dormitory at Walter E. Fernald State School to the laboratory at Metropolitan State Hospital for one-hour experimental sessions once a week during successive weeks. Before the start of the first session, each child was introduced to the "machine" by E showing him the two knobs and explaining that when the machine was on one of the lights would go on. He was also shown the reinforcement delivery tray and told that he could learn to work the machine so that some of the time he would get a penny or a piece of candy. No further explanation was given. If by the end of 10 minutes the child had not responded on either of the knobs, he was told that he would have to "work" on the machine to get his candies. Only two children failed to respond until given a demonstration of how to pull the knobs. At no time did a demonstration include running off a ratio to obtain a reinforcement.

The number of experimental sessions per child was not preset. The purpose was, rather, to use the apparatus as a vehicle for observing the behavior of each child in this fully controlled experimental environment and to determine whether the method would yield relevant data on the ability of each child to differentiate two responses and to discriminate two stimuli. No experimental changes were introduced until the behavior baselines generated by the previously described pattern of differential reinforcement had stabilized over a number of experimental sessions. The nature of procedural changes was decided on the basis of questions raised by emerging data from each individual.

RESULTS

The patterns of acquisition revealed to date range from rapid acquisition, which is characteristic of the normal adult (Lindsley, 1958a, 1958b, 1962), through delayed acquisition, to no acquisition in adequately motivated subjects in as many as 40 weekly one-hour sessions. Stability in the behavior processes of some children has not been reached in as many as 60 weekly sessions. Initial differential responding of a "superstitious" nature appeared in some of the older children, and marked response stereotypes were immediately shown by others. In those children who eventually reached an optimal level of performance, response differentiation occurred before stimulus discrimination, and the last stage of learning involved the elimination of the overgeneralized response of relatively high rates on C2M2, or "pulling the knob under the light" (Barrett, 1962).

While the above are general summary statements describing the commonalities in the data, the most significant findings are the highly individualized response patterns, many of which were revealed only after months of baseline observation. These deviations from the more general patterns were focused upon in an effort to locate and functionally define specific behavior deficits. Some examples of these specific deficits in discrimination and differentiation are described below.

Initial rapid learning followed by slow loss. Although cumulative records of responses during his first hour showed rapid acquisition (increased rate of the reinforced C1M1 reflex and marked drop in the rate of the nonreinforced reflexes: C1M2, C2M1, and C2M2), one child began to reveal slow sporadic losses in stimulus discrimination through successive hours. This was shown by session to session irregularities in the

C2M1 reflex rates relative to the reinforced C1M1 rates and is seen in the irregular decline in the discrimination index from Session 4 through Session 17 in the upper graph in Figure 3[6]. His discrimination losses occurred not only from session to session but frequently within sessions. There were several successive hours when his discrimination failures occurred only at the beginning of each session, suggesting the possibility that forgetting necessitated reacquisition each week.

As this child's experimental history grew, it became apparent that successive reacquisition within sessions was not sufficient for him to reach a stable performance with respect to this discrimination function. His differentiation of responses (differentiation index: lower rate on C1M2 relative to C1M1) was considerably more stable, although it was subject to occasional temporary loss (Sessions 10, 19, and 23). Nevertheless, this child permanently eliminated the superstitious overgeneralization response (high C2M2 rate) by the third hour.

While there was some fluctuation in his motivational level from session to session (total responses per hour and number of reinforced responses per session in lower graph in Figure 3), his discrimination losses can not be explained on this basis. Intrasession loss, especially when occurring in the middle of a session within a controlled environment, can be attributed to neither

[6] The rate index was devised (Jetter, Lindsley, & Wohlwill, 1953) to quantify the relationship between two rates of response. It is defined as the difference between two rates divided by their sum. Thus, referring to the rate comparisons diagrammed in Figure 2, a child's discrimination index for a given experimental session is the difference between his C1M1 rate and his C2M1 rate divided by their sum; his differentiation index, the difference between his C1M1 rate and his C1M2 rate divided by their sum; etc. Absence of differential behavior is represented by zero, maximum differential behavior by ±1.00. Positive values represent higher rates of the reinforced reflex than of the nonreinforced reflex; negative values represent higher rates of the non-reinforced compared with the reinforced reflex.

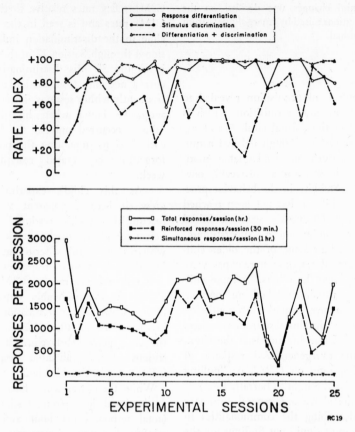

FIGURE 3   Slow, sporadic loss of discrimination and infrequent losses of differentiation, neither of which is correlated with the total behavior output of this child.

extra-experimental factors nor intersession memory loss. Neither can it be attributed to experimental variables, because they were held constant.

The fact that this was the only child in the group whose mental retardation was attributed to emotional factors may be of considerable significance. Observational data from the laboratory suggest that sharp drops in his discrimination tended to occur on days when clinical symptoms were most obvious. It is clear from these data that, in order to know the range and patterns of variability in this child's baseline behaviors, prolonged controlled observations are necessary. His experimental history to date demonstrates a phenomenon often seen in the clinic, namely

that the patient who may appear fairly intact during the first hour may subsequently reveal pathology over a number of months. A one-hour evaluation of this child may be grossly unreliable in predicting his behavior.

Abrupt intrasession loss. After 14 hours of conditioning, one boy proceeded through half of Session 15 in a manner indicating he had learned all the requirements of the task (Figure 4). After approximately 40 minutes, with no change in the apparatus or the experimental enclosure, he suddenly started pulling both knobs simultaneously under the C5 light configuration associated with reinforcement of only one response (see abrupt onset of responding on cumulative records of M1M2 and C5M2 in Figure 4).[7] Within the next 2 minutes, this double responding began to occur under the C6 configuration associated with no reinforcement, though somewhat less continuously (see sudden onset of responding on both C6 records in Figure 4). This abrupt and complete loss of response differentiation rapidly followed by equally abrupt but less complete loss of stimulus discrimination, lasted throughout the remainder of the experimental session. Without continuous functional recording of this boy's behavior, such findings would not have come to light. The implications of these findings in terms of this boy's ability to sustain performance on a learned task are obvious. The fact that he is subject to unilateral focal myoclonic seizures which are barely perceptible clinically, raises a variety of questions which can only be answered experimentally with appropriate devices for simultaneous measurement.

Initial differential responding. The most extreme pattern of initial differential responding was that of pulling only the plunger under the light at very high rates. This apparently prepotent pattern is grossly deviant from the initial undifferentiated responding shown by most subjects. In those children who showed it, the excessive generalization (pulling the plunger under each light when only responses on the left plunger under the left light were reinforced) appeared immediately at the beginning of the first experimental session (see RC 11 in Figure 5). Since it was displayed only by subjects who were among the oldest in the group, it was probably a pattern generated outside of the experimental environment as, for example, by vending machines. This

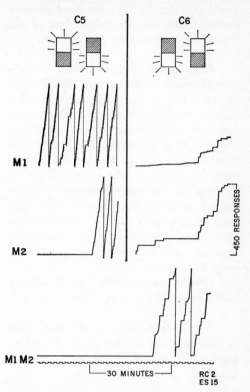

FIGURE 4   Simultaneous cumulative records showing abrupt and complete intrasession loss of differentiation (C5M2) followed by equally abrupt but less complete loss of discrimination (C6M1) and sudden overgeneralization (C6M2) within a single session in a fully controlled environment.[8]

pattern is very resistant to change under differential reinforcement, but in some cases it can be broken up by programing different stimulus configurations (such as the C5–C6 alternation shown in Figure 4), though sometimes at the expense of other behavior previously stable in the experimental setting. Experiments in which reinforcement is programed for responses under each of the lights

[7] In his first five sessions this boy showed little change in his initial differential reflex pattern which was marked by high C1M1 and C2M2 rates with few other responses. Beginning with the sixth session, the stimulus conditions were changed to C5 alternating with C6 as shown in Figure 4. There was no change in the reinforcement contingency. C5M1 responding was reinforced on FR 10 and all other reflexes were programed on extinction.

[8] Hatch marks indicate delivery of reinforcement for every tenth C5M1 response. The M1M2 record continuously monitors the occurrence of simultaneous responses (within 125 ms. of each other) on both manipulanda throughout the entire experimental session. The lower event marker on this record is depressed during C5 presentations.

would capitalize on this generalized response pattern which may be independent of the experimental contingency arrangement.

Response stereotypy.   Another immediately observable initial pattern which is even more resistant to control is that of pulling the two manipulanda in regular single alternation regardless of the stimulus conditions (see RC 10 in Figure 5). While successive discrimination may be brought about eventually by changes in the nature of the C2 stimulus, the single alternation pattern under the C1 condition may remain unchanged even when force is added to the right manipulandum (M2) or when an aversive consequence such as shock is programed for every M2 response. Without the independent and simultaneous recording of all reflexes, such data would not be available for analysis.

Long-term highly variable acquisition. A number of the children provided good examples of long-term acquisition with either temporary or progressive losses in either

differentiation or discrimination ability. There is one child, however, whose experimental history reveals a number of surprising facts. This girl carries the diagnosis of congenital cerebral spastic hemiplegia. With decided spasticity of the right hand, she would probably be excluded from other less exploratory experiments involving manual responding. Despite her physical handicap, 80 per cent of this girl's responses during the first experimental session were with her right hand on the right manipulandum (M2), which never produced a reinforcement. During her second hour this dominance reversed to the left manipulandum (M1). However, during this same hour a high rate of simultaneous responding (M1M2) began. The majority of these double responses occurred under the C2 light condition, which is associated with non-reinforcement of both responses. This double responding in a right hemiplegic child predominantly during the extinction component of the schedule did not dissipate until 15 sessions later when response differentiation began to form. It

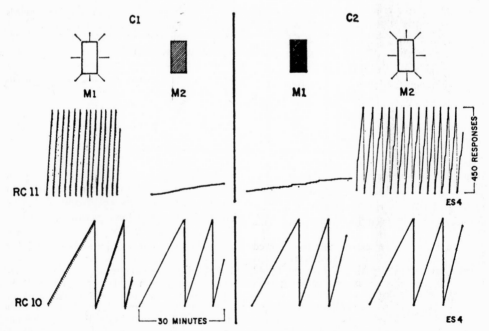

FIGURE 5   Cumulative response records of two children showing two different types of persisting prepotent response patterns.

would appear that during periods when no responding pays off, this child expends excessive amounts of energy involving her handicapped limb. This finding suggests that physical therapy procedures with this child which provide prolonged periods of extinction with brief periods of reinforcement would produce greater exercise of the spastic hand than would the opposite arrangement. In addition, it may be that more right hand activity would occur if the opportunity to use both hands together were present. This, of course, is subject to experimental test.

Abnormally low response rates. Three children, all of whom were on anticonvulsants, responded at abnormally low rates.

One of these children also displayed clinically evident psychotic symptoms, the second produced higher rates when his medication was reduced, and the third required a lower ratio of reinforcement to maintain sufficient behavior for a differential response pattern to emerge. The plotted data for this third child are presented in Figure 6. Response rates during the first six sessions under fixed-ratio 10 (FR 10) were uniformly low (see lower graph of responses per session for each of the four reflexes), and no differential pattern was shown (see rate index graph). The next three sessions were programed to determine effects of lower ratio requirements. Reinforcement of every C1M1 reflex (FR 1) took two sessions to show an effect (Sessions 7 and 8

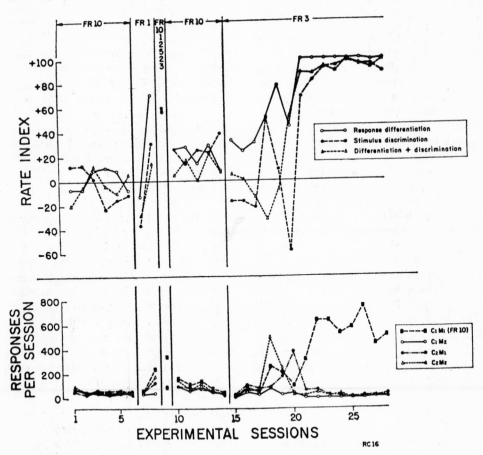

FIGURE 6 The delayed effects of lowered ratios of reinforcement on one child's differential responding and response rates.

in Figure 6). Return to FR 10 at the beginning of Session 9 produced a drop in response rate to the level shown in the first six sessions. Obviously the effects of two sessions on FR 1 was not maintained. Cumulative records of Session 9 showing effects of successive intrasession ratio changes indicated that this boy responded at higher rates on lower ratios. This is most readily seen in the long range effects of FR 10 during Sessions 10 through 14 followed by change to FR 3 for Sessions 15 through 28 (Figure 6). Under FR 10, rates of all four reflexes progressively declined and the previously shown differential responding disappeared. The change to FR 3 produced a marked facilitative effect both on total behavior output and on differential responding. Note, however, that this effect was quite delayed and was preceded by three sessions of no change followed by disruption, as indicated in the increased rate of first C2M2 and then C2M1, before this child's optimal differential pattern was shown.

It is not surprising that the lower ratio of reinforcements enabled this child to learn the differentiation and discrimination task. Its effect on his rate of responding is unusual enough to have possible implications for his deficit. Higher ratios most often produce faster rates of response, provided the nature of the reinforcement is appropriate. In this case, the behavior deficiency is not attributable to a poor reinforcing agent but may be a function of its intermittent delivery, for he works harder and learns more rapidly when it is delivered more frequently. Also, he may not be capable of "feeling" ratios above 5. The reliability of these findings will be further tested. At this point, however, the data clearly show that, in order to produce best results with this child, training procedures should provide more frequent reinforcement than is practical in most classroom situations.

DISCUSSION

The examples described above are but a few of the more striking deficits shown in the group of retarded children who continue to serve as subjects in the ongoing investigation. The data indicate that the device and the programing are sensitive to individual response patterns. The experimental procedure locates and automatically measures some basic behavioral excesses and deficiencies which interfere with efficient differential response to immediate contingencies in a controlled environment. Because it makes no demands of language comprehension on the part of the subject, it may be used to study the behavior of severely retarded nonverbal children who are often excluded from other experimental procedures and whose deficits are usually beyond the range of sensitivity of current clinical tests. The use of indestructible equipment in sturdily built experimental rooms permits the investigation of extremely disturbed and assaultive patients who are "untestable" by other behavior measures.

The examples described here represent a variety of deficits in the interaction between individual children and the same controlled environment. Except for the prepotent response patterns (shown in Figure 5), none appeared without continuously and functionally measured, controlled laboratory observations over a number of months. Whether similar information could have been obtained in a shorter span of time with daily sessions is a question which can only be answered experimentally. In any event, the nature and amount of daily intrasubject variability is likely to be more related to problems of diagnosis, training, and management than is weekly variability. In cases which show intrasession variability, especially severe and abrupt losses (shown in Figure 4), the question of recovery time could be answered by lengthening the duration of experimental sessions. It is also conceivable that longer sessions for children showing such patterns might reveal more severe disruption as a function of time spent in the experimental room.

A given duration of experimental session may be appropriate for one child but not for another. Strategically, the question is: appropriate for what purpose? Selection of an

experimental period for the purpose of showing optimal and stable performance in a
given subject is substantially different from
adjusting the duration of the subject's sessions to obtain maximal exposure of a behavior deficit. The same is true of the
timing and selection of procedural variations
which might produce changes in the performance of a subject. If the interest is in
producing therapeutic behavior modification,
a series of apparatus and programing changes
may be instituted in rapid succession to
achieve the desired results as quickly as possible. On the other hand, if diagnostic functional analysis is the major concern, sufficient
time must be allowed for the natural properties of the behavior to emerge prior to experimental changes.

Some of the data presented here (see
Figures 3 and 4) indicate that intrasubject
variability in the behaviors being measured
may be of major importance in characterizing various deficits. In order to evaluate
the effects of later introduction of experimental changes, the nature and amount of
this baseline variability must be known (see
Sidman, 1961). Also, it is entirely conceivable
that extra-experimental factors may produce
some of the variability. It this can be shown
in a systematic manner, it may be possible
to evaluate differential reactions of certain
children to such events as parental visit,
reprimand on the ward, and administration
of certain drugs.

The sensitivity of this method permits
using individual children as their own controls in an experimental analysis which will
yield conclusions with respect to these individuals. Furthermore, the data have shown
that, unlike techniques which suffer from
observer bias, the method does not lose sensitivity with repeated measurement. It is therefore possible to conduct experimental analyses
over a long enough time span to reveal
pertinent temporal dimensions of behavior.
Continuous, independent, simultaneous measurement of two behavioral processes, permits
direct observation of their spontaneous or
experimentally induced interaction.

SUMMARY

This report has described some of the
findings from the first year of a continuing
laboratory investigation of the operant behavior of a representative group of institutionalized retarded children. The research
focused on the location and automatic measurement of clinically and educationally relevant behavior deficits in a controlled experimental environment. The method of simultaneous and independent measurement of
response differentiation and stimulus discrimination was sensitive to a variety of
reliable individual response patterns including a wide range of deficits. Most of these
deficits were revealed only through repeated,
continuously recorded, controlled observations over many experimental sessions. Individual variability—both intersession and
intrasession—is extreme enough in some
cases to demand prolonged study. Because
of our focus on diagnostically oriented experimental analysis rather than on rapid pros-
thesis, the nature and amount of individual
variability emerges as an important and basic
datum rather than as statistical "noise" or
therapeutic failure.

REFERENCES

BARRETT, B. H. Acquisition of operant differentiation and discrimination in institutionalized retarded children. Paper read
at Eastern Psychol. Assoc., Atlantic City,
April 1962.
BIJOU, S. W., & ORLANDO, R. Rapid development of multiple-schedule performances
with retarded children. *J. exp. Anal.
Behav.*, 1961, 4, 7–16.
ELLIS, N. R., BARNETT, C. D., & PRYER, M. W.
Operant behavior in mental defectives:
exploratory studies. *J. exp. Anal. Behav.*,
1960, 3, 63–69.
JETTER, W. W., LINDSLEY, O. R., & WOHLWILL,
F. J. The effects of x-irradiation on
physical exercise and behavior in the
dog; related hematological and patho-

logical control studies. Boston Univer. Medical School, 1953. Microcard No. NYO–4548; Final Report (1953) AEC contract AT (30–1) 1201

LINDSLEY, O. R. Analysis of operant discrimination and differentiation in chronic psychotics. Paper read at Eastern Psychol. Assoc., Atlantic City, April, 1958. (a)

LINDSLEY, O. R. *An experimental analysis of psychotic behavior.* Detailed progress report II for period June, 1956–November, 1958. Behavior Research Laboratory, Metropolitan State Hospital, Waltham, Mass. (b)

LINDSLEY, O. R. Characteristics of the behavior of chronic psychotics as revealed by free-operant conditioning methods. *Dis. nerv. Syst.,* monogr. suppl., 1960, 21, 66–78.

LINDSLEY, O. R. Operant conditioning methods in diagnosis. *First Hahnemann symposium on psychosomatic medicine.* Philadelphia: Lea & Febiger, 1962.

ORLANDO, R. The functional role of discriminative stimuli in free operant performance of developmentally retarded children. *Psychol. Rec.,* 1961, 11, 153–161. (a)

ORLANDO, R. Component behaviors in free operant temporal discrimination. *Amer. J. ment. Def.,* 1961, 65, 615–619. (b)

ORLANDO, R., & BIJOU, S. W. Single and multiple schedules of reinforcement in developmentally retarded children. *J. exp. Anal. Behav.,* 1960, 3, 339–348.

SIDMAN, M. *The tactics of scientific research.* New York: Basic Books, 1961.

SKINNER, B. F. Teaching machines. *Scient. Amer.,* 1961, 205, No. 5, 90–102.

ZEAMAN, D. *Learning and transfer in mental defectives.* Progress Rep. Nos. 1 & 2, Univer. Conn. Dept. Psychol., 1957 & 1960.

47   PROGRAMED INSTRUCTION IN THE CLASSROOM[1]

Jay S. Birnbrauer • Sidney W. Bijou • Montrose M. Wolf • J. D. Kidder[2]

If you were to visit Rainier School, your tour would include the "Programed Learning Classroom" shown schematically in Figure

1. The physical layout of the classroom is not unusual except for three individual instruction rooms at one end and an observational room at the other. What *is* unusual is the way in which the class is operated and the relaxed, but busy, atmosphere. Typically, you would see one pupil working at a table in the writing area with or without the aid of a teacher, other pupils studying at their desks, and pupils and teachers going to and coming from the individual instruction rooms.

Perhaps the best way to describe how this class functions is to follow one pupil, Hugh, through his daily schedule. Hugh was selected as our example because he was the median pupil at the end of the school year and was the least promising at the beginning. He was eleven-years-old and diag-

[1] This is an amended version of a paper read by the senior author at the American Association on Mental Deficiency convention, Portland, Oregon, May 1963. The project described is conducted jointly by Rainier School (C. H. Martin, Superintendent), the White River School District (Paul C. Webb, Superintendent), and the University of Washington. It has been supported in part by National Institute of Mental Health Research Grant M-2232 and Project Grant MH-01366.

[2] We wish to acknowledge our debt to Nancy Heid, W. H. Heid, R. F. Peterson, and Judith Thoft, who assisted in the preparation of programs and in the selection and evaluation of the pupils. Special thanks are due Cecilia Tague, whose contributions to every aspect of this project, as an Assistant Teacher, are too numerous to list.

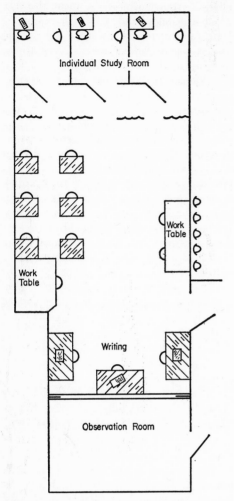

1. He takes a seat in the hallway.
2. When invited to do so, he quickly moves to his desk.
3. A teacher, after placing a number on his desk, says, "Hugh, you may bring your number and star box to the booth now."
4. Hugh practically runs to the booth, possibly saying something like, "What do we have today, reading?"
5. After about twenty minutes, he emerges and returns to his desk where he begins pasting stars into booklets. (He may comment about how many stars he has earned or the new words he has learned, but he "settles down" in a matter of seconds.)
6. A teacher instructs Hugh on a work assignment to be done at his desk.
7. After about fifteen minutes of studying, Hugh raises his hand, whereupon a teacher checks his work and reinforces correct answers with stars and praise.
8. A teacher gives him his next assignment and Hugh moves to the designated location, for example, a writing table.

The above sequence continues until he has completed all of his assignments. Occasionally, he may request some homework before leaving.

While Hugh is going through these procedures, each of the other pupils is following a similar schedule of studies.

The routine, classroom, and, of course, the pupils are part of a project established for the following purposes:

1. To develop materials according to the principles of programed instruction (*PI*) (Green, 1962; Skinner, 1958) in primary academic subjects for educable retarded children and
2. To develop procedures whereby motivation, good study habits, cooperation, perseverance, and concentration can be developed and strengthened. The procedures are based on reinforcement principles (Bijou and Baer, 1961; Skinner, 1953) and are constantly being tested and revised. Our basic assumption is that if the children do not learn or learn slowly, our procedures are ineffective, or at best inefficient.

FIGURE I   The Rainier School Programed Learning Classroom.

nosed as brain-damaged. He often had temper tantrums when thwarted or given instructions. His achievement scores were mostly zero despite five years of school attendance. More specifically, he could count only to fifteen, print little more than his name (Fig. 2, Ex. 1) and read virtually nothing.

After about five months in the class you could have observed Hugh cheerfully proceeding through the following daily routine for from sixty to ninety minutes per day:

The project was started because of the need to find ways in which teachers can reach more retarded children without sacrificing the extent and intensity of the education that each pupil receives. *PI,* if it can be made self-instructional, offers a way of accomplishing this end. However, writing good programed materials is only one of many steps that are necessary. As you have seen, a special classroom and routine that would permit children to follow independent, staggered schedules were designed. The children had to be taught this routine, and disruptive reactions to failure and requests to work, for example Hugh's temper tantrums, had to be eliminated. In other words, a decision to use *PI* does not obviate the necessity for considering many standard classroom problems.

Our strategy was to assign a representative group of young educable pupils to the Programed Learning Classroom for instruction in primary academic subjects, that is, reading, writing, arithmetic, and related practical skills, such as time-telling and use of measuring instruments, and to regular classes in art, crafts, music, and physical education. Eight boys were selected. They ranged in age from nine to thirteen years, in mental age from 5–5 to 7–3 (Peabody Picture Vocabulary Test), and in previous education from six months to five years. Academically, most of their achievement scores were zero. Their clinical diagnoses included retardation associated with brain damage and familial retardation.

Three teachers assumed responsibility for preparing, evaluating, and revising the programed materials, conducting the classroom, and coping with whatever behavior problems arose under the circumstances.

Behavior problems did occur frequently and most of the boys had not learned to study persistently by themselves. Behavior problems were handled almost exclusively by extinction, that is, in this case, by ignoring instances of inappropriate behavior, and positively reinforcing approximations to desired behaviors. In other words, the emphasis was upon strengthening the desirable behavior by positively reinforcing it. Praise and token reinforcers (stars) were used. The

physical arrangement of the room, the staggered schedules, and the high teacher-to-pupil ratio permitted disruptive behavior to run its course without unduly affecting the studying of the other children.

A token reinforcement system was instituted after we discovered that these pupils would not work steadily for only social approval and knowledge of results. It appeared as if incorrect and correct answers were one and the same to them, and often the children did not even look at the answers provided in the teaching programs. Learning academic subjects had little value to them and in the light of their histories there are very few reasons why it should. Therefore, stars, together with verbal approval, were given when a pupil behaved acceptably or answered questions correctly. The criteria for acceptable behavior and the ratio of correct responses to tokens were increased gradually.

The stars were saved in booklets that were exchanged for anything the pupils chose, for example, a nickel, credit toward a larger sum of money and an opportunity to spend it in town, or airplane models. Red, green, and silver stars were given randomly to avoid the work-lulls that often follow completing a project or attaining a goal. That is, the pupils could obtain another prize shortly if they continued to work.[3]

Although we have not experimentally evaluated these reinforcement procedures as yet, we are inclined to think that the boys would not have learned the classroom routine described earlier and would not have acquired better study habits as quickly without

[3] Two changes have been made recently in the reinforcement procedures. The stars have been replaced by check marks which the teachers make in the pupils' booklets. This rather simple and easily administered procedure appears to be equally effective. Secondly, since extinction is often difficult to implement effectively in a classroom, a procedure consisting of briefly removing the child from the classroom contingent upon misbehavior is being used also. "Time-out" from opportunities to engage in positively reinforcing activities has been used effectively to eliminate disruptive behaviors by Holz, Azrin, and Ayllon (1963) and Wolf, Risley, and Mees (12).

some sort of tangible reinforcer system. Within 5 months, 7 of the 8 pupils could be described as good students. They studied independently for longer periods and accomplished much more work in spite of the activities of the other pupils. Disruptive behaviors were virtually eliminated, thus making the classroom quite reinforcing to the teachers. For example, in October, Hugh spent, on the average 60 minutes in class (Table 1). While he ostensibly was working for 50 of these 60 minutes, he accomplished only 50 items during that time. One

TABLE I   Summary of Hugh's Average Performance in October and March

	Oct.	Mar.
Class Time (minutes)	60	90
Productive Time (minutes)	50	68
Total Items	50	152
Reading (minutes)	20	17
Errors/Total	1/13	2/36
Arithmetic (minutes)	18	12
Errors/Total	2/12	0/25
Writing (minutes)	12	20
Letters Correct	25	64
"Desk Work" (minutes)	—	19
Items	—	27
Homework Items	—	52

item per minute is an extremely slow rate for the kind of material being presented at that time, and indicates that Hugh was quite inefficient. By March, although Hugh was spending only 18 minutes more per day in "productive study," his rate of completing items increased 200 percent, while his error rate did not change. In addition, he was accomplishing substantial amounts of homework, which, as was mentioned above, was only given when requested. The "desk work" is also significant because these activities, which were not always supervised, involved delayed token and social reinforcement, and were done in the classroom proper, where distractions occurred.

Hugh and his classmates indicate that PI can be used in a classroom daily for an extended period if a suitable environment is

provided and systematic procedures are used to strengthen appropriate social and study behavior. While it is true that the pupil-to-teacher ratio was frequently one-to-one during the school year, many of the functions of the teachers could have been accomplished by automatic equipment—once the children were motivated to study and had learned the necessary social and emotional control. Another potential saving of teacher-time rests in the fact that the pupils learned to accomplish a greater amount of study in a shorter period of time. Thus, teachers could spend less time per pupil with no loss and probably a considerable gain in rate of progress.

Although the programs used to teach reading, cursive writing, and arithmetic differed in format and type of equipment used, they had the following characteristics in common:

1. Each began at or below the first-grade level.
2. Recordable responses were required to all items (questions, problems).
3. Confirmation or knowledge of results followed every response or sequence of responses, and token reinforcers and praise were given according to an unsystematic variable schedule of correct answers.
4. The sequence of items was arranged so that new material was presented only when the pupil was adequately prepared. (This was determined from daily analyses of errors.)
5. Each program, administered with or without the aid of automatic equipment, was designed to help the pupils teach themselves.

Although the children learned the prerequisite study and social skills for self-instruction, it is difficult to assess, in the absence of comparative data, how much content was acquired from the programs. Also, it is apparent that the reading and arithmetic programs developed need extensive revisions. However, the results in cursive writing indicate that the general approach may be fruitful. We shall, therefore, outline this program and show Hugh's progress in it.[4] Cursive

[4] The reader may compare Hugh's performance with that expected of normal third-grade children during their first year of writing instruction.

writing was taught in lieu of script because of the greater utility of this skill.

The program consisted of three major stages—Tracing, Tracing and Copying, and Copying. An illuminated tracing box was used to ensure that the model being traced was clear and to provide a means of controlling the amount of time that the pupil could see and trace the model. At first, the light was on almost continuously, thus providing continuous information about the lines to be traced. Then, the proportion of light-on time was decreased to "wean" the child from tracing and to transfer control to lines on the paper and other cues used in free handwriting.

The program began with tracing simple strokes which permitted a wide margin of error. Figure 2, Example 1, shows how Hugh managed for the most part to keep his pencil line within the simple model.[5] Then, the margin of error was gradually decreased and the complexity of the models was increased to include letters and letter groups. (Fig. 2, Exs. 2 and 3). When the pupil traced these models competently, with reduced light-on time, the second stage began.[6]

During the Tracing and Copying stage, two types of items were presented, one providing both a model to trace and one to copy; the other, only a model to copy. The latter served as tests of the acquisition of copying. For example, in Figure 2, Example 4, Hugh traced his name but could have either traced the "b," "ba," and "baby," copied them from the versions above them, or a little of both. In Example 5, he wrote his name with only the lines on the paper as aids, either traced or copied the left "nz," and copied the right "nz" from the model labeled "T."

[5] The revised program includes only the strokes which are components of English letters. The margin of error in the nonsense model shown in Example 1 is, however, still accurate.

[6] We omit the actual variations in the light-on time, because it is not at all clear what the proportions should be or even whether this procedure is superior to continuous tracing. The procedures are being compared experimentally.

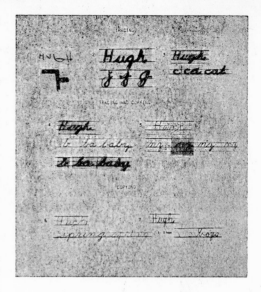

FIGURE 2   Examples from each stage in the cursive writing program. The heavy black lines are models which can be seen only when the tracing box is illuminated. The lines on the paper and the dots can be seen at all times. Hugh could have either traced or copied the nearby models in 4 and 5, except for the "nz" at the far right.

The third stage, Copying, probably is self-explanatory, although it should be pointed out that the models are still further removed and more complex (Fig. 2, Ex. 6). Script models that the pupil translated into cursive were also introduced (Ex. 7). After this stage, for the most part, writing practice was incorporated into other exercises. An example of combined writing and comprehension done by a more advanced student than Hugh is shown in Figure 3. First, the pupil copied instructions, such as "Put 11 dogs in box 5," from a script model, and then demonstrated comprehension by carrying them out.

In summary, we have described a classroom for retarded children in which *PI* methods and reinforcement principles were applied for an academic year. Although *PI* may never be regarded as a technology that can stand alone, this is especially apparent

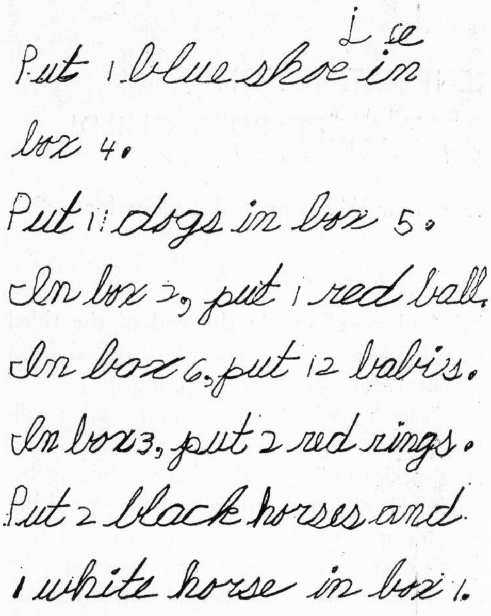

Put 1 blue shoe in box 4.
Put 11 dogs in box 5.
In box 2, put 1 red ball.
In box 6, put 12 babies.
In box 3, put 2 red rings.
Put 2 black horses and 1 white horse in box 1.

FIGURE 3 An example of combined writing practice and reading and arithmetic comprehension. After copying these instructions from a script version, the pupil carried them out.

when the pupils involved are not motivated to learn and have not acquired the prerequisite attentional and study skills. We have described the programs used on eight pupils who demonstrated that they could acquire these skills and were capable of contributing considerably to their own education.

The token reinforcement system used to maintain studying and cooperation has the flexibility needed in dealing with a group of individuals whose histories vary over a wide range. Tokens may also be dispensed automatically and in large quantities at practically no expense. Rarely did the children earn more than the equivalent of about five cents a week.

Currently, we are repeating these procedures with revised programs on the group of pupils described here, and on another similar group. In general, the new group is making greater progress. While this accelerated progress may be due to selection factors, it may also be attributable to the substantial amount of time that Hugh and his classmates spent during the past year in teaching us.

REFERENCES

BIJOU, S. W. and D. M. BAER. *Child development. Vol. I: A systematic and empirical theory.* New York: Appleton, 1961.

GREEN, E. J. *The learning process and programmed instruction.* New York: Holt, Rinehart and Winston, Inc., 1962.

HOLZ, W. C., N. H. AZRIN, and T. AYLLON. Elimination of behavior of mental patients by response-produced extinction. *J. exp. Anal. Behav.,* 1963, **6**, 407–412.

SKINNER, B. F. *Science and human behavior.* New York: Macmillan, 1953.

SKINNER, B. F. Teaching machines. *Science,* 1958, **128**, 969–977.

WOLF, M. M., T. R. RISLEY, and H. L. MEES. Application of operant conditioning procedures to the behavior problems of an autistic child. *Behav. Res. Ther.* 1964, **1**, 305–312.

48   A NOTE ON APPARENT EXTINCTION
OF THE VOMITING BEHAVIOR OF A RETARDED CHILD[1]

Montrose M. Wolf • Jay S. Birnbrauer • Tom Williams • Julia Lawler

Vomiting is usually classified as respondent behavior that is elicited by a class of unconditioned stimuli (emetics) and presumably, given the necessary history, by conditioned stimuli. Several reports in the medical literature describing a childhood "syndrome" characterized by a high rate of vomiting behavior were reviewed by Hoyt and Stickler (1960), who concluded that "the cause of the syndrome of recurrent vomiting, while possibly psychogenic is not known definitely."

Laura was a nine-year-old girl diagnosed as suffering from mental retardation, cerebral palsy, aphasia, hyperirritability, and brain damage. She was admitted to Rainier School, an institution for the retarded, about ten months before our observations began. According to Laura's dormitory nurse, Laura vomited at a moderate rate upon admission, but within a few weeks the rate declined to its present level of "a couple of times a month."

Approximately six months after admission, Laura was enrolled in the school program in a developmental level class, which met three hours a day. After about a month, Laura began to vomit occasionally in class, and within three months, vomiting became practically an everyday occurrence. Among other consequences, the teacher returned Laura to her dormitory whenever Laura vomited on her own dress, which happened fairly frequently. Drug therapy was initiated

[1] The assistance, under aversive data-gathering conditions, of Larry Hakala and John Nonnenmacher is gratefully acknowledged. This study was supported in part by research grants (M-2232 and MH-01366) from the National Institutes of Health.

but had no effect. At the end of the third month Laura was temporarily dropped from school because of her vomiting.

Two months later a second teacher volunteered to work with Laura and to attempt an experimental analysis of the vomiting behavior. It was our guess that the vomiting was an operant. The first step in our design was to try to decrease Laura's vomiting by operant extinction, by not allowing her access to possible reinforcers during the vomiting episodes. Our hunch was that return to the dormitory had been the reinforcing consequence responsible for maintaining the behavior.

Our planned second step was to reinstate the vomiting after the extinction rate reached a stable low level by presenting the apparent reinforcer contingent upon vomiting, that is, allowing her to return to her dormitory. The new teacher was asked to record (with the help of an observer) the number of times Laura vomited each day in class, to make every effort to continue the class as usual, and not to send Laura back to the dormitory till class had ended. The teacher also attempted to shape desirable behavior using M&M's and praise as reinforcers. These positive reinforcement procedures were discontinued during the vomiting episodes.

The course of Laura's vomiting behavior throughout the semester is presented cumulatively in Figure 1. As can be seen, the rate of vomiting declined to zero in an orderly manner over a period of thirty class days, or six calendar weeks. Twenty-one vomits was the highest number recorded on any one day. Laura was absent two Fridays

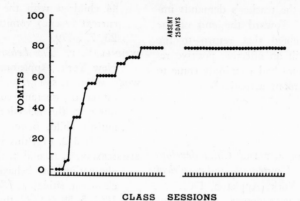

FIGURE 1   A cumulative record showing the cessation of vomiting behavior of a retarded girl.

during the first six weeks and was later absent twenty-five days, as shown in Figure 1, as a result of her dormitory's being quarantined.

The vomiting responses were not equally distributed throughout the days of the week. The total for Mondays was thirty-five, Tuesdays twenty-six, Wednesdays twelve, Thursdays five, and Fridays one. This relationship between the day of the week and the number of vomits resembles that typically described as spontaneous recovery.

Our original plan, attempting to increase the vomiting rate by positive reinforcement after a stable rate was reached during extinction, was foiled by the fact that the rate remained at zero, leaving us with no response to reinforce. Without the important step of reinstatement, the probable nature of the conditioning history, operant or respondent, cannot be accurately inferred. Although this detracts from the analytical value of the data, it is irrelevant for the practical value of the extinction technique. It is probable that the classroom procedure would have been equally effective in extinguishing the behavior regardless of the type of conditioning history.

If the vomiting had clearly been the result of respondent conditioning, the extinction procedure would have been carried out in much the same manner. The same care would have been taken not to positively reinforce the respondent behavior, since such a procedure might result in an increase in the behavior through operant control (Bijou and Baer, 1961; Skinner, 1938). Laura would still have been sent to class and forced to remain in the presence of the conditioned eliciting stimuli in order for respondent extinction to occur. The existence of certain correlated operant behavior suggested, however, that Laura's vomiting was operant or perhaps operantly controlled respondent behavior (Bijou and Baer, 1961; Skinner, 1938). Concurrent with virtually every vomiting episode, Laura screamed, tore her clothes, and destroyed property. Such behaviors in other abnormal children have succumbed to operant response controlling techniques (Wolf, Risley, and Mees, 12; Zimmerman and Zimmerman, 42). Frequently during these tantrums, Laura escaped from her classroom and attempted to return to her dormitory; she was returned to the classroom each time. The vomiting itself also had certain operant components, such as the selection of targets: the teacher's desk (on one occasion, a neighboring teacher's desk), the table at which the class was seated, and her own clothes when she had taken them off.

The tantrumlike behaviors decreased in frequency to zero along with the vomiting, while Laura's productive classroom behavior apparently increased. Her appearance and responsiveness to the teacher's demands improved markedly. Toward the end of the semester, we doubted that return to the dormitory was still an effective positive reinforcer, since Laura had seemingly come to "enjoy" her classroom activities.[2]

REFERENCES

BIJOU, S. W. and D. M. BAER. *Child development*. Vol. I: *A systematic and empirical theory*. New York: Appleton, 1961.

HOYT, C. S. and G. B. STICKLER. A study of 44 children with the syndrome of recurrent (cyclic) vomiting. *Pediat.*, 1960, **25**, 775–779.

SKINNER, B. F. *The behavior of organisms*. New York: Appleton, 1938.

WOLF, M. M., T. RISLEY, and H. MEES. Application of operant conditioning procedures to the behavior problems of an autistic child. *Behav. Res. Ther.*, 1964, **1**, 305–312. (12, this volume.)

ZIMMERMAN, E. H. and J. ZIMMERMAN. The alternation of behavior in a special classroom situation. *J. exp. Anal. Behav.*, 1962, **5**, 59–60. (42, this volume.)

[2] Editors' note. Additional information which was obtained after completion of the article was summarized by the authors as follows: We continued taking data on the subject's vomiting behavior throughout the school year following the one described above. The general class conditions were similar to the previous year's including the same teacher and many of the same students. About a month after the beginning of the fall term the subject vomited once in class and was immediately returned to her dormitory. During the next three months, each time the subject vomited she was returned to her dormitory. Vomiting occurred in over one-third of the class sessions. At that point we returned to the extinction procedure. The subject was kept in the classroom the entire session regardless of whether or not she vomited. During the next few months the vomiting decreased in an orderly manner from a high rate (twenty-nine being the most responses in any one session) to only one vomit in class during the last two months of the school year. The resulting extinction curve was similar to that of the previous year.

49   A PROCEDURE FOR SHAPING VOCALIZATIONS IN A MUTE CHILD

Nancy Kerr • Lee Meyerson • Jack Michael[1]

INTRODUCTION

One of the most difficult diagnostic and treatment problems seen in rehabilitation centers for children is the young mute child. Sometimes no physical or behavioral anomaly can be found except for the delayed speech, and sometimes deafness is clearly indicated. In other cases, however, the pattern of behavior is grossly divergent and a

[1] The authors acknowledge with gratitude the assistance provided by NIMH and VRA Training Grants and the courtesies offered by the administrators and staff of the Samuel Gompers Memorial Rehabilitation Center.

diagnosis of impaired hearing, mental retardation, aphasia, autism, psychosis, "brain damage"—or some combination of these—is possible.

Present clinical practice is to place great emphasis upon diagnosis prior to attempting treatment. Since test results are not infrequently "inconclusive" the parent is advised to "bring the child back for retest in six months," and nothing is done in the interim. This procedure seems to hold particularly for children who lack echoic behavior, for psychotherapists often feel inadequate if they cannot communicate with a client at least at some primitive level, and speech therapists generally require that the child be willing to "try" to imitate the sounds presented to him.

From a behavior theory standpoint, the lack of a diagnosis is not a barrier to initiating treatment. Behavior that is reinforced will be engaged in with distinctive frequency, according to the schedule of reinforcement and the stimulus conditions, up to the limits of capability of the organism. If a specific behavior cannot be obtained in one way, perhaps it can be obtained in another way. The appearance of the desired behavior is evidence of success. If treatment is temporarily or relatively unsuccessful, the cumulative record of responses under varied conditions will provide evidence of behavioral deficits that will contribute to diagnosis. In general, the diagnostic problem can be recast, in behavioral terms, as the specification of the conditions under which a specific behavior can be obtained. Since not every effort to shape behavior will be successful, the behavioral engineering process may also specify the conditions under which a response cannot be obtained and indicate the deficit that is responsible. For example, if a child's suitably reinforced lever pressing behavior cannot be brought under the control of a pure tone auditory stimulus but is readily brought under the control of a visual stimulus, he is deaf.

The task of the behavioral engineer when confronted with a young mute child is to develop speech. Sometimes the child already possesses at least a minimal echoic repertoire. For example, upon hearing the sound "moo," an infant often will say "moo" or make some utterance that sounds vaguely like "moo." Skinner (1957) offers an analysis of the conditions under which such a minimal repertoire may be increased, refined, and maintained. A much more difficult problem is presented if a child fails to show any echoic behavior. If a child is to learn to speak, it seems necessary not only that he vocalize but also that his vocalizations be brought under the control of the vocal

stimuli of others. In the developmental process, it is only as echoics are selectively reinforced that a complex verbal repertoire develops.[2]

PROBLEM

Jane was a mute, three-year-old female who had been diagnosed as a severely mentally retarded (M.A. nine months), cerebral palsied, epileptic, emotionally disturbed child. Her history indicated that she had been subjected to serious maternal, social and sensory deprivation. When the child was ten months old, her mother had been hospitalized or acutely, physically ill for approximately a half-year, and during this time, except for minimal and often delayed attention to diapering and feeding, the infant had been left unattended in her crib.

At the time she was first seen, she did not walk, talk, laugh, cry, or respond to people except by avoidance behavior. Most of her nourishment came from milk, taken from a baby bottle, which she drank without help. She threw or tried to destroy any manipulable object that came into her hands, and she made scratching movements on larger, heavier objects.

Exposure to a well organized preschool class for orthopedically handicapped children, and other services of the rehabilitation center, for a period of three months resulted in considerable physical gains. She learned to walk well with the aid of a brace, and her seizures were controlled by medication. Other behavior, however, was relatively un-

[2]Theoretically, it would seem possible to shape emitted vocalizations by selective reinforcement also. Under these conditions, it would be necessary to shape each utterance into a word which would then be brought under the control of the proper stimulus conditions. For example, one might teach a child to say "water" in the presence of water and not to say it under other stimulus conditions. The same procedure would then be followed for each new word to be learned. It does not appear, however, that this is the process that occurs in natural speech development nor does it seem a feasible procedure for beginning speech therapy.

changed. The child remained mute, for example, but "having reached maximum medical benefit," as the euphemism runs, was about to be discharged with a recommendation for custodial institutionalization.

EXPERIMENTAL WORK

Phase 1

In an experiment reported elsewhere (Kerr and Meyerson, 1964) six 20-minute sessions of selective reinforcement of the child's faint vocal grunts were sufficient to shape up vocalization.

The child was held on the experimenter's lap and reinforced after each appropriate vocal response by being joggled up and down gently while the experimenter sang a verse of a nursery song. The joggling and singing lasted about five to seven seconds. In the final session, the child responded with an average of seven clear vocalization responses per minute (after reinforcement time was removed from the record).

Phase 2

Following a lapse of several months, the child returned for further work. The rate of vocalization under the conditions of Phase 1 was readily reinstated, and an attempt was made now to introduce stimuli that would facilitate the development of echoic behavior. The experimenter began to vocalize every ten seconds. The plan was to reinforce the child's vocalizations, when they occurred soon after the experimenter's vocalizations, but not at other times. In this way the experimenter's vocalizations might become S^Ds for the child's vocal behavior. Under these conditions, however, the child's vocal output, in several sessions, dropped sharply to almost zero. This behavior was characteristic of her everyday life. Any actions of another that appeared to be directed toward her, froze her into near immobility. What were intended to become S^Ds for vocal behavior by the child appeared to be functioning as conditioned aversive stimuli.

Phase 3

The experimenter ceased introducing vocal stimuli that were different from the singing sounds that were used in reinforcing the child. The original experimental conditions of continuously reinforcing the child's vocal behavior were reinstated. Within three 20-minute sessions, the child's vocal output was as high as it had been at the termination of Phase 1.

A renewed attempt was then made to introduce the experimenter's vocalizations of sounds, words or phrases without interfering with the child's rate of vocal output. Again, the intent was to create an S^D for echoic behavior. The process was one of fading-in the stimuli. In the first few sessions, only one soft vocalization, gradually increasing in loudness, was presented. The number of experimenter vocalizations increased gradually in each succeeding session but fluctuated in rate roughly according to the child's performance. The experimenter vocalized often when the child's rate of responding was high and with less frequency or not at all when the child's rate of responding was low. In each session, of course, the child was reinforced as usual for her own vocalizations.

From the 35th to the 40th session, it was possible for the experimenter to present a vocal stimulus every 10 to 15 seconds, or 80 to 100 stimuli in each session, without interfering markedly with the child's vocal output.

Phase 4

This phase was intended to establish the experimenter's vocalizations as S^Ds with reinforcement available under ten-second and, later, five-second limited-hold contingencies. Vocalization by the child, but not echoic behavior, was required for reinforcement.

The experimenter made a sound, usually a single word, every fifteen seconds. If the child vocalized within ten seconds after the S^D, she was reinforced with ten seconds of joggling and song. If she made no response, or if she responded only during the final

five seconds of the period, she was not reinforced. Nine 15-minute, semi-weekly sessions were held under these contingencies.
In an additional nine 15-minute, semi-weekly
sessions, the limited hold contingency for
reinforcement was reduced to five seconds.
The S^Ds were still presented every fifteen
seconds, but only responses that occurred
within five seconds were reinforced.

RESULTS

The results are shown in Figure 1. It
will be seen that the best performance under

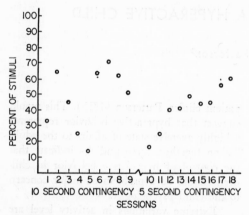

FIGURE 1   Percent of stimuli to which response was made within limited-hold contingency when number of stimuli varied between
60 to 70 per session.

the ten second limited hold occurred in
the seventh session when an appropriate response to the S^D was made within the time
contingency seventy percent of the time.
The shape of the curve, however, is grossly
irregular. Performance under the five-second
contingency was much more regular. The
graph shows the expected improvement of
responding until in the final session sixty
percent of the S^Ds were followed almost
immediately by an appropriate vocal response.

These results are hardly adequate in
comparison to those that are regularly ob-

tained in highly controlled laboratory studies.
They are by no means inadequate, however,
for the conditions that exist in an unprotected,
free-field study in which many possibly
important variables are not under the experimenter's control. For example, in Sessions
3, 4 and 5, the subject's medication for the
control of seizures was being adjusted and
she was extremely drowsy. Similarly, the
final experiment of this series in which only
echoic behavior would have been reinforced
has been delayed by an experimentally-
irrelevant situation. These are the conditions,
however, under which a good deal of beginning experimental work in applying behavior principles to human beings may have
to be done.

On the other hand, the gains are not
small. We have taken what might be called
a psychological "terminal case" and in a relatively brief period, as clinical time is measured, altered her mute, antisocial behavior
in the direction of spontaneous vocalizations
under the control of adult vocal stimuli and
a first approximation to true echoic behavior.
We have no doubt that additional gains can
be made with this child and that the procedures described are worthy of additional
study with other mute children.

SUMMARY

Attempts to modify or remove behavioral deficits of handicapped children need
not wait upon full and precise diagnosis. A
case study was presented in which an effort
was made to establish the conditions under
which a mute, three-year-old child—who
had other serious physical handicaps and
behavioral deficits of unknown origin and
scope—could exhibit the precursor to imitative behavior; namely, to make a sound
within a short interval after the experimenter
had made a sound.

Applying the general behavioral principle of reinforcement for an appropriate
response, the child learned to vocalize freely
after two hours of intermittent exposure to

the reinforcement contingency. A strong tendency to cease vocalizing in response to the experimenter's vocalizations was altered by a fading-in procedure. An additional four and one-half hours of operant conditioning therapy was sufficient to establish the experimenter's vocalizations as an S^D to which the child gave a quick response 60 percent of the time by making a vocalization of her own. Additional progress in this case and applicability of the procedures to other cases of muteness were predicted.

REFERENCES

SKINNER, B. F. *Verbal behavior.* New York: Appleton, 1957.
KERR, NANCY, and L. MEYERSON. *Learning theory and rehabilitation.* New York: Random House, Inc., 1964.

50 AN APPLICATION OF CONDITIONING TECHNIQUES TO THE CONTROL OF A HYPERACTIVE CHILD

Gerald R. Patterson[1]

This report describes a technique for controlling the behavior of a hyperactive child in the classroom setting. Social and nonsocial reinforcers were used to increase the rate of occurrence of a broad class of behaviors appropriate to a classroom setting. The data show that this procedure was effective in reducing the rate of occurrence of behaviors inappropriate to the classroom.

The ubiquitous presence of an activity variable is shown in the earlier factor analytic work of Baldwin (1948), Walker's (1962) observation of nursery school behaviors, and both Patterson (1964) and Dreger and Dreger's analysis (1962) of children's disturbed behavior. High rates of activity in the behavior of children are one of the most frequent complaints made by adults in referring children to child out-

[1] The writer gratefully acknowledges the patient cooperation of the staff at the Malabon School for permitting the introduction of these rather unusual procedures into the classroom setting. Many of the actual procedures were worked out and modified as a result of discussions with I. Hunter, Dr. J. Straughan, and R. Lane; Hunter and Lane also served as experimenters.

patient clinics, Patterson (1955). This would suggest that hyperactive behavior represents a highly aversive state of affairs to the adult. Taken together, these findings indicate that the control of hyperactive behavior in children should be a problem of major concern to the child psychologist.

Extreme variations in activity level are of further interest because of its association with both anoxic births, Parmelee (1962), Graham, Ernhart, Thurston, and Croft (1962) and with premature births, Shirely (1939), Knobloch and Pasamanick (1962), Dunn, Levine, and New, (1958). For these children, the assumption has been that the high rate of activity is a function of some unspecified neurological damage. In the presence of these antecedents, the suggested techniques for controlling hyperactive behavior have been either the administration of drugs or reducing the amount of external stimulation presented to the child.

This latter approach is best summarized in the publication by Strauss and Lehtinen (1950). Their dual approach of reducing sensory input and "educating the child in self control" is also reflected in the contemporary writings of Stone (1960), Bradley (1957), and Hareng and Phillips (1962).

Many of the responses that characterize the hyperactive child are not, in and of themselves, aversive. The aversive characteristic, however, is inherent in the extremely high rate of emission of these behaviors. The conditioning procedures described below are based upon the assumption that, regardless of etiology, hyperactive behaviors can be controlled by the application of general principles from learning theories outlined by Skinner (1958), and by Guthrie (1935). In this application, it is assumed that both environmental and internal stimuli have become conditioned elicitors of such behaviors as: squirming, looking "around," pinching, tapping, and walking about the room. Theoretically, it should be possible to condition a set of responses to these same stimulus matrices that would interfere with the occurrence of these "hyperactive behaviors." In the classroom setting, such interference could be achieved by strengthening any one of a number of appropriate "attending" responses such as: looking at the book, looking at the arithmetic problem, or listening to the teacher. Because of the relatively high strength of the "hyperactive" behaviors, it is necessary to introduce a procedure for strengthening the associations among the stimuli present in the classroom setting and the "interfering" responses. Skinner (1958) and other theorists would place particular emphasis upon the necessity of making reinforcing stimuli contingent upon the occurrence of these responses. In addition, the latency between the occurrence of one of these desirable responses and the occurrence of the reinforcing stimulus must be very short. For the present application, the reinforcer must also be dispensed in such a way as to provide the least amount of disruption for the other children in the classroom. The apparatus and procedure for providing these contingencies are described below. Data is also presented showing the effect of this procedure in controlling the behavior of a hyperactive boy.

METHOD

The Subject

Earl was a nine-year-old boy in the second grade. He was referred to the University Psychology Clinic because of marked hyperactive behavior and academic retardation. He was described as being in almost continuous motion in the classroom and impossible to control unless he was in the immediate presence of the teacher. Easily distracted, he would work upon his lessons for only short periods of time and then leave his desk to wander about the classroom. Occasionally he would literally move his desk "through" the classroom, scattering children and desks as he did so. Frequently his behavior was aggressive. For no apparent reason he would hit, pinch, or hurtle himself into a group of children and as a consequence demolish the group. Although the other children occasionally found these behaviors amusing, by and large they avoided him.

Previous to his adoption, at the age of three, he had been treated with extreme brutality by his natural parents, and later by the grandparents. His medical records show a skull fracture received when he was less than one year of age. At the age of four he was referred for a neurological examination because of reoccurring convulsions and some minor incoordination. The subsequent medical report indicated an abnormal EEG and pneumoencephalogram; these taken in conjunction with other neurological signs led to the diagnosis of minimal brain damage. Psychological tests given to Earl when he was eight showed him to be of borderline intelligence and also indicated some significant perceptual motor impairments on the Bender Gestalt.

His parents, by adoption, were dedicated in their care of this child and eventually achieved some control over his behavior when he was in the home. This was achieved by the mother's constant surveillance and by her ability to anticipate situations that would elicit uncontrolled behavior.

Procedures

After several hours of observing Earl's behavior both at home and in the school, it was decided that most of his "hyperactivity" could be described by the inappropriate occurrence of the following behaviors: talking, pushing, hitting, pinching, looking about the room, looking out of the window, moving out of location (walking or moving desk), and moving in location (tapping, squirming, handling objects).

The frequency of occurrence of each of these responses was tabulated for each thirty second interval. During this interval, a tabulation was made for each second during which a response persisted. For example, if Earl were walking about the room (when he was supposed to be studying) he received one check for each second during which he was walking.

Prior to each conditioning session, Earl was observed for twenty minutes to establish a baseline rate of estimate for the occurrence of the undesirable behaviors. The estimate of rate was calculated by dividing the total number of tabulations by the number of minutes during which the observations were made.

Following the tabulation of the baseline observations, a conditioning session was initiated. The amount of time directly involved in the conditioning sessions varied somewhat from one day to the next. The first conditioning trial lasted five minutes. By the end of the fifteen sessions, the time interval had been extended to twenty or thirty minutes. The observation data described above were also tabulated during the conditioning session. The data were collected by three experimenters who worked on alternate days, and were collected at roughly the same time on each day (10:30) over a four week period.

The apparatus consisted of a small box six by eight by five inches. A small flashlight bulb was mounted on top of the box; the dial of an electric counter could also be observed in the top of the box. The light and counter were controlled by the experimenter who sat across the room from Earl. Before the conditioning trials began, Earl was given several short trial runs with the apparatus. During the pretraining sessions, Earl was given a book to look at. During each ten second interval when only "attend-

ing" behaviors occurred, the light would flash on, the counter click, and the experimenter deposited one M&M candy on the desk. It was explained to Earl that each time the light went on in the trials that would follow it meant he had "earned" one candy or one penny. The counter would keep score for him and he would get the candy or pennies at the end of each "lesson."

At the beginning of the first conditioning trial the following instructions were given to the class, in Earl's presence.

Earl has some trouble in learning things here in school because he is always moving around. This is a magic teaching machine that is going to teach Earl to sit still so that he can learn like other children. Each time that the light flashes on it means that Earl has been sitting still. It also means that he has earned one piece of candy (penny). The counter here will keep score. At the end of the lesson we will take the candy (pennies) and divide it up among all of you. If you want to help Earl earn the candy you can do so by not paying any attention to him when he is 'working.'

The classroom situations during which the conditioning was carried out varied from silent reading and art work at the desk, reading or arithmetic in small groups, and class recitation.

During the conditioning sessions, an average of 60 to 100 reinforcers were dispensed by the experimenter. During the initial conditioning sessions, M&M candies were used; during later sessions the candy was alternated with pennies as reinforcers.

It should be noted, however, that the peer group proved to be a source of social reinforcers that undoubtedly had some effect upon Earl's behavior. For example, at the end of each conditioning session when the score was announced to the class, they would typically applaud Earl for his performance earnings. They also frequently walked by his desk and peered at the counter to see how well he was doing. During breaks in the classroom routine, for example at recess, the experimenters overheard frequent comments such as, "You sure are doing good; you get better every day." There seems little reason to deny that these reinforcers had some effect; in fact, the procedure was structured in such a way as to maximize the possibility of their occurrence.

RESULTS

There was a significant decrease in the number of responses per minute when comparing the base operant with the conditioning scores. The average drop of 8.4 responses per minute was significant at p less than .01 level.

It was, of course, of prime importance to show that Earl's behavior was affected during the conditioning trials. It is of even greater interest to note that some of the stimuli associated with the conditioning procedure acquired the status of a discriminative stimulus. In this case, the presence of the experimenter in the classroom served to elicit attending behaviors. In the initial conditioning trials, there would be a brief reduction in the overall rate of activity during the first few minutes of the experimenter's entering the classroom and making his baseline observations. As the trials progressed, the duration of these periods increased as shown in Figure 1 below.

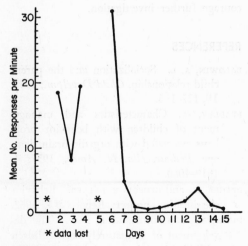

FIGURE I   The experimenter as a discriminative stimulus.

These data show that the presence of the experimenter is operating as a discriminative stimulus that elicits attending (non-hyperactive) behaviors. Toward the end of the experiment, the writer observed Earl for a two hour period in which he was the "best behaved child in the class." Observations of three other boys (twenty minutes each) showed a mean of 3.2 responses per minute (same behaviors being recorded for each). Earl's behavior toward the end of the conditioning compares very well with this figure.

Because of the fact that school had closed it was not possible to continue this experiment. At the end of the series of trials, the teacher reported that he was not as hyperactive and destructive on the playground and that he seemed to actually "play with other children" rather than hurtle himself at them. She felt that there was some minor reduction in his over-all behavior rate in the classroom, but at this point she was much more concerned with his continued difficulty in learning than with his classroom adjustment. Her report could not be taken as support for the hope that the behavior control manifest in the presence of the experimenter characterized his behavior during the remainder of the day.

A telephone call to the parents four months after the study indicated that the teachers in the school reported him to be much "quieter." For the first time, other children come to his home to play, and he is making progress in a remedial reading program.

DISCUSSION

These data offer support for the hypothesis that it is in fact possible to manipulate "high rate" behaviors occurring in the classroom setting. There is little doubt that, however effective they are, the present procedures are rather crude. Our preliminary experience with the procedure suggests several changes that would make the application more efficient.

The major problem in this (all) application of conditioning procedures is to ensure generalization from the conditioning periods to behavior occurring outside of the conditioning sessions. The concept of stimulus generalization would suggest that the conditioning sessions should occur in as wide a variety of stimulus settings as possible. Presumably such a sampling of settings would ensure a wider range of stimuli which would be conditioned to the "attending behaviors." In Earl's case, the conditioning periods occurred at the same time of day and typically involved his participation in only a limited number of activities. Generalization would have been more likely to occur if the conditioning sessions were distributed throughout the day.

The "teaching machine" used in the present study also introduces some severe limitations upon the settings in which conditioning can be carried out. It was necessary, because of these limitations, to carry out the conditioning procedures only when Earl was seated at his desk. This would mean that none of the settings in which free movement can occur, that is, recess, can be used for conditioning purposes. Because of the undoubted importance of sampling social stimuli arising from this type of interaction, a new apparatus has been developed for research now underway. This is a radio control device which can dispense an auditory stimulus through a microphone in the child's ear even though he is sixty yards distant from the experimenter. With this improved apparatus, conditioning can take place in almost any social setting; presumably this greater flexibility will enhance the generalization.

In the last two conditioning trials, a procedure was introduced which would also tend to increase the spread of effect. This procedure involved the introduction of a type of discrimination learning paradigm. It was assumed that greater behavior change would occur if the child were first taught to use appropriate labels in describing behaviors inappropriate to the classroom setting. As a second step he was to be taught the contingencies holding between the occur-

rence of these behaviors and reinforcers. Earl was presented with a clip board and told to observe his classmates. Whenever he observed any of the following behaviors he was to first identify it (verbally) and then make a check upon the data sheet: talking, walking around, not listening to the teacher, squirming, tapping, or staring out the window. On each occasion in which he correctly labeled such behavior the light on the teaching machine was activated. Of all of the procedures attempted, Earl was undoubtedly most enthusiastic about this one. His dedication to locating behavioral sins made the policeman, Javert, of *Les Miserables* apathetic by comparison. Because the experiment was terminated, there is no way of knowing whether this process generalized to Earl's labeling his own behavior or to his learning to discriminate among behaviors that lead to rewards.

It is quite clear that the present procedure seriously confounds the effect of several experimental variables. There is no way of identifying which of the following variables produced the effect: candy and pennies as reinforcer, social approval dispensed by the peer group as a reinforcer, preliminary attempts at discrimination training. Better controlled studies, now under way, will attempt to identify the relative contribution of each of these variables. For the present, however, these preliminary results seem to encourage further investigation.

REFERENCES

BALDWIN, A. L. Socialization and the parent child relationship. *Child Develpm.*, 1948, **19**, 127–136.

BRADLEY, C. Characteristics and management of children with behavior problems associated with organic brain damage. *Pediatr. clin. N. Amer.*, 1957, **4**, 1019–1060.

DREGER, R., and GEORGIA E. DREGER. Behavior classification project: Report #1, 1962.

DUNN, M., S. LEVINE and E. NEW. The development of prematurely born children with birth weights or minimal post natal weights of 1000 grams or less. *Pediatrics,* 1958, **22,** 1037–1053.

GRAHAM, F. K., CLAIRE B. ERNHART, D. THURSTON, and MARGUERITE CROFT. Development three years after perinatal anoxia and other potentially damaging newborn experiences. *Psychol. Monogr.,* 1962, **76.** (3, Whole No. 522).

GUTHRIE, E. R. *The psychology of learning.* New York: Harper & Row, 1935.

HARENG, N. and E. L. PHILLIPS. *Educating emotionally disturbed children.* New York: McGraw-Hill, 1962.

KNOBLOCH, HILDA, and B. PASAMANICK. The developmental behavioral approach to the neurologic examination in infancy. *Child Develpm.,* 1962, **33,** 181–198.

PARMELLE, A. H. European neurological studies of the newborn. *Child Develpm.,* 1962, **33,** 169–180.

PATTERSON, G. R. A tentative approach to the classification of children's behavior problems. Unpublished doctoral dissertation. University of Minnesota, 1955.

PATTERSON, G. R. An empirical approach to the classification of disturbed children. *J. clin. Psychol.,* 1964, **20,** 326–337.

SHIRELY, MAY. A behavior syndrome characterizing prematurely-born children. *Child Develpm.,* 1939, **10,** 115–128.

SKINNER, B. F. *Science and human behavior.* New York: Macmillan, 1958.

STONE, F. H. Psychodynamics of brain-damaged children: a preliminary report. *J. child psychol. Psychiatr.,* 1960, **1,** 203–214.

STRAUSS, A. A., and L. LEHTINEN. *Psychopathology and education of the brain-injured child.* New York: Grune & Stratton, 1950.

WALKER, R. N. Body build and behavior in young children. *Monogr. Soc. Res. Child Develpm.,* 1962, **27,** No. 3.

REFERENCES

ADAMS, H. E., J. R. BUTLER, and C. D. NOBLIN. Effects of psychoanalytically-derived interpretations: a verbal conditioning paradigm? *Psychol. Rep.,* 1962, **10,** 691–694.

ALEXANDER, F., and T. M. FRENCH. *Psychoanalytic therapy.* New York: Ronald, 1946.

AMERICAN PSYCHIATRIC ASSOCIATION. *Diagnostic and statistical manual of mental disorders.* Washington, D.C.: Author, 1952.

APTER, I. N. On the psychotherapy of psychogenic impotence. In R. B. Winn (Ed.), *Psychotherapy in the Soviet Union.* New York: Philosophical Library, Inc., 1961.

ASH, P. The reliability of psychiatric diagnoses. *J. abnorm. soc. Psychol.,* 1949, **44,** 272–276.

ASHEM, B. The treatment of disaster phobia by systematic desensitization. *Behav. Res. Ther.,* 1963, **1,** 81–84.

ASTIN, A. W. The functional autonomy of psychotherapy. *Amer. Psychologist,* 1961, **16,** 75–78.

AYLLON, T., and E. HAUGHTON. Control of the behavior of schizophrenic patients by food. *J. exp. Anal. Behav.,* 1962, **5,** 343–352.

AYLLON, T., and E. HAUGHTON. Modification of symptomatic verbal behavior of mental patients. *Behav. Res. Ther.,* 1964, **2,** 87–97.

BACHRACH, A. J. (Ed.) *Experimental foundations of clinical psychology.* New York: Basic Books, 1962.

BANDURA, A. Psychotherapist's anxiety level, self-insight and psychotherapeutic competence. *J. abnorm. soc. Psychol.,* 1956, **52,** 333–337.

BANDURA, A. Psychotherapy as a learning process. *Psychol. Bull.,* 1961, **58,** 143–159.

BANDURA, A. Behavioral modification through modeling procedures. In L. Krasner, and L. P. Ullmann (Eds.), *Research in behavior modification.* New York: Holt, Rinehart and Winston, Inc., 1965.

BANDURA, A., D. H. LIPSHER, and PAULA E. MILLER. Psychotherapists' approach-avoidance reactions to patients' expressions of hostility. *J. consult. Psychol.,* 1960, **24,** 1–8.

BANDURA, A., and R. H. WALTERS. *Social learning and personality development.* New York: Holt, Rinehart and Winston. Inc., 1963.

BANGS, J. L., and A. FREIDINGER. Diagnosis and treatment of a case of hysterical aphonia in a thirteen-year-old girl. *J. speech hearing Dis.,* 1949, **14,** 312–317.

BANGS, J. L., and A. FREIDINGER. A case of hysterical dysphonia in an adult. *J. speech hearing Dis.,* 1950, **15,** 316–323.

BARBER, T. X., and L. B. GLASS. Significant factors in hypnotic behavior. *J. abnorm. soc. Psychol.,* 1962, **64,** 222–228.

BARNETT, C. D., MARGARET W. PRYER, and N. R. ELLIS. Experimental manipulation of verbal behavior in defectives. *Psychol. Rep.,* 1959, **5,** 593–596.

BEECH, H. R. The symptomatic treatment of writer's cramp. In H. J. Eysenck (Ed.), *Behaviour therapy and the neuroses.* New York: Pergamon, 1960, 349–372.

BELKNAP, I. *Human problems of a state mental hospital.* New York: McGraw-Hill, 1956.

BERG, I. A., and B. M. BASS (Eds.) *Conformity and deviation.* New York: Harper & Row, 1961.

BERGER, S. M. Incidental learning through vicarious reinforcement. *Psychol. Rep.,* 1961, **9**, 477–491.

BEVAN, J. R. Learning theory applied to the treatment of a patient with obsessional ruminations. In H. J. Eysenck (Ed.), *Behaviour therapy and the neuroses.* New York: Pergamon, 1960, 165–169.

BIDERMAN, A. A., and H. ZIMMER (Eds.) *The manipulation of human behavior.* New York: Wiley, 1961.

BIJOU, S. W. Theory and research in mental (developmental) retardation. *Psychol. Rec.,* 1963, **13**, 95–110.

BIJOU, S. W. Experimental studies of child behavior, normal and deviant. In L. Krasner and L. P. Ullmann (Eds.) *Research in Behavior Modification.* New York: Holt, Rinehart and Winston, Inc., 1965.

BIJOU, S. W., and BARBARA OBLINGER. Responses of normal and retarded children as a function of the experimental situation. *Psychol. Rep.,* 1960, **6**, 447–454.

BIJOU, S. W., and R. ORLANDO. Rapid development of multiple-schedule performances with retarded children. *J. exp. Anal. Behav.,* 1961, **4**, 7–16.

BLACKER, K. H., and G. C. STONE. Adaptation of operant conditioning techniques for use with mental patients: 1. Exploratory studies. *Calif. Ment. Health,* 1963, **1**, 3, 32–33.

BLAKEMORE, C. B., J. G. THORPE, J. C. BARKER, C. G. CONWAY, and N. T. LAVIN. The application of faradic aversion conditioning in a case of transvestism. *Behav. Res. Ther.,* 1963, **1**, 29–34. (a)

BLAKEMORE, C. B., J. G. THORPE, J. C. BARKER, C. G. CONWAY, and N. T. LAVIN. Follow up note to: the application of faradic aversion conditioning in the case of transvestism. *Behav. Res. Ther.,* 1963, **1**, 191. (b)

BOCKOVEN, J. S. *Moral treatment in American psychiatry.* New York: Springer Publishing Co., 1963.

BRACKBILL, YVONNE. Extinction of the smiling response in infants as a function of reinforcement schedule. *Child Develpm.,* 1958, **29**, 115–124.

BRONFENBRENNER, U. Soviet methods of character education: some implications for research. *Amer. Psychologist,* 1962, **17**, 550–564.

BROUSSEAU, KATE. The effect of suggestion on a case of traumatic hysteria. *J. abnorm. Psychol.,* 1923, **17**, 346–349.

BURNHAM, W. H. *The normal mind.* New York: Appleton, 1924.

CAMERON, N. A. *Personality development and psychopathology.* Boston: Houghton Mifflin, 1963.

CASE, H. W. Therapeutic methods in stuttering and speech blocking. In H. J. Eysenck (Ed.), *Behaviour therapy and the neuroses.* New York: Pergamon, 1960, 207–220.

CHERRY, C., and B. MCA. SAYERS. Experiments upon the total inhibition of stammering by external control, and some clinical results. *J. psychosom. Res.,* 1956, **1**, 233–246. (In Eysenck, 1960a).

CLARK, D. F. The treatment of monosymptomatic phobia by systematic desensitization. *Behav. Res. Ther.,* 1963, **1**, 63–68. (a)

CLARK, D. F. The treatment of hysterical spasm and agoraphobia by behaviour therapy. *Behav. Res. Ther.,* 1963, **1**, 245–250. (b)

CLARK, D. F. Fetishism treated by negative conditioning. *Brit. J. Psychiat.,* 1963, **109**, 404–407. (c)

COLBY, K. M. Things to come: designing neurotic computers. In L. Krasner, and L. P. Ullmann (Eds.), *Research in behavior modification*. New York: Holt, Rinehart and Winston, Inc., 1965.

COLEMAN, J. C.   *Abnormal psychology and modern life* (2nd ed.). Chicago: Scott, Foresman, 1956.

COOPER, A. J.   A case of bronchial asthma treated by behaviour therapy. *Behav. Res. Ther.,* 1964, **1**, 351–356.

COOPER, J. E.   A study of behaviour therapy in thirty psychiatric patients. *Lancet,* 1963, **1**, 411–415.

COSTELLO, C. G.   Behaviour therapy: criticisms and confusions. *Behav. Res. Ther.,* 1963, **1**, 159–161.

COSTELLO, C. G.   LSD as an adjunct to behavior therapy: treatment of a case of claustrophobia. Unpublished manuscript, 1964.

CRADDICK, R. A., and M. R. STERN.   Verbal conditioning: the effect of partial reinforcement upon the recall of early memories. *J. abnorm. soc. Psychol.,* 1964, **68**, 353–355.

CURRAN, D., and M. PARTRIDGE.   *Psychological medicine: a short introduction to psychiatry.* (4th ed.) Baltimore: Williams and Wilkins, 1955.

DAILEY, C. A.   An experimental method for improving interpersonal understanding. *Psychol. Rep.,* 1963, **13**, 240.

DAVIDSON, J. R., and E. DOUGLASS.   Nocturnal enuresis: a special approach to treatment. *Brit. Med. J.,* 1950, **1**, 1345–1347.

DINOFF, M., R. F. HORNER, B. S. KURPIEWSKI, H. C. RICKARD, and E. O. TIMMONS.   Conditioning verbal behavior of a psychiatric population in a group therapy-like situation. *J. clin. Psychol.,* 1960, **16**, 371–372.

DINOFF, M., H. C. RICKARD, H. SALZBERG, and C. N. SIPPRELLE.   An experimental analogue of three psychotherapeutic approaches. *J. clin. Psychol.,* 1960, **16**, 70–73.

DOLLARD, J., and N. E. MILLER.   *Personality and psychotherapy.* New York: McGraw-Hill, 1950.

DREGER, R. M., P. M. LEWIS, T. A. RICH, K. S. MILLER, M. P. REID, D. C. OVERLADE, C. TAFFEL, and E. L. FLEMMING.   Behavioral classification project. *J. consult. Psychol.* 1964, **28**, 1–13.

DUNHAM, H. W., and S. K. WEINBERG.   *The culture of the state mental hospital.* Detroit: Wayne State University Press, 1960.

DUNLAP, K.   A revision of the fundamental law of habit formation. *Science,* 1928, **67**, 360–362.

DUNLAP, K.   Repetition in the breaking of habits. *Scient. Mo.,* 1930, **30**, 66–70.

DUNLAP, K.   *Habits: their making and unmaking.* New York: Liveright, 1932.

DUNLAP, K.   *Personal adjustment.* New York: McGraw-Hill, 1946.

EFRON, R.   The conditioned inhibition of uncinate fits. *Brain.* 1957, **80**, 251–262.

EKMAN, P.   A comparison of verbal and nonverbal behavior as reinforcing stimuli of opinion responses. Unpublished doctoral dissertation, Adelphi College, 1958.

EKMAN, P.   Body position, facial expression and verbal behavior during interviews. *J. abnorm. soc. Psychol.,* 1964, **68**, 295–301. (a)

EKMAN, P.   Judgements of body position and facial expression. Paper presented to West. Psychol. Assoc., Portland, Oregon, April, 1964. (b)

ELLIS, A.   *Reason and emotion in psychotherapy.* New York: Lyle Stuart, Inc., 1962.

ELLIS, A.   *The theory and practice of rational-emotive psychotherapy.* New York: Lyle Stuart, Inc., 1964.

ELLIS, N. R.   Amount of reward and operant behavior in mental defectives. *Amer. J. ment. Defic.,* 1962, **66**, 595–599.

ELLIS, N. R., C. D. BARNETT, and MARGARET W. PRYER.   Operant behavior in mental defectives: exploratory studies. *J. exp. Anal. Behav.,* 1960, **3**, 63–69.

ELLIS, N. R. and MARGARET W. PRYER.   Primary versus secondary reinforcement in simple discrimination learning of mental defectives. *Psychol. Rep.,* 1958, **4**, 67–70.

ENGLISH, H. B., and AVA C. ENGLISH. *A comprehensive dictionary of psychological and psycho-analytical terms: a guide to usage.* New York: Longmans, 1958.

EYSENCK, H. J. The effects of psychotherapy: an evaluation. *J. consult. Psychol.,* 1952, **16,** 319–324.

EYSENCK, H. J. Learning theory and behaviour therapy. *J. ment. Sci.,* 1959, **105,** 61–75. (In Eysenck, 1960a)

EYSENCK, H. J. (Ed.) *Behaviour therapy and the neuroses.* New York: Pergamon, 1960. (a)

EYSENCK, H. J. Personality and behaviour therapy. *Proc. royal Soc. Med.,* 1960, **53,** 504–508. (b)

EYSENCK, H. J. The effects of psychotherapy. In H. J. Eysenck (Ed.), *Handbook of abnormal psychology.* New York: Basic Books, 1961, 697–725.

EYSENCK, H. J. Conditioning and personality. *Brit. J. Psychol.,* 1962, **53,** 299–305.

EYSENCK, H. J. Behaviour therapy, spontaneous remission and transference in neurotics. *Amer. J. Psychiat.,* 1963, **119,** 867–871. (a)

EYSENCK, H. J. Behaviour therapy, extinction and relapse in neurosis. *Brit. J. Psychiat.,* 1963, **109,** 12–18. (b)

FENICHEL, O. *The psychoanalytic theory of neurosis.* New York: Norton, 1945.

FERSTER, C. B., J. I. NURNBERGER, and E. B. LEVITT. The control of eating. *J. Mathetics,* 1962, **1,** 87–109.

FIEDLER, F. E. Quantitative studies on the role of the therapists' feelings toward their patients. In O. H. Mowrer (Ed.), *Psychotherapy: theory and research.* New York: Ronald, 1953, 296–315.

FLANAGAN, B., I. GOLDIAMOND, and N. H. AZRIN. Instatement of stuttering in normally fluent individuals through operant procedures. *Science,* 1959, **130,** 979–981.

FLETCHER, J. M. An experimental study of stuttering. *Amer. J. Psychol.,* 1914, **25,** 201–252.

FLETCHER, J. M. *The problem of stuttering.* New York: Longmans, 1928.

FRANK, J. D. *Persuasion and healing.* Baltimore: Johns Hopkins Press, 1961.

FRANKS, C. M. Alcohol, alcoholism and conditioning: a review of the literature and some theoretical considerations. *J. ment. Sci.,* 1958, **104,** 14–33. (In Eysenck, 1960a)

FRANKS, C. M. Conditioning and abnormal behaviour. In H. J. Eysenck (Ed.), *Handbook of abnormal psychology.* New York: Basic Books, 1961, 457–487.

FREEMAN, H. L., and D. C. KENDRICK. A case of cat phobia: treatment by a method derived from experimental psychology. *Brit. med. J.,* 1960, **2,** 497–502.

FRENCH, T. M. Interrelations between psychoanalysis and the experimental work of Pavlov. *Amer. J. Psychiat.,* 1933, **12,** 1165–1203.

FREUND, K. Some problems in the treatment of homosexuality. In H. J. Eysenck (Ed.), *Behaviour therapy and the neuroses.* New York: Pergamon, 1960, 312–326.

FREUND, K. A laboratory method for diagnosing predominance of homo- or hetero-erotic interest in the male. *Behav. Res. Ther.,* 1963, **1,** 85–93.

GEHRING, J. G. *The hope of the variant.* New York: Scribner, 1893.

GEPPERT, T. V. Management of nocturnal enuresis by conditioned response. *J. Amer. med. Ass.,* 1953, **152,** 381–383.

GLYNN, J. D., and P. HARPER. Behaviour therapy in transvestism. *Lancet,* 1961, **1,** 619.

GOFFMAN, E. *Asylums.* New York: Anchor Books, 1961.

GOLDIAMOND, I. The maintenance of ongoing fluent verbal behavior and stuttering. *J. Mathetics,* 1962, **1,** 57–95.

GOLDIAMOND, I. *Stuttering and fluency as maniputable operant response classes.* In L. Krasner, and L. P. Ullmann (Eds.), *Research in behavior modification.* New York: Holt, Rinehart and Winston, Inc., 1965.

GOLDSTEIN, A. P.   *Therapist-patient expectancies in psychotherapy.* New York: Pergamon, 1962.

GORDOVA, T. N., and N. K. KOVALEVE.   Unique factors in the hypnotic treatment of chronic alcoholism. In R. B. Winn (Ed.), *Psychotherapy in the Soviet Union.* New York: Philosophical Library, Inc., 1961, 136–140.

GROSSBERG, J. M.   Behavior therapy: a review. *Psychol. Bull.,* 1964, **62**, 73–88.

GUTHRIE, E. R.   The psychology of human conflict. New York: Harper & Row, 1938.

HABERMAN, J. V.   Probing the mind, normal and abnormal. First report. Feeling, association, and the psychoreflex. *Medical Records,* 1917, **92**, 927–933.

HAUGEN, G. B., H. H. DIXON, and H. A. DICKEL.   *A therapy for anxiety tension reactions.* New York: Macmillan, 1958.

HAYES, K. J.   Genes, drives, and intellect. *Psychol. Rep.,* 1962, **10**, 299–342.

HEFFERLINE, R. F.   Learning theory and clinical psychology—an eventual symbiosis? In A. J. Bachrach (Ed.), *Experimental foundations of clinical psychology.* New York: Basic Books, 1962, 97–138.

HEILBRUNN, G.   Results with psychoanalytic therapy. *Amer. J. Psychother.,* 1963, **17**, 427–435.

HELLER, K., R. A. MYERS, and LINDA V. KLINE.   Interviewer behavior as a function of standardized client roles. *J. consult. Psychol.,* 1963, **27**, 117–122.

HERRON, W. G.   The process-reactive classification of schizophrenia. *Psychol. Bull.,* 1962, **59**, 329–343.

HERZBERG, A.   Short treatment of neuroses by graduated tasks. *Brit. J. med. Psychol.,* 1941, **19**, 36–51.

HILGARD, E. R.   *Introduction to psychology* (3rd ed.). New York: Harcourt, 1962.

HILGARD, E. R., and D. G. MARQUIS.   *Conditioning and learning.* New York: Appleton, 1940.

HOLLINGSHEAD, A. B., and F. C. REDLICH.   *Social class and mental illness.* New York: Wiley, 1958.

HOLLINGWORTH, H. L.   *Abnormal psychology.* New York: Ronald, 1930.

HOLZ, W. C., N. H. AZRIN, and T. AYLLON.   Elimination of behavior of mental patients by response-produced extinction. *J. exp. Anal. Behav.,* 1963, **6**, 407–412.

HOMME, L. E., P. C. DEBACA, J. V. DEVINE, R. STEINHORST, and E. J. RICKERT.   Use of the Premack principle in controlling the behavior of nursery school children. *J. exp. Anal. Behav.,* 1963, **6**, 544.

HUTT, M. L., and R. G. GIBBY.   *Patterns of abnormal behavior.* Boston: Allyn and Bacon, 1957.

HUXLEY, A.   *Brave New World.* New York: Harper and Row, 1932.

JACOBSON, E.   *Progressive relaxation.* Chicago: University of Chicago Press, 1938.

JAMES, B.   Case of homosexuality treated by aversion therapy. *Brit. med. J.,* 1962, **1**, 768–770.

JERSILD, A. T., and FRANCES B. HOLMES.   Methods of overcoming children's fears. *J. Psychol.,* 1935, **1**, 75–104.

JONES, E.   *The life and work of Sigmund Freud. Vol. I.* New York: Basic Books, 1953.

JONES, H. G.   Continuation of Yates' treatment of a tiqueur. In H. J. Eysenck (Ed.), *Behaviour therapy and the neuroses.* New York: Pergamon, 1960, 250–256. (a)

JONES, H. G.   The behavioural treatment of enuresis nocturna. In H. Eysenck (Ed.), *Behaviour therapy and the neuroses.* New York: Pergamon, 1960, 377–403. (b)

JONES, MARY C.   The elimination of children's fears. *J. exp. Psychol.,* 1924, **7**, 382–390. (In Eysenck, 1960a). (a)

JONES, MARY C.   A laboratory study of fear: the case of Peter. *Ped. Sem.,* 1924, **31**, 308–315. (In Eysenck, 1960a). (b)

JOURARD, S. M.   I—thou relationship versus manipulation in counseling and psychotherapy. *J. indiv. Psychol.,* 1959, **15**, 174–179.

KALISH, H. I. Behavior therapy. In B. B. Wolman (Ed.), *Handbook of clinical psychology.* New York: McGraw-Hill, in press.

KANFER, F. H. Vicarious human reinforcements: a glimpse into the black box. In L. Krasner, and L. P. Ullmann (Eds.), *Research in behavior modification.* New York: Holt, Rinehart and Winston, Inc., 1965.

KANFER, F. H., and A. R. MARSTON. Human reinforcement: vicarious and direct. *J. exp. Psychol.,* 1963, **65**, 292–296.

KANTOR, R. E., J. M. WALLNER, and C. L. WINDER. Process and reactive schizophrenia. *J. consult. Psychol.,* 1953, **17**, 157–162.

KANTOROVICH, N. An attempt at associative-reflex therapy in alcoholism. *Nov. refl. fiziol. nerv. sist.,* 1929, **3**, 436–447. (*Psychol. Abstr.,* 1930, **4**, 493.)

KELLY, G. A. *The psychology of personal constructs.* New York: Norton, 1955. 2 vols.

KENDLER, H. K. *Basic psychology.* New York: Appleton, 1962.

KETY, S. S. Recent biochemical theories of schizophrenia. In D. D. Jackson (Ed.), *The etiology of schizophrenia.* New York: Basic Books, 1960.

KING, G. F. Differential autonomic responsiveness in the process-reactive classification of schizophrenia. *J. abnorm. soc. Psychol.,* 1958, **56**, 160–164.

KIRK, S. A. *Educating exceptional children.* Boston: Houghton Mifflin, 1962.

KRAINES, S. H. *The therapy of the neuroses and psychoses.* Philadelphia: Lea and Febiger, 1941.

KRASNER, L. The use of generalized reinforcers in psychotherapy research. *Psychol. Rep.* 1955, **1**, 19–25.

KRASNER, L. Studies of the conditioning of verbal behavior. *Psychol. Bull.,* 1958, **55**, 148–170. (a)

KRASNER, L. A technique for investigating the relationships between the behavior cues of the examiner and the verbal behavior of the patient. *J. consult. Psychol.,* 1958, **22**, 364–366. (b)

KRASNER, L. The therapist as a social reinforcement machine. In H. H. Strupp, and L. Luborsky (Eds.), *Research in psychotherapy.* Washington, D.C.: Amer. Psychol. Assoc., 1962, vol. 2, 61–94. (a)

KRASNER, L. Behavior control and social responsibility. *Amer. Psychologist,* 1962, **17**, 199–204. (b)

KRASNER, L. The therapist as a social reinforcer: man or machine. Paper presented to Amer. Psychol. Assoc., Philadelphia, Sept. 1963. (a)

KRASNER, L. The behavioral scientist and social responsibility: no place to hide. Paper presented to Amer. Psychol. Assoc., Philadelphia, Sept. 1963. (b)

KRASNER, L., J. B. KNOWLES, and L. P. ULLMANN. The effect of verbal conditioning of attitude on subsequent motor performance. Paper presented to Amer. Psychol., Assoc., Los Angeles, Sept. 1964.

KRASNER, L., and L. P. ULLMANN. *Research in behavior modification.* Holt, Rinehart and Winston, Inc., 1965.

KRASNER, L., L. P. ULLMANN, and D. FISHER. Changes in performance as related to verbal conditioning of attitudes toward the examiner. *Percept. Motor Skills,* 1964, **19**, 811–816.

KUBIE, L. S. Relation of the conditioned reflex to psychoanalytic technic. *AMA Arch. Neurol. Psychiat.,* 1934, **32**, 1137–1142.

LANE, H. Operant control of vocalizing in the chicken. *J. exp. Anal. Behav.,* 1961, **4**, 171–177.

LAVIN, N. I., J. G. THORPE, J. C. BARKER, C. B. BLAKEMORE, and C. G. CONWAY. Behavior therapy in a case of transvestism. *J. nerv. ment. Dis.,* 1961, **133**, 346–353.

LAZARUS, A. A. New methods in psychotherapy: a case study. *S. Afr. med. J.*, 1958, **32**, 660–664.

LAZARUS, A. A. The elimination of children's phobias by deconditioning. *Med. Proc. S. Afr.*, 1959, **5**, 261–265. (In Eysenck, 1960a)

LAZARUS, A. A. Sensory deprivation under hypnosis in the treatment of pervasive ("free-floating") anxiety: a preliminary impression. *S. Afr. med. J.*, 1963, **37**, 136–139. (a)

LAZARUS, A. A. The results of behaviour therapy in 126 cases of severe neurosis. *Behav. Res. Ther.*, 1963, **1**, 69–79. (b)

LAZARUS, A. A. The treatment of chronic frigidity by systematic desensitization. *J. nerv. ment. Dis.*, 1963, **136**, 272–278. (c)

LAZARUS, A. A. Behaviour therapy with identical twins. *Behav. Res. Ther.*, 1964, **1**, 313–319.

LAZARUS, A. A., and S. RACHMAN. The use of systematic desensitization in psychotherapy. *S. Afr. med. J.*, 1957, **31**, 934–937. (In Eysenck, 1960a.)

LEHNER, G. F. Negative practice as a psychotherapeutic technique. *J. gen. Psychol.*. 1954, **51**, 69–82.

LEHRMAN, N. S. Do our hospitals help make acute schizophrenia chronic? *Dis. nerv. Syst.*, 1961, **22**, 489–493.

LEMERE, F., W. L. VOEGTLIN, W. R. BROZ, P. O'HALLAREN, and W. E. TUPPER. The conditioned reflex treatment of chronic alcoholism: VIII: A review of six years' experience with this treatment of 1526 patients. *J. Amer. med. Assoc.*, 1942, **120**, 269–270.

LENNARD, H. L., and A. BERNSTEIN. *The anatomy of psychotherapy*. New York: Columbia University Press, 1960.

LEVITT, E. E. The results of psychotherapy with children: an evaluation. *J. consult. Psychol.*, 1957, **21**, 189–196.

LEVITT, E. E. Psychotherapy with children: a further evaluation. *Behav. Res. Ther.*, 1963, **1**, 45–51.

LINDSLEY, O. R. Operant conditioning methods applied to research in chronic schizophrenia. *Psychiat. Res. Rep.*, 1956, **5**, 118–139.

LINDSLEY, O. R. Characteristics of the behavior of chronic psychotics as revealed by free-operant conditioning methods. *Dis. nerv. Syst.*, 1960, **21**, 66–78.

LINDSLEY, O. R. Direct measurement and functional definition of vocal hallucinatory symptoms. *J. nerv. ment. Dis.*, 1963, **136**, 293–297. (a)

LINDSLEY, O. R. Experimental analysis of social reinforcement: terms and methods. *Amer. J. Orthopsychiat.*, 1963, **33**, 624–633. (b)

LINDSLEY, O. R. Free-operant conditioning and psychotherapy. *Current psychiatric therapies.* New York: Grune and Stratton, 1963. (c)

LIVERSEDGE, L. A., and J. D. SYLVESTER. Conditioning techniques in the treatment of writer's cramp. *Lancet.* 1955, **1**, 1147–1149. (In Eysenck, 1960a)

LORR, M., D. M. MCNAIR, C. J. KLETT, and J. J. LASKY. Evidence of ten psychotic syndromes. *J. consult. Psychol.*, 1962, **26**, 185–189

LOVIBOND, S. H. The mechanism of conditioning treatment of enuresis. *Behav. Res. Ther.*, 1963, **1**, 17–21. (a)

LOVIBOND, S. H. Intermittent reinforcement in behaviour therapy. *Behav. Res. Ther.*, 1963, **1**, 127–132. (b)

LURIA, A. R. *The role of speech in the regulation of normal and abnormal behavior*. London: Pergamon, 1961.

MC REYNOLDS, P. The Rorschach concept evaluation technique. *J. proj. Tech.*, 1954, **18**, 60–74.

MC REYNOLDS, P., MARY ACKER, and J. DAILY. On the effects of perceptual enhancement on certain schizophrenic symptoms. *Res. Rept. VA Palo Alto,* 1959, No. 1.

MAKARENKO, A. S. *Road to life.* London: Stanley Nott, 1936.

MAKARENKO, A. S. *Learning to live.* Moscow: Foreign Languages Publishing House, 1953.

MALLESON, N. Panic and phobia. A possible method of treatment. *Lancet,* 1959, **1**, 225–227.

MALMO, R. B., J. F. DAVIS, and S. BARZA. Total hysterical deafness: an experimental case study. *J. Pers.,* 1952, **21**, 188–204. (In Eysenck, 1960a)

MAGARET, ANN. Generalization in successful psychotherapy. *J. consult. Psychol.,* 1950, **14**, 64–70.

MARMOR, J. Psychoanalytic therapy as an educational process. Paper presented at Academy of Psychoanalysis. Chicago, May, 1961. In J. H. Masserman (Ed.), *Psychoanalytic education.* New York: Grune and Stratton, 1962.

MASLING, J. The influence of situational and interpersonal variables in projective testing. *Psychol. Bull.,* 1960, **57**, 65–85.

MAX, L. W. Breaking up a homosexual fixation by the conditioned reaction technique: a case study. *Psychol. Bull.,* 1935, **32**, 734. (abstract).

MEDNICK, MARTHA T., and O. R. LINDSLEY. Some clinical correlates of operant behavior. *J. abnorm. soc. Psychol.,* 1958, **57**, 13–16.

MEEHL, P. E. *Clinical versus statistical prediction.* Minneapolis: University of Minnesota Press, 1954.

MEES, H. How to create a monster. Unpublished manuscript, 1964.

MERTENS, G. C. *Willmar handbook of conditioning therapy.* Willmar, Minn.: Willmar State Hospital, 1963.

MERTENS, G. C. The therapist's manual: a manual for assisting an alcoholic in his development of self-control. Willmar, Minn.: Willmar State Hospital, 1964. (a)

MERTENS, G. C. The manual for the alcoholic. Willmar, Minn.: Willmar State Hospital, 1964. (b)

MERTENS, G. C., and G. B. FULLER. Conditioning of molar behavior in "regressed" psychotics: I. An objective measure of personal habit training with "regressed" psychotics. *J. clin. Psychol.,* 1963, **19**, 333–337.

METZNER, R. Learning theory and the therapy of the neuroses. *Brit. J. Psychol.,* 1961, Monogr. Suppl. 33.

MEYER, V. The treatment of two phobic patients on the basis of learning principles: case report. *J. abnorm. soc. Psychol.,* 1957, **55**, 261–266. (In Eysenck, 1960a)

MEYER, V., and M. G. GELDER. Behaviour therapy and phobic disorders. *Brit. J. Psychiat.,* 1963, **109**, 19–28.

MEYER, V., and J. M. M. MAIR. A new technique to control stammering: a preliminary report. *Behav. Res. Ther.,* 1963, **1**, 251–254.

MICHAEL, J. Behavioral approaches to rehabilitation. Paper presented at Stanford Medical School, 1963.

MILLER, N. E., and J. DOLLARD. *Social learning and imitation.* New Haven: Yale University Press, 1941.

MOLLIVER, M. E. Operant control of vocal behavior in the cat. *J. exp. Anal. Behav.,* 1963, **6**, 197–202.

MORGAN, C. T. *Introduction to psychology.* (2nd ed.) New York: McGraw-Hill, 1961.

MORGAN, J. J. B., and FRANCES J. WITMER. The treatment of enuresis by the conditioned reaction technique. *J. genet. Psychol.,* 1939, **55**, 59–65.

MOSS, F. A. Note on building likes and dislikes in children. *J. exp. Psychol.,* 1924, **7**, 475–478.

MOWRER, O. H. *Learning theory and personality dynamics.* New York: Ronald, 1950.

MOWRER, O. H. *The new group therapy.* Princeton, N.J.: Van Nostrand, 1964.

MOWRER, O. H. Learning theory and behavior therapy. In B. B. Wolman (Ed.), *Handbook of clinical psychology.* New York: McGraw-Hill, in press.

MOWRER, O. H., and WILLIE M. MOWRER. Enuresis: a method for its study and treatment. *Amer. J. Orthopsychiat.,* 1938, **8**, 436–459.

MOWRER, O. H., and P. VIEK.   An experimental analogue of fear from a sense of helplessness. *J. abnorm. soc. Psychol.,* 1948, **43,** 193–200.

MUNN, N. L.   *Psychology.* (4th ed.) New York: Houghton Mifflin, 1961.

MURRAY, E. J.   A content-analysis method for studying psychotherapy. *Psychol. Monogr.,* 1956, **70,** 1–32, (13, whole No., 420).

MURRAY, E. J.   Direct analysis from the viewpoint of learning theory. *J. consult. Psychol.,* 1962, **26,** 226–231.

NARROL, H. G.   Toward a life-like operant technology for alcoholic rehabilitation. Unpublished manuscript, 1963.

NEALE, D. H.   Behaviour therapy and encopresis in children. *Behav. Res. Ther.,* 1963, **1,** 139–149.

NOYES, A. P., and L. C. KOLB.   *Modern clinical psychiatry.* (5th ed.) Philadelphia: Saunders, 1958.

ORLANDO, R., S. W. BIJOU, R. M. TYLER, and D. A. MARSHALL.   A laboratory for the experimental analysis of developmentally retarded children. *Psychol. Rep.,* 1960, **7,** 261–267.

ORNE, M. T.   On the social psychology of the psychological experiment: with particular reference to demand characteristics and their implications. *Amer. Psychologist,* 1962, **17,** 776–783.

ORWELL, G.   *1984.* New York: New American Library, 1954.

OSGOOD, C. E.   *An alternative to war or surrender.* Urbana, Ill.: University of Illinois Press, 1962.

OSWALD, I.   Induction of illusory and hallucinatory voices with considerations of behaviour therapy. *J. ment. Sci.,* 1962, **108,** 196–212.

PASCAL, G. R.   The use of relaxation in short-term psychotherapy. *J. abnorm. soc. Psychol.,* 1947, **42,** 226–242.

PAUL, G. L.   Modifications of systematic desensitization based on case study. Paper presented to West. Psychol. Assoc., Portland, Oreg., Apr. 1964. (a)

PAUL, G. L.   Comparative psychotherapeutic effectiveness in the treatment of performance anxiety: stress condition results. Paper presented to Midwest. Psychol. Assoc., May, 1964. (b)

PHILLIPS, E. L.   *Psychotherapy: a modern theory and practice.* Englewood Cliffs, N.J.: Prentice-Hall, 1956.

PHILLIPS, E. L.   Parent-child psychotherapy: a follow-up study comparing two techniques. *J. Psychol.,* 1960, **49,** 195–202.

PHILLIPS, L.   Case history data and prognosis in schizophrenia. *J. nerv. ment. Dis.,* 1953, **117,** 515–525.

PLATONOV, H. I.   *The word as a psychological and therapeutic factor.* Moscow: Foreign Languages Publishing House, 1959.

QUAY, H.   The effect of verbal reinforcement on the recall of early memories. *J. abnorm. soc. Psychol.,* 1959, **59,** 254–257.

QUAY, H. (Ed.)   *Research in psychopathology.* Princeton, N.J.: Van Nostrand, 1963.

RACHMAN, S.   The treatment of anxiety and phobic reactions by systematic desensitization psychotherapy. *J. abnorm. soc. Psychol.,* 1959, **58,** 259–263.

RACHMAN, S.   Sexual disorders and behavior therapy. *Amer. J. Psychiat.,* 1961, **118,** 235–240.

RACHMAN, S.   Introduction to behaviour therapy. *Behav. Res. Ther.,* 1963, **1,** 3–15. (a)

RACHMAN, S. Spontaneous remission and latent learning. *Behav. Res. Ther.,* 1963, **1,** 133–137. (b)

RACHMAN, S., and C. G. COSTELLO. The aetiology and treatment of children's phobias: a review. *Amer. J. Psychiat.,* 1961, **118,** 97–105.

RAIMY, V. C. (Ed.) *Training in clinical psychology.* Englewood Cliffs, N.J.: Prentice-Hall, 1950.

RAYMOND, M. J. Case of fetishism treated by aversion therapy. *Brit. Med. J.,* 1956, **2,** 854–857. (In Eysenck, 1960a.)

RAYMOND, M. J. The treatment of addiction by aversion conditioning with apomorphine. *Behav. Res. Ther.,* 1964, **1,** 287–291.

RHEINGOLD, HARRIET L., J. L. GERWITZ, and HELEN W. ROSS. Social conditioning of vocalizations in the infant. *J. comp. physiol. Psychol.,* 1959, **52,** 68–73.

ROGERS, C. R. *Client-centered therapy.* Boston: Houghton Mifflin, 1951.

ROGERS, J. M. Operant conditioning in a quasi-therapy setting. *J. abnorm. soc. Psychol.,* 1960, **60,** 247–252.

ROSENTHAL, R. On the social psychology of the psychological experiment: the experimenter's hypothesis as unintended determinant of experimental results. *Amer. Sci.,* 1963, **51,** 268–282.

ROTTER, J. B. *Clinical psychology.* Englewood Cliffs, N.J.: Prentice-Hall, 1964.

RUBENSTEIN, C. The treatment of morphine addiction in tuberculosis by Pavlov's conditioning method. *Amer. Rev. Tubercul.,* 1931, **24,** 682–685.

SALTER, A. *Conditioned reflex therapy.* New York: Putnam, 1961.

SALZBERG, H. C. Manipulation of verbal behavior in a group psychotherapeutic setting. *Psychol. Rep.,* 1961, **9,** 183–186.

SALZINGER, K. Experimental manipulation of verbal behavior: a review. *J. gen. Psych.,* 1959, **61,** 65–94.

SALZINGER, K., and STEPHANIE PISONI. Reinforcement of affect responses of schizophrenics during the clinical interview. *J. abnorm. soc. Psychol.,* 1958, **57,** 84–90.

SALZINGER, K., and STEPHANIE PISONI. Some parameters of the conditioning of verbal affect responses in schizophrenic subjects. *J. abnorm. soc. Psychol.,* 1961, **63,** 511–516.

SALZINGER, K., and M. B. WALLER. The operant control of vocalization in the dog. *J. exp. Anal. Behav.,* 1962, **5,** 383–389.

SARASON, I. G. The human reinforcer in verbal behavior research. In L. Krasner, and L. P. Ullmann (Eds.), *Research in behavior modification.* New York: Holt, Rinehart and Winston, Inc., 1965.

SARBIN, T. R. (Ed.) *Studies in behavior pathology.* New York: Holt, Rinehart and Winston, Inc., 1961.

SARBIN, T. R. Anxiety: the reification of a metaphor. Paper presented to West. Psychiat. Assoc., San Francisco, Sept. 1963.

SARBIN, T. R. Hypnosis as a behavior modification technique. In L. Krasner, and L. P. Ullmann (Eds.), *Research in behavior modification.* New York: Holt, Rinehart and Winston, Inc., 1965.

SARBIN, T. R., and C. D. HARDYCK. Conformance in role perception as a personality variable. *J. consult. Psychol.,* 1955, **19,** 109–111.

SAUL, L. T., H. ROME, and E. LEUSER. Desensitization of combat fatigue patients. *Amer. J. Psychiat.,* 1946, **102,** 476–478.

SCHMIDT, H. O., and C. P. FONDA. The reliability of psychiatric diagnosis: a new look. *J. abnorm. soc. Psychol.,* 1956, **52,** 262–267.

SCHREIBER, Y. L. The method of indirect suggestion as used in hysteria. In R. B. Winn (Ed.), *Psychotherapy in the Soviet Union.* New York: Philosophical Library, Inc. 1961.

SCHROEDER, W. W.   The effect of reinforcement counseling and model-reinforcement counseling on information-seeking behavior of high school students. Unpublished doctoral dissertation, Stanford University, 1964.

SCHWITZGEBEL, R., and D. A. KOLB.   Inducing behaviour change in adolescent delinquents. *Behav. Res. Ther.*, 1964, 1, 297–304.

SCOTT, W. A.   Research definitions of mental health and mental illness. *Psychol. Bull.*, 1958, 55, 29–45.

SEARS, R. R., and L. H. COHEN.   Hysterical anesthesia, analgesia, and astereognosis. *Arch. Neurol. Psychiat.*, 1933, 29, 260–271. (In Eysenck, 1960a)

SHAPIRO, A. K.   A contribution to a history of the placebo effect. *Behav. Sci.*, 1960, 5, 109–135.

SHAW, F. J.   A stimulus-response analysis of repression and insight in psychotherapy. *Psychol. Rev.*, 1946, 53, 36–42.

SHAW, F. J.   Some postulates concerning psychotherapy. *J. consult. Psychol.*, 1948, 12, 426–431.

SHEEHAN, J. G.   The modification of stuttering through non-reinforcement. *J. abnorm. soc. Psychol.*, 1951, 46, 51–63.

SHEPHARD, M., and G. M. GRUENBERG.   The age for neuroses. *Millbank Mem. Quart. Bull.*, 1957, 35, 258–265.

SHOBEN, E. J.   Psychotherapy as a problem in learning theory. *Psychol. Bull.*, 1949, 46, 366–392.

SINGER, R. D.   Verbal conditioning and generalization of prodemocratic responses. *J. abnorm. soc. Psychol.*, 1961, 63, 43–46.

SKINNER, B. F.   *Walden two.* New York: Macmillan, 1948.

SKINNER, B. F.   *Science and human behavior.* New York: Macmillan, 1953.

SKINNER, B. F.   Teaching machines. *Science,* 1958, 128, 969–977.

SKINNER, B. F.   Operant behavior. *Amer. Psychologist*, 1963, 18, 503–515.

SMITH, S., and E. GUTHRIE.   Exhibitionism. *J. abnorm. soc. Psychol.*, 1922, 17, 206–209.

SOMMER, R., GWYNNETH WITNEY, and H. OSMOND.   Teaching common associations to schizophrenics. *J. abnorm. soc. Psychol.*, 1962, 65, 58–61.

STANTON, A. H., and M. S. SCHWARTZ.   *The mental hospital.* New York: Basic Books, 1954.

STEVENSON, I.   Direct instigation of behavioral changes in psychotherapy. *AMA Arch. gen. Psychiat.*, 1959, 1, 99–107.

STEVENSON, I., and J. WOLPE.   Recovery from sexual deviations through overcoming non-sexual neurotic responses. *Amer. J. Psychiat.*, 1960, 116, 737–742.

SYLVESTER, J. D., and L. A. LIVERSEDGE.   Conditioning and the occupational cramps. In H. J. Eysenck (Ed.), *Behaviour therapy and the neuroses.* New York: Pergamon, 1960, 334–348.

SZASZ, T. S.   The myth of mental illness. *Amer. Psychologist,* 1960, 15, 113–118.

SZASZ, T. S.   The uses of naming and the origin of the myth of mental illness. *Amer. Psychologist,* 1961, 16, 59–65. (a)

SZASZ, T. S.   *The myth of mental illness.* New York: Hoeber, 1961. (b)

SZASZ, T. S.   *Law, liberty and psychiatry.* New York: Macmillan, 1963.

THORPE, J. G., and E. SCHMIDT.   Therapeutic failure in a case of aversion therapy. *Behav. Res. Ther.*, 1964, 1, 293–296.

THORPE, J. G., E. SCHMIDT, and D. CASTELL.   A comparison of positive and negative (aversive) conditioning in the treatment of homosexuality. *Behav. Res. Ther.*, 1963, 1, 357–362.

THORPE, L. P., and B. KATZ.   *The psychology of abnormal behavior.* New York: Ronald, 1948.

ULLMANN, L. P., and JEANNE M. GIOVANNONI.   The development of a self-report measure of the process-reactive continuum. *J. nerv. ment. Dis.*, 1964, 138, 38–42.

ULLMANN, L. P., and W. A. HUNRICHS. The role of anxiety in psychodiagnosis: replication and extension. *J. clin. Psychol.,* 1958, **14**, 276–279.

ULLMANN, L. P., L. KRASNER, and BEVERLY COLLINS. Modification of behavior through verbal conditioning: effects in group therapy. *J. abnorm. soc. Psychol.,* 1961, **62**, 128–132.

ULLMANN, L. P., L. KRASNER, and R. L. EDINGER. Verbal conditioning of common associations in long-term schizophrenic patients. *Behav. Res. Ther.,* 1964, **2**, 15–18.

ULLMANN, L. P., L. KRASNER, and P. EKMAN. Verbal conditioning of emotional words: effects on behavior in group therapy. *Res. Rep. VA Palo Alto,* No. 15, June 1961.

ULLMANN, L. P., L. KRASNER, and DONNA M. GELFAND. Changed content within a reinforced response class. *Psychol. Rep.,* 1963, **12**, 819–829.

ULLMANN, L. P., R. L. WEISS, and L. KRASNER. The effect of verbal conditioning of emotional words on recognition of threatening stimuli. *J. clin. Psychol.,* 1963, **19**, 182–183.

VERPLANCK, W. S. The control of the content of conversation: reinforcement of statements of opinion. *J. abnorm. soc. Psychol.,* 1955, **51**, 668–676.

VOEGTLIN, W. L. The treatment of alcoholism by establishing a conditioned reflex. *Amer. J. med. Sci.,* 1940, **199**, 802–809.

WALTON, D. The relevance of learning theory to the treatment of an obsessive-compulsive state. In H. J. Eysenck (Ed.), *Behaviour therapy and the neuroses.* New York: Pergamon, 1960, 153–164. (a)

WALTON, D. Strengthening of incompatible reactions and the treatment of a phobic state in a schizophrenic patient. In H. J. Eysenck (Ed.), *Behaviour therapy and the neuroses.* New York: Pergamon, 1960, 170–180. (b)

WALTON, D. The application of learning theory to the treatment of a case of bronchial asthma. In H. J. Eysenck (Ed.), *Behaviour therapy and the neuroses.* New York: Pergamon, 1960, 188–189. (c)

WALTON, D. The application of learning theory to the treatment of a case of neurodermatitis. In H. J. Eysenck (Ed.), *Behaviour therapy and the neuroses.* New York: Pergamon, 1960, 272–274. (d)

WALTON, D. The application of learning theory to the treatment of a case of somnambulism. *J. clin. Psychol.,* 1961, **17**, 96–99. (a)

WALTON, D. Experimental psychology and the treatment of a ticquer. *J. child psychol. Psychiat.,* 1961, **2**, 148–155. (b)

WALTON, D., and D. A. BLACK. The application of learning theory to the treatment of stammering. *J. psychosom. Res.,* 1958, **3**, 170–179. (In Eysenck, 1960a.)

WALTON, D., and D. A. BLACK. The application of modern learning theory to the treatment of chronic hysterical aphonia. *J. psychosom. Res.,* 1959, **3**, 303–311. (In Eysenck, 1960a.)

WALTON, D., and M. D. MATHER. The relevance of generalization techniques to the treatment of stammering and phobic symptoms. *Behav. Res. Ther.,* 1963, **1**, 121–125. (a)

WALTON, D., and M. D. MATHER. The application of learning principles to the treatment of obsessive-compulsive states in the acute and chronic phases of illness. *Behav. Res. Ther.,* 1963, **1**, 163–174. (b)

WATSON, J. B., and ROSALIE RAYNER. Conditioned emotional reactions. *J. exp. Psychol.,* 1920, **3**, 1–14. (In Eysenck, 1960a).

WATSON, R. I. The experimental tradition and clinical psychology. In A. J. Bachrach, (Ed.), *Experimental foundations of clinical psychology.* New York: Basic Books, 1962, 3–25.

WEINER, N. *Cybernetics,* (2nd ed.) Cambridge, Mass.: M.I.T. Press, 1961.

WEISS, R., L. KRASNER, and L. P. ULLMANN. Responsivity of psychiatric patients to verbal conditioning: "success" and "failure" conditions and pattern of reinforced trials. *Psychol. Rep.,* 1963, **12**, 423–426.

WHITE, R. W.   *The abnormal personality.* (2nd ed.) New York: Ronald, 1956.

WILDER, J.   Facts and figures on psychotherapy. *J. clin. Psychopath.,* 1945, **7**, 311–347.

WILLOUGHBY, R. R.   Some properties of the Thurstone Personality Schedule and a suggested revision. *J. soc. Psychol.,* 1932, **3**, 401–424.

WILLOUGHBY, R. R.   Norms for the Clark-Thurstone inventory. *J. soc. Psychol.,* 1934, **5**, 91–97.

WITTENBORN, J. R., J. D. HOLZBERG, and B. SIMON.   Symptom correlates for descriptive diagnosis. *Genet. Psychol. Monogr.,* 1953, **47**, 237–302.

WOLFE, B.   *Limbo.* New York: Random House, Inc. 1952.

WOLPE, J.   Experimental neuroses as learned behaviour. *Brit. J. Psychol.,* 1952, **43**, 243–268.

WOLPE, J.   Reciprocal inhibition as the main basis of psychotherapeutic effects. *AMA Arch. Neurol. Psychiat.,* 1954, **72**, 205–226. (In Eysenck, 1960a)

WOLPE, J.   Learning versus lesions as the basis of neurotic behavior. *Amer. J. Psychiat.,* 1956, **112**, 923–927.

WOLPE, J.   *Psychotherapy by reciprocal inhibition.* Stanford, Calif.: Stanford University Press, 1958.

WOLPE, J.   The systematic desensitization treatment of neuroses. *J. nerv. ment. Dis.,* 1961, **132**, 189–203.

WOLPE, J.   The experimental foundations of some new psychotherapeutic methods. In A. J. Bachrach (Ed.), *Experimental foundations of clinical psychology.* New York: Basic Books, 1962, 554–575.

WOLPE, J.   Psychotherapy: the nonscientific heritage and the new science. *Behav. Res. Ther.,* 1963, **1**, 23–28.

WOLPE, J., and S. RACHMAN.   Psychoanalytic "evidence": a critique based on Freud's case of Little Hans. *J. nerv. ment. Dis.,* 1960, **130**, 135–148.

YATES, A. J.   Symptoms and symptom substitution. *Psychol. Rev.,* 1958, **65**, 371–374. (In Eysenck, 1960a). (a)

YATES, A. J.   The application of learning theory to the treatment of tics. *J. abnorm. soc. Psychol.,* 1958, **56**, 175–182. (b)

YATES, A. J.   Recent empirical and theoretical approaches to the experimental manipulation of speech in normal subjects and in stammerers. *Behav. Res. Ther.,* 1963, **1**, 95–119.

ZIGLER, E., and L. PHILLIPS.   Psychiatric diagnosis and symptomatology. *J. abnorm. soc. Psychol.,* 1961, **63**, 69–75.

ZILBOORG, G., and G. W. HENRY.   *A history of medical psychology.* New York: Norton, 1941.

ZIMET, C. N., and G. A. BRACKBILL.   The role of anxiety in psychodiagnosis. *J. clin. Psychol.,* 1956, **12**, 173–177.

SUBJECT INDEX